Dianying   Electric Shadows

An Account of Films
and the Film Audience
in China

On this book's title: the two characters *dian ying* translate as "electric
shadows," the term for cinema in
Chinese. However, *dian-ying* is not the
"official" latinizing of the characters;
this would be *tien-yin*, but the long
continued usage of *dianying* in publications of the Foreign Languages
Press and elsewhere requires that
spelling in this book. To increase the
tangle, neither of these *sounds* would
be understood by a Peking citizen. He
pronounces this "dyan-yer."

电影

The MIT Press
Cambridge, Massachusetts,
and London, England

Dianying

An Account of Films
and the Film Audience
in China

Jay Leyda

"I have at times [thought Kyo] found
myself in front of a mirror, unexpectedly, and not known who I was . . ."
— André Malraux

"Is it possible," cried Chou, "that I
didn't know my own face?"
— P'u Sung-ling

Library of Congress Cataloging in Publication Data

Leyda, Jay, 1910—
    Dianying.

    Bibliography: p.
    1. Moving-pictures — China — History.
    I. Title.
PN1993.5.C4L4   791.43'0951   78—175719
ISBN 0—262—12046—1 (hard cover)

by Jay Leyda

Film Notes (with Iris Barry)

Kino, A History of the Russian and
Soviet Film

Films Beget Films

Sergei Rachmaninoff, A Lifetime in
Music (with Sergei Bertensson)

Translations

The Film Sense, by Sergei Eisenstein

Film Form, by Sergei Eisenstein

Film Essays, by Sergei Eisenstein

The Mussorgsky Reader (with Sergei
Bertensson)

Lessons with Eisenstein, by Vladimir
Nizhny (with Ivor Montagu)

and

The Melville Log, A Documentary Life
of Herman Melville

The Portable Melville

The Complete Stories of Herman
Melville

The Years and Hours of Emily
Dickinson

Robert Flaherty (with Wolfgang
Klaue)

Bartleby, libretto for the opera by
Walter Aschaffenburg

Meinen Kollegen und Genossen
in den Filmarchiven
von Peking und Berlin
gewidmet

Contents

Foreword

This account was begun in the summer of 1963, a year before I left China. Since my arrival in Peking in 1959, to take employment on the fringe of the film industry, I had not thought of attempting any sort of history of Chinese films, for I learned then that a detailed history was in preparation by a responsible group headed by Cheng Chi-hua. One history seemed enough, and I was content to offer my help whenever the work would be finished and an English translation contemplated.

My chief duty was at the Film Archive of China where, though I was supposed to concentrate on the examination and cataloging of their foreign films, it was inevitable that I should see, without any particular system or plan, a large part of the Chinese collection. This I did with great enjoyment, no matter whether the films were good or poor, because they showed me a range and depth of problems that were still visible in the new films being made. The Chinese films of the past helped me understand the Chinese films of the present.

When my wife and I returned from spending the winter of 1962–1963 in London, we found that in six months many changes in cultural policy had taken place that affected our respective jobs, leaving us both only partially employed. Also while we were away two volumes of Cheng Chi-hua's history had been published, and soon after our return, and in my comparative idleness, friends translated sections of it for me. Hearing these made me feel relief that my editorial offer had been politely declined, and also made me feel impatience that the values and problems I had sensed in Chinese films of the past, even of the recent past, had been left so unexplored. As I heard this translation of a history so extremely orthodox in attitude and in structure, I began to imagine another history of Chinese films, looser in both attitude and structure, less anxious to subscribe to habits and taboos, and that is what I began to write. From the beginning it was embarrassingly clear to me that regardless of the reservations I had on the one history already partially published, I would be greatly dependent on its data and research.

Even for such an unorthodox history (conscience has forced me to call it an "account") I was conspicuously unprepared. To begin with, during my five years in China, I could not learn to read Chinese, my speaking knowledge was lower than kindergarten level, and I could do little without the assistance of interpreters and translators. I had come to China with no special grounding in Chinese history or culture. These failings made me half-blind and half-deaf in my first months in China, but the disabilities also tended to increase my alertness to what I saw on the screen: pictures often revealed motives that were concealed by the words. Another barrier also had to be overcome, though only partially, by what could be deduced from completed films: I grew increasingly aware of the importance of the Chinese spectator in any analysis of Chinese film history, yet the peculiar position of all foreigners in China while I was there made *any* communication with the chance man-on-the-street, or woman in the theater seat next to me, or child in the foyer, quite impossible, even with the best-willed interpreter. And, in spite of my working relation to the Film Bureau, I was able to have brief conversations with only three filmmakers in my first four years there. Nor was I allowed to see a studio film being made until two months before our departure. A more sensible person would have withdrawn from such an ambitious project as I had outlined for myself, but by that time I was too excited by its possibilities to be sensible.

Ambitious and quixotic — to illuminate our notions of modern Chinese history and culture through its least regarded, least respected, and, at present, most controlled art. Chinese governments of the past fifty years are not, of course, the only governments of the world that wish to use films with neither understanding nor trust. That attitude is now so taken for granted that any evidence of a decent relationship between authority and cinema is considered remarkable, even suspect. The good aspect of this negative attitude, from the viewpoint of any type of investigation, is that a lack of respect can offset the otherwise disadvantageous caution and extreme control applied to a national film industry. No matter how hemmed in or guarded against, revelations of reality do emerge, even in the work of timid or scared filmmakers. Thus — *more* supervision, always less effective than imagined by the supervisors. Nevertheless, to quote Nagel's latest *Encyclopedia-Guide* to China, the cinema is "more strictly organized than any other branch of cultural activity."

No one, after a moment's thought, would deny that films can reveal more than appears on their surface. But isn't it exaggerated to speak of "history" and "culture" as being opened to us through a country's films? Few of us, in our own filmgoing, look for such manifestations in single films, but all of us tend to draw general conclusions about both modern history and culture after seeing a group of films from a foreign country (it is more difficult to draw such conclusions from one's native films) — and that is all that I am proposing be looked for in the films of China, past and present. I have only tried to give detail and particulars to the more visible generalizations. A wealth of evidence awaits examination, and this book will have achieved one of its purposes if the existence of this wealth is recognized.

This foreword says so much about *meaning* that I may have to draw attention to an aspect of Chinese films that is of equal importance to me — the *quality* of these films. The links between meaning and quality in them are, by the way, neither simple nor mechanical — they are occasionally in conflict. Many of the films, including some made recently, contain passages of such original, expressive power that I deeply regret the circumstances — geographic, temperamental, political — that have prevented the Chinese cinema from contributing more to international film history. Time may alter these circumstances to give us all the opportunity to enjoy and judge Chinese films.

A reader would be justified to insist on a clearer definition of this book's relation to Cheng Chi-hua's history.* In his work, alongside information that I want and need is a viewpoint that I distrust and consider harmful, to filmmaker as well as to reader, and it is not easy to separate these poles of attraction and repulsion. This makes for an account that the reader must not accept at face value — especially as it concerns films that the reader has, most likely, not seen, and filmmakers whose names are being encountered for the first time here. The number of unfamiliarities — more than in any other work of film history, and including incredible motivation and fantastically alien attitudes — has presented a series of problems that, I admit, added to my excitement with the book.

Most of this book, all the period covered by Cheng Chi-hua's two volumes (which break off at 1949), was written by April 1966, when *Renmin Ribao* published its blistering condemnation of Cheng and his history.† Whatever the larger motive for this attack (obviously a reinforcement of the earlier attack on Hsia Yen and all film work identified with his party activity — and possibly a threat of broader attacks on all Shanghai-based culture or non-Yenan-inspired art), one result was certain: Cheng Chi-hua's book was transformed from an official history to an officially declared instrument of the "enemy." This is an important symptom that I have discussed in Chapter 12. In another sense, how has this affected my use of Cheng's work? I have, of course, reexamined all my references to it, now that it must be seen in the light of a document recording a past attitude rather than a current official position. *Renmin Ribao* has announced that the book will be used for capitalist distortion. I'd like to protect the helpless author from a confirmation of this prophecy, but if he were my first consideration I should have to put aside all thought of writing my book. With or without a new history to embody the "correct" Chinese point of view, any

---

* *History of the Development of Chinese Cinema* (Zhong guo dianying fa zhan shi). All other chronicles of Chinese film history that I have consulted—Tsai Chu-sheng, Zalman, Casiraghi, Sadoul, Scott, Bergeron, Lerchenthal—apart from their critical worth, have been too brief and condensed and indirect to replace Cheng Chi-hua.
† 19 April 1966, "Let Us Destroy the Mystic Belief in the Films of the Thirties," signed by "Tien Hsin." The *Renmin Ribao* attack on Hsia Yen appeared 29 May 1965.

voice — mine, for example — that doesn't agree with it will be dismissed as bourgeois or revisionist distortion. This is a situation that makes it necessary again to quote Malraux:

What runs counter to the revolutionary convention is, in revolutionary histories, suppressed more imperiously than embarrassing episodes in private memoirs, and by the same obscure forces. . . .*

In this case the suppression is so complete and the obscurity of motive so thick that it will be many years before any other film history can appear in China.

In approaching the involved issues of this history, I've allowed my personal feelings, aesthetically as well as socially, to intrude so often as to make any pretence of objectivity ridiculous. My substitute for objectivity here is a quantity of material that enables a reader to *want* to form his own attitudes, possibly quite opposed to my own. And to counter the numerous ambiguities of attitude to China and Chinese traditions, I want to make my sympathies clear: I'm sorry for the talented filmmakers, many of whom will disappear or die without showing what they were capable of, and I'm sorry for the Chinese audience, who are fed so watery a film diet when they need the most robust of dramatic forms.

A book about films must rely, first of all, on the films themselves as its primary source, and most of my printed sources are used to fill gaps in my film seeing, often — in the case of Chinese film history — caused by the loss of films. I hope the reader will not be disturbed by the strange variety of printed sources that are quoted; writers who were not particularly concerned with the fate of the Chinese cinema have provided some of the most valuable comments on their chancy filmgoing in China.

This time of extreme crisis in all Chinese society and arts may seem an inappropriate occasion to draw attention to a medium that in the best of times is snubbed by most historians, and in countries far from China. My suggestion that in not looking closely at Chinese films we are neglecting a treasure of information about twentieth-century China will be questioned (first, How are we to see them?), as it has become clear that except for newsreels fewer films are now being made in China than at any time since the beginning there of film production. It would be premature to assume that all that has happened in Chinese cinema has been closed and locked up forever, no matter how thorough the demolition by the Great Proletarian Cultural Revolution. It is still possible to see

---

* "Lawrence and the Demon of the Absolute," *The Hudson Review*, Winter 1956; the essay was written in 1941 as a chapter of an unpublished book.

(in *Western* countries, under the auspices of political friendship organizations) some Chinese films made since 1949, and to find (in film archives) an occasional Chinese film made before that date and shipped abroad. Of greater importance are the Chinese films acquired by the Pacific Film Archive at the Berkeley campus of the University of California, but these are not yet ready for examination. Most of the former audience for Chinese films abroad (in the socialist countries of Europe and Asia) are seeing fewer or no Chinese films, but that, too, need not be thought an end; as I write this, in the summer of 1968, a West German television network is showing *Red Detachment of Women* (1961). For most viewers it is their first Chinese film.

In one battle I have to admit nearly total defeat: consistency of transliteration. One excuse is the use of varied transliteration methods in my European and American sources. A more valid difficulty would result from the choice of one method into which all Chinese names would be fitted, making many familiar names incomprehensible to most readers. There are, however, two parts of the book where clarity and consistency have been more strictly applied — Appendix 1 (the biographical sketches) and the Index. I trust these will make some inconsistencies of transliteration in the text less awkward.

Many of the people, the Chinese certainly, who have helped me in the work on this book would prefer not to be thanked publicly. Otherwise I'm glad to show my appreciation for many kinds of help to an often discouraged researcher — from Nikolai Abramov, J. F. Aranda, W. H. Auden, Ion Barna, Ted Brake, W. Slade Bungey, Ernest Callenbach, Eileen Chang, Nan Green, John Grierson, C. T. Hsia, Akira Iwasaki, Eckart Jahnke, Wolfgang Klaue, Naum Kleiman, John Kuiper, Gerhard Lamprecht, Standish and Ursula Lawder, John Howard Lawson, Sidney Meyers, Marion Michelle, Ivor Montagu, David Morris, Jan Myrdal, Vanda Perretta, Doris Schirmer, Harry Sichrovsky, G. M. Shillinglaw, Helen Snow, Jonathan Spence, Heinz Steinberg, Daniel Topolski, Herman Weinberg, Monica Whyte, Charles Willemen, Lili Williams, Morris Wills, Alan Winnington, Kazuo Yamada. Other help was given by East Asian Studies and the many libraries at Yale University. The film archives of China, the German Democratic Republic, the Soviet Union, Austria, Romania, Czechoslovakia, the Netherlands, Belgium, and Great Britain have been generous with films, documents, and some encouragement. The former director of the Film Archive of China was the first to suggest to me that there might be value in a Chinese film history written from an outside point of view.

J. L.

Peking — New Haven

1

Preliminaries
1896–1911

> You may consider the performance as true or false. It is always an image of life and its conclusions.
>
> — inscription in an old Peking theater

The device for making money easily — by throwing gray shadows on a white screen — had been brought in from the outside, from where so many other dubious devices had come. These were not the familiar shadowplays of heroic generals and vulnerable heroines. No one knows if spirits and ancestors had been properly propitiated, but as their influence was weakest in the treaty ports, probably not. Certainly the introduction of films to China came in such an unlucky decade that Chinese audiences shunned anything untraditional.

The hopeless war with Japan in 1894 had resulted in the Manchu government's cessions of Chinese territory in 1895, increasing the appetites of the Western powers who were already well entrenched in the bewildered continent. English, French, German, and Russian gains of "spheres of influence" kept pace with Japan's. The United States concentrated on industrial concessions, using "the cheapest labor in the world." All these countries, with the exception of Russia, gained film footholds in China from the earliest years of the invention's exploitation.

It may have been one of the several Lumière cameramen-showmen who first brought films to Chinese audiences. On 11 August 1896, Shanghai, future center of the Chinese film industry, saw its first film program, as one "number" in the variety show at the Hsu Gardens that included a magician, acrobats, and a juggler with fireworks.[1] * Beyond two advertisements nothing is known about either the showman who brought this program to China or the source of his films, but tradition says that both were French. (The Lumière records name no assignment to the China concession. Marius Sestier, representing the Lumière Brothers, showed their films in Bombay [at Watson's Hotel and Novelty Theatre] from 7 July to 15 August, and he seems to have been on his way to Australia,[2] all of which makes him an unlikely candidate for the Shanghai showman.) As all the Lumière travelers made new films with the same apparatus used for their screenings, it should be noted that films of China do not appear in the Lumière catalogs.†

---

* All numbered source notes are at the end of the book.
† Though these catalogs list films from Australia (1896?), Japan (1897–1899), and Indo-China (1900–1901), according to Sadoul, *Louis Lumière* (1964). A Lumière cameraman, Francis Doublier, has said that he was in China in 1899, but gave no details of what he did there.

The next film showman to reach Shanghai was an American, James Ricalton of Maplewood, New Jersey, bringing a program of Edison films that he exhibited in teahouses and amusement parks in July 1897. His attraction lasted ten evenings at the Tien Hua Tea Garden, where admission was 50 cents for seats in the front row, with prices receding to 10 cents for seats in the last rows. The tea garden advertised the listed program vigorously:

This show is entirely mechanised, but it is as vivid as life itself. In the great variety of items the spectator will find as many things to please his eye as on the Shanying Highway.[3]

The final allusion is to a Tsin Dynasty poem, though neither Czar Nikolai II (shown visiting Paris) nor Little Egypt, the belly dancer of the Chicago World's Fair, could be easily imagined in fourth-century China. In Ricalton's miscellany, however, there was one item that would have looked vaguely familiar to a Chinese audience: Annabelle dancing the serpentine dance that Loie Fuller had adapted from the ribbon dance brought by Chinese performers to the Paris Exposition of 1889.

Ricalton's programs evoked the earliest Chinese film journalism. In September *The Amusement Paper* (Yo-shi Bao) published an unsigned appreciation entitled "Seeing American Films":

Last night, in the cool of the evening following a shower of rain, my friends took me to the Chi Gardens to see a show. After the audience gathered, the lights were put out and the performance began. On the screen before us we saw a picture — two occidental girls dancing, with puffed-up yellow hair, looking rather silly. Then another scene, two occidentals boxing. Then a woman bathing in a tub. . . . In another scene* a man puts out the light and goes to bed, but he is disturbed by a bedbug. To catch it he throws off all the bedding, and when he finally puts it in the chamber pot he looks very funny. . . .

One wonderful scene, which was repeated, is a bicycle race. One man rides in from the east, another from the west. They collide, one man falls down and when the other tries to help, he falls down, too. Suddenly many bicycles come in and all fall down, making the audience clap their hands and laugh out loud. . . .

Another scene is an American street [Fifth Avenue] with tall street lamps, carriages going to and fro, and pedestrians in great numbers walking along. The spectators feel as though they are actually present, and this is exhilarating. Suddenly the lights come on again and all the images vanish. It was indeed a miraculous spectacle.[4]

---

* *Now I Lay Me Down to Sleep*, copyright in April 1897.

Ricalton was filming as well as showing: the Edison catalog of 1898 offers six short scenes of Hong Kong, Shanghai, and Canton. He may have hung on until the following spring, helped by fresh supplies from home, for the *Fun Paper* (Tzu Bao) of 20 May 1898 described a visit to a film show at the Hsu Gardens (scene of the earliest show), where the writer saw an almost entirely new program, with the piquant items and sports views that were the specialty of the Edison Company.

In 1899 a new nationality entered the Shanghai contest: a Spanish showman, Galen Bocca (?), showed films in a teahouse, a skating rink, and a restaurant, but with so little success, especially after his single program began to show signs of wear, that he turned over his films and apparatus to a friend, Antonio Ramos, whose more persistent efforts in the Ching-Lin-Ko [Tsing Lien Ko?] teahouse (beginning in 1903) established the first steadily profitable film enterprise in China. A writer in 1936 mentions, tantalizingly, that Ramos's effort to introduce regular film shows was followed by that of "several Christian missionaries at Hong Kong and Canton in the following year."[5]

The nineteenth century had also brought to China a mounting series of humiliations that influence Chinese attitudes and films to this day.* The culminating clash between China and the West came in 1900, opening in Shantung where the feeling against the German concessions was particularly acute:

Towards the close of the nineteenth century the Yi Ho Chuan [Society of Righteous and Harmonious Fists] in Shantung, under the slogan of "Oppose the Manchus and revive the Ming [dynasty] ," had organized armed uprisings. It defeated the Manchu troops and forced [the governor of Shantung] to recognize the Yi Ho Chuan as a legal society. Then it was renamed Yi Ho Tuan [omitting the fists] . To meet the people's pressing demand for fighting imperialist aggressors, the Yi Ho Tuan changed its slogan . . . to "Cherish the dynasty and exterminate the foreigners."

. . . In April 1900 the Yi Ho Tuan poured into Peking, putting up anti-foreigner catchwords around the churches and raiding the missions . . . the Empress Dowager received the leaders of the Yi Ho Tuan in audience and conferred on them the title of "righteous people." She promised to give support to their activities.

In June 1900 the Manchu government declared war on the imperialist powers. The Manchu troops, in collaboration with the Yi Ho Tuan patriots, launched onslaughts on the legations in Peking.[6]

---

* The psychological need to "humiliate the foreigner" is still a dominant ingredient of historical films, whether of the far or the recent past.

It is difficult to find or to imagine an objective historical account of this most deeply disturbing of all conflicts between China and the outside world. With rare exceptions European historians see in this nothing but Chinese hatred. With no exception Chinese historians see in it nothing but heroic patriotism. Even less possible is an unprejudiced film treatment of the Boxer Rebellion. One of the results of the subsequent foreign control of many areas of Chinese life was that for forty years of Chinese filmmaking there could be only indirect and veiled references on the screen to this crucial episode, though the Boxers could sometimes be shown in plays and operas. Historical confusion, even embarrassment, has also contributed to this silence. Even after liberation, when other clashes, such as the first Opium War, could be treated in some film fashion, the contradictions of the Boxers have not yet been faced.

Outside China, however, the Boxer Rebellion became material that could be manipulated into any form of film fiction that dramatic or propaganda purposes suggested. The following chapter mentions some of the many variations and echoes of the Boxers that the American film industry employed in its most anti-Chinese period, before 1923, and these filmic echoes reverberate to the present. From a propaganda viewpoint it is the immediate reactions that count for most. The most significant film treatments of the Boxers (lasting long in some spectators' memories) were produced by European and American firms as soon as the news reached and horrified foreign newspaper readers. These films were reconstructions — on Brighton lawns, in French parks, and on New Jersey farms — of the recent events in and near Peking and were presented to audiences as authentic records of those events. A few of these early propaganda efforts have survived; I have seen two of the British fakes, preserved in the National Film Archive: *Beheading a Chinese Boxer* and *Boxer Attack on a Missionary Outpost*, ca. 1900.[7]

A few other "reconstructions" of Boxer incidents have been preserved. The English firm of Walturdaw (Walker-Turner-Dawson) distributed in 1901 an *Attempted Capture of an English Nursery and Child by Boxers* and *Assassination of an English Citizen by Boxers*. All of these appear to be imitations of James Williamson's success, *Attack on a Chinese Mission* (partially preserved), which Georges Sadoul regards as equal in importance with the later *Life of an American Fireman* and *The Great Train Robbery* in the development of film narrative methods. It was made in the winter of 1900–1901 at the Brighton villa where the Williamson family was then living, and the roles of heroic Britons and villainous Chinese were all played by the family and friends. Brighton, as a center of the British vogue in chinoiserie at the start of the nineteenth century, was able to furnish all the Chinese costumes and properties that were wanted.

The scene opens with the outer gate of the premises; a Chinaman with flourishing sword approaches and tries the gate. Finding it fastened, he calls the others, who come rushing up; one leaps over the gate, and the combined attack results in forcing it open; nine Boxers in Chinese costumes of varied character now swarm in, stopping occasionally to fire in the direction of the house.

The second scene shows the front of the house — the missionary walking in front with a young lady; wife and child are seated a little way further off. At the first alarm, the missionary drops his book and sends the young lady into the house to fetch rifle and pistol; he then rushes to his wife and child, and sees them safely into the house; takes cover behind some bushes, discharges his revolver at the Boxers advancing in different directions, kills one, then picks up rifle and discharges it at another; his ammunition exhausted, he comes to close quarters with another Boxer armed with a sword, and, after an exciting fight, is overcome, and left presumably killed. Meanwhile, others of the attacking party have closed round the young lady and followed her, retreating into the house.

Missionary's wife now appears waving handkerchief on the balcony; the scene changes and shows party of bluejackets advancing from the distance, leaping over a fence, coming through the gate, kneeling and firing in fours, and running forward to the rescue, under command of a mounted officer.

The fourth scene is a continuation of the second. The Boxers are dragging the young lady out of the house, which they have set on fire, at the moment the bluejackets appear; a struggle takes place with the Boxers; mounted officer rides up and carries off the young lady out of the mêlée.

The missionary's wife now rushes out of the house pointing to the balcony, where she has left her child; a bluejacket has secured it, but his passage down the stairs being blocked, three sailors mount on each other's shoulders and land the child safely in the mother's arms.

The struggle with the Boxers continues, but they are finally overcome and taken prisoners.

This sensational subject is full of interest and excitement from start to finish and is everywhere received with great applause.[8]

There are less significant reflections of the Boxer crisis in the "film allegories" characteristic of the first years of film history, when the slight movement of a theatrical tableau was enough to make a film program item. After Georges Méliès staged and filmed *La Chine contre les Allies* in 1900,* the Vitagraph Company in the United States imitated it, adding a patriotic variant. This is described in the flowery vulgarity of Vitagraph's historian:

Blackton and Smith took advantage of the Boxer uprising to concoct a noble gusher of emotional oil called *The Congress of Nations*. This fifty foot masterpiece depicted a tiny Chinaman standing in abject supplication, surrounded by a

---

* No. 327 in the Méliès catalog.

group . . . of towering figures representing the various nations involved in this shameful embroglio: John Bull, La Belle France, Germania, and so forth. At a given signal from the cameraman, Smith, . . . the Great Powers made a concerted grab for the little Chink who was, it must be admitted, dressed like a laundry-man rather than as a mandarin dignitary. But lo! before the grasping hands could dismember the unfortunate Chinaman he was magically dissolved into an animated Statue of Liberty, before whom the disgruntled Congress of Nations fell back. . . . In their places there appeared, fluttering in amity with the American flag, which was uppermost in the background, the flags of all the Nations, with Miss Liberty smiling complacently around. The dual role . . . of the little Chinaman and the giant Miss Liberty was played by the Vitagraph clerk, Morris Brenner. . . .[9]

The National Film Archive has preserved, through the gift of Joseph Rosenthal, the earliest English document of China. Rosenthal, working for the Warwick Company, was the first cameraman to reach China after the bloody suppression of the Boxers, coming directly from South Africa, where he had filmed the Boer War (becoming the "first professional war cameraman"):

From there I went to Pekin, with the expedition during the Boxer trouble. I saw the whole place smashed up and went through the Forbidden City. Really, the thing wasn't as bad as the press made it out. Next I went to the Philippines.[10]

If he took films in Peking there is no trace of them now.* But one of his short valuable records, listed as "Nankin Road, Shanghai" in the Warwick catalog of April 1901, has survived in this collection. It is a crowded street scene showing pedestrians, rickshaws, sedan chairs, a European lady on a bicycle, a detachment of Sikhs, and two German officers.[11]

Traces will surely come to light of other Rosenthal films made in Peking. Meanwhile we have copies (from paper prints registered for copyright) of the films made by two American cameramen working in China for Biograph in 1901.[12] The films sent home by Ackerman and Bonine include what is possibly the first staged film made in China: Ackerman's reconstruction of the Sixth Cavalry's assault on the South Gate, a turning point in the defeat of the Boxer Uprising (Plate 2a). Ackerman himself briefly appears in his presentation of a Mutoscope apparatus to Li Hung-shang. This was the year of the noted statesman's death (Plate 2b).

---

* British film historians write that his only work in Peking was "a series of non-action pictures." Low and Manvell, *The History of the British Film*, Vol. I (London: Fernhill, 1948), p. 26.

Another American cameraman, Oscar Depue, was on the scene in 1901:

From Seoul we went to Peking where the Boxer Rebellion had just been sub-
dued. We saw troops of all the allies that took part in the siege — they were still
there and in other parts of China. It was an opportune time for our visit because
we were allowed, through the aid of our own troops, to see and film things that
might not have been available to us otherwise . . . a company of American troops
from Indiana guarded the north half of the Emperor's Palace in the Forbidden
City.[13]

Burton Holmes, who made a career of travel film lectures, visited Peking a year
after the Boxer crisis, and his scenes of Peking are among the few early film
records of the imperial capital. He filmed places that his lecture audiences had
heard of, as associated with the defense of the Legation Quarter, and various
personages, including the Dowager Empress.

Peking saw its first films in January 1902. "A foreigner" hired Fu Sho Hall in
the "Chinese City's" theater district, and showed a program that sounds like the
American Mutoscope catalog of 1897: a beautiful woman turning her head to us
and smiling, women dancing like butterflies, a Negro eating watermelon, a
bicycle race, a horse scaling a wall and climbing to a roof.

The thorough Pathé Frères ("We Cover the World") stationed a cameraman in
China. He travelled extensively from 1907 to 1909 and sent back footage of the
Grand Canal, the boat families of Canton, and the streets and theaters of
Peking.* A cameraman for Charles Urban also reached Peking in 1909.† A
Neapolitan showman, Enrico Lauro, who came to Shanghai to show films in
1907, bought an Ernemann camera and provided footage both for export and
for local showings. His records continued throughout the overthrow of the im-
perial power; among them are

Shanghai's First Tramway (1908)
Imperial Funeral Procession in Peking (1908) [for both dowager and
emperor son]
Lovely Views in Shanghai Concessions (1909)
Cutting Pigtails by Force (1911)[14]

Lauro's interest in Chinese showings for his records is almost unique among
foreign cameramen. Here was a situation that prevailed in no other film-
producing country, with the possible exception of India: of the enormous

---

* These Pathé films preserved in the National Film Archive are listed in Appendix 2.
† In the National Film Archive: *Modern China* (456 ft), released in April 1910.

quantity of documentary material filmed in China by foreigners, from the earliest travels of film showmen to liberation, most of it was never seen by Chinese audiences.

The earliest recorded Chinese to enter this growing film business was Lin Chu-shan. In 1903 he brought back from America a projector and a film program and rented the Tien Lo teahouse in Peking's theater district for his show;[15] what he did after his films were worn out is not recorded.

In Peking's upper levels — the topmost, indeed — two incidents determined official attitudes to the unlucky cinema. In 1904 for the seventieth birthday of the Empress Dowager the British Minister, Sir Ernest Mason Satow, presented her with an English projection apparatus and a program of several English films. Something unpleasant took place on this occasion, but stories vary as to its seriousness; published official records, both Chinese and British, maintain a dignified silence. Another incident confirmed the worst suspicions of the electric shadows. Among the entourage of a Manchu official, Tuan Fang, sent in 1905 on a mission to Europe and America, there were adventurous aides who persuaded him to take home a film projector and some American films. By 1906 the un-fortunate birthday program of 1904 was dim enough a memory for Tuan Fang to plan another film entertainment for the Empress Dowager; to make sure that everything was safe there was a full dress rehearsal, to which Ho Tza-hua, an official gifted in languages, was invited to deliver a Chinese explanation of the films shown. The rehearsal ended abruptly with an explosion of the projector that blew off Ho's leg. The planned court presentation was cancelled.

Despite these portents and social setbacks the attraction of Peking's public to films increased. In the big bazaars both teahouses and actual theaters were rented for very profitable film shows.

In Hong Kong, which was soon to become a world film center, the introduction of films was discouraged by superstition and habit. Following a visit to Hong Kong and South China, Burton Holmes passed on a story told him in Hong Kong about the first cinema there for a Chinese audience:

An Englishman opened an attractive theater in Hong Kong, but the inhabitants [described in the *Chicago Daily News* headline as "Mongolians"] could not be persuaded to support it. They were over-awed by the idea of objects in motion on the screen, and, being superstitious, feared the consequences of encouraging the new art. This man struck a happy plan to secure patronage, and to-day operates ten theaters successfully. He hired audiences to attend at his playhouse

for three successive weeks, paying each patron a stipulated sum each day for his
or her attendance until the superstitious fear aroused by the "movies" had worn
off, and the attractiveness of motion pictures became a household discussion,
after which his business began to prosper.[16]

In Shanghai films were even more popular, to the point of arousing the concern
of the city government. In June 1911 near the empire's end, regulations were
published for the control of film shows: permits were required to open a film
theater, the seats for men and women must be kept separate, immoral films were
forbidden, all shows must end by midnight, and offenders would lose their permits and could expect punishment.[17] These regulations, the foundation of film
censorship in China, were maintained by Shanghai's municipal council after the
establishment of the republic.

Inevitably the imperialist powers' rivalry for privileges and concessions in China
came to open blows on battlefields. The Russo-Japanese War, beginning in 1904,
was fought on Chinese territory that each of the powers hoped to control. Again
in the words of the official history of 1958:

Despite this, the Manchu government shamelessly declared strict neutrality. It
made not the least endeavour to defend China's territory and sovereign rights.
The war lasted more than a year and Japan finally defeated Russia.

In 1905, Japan and Russia signed a treaty of peace under which Russia agreed to
transfer to Japan a portion of the interest she had grabbed from north-east
China. Thus began Japan's penetration into the north-east.[18]

Britain had openly favored the Japanese side in the struggle, and when British
film companies covered the war from both sides (an American cameraman,
George Rogers, with the Russian army, while Rosenthal remained with the
Japanese), the propaganda was heavily weighted with Japanese sympathies.* The
cameramen of Charles Urban gladly staged any episodes difficult to film (or even
to find) in reality, and when the home office put together a whole program on
the war it was an unreliable mixture of document and invention. The Russian
film industry was not yet ready for any organized coverage of the war, but some
amateur cameramen filmed activities with the Russian authorities in Manchuria.†

---

* Films taken by Joseph Rosenthal of the Russo-Japanese War were projected at the
Japanese Legation in London 20 April 1905.
† When their footage was sold to Pathé or Italian firms it achieved a world distribution equal
to that of the British footage, and even reached Japan, where titles were easily altered to
conform to propaganda needs. Pathé also appreciated this flexibility: its catalog offered its
"reconstruction" of the Port Arthur naval battle with alternative final titles — you could
have either *Vive la Russie!* or *Vive le Japon!*

Between 1905 and 1908 the Feng Tai Photography Shop in Peking had the
initiative to film popular actors in Peking opera scenes with a French camera and
film bought from a German photography supply shop in Peking. The most
important of these, the first dramatic Chinese film, was *Tingchun Mountain*, an
episode from *The Three Kingdoms*, with T'an Hsin-p'ei (the Empress Dowager's
favored actor) playing the heroic role of General Huang Chung. There is an
eyewitness account of this filming, preserved by Mei Lan-fang in his theater
memoirs:[19]

My old friend Wu Chen-hsiu accidentally observed the filming of *Ting-chun-
shan* . . . and this is what he told me —

"At the end of the Kuang-hsu period I was teaching in the normal school of
Peking College. After class I often visited Liulichang to browse among the
various bookshops. . . . One day, I think in autumn, I was in Liulichang and as I
passed the open square near the Feng Tai Photography Shop I happened to
notice, on the far side of the square, that a large piece of white cloth had been
hung up and that people were taking pictures. When I came closer, I found they
were not taking photographs but a film. And there was one of our most celebrated old actors — T'an Hsin-p'ei. He was wearing the yellow robes of a warrior,
and carried a golden sword. After going through the fighting movements of the
opera *Ting-chun-shan*, he left. Standing near by were relatives and friends of Mr.
T'an; but otherwise there were not many people about. The manager of the
photography shop, a big fellow who knew me very well, was also helping. Unfortunately they did not take many shots, and it was soon over. Later the film
was publicly shown in the Ta-kuan-lou Cinema. This must be the earliest
instance of filming Peking opera."*

A print of this key film survived until after 1949, but by the time the Film
Archive of China was organized in 1957 that copy had disappeared.† It was said
to have been three reels in length, but thirty minutes would have been such an
extraordinary length for that time that it makes one wonder if its "three scenes"
were not actually contained within one reel. There is no other record of its exhibition or distribution, though some of the Feng Tai's work was shown in Kiangsi
and Fukien provinces.

Another pioneer effort, slightly more documented, was the Asia Film Company,
organized in Hong Kong by an enterprising American named Benjamin Polaski.

---

* Mei Lan-fang mentions other Peking opera scenes filmed at the Feng Tai Photography
Shop; Yu Chu-sheng and Chu Wen-ying in the fighting scenes of *Ching-shih-shan* (Green
Rock Mountain), Yu Chen-t'ing in *Pai-shui-tan* (White Water Bay) and in *Chin-chien-pao*
(Golden Spotted Leopard).
† Probably in a disposal fire about six months before Cheng Chi-hua, in 1953, interviewed
the surviving employees of the Feng Tai shop.

He is known to have made four short films there, all based on theater works, in 1909 (*The Widowed Empress, The Unfilial Son, Revealed by the Pot, Stealing the Cooked Ducks*), and then there is a curious hiatus in the history of this company until 1912, when it reappeared in Shanghai.

In 1905, the year of the first organized popular uprising in Russia, the several anti-Manchu societies, scattered in Japanese exile, united their forces under the leadership of Dr. Sun Yat-sen, and China's first bourgeois nationalist party was formed. With its contacts at home, most importantly among the young intellectuals in the army, the party pushed here and there at the crumbling edifice of the Ching dynasty. There were trials and failures, and on the night of 10 October 1911 the New Army rose and seized Wuchang from fleeing Manchu officials. There is the possibility that a film record of this victory's immediate aftermath may come to light: *War in Wuhan* is a 1911 film, made by Chu Lian-kui, a well-known acrobat, in collaboration with a foreign firm, the Mei Li (Mary?) Company. I am inclined to believe, however, that this is the same film that was registered for U.S. copyright in 1912 as *The Chinese Revolution*. Fortunately a print survives in the Copyright Office of the Library of Congress (see Plate 3) of this staged reconstruction. The film tries hard to please everybody: the "rebels" are shown both as marauding bandits and revolutionary heroes. The Manchu officials likewise alternate as patriotic heroes and pitiless judges. This was clearly intended for overseas audiences as well as distribution in China; the titles are in both Chinese and awkward English. Could this have been another of Polaski's enterprises?

THE CHINESE REVOLUTION, produced in Hong Kong by Oriental Film Company (preserved in the Louise G. Ernst Collection, Library of Congress)

1. Manchu Headquarters outside wall of Hankow.
2. Boy Revolutionist receiving sentence of death.
3. Fourteen year old boy executed outside of city.
4. Broken-hearted father viewing remains of his boy, a Martyr to Liberty.
5. Rich Mandarin attacked by group of Revolutionists.
6. Taking to prison of Rioting Revolutionists.
7. Swift trial and Judgement.
8. Revolutionaries waiting for the coming death.
9. Even Women were not spared.
10. Sample of Manchu Judges.
11. The bodies of the dead strewn along the ruins.
12. Basket in which daring camera man was carried.
    Passing sentries and firing line while taking pictures.

Newspaper advertisement for *War in Wuhan* (1911)

Though the monarchy was shortly abolished forever, its abolition did not remove deeply ingrained habits and patterns of thought; these persist, even in
areas — such as the Chinese cinema — that had not even existed under the old
Empire.

One newsreel helped to change modern Chinese history. In 1902 a 21-year-old
Shaohsing student named Chou Shu-jen went to Japan to study in the Medical
College at Sendai. The young man was passionately concerned with the welfare
of his country: he had, in fact, chosen to study medicine because he was convinced that with medical science he could help the Chinese people. But in 1906 a
chance incident at the college changed his mind:

I do not know what advanced methods are now used to teach micro-biology, but
at that time lantern slides were used to show the microbes; and if the lecture
ended early, the instructor might show lantern slides or films of natural scenery
or news to fill up the hour. This was during the Russo-Japanese War, so there
were many war films, and I had to join in the clapping and cheering in the
lecture hall along with the other students. It was a long time since I had seen any
of my countrymen, but one day I saw a film showing some Chinese, one of
whom was bound, while others stood around him. They were all strong fellows
but appeared completely apathetic. According to the information in the subtitles, the one with his hands bound was a spy working for the Russians, who
was to have his head cut off by the Japanese military as a warning to others,
while the Chinese beside him had come to enjoy the spectacle.*

Before the term was over I had left for Tokyo, because after this film I felt that
medical science was not so important after all. The people of a weak and backward country, however strong and healthy they may be, can only serve to be
made examples of, or to witness such futile spectacles; and it is not necessarily
deplorable no matter how many of them die of illness. The most important
thing, therefore, was to change their spirit, and since at that time I felt that
literature was the best means to this end, I determined to promote a literary
movement.[20]

---

* Romil Sobolev's *People and Films of Russia's Pre-Revolutionary Cinema* (Moscow, 1961)
provides an identifying hint for this newsreel: "By the time of the Russo-Japanese War
the number of amateur cameramen in Russia was already considerable. Some of them worked as camera-correspondents for the French firms of Pathé or Gaumont, some worked as
freelances, selling their most interesting subjects to the French, or occasionally to the Italians or Americans. Ordinarily the exposed film would be sent to Paris, for development
and printing. . . . Cameraman P. Kobtsov, for instance, sent Pathé the footage that he took
in Manchuria of the execution of the *hung-hu* ["red-beard," meaning bandit] . . . ." (p. 11)
The Charles Urban Trading Company's catalog of 1904 reproduced the photograph shown
in Plate 3. Examining it, one can well understand the revulsion of the young Chinese
medical student.

In Tokyo Chou joined the revolutionary anti-Manchu party, found other Chinese students to work with him in translating European literature and planning a magazine, and returned to China in 1909. At home he taught school and after the overthrow of the Ching dynasty he accepted an educational post in the new government. When he saw that the revolution had changed little fundamentally, hopelessness forced his retirement from public activity for a few years. Hope returned, the hope that he could change people through literature — as a "spiritual physician" — and in April 1918 he published his first short story, using the pen name of Lu Hsun.

2

With monkey-shadows on the screen
You mock me now, but I can wait.

— William Plomer

"There is no racial discrimination. It is all a question of price," says Mr. Hoyt.

Though a more or less continuous line of Chinese film production did not begin until 1916, several efforts that deserve mention were made in 1913.

Politically 1913 was a year of hopes and broken illusions. After the successful uprising of 1911 and the abdication of the Manchus in 1912, Sun Yat-sen's principle of uniting the country influenced his decision to turn over the presidency of the republic to a man who was favored by all "respectable" levels of society as well as by foreign governments and financiers — Yuan Shih-kai. When by 1913 Yuan's personal ambitions (before his death in 1916 he schemed to be named emperor and to found a dynasty) and his coolness to all forms of democracy became open, Dr. Sun supported a movement in the newly formed Kuomintang party to remove Yuan. In the summer some Kuomintang governors and sectors of the army declared their opposition to Yuan, but after two months of sporadic fighting this "Second Revolution" failed. The July fighting in Shanghai, when the revolutionary forces attacked the arsenal and the Woosung forts, was recorded on film by the Asia Company, revived in Shanghai just in time for this moment in history. Their film, *War in Shanghai,* was ready to be exhibited at the end of September, along with their first Shanghai fictional film.

In 1912 Benjamin Polaski, discouraged that his Hong Kong productions had not made it possible to establish himself in Shanghai, transferred his company's name and equipment (perhaps not voluntarily) to the American managers (Essler and Lehrmann) of the Nanyang Insurance Company. Willing to squeeze some profit from these new possessions, they employed two Chinese to make films for them. One, Chang Shih-chuan, was an efficient clerk with no theater experience but clever at adapting himself to new problems. The other, Cheng Chen-chiu, was a friend of Chang's, a theater lover with some experience as a critic. Word of the new company reached Europe late in 1913:

In the Central Kingdom there have already been numerous film theaters in Shanghai, Hong Kong, and other cities. Now an organization has been founded by three Chinese and four Europeans which is intended to form additional establishments in the Empire in order to show their own films, among others. Chinese writers and performers were engaged, and studios with modern equipment are already under construction.[1]

Cheng, a Cantonese in sympathy with the political progressives of the South, proposed for their first film an idea about feudal marriage customs of his native province. *The Difficult Couple* (or *Wedding Night*), with Cheng's scenario, became the first Chinese fictional film that did not rely on the mere recording of popular theater scenes. The work was so new to both men that they had the sensation of inventing it; according to Chang,

We discussed the division of the directorial work between us. Cheng was to direct the facial expressions and body movements of the actors and I would direct the placing and changing of the camera.[2]

The actors (with men in the female roles, too) played their scenes in the court-yard of the Asia Film Company; whenever the 200-foot rolls ended, the actors froze in their positions, ready to make the action continue onto the next roll. One of the foreign managers of the insurance company operated the camera. *The Difficult Couple* was shown at the end of September, 1913, along with *War in Shanghai.*

Because of some dissatisfaction, either with the reception of his work or with the money he received for it, Cheng Chen-chiu left the Asia Film Company and did not return to filmmaking again until 1922. Without Cheng's standards and taste Chang Shih-chuan turned out mere "products," short films made with the actors of a new drama group who filmed by day and played, more seriously, by night. The titles[3] give us a glimpse of their ideals in the winter of 1913–1914:

The Living Ghost (or *Bride in Sedan-chair Meets a Live Ghost*)
Five Raps on the Door (or *The Romantic Monks*)
Gabby Visits the City Temple
A Restless Night [a bedbug farce modeled on the Edison farce shown in Shanghai, 1897]
The Murdered Son (or *Blood of the Family*)
The Shop Salesman Loses the Lottery Ticket (or *Sudden Wealth*)
The Bicycle Accident [another imitation of an 1897 success]
Slapping the City Buddha (or *Three Thieves*)
Blind Man Catches the Adulterers
Gambler Pretends Death (or *Dead Men Steal Money*)
The New Camille (in 3 reels)

All of these were made to function as interludes in the theater of the new drama group.* This limited their income to a single Shanghai theater, fatal as film

---

* Even in these superficial subjects there was a progressive step — most of them were set in the present. It was a retrogressive step when the Asia Company capitulated to tradition and ended its career with several opera scenes; *Chang Ban Po, Sacrifice at the Yangtze, Return of the Corrupt Official, Blind Husband Catches the Lover.*

practice, and too late it was discovered that they could make more money by sending them to other communities. Too late, for there was no more film to make prints of them.

Until 1960 the Chinese film industry was either wholly or largely dependent on foreign manufacturers for its equipment and raw film stock. In the early years of the industry this link was so tenuous that the entire industry could be brought to a halt by a crisis at the point of manufacture. When World War I cut off Shanghai's supply of German raw film, the production activity of the Asia Company ceased abruptly. Film production in Shanghai could not resume until 1916, with raw film then supplied from the United States.

Benjamin Polaski, though discouraged, was not yet finished with Chinese film dreams. As he was returning to the United States in 1913 through Hong Kong, he met Li Ming-wei, the actor-manager of a drama company. Their talk resulted in Polaski agreeing to supply the capital and equipment for a film while Li furnished the scenery and actors. The first and only production of the Hua Mei (Sino-American) Film Company was *Chuang-tze Tests His Wife* (*Cosi Fan Tutte* with a macabre ending). Li played the leading role of the wife, and *his* wife, in the small role of a maid, made Chinese film history by being the first Chinese actress to appear on the Chinese screen. The two-reel film was successful, even from Polaski's point of view: he took it to the States, the first dramatic Chinese film to be shown there.

In Shanghai the first producer to take advantage of the newly available American raw film in 1916 was the efficient Chang Shih-chuan. When working for the Asia Company he had tried to negotiate the filming of *Wronged Ghosts in an Opium Den*, a popular and sensational play that disguised itself as a moral tract; in 1913 the successful theater asked more money than Chang or the Asia people could afford. By 1916 the theater and Chang came to terms; he collected capital from several sources to form the Huei Hsi (Dream Fairy) Film Company, to film *Wronged Ghosts* — this was Shanghai's first *Chinese* production company. Lauro, who furnished camera and studio, also worked as cameraman. Chang himself played the principal role of the tragedy:

A wealthy miser has a son who is enthusiastic about public welfare and gives money generously to relieve the poor. His father fears that the family fortune will be wasted in the son's hands and he persuades the son to start smoking opium, hoping that this will keep him idle and at home. The son resists the habit but finally succumbs, spending his days on the opium couch and growing lazy and careless in all matters. Seeing the state of his son, the father realizes that there will be no one to manage the family fortune; he dies of remorse. When the son's wife repeatedly appeals to him to give up opium and watch over the family's affairs, he treats her brutally. Their infant son finds some opium, mistakes it for candy and poisons himself. The opium-smoker's mother is horrified by the deaths of her husband and grandson; she also dies. Meanwhile two shop assistants get their hands on the family wealth and begin to spend it. But the son continues his smoking. When the pleas of his wife are answered by beatings and curses, she drowns herself in the river. After her death the shop assistants sell the property. Plotting with a maid servant they kidnap the opium-smoker's daughter to sell her to a brothel. Then the shop assistants cheat the smoker out of his last funds. Heavily in debt he becomes a beggar, though he manages to earn a little money as a rickshaw coolie. One day his prostitute daughter calls his rickshaw. When they recognize each other they weep, until the mistress of the brothel takes the girl away. He is left by the City Gate where he collapses and dies.[4]

Such an inexorable heaping of disasters behind a screen of social purpose is still a hallmark of the Chinese film. Even in such a "normal" film as *Land Aflame* (1961) the death of a father in a walled-up mine is followed by the arrest and bloody punishment of his son, threats to sell the son's fiancée to prostitution to pay the father's debts, her suicide, a threatened murder with a prominent meat chopper —before the son sees his revolutionary duty. The major change since 1949 is the invariably optimistic, though often forced conclusion.

Wronged Ghosts was still being shown in Shanghai and other cities seven years after its premiere — even by later standards a notable success for a Chinese film — but the Dream Fairy Film Company had vanished.

A more solid Chinese production enterprise began with the failure of an American showman in Nanking. He had brought equipment and films there, "but unacquainted with Chinese conditions" (a pregnant phrase*), he went bankrupt. A friend of his asked the advice of the thriving Commercial Press, a Shanghai publisher and bookshop founded in 1897, and the upshot was that for less than 3,000 yuan the Commercial Press, in the autumn of 1917, opened a Film Department graced by an almost new Pathé camera. Their first employee was Yeh Shian-rung, a student just returned from the United States, who began his documentary photography with "End of Work-Day at the Commercial Press" (an innocent publicity echo of the first Lumière program), and a subject that

---

* An advertisement in the *Moving Picture World* (6 Nov. 1920): "Do you know that you and you and YOU can make money in this market if you approach it properly — if you don't build theatres next to graveyards? China, ever superstitious, is more so over its dead than anything else.

"I have lived in the Orient nine years. I know the traditions, the customs, the creeds a foreigner must know if he is to suceed in business. . . . I can point the way to financial success in China and India."

was to become traditional in Chinese newsreels, the expensive funeral,* in this case that of a Shanghai businessman. At the same time the head of the Press, Pao Ch'ing-chia, had the idea of sending men abroad to learn film technique.

It was just at the propitious moment when these returning trainees were extending the interests of the Commercial Press into profitable drama that China's greatest actor joined forces with them. Mei Lan-fang remembers the accidental encounter:

It was in 1920 that I made films for the first time. At the end of that year's spring our [Peking] troupe went to Shanghai to perform in the Tien Chan Theatre. I was acquainted with the assistant manager of the Commercial Press, Li Pa-ke. At a dinner-party he mentioned that the bookshop's photographic department had recently imported some film apparatus from the United States. "If you are interested, you are welcome to try your hand at filming." I replied, "I've never had any experience in making films, but I'd like to try." . . .

Some days later Mr. Li Pa-ke introduced me to people working in the photographic department of the Press. Exchanging general opinions on filming, we fixed a date to film "Spring Fragrance Disturbs the Study."† We started work just after the Dragon Boat Festival, using a large glassed-in shed, big enough and with equipment good enough. . . . We made our first film without any especially trained film director. The cameraman [Liao Un-so] indicated the space for our playing, and left the rest to us. . . .

For an opening close-up I covered my face with a fan, slowly lowering it to show my face, mischievously smiling. The day we filmed that shot a friend who worked in a foreign film company visited our improvised stage, and complimented us on the idea of this opening.[5]

The first glass-enclosed studio of the Press was on its fourth floor, but before filming the two plays by Mei several improvements had been made. One inadvertent donor had been Carl Laemmle, president of the Universal Film Company, who early in 1919 made a suspiciously virtuous statement: "the Universal is taking upon itself to aid in the moral uplift of China, India and Japan," yet adding a touch of proud realism : "It may be mentioned here that the Universal is now distributing more pictures over those three countries than it does in the United States."[6] Some pin must have pricked his philanthropic balloon, for I have traced no Universal production being filmed then in China except a serial, *The Dragon's Net*, whose eleventh episode used the Great Wall

---

* Eventually a film record of an expensive funeral (at least in Shanghai) became an accepted item of funeral expenses.
† A scene extracted trom the Ming dynasty play, *The Peony Pavilion*, by Tang Xian-zu. At this age and for this film Mei played the role of the maidservant, Chung-xiang (Spring Fragrance).

and the Temple of Heaven as backgrounds; I can detect no particular moral uplift in its synopsis. It may, however, have been in this location work that the Commercial Press staff rendered Universal sufficient service for the American crew to leave some of their equipment (probably glad to get rid of it at that point) with the Press. Early in 1920 more American apparatus was imported and the Press built a larger studio (60 x 80 feet) under glass, with artificial lighting. This was the studio where Mei Lan-fang filmed "Spring Fragrance Disturbs the Study" (in two reels) and "Heavenly Maiden Strews Blossoms" (in one reel):

Filming technique was quite primitive then, and that is why we used so many uncut scenes in long shot, and so few close shots. Artificial light was just then being introduced, and our use of natural light was not always satisfactory. . . .

On completing these two films I returned to Peking. During the next year (1921) I heard from Shanghai friends that both our films were being shown in cinemas there, along with other productions of the Commercial Press. After a time these same programmes appeared in Peking, at the Gaumont Cinema. Later, I met Mr. Li Pa-ke again and he told me that after Shanghai and Peking our films had been sent to other cities in China, and also to commercial ports in the Pacific, where Chinese overseas audiences had liked them very much. Technically, both films . . . made little artistic contribution to the question of combining the arts of classical opera and cinema, but they had played a role in helping the Commercial Press to build the Chinese film industry.[7]

Mei's encouraging voice has to be heard against some evidence of the Commercial Press's aims. Here, for example, is the synopsis of *Murder in a Good Cause* (a Press film of 1922 that was given the more polite English title of *A Secret Told at Last*):

The niece of a Chinese Cabinet Minister is rescued from drowning by Ming Wei [the hero] . . . . On being rescued, the girl is taken to a farmer's house where the usual post-rescue attachment is established. Ming Wei's entrance into the Minister's family is secured by an introduction, and the hero now pays constant court to the girl until her heart is won.

The uncle is discovered to be a traitor to his country by the hero, who overhears a foreigner offer a million dollar bribe for the signing of a contract. As Ming Wei is a member of a secret patriotic society, he reports his discovery to this fraternity, which decides that the hero must assassinate the uncle. This work he enters upon with grief. . . .

Patriotism, however, conquers, and the uncle is assassinated. Ming Wei is caught and sentenced to death. The girl . . . hesitates to support the condemned man, although she knows that the uncle was engaged in nefarious operations. . . . At length she is persuaded to stand by her lover by a faithful servant who tells her that her uncle poisoned her own father to secure his property. This . . . sends her to the rescue of the condemned man.

Pardon for the lover is secured from the President of China who signs the document while reviewing troops. The story ends with a race with the pardon papers
to the execution ground where Ming Wei in another second would have been
shot.[8]

This is clearly based upon a foreign film model (possibly an American film about
Czarist Russia), as were most of the dramas and comedies filmed by the Press.
More promising for the future were the Press adaptations of P'u Sung-ling's
seventeenth-century *Strange Tales of Liao-chai*, and various old operas — but Mei
did not again work with the Commercial Press.

Another, shorter-lived enterprise was the Peking studio opened in 1920 by a
Frenchman, F. Martin,[9] but the official histories are silent on his efforts or
success. As with other Peking tries before 1937 Martin's studio did not survive
for long: it made one film, *Flight*.

In these first years after the European war several Chinese artists and businessmen, sometimes even realizing that they had to work together, took an initiative
toward film production. Though not in reference to a film industry specifically,
Joseph Needham shows the logic of this timing:

It was not until the first World War, when the European powers temporarily
relaxed their profit-making activities in China, that indigenous Chinese capitalist
industry got a chance to develop. . . . Even so, it never conquered sectors wider
than those of light industry. . . .[10]

The China Film Company was begun in 1919 on a relatively grand scale, with
100,000 yuan invested by a group of businessmen led by Tsang Chi-shih, an
enterprising scholar who had turned his talents into money and political influence. Tsang did everything that was thought necessary — starting a dramatic
school, importing an American cameraman and equipment, building a new
studio outside the city, hiring young talents from the theater* — but the company collapsed after making one Peking opera film, *Four-Gallon Village*; a short
comedy, *The Glutton*; and some newsreels.

Two other equally short-lived companies each made one successful film (with
the help of the Commercial Press studio) before expiring. The China Film

---

* Among them, Hung Shen, just returned from a year with George Pierce Baker in 1924, the
year that Baker moved "The 47 Workshop" from Harvard to Yale; the China Film Company
went to pieces before Hung Shen did any work for it.

Research Society made a ten-reel melodrama, *Yen Rei-hsun*, from a play based on a recent crime (a young embezzler murders a prostitute for her money), sharing production expenses with the theater that staged the play. *Yen Rei-hsun* opened at Ramos' Olympic Cinema in July 1921, made 1,300 yuan in one day (and averaged over 4,000 yuan a week), but the group was unable to make a second film. Kuan Hai-feng, who had worked as assistant on *Wronged Ghosts*, organized the Hsin Ya (New Asia) Film Company and wrote and directed its only film, *Beauties and Skeletons* (English title: *Vampire's Prey*), modeled on a foreign crime film, *Ten Sisters*.* Its low subject matter and imitativeness have doomed *Beauties and Skeletons* to a low place in Chinese film history, but it sounds more spirited and less bound to the theater than all previous Chinese films. The least pretentious but most enduring of the several companies formed in 1919–1920 was the Shanghai Film Company: it was begun by a calendar artist named Tan Du-yu who collected 1000 yuan to buy a camera (from a foreigner leaving China), with no other assets beyond his determination to make films that could compete with foreign films. He directed, photographed, and did his own laboratory work on his first film, *Sea Oath*, with a painter-hero, a happy end, foreign clothes and settings, and subtitles written in classical Chinese verse.†

But a film industry requires more than film production. Films are made to be shown, seen, and paid for, if there is to be any continuity of production. The isolation of the successful *Yen Rei-hsun* or *Beauties and Skeletons* may be explained simply by someone pocketing the profits and going into some other business, but it is more likely that the producing companies were forced into poor distribution or exhibition deals. With some foreign investment most of Chinese film production remained in Chinese control, but the management of income, the theaters, continued in foreign control, especially in Shanghai, already recognized as China's film center. Shanghai's dominant film theaters were under foreign management: Antonio Ramos expanded the enterprises that he began in 1903 with costumed doormen and beating drums until the giant Ramos Amusement Corporation controlled half of Shanghai's cinemas; another Spaniard, B. Goldenberg, a Portuguese, S. G. Hertzberg, and the pioneer Italian, Enrico Lauro, owned other large cinemas in Shanghai; Japanese and British businessmen completed this postwar control.

---

* I have not yet identified this source. Its plot of unsubtle physical action (a gang uses beautiful women as bait for its insurance racket) sounds like a serial film ca. 1916, though it may also have been a serial novel. In 1922 the script was credited to a son of Yuan Shih-kai, but his name was bought for $500 to give "prestige" to the new film.
† One account explains the popularity of *Sea Oath* with an innuendo — its heroine was played by "one of Shanghai's fashionable set."

Advertisement (in the Shanghai *Shun-Bao*, 29 July 1921) for the opening of *Yen Rei-hsun* at the Olympic Cinema on Ching-An Temple Road.

This play, who would not enjoy seeing it? This shadow-play, who would not welcome it?

Whenever the play *Yen Rei-hsun* is shown on any stage, it always takes a great deal of your time. And you must continue to watch it for two or three nights before you reach the end of it. Each spectator's backside becomes sore and his legs go to sleep painfully even before getting halfway through it. But we now employ the most economical method of presenting this play: with one visit you can see it all. Furthermore, the seats are comfortable, and we are positive that the spectator will sing the praises of all these matters.

Our play has ten great chapters. We invested more than six months of effort and a few ten thousands of yuan. The essence of the heart and blood of more than one hundred persons has been concentrated in this production, and the acting stars all enjoyed a superior education; in addition to this, the two characters of YEN REI-HSUN and LIEN YING look exactly alike.

All settings . . . were made and filmed in their real places, and cannot be compared with painted backgrounds . . . [ornament around edge: *shadow play shadow play shadow play . . .*]

Examining contemporary records of film theaters in China after the First World War brings to light a fascinating if somewhat hazardous and confusing commerce. Of the three levels of film audiences the top level, composed of foreigners (business and diplomatic families) and certain Chinese who wished to see foreign films for reasons of official position, financial capacity, educational background, or merely status or "for the recuperation of jaded minds,"* attended film theaters (operated by foreigners and showing foreign, chiefly American, films) in the foreign concessions of the treaty ports. Most of these theaters never considered showing anything but American and European films until the Japanese occupation changed their management.

The English general manager of China Theatres, Ltd., F. Marshall Sanderson, visited the United States in the spring of 1919, chiefly for the purpose of bringing down the prices charged him by American film distributors.† The interviews he gave on that occasion show us the two widely contrasting types of film theater that he operated in North China, for of his fourteen theaters ten "are Chinese houses exclusively. The other four cater to the cosmopolitan element consisting mainly of foreign business men and the staffs attached to the various legations."[1] The Empire Theater in Tientsin had been built two years before by Abdul Bari, a British-Indian subject, and Sanderson added a bar, a café and "a cabaret with a Russian stringed orchestra of five pieces, led by an American." Sanderson proudly reported: "Even the Chinese women are dancing now, a thing undreamed of five years ago." The Pavilion, in Peking, sounds somewhat more conservative in its upperclassness. It had

. . . so consistent a patronage in the legation attachés and their families that certain rows of seats in the house amount to another set of family pews. After dinner in the evening, they come around to see the one show starting at 9 p.m.,‡ and occupy the same seats night after night. The president of China [Hsü Shih-ch'ang who also lent his presence to the happy finale of *Murder in a Good Cause*] is a frequent viewer of the Pavilion's pictures. The patrons pay their four dollars "Mex" or two dollars American money for the big feature pictures. . . .

Sanderson even revealed that of the Chinese staffs in all his theaters the projectionists "sleep in quarters provided by the theatre and are happy on a salary of

---

* The only function for films suggested by an English-educated Chinese writer, Tyau, writing in 1920 (M.-c.T.Z. Tyau, *China Awakened*, [New York: Macmillan, 1922]).
† "American producers have the idea that the whole of China is nothing but a mint turning out money for the moving picture men. . . . They say, 'With four hundred millions of people out there, they must be harvesting money.' So the prices for their films are almost unbelievable."
‡ " . . . the foreigners are all business men and can only find time for pictures after dinner in the evening." — *Moving Picture World*, 14 Aug. 1920.

five dollars 'Mex' per month." Any American film salesman who compared
Sanderson's ticket price with his projectionists' salary would surely be reluctant
to reduce his film fees for Sanderson.

Sanderson's "Chinese houses" were operated in a quite different style:

Mr. Chinaman has queer ideas on the pay-as-you-enter proposition. You don't
catch him paying for anything he can't see. Accordingly such a thing as selling
him a ticket for a movie show is out of the question. You must open your doors
to the crowd, let it surge in, and then start your show.

"After the picture has run for a few hundred feet and we have their interest, we
stop the projection, put up the lights, and take up the money in big baskets,"
said Mr. Sanderson. "The Chinaman puts in his coppers, 3, 10, or 20, according
to the price on the seat he is occupying. Then the lights go out and the picture
goes on." . . .

The Chinaman, Mr. Sanderson finds, cannot sit through a picture show for an
hour and a half without frequent cups of tea and cold towels. Accordingly, the
picture is stopped about every reel for an interval to permit him to imbibe and
to whizz his towel across to an attendant in the aisle, who immediately wets it in
icy water and whizzes it back.

A visitor to Peking in May, 1919, found the film business flourishing:

The cinema was immensely popular and there was an average daily attendance of
three thousand at the half dozen picture palaces established in Peking, in spite of
the fact that the films all depicted Occidental life, or a strange version of it, and
had their captions in English. In the New World [an amusement center north of
the Temple of Agriculture] admission to the cinema was included in the entrance fee [thirty copper cash] but elsewhere the price was about eight copper
cash although the most expensive cinema of all, largely patronized by foreigners,
oost $1.50. . . . As an economical entertainment the cinema already had the
advantage [over the theater].[12]

The United States Trade Commissioner at Shanghai, Lansing W. Hoyt (reporting
in 1923), adds more clarity to the distinction between the two kinds of film
theater:

The average theatre for Chinese patrons charges ten and twenty cents [copper
cash]. If a Chinaman goes to a foreign neighborhood theatre he pays what the
foreigners do, usually $1, or more. A foreigner pays only ten or twenty cents,
however, in a native theatre. "There is no racial discrimination. It is all a question of price," says Mr. Hoyt.[13]

Foreign efforts to extend film showings beyond the treaty ports were constantly
being made and constantly rebuffed. Enterprising Americans never tired of
describing their unexpected difficulties.

There are untold difficulties to contend with in reaching the Chinese in purely Chinese territory, i.e., anywhere except in the Treaty Ports, which at present makes it impossible to carry the picture show to the Chinese in their own cities[!].[14]

This account of 1920 blames "minor officials and the general unsettled state of the country." When a salesman for the Famous Players-Lasky Corporation visited China in 1916—1917 he was given a more circumstantial explanation why there was only "one theatre for every 10,000,000 inhabitants":

It is next to impossible to establish a theatre in the interior of China. The Chinese do not want conflict between the civil and military authorities, and the soldiers insist upon free admission. If this were allowed the theatre would be full of soldiers all the time. When it is refused sufficient soldiers pay for admission to get inside and wreck the house. The civil authorities refuse to interfere . . . the motion picture theatre for the interior of China is a long way off.[15]

Cinema's penetration of China's interior was indeed very slow and troubled. It was not until the summer of 1922 that Kiangchow (Shansi Province), a large town about 900 miles north of Shanghai, saw its first films:

Here, with a tanner's yard as the setting, a projection machine of ancient vintage cast flickering images on a sheet supported by clothes props for the benefit of an audience which had paid a little less than 2 cents a head for the privilege of seeing the new magic. The projection apparatus was supported by a pile of boxes and a shaky table, correct elevation being attained by the addition of broken tiles and old shoes.[16]

Often the first films that reached communities in the interior could not be called "entertainment" in the strictest sense of the word. Here is the sad history, in the mid-twenties, of one advertising agency's bright idea, advertising boats in the interior:

A boat would start out with perhaps six advertising films and these would be exhibited in various small towns along the river or canals. Sometimes the expense of the trip was prorated among the various firms interested and other times a flat rate of 100 taels a month was charged for the exhibition of a film. When the boat reached a suitable village the moving-picture apparatus was set up on deck, a screen adjusted, and the pictures were viewed by the audience from the bank of the canal. Sometimes samples were distributed among the Chinese. This line of activity has, however, been discontinued, because it was not considered to be obtaining the results that the same amount of money expended in other advertising would. The higher-class Chinese thought he was losing "face" if he mixed with a crowd of coolies on the river bank, so he refused to attend free exhibitions and thus it was usually just the curious who were attracted. Then, too, free distribution of samples has not been productive of good results among

the Chinese, as they do not value something they get for nothing; if but a copper
or a postage stamp is required the sample is more appreciated.[17]

There were, however, two foreign nationalities that made an extra effort to
reach the millions of cash admissions in China's interior. A note in 1921:

According to recent reports which I received from a friend — an official stationed in the interior — picture theatres, although but primitively equipped with
portable projectors, are putting in an appearance, showing mostly German and
Japanese pictures.

Of these pictures very little is read in official reports. The American producer
has read that 95 per cent. of the pictures exported to China are American, but he
forgets that these pictures stay in the treaty ports, where the public is of an
entirely different nature than it is in the interior, where now the Germans and
the Japanese are doing the pioneer work and will finally cop the trade. . . .[18]

This successful "copping" may have begun quite early in the century; even
before the World War an English journalist made this comment: "The cinemato-
graph has caught the Chinese taste to such an extent that German and Japanese
firms are making enormous sums in China with moving picture shows."[19] It was
probably in northeast China where they were less disliked that the Japanese
concentrated their commercial enterprise; historians of the Japanese cinema
mention that "Movies were first shown in Manchuria in 1910. They were largely
the products of French Pathé and were shown mainly to the Russians living in
Harbin."[20] And Pathé programs penetrated more deeply into China: in Berlin,
in Gerhard Lamprecht's rich collection of early film apparatus there is a projector that was taken through the interior of China in 1909 by a traveling
Munich showman; with it came a roll of Chinese announcements — all for Pathé
films, carefully retitled to appeal to the publics of small towns and villages. This
energetic traffic by privately enterprising German and Japanese showmen continued well into the 1920s, possibly discouraged only by the increasing hazards
of Chinese travel then.

Of course no German showman would be so careless as to show Chinese audiences any of the German films being made about China. After the normal
number of "Chinese" films made in Germany before the first war, the strange
effect on German films by the loss of her Chinese concessions (beginning with
Japan's prompt seizure of Tsingtao in November 1914) was to *increase* her attention to that part of the world. In general Asian subjects exerted a powerful
attraction for German filmmakers and spectators (escape from the uncomfort-
ably close problems of war, food, and coal may have been one reason for this
interest), but China had a special lure that put the maharajahs and dancing girls

A scholar was hired to give attractive and poetic Chinese titles to these Pathé films, ca. 1909; their original French titles may never be ascertained.

The vertical poster advertises "Easy for an Amateur to Give Commands" (a comedy?) The horizontal poster advertises "Same Heaven, Same Sun" (meaning "Sharing the Same Fate" — a tragedy?)

of India in second place as dramatic material. A symptom of something peculiar about the increased attention to China is that the foreigners who figure in these stories rarely represent Germans: they are British (primarily), Danes, Americans; but *German* heroes battling Chinese intrigue had to wait for Hitler and the Axis.

Many of the best actors of the German silent film seem to have acquired their basic film training beneath Oriental makeup: Krauss, Wegener, Veidt, Goetzke, Lupu Pick all played their Oriental roles with a stylistic gusto that crept into their Occidental roles as well. In *Der Fremde* (1917), a Chinese drama, Werner Krauss (playing a Tibetan prince) and Lupu Pick look quite un-European in the photos I've seen. After the effective exaggerations of his *Homunculus* serial Robert Reinert's *Opium* (1919) looks almost realistic: the Oriental skulduggery of Krauss is given an international range and setting. Only the first "act" is supposed to represent China, actually an ornate Chinese nightmare. One of the last of this cycle was also the most important, artistically: *Die Puppenmacher von Kiang-Ning* (1923), with a scenario by Carl Mayer that probably used China only as an exotic setting for his fable.

Adventure films were even less inhibited. In *Schiffe und Menschen* (1920) an American journalist rescues a young engineer from a Singapore opium den, and at his next port snatches a European bride from Li, "greatest merchant in China" (she has to marry Li to save her debtor-father). Taylor helps Helen to escape by ship, but then has to put down a mutiny — yellows vs. whites. His radio message is memorable:

Can only hold out two more hours. Three cheers for America. Taylor

The mutiny is quelled, the ship reaches New York where Li follows Helen; he tries to poison her, but the film ends with Li's suicide — another scoop for Taylor.[21] In *Die Jagd nach dem Tode*, a serial in four chapters,* the adventurers chased through a fictional Tibet and Turkestan.

Fritz Lang's first work as director was on an adventure serial, *Die Spinnen*, about a powerful international gang of criminals in which a mandarin (!) figures prominently. San Francisco's Chinatown is represented as a complete underground city with secret entrances. A more ambitious, but less inventive serial is *Die Herrin der Welt*, in eight full-length installments that range freely about Asia, Africa, and New York. The heroine is an accident-prone Danish girl (played by

---

* Possibly identical with *Der Tod und die Liebe*, a film about Tibet that was distributed in America in 1921 as *Tradition*.

Mia May, wife of the film's director Joe May) who in Part I (*Die Freundin des gelben Mannes*) arrives in Canton to take a dignified post in a rich Chinese family, but lands instead in a brothel where she is tortured and held prisoner until rescued by the Danish Consul, helped by an overseas Chinese (played by Henry Sze) whom she had met on the ship. Canton is described as "an ant-heap of two million yellow people, scrambling, fighting, toiling ants, a maze of dark alleys, secrets, orgies, horrors, miseries. . . ." What amazed me when I saw it at the Staatliches Filmarchiv der DDR is that Part I including its interiors (rich homes, brothel rooms, etc.) reconstructed Canton with scrupulous care, with all Chinese characters played by Chinese. It was startling to see reproductions of the Pearl River waterfront and Shameen Island (built, I learn, in Potsdamer Havel) where I had expected an Oriental fantasy, and there is something compelling about even the silliest fiction when the backgrounds look so believable. Another by-product of this involuntary belief is that it makes it difficult to dismiss all the fictional cruelties, treacheries, lies, violence. Underneath the fiction, many realities seem waiting to be brought to light.

At the end of the war California was not only the center of the world's film industry, it was also the center of a well-organized and heavily financed campaign against "the yellow races." The expanding industrial farmers of the West Coast wanted no competition from the large numbers of vigorous Chinese and Japanese immigrants, who "should be kept in their place" as a cheap labor force, and William Randolph Hearst adopted the anti-Asian cause as an expedient to help his political ambitions. The newspaper magnate was then beginning to invest in film production and all his interests merged in a serial thriller called *Patria*, with Irene Castle and Milton Sills battling the evil Oriental forces (personified by Warner Oland[*]), who are threatening the security of the United States and the purity of Mrs. Castle. In 1917 Oriental mystery and intrigue were not novel ingredients for films; *Broken Fetters* had had a piteous Chinese heroine whose struggle was resolved only when she turned out to be a white family's lost child, thus breaking the Oriental fetters holding her from her true (white) love, and an earlier serial had the specific title of *The Yellow Menace*. But *Patria*, possibly because of its professional scenario by Louis Joseph Vance, established a pattern that colored the next few film years with threatening mandarins, smoking idols, long silhouetted fingernails, opium pipes, pigtails, and miracles of makeup. By 1919 these elements were inflated to spectacle proportions in *The Red Lantern*:

---

[*] In *The Portrayal of China and India on the American Screen, 1896–1955* (Cambridge, Mass.: Massachusetts Institute of Technology. Center for International Studies, Communications Program, 1955), Dorothy B. Jones describes the steps in the evolution of Hollywood's "Oriental type." (p. 28)

In preparation for the filming of the spectacle Director [Albert] Capellani, his art director, Henri Ménessier, who designed the massive and picturesque Pekin street "set," and Eugene Gaudio, the cameraman, made elaborate tests of the lighting of the street the night before the scenes were "shot." . . .

There were 500 lamps in the Chinese lanterns which hung from every post and from the windows of the Chinese houses. Coolies carried other lamps on poles — seventy-five of them. In the huge red lantern on the palanquin used to carry Nazimova were five 1000-watt bulbs. Besides there were seventy "Broadsides," twenty-five "spots" and a powerful searchlight [to follow the principal players]. . . .

Eight hundred Chinese "extras," imported from all parts of California and garbed at the Nazimova studios, filled the street. . . .

The episode had to do with the sudden, seemingly miraculous appearance of the Goddess of the Red Lantern, borne on a gilded palanquin carried by sixteen men. . . . To the Chinese this meant that she was to be a deliverer. The Boxers seized upon the circumstance to put her, like a Joan of Arc, at the head of their forces which sought to drive Europeans from China.[22]

Nazimova's half-Oriental heroine, recalling *Broken Fetters* and many films since, could not marry her true (white) love, and chose suicide.

Each of the big film-producing countries contributed an adaptation of *Mr. Wu*, an English play by Harry Maurice Vernon and Harold Owen, which had come to mean "China" to the Western world: in 1918 Lupu Pick directed Carl Meinhard as Wu, and Maurice Elvey directed the English version with Matheson Lang in 1920; American studios were as continuously attached to Wu as to Fu Manchu.* Chinese authorities banned the uninhibited Part I of *Die Herrin der Welt* at the same time that they stopped the Peking showing of a French film, *Li-Hang le Cruel* (1920), "because the Chinese are represented in it as a people who are unusually cruel and vengeful."[23] The largest quantity and most pointedly obsessive of Oriental nightmares continued to come from Hollywood. The titles tell much: *Mandarin's Gold, Crooked Streets, The Yellow Arm, A Tale of Two Worlds, The House of Darkened Shadows, Yellow Men and Gold.*

"American Pictures Are Unjust to China," is the title of an incoherent but justified protest by a retired Chinese major living in America. For the sake of the film trade paper that printed it his title is completed: "— Which Is Potentially Great Film Market."

---

* English audiences were also addicted to Sax Rohmer's original villain through a series of films made in 1923—1924: *Mystery of Dr. Fu-Manchu.*

The reason why of all nations of the world the Chinese are picked to be vilified in pictures and much cheap fiction is rather obvious.

The diplomatic representative of any other power would instantly raise objections in Washington were he to notice persistent abuse of his co-nationals in pictures. The Chinese government though . . . has not done so, but the people nourish their grudge deeply in their hearts. . . .[24]

Major Ko does not assume that any of the offensive films actually reached Chinese audiences, but he points out that the number and key posts of Chinese spectators in American audiences were sufficient for the harm to be done at home. Some official objections may have been raised at about this time, for 1921—1922 marks the end of the uninhibited film use of Chinese characters for "negative" roles. A multitude of other, less substantial factors may also have contributed to this perceptible change. In 1921 I was, at the age of eleven, a fully committed Ohio filmgoer; my image of China was already a contradictory one, and I had to reconcile the scheming fiends of serials and dramas with the different, agonized China of the newsreels:

What are said to be the first motion pictures to reach America showing the famine-swept districts in the interior of China are in the current issue of Fox News, Vol. 2, No. 59 [May 1921]. Deserted villages, abandoned even by the vultures which haunted the air day and night during the early days of the famine; river boats crowded with starving refugees, making their way to the coast; relief stations thronged with hungry supplicants, and many other features of the famine are shown, the picture as a whole telling more graphically than any newspaper and magazine articles the story of China's gigantic tragedy. . . .

The picture as shown in American theatres is suited to all classes of audiences, it is said, the element of horror being minimized by careful editing and titling.[25]

Among the filmed sensations of Oriental evil and intrigue only one lyrical and tragic image stood out, The Yellow Man played by Richard Barthelmess in *Broken Blossoms* (1919) by D. W. Griffith, based on the Limehouse stories of Thomas Burke. His gentle, meditative, determined hero is the central force of this American masterpiece. Nevertheless I have seen no reference to this film being shown in China.

Even the most "sympathetic" film treatments of Chinese life — such as the series made in 1921—1922 by the Film Booking Office with its only Oriental star: *The First Born, Where Lights Are Low, The Swamp, Five Days to Live, The Vermillion Pencil* — could never reach China, even through Mr. Sanderson's least Chinese theaters there, for the star was the Japanese Sessue Hayakawa, and only outside China would he be accepted in Chinese roles. Among the last of this period's American chinoiserie: Lon Chaney as Yen Sin in *Shadows* (adapted from a popular story, "Ching, Ching Chinaman"); *East is West* with Constance Talmadge as Ming Toy, a Chinese heroine (finally revealed to be a white girl stolen from missionaries, so that her love for the American hero can be moral), against a background of rather light-surfaced stereotypes; *The Toll of the Sea*, an early Technicolor experiment with the newly discovered Anna May Wong as a Chinese Madame Butterfly (*her* American "eventually leaves her for a girl of his own race").*

This whole disgraceful epoch was summed up by Richard Griffith and Arthur Mayer in 1957:

Defying Rudyard Kipling, East and West met constantly in screen dramas of the Mysterious East. Met and mingled, but rarely blended. Miscegenation or some hint or threat thereof hung over these films like a miasma, but it was usually unmasked or nobly renounced in the last reel. For the rest, the East was neither the emergent Asia we know nor the Yellow Peril of William Randolph Hearst's imagining, but simply a stamping ground for vice — opium dens, gambling hells, white slavery, torture cells, and the like. On the whole it was a not inaccurate portrayal of colonial Asia of three generations ago, a place where the representatives of two colliding cultures corrupted each other.[26]

In the same way that Chinese worried about the portrayal of Chinese in foreign films, Europeans worried about the opportunity to see European and American self-portraits on Asian screens. In a feverish report of 1934, entitled "L'influence pernicieuse du cinéma sur les peuples de l'Orient,"[27] two "colonial experts" point to the same danger. The first is Sir Hesketh Bell, writing in 1928:

While the subversive influences of Bolshevic agents may have played a great part in the general unrest that is pervading nearly every country in Southeastern Asia, another new and even more powerful agency has been gradually undermining the prestige of the white race. It is the cinema.[28]

Sir Hesketh quotes an article that he wrote on this danger for *The Times*, two years before; after going into some detail on the effect of kisses and other "erotic exhibitions" on the status of "the white man and, worse still, of the white woman," he proceeds to the foreign (especially American) film's inspiration for local crime:

The simple native has a positive genius for picking up false impressions and is very deficient in the sense of proportion. . . . The police authorities in the East are unanimous in attributing many of the more important and complicated

---

* Short comedy series, ever watchful for satirical targets, made parodies of these "Chinese" films: *The Chink, Chop Suey, West Is East, Dragon Alley*, etc.

crimes to the suggestions of the cinema. It is, in fact, not necessary for the
people to pay to see the most striking of the violent episodes of a film. Posters
outside a cinema display, with every possible exaggeration, scenes of battle,
murder, and sudden death. . . . To the vast majority of those who pay to see the
show the plot of the film is often quite incomprehensible. Most of the scenes
depict things and situations that they have never even imagined and cannot
understand. But the vivid actions of the actors are clear enough to their
minds. . . .

In *L'Asie contre l'Europe* M. Legendre also grows nervous at the exposure of
simple Asian natives to American film kisses:

One sees attractive ladies, décolleté to their navels, playing with revolvers or
offering themselves to anyone at all with gestures that are all too expressive. One
sees an excess of lovely young girls, their faces and souls evidently open, throwing themselves at a young man, embracing him and pressing an endless kiss on his
lips.[29]

Via the hazards for "la femme blanche" M. Legendre comes to conclusions
identical with those of Sir Hesketh:

. . . the ultimate conclusion that impinges on the narrow mind of the native is
that the *Protector*, the powerful master of white race, is by no means the great
moral figure, the demigod, which he had pictured to himself, and furthermore
that his wife and his daughter did not rise above the low level of indigenous
society with any more shamelessness. This is undeniably the unfortunate result
of the cinema as it has been introduced in Asia and a few parts of Africa. Besides
demoralizing the native and arousing his brute instincts, it delivers the most
severe blow to our race and our prestige, opening the door to Communism and
the agents of Moscow.

The author of the article that quotes these works is A. J. W. Harloff, Ancien
Membre du Conseil des Indes. His proposed solutions are sweeping, including the
total control by each colonial government *lui-même* of all films intended to be
shown to the *indigènes*, and some encouragement (also controlled) of native film
production. Naturally there should be cinemas to please the taste of the Occidental, from which all natives are to be excluded. And finally, to reduce this
"veritable poison for the colonial population and danger for the colonial development work," Mr. Harloff declares:

"Posters of the 'American sensational type' should not be permitted."

Though these unfortunate self-portraits continued to reach Chinese screens,
there is an indication that Hollywood's irresponsible cycle of Chinese subjects
and characters was well over by May 1924 (though the Mah-Jongg craze was at

its height) when the Broadway reviewer for *Moving Picture World* thus recommended a play for film adaptation:

A story of much intrigue is always good picture material, but the question is, is
the public interested in pictures of old China? There hasn't been a good picture
produced along these lines in many years. Perhaps it is about time for the cycle
to come around again.[30]

Fortunately, this reviewer's advice was not heeded, and "to come around again,"
the cycle had to wait twenty-five years for political change in China and Korea.
It may even have been the narrow monotony of Hollywood's treatment of
Chinese subjects that killed them.

One section of this formula — the barriers between East and West — is left curiously untouched in Chinese films of this and even later periods. Except for the
western costumes, overstuffed furniture, plaster Venuses, and fox-trots of Shanghai high life, one never sees even the threat of a dramatic element, "West," that
might come into conflict with "East." Occasional western characters — night-
club musicians who could be either Russian or German, or the "Italians" with
pointed putty noses and blonde curls in the later wartime *Secret Agent of
Japan* — figure in the action, without producing the emotional upheavals of
Broken Fetters or *The Red Lantern*. It is true that many Chinese filmmakers
had European or American training, and that they employed a quantity of Western literary and dramatic sources, all of which might have damped any wish to
reveal East-West antagonisms. This noticeable *absence* of the West from Chinese
films of the twenties and thirties could be interpreted as another, possibly
deeper expression of a conflict felt so painfully by Chinese that even tokens of
it could not find their way into Chinese films. All of this, of course, changed
abruptly after Liberation, or, more accurately, after the Korean War; then every
historical film was employed to dramatize every antagonism for multifarious
purposes: if Manchu officials betray the national interest, see the foreign
advisors standing behind them; if decent reforms are hindered, see the foreign
merchants who stand in their way.

In Shanghai studios the search for the right subject was almost as frantic as the
search for money. In 1921, during one of the many inflationary periods that
swept over the port, it was rumored that the film business could bring fortunes
to courageous investors. Within nine months 140 new "film production" firms
were registered, but by March 1922 only twelve of these were still in business —
the speculators had found other ways to invest their money. Another revival of
hope in film investment as a quick way to wealth struck Shanghai in 1925; of
the 175 film companies formed in China, 141 had Shanghai addresses, but most

of these were no more than an address, an office with a hopeful signboard hanging outside. Operating on the principle that "any kind of film will do," that people were willing to buy cheap tickets for any entertainment, forty of these firms had actually produced at least one film by the end of 1926, though some of these were made in rented hotel rooms (with windows facing south) in less than two weeks, and sometimes using the cheaper positive film for their negative. Throughout the inflated, disturbed twenties the swift turnover produced a curious procession: the "businessmen" and "artists" who found a temporary haven together in film dreams were usually on their way from something poor to something worse. Writers, discarded by literature and looking for another profession, were eager to offer their services for scenarios, publicity, advertisements in verse, even the composition of a highly moral prospectus to attract investors — anything to keep the pot boiling. How to translate the feudal ethics of "beautiful thoughts" and semipornography into profitable films was the main problem.

This newly intense film activity, largely hollow as it was, was nevertheless reported in 1922 to the U.S. Department of Commerce by a recently returned visitor to Shanghai:

The Chinese are so enthusiastic over motion pictures that they have begun producing films themselves. Last year the first Chinese dramatic film [probably *Yen Rei-hsun*] was shown in Shanghai. This was produced, acted, filmed and exhibited by Chinese, and the results were surprisingly good, it is stated.[31]

But Chinese upper circles, as with upper circles everywhere, preferred to ignore native film activities. When a party of prominent Chinese officials (including the current Minister of Finance, Chou Tzu-ch'i) visited the New York studio of William Fox at the beginning of 1922,[32] their spokesman, Mr. Y. C. Kuang, made the position clear: "The American pictures are so much the favorite that the others are hardly worth mentioning."

Asked if there had been any attempt to produce by Chinese companies, Mr. Kuang said there had been such an undertaking. "But I do not know much about it," he added. "Personally I have never seen a motion picture made by a Chinese company. I have heard of two or three companies who attempted it, and understand the results were very crude."

All the filmmakers of China then might have concurred in the description of "crude," but that would not have discouraged them.

Comedy was for a while considered a cure-all for the financial ills of film firms. When the Ming Hsing (Star) Film Company began its activity in March 1922, its director, the tireless Chang Shih-chuan, found Richard Bell, a British resident in Shanghai who gave Chaplin imitations at parties, to play the role of Chaplin in three reels of *The King of Comedy Visits China*, and in *Disturbance at a Peculiar Theater* (where "Chaplin" is joined by "Lonesome Luke" — Harold Lloyd). The first of these had a British cameraman, too (though I cannot penetrate the Chinese characters of his name, Ko-ta-ya — Goodyear?), and the other an American cameraman, Carl Gregory.* As for all the first productions of the Star, Cheng Chen-chiu wrote the scripts, and played small roles, along with actors from the modern drama theater groups and students from the Star Film Acting School, founded at the same time to bolster the company's income.

The third of the Star three-reel comedies of 1922 was *Romance of a Fruit-Peddler* (or *Love's Labor*), with the same director and writer and a Chinese cameraman, Chang Wei-tao. This is the earliest Chinese fictional film that I've seen, and I enjoyed it immensely. Its whole tone is very fresh, as if its makers were excitedly discovering the film medium. It presents a comic view of reality, but it is so clearly *reality* that its actual places and behavior can be considered documentary. Many camera setups give movement and there is only one *stage* scene, an overelaborated fight. There are extended solo pantomimes that do not disturb its film quality, and there is necessarily a certain amount of improvisation (you can detect that economy restrained repeated takes), all to the good. Some action is speeded up "comically," and there is also some purposeful optical distortion. The subtitles are in Chinese and English, and the story is simple: the fruit-peddler sweetheart of a street doctor's daughter arranges more business for his future father-in-law by "fixing" the steps leading to a Mah-Jongg room ("The Whole Night Club"), so that its falling members require the waiting doctor's services; the peddler gets the girl.

Unfortunately, Chang Shih-chuan's ambitions could not be satisfied with such minor works. With the success of *Yen Rei-hsun* as his ideal, he seized upon a new play, *Chuang Hsing-hsun*, also based on an actual crime, to make an eight-reel frightener: Chuang, in need of money, kills his father, cuts him up, stews the pieces and scrapes the flesh from the bones to scatter the corpus delicti. This time Chang went too far into gore and horror, the film's exhibition was prohibited, and the Star Film Company was on the brink of ruin. British and American collaborators withdrew hastily and Cheng Chen-chiu proposed that their remaining funds be concentrated on a safe project, sentimental, moral, and

---

* Then completing his textbook, *Motion Picture Photography* (New York: Falk Publishing Co., 1927).

long. Eight months in production, *Orphan Rescues Grandfather* also rescued the Star Company. It enjoyed all the success that was prayed for,* and the company's future was founded on it. It uses some elements from *Wronged Ghosts*, combined with basic appeals that can be recognized as standard fare in all film-producing countries:

A wealthy son is killed while horseback-riding and his father is left without an heir. A wicked nephew schemes to be made his heir, and invites an equally unscrupulous relative to advise him and share the comforts of the rich old man's household. This relative is attracted by the young widow of the dead son and learns that she is pregnant. The nephew recognizes this as a threat to his future fortune and the evil partners slander her so that her father-in-law drives her from the house. She returns to her father's household and gives birth to a son. Her father dies and she raises her son in poverty and righteousness. Meanwhile the remorseful old man, realizing the true character of the spongers living with him, moves to a school where he invests his money. Unaware of their relationship his ten-year-old grandson [played by Cheng's son] attends the school and becomes a clever scholar, a favorite of the old man. When the grandfather refuses to give any more money to the evil partners, they plot to murder him. It is the little boy who saves his grandfather's life, and he and his mother are restored to their rightful place. With the young widow's share of the family wealth she also opens a free school for the children of the poor.[33]

Aside from the reasons for success clearly visible in this synopsis, *Orphan Rescues Grandfather* appears to have attracted favorable attention — and paying customers — through its careful production: there were comments on its pleasantly contrasted changes of mood and its coherently connected scenes. Today it is looked down upon for the "feudal" determination of its good and evil characters, and for its "bourgeois reformism." Yet severe left critics might note that it was such sentimental stories that established the Star Company so solidly that five years later, when left-wing writers took a serious interest in filmmaking, it was the Star that employed them and became the center of their film activities.

Profits and markets were growing more regular in 1923. *The Chinese Economic Monthly* published a glowing account of the large number of new companies formed for film production in Shanghai, though it added realistically, "As in other lines of business, there have been many failures." Present limits were also defined, but with the usual alluring bait attached:

With the number of show places in the country where Chinese films may be shown limited to about seventy, opportunities for financial gain are not encour-

---

* "Chou Chien-yun, the vice-president, was rumoured to have borrowed his wife's dowry to subsidise the production." A. C. Scott, *Literature and the Arts in Twentieth Century China* (London: Allen & Unwin, 1965), p. 67.

aging. A manager of one of the leading companies in Shanghai estimates that the manufacturing costs of a drama in which a fairly large cast is used would just be covered if the film were exhibited in all these theatres. The profit would be the returns from those theatres outside China where there are large Chinese settlements, as in the Straits Settlements, the Philippines, etc.[34]

In years to come these overseas audiences played an increasingly decisive role in the choice of subjects. They and the city audiences far outweighed the millions in China's harder-to-reach interior. This business account also gives encouraging details of the backing for the Commercial Press Film Department, the Star Motion Picture Company (begun "with a capital of $50,000, recently extended to $100,000 and shares at a par value of $10 each were sold"), the Shanghai Motion Picture Company (the only one of these located in the Chapei District outside the concessions — "Most of the actors are taken from Mr. Tang's circle of friends"), and the British-American Tobacco Company's new film interests. Two companies had recently been incorporated in the United States, the Great Wall Film Company ("with capital of U.S. $200,000 — all shareholders are Chinese overseas merchants") and the Peacock Motion Picture Company, a Sino-American corporation, under the laws of Delaware (capital U.S. $5,000,000) with very big guns among its promoters: an ex-Premier of China and former governor of Shantung Province (Chou Tzu-ch'i), an admiral (Tsai Ting-kan) and twelve others whose names must have looked splendid on the stationery.

In Peking the President of China was not the only exalted personage to patronize the cinema. The Manchu dynasty had never been totally dethroned and the Emperor of China, Henry P'u Yi, was still maintained in the Imperial Palace, where films were brought to him.

Henry . . . was always glad of an excuse for enjoying a quiet hour or two watching a film. A small theatre in the Palace of Established Happiness had been fitted up as a cinema, and few American films made their way through Peking without the honour of a private viewing. Charlie Chaplin and Fatty Arbuckle had been the favourites, but Harold Lloyd had now taken their place, and some Chinese have pretended to trace from this source the curiously owlish style of P'u Yi's horn-rimmed glasses, which thenceforward became his most noticeable feature.[35]

When the Palace of Established Happiness caught fire in June 1923 the eunuchs were quick to blame Harold Lloyd and the cinema wiring — the palace's ill luck with the electric shadows, a tradition established by the Empress Dowager, was continuing.

In these years no central government could claim authority over all parts of China. As foreign powers adopted different warlords to protect their Chinese investment, it was inevitable that each warlord would use his backer to extend his military domain. With big merchants paying the bills, small merchants were bound to suffer. Outside the treaty ports the tangle of civil strife continued to make film showing a perilous career. A theater equipment salesman from San Francisco felt that the business in 1922 was too great a gamble:

In China the war is raising hob with the [film] theatres in Canton and Tientsin. This is no comic opera conflict, but three hundred thousand fully equipped men in the field. The exhibitors simply have to shut up shop in the provinces where the fighting occurs. If one side wins, the money they take in is all right. If the other side happens to come out ahead, the other money makes fine cigar lighters. There are only about fifty theatres in all of China and these along the coast. So it does not take much to put a crimp in the exhibition game in Quaint Cathay.[36]

By 1924 the situation looked even more hopeless to an English proprietor of cinemas in Hong Kong and Canton:

Mr. Ray said that present conditions in China are very unsettled and this is having an effect on theatre patronage. There is scarcely a town, he says, that does not have a little war of its own at least once a month. It is unsafe to travel from one district to another.[37]

Though some of Canton's and Hong Kong's wealth was supporting Dr. Sun Yat-sen's revolutionary activity in the South, many small enterprises, including film distribution and production firms, left for calmer regions. Shanghai, especially its foreign concessions, became the safest place to show films and to make them.

From Yuan Shih-kai and, after his death, from the power struggles of the provincial warlords, Dr. Sun had learned that no help from that direction could be expected for the strengthening of China as a modern nation. He and his Kuomintang party sought new alliances, with the trade unions, with the Chinese Communist Party (formed in 1921), and with the Soviet Union, where the civil war had ended in a consolidated and independent country that was close to Sun's ideal for China. When the First National Congress of the Kuomintang convened in Canton in January 1924, these alliances were publicly announced.

The revival of the Kuomintang gave new spirit to a pioneer of Chinese films — Li Ming-wei, associated in Polaski's Hong Kong venture of 1913. After that fiasco Li waited until 1921 when he and his brothers collected 50,000 Hong Kong dollars to invest in a film theater and, two years later, to begin film production. Their company, Min Hsin (New People), began modestly, with newsreels of Hong Kong and then, daringly, bought studio equipment from abroad, lured a

German cameraman and an American advisor from Hollywood (his Chinese name: Kuan Wen-ching) with the promise of high wages, only to have all this ambition tumble down with the Crown Colony's rejection of his application to build a studio. Instead he took some of his apparatus to Canton, where he joined the Kuomintang party and became its regular newsreel reporter, beginning an important year of work by filming the First Congress in January 1924.

This last year of Dr. Sun's activity, at least in its public manifestations, was recorded by Li Ming-wei in these newsreels[38] of the Canton government. Some, though not all, have been preserved; except where noted, these are single reels:

International Women's Festival [in March]
Opening of the Yunnan Province School for Cadres; Speech by Sun Yat-sen*
Mr. Liao Chung-kai† at the Canton Arms Factory; opening of Young Workers' School
Generalissimo Sun Yat-sen Reviews Canton's Police, Army and Commercial Police (2 reels)
Generalissimo Sun Yat-sen Visits the North East of Kuangtung Province (2 reels)
Dr. Sun Yat-sen Leaves for the North

Dr. Sun's new alliances disturbed the old guard and their foreign backers. The warlord who controlled Peking, Chang Tso-lin, invited Sun to come north to "negotiate." When Sun's party left Canton for Peking late in 1924, Li Ming-wei also left, on a mission of his own. He was to photograph for the North China Film Company five short scenes of Peking opera performed by Mei Lan-fang.‡ Part of Li's payment was in copies of these, edited into two reels, and when no further projects materialized in Peking, Li Ming-wei went home to sell the Mei reels through the South. This was enough to revive his production enthusiasm: the Li brothers built a filming stage in Canton and planned to use Hong Kong for their raw materials and laboratory work. One film was made, *Rouge*, a modern-dress adaptation of a story from P'u Sung-ling's *Strange Tales of Liao-chai*; it was well received by the Canton public, but its release in the spring of 1925 was soon followed by political and economic difficulties for the Li organization that forced them to leave for Shanghai.

---

* This contained the shot of Sun speaking vigorously (see Plate 4) which became familiar in foreign use. At some showings of this film, a wax disk recording of Sun's speech was played with the film.
† Assassinated the following year; father of Liao Cheng-chih
‡ The Feather Dance from *Xi Shi the Beauty*, the Sword Dance from *The Emperor's Farewell to His Favorite*, the Brush Dance from *Madame Shang Huan*, the Walking Dance from *Mu Lan Goes to War*, and "Dai Yu Buries the Flowers," from the novel *Dream of the Red Chamber*. The first four were filmed in an open-air studio improvised on the roof of Peking's Gaumont Cinema; the last scene was filmed in the handsome garden of Mei's friend, Mr. Feng, who occupied the home of a Ching prince. ("The Filming of a Tradition," *Eastern Horizon,* July 1965, p. 16.)

In 1925 the Shanghai film boom was on again. Most of the new companies fell
by the wayside with nothing but beautiful statements to show for their short
careers. The Li brothers and Min Hsin might also have been lost in the frenzy
had it not been for the calculating ambitions of another brother Li (who owned
a jewelry shop in the French Concession) and the several women of his family,
including two wives, a concubine, a mistress, and a daughter.[39] He advised that
Min Hsin turn for a few months to film distribution before venturing into production again. Planning was to be careful, for roles had to be found for each of
his women.

The excitement of film gambling affected Shanghai's foreigners, too. The accu-
mulated Spanish resources of the Ramos Amusement Enterprises were diverted
into production, but quickly withdrawn in 1924 after one unsuccessful drama,
Vengeful Tide — an ominous title — and a short comedy, *The Foolish Policeman*.
The largest Japanese-owned film theater organized the T'ung P'eng (Com-
panionable!) Film Company. American money went into the American-Oriental
Pictures Company (*Shattered Jade Fated to be Re-united*; see Plate 5), and
English money into the China Film Production Company (the only identifica-
tion we have for its unlucky English manager is his Chinese name, Lin Fa Ban –
Ben Renfer?). Even the hardiest of these was out of business by the end of 1925.
In 1922 the advertising department of the British-American Tobacco Company
(a skillfully and intensely managed monopoly begun in China in 1902) employed
William H. Jansen, a wandering English cameraman who was trying his luck in
Shanghai, to make their first advertising film:

I was just on the point of making my departure for more fertile soil, when I
received a note requesting my presence at the office of the British-American
Tobacco Company. . . . I was asked whether I would consider remaining in China
if a satisfactory offer were made [and] I was asked whether I could make
cartoons. . . .

Without knowing the first thing about cartoon making, I found space in a garage,
setting up my equipment . . . and proceeded to solve the mystery of mechanical
action on the screen. Three months was the time agreed upon to produce my
first cartoon . . . the subject of which was a donkey wagging its ears and refusing
to move until it smelled the smoke of a cigarette its Chinese leader lit; the smoke
spelling the name of the cigarette in the air. . . .[40]

The next step was to make simple short films, variously labeled as "town
topics," "scenics," and "educationals," into which the more open advertisements could be inserted and offered free to Shanghai and Tientsin cinemas.
In 1924 this department could afford to buy its own film theaters; it also
financed Jansen to make more ambitious fictional films for it in a carefully

Poster for *Resurrection of the Rose* (1927)

equipped new plant, "one of the most modern and best motion picture studios that at that time could be found anywhere in the world outside of the United States of America." Kuan Hai-feng, the director of *Beauties and Skeletons*, was employed to direct the comedy program; among the cameramen were Emile L. Lauste and a young Russian émigré, Georgi Krainukov.[41]

Two companies financed by overseas Chinese opened Shanghai offices before the profit fevers of 1925. One of these, the Great Wall Film Company, had been formed in New York out of sheer irritation with the picture of Chinese life given in such films as *The Red Lantern* and *The First Born*. The initiative for this venture came from a prosperous Chinese merchant in South Brooklyn, Hon Sang Lum, who excited a few wealthy friends in Brooklyn and Manhattan's China-town to join him in financing a production company, and then visited New York film studios to learn the film business and find technical assistance. At the studio making Rube Goldberg's animated cartoons Mr. Lum met Harry Grogin, who had more enthusiasm than experience to contribute to the new company; he was, nevertheless, a help, according to Mr. Lum:

In the short space of one year Mr. Grogin built and equipped a motion picture studio, instructed a dozen of our men in studio technique and placed us in a position to realize our ambition to go to China and produce Chinese films.[42]

In this studio two short films were made (on Chinese costume and shadowboxing), and the younger Chinese in the company took work in older New York film studios and factories that produced studio and laboratory equipment, to have more experience to take to China.

Grogin went to Hollywood to study the inside of an industry in which he was as yet scarcely more than an amateur. There he met Zeuling L. Loo, a rich, 300-pound Chinaman educated in this country, who, also, had conceived the idea of making Chinese pictures in China.

The outcome was that Grogin signed a contract with Zeuling L. Loo on Dec. 31, 1921, and they landed in Shanghai in February, 1922, with all the latest im-proved movie machinery. . . . Loo succeeded in interesting Chang Chien, a wealthy industrial magnate, who guaranteed ample financial backing.[42]

Grogin and two Chinese university graduates wrote their first film script, a com-edy, *Fool*; for its cast he lured Loo to imitate Fatty Arbuckle, and found his heroine, Miss Margaret Yung, in a missionary school.

The comedy was successful enough, but no second film was begun until 1924, when the company opened an office and studio in the French Concession. A fresh group of intellectuals came in at this time, bringing with them principles and stories from abroad that were only to a limited degree useful or entertaining for Chinese audiences. Ibsen was their guide: "Art must criticize life and blend with life." Their first film in 1924, *Divorcée*, was adapted by Hou Yao, a recent graduate from Tung Nan University, from his own play on women's rights:

A rich young wife divorces her philandering husband and seeks employment as an independent woman. She finds work in a bookshop but she is insulted by the proprietor. Her maid tries to study but is looked down upon by the other students. The *divorcée* realizes the necessity for struggle and becomes Chairwoman of the Women's Suffrage Association. When her ex-husband seeks a reconciliation with her and is rejected, his anger leads him to join a gang of villainous men-about-town in trying to disrupt her work. He disgraces her by calling her a runaway and anarchist, and succeeds in driving her into seclusion. There she is robbed and dies of shock.[43]

Hou Yao's later scenarios for Great Wall drew upon a variety of European writers, not always acknowledged: *The Pearl Necklace* (1925) is taken directly from Maupassant, with the bite removed from the end; *The Star-Plucking Girl* (1925) uses the plot of Sardou's *Tosca*, with a happy ending; *The Hypocrite* (1926), his last for Great Wall, combines *Pillars of Society* with *Tartuffe*. Only in *The Virgin's Vision* (1925) was he inspired both by Chinese literature and direct experience: the suffering that he saw in traveling through war-torn provinces was the direct impetus for this film against war.[44]

The other group that was chiefly supported by overseas Chinese was the Shen Chou (Wonderful Continent) Film Company. It was incorporated with less than 50,000 yuan in 1924 by Wang Shü-ch'ang, a wealthy young man who had studied film production in France. He began his professional career as chief cameraman for the Star Company, and then issued a manifesto for a new company that was to make films around "a concealed message." The power of manifestos! This term is permanently attached to the two years of Shen Chou's productions, though their "message" is no more concealed than in other Chinese films of the twenties. Whatever the message of their first film, *Unbearable to Look Back* (1925), it cannot be called concealed:

The daughter of a vegetable peddler helps a destitute young gentleman, and they fall in love. Tempted by women and luxury, he leaves her and she becomes ill. His rich girl friend kicks him out and he returns to the poor girl — but too late: she is dying. He is left alone, broken, desolate, picking up the poor girl's things — her needle and thread —to look at these relics of his love. The final title:

The things of the past are like smoke
And I cannot bear to look back . . .

and he staggers out of the room.[45]

The needle and thread is an emotional detail with a pure film quality, but the
film is burdened with a mass of symbolism that was already too familiar in
1925: doves of innocence, and overflowing teacups of forgetfulness. Yet the use
of *any* details within such a simple story line was a notable victory for Chinese
films of the time.*

On Dr. Sun's way North it had become clear that he was seriously, fatally ill
with cancer, and on 12 March 1925 he died in Peking. The revival of the Kuomintang might have been expected to subside back into talk after Sun Yat-sen's
death, but instead the loss of their leader became a rallying call to action, and
their left alliances put bone into the action. In Shanghai a strike in a Japanese-
owned cotton mill expanded into direct challenge to the authority of the International Settlement. Students joined the demonstrations and on 30 May 1925
thirteen students were killed attacking a police station in Nanking Road. An
hour after the shooting a film crew of the Yu Lien Film Company arrived on the
scene. There was still some struggling between police and students to be filmed,
and this opens the two-reel film that was soon edited, *The May 30 Tide in
Shanghai*. Also shown were the funeral ceremonies, the following demonstrations, the student activities with leaflets and meetings, and the wounded in the
well-guarded hospitals (the doctors disguised the crew as internes and nurses, and
smuggled in the cameras as medical equipment!). The completed film was forbidden public showings in the International Settlement, but the film found its eager
audience, somehow.

In response to the "May 30 Massacre" the dock workers of Hong Kong began a
strike that spread to Canton. On 23 June police of the British and French communities fired on a Canton demonstration and the long murmured indignation
against the imperialist powers' occupation of Chinese territory exploded. The
Canton—Hong Kong strike lasted for sixteen months and gave new powers and
fresh dreams to the National Government that Dr. Sun's followers formed in
Canton. Its army was headed by Chiang Kai-shek.

Little of this history was recorded by either Chinese or foreign newsreel cameramen. Li Ming-wei had left Canton, and the European and American newsreel
companies kept their employees and free-lance cameramen close to the official
center of China's government, Peking, with an eye on Shanghai. Only the Hearst
organization, its Yellow Peril campaign not quite forgotten, had the imagination

---

* I must remind the reader that, here, as with most of the cited films of the twenties, I am
dependent on Cheng Chi-hua's description. I have not seen this film, and I'm not sure that
he has either.

to assign a cameraman of ingenuity and initiative to the new revolution stirring in the South. Edgar B. Hatrick, in charge of Hearst's film interests, took the responsibility of sending Ariel L. Varges to follow the military and political movements spreading from Canton and, in the words of later publicity, "to wait for the lid to blow off." Whatever Hatrick's motive, it is to him and to Varges that historians now owe their opportunity to see, in some degree of actuality, critical Chinese events of the next two years.

A less continuous but equally important newsreel source for the events of 1925 was given by a Soviet crew that happened to be in China that year. The original reason for the presence there of director Vladimir Schneiderov and cameraman Georgi Blum was to accompany and record the historic flight from Moscow to

Peking via Mongolia. But once they arrived in Peking they decided to ask permission to travel and film more widely in China, to work in Peking, Tientsin, Nanking, Shanghai, and Canton. This film, entitled *Civil War in China*, far outweighed in interest their planned film, *The Great Flight* — both shown in Soviet cinemas before the end of 1925. The *Civil War* film preserves a record of demonstrations in Shanghai, of foreign intervention armies, and the people's military defense against counterrevolution in Canton. Considering its historic value, it is surprising that so little use has been made of this precious footage (both the Schneiderov-Blum films have been preserved in the Moscow archives).

The bitter feelings towards foreigners, and especially the British, caused by the Canton—Hong Kong strike and the actions of the foreign police of Canton, found an economic expression: a boycott of British and other foreign goods. This popular movement spread quickly to Shanghai where the boycott pinched British merchants even more painfully. The British-American Tobacco Company suddenly discovered that people were not smoking the cigarettes advertised by

the expensive films shown in their newly purchased theaters. Their first fictional films, a full-length comedy, *One Yuan*, and a shorter fantasy, *The Wonder-
working Priest*, had the bad luck to be released on the eve of the May 30 shooting in Shanghai, and these films, made with the profits of a foreign tobacco
monopoly, found themselves, along with the English-backed *Mirror of Youth*,
under a barrage of attacks, as "cultural aggression" products. The article, "A
Frank Warning to the British-Americans and to Lin Fa," threatened that if these
foreign-controlled films do not show Chinese in a more polite light, "we will
take mass measures to control foreigners who make films in China."[46] From
then on the film enterprises of the British-American Tobacco Company fought a
losing war against the angry magazines, heartened by the spreading boycott. The
studio turned from dangerous comedy to safer classic subjects, but it was hopeless. The critics turned on Jansen, now directing these, for wearing a Ching
dynasty robe during the filming. Two decades later, the only pleasing gesture a
foreigner could make was departure, but Jansen took his last film, *Willow Tree
and Butterfly Marriage*, and sold it energetically abroad as *Legend of the Willow
Pattern Plate*,* and with the proceeds established a new Shanghai firm with an
extremely flexible program, Industrial and Educational Films, Inc.

As the National Army started in the summer of 1926 on what came to be known
as the "Northern Expedition" and the "First Revolutionary Civil War," the
Hearst cameras seem to have been the only ones to cover the series of victories.
(Later in 1927 several film companies issued grandiloquently advertised "documentary" films of the Northern Expedition, but these showed little of the
expedition except in adulatory subtitles about Chiang Kai-shek. Li Ming-wei put
together his Cantonese newsreels of Sun Yat-sen under the not quite honest title
of *Record of the Revolutionary Army's Battles on Land, Sea and in the Air*;
other companies issued films entitled *Military History of the Revolutionary
Army, History of the Great Northern Expeditionary War, Record of the Revolutionary Army's Northern Expedition*, but at this distance we must be suspicious
of their pretensions.†) Sometimes Varges set up his camera behind Chiang's

---

* It was first shown "in London before Her Majesty Queen Mary and other members of the
royal family. This film had a record of 263 bookings in Great Britain and Ireland alone, and
in March, 1930, was still being shown at the Piccadilly Theatre in London, four years after its
original release in the city." — Jansen, in *American Cinematographer*, Feb. 1931.
† No direct reference to the Northern Expedition in fictional films of the time is known.
Aside from later oblique plot uses of the Canton revolutionary base, as in *Daybreak* (1933),
Statue of Liberty (1935), *Unchanged Heart in Life and Death* (1936), and *The Way to Love*
(1949), there continues to be almost as complete a film silence on both the victories and
defeats of 1926—1927 as on the Boxer Uprising of 1900. I have seen only one film to treat
this period in any detail, *A Revolutionary Family* (1960), based on the memoirs of a woman
participant, Tao Cheng.

increasingly confident armies, but more often he moved with the permits of the retreating warlords, who were in a better position to know the value of a favored newsreel cameraman.* The efficient organization and ample funds even made it possible to hire promising Chinese cameramen (the later famous "Newsreel" Wong began his career here), equip them with good cameras and supply lines, so that International Newsreel could cover *both* sides of a battle or siege. In February 1927 they arrived in Hankow along with the victorious Kuomintang soldiers, so that the startling news going abroad that the British had been forced to leave their concession there was almost immediately followed† by Varges's record of Hankow crowds entering the sacred shops and banks, and of the foreigners hurrying to their gunboats in the river. British prestige in China never fully recovered from the Chen-O'Malley agreement that, for the first time since the Opium Wars, brought a foreign concession back to China. And Britain's Foreign Office never forgave Eugene Chen, the overseas Chinese from the British colony of Trinidad, the author of the agreement and initiator of the earlier anti-British boycott.

In the face of the approaching revolutionary tide the Shanghai film industry grew not only less revolutionary, but less real. This was the period of the first attention of the entire film industry to Chinese literary sources little noticed before: classical novels and stories, Peking opera, fairy tales, myths, and folklore. On the surface this looks like the escapist tendency of a speculative industry: for this reason Chinese film historians view this period with abhorrence (regardless of the fact that these same classic materials are used by Chinese films today). But these "old subjects" were so extremely popular with film audiences then that we are forced to look beneath the "escapist" surface and beyond the ticket-buyer's wish to forget for a couple of hours the huge political issues and

---

* At the end of 1923 the British-American Tobacco cameraman made a film in the Northeast for Chang Tso-lin's benefit, *Autumn Manoeuvres of the Army*. Most of the existing Chinese newsreels of this period were obviously made as flattering gestures to him and other warlords. An American traveler-photographer, Harry A. Franck, noticed Chang Tso-lin's camera nerves on this occasion: "When another American, armed with a motion-picture outfit and full credentials, was introduced into the war lord's residence by one of his most trusted officials, General Chang the younger, his son and commander-in-chief of his armies, came to look things over in person, and even then the father cautiously examined the camera when he appeared, and a dozen of his personal body-guard . . . stood behind the camera-man with rifles loosely slung in the crook of their elbows during the filming." *Wandering in China,* 1923, p. 77.
† "There are no railroads running out of Hankow to Shanghai, and Varges sent the [negatives] by boat down the Yangtze river to Shanghai, a distance of more than six hundred miles, where they were placed aboard a steamer for Vancouver, B.C. In the latter city the films were taken off the steamer and sent by airplane to New York, with the result that they were shown [in U.S. theaters a little over three weeks after] the disorders started." — *Exhibitors Herald*, 26 Feb. 1927.

the prospect of disturbing change that were coming down upon Shanghai. It seems to me more significant that the *other* kinds of films, those of "modern" subjects, had even less connection with their audiences: rarely drawn from modern Chinese life, they were usually content to give Chinese backgrounds and costumes to imitations of foreign, usually American, films. To turn from these could be interpreted as a healthy tendency of the audience. Less healthy, perhaps, is the Chinese spectator's love of tradition, with all the security and serenity that tradition represents; in that light it is remarkable that the film industry waited this long to turn backwards. Whether the motive now was merely money or a countering of the approaching revolutionary threat, the choice was a wise, if not bold one. It was a wise artistic choice, too, for classical Chinese literature is conspicuously "visual" and can be ranked with the imagery of Elizabethan writing for the theater.*

Before the general rush to these new (old) sources, the few established companies increased their product without any better defined aim than before, and the dozens of new companies mushrooming in 1925 added to the confusion. After the success of *Orphan Rescues Grandfather* the Star staff pursued a well-intentioned but maudlin-sounding series on the difficult life of Chinese women: *The Soul of Yu Li* (1924), *The Last Kind Gesture* (1925), *A Woman of Shanghai, The Blind Orphan Girl*. The plots do not sound original and, in Cheng Chi-hua's words, they "touch social phenomena, but only as a surface to float upon." At least the dramatic solidity of this company was reinforced by the employment of Hung Shen, recently arrived from George Pierce Baker's play-writing class. His scenarios for *Young Master Feng* (1925) and *Give Early Birth to Noble Son* (1925), both of which he also directed for Star, sound like personal observations. He neglected his plays and left a post as teacher of English; his friends and colleagues all opposed his new work. A professor warned him, "The ethics of the film world are very thin, not to mention Shanghai's own ethics — no better than Hollywood." He even received anonymous letters of advice: one student blurted, "Hung Shen has prostituted his art." Ten years later in a too elaborate apologia for his choice, Hung Shen wrote, "I consider film-making a proper occupation, where I can work hard to feed myself, just as a rickshaw coolie sweats for a few coppers to buy food — there's nothing disgraceful about that."[47]

Another lasting contributor entered Chinese films at this time. Ouyang Yu-chien was a talented, happy-go-lucky Peking opera actor and playwright who wandered into films less decisively than Hung Shen, but in the same way — writing flowery

---

* See Chapter 12.

announcements of some new film company's ideals. When the Li brothers resumed Min Hsin's production, they hired both Ouyang and the exile from Great Wall, Hou Yao, to write their first scenarios. Ouyang's first attempt, *Pure as Jade, Clear as Ice*, was, normally for that time, a Chinese variation on a familiar plot. But he became excited by the new medium and his next scenario, which he was allowed to direct, was a completely original work. *After Three Years* (1926), a story of a large family, grew out of a passionate feeling: "I hated the big feudal family system," Ouyang later explained. He took his direction job seriously: "It's easy to call 'Camera!' but I didn't know when to call 'Cut!,' and I found it was even more difficult in the cutting room to decide *where* to cut," and thinking about his problems kept him awake at night. The production had to be hurried at the end as some gentleman near their Nantung studio, outside Shanghai, accused Ouyang, who was from the South, of being a communist and sympathetic to the southern revolutionary army.[48]

At the Commercial Press a young writer also tried to break the tight pattern. Yang Hsiao-tsun, a clerk there who wrote stories in his leisure time, was given the chance to direct a scenario of his own. Despite its title, *The Drunkard's Remorse* (1925) deserves attention. Yang declined to use professional actors and cast the film with teachers and university students whom he met at discussions of a film society. It was six months in production and not a success, but the enthusiastic amateurs felt rewarded for their efforts.[49]

The most explicitly reactionary stories came from the merger of the Great China and Bai Ho (White Lily) studios. Formed in 1924, the one by a successful speculator, the other by a dye merchant, each company showed its hand with its first production. Great China's first film was *Hearts of the People*:

The owner of a textile mill has a son who marries secretly. When a child is born, the mill owner learns of the wife and forces his son to leave her. Later a strike at the mill is planned; the deserted wife overhears the plans and immediately informs an army officer, who brings troops to suppress the strike. This delights the father-in-law and he allows the young couple to resume their marriage.[50]

Bai Ho's first film was *The Girl Tea-Leaf Picker*:

A rich young gentleman falls in love with a tea-leaf picker. His father opposes this match on social grounds, and chooses the daughter of a rich family for his son's wife. It is eventually disclosed that the poor girl also comes from this family, so the young lovers are allowed to marry.*

---

* This was adapted from a modern novel, *The Mulberry-Leaf Picker*, but more was changed than its title: in the novel the obstacle of the different social positions of the lovers leads to their suicide.

In June 1925 the two companies joined forces with more stories of the same sort: *The Little Foreman* (1925), *Naked Shanghai* (1926), *Father-in-Law Visits Father-in-Law* (poor country folk misbehave when they visit city relatives), *Circle of Debt* (three sets of couples indulge in clearly described exchanges of partners), and so on until 1929.

The Tien Yi (First Under Heaven) Film Company was formed in June 1925 by a wealthy lawyer, Hsiao Tsai-weng, who wanted to invest his money and, what is more unusual, wanted a chance to direct films. His first films have a distinct moral though silly tendency, always with a Buddhist inclination. *Instantaneous Transfiguration* shows a warlord's reform under the influence of Buddhist principles: slay not, steal not, lust not, be not light in conversation, drink no intoxicants. Attaining enlightenment, he first reforms his army by setting them onto road building, while he himself, after sending away his wives and concubines and dispersing his wealth, goes "into the mountains" to become a hermit. It's hard to realize that such a film could be made seriously in 1925,[*] though the Moral Rearmament films of today are peculiarly similar. It was the Tien Yi Company that initiated the classical subjects that characterize the Shanghai films of 1926 and the next few years.

When the British-American Tobacco films closed shop at the end of 1925, the Tien Yi studio bought their junked equipment and expanded its production program. The Buddhist tendency of their first films led lawyer-director Hsiao and his scenarist brother to look for subjects in classical Chinese, often Buddhist literature. During 1926 ten films were made whose immediate success forced all studios to follow suit:

The Tragic History of Lian Shan-po and Chu Ying-tai was a tale of faithful lovers that can be found in the repertoire of every Chinese opera troupe.

The Pearl Pagoda (made in two parts) derived from an ancient popular ballad.

Tale of White Snake, the Constant Spirit (made in three parts) was a legend also to be found in many Chinese opera variants.

Lady Meng Chiang was the legendary widow who sought revenge on the emperor who had killed her husband, an engineer of the Great Wall.

Monkey Fights Golden Leopard was an episode from the great comic novel by Wu Cheng-en, *Pilgrimage to the West*, translated into English by Arthur Waley as *Monkey*.

---

[*] By coincidence(?) General Chin Yun-p'eng's military career ended in 1926, when failure sent him into retirement in the British concession in Tientsin. In the summer of 1931 he became a Buddhist monk.

Tang Bo-hu Burns the Incense [or, *Marriage of Three Smiles*] (in two parts) was the story (found in several forms) of a Ming dynasty painter whose persistence won him the wife he wanted.

Shanghai producers combed Peking opera repertoires, ransacked Ming and Ching storybooks, but never went very far from the successful territory staked out by the Tien Yi innovators. *Pilgrimage to the West* remained the favorite source, with *Shuei Hu Chuan* (*Water Margin*, or *All Men are Brothers*) and *Romance of the Three Kingdoms* furnishing some of the most cinematic plots.* Later productions did go further, however, in the matter of looking like the past, for Tien Yi's films had usually worn any clothes that were at hand. Now the renters of Peking opera costumes did great business with the film companies, and the "opium films" were more scrupulously dressed. There was only a smattering at this time of the fantastic and the supernatural — the demons and ghosts were waiting offstage for a darker period of Chinese history.

The years 1926—1927 seemed a dark enough winter to the Shanghai entrepreneurs and speculators. The approaching revolution promised nameless terrors for them. Antonio Ramos liquidated the assets of the Shanghai Amusement Corp. and took his money back home to Spain. An attempted uprising in February was met with executions and torture. The International Settlement was so nervous that Cecil De Mille's *Volga Boatman* was barred from their theaters by "the Constitutional Defense League, which charged the Russian revolutionary scenes might be provocative of Chinese disturbances."[51] When the Embassy Theatre orchestra, accompanying the first and last Chinese performance of *The Volga Boatman*, played the Marseillaise, outraged Frenchmen hurled cushions at the musicians.

Toward the end of March the army, Blues and Reds still together, was outside Shanghai, and the Varges organization was already inside the city.

Shanghai's confusion of soldiers, refugees and lost children is depicted by International Newsreel in Issue No. 26. . . .

The pictures portray the terror that reigns in Shanghai, and the wild scenes as the besieged city awaited its fate. It is difficult to describe the abject horror depicted upon the faces of the luckless Chinese, rushing for protection behind the barbed wire entanglements. Some idea of what brings this horror upon them is shown in brief glimpses of the "street of death," in the heart of the native district. The toll that has been taken by the broadsword of the executioner is

---

* Note that it was essential for the stories to be *familiar;* it was several years before the tales in *1001 Nights*, easily adapted into Chinese terms, were touched by Chinese studios.

apparent from "bird cages" strung on telegraph poles, which contain grim and gruesome reminders of the vengeance of the mobs.

. . . Meantime two native Chinese cameramen, Wong and Liu, were obtaining scenes of the horrors enacted in the native portions of the city, into which a white man would not have dared to venture. Other native cameramen, later assisted by Wong and Liu, covered the development at Nanking and points to the North of Shanghai.[52]

The "developments at Nanking" were more violent than at either Hankow or Shanghai. The subtitle of an English newsreel (Topical Budget) describes the state of mind precisely:

CHINA, THE REIGN OF TERROR: English and American Refugees Take to the Shelter of Warships at Nanking as Chinese Wrath Flames Against All Foreigners.[53]

It was only outside the Chinese film industry that any attempt was made to reflect in films the revolutionary wave moving northward from Canton. Yet so long as material and other reasons hampered amateur film enthusiasts in Shanghai, this could be no more than a gesture. Operating on excitement instead of money the South China Film Drama Society took its name from an equally brave journal that was paid for by a poor young editor, T'ien Han, working in a publishing firm. He was always proud of the fact that he had become nearsighted seeing too many films in Tokyo (where he was supposed to be busy preparing for a teaching career), and when the publication of his first play, *Violins and Red Roses*, led young film people to invite him to work with them, he leapt at the opportunity: "It was like finding a new love, and I temporarily put aside my ideological depression." The young society issued a charter whose preamble, written by T'ien Han, is a heady mixture of modern Japanese aesthetics and Chinese idealism:

Wine, music, and cinema are the three great creations of humanity. Of these the cinema is the youngest and most powerful. It can stimulate minds into day-dreaming. Dream is the free movement of the heart and it mirrors the sadness of the oppressive world. There is no limit to the cinema's ability to spread ideas. . . . The aim of this organization is to show through film the deep sadness of our people. We'll apply our collective strength and our pure attitude to achieve this. We'll work hard and hope for success.[54]

T'ien Han developed this ecstatic note in a much reprinted manifesto entitled "The Silvery Dream." The first action of the Society was to recover a scenario that he had written for the Shen Chou Company, who had shelved it. This was called *To the People!*, directly inspired by a Japanese poem hailing the nine-teenth-century Russian *narodnik* movement (intellectuals volunteering to teach the peasants) as a model for young Japanese intellectuals to follow. This rather confused background was matched by a scenario of wordy ideals but little action: it opens on young Chinese university students in a café welcoming a revolutionary Russian poet who describes his travels through the Orient and stirs the students' minds! But it is the only film of the period that seems to welcome the revolution rather than resist or ignore it, the only attitudes of the film industry in 1926 and 1927. Unfortunately, but not entirely surprisingly, it was never completed. By selling or pawning personal belongings, the young people raised 200 yuan, and when this was spent, after a sporadic year of production, the film stopped. T'ien Han, who was also directing, even hurried out another scenario for the Star Company (*Dream by the Lake*), in order to pay for a few more feet of *To the People!* He describes this failure as "a tragedy of the times," but it is good to know of such an effort* in those difficult days.

The climax of tragedy can be told in Felix Greene's even-tempered words:

When, in 1927, two years after Sun's death, the revolutionary armies under Chiang Kai-shek approached Shanghai in the great 'northern drive' to unify China, Shanghai's workers, then under Communist leadership, seized the city and opened the gates to Chiang's forces.

. . . immediately after the occupation of Shanghai . . . Chiang broke with the Communists. Shanghai trade unions were dissolved, twelve thousand workers, supposedly Communists, were executed in three weeks, and another fifty thousand imprisoned or put to death within the year. By a curious stroke of fate Chou En-lai, who had helped to plan the rising of the workers, was one of the few Communist leaders to escape from Shanghai.[55]

Chiang's big triumphant deal with the foreign and Chinese lords of China might be thought guarantee enough for the Shanghai foreigners' safety, but the large number of cameramen already there and arriving daily to cover this bloody chapter were still given a fright or two:

Surrounded by a mob of angry Cantonese sympathizers at Yu Yuen Road and the Shanghai-Hangchow Railway, three American photographers were robbed, pelted with stones, beaten with bamboo poles and rescued from certain death by a Cantonese officer and a number of Cantonese soldiers on Tuesday afternoon.†

---

* The Society continued its efforts, both in unfinished films and on the stage, until 1930 when the Kuomintang authorities saw T'ien Han's "slightly altered" version of the opera, *Carmen*, and abruptly dissolved the Society. Much later (August 1966) both T'ien Han and *Carmen* were attacked by Chinese Communist authorities: Bizet was solely concerned with selling "the cult of sex and individualism."

† An April news item from the *Shanghai Times* quoted in the *Motion Picture News*, 6 May 1927. The photographers were G. T. Rucker of Pathé News, James Seeback of Fox News, and T. E. Grant of the London *Daily Mirror*.

In Canton the revolution held out longer, but when Chiang's forces wiped out
the Canton Commune the persistent Jansen was on hand to record the tragedy —
just another item for the newsreel:

[Jansen] took many moving pictures of executions in China in connection with
the Canton Red uprising, and he says that man after man just about to be shot
by the executioner would direct his last glance to the lens of the camera and
assume the best possible pose. Mr. Jansen used an Eyemo movie camera all
through those turbulent Canton days. He says things were frequently moving too
fast . . . to set up a tripod.[56]

In 1926 Russian advisors and the Soviet orientation of the Kuomintang movement produced four events of considerable interest but of little influence on
either the Chinese film industry or the Chinese audience.* In December an auditorium in Canton was crowded with the leaders and members of the revolutionary government to see a new Soviet film that had gained a world reputation in
the past year. The already strong Soong family, including the widow of Sun Yat-
sen, was present. Two of the sophisticated children of the Foreign Minister,
Eugene Chen, had just arrived from England and anticipated little to interest
them in the film to be shown. The propaganda workers in the Whampoa Military
Academy waited with more excitement; one of these may have been Chou
En-lai. Whatever this audience expected, they were swept off their feet by
Battleship Potemkin: they cheered the red flag of the successful mutiny and at
the film's conclusion they stood in ovation to the sailors of the *Potemkin*, to the
Soviet Union, to the power of films, and to Eisenstein. In Shanghai the Soviet
Consulate arranged another screening of *Potemkin* for Chinese writers and
artists.[57]

It was at about this same time that Eisenstein, in Moscow, was reluctantly
relinquishing the project of a film to be made in China. Sergei Tretyakov had
brought back from his teaching years in Peking University (at the same time Lu
Hsun taught there) a determination to take a Soviet film crew to China, and in
the enthusiasm of persuading the makers of *Strike* and *Potemkin* (Tretyakov and
Eisenstein had worked together in the Proletcult Theater) to join his project, his
script outline had swollen to a film trilogy, *Zhung-guo*, covering all the most

---

* The first Soviet films known to have been shown in China were seen, but not publicly, in
1920 in Harbin by the staff of the Trans-Siberian Railroad. A film of Lenin's funeral was
shown at memorial services in 1924 and 1925 in Peking, Tientsin, and Canton, but its
significance *as a film* may be gauged by the fact that Chinese historians do not know that it
was made by Vertov.

dramatic aspects of modern Chinese history, most of which Tretyakov had himself witnessed.*

The proposed title for the first part of *Zhung-guo* was "The Yellow Peril":

General idea — China tortured from two sides, by the Five Imperialists and by its own generals and bureaucrats, sometimes bursting with individual chaotic protests.[58]

Its story follows Soldier Li through Peking's history in the early twenties, the warlord period. An introductory paragraph of the outline shows Li's earlier job, as boatman on the Yangtze at Wanhsien:

A cargo boatman at the Wanhsien docks indirectly causes the death of Hawley, an American exporter and shipping agent. The boatman [Li] saves himself by running away and by selling his daughter to a dealer in children. An English gunboat aims its guns at Wanhsien, to enforce its demands on the city authorities: a ceremonial guard for Hawley's funeral, a monument to be erected in his memory, and the execution of two members of the boatmen's union. Petitions from the city are of no use and sailors [from the gunboat] seize the telegraph, and carry out the execution. The gunboat's captain, who had taken part in the suppression of the Boxer uprising, describes the uprising to the Europeans who have sought refuge on his ship. As a protest a Chinese boy-servant hangs himself in the door-way of the captain's cabin . . .

The title of the second film was to be "The Blue Express":

General ideas — China ceases to be afraid of foreigners and spontaneously defies them. Basic material — the China of countryside and of the city bourgeoisie. The China of declassed bandits.

The setting of this part was to be Shanghai, the countryside, and the train:

Through the flooded provinces of China runs "The Blue Express" — from Shanghai to Tientsin. Floods drive crowds into cities. Beggars appeal at every side. Unemployed besiege the American-owned mines, bring down wages and create conflicts among the workers. . . . Some of the peasants form outlaw bands. . . .

At the station [in Shanghai], surrounded by missionaries, directors, agents and Chinese compradors, the American billionaire's niece amuses herself by flinging coppers to children, who can reach them only by crawling through barbed-wire barriers.

---

* In newsreels of Sun Yat-sen's funeral Tretyakov can be seen walking behind the Soviet Ambassador, Karakhan.

Night. The locomotive. The European engineer quarrels with the Chinese fireman. [The bandit] Yu climbs on the locomotive. With the silent consent of the
fireman the engineer is immobilized. . . .

This part ends with Yu being advised by the Russian on the train to "go to
Canton if you want to fight," and the third film of the trilogy — entitled "China
Roars" — is chiefly set in revolutionary Canton, with a comprador's family divided between clinging to the past and embracing the dangerous but hopeful
future.

This was Tretyakov's panorama of China up to 1926, the year of the *Zhung-guo*
project. A production plan preserved with the outline shows a schedule of 2½
years. It is impossible now to determine how Eisenstein would have chosen and
transformed this bulk of material, for he was assigned instead to a film about the
Soviet Union's agricultural policy, and Tretyakov had to find other uses for his
Chinese experiences and dramatic conflicts. He first used the title of the third
film, but strengthened to "Roar, China!," for a poem, and then for a play about
the Wanhsien incident (which actually recurred in August 1926), used as an
opening for the first film, quoted above.* The main title, *Zhung-guo*, was employed in 1927 for Tretyakov's memoir on his life in China. Somewhat later
the title and the quoted part of the second film found their way to the screen as
The Blue Express, a film about the Chinese revolution that has not yet been seen
in China.†

One of the makers of *Potemkin* did get to China, however. In the winter of
1926–1927 Yakov Bliokh, production manager of the *Potemkin* staff made a
notable actuality film called *Shanghai Document* (see Plate 3), known all over
the world except in China until recent years.

This was the first film of social analysis made in China, and the first (and
possibly last) film to show, realistically, social relations between Chinese and
foreigners. A glimpse of the bloody consequences in Shanghai of Chiang Kai-
shek's coup d'état in the spring of 1927 forms the conclusion to *Shanghai
Document*.

---

* The play *Roar China!* was first staged in January 1926 (the month of *Potemkin's* first
showing) at the Meyerhold Theater.
† *Goluboi Ekspress* (1929), directed by Ilya Trauberg, is also known in Europe and America
as *China Express*. Tretyakov's film idea was also flattered by an American imitation,
Shanghai Express (1931), which *was* shown in China (see page 82). It was Harry Hervey
who sold this to Paramount as his "idea" for a film.

Before Chiang claimed China for himself one Soviet film was bought and shown, briefly, commercially. This was *Little Red Devils* (or *Red Imps*), about a group of brave children who helped the Red Army during the Civil War in 1920. This film left one curious trace — the boys and girls (usually orphans) who lived and worked with the Chinese Red Army from 1927 to Yenan were called "Little Red Devils."*

A "little red devil" drawn at Yenan in 1937 by Liao Ch'eng-chih. He used his Yenan pseudonym as signature here.

---

* Since the liberation these fighting children have been the subject of films made in China (*Letter with Feather,* and others) and Korea (*Fighting for the Fatherland*).

No film may be shown which is in violation of the political principles of Kuomintang or which might affect the prestige of the nation.

The Committee must refuse license to any film, or any part of film which may be disadvantageous to morality or to the public peace.

License will be refused to all pictures which might conduce to superstitious practices, or might encourage feudalism.

These three regulations, to go into effect on 1 January 1930, were issued by the Ministry of the Interior, at the same time that the Shanghai Special District Film Censorship Committee was established. From a Chinese viewpoint the regulations strike the perfect note: handsome and high-minded while open to as many interpretations as there can be occasions. "Under such conditions," declared a leading Chinese distributor (probably Luther Jee), "the actual footage taken from any films would depend entirely upon the personal reaction of the members of the censorship committee. We could not say in advance that this picture or that picture would be passed or rejected. . . ."[1] An American reporter commented

The mandate has some interesting angles. Obscenity, nudity, suggestion and the seventeen other points which are kept in view by the American film censor boards are conspicuously absent. The Chinese cover that entire field with one word, "morality," and leave the committee and the distributors to fight it out. Manifestly, the first object of the censorship is political rather than moral. . . .

But, while the "principles" of this censorship are rather vague, its provisions for application are concrete and detailed.

In the case of Chinese film, the producing companies must submit their stories to the censor board, in detail, before any of the picture is made, and the finished product also must be sent up for censorship,

and the German film business was alerted:

For years and years a lively agitation against foreign films has been evident in the Chinese press and among the public and has found its climax in demands for import restrictions. Censorship is very rigidly enforced.[2]

At 50 cents (Mexican) a reel for distribution and exhibition license the new committee surprised no one by deciding that all foreign film in Shanghai imported before 1 January (about 3,000 reels) also required licenses. Furthermore — and this did startle both distributors and producers — the license was good for only three years, when each film would have to be again submitted to the machinery. "China is a changing country," explained the Ministry of the Interior, "and it is quite possible that something which was in accord with the

present political and social conditions might be out of date and subversive within
three years. . . ."

Subversive is the key word.* Yet the ultimate effect of these carefully loose
regulations was not that intended by their authors. Though everyone bitterly
protested the regulations, whose political objective was clear to all, we can now
see that they nourished the very tendencies they sought to annihilate: they
helped to consolidate left-wing filmmakers and made them more ingenious in
outwitting or evading the censors. And within this dual maneuver of consolida-
tion and evasion, focused on carrying a fighting message to the protected
millions, the power and art of the Chinese film were taken forward to heights
unsuspected in the unprotected 1920s. Lu Hsun helped move this campaign, too,
with his translation from the Japanese of Iwasaki's "Films as a Means of
Propaganda," with a changed title, "Modern Film and the Bourgeoisie." Lu
Hsun's translation carries a postscript, dated 16 January 1930, that concludes

European and U.S. imperialists dispose of their old guns to give us war and
unrest, then they use old films to astound us and stupefy us. After the films and
guns get even older, they will be sent to the interior of China, to enlarge their
potency of making people foolish.[3]

After the tragedy of 1927 all phases of intellectual life in China went into
cautious retreat. Even the cinema, least intellectually demanding of China's arts,
found it possible to retreat further from ideas and real life. By the time the new
censorship regulations came into effect in 1930, it is hard to find a concrete target
for the government's fears, for the classical subjects that were in vogue in 1926
had been replaced, and stayed replaced for the next four years, by a Chinese
version of the most popular of all American film forms, the "western." The
central figure (usually male, but not invariably) was a hero of some undefined
period in the past, a synthesis of a medieval knight-errant, a Japanese samurai,
the French Fantômas, and old reliable Robin Hood (who *might* have made the
Kuomintang censors nervous). His (or her) impetuous, death-defying exploits
could be infinitely prolonged, unbounded by any discipline beyond "pure entertainment," which, of course, always involved rather continuous violence, usually
swordplay, with intervals of romance and/or exposed flesh. His (or her) antagonists could be rich or evil, demons or ghosts: for all the spooky techniques of
the foreign mystery film were also thrown into the stew. Of the approximately
four hundred films produced by the more than fifty Shanghai film producers

---

* In January 1939 the Chinese censor was disturbed by M-G-M's *Marie Antoinette*! "Delete
all footage which made Louis XVI appear ridiculous or showed royalty in an unfavorable
light or urged freedom from oppression." Quoted in *World-Wide Influences of the Cinema*,
by John Eugene Harley (Los Angeles, 1940), p. 112.

between January 1928 and December 1931, about two hundred fifty films were
of this swordplay-cum-mystery type, and all the financial successes of the
period — except for the first Chinese sound novelties — were in this group.[4]

The literary base for these films was the newspaper adventure serial, and its
derivative, the picture books (or comics) that have never lost their popularity in
China. It was one of these many serials, *Strange Tales of the Adventurer in the
Wild Country* by Shang K'ai-jan, that the alert Cheng Chen-chiu and Chang
Shih-chuan of the Star Film Company adapted as *The Burning of Red Lotus
Temple.* Its release in May 1928 was received "with a roar": Cheng Chi-hua says
that "in the flashing of its swords the era of the adventurer film burst upon us."
Over the next three years Star made *eighteen* parts[*] of *The Burning of Red
Lotus Temple* — eighteen films in praise of strength and cunning: what a direct
reflection of Chiang's murdering victory! Other companies had to have their
burnings, too: *The Burning of Black Dragon Temple, The Burning of White
Flower Terrace, The Burning of Sword-Peak Fortress, of Nine-Dragon Mountain,
of P'ing Yang Village* (in seven installments), *of Seven Star Lodge, of White
Sparrow Temple, of Darkened Soul Temple, of Han Family Village, of White
Lotus Temple, of the Hundred Flower Stage.* With China's shortage of lumber it
must have cost plenty of money and influence to erect so many inflammable
sets.

The titles of 1928 and 1929 sound like a torrent sweeping all other production
plans before it:

Lady Adventuress on Wild River (in 13 parts)
Great Adventurer East of the Pass (in 13 parts)
Red Butterfly, Adventuress (in 4 parts)
Tale of Mysterious Adventurer, Savior of the Country
Lord of Ten Thousand Adventurers
Three Champions Struggle for the Beauty
Hero Who Disturbs the World
Lady Champion in Black
Phantom Light and Heroic Shadow
Wrest-Life-from-Tiger's-Mouth
Iron-Blood Hero
Lady Pirate

There were extreme variations that begin to sound like parodies of the pattern:
Playboy Swordsman, Harebrained Hero, Absurd General, Woman Champion

---

* These were not the program-filler installments of the U.S. serial film: each "part" was a
full-length sequel of an hour and a half. Some desperate theaters would combine several
parts to make an all-day treat. My wife and her sister, in Hankow in 1927, saw one of these
"endless" serials.

Saves Woman, Hero of the Empty Wish, Romantic Champion of Cinema.
Novelty was not much sought after, but the form absorbed any foreign devices
or plots that caught the fancy of the Chinese spectator or filmmaker: *Flying
Bandit* was modeled on *The Thief of Bagdad; The Money King* borrowed its
daring nakednesses and "futurist" sets from *Metropolis.* In some films the
costumes looked more like Texas than Szechuan.

One actress of these adventurer-heroines has recorded memories of her hectic
career. Fan Hsueh-peng came from a well-to-do family of Kiangsu Province
whose declining fortunes compelled their daughter to look for work in Shanghai
when she was seventeen. "Robust youth and natural agility" found her an acting
job at the small United Friends Company; when not acting she worked as a film-
cutter and general handy-girl about the place. Real locations and sunlight were
relied upon to save money. Once while filming in Soochow one of the crew
happened to read the eighteenth century novel, *Heroic Sons and Daughters*,
proposed it as a film subject, and one episode (that cost 4,000 yuan) was so
successful that it led to a seemingly endless series of sequels. Fan Hsueh-peng,
who played its heroine, recalls the increasingly haphazard way the series was
filmed:

At that time there was no special photographic technique for filming unusual
feats of daring. When I had to fly through the air, a rope was tied around my
waist and I was hoisted up high above the floor. The shaky ceiling of the studio
threatened to fall and there was no safety net to catch me. . . .

For the fighting scenes, the studio hired ricksha pullers, pole-carriers and others
who had never had any training in either sword-fighting or picture-making.
Brandishing wooden broadswords and spears, they would strike blindly at me. I
emerged from every shooting covered with bruises. . . .

On paper my salary was impressive, but I only received a part of it, the rest being
kept on account by the boss. If there was an idle period in the studio and I
signed up elsewhere, all the money credited to me was confiscated.[5]

One important and lasting film talent developed in this unpromising period. Shih
Tung-shan was in the group of young people that helped in 1921 to form Tan
Tu-yu's Shanghai Film Company, where Shih worked as designer and actor. He
wrote and directed one film, *Willow Fluff* (1925), before leaving this quasi-
amateur studio to join the recent merger of the two most commercial film
companies, Great China and Bai Ho. And it was in this unlikely setting that Shih
Tung-shan enunciated his esthetic of film: that all the beauties of the visible
world can be used to express feelings and drama. The Japanese sound of this
manifesto may have been influenced by the Japanese cameraman who worked
on *Willow Fluff.* At the more commercial studio Shih also managed to work

with a Japanese cameraman, and this emphasis on pictorial beauty as a proper vehicle for film drama reminds one of Mizoguchi's principles. For such a director as Mizoguchi or Shih Tung-shan, subjects of action and violence can spur him to great beauties, and films of lasting value can grow from a disturbing clash of loveliness and brutality: Mizoguchi's *47 Loyal Ronin* is such a film. And the adventurer vogue gave Shih a similar opportunity. *Four Champions of the Wang Family* (1927) did not enjoy the tremendous success of *The Burning of Red Lotus Temple*, released a few months later, but critics of the time were surprised to see its elegant interior scenes and well-composed exteriors, its unusual attention to acting details, and an always perfect relation between camera and subject. We'll have to take their word for these qualities, as no copy of this film has survived. It is still possible that copies of this or his later films in the cycle — *Hero Chun Kills the Tiger* and *Two Heroes at Swords-point* (in 1929, for the Tien Yi Company) — may turn up to confirm the early reputation of Shih Tung-shan.

Aside from the work of Shih Tung-shan and the possibilities for varying their experience given to other filmmakers, the adventurer cycle had little to be proud of. It was the most completely escapist period in China's film history. The stream of endless variations on a few fantastic, erotic, and violent themes was helped to its end by the sound film, for in its earliest stage the sound film was obliged to sound real, if not realistic.

America's sound films won the race to monopolize Shanghai's best theaters* (China's film theaters had doubled in number since 1927): 90% of the films shown in China in 1929 were American-made. The limitations of the American sound film were taken over wholesale by Chinese producers when they finally achieved sound productions of their own, and it cannot be said that Chinese films have yet escaped from their entangling admiration of the efficient American film.

By 1929 it was clear to Shanghai's film theaters and filmmakers that the sound film was here to stay, yet it was far from clear how China was to make sound films, either for its own consumption or for export. None of Shanghai's film companies could face the huge expenditure that the changeover from silent to

---

* The first sound (or, rather, talking) films shown in Shanghai began with *The Jazz Singer* (as "Song of Pious Son"), followed by "Flying General" (*Hell's Angels?*), "Singable and Cryable" (*The Singing Fool?*), *The Broadway Melody*, "Murder Case of the Dancing Girl" (*Tenderloin?*), "Hidden Things Revealed" (*Bulldog Drummond?*) and "Tranquillity of Song and Dance" (*Sunny Side Up?*). The first sound films in Peking and Tientsin were shown at a nicely named theater—the Ping An, Peace and Quiet!

sound filming required, and the technical problem alone seemed insuperable. Nevertheless, the three largest companies were impatient to take some risk, for the winner of the race was sure to make a resounding profit. To be the producer of "China's First Sound Film" was the dream that drove other dreams into the background in 1929 and 1930. One studio sent a team of technicians to bribe their way into the well-guarded projection booth in the theater where *Three Famous Actors* [*The Royal Family of Broadway?*] was being shown, to see how the synchronization of disk and film was managed. Another studio started negotiations with a Japanese company that had made a workable imitation of Western Electric apparatus, but a required down payment of 200 ounces of gold stopped that move abruptly. Another start, more hopeful, was based on the fact that one of the Chinese managers of the Shanghai branch of Pathé Gramophone Records was also an investor in the Star Film Company. With Pathé to take care of the sound and Star the filming, the future looked bright and a new company was launched that promised to make twelve sound films. Only two of these were actually made, but Chinese sound films were no longer a dream.[6]

The pains of this beginning were hard, but the Star-Pathé technicians had some comfort in knowing that the introduction of sound films into each producing country had gone through similar pains. Under a pseudonym Hung Shen wrote this first scenario, *Singsong Girl Red Peony*, to be photographed first and recorded afterward. The scenes had to be fitted onto 600-foot lengths of film, to fit the disks they were using.* Four times the synchronization failed, but the fifth time it was satisfactory. The audience being promised plenty of talk, there was almost no sound but songs and dialogue, and these were continuous. Its story did not disturb Chinese film patterns in the slightest:

The story was about Red Peony [played by Butterfly Wu], an actress blessed with both beauty and a fine singing voice. Her mother prevented her marrying her lover, a fur dealer, and insisted on a union with the brother of the theatre owner who employed Red Peony. The new bridegroom immediately began sponging on his wife and eventually stole her jewellery to give to his cabaret-girl paramour. Red Peony was so distressed when she found out that she became sick, lost her voice, and, in consequence, her employment. On the advice of an evil friend, her husband then sold their daughter to a sing-song house, but was smitten with remorse and helped his wife get the child back. He killed his evil counselor, and was imprisoned for the crime. The three-hour film ended with a shot of Red Peony, escorted by her faithful lover, the fur dealer, sadly embarking to take a job in Dairen.[7]

---

* This also made life difficult for the projectionists, who had to race to change eighteen 600-foot reels and watch over eighteen disks.

There was a trial screening in January 1931; between then and its public release
on 15 March, most of its production expense was recovered through sales to the
Philippines (18,000 yuan) and Indonesia (16,000 yuan).* The success of the
novelty was all that its makers could have wished.

While Hung Shen was sent to America to learn everything he could pick up
about sound-film recording, the Star-Pathé group began their next film. *The
Beauty Yu* combined Peking opera (*The Emperor's Farewell to His Favorite*†)
with a story of backstage life. The arias and set speeches of the opera made it
possible to record the voices first, with the filming to be matched afterwards.
The synchronizing motor that they rigged up couldn't be adjusted to the variable
electric current of the studio they rented, and then they had to find a theater
whose equipment could be altered (Western Electric forbade any tampering) to
fit their improvisation, but the finished film showed a profit.

The third sound film was a combined effort involving two Chinese studios,
Japanese sound equipment, and an American cameraman, K. Henry. To make
After Rain, Clear Sky (this title conveys the whole story: girl abandoned
by husband attracted to loose woman, is finally reunited with him), a cast and
crew were taken in March 1931 to Tokyo, where the film was made (with
Minatoki sound equipment), cut, and tried out at the Chinese Embassy. At this
showing someone named Grant (?), representing "a Broadway theater," is
reported to have paid $57,000 for the American rights, but I've seen no reference
to an American showing. The film was brought from Tokyo to Shanghai in May
and shown to an invited audience on 21 June 1931. Its Japanese origin was
concealed behind publicity about "977 occasions for dialogue, 6,935 sentences
are spoken," but the truth leaked out just as the Japanese army moved into
Manchuria (on the pretext that their nationals in Mukden must be protected),
and the film was avoided by patriotic citizens.

The fourth sound film, *Spring Colors* [meaning a love story] *in the Music Hall,*
was made by the Tien Yi Film Company and directed by its show-business
lawyer, Hsiao. Its literary origins are still argued — was it a newspaper serial,
Women, Women, by Yao Ssu-feng, or a stage comedy, *The Dancing Beauty,
Mei*? — but it managed to present a full package: singers, dancers, theater stars,
and a miscellany of well-known personages (appealing, fictionally, for flood
victims). It was the first Chinese sound-on-film effort, and the two recording

---

* Compare with 1,000- and 2,000-yuan sales for these rights to silent films.
† A good description of this play is given by Claude Roy, *Into China* (London: McKibbon &
Kee, 1955), pp. 345–349.

technicians, British Bryan Guerin and American Charles Hugo, nearly wrecked the company with their combined monthly salary of 10,000 yuan in silver. But Chinese assistants replaced them and the American cameraman, Bert Cann, on the next job.

From America Hung Shen brought back more than information and equipment: along with him came a cameraman, Jack Smith, and fifteen assistants. The equipment turned out to be faulty (though advertised by Star as "Startone"), and *Old, Prosperous Peking*, with locations filmed in the old capital, was made against a background of constant quarreling. The foreign crew and quarrels cost 100,000 yuan before the production ended, and the Americans scattered. Hung Shen's scenario, on the decline of an aristocratic family in the last years of the Ching dynasty, was considered one of his best. But the novelty of Chinese sound films was wearing thin, the fighting in the north discouraged film attendance, and *Old, Prosperous Peking* did merely normal business. At the time of its release, January 1932, Chinese cinema history had taken a turn more important than the introduction of sound.

The first sound films took a cultural step of more significance than was realized at the time: though made by Shanghai companies, the language spoken in all of them was not the ordinary speech of Shanghai (a city thought of as "Southern"), but the language of the north, the Peking dialect known as "Mandarin," and politically known as *pai-hua*, the national language. So long as films were silent, no such decision had to be made: written Chinese subtitles could be read by all literate Chinese, no matter where they were born. It was, perhaps, for this reason that it took several years for the whole industry to commit itself to sound production; silent films continued to be made and sold until the mid-thirties,* with only a sprinkling of sound novelties. Yet whenever the various companies of Shanghai decided to use speech, Mandarin was the single, unifying dialect. In a period when the nation was in need of all unities, the film industry contributed its mite.

It was at this time that another kind of unity was attempted, the unity that is more accurately called monopoly. The ambition of Lo Ming-yü, owner of a widespread chain of cinemas (principally in Northern cities), was to bring all the studios and film companies together in one huge omnipotent enterprise, with himself, naturally, at the head of it. Starting with a prestigious letterhead

---

* In 1931 Hankow theaters were being offered plenty of *cheap, silent* films (*Film Daily*, 9 Aug. 1931); China was one of several dumping grounds for the scrapped American silent films made obsolete by conversion to sound at home.

(decorated by a former prime minister, a chief justice, and Sir Robert Ho Tung, described as a former governor of Hong Kong!), Lo took over Li Ming-wei's Min Hsin Company in November 1929, and formed a new company, the North China Film Company. Lo also collaborated on the script of their first film, *Spring Dream in the Old Capital*, a curious mixture of exposures and evasions:

It is set in the warlords' period in Peking. A private tutor is ambitious to obtain an official appointment, and with the aid of an attractive prostitute, Yen Yen, he is made head of a customs office. He amasses a fortune, most of which is spent in debauchery and drink. Yen Yen becomes his concubine and he neglects his wife and daughters. Concubine and wife come to an understanding and agree in criticizing their husband's evil ways. Yen Yen lures the elder daughter into "gay places," and the frightened wife takes the younger daughter away to her old home. With a change in government the [anti-] hero loses his post and is thrown into jail. Yen Yen and her lover (one of the servants) grab all they can, and run, deserting the elder daughter. Her father is finally released and returns to his home that he finds plundered and covered with dust. He dreams of the glamor and luxury of its past. As snow falls he goes to his wife's home to ask forgiveness.[8]

The absorption of the Min Hsin Company had made the films of Mei Lan-fang (photographed by Li Ming-wei in 1925) available to the new company, and one of these, *The Emperor's Farewell to His Favorite,* was somehow incorporated into *Spring Dream* to make it more attractive. The film consolidated Lo Ming-yü's ambitions and established Sun Yu as a director.

In August 1930 Lo acquired the combined Great China and Bai Ho companies, along with their studios and personnel (including Shih Tung-shan), and the enlarged company was called Lien Hua, the United China Film Company. On his way to building a film city somewhere, and absorbing the entire Chinese film industry, Lo established branch offices in four centers of China and started a technicians' training group in Peking and a song-and-dance class in Shanghai.

In his first two years of business Lo made twelve films; the most successful of these were directed by Sun Yu and Shih Tung-shan. Sun Yu was a scholar's son, born in Chungking, and given a good education in Tientsin and Peking. He had an interest in theater, and continued to study it at the University of Wisconsin, in New York at a class conducted by David Belasco, and in an evening course at Columbia University. When he returned to China in 1927 he worked for the Great Wall Company and for Min Hsin (where he made the obligatory swords-men films), before melting into Lo's great combine. While working on the phenomenally successful *Spring Dream* he found time to make a short comedy, *Suicide Pact*, and the commercial impulse of his work grew increasingly obvious.

His next film, *Wild Grass*, (he himself confessed) was a makeshift combination of *La Dame aux Camélias* and a popular American film, *Seventh Heaven*. This was followed by a superficial scenario set against a background of the 1911 Revolution, *Free Soul*, directed by another of Lo's young men. Sun Yu had talent, but it remained buried until the cinema's left-wing movement enlisted him.

Shih Tung-shan's was a more original and more consistent talent, yet even he showed signs of capitulating to the manufacturing pressures of the Lien Hua Company. His films for this studio made money but they did not stir the critical admiration that his sword fights had. The photographs of *Hung Niang* (An Ordinary Woman) show a glossy smartness that must have cleverly emphasized his device of bringing *Tale of West Chamber* into a modern setting. His next film for Lien Hua, *Two Stars from the Milky Way*, seemed to me a work of minimum interest — as it possibly may have been to him, too. I must confess that I expected too much of it, as I tend to do of any film whose story touches filmmaking. By its third reel *Two Stars* had forgotten that it had begun in a film studio, and had settled down into a more ancient pattern, but I still remember the dialogue (the titles were in both Chinese and English) during a production conference: their high moral and artistic principles expressed in *words* had a peculiar tone in this quite unprincipled film. Was this a private joke of Shih Tung-shan?

China as the top newsreel story of 1927 was pushed off foreign screens by Lindbergh's flight and the Mississippi flood, but before the year ended the excitement over events in China had been echoed in Hollywood by a flurry of Chinese stories. The most significant of these was *Foreign Devils*, an M-G-M film with Tim McCoy as an attaché at the American Embassy in Peking at the time of the Boxer Rebellion — a story by Peter B. Kyne that was to reappear in fancier dress thirty-five years later. I must have missed this, because I'm sure I'd remember Emily Fitzroy in the role of the Dowager Empress. The other films of this short-lived excitement were *Shanghai Bound*, about a Yangtze steamer (captained by Richard Dix) caught in the civil war; *The Warning*, with the evil occupants of a temple wiped out by explosion; and *Shanghai Streets*. Then the greater Hollywood excitement of sound captured all attention, and subjects rarely strayed outside small soundproof rooms. Perhaps fortunately, there was not another important Chinese subject filmed in Hollywood for ten years.

German film interest in China also revived with the 1926—1927 crisis. *Die Gefangene von Schanghai*, released toward the end of 1927, concerns the young

English consul's wife who arrives in Shanghai to join him just as he is arrested by the nationalist troops charged with supporting the "enemy" (undefined). Mary is also arrested and her device of pretending to be a Russian agitatress doesn't work: the Chinese general (Bernhard Goetzke) has seen a photo of Ralph's wife. Ralph is also loved by a half-Chinese woman, but her attempt to free him results only in the preparations for her execution by his side. Ralph's freedom is offered by the general in exchange for the possession of Mary, but before this awful bargain is concluded, the British fleet shells the general's headquarters. He dies, a glass of champagne held aloft: "To China, the country that is strong enough to wait for more centuries."[9] That was produced by Bayrische, while UFA made *Die Hölle von Fu-Tschang-Ku*, released in mid-1928. The leading English merchant in this southern Chinese "hell" is preparing his daughter's marriage, while the community is preparing an uprising to wipe out all foreigners. Thereafter the action follows predictable lines, with British airplanes and a pilot who becomes a rival for the daughter's hand. The uprising becomes no more than a dangerous background and a means of testing the two heroic rivals. British films, on the other hand, remained remarkably reticent about the nationalist threat to British property and lives. It may have been either *Die Gefangene* or *Die Hölle* that was mentioned later in a Shanghai magazine:

A few years ago, a certain German film was about to be exported to China. When rumor had it that it contained much that was humiliating to the Chinese, our students in Germany began to denounce it and to make arrangements to prevent its exportation.[10]

I like to think that Chu Teh, then studying in Berlin, was one of those students.

Only one Chinese film company then made any effort to sell its films to European audiences. This was Min Hsin, still headed by the indefatigable Li Ming-wei. Through his brother's contacts with Paris merchants three of Min Hsin's 1927 productions were shown in Paris, as *Le Poème de la Mer, La Rose qui meurt,* and *La Rose de Pu Shui.** It was the last of these that had some success, and considerable circulation through Europe. After it was prepared for foreign customers (in the process of which its eleven reels were reduced to five) its European career began in 1928 at the distinguished Paris cinema "Studio 28," from where it moved to Geneva, London, Berlin, and elsewhere. A Geneva critic summed up its values:

This is a film of genuine interest. The shooting technique is primitive to be sure, but the actors' interpretations and the acting itself are not lacking in sincerity.[11]

---

* The two first were both written by Hou Yao; *La Rose de Pu Shui* was his adaptation of *Tale of Western Chamber*, also made in 1927. "Pu Shui" must be a stab at Pu Chiu Ssu, the actual setting of *The Tale*.

Fortunately a copy of this enjoyed film has been preserved in the Nederlands Filmmuseum. The copy is, of course, in the abbreviated European version, and its obvious qualities of childishness and charm may have been helped by the shortening, though the shorteners have not always been logical in their compression of the simple tale. A student, who has stopped at the monastery of Pu Shui to rest and study, is distracted by the beauty of a girl staying in another wing (she is the daughter of a recently dead prime minister, for whom she is offering prayers). The military terror of the province hears of her unprotected presence in the monastery and arrives, backed by his army in Peking opera uniforms, to demand her. The student proposes a ruse: to request a delay of three days, ostensibly to complete the girl's mourning, but actually to send a message to another, more noble general, who arrives in time to scatter the evil army and to unite girl and student. The scenes of armies and fighting depend for their effectiveness on the quantity of extras, but the rest of the film is expressively photographed (I disagree with the Geneva critic), and the exteriors were apparently filmed in Suchow and Hangchow. There are some fine moments that dramatize the *spectator's* reactions. The hero has a dream of the heroine that begins awkwardly but improves when his writing brush is transformed into a weapon and then a vehicle! The film also plays little jokes on the characters (possibly improved by the European cutters), such as the parallel scenes of hero and heroine getting into their makeup and marriage regalia.

For me the most dramatic, and the most astonishing, period of Chinese film history is the maintenance of an active underground movement in the film industry for almost twenty years. More than any other factor this record distinguishes Chinese films from the films of other countries. Under the threat of two of the most repressive political systems in modern history, the Kuomintang and the Japanese occupation, a group of Chinese revolutionaries made films that continued to reach a large public. The mechanics of this operation have their own fascination. What is of greater significance in the history of twentieth-century arts is that these exceptional, bitter, difficult, and often bloody circumstances resulted in the most interesting and lasting Chinese films, superior to what came before, to what was going on above ground at the same time, and, in many important respects, superior to the Chinese films made in the years well after the triumph of the Chinese revolution — whether in Peking, Shanghai, or Hong Kong — even though some of the same artists are still making films.

The necessary setting was crisis, a national crisis that bulked larger than any social or economic crisis, which could indeed absorb all crises into its current. On 18 September 1931 the Japanese moved into Manchuria, and then

On January 18, 1932, they were given the chance to go into Shanghai, when a mob there killed a Japanese. The Japanese navy moved swiftly in and landed marines, who fought the Chinese for some weeks, until the Chinese forces retreated on March 1.[12]

The Japanese had boasted that they could take the city in four hours, and their failure gave a great boost to Chinese morale. The Italian newsreel company, L.U.C.E., made one of the several records of the Shanghai battles, *Le Giornate di Fuoco a Shanghai*, and its producer wrote an account of its making:

Nanking Road, luxurious and colorful, no longer belongs to the elegant and carefree elite of the white world. It is now invaded by a native mass that does not speak, does not smile, but only runs, pushes, shoves, jolts, stops — looking for some shelter, a better destiny. . . . Beyond Soochow Street there is a haze enveloped in dense, black smoke. It is the fire that has been burning for days, destroying a densely populated area where thousands of huts of mud and wood are mingled with such splendid buildings as the North Station and the Commercial Press. . . .

The production of the film has been difficult and dangerous. The Japanese authorities, who either have a prejudice against newsreels or sought to avoid international incidents that would become complicated, were very severe with us. . . . The filming of the North Station, which the Chinese held under continuous enemy fire, was particularly nerve-wracking. The Japanese had refused to give permission for either films or photos, declaring that the presence of cameramen from a neutral country would not interrupt their fire. On one occasion an American cameraman near Craveri's position tried to film the action with a hand camera. A Japanese officer, followed by a few sailors, rushed at him, his camera was seized and he was escorted to the high command. Then the officer turned to Craveri, who quickly tossed camera and equipment into our bus, locked its doors and sped away.[13]

In the 1931 invasion the Chinese industry had the great Manchurian corner of its audience and its theater chains cut away, and it then seemed forever. When the 1932 bombing and burning in Shanghai destroyed much of the film industry's property, many small companies were forced out of business. Thirty companies had to stop production, including the fourth studio of Lien Hua. Lo hastily placed his whole enterprise in the care of a Hong Kong trust company, and moved his first studio to Hong Kong. Before the clash on 28 January, there were thirty-nine film theaters in Shanghai, and sixteen were destroyed in the bombing; most of these sixteen were showing only Chinese films. In some areas of the industry morale and patriotic spirit were high: several companies issued news films of the battles, and their popularity showed them a direction to take in their private crisis. Even semi-animated cartoons (*The Rapid Awakening of Our People* and *Blood-stained Money*) were made and out before the dust of those battles had settled. The employees of Star and those of Lien Hua who were left behind in Lo's escape to Hong Kong collected money for a "Save the Country Group" and helped the spreading boycott of Japanese goods.

Of the stable companies Star (Ming Hsing) was the most seriously affected, with damage to its studio and the withdrawal of available capital. Patriotic films might be the answer, but how could they be *sure* that they were making the kind that people would be eager to spend money to see? Their way of studying changed audience demands was to send Chou Chien-yun in search of his country-man Ah Ying, and to ask him to introduce them to Hsia Yen and other leaders of the left-wing art movement.

Hsia Yen (pen-name for Shen Tuan-hsien) was born to a poor family of Hang County, Chekiang Province, in 1900. When he was three, his father died, and from then on each step of his education was a struggle, helped only by his superior intelligence and persistence. On finishing primary school he was apprenticed to a dye shop; his school was proud of his record and sent him instead to a first-class vocational school in Hangchow. In the tide of the May Fourth movement the student joined a Marxist group and worked on the first publications in the province to advance Marxism. Graduating at the top of his class he was given a scholarship to study abroad. He chose Japan (the Kyushu Engineering School), where his love of philosophy and literature developed, but in 1927 he had to return to China where he joined the Chinese Communist Party in Shanghai and directed workers' activities in the dangerous period that followed Chiang's coup d'etat. In the autumn of 1929 the underground organiza-tion ordered his transfer to work in the Left-Wing Writers' League; he also became a responsible leader in the Left-Wing Dramatists' League, and chief editor of the Art Society's publications, *Art* and *Sha Lun.* If the heads of Star sought the support of the leading left-wing organizations they found the right man in Hsia Yen. Much later, when all this had stiffened into history, Hsia Yen wrote an account of this meeting and his subsequent moves:

After the battle of 28 January a film company invited me, Ah Ying, and Cheng Bo-shi to write scenarios. Confronted with this proposal, we brought it up for discussion at a [party] meeting. A few comrades opposed the idea and he [Ch'ü Ch'iu-pai] also was apprehensive for some time. He asked, "Only you three?"

I replied, "They also plan to invite a number of modern drama people."

Suddenly he thought of another aspect to it, saying, "We ourselves should be able to make films. At present, though, there are too many difficulties. But we must have this capability in the future."

After much discussion, and after all had aired their views, he summed up: "Very well, it won't hurt to experiment. To get to know a few of these people and to do a little of this work will help us to train our own forces in this field. However, we must not expect immediate or great successes. There are still many difficulties." Then, after a pause, he said the following significant words, words that I will never forget: "But you must be careful."

This meant that he wanted us to be on the alert. Films are the sharpest ideological weapon of the class struggle, and the enemy would certainly not let us grasp this weapon easily. That is why we would have many difficulties. We also understood from what he said that the situation in film circles at present was extremely confused. Alongside the bureaucrat-compradors who were grabbing at profits there were others who were even more dangerous to us newly active art workers with little social experience — dangerous entrepreneurs, scoundrels, and other rotten forces. Following his instructions we began carefully to wrest a way for ourselves in the film industry.[14]

A party film team was set up and Hsia Yen was made responsible for its work; his and their first task was the writing of scenarios.* In addition to the scenarios, to which Cheng Chi-hua refers as "the soul of film art," he goes on to say that "the film team also distributed their cadres to various posts in order to strengthen the left-wing creative forces in each company."[15] These efforts were concentrated on three companies, Ming Hsing, Yi Hua, and Lien Hua. For the next few years these companies were the bases for the party's film team, until it was forced to go more deeply underground, into wholly clandestine companies.

The emphasis then (as now) was on the writer rather than on the director: he could be more trusted to have the right content and the right words, which could be discussed and approved *outside the studio* before the less reliable director and cameraman went to work. Only later were filmmakers in nonwriting jobs recruited in the work of the party's film team. After thirty years of military and ideological war it is not easy to establish the exact personnel of the writing group, or who did which films. Certain names have been completely erased from

---

* A document relevant to the formation and work of the film team must be quoted here. It is "Present Program of Action," adopted by the Left-Wing Dramatists' League in September 1931. Its first article defines the tasks of the left-wing dramatic movement, including themes to be used: ". . . it should show what the Chinese proletariat must stand for and what it must oppose [imperialism, pornography, and right deviations], it must defend the Soviet Union, the Soviet Areas of China and Red Army . . . it should expose the dilemma of China's small agricultural holdings that go bankrupt under the pressure of aggressive foreign capital; it should tell the people to oppose their enemies and strive for today's stage of development — complete democracy." The final article deals specifically with cinema: "Members [of the League] must produce scripts for the filmmakers; join in the film production of the various companies; accumulate capital for our own film productions; organize a society for film research and bring together progressive actors and technicians to form a base for China's left-wing film movement; and we must criticize and analyze the present state of the Chinese cinema. . . . " (quoted by Cheng Chi-hua, vol. I.) Within the year most of this program was well under way.

modern texts. For example, Cheng Chi-hua, neither in his history nor in his appended filmography, mentions the name of Ting Ling, an important revolutionary writer (still alive and in China) whose conflict with official policy has ended her professional career. But a contemporary article about Ting Ling places her in the center of underground film activity:

In 1932 Ting Ling published a short novel, built around the great Yangtze floods which were caused in part by the fact that money earmarked for the repair of dykes always found its way into the pockets of the officials. Much of her material was used in a motion picture on floods, and she became one of a small nucleus of left writers and artists trying to develop a new social cinema in China.[16]

The scenario of *Wild Torrent* (shown in February 1933; see Plate 5) is now credited solely to Hsia Yen, and it is quite possible that he was more prepared than she was to wrestle with the new medium and the "rotten forces" that had to be cajoled into financing production. Nevertheless, a recent description of *Wild Torrent's* action sounds remarkably close to Ting Ling's no-longer-mentioned novel.

Against a background of the disastrous flood in the Yangtse Valley after the Japanese imperialists had invaded and occupied China's three north-eastern provinces in 1931, the film shows how landlords use "refugee relief" as a pretext to extort money from the peasants and join hands with the local authorities to oppress them. The peasants rise in revolt and take the landlords' timber to repair the dykes.[17]

Hsia Yen's intense scenario activity, uninterrupted by war or administrative posts, undoubtedly began at this time. Another, even more experienced dramatist, T'ien Han, provided two scenarios at once: *Three Modern Girls* and *Survival of the Nation.* Yang Han-sheng contributed *Angry Tide of China's Sea.*

T'ien Han was also responsible for the recruiting into progressive film work of a young Kunming musician, lately arrived in Shanghai, Hso Hsing. T'ien Han described their first meeting, in 1931, at the Bright Moon Variety Troupe:

Their premises were crowded and noisy, but we found a quiet room and had a good talk. . . . Upon graduating from secondary school he left home to roam the country. He served as a soldier in Hunan and Kwangsi, and studied for a short time in Kwangtung at the Institute of Drama under the direction of the dramatist Ouyang Yu-chien. Two years before our meeting he had come with a Yunnan merchant to Shanghai and been taken on as a violinist by the popular Bright Moon Variety Troupe. . . .

Like many students from poor families, he thirsted for revolution. A progressive friend introduced him to the Shanghai Anti-Imperialist League and he took part in mass work in the western district of Shanghai. . . . He wanted to know how he could use his music in the service of the revolution.[18]

T'ien Han introduced him to other left musicians, and one effect of this was to strengthen his resolve to study composition seriously, but his efforts to enter the College of Arts' music department at Peking's National University were rebuffed, and in 1932 he returned jobless to Shanghai. At this point T'ien Han found him a clerk's job at the Lien Hua Studio, recruited him into the Communist Party, and took a further step to help him: T'ien Han's script for *Light of Motherhood* required two songs, and the new clerk was asked to write them. He changed his name to Nieh Erh, and composed a militant song for the hero's memory of his mining days abroad (it could be Malaya or Indonesia), a song that has had a longer life than its film: *Light of Motherhood* was stopped by the Canton censors in its third day there, but "The Miners' Song" went on. Thus began the brief but intense film career of Nieh Erh: the many film songs he composed in his remaining three years became a mainstay of the left Chinese cinema in its bravest period.

The team gave equal organizational attention to another field, journalism and criticism, where words had weight, free of slippery images.* Using contacts in some of the most reactionary newspaper offices of Shanghai, the team brought into being "film supplements" to these major papers. The left-wing tone of these supplements, which began to appear in May 1932, was not even muffled. It was at about this time that Lu Hsun described the strategy clearly enough to be understood by anyone, either among newspaper owners or the Kuomintang police, who bothered to read his essay:

The air over a major battlefront is always full of black smoke — nothing can be seen clearly. We could not print our own paper, nor was there any paper that was quite clean — but we had to find a corner, somewhere, to speak our piece. Yet we had to be alert, to make no retreat in principle.[19]

On 18 June a manifesto, signed by fifteen left-wing film critics, appeared in one of the supplements: "Our Policy in Future Criticism." Two weeks later the first issue of *Film Art* appeared, the first Chinese journal of film theory and criticism. It survived only four weekly issues before it was banned, but it was a victory for the team. A sensational issue was aired in July when it was discovered that a

---

* Reversal had already begun of the ancient and familiar saying about a picture being worth several hundred words. Lu Hsun was perhaps the only revolutionary writer who promoted actively an interest in creating a new graphic art for China as well as in creating a new literature.

Chinese registration had been made for an American sound-film company. I
cannot learn the details of this "plot" to set up a Shanghai Hollywood, producing "typical Chinese films," but it may have been a convenient straw man at
this revolutionary moment. There were a dozen frightening attacks in the special
film supplements: Hung Shen's article of 21 July said that "this is even worse
than the Japanese ownership of Shanghai's textile mills," and that "film theaters
will become schools for slaves", the next day the third number of *Film Art*
advised "How to Break Out of the Present Crisis Provoked by an Invasion of
U.S. Capital into Chinese Film Industry." Cheng Chi-hua records that leading
artists rejected tempting offers from this new company and that in four months
its stock was no longer advertised — "a brilliant victory for the film criticism of
left-wing organizations."

The first stage of intense left-wing activity in the film studios had a success that
went beyond the hopes of the party film team and its advisor, Ch'ü Ch'iu-pei.
Thanks to Japanese marines and cannon the party's policy of anti-imperialism
had the support of most of the country, or at least those parts of the country
that read newspapers or had been directly in the Japanese line of march.
Shanghai, center of China's revolution, was now the focus of the country's
patriotism, and Shanghai, as the center of China's film industry, soon presented
a full-scale display of the Communist Party's new concentration.

The films made in 1932 and 1933 were schematic but effective. The combination of revolutionary fervor and patriotic excitement with which they were
made gave them a strength and an element of art that are hard to detect in
synopses of their action. It is easy to believe that some of those that have been
preserved — and can thus be checked (though only partially, separated as they
now are from the circumstances of 1932) — moved audiences then. Audiences so
moved mean financial success as well, and we can note a reflection of the general
tendency towards "economically reasonable patriotism" even in the products of
companies that were not in direct contact with the party's film team. Tien
Yi abandoned its Robin Hood formula, or more accurately, abandoned the
formula's old costumes: the old hero can still be detected in the unjustly jailed
farmer who is released after 28 January to join the volunteers and to die, with a
confident smile on his face, after a defiant solo attack on a Japanese tank
(*Struggle*), or in the superheroes of *Morning Sacrifice* (Jieh Hsing Company) who
lead a mining village with swords against the Japanese invaders. Other familiar
structures were given new patriotic props: in *Poem on a Palm Leaf* a song and
dance group (old base) attempt to organize a women's regiment (new attitude,
and with smart uniforms). In the general enthusiasm the Moon is Clear Company produced a rare piece of symbolism, *Bad Neighbor*: two young scholars

(representing the Chinese people) are cheated by a nasty, small neighbor to the East (Japan) and an equally nasty white neighbor to the West (European and American merchants), and only one of the scholars' wives (the Chinese spirit) can settle their quarrel; in the course of the symbolic action the white neighbor, named Economist, tramples underfoot a volume of Mencius, and a subtitle argues: "Without the Chinese spirit China is lost." I deeply regret that this film (which lasted for three days at the Carlton Theater before the Shanghai censors realized what was going on) has not been preserved — I can't even imagine its style and effect, it is so outside the Chinese film norm.

The only Ming Hsing production of this period that the supplements had to fight rather than support was a film called *Humanity*, released in June 1932. Drought and hunger figure properly in the story but its unforgivable resolution — the deathbed enlightenment of a greedy comprador who contributes part of his wealth to a fund for the drought-stricken area — appalled the party film team and the left-wing critics. But it was so popular that, to quote Cheng Chi-hua, "it was necessary to neutralize its effect," and readers were told how poisonous it was. Another film of 1932, from a smaller studio, was despised by left critics, but they said little about it, for *Romance in the Yao Mountains* touched the delicate problem of China's minorities. Lu Hsun, however, always enjoyed "untouchable" subjects and his sharp pen went to work on the film and its audience; he spared nobody:

The idea of this film is to enlighten the Yao minority. The main story line — someone marries a Yao princess. That brings to mind certain operas with a similar subject. Nowadays one rarely hears big talk about Chinese civilization controlling the whole world. So when we have the urge to enlighten others, we have to resort to Yaos and Miaos. And to accomplish this great deed, we must first marry them. The descendants of the Yellow Emperor cannot possibly marry the princesses of Europe, so we have to propagate our spiritual civilization nearer home.[20]

The other successes at Ming Hsing were all initiated and approved by the team. After *Wild Torrent*, "the first red flag raised by the party in filmmaking," Hsia Yen's next script was one of his best, *24 Hours of Shanghai*, so good indeed that the censors held up its release until December 1934 — the authorities had also seen the newly raised red flag. Several other scripts by Hsia Yen were produced and seen sooner. *Spring Silkworms* was an adaptation of a newly published story by Mao Tun about a Chekiang village whose crop for uncounted generations has been silk cocoons to be sold annually; our family does everything to ensure success, but a drop in the silk market ruins them, along with hundreds of others. A film whose material and attitude are stronger than its formula; while most left-wing films were content to apply fresh settings to familiar conflicts, the scripts by Hsia Yen, T'ien Han, and Hung Shen appear to bring both political and artistic responsibility to their difficult task. For *Spring Silkworms* Hsia Yen had the extra strength of Mao Tun's story,* one of the best of a period that Lu Hsun's guidance made into a high point of Chinese literature. The story's people (and most of the film's people) are credible without depending exclusively on naturalism. It taught without the bullying tone of a lesson: the film used animated diagrams in an introduction (now missing) to explain the silk industry's predicament, but even this could not have dimmed the film's vivacity. Only the hodgepodge of random music recordings added to make an accompaniment weakens the effect of the film today.† Even the enthusiastic but untalented actor who plays the head of the family does not hurt the good will of the film.

The left-wing film's concentration on peasant life, from *Wild Torrent* through *Spring Silkworms* to many more such themes before 1938, was an important task. Ever since the break with the Kuomintang in 1927 the Communist Party had placed increasing reliance, both practically and theoretically, on China's peasantry as the revolution's base; and the peasants gave political support and material protection to the Red Army's southern stronghold that effectively frustrated Chiang Kai-shek's repeated "extermination" attempts. The slogan, "internal pacification before resistance to external attack," was Chiang's answer to the Japanese aggressions in North China, and this also cost him the support of patriots and the peasants. Though the mass of peasants were only lightly touched by films of any kind, the portrayal of peasant problems was nevertheless a crucial revolutionary claim for the left filmmakers to emphasize. It was necessary to drive home this point to the intellectual or proletarian filmgoers of the cities, nor was it forgotten that many city families had come there recently from the countryside: most of the protagonists of these left films were shown as peasants forced to leave village miseries to endure city miseries. This change of locales, usually in reel one or two, was a help to actors who had difficulty pretending to be peasants (even when they had known this life at first hand), but over the years Shanghai actors evolved certain formulas for the representation of

---

* Described by C. T. Hsia (in his *History of Modern Chinese Fiction 1917–1957*, [New Haven: Yale University Press, 1961]) as "Mao Tun's best story and perhaps the outstanding achievement in Chinese proletarian fiction . . . one feels that Mao Tun is celebrating in his tale the dignity of labor."

† Released as a sound film, it is fairer to see *Spring Silkworms* without its meaningless soundtrack: dinner music, Parisian and Viennese operettas, jazz, "Old Black Joe," Aloha, church hymns make no attempt to reflect or to comment on the film's action or meaning. Why did the serious group ignore the problem of finding the right music for their good film? Perhaps the Chinese film industry of tomorrow could honor this ancestor with an especially composed score.

peasant characters, formulas that have not yet been eradicated from Chinese films. Convincing portrayals of workers were also rare, but more possible.

Hsia Yen has recently commented on the aim and failure of his next scenario, *Outcry of the Women*. In 1935 he published a vivid and unexaggerated reportage, "Contract Labor," of his earlier observation of the life of textile mill girls in Shanghai; in 1959 he wrote a postscript to this, speaking of the film:

After the Japanese attack on Shanghai in 1932, when the film director Shen Hsi-ling decided to write a scenario dealing with girl workers in Shanghai, I told him about this contract labor. Later the Shanghai Ming Hsing Film Studio made it the subject of the film *Outcry of the Women*. To write the script, however, I collected more material about contract labor and gained a deeper insight into the inhuman sufferings of these girls, which left me and other intellectuals like me aghast. This was the first attempt by Chinese writers to deal with "contract labor," but owing to our lack of first-hand knowledge of the subject, as well as to the limitations imposed on us and the cuts made by the Kuomintang censors, the film was not too successful.[21]

Another, more tangible reason for the film's weakness was that its dramatic center, the working conditions in the mills, could not be shown: no mill owner would have allowed a cameraman to record these conditions (though cleverer newsreel cameramen later found pretexts to record some shocking glimpses).

Shen Hsi-ling's next film was a more serious frustration. Written by Hsia Yen just after *Wild Torrent, 24 Hours of Shanghai* was his first use of a form that he was to fill often and interestingly: widely different lives crisscross at unexpected points, occasionally split up into a sequence of short story films. Even a loose adherence to a unity of time or place of this sort makes an effective film base (*vide* the films of Jeanne d'Arc's trial and execution, and *Grand Hotel*, to mention extremes). *24 Hours* begins at 4 P.M., with the serious injury of a child worker, and the telephone call of the comprador mill owner to his wife, inviting her to a cinema; she says she has a Mah-Jongg date, though she is really meeting her lover. From these two points spreads a line of action that involves the child's family and their neighbors in the tenement, the intrigues of the comprador's family, with his wife's gambling and love affairs, and the comprador's visit to the textile mill to remove foreign labels. The film ends at 4 P.M. the next day, with the death of the boy and the waking of the comprador's wife from her long nap as she plans her next night's enjoyment. The film was completed in three months, but it took more than a year, and ten checks by the censor, before it could be released. Even during its production, "observers" were sent to the studio, and their anxieties were partially soothed by cuts and reshooting. When the finished film was first submitted to the Kuomintang censors, they declared

The only solution to the contradictions between capital and labor that this film suggests, leads to, and propagates is, in its method and tendency, neither human nor suitable to our national situation.[22]

The party film team was accomplishing underground miracles, but this first serious conflict with the authorities was to lead to a complete change of method. Hsia Yen and his comrades were hardier and more flexible in the face of adversity. Shen Hsi-ling however, was so discouraged by his drastically altered film that he left film work altogether for some time.

One foreign observer[23] attended Chinese films of various tendencies, and her report on audience reactions is probably typical. Her first Chinese film, seen in Nanking, was an unconscious caricature of a poor American film, with all the standard ingredients, and the audience was as unenthusiastic as she was:

The lights flashed on; seats banged; and the audience made slowly for the exits. Women from the country in wadded jacket and trousers, a few city girls wrapped in furs, students in overcoats and spectacles. Not over fifty spectators all told.

When she showed doubt to the student with her, he explained:

"It's the sort people high up prefer. You see, such films don't stir up any unpleasant problems and besides, they're so European. . . . Yes, our producers have made other movies, but you won't see them very often; that is, not outside the International Settlement. This is one of the cases when extraterritoriality has its advantages."

So she found her second film, *Spring Silkworms*, in a tiny hall in the International Settlement of Shanghai that was encouragingly packed by Chinese spectators from the neighborhood who "gave the film concentrated and silent attention. No applause, but occasionally a guttural 'Hao!' (Good!) the usual sign of approval in the Chinese theater." One director, interviewed, explained the production of the "Nanking type" of film:

"If the film touches on any serious aspect of China today, someone high up is sure to find something that can be interpreted as criticism of the regime."

When *Bloody Cry* was ready for the screen, the Censors banned the film because the villain of the picture bore a certain physical resemblance to Chiang Kai-shek. *Salt Tide*, a film on the Fukien salt-marshes, had its whole ending amputated and was eventually suppressed.

One of the film team's problems was to identify the anti-Japanese struggle with a broader anti-imperialist movement, no matter how watchful the Kuomintang censors were. Some scripts, such as that for *Two to One* in which a foreign foot-ball team attempts to bribe the Chinese team, an attempt defeated by patriotic emotion and superior playing, brought this identity, though somewhat indirectly, to the film spectator.

But the party group had to do something to shame the large Chinese audience attending American films, and they chose their most vulnerable aspect, scenes involving Chinese characters. These had always been a risk in China: even in 1930 Harold Lloyd's *Welcome Danger* was banned because its scenes in San Francisco's Chinatown hurt "national feeling,"*[24] and *The China Critic*, a mod-erate Shanghai weekly, published an article by Frederick Hung, "Racial Mockery in Motion Pictures," in its Christmas issue. Early in 1932, as the patriotic revolutionary fervor was at its height, after the January cannonades and humil-iations by the Japanese, Paramount was so ill advised as to bring *Shanghai Ex-press* to Shanghai. Even under the carefully selected Chinese title, *Not Afraid of Death*, the opportunities it offered Chinese sensibilities to be insulted were generous. Based on a Soviet film that the left-wing critics had not seen, it touched subjects that were not even permissible in a Chinese film, no matter how rooted in reality they might have been: warlords, and peasant revolu-tionaries who are regarded as bandits by the train's passengers. The film's run ended in the middle of its first evening, when Hung Shen, eluding the ushers, reached the stage to make his protest clear before leading a student demonstra-tion outside the theater. The whole action was so successful that no other film of Sternberg or Marlene Dietrich ever had an easy career in China.†

Hung Shen's varied activities were a credit to the film team. His main respon-sibility was to the now strong left wing of Ming Hsing. His two scenarios of this time were among the most openly militant being produced, but their synopses[25]

---

* Lloyd sent his sincere apologies to the Chinese Consul-General at Los Angeles, H. K. Chang: "When we started to produce *Welcome Danger*, we engaged a staff of Chinese experts to guide us in a path that we felt would prevent us from casting any reflection on China as a nation or its people as individuals.. . . . I felt that our entire action was laid in a comedy premise and would be accepted as such. Since I have learned of the objection on the part of the Chinese to what was intended to be an innocent bit of fun, I have ordered its complete withdrawal from China." (published in *The China Critic,* 7 Aug. 1930). Harry Alan Potamkin, however, agreed with the Chinese censors: "A presumably wholesome (since farcical) film like Harold Lloyd's *Welcome Danger!* is a thousand times more vicious in its picturing of fiendish Chinaman and Negro than the vilest sex-film." — "The Cinematized Child," written in 1930, published posthumously in *Films*, November 1939.
† From Sternberg's memoirs: "I was told that if ever I appeared in China I would be arrested and punished. Nevertheless, some years later I managed to enter that extraordinary country, after the train that brought me there was delayed by bandits soon after crossing the Manchurian border." *Fun in a Chinese Laundry* (New York: Macmillan, 1965), p. 263.

(I have seen neither film) sound dangerously alike, both in "typical" characters and "basic" conflicts. A *Beauty of Perfumed Grasses*: farmer and family come to Shanghai — find work in cigarette factory — wife loses her job — daughter rejects employer's advances — loses her job, too — factory conditions worsen — husband wants to strike, but conservative brother restrains him — he is fired, anyway — daughter becomes prostitute — wife takes daughter away from city — leaves child at home — child dies, "punished by life" — husband sees display of foreign cigarettes in shop window — breaks window and is arrested — in jail meets a worker who shows him the correct way. . . . The story is framed by the hero's testimony at his trial, with which the film opens. It used a cartoon sequence of oppressive dollars and of foreign products (shown as a heavy, black smoke) filling the Chinese landscape. Soon after the film opened in a concession cinema in November 1933, the theater received an order from the concession authorities to stop the film.

Hung Shen's next scenario, *Oppression*: manager of textile mill is oppressed by bigger capitalist, forced to close mill — worker of weak character one of those who lose jobs — difficulties of his unemployment — wife works as servant in the big capitalist's house — she is abducted by private guard of house — worker's mother and child die of cold and hunger — he gets job in factory owned by the big capitalist, but foreign capitalist forces this factory to lower wages — strike — worker denounced by private guard — arrest of both man and abducted wife. . . . The authorities insisted on a "tail" being added to take sting out of the film's intention:* a court establishes the innocence of the couple.

Both these synopses sound like setups, dry, easy arrangements of politically necessary ingredients. Yet Hung Shen's art can be detected here, too, in his insistence on a weak-willed worker as the protagonist of *Oppression*, a possibly more credible (and less repetitious) character than the "correct type" of determined worker that dogma required. This character is, indeed, regarded by Cheng Chi-hua as Hung Shen's most serious "mistake" in this period.

Unfortunately there were few such "mistakes" in these victorious months of the party's film team. Riding on the year's wave of patriotic feeling the energetic left-wingers at Ming Hsing and the other two studios under the film team's influence grew overconfident, making their films not only more openly a summons

---

* This alteration may have been self-censorship within the studio, not from the authorities outside, for in an interview with the film's director, Gao Li-hun, he merely talks about the change without even hinting at external pressure. (*Shun Bao*, special film supplement, 23 Aug. 1933)

to struggle (along lines that had swiftly become traditional), but also less inventive and expressive as art, as drama, as reality. Apparently these values require more obstacles and conflict; and these were to come. So long as the Kuomintang authorities wished to identify themselves also with the patriotic movement, and before the later bargaining stages of their negotiations with the Japanese arrived, the left wing in all Shanghai arts had things much their own way. "Anti-imperialism" and even "revolution" became acceptable words and attitudes, and a host of second- and third-rate artists, especially in the new field of films, adopted this tone as the required mode of the moment.* The more left films made the more flatly ordinary they became, despite Hsia Yen's efforts to maintain high standards of filmwriting and direction. *Quantity* was also of interest to the underground leaders, especially as they thrilled to see so many of *their* films reaching the public; but this quantity, with its increasing openness and repetition, turned into a self-destructive factor.

The Lien Hua Company was the second large studio to be penetrated by the film team. Lien Hua was less easy, even though it too had been hurt economically by Japanese aggression: its Peking branch had been closed down (along with all of Lo Ming-yü's ambitious training programs), and the company tottered along on its No. 1 base in Hong Kong and its No. 2 base in Shanghai. For a man of Lo's grand schemes it is not surprising that he would wish to maintain all his government contacts, so the film team did not find their entrance into his No. 2 plant so easy. His slogan of The Four Nationalisms,† and his support of the Association of Chinese Educational Films, newly created by the Kuomintang government to dilute left-wing influence, made him a formidable opponent to the team, but they had history (for a while) on their side. Soon after the critical violence of 28 January 1932 Lien Hua issued a three-reel actuality film,‡ *How the 19th Army Fought the Japanese*, "a textbook to arouse the people's patriotism," and this was immediately followed by an equally rousing fictional film, *Share the Burden of the National Crisis*: story discussions began on 18 February,

---

* "It became more and more the habit, particularly of the inferior sorts of literati, to make up for the want of cleverness in their productions, by political allusions which were sure to attract attention. Poetry, novels, reviews, the drama, every literary production teemed with what was called "tendency," that is with more or less timid exhibitions of an anti-governmental spirit." — Friedrich Engels, *Revolution and Counter-Revolution in Germany.*
† "Save National Films, Propagate National Spirit, Develop National Enterprise, Serve National State."
‡ In 1926, for a Chicago review of *Moana*, John Grierson imported from France the term *documentaire*, and gave the name of "documentary" to the British movement he championed and led. But in six years he worried about the term: "Documentary is a clumsy description, but let it stand." I am more bothered by the increasingly loose use of the term, and I propose another French import that is closer to reality — *actualité,* actuality films.

shooting began 27 February, and the film was completed in mid-April and shown publicly on 19 August. Regardless of its political errors,* too easily pointed out at this distance in time, its success was the entering wedge for the film team.

For two years T'ien Han had written plays that were seen by few, if any spectators, and film scenarios that were swiftly rejected (including one, *China Roars*, that was probably an adaptation of Tretyakov's play), but under one of his pseudonyms T'ien Han's script for *Three Modern Girls* was brought to Lien Hua by the film team, and the result, a popular and valuable film, was the pride of the film team and Lien Hua's bookkeeping department; its plot was tangled but original:

The center of the story, around which the three females circle, is a young man who becomes a popular film star.† As a student he had not agreed with the marriage arranged for him, and he escaped to the city where he found fame and fortune. Unknown to him the fiancée of his arranged marriage also escaped to Shanghai where she becomes a telephone operator. The film star now loves a girl from South China. After the January crisis his love films are less popular and he receives a warning telephone call that he must stop making such films. He discovers that it is his former fiancée who called him. In spite of an infatuated fan from the South who contrives to meet him, he joins the army and goes to the front. He is wounded, and at the hospital his fiancée turns up as a nurse, but she makes it clear that she is no longer interested in their marriage. When he returns to the studio his first Southern sweetheart is widowed and cannot act with him, so he agrees to make a film with his second Southern sweetheart: in a scene where she is supposed to kill herself, she really does so. The star finds his former fiancée, and she introduces him to parts of the city he never knew before: the port, the factories, the slums and poor schools. He meets her friends and there is progress in his political development. For her participation in a strike at the telephone company she loses her job, but he is by her side.

The mixture of appealing ingredients with instructional ones worked more smoothly in *Three Modern Girls* than with anything else produced by the film team at Lien Hua. T'ien Han's responsibility for this success was rewarded by his being given artistic charge of a whole small new studio that had been formed at

---

* Cheng Chi-hua: "Peasants and proletarians are missing from the film, and anti-Japanese leadership is not clear."
† Played by Kim Yen (King Shan in Chinese), a Korean whose father had participated in the anti-Japanese struggle in 1911 before escaping to Northeast China.

this critical time, Yi Hua. Despite its thin finance and minimum equipment T'ien Han plunged into the new work with enthusiasm, writing twice as many films as were produced, and directing the new studio's first production, *Existence of the Nation,** avoiding studio scenes because no sets could be built, nor was there a stage to build them on: T'ien Han's long experience with impoverished theater groups had prepared him for Yi Hua. The company's financial base was precarious, and the circumstances of its birth tell us something about the dozens of fly-by-night companies that came and went in Shanghai each year: the money came from Yen Chun-tang, the intimate of a wealthy opium-dealing gangster; Yen was able to get enough money from him to help out another friend of his, an unemployed fellow who had an acquaintance in the film team, and thus a new film company was formed, with talent supplied by the team. Yi Hua's public declaration was "to make realistic films which will realize the historical task and express the people's suffering"—a statement that must have amused the gangster who supplied the founding money. Yen, however, by the summer of 1933, observed that left-wing films made money, increased his investment in Yi Hua, and dreamed about cornering stars and directors. There was even enough money to build one filming stage.

Along with other American film habits Ming Hsing and the other companies guided by the film team gladly used the star system. Even today a Chinese film not based on a star is a rare thing. Chiefly because Yi Hua couldn't afford them, T'ien Han's *Existence* was a rare and suggestive example of a film without stars, or rather, with the whole group of actors on one level of importance. Custom, however, was pushed in the opposite direction, with the promotion of individually attractive actors and, especially, actresses. The selection of star faces in the front offices must have been a peculiar process: male stars, of course, had to be handsome (except those who wrote or directed their own films), but there was not the great gulf here between faces on a Chinese street and faces on a Chinese screen as is so conspicuous among female stars. Only on Chinese calendars of modern beauties can one find counterparts of the ladies who were "developed" to attract film audiences of the treaty ports in the 1930s, and these standards have changed little since then. If you seek a film actress who resembles the uniquely Chinese beauty that one can see in ancient frescoes or in the modern countryside, you will find her, if at all, playing a "character" or "negative" role. The Shanghai standard for film beauty is one thing left unchanged by revolution.

Ming Hsing's trump card was Wu Hu-tieh, a plump, soft creature who wisely did not try to act. Her English name (this was the mark of the true star) was Miss

---

* This was the title finally passed by the censors; T'ien Han's first and forbidden titles were *China's Homeless People* and *Where Can We Go?*

Butterfly Wu. She specialized in persecuted heroines, for the sight of a tear rolling over that round cheek shook filmgoers. She was part of the film team's plan, if not of the film team itself, from its entrance into Ming Hsing, playing the frustrated daughter in *Wild Torrent*, the salt worker's daughter in *Salty Tide*, the put-upon salesgirl in *Rouge and Powder Market* — more than thirty films for this one studio. Her best remembered film (filling its first theater for sixty days) was *Twin Sisters*, in which she played both the poor, honest carpenter's wife and the haughty No. 7 wife of a warlord (see Plate 6). Left critics were proud of this success, but Lu Hsun saw through its social pretentions, commenting sharply and with distressing frankness that this film was intended "to tell people to be content with poverty."[26] The permanent stars of Lien Hua were Wang Ren-mei (known as the Tiger Cat), who played the trapped poor girl in *Dawn Over the Metropolis*, and Li Li-li (Lily Lee), who played in *Volcano in the Blood*, *Daybreak*, and many other films.

There is one film actress of the 1930s who must be clearly separated from these popular creatures. Ruan Ling-yu was also popular, but any one of her films, even one of her worst, will support my opinion that here was one of the great actresses of film history, as perfectly and peculiarly adapted to the film as we recognize Greta Garbo to be. Most of her Chinese admirers (I do not know that any of her films found an audience elsewhere) explain her special place in their memories as somehow attached to her tragic, early death in 1935, but I can say that I was impressed by her art before I knew of her death. The earliest of her films in which I was conscious of an unusual presence was an undramatically harrowing variant on Pushkin's "Station Master" that depended entirely on our interest in the betrayed girl: *The Peach Blossom Weeps Tears of Blood* (1931); Ruan Ling-yu was then twenty-one years old. After that screening I took special pleasure in observing, from film to film, the maturing consciousness of her own style (or method), a delicate mixture of naturalism and stylization that seems the basis of the best film acting in all countries. Like Garbo she had the capacity of transforming the banal and cheap materials given to her in the early 1930s (though nothing worse than *Susan Lenox* or *Mata Hari*!), and making you believe that you were witnessing genuine joy and suffering. When there was an interesting script (she played the strong-minded fiancée in *Three Modern Girls*) her serious work was extremely effective. The value of Ruan Ling-yu to the film team at Lien Hua, especially in their next, less open period, was immense. Her work in their films has not yet lost its power.

In November 1933 Hung Shen wrote an article (published later, in *Culture*[27]) on the extraordinary achievements of progressive Chinese films that year: "After the Japanese attack on Shanghai in 1932, dancing girls disappeared from our

cinema, and we started on the new road of courage. . . . " He described Lien
Hua's *Three Modern Girls* as "a public explosion — a *sensation*," and named *Wild
Torrent, Volcano in the Blood, Daybreak,* and *Dawn Over the Metropolis* as "four
more bombs." But on the morning of 12 November there were some non-
metaphorical explosions that changed the course of progressive Chinese films:
thirty members of the Blue Robe Society arrived at the gates of the Yi Hua
studio, a whistle blew, and the gang proceeded systematically to wreck the entire
establishment. Of the three studios where the left wing had been particularly
active and successful, the fascist organization chose the smallest and weakest for
their example, and their meaning was not lost on the managements of Ming
Hsing and Lien Hua. So that there would be no ambiguity in the action, a letter
was sent to all Shanghai cinemas the next day, threatening generally and specifically:

Films made by T'ien Han [and others, named] that promote class struggle, pit
poor against rich — such reactionary films may not be shown. If they are shown,
there will be violence and we cannot assure you that what happened to the Yi
Hua Company will not happen to you.

The letter was signed by the Committee to Destroy Communists. Their blows
and threats were not confined to film studios and theaters. A left-wing publishing house, the offices and printshops of left-wing journals and several bookshops
were thoroughly wrecked, and leaflets were left behind: "WARNING! . . . We
intend to cleanse the cultural world. . . . We are carefully examining all publications. . . . " The Blue Robes and their employers were testing the successful
terrors used by black and brown shirts abroad.

The effect of this violence was sudden, yet a movement towards Kuomintang
control of films had been under way ever since the film team entered the
studios. In 1932, even before the team's arrival at Ming Hsing, that studio's production of *Blood Debt* had been totally forbidden by the censors. The organs of
control, already alert, were prodded into firmer action by the political situation,
especially by Kuomintang efforts to soothe and soften the Japanese authorities.
The Shanghai Treaty with Japan agreed to suppress anti-Japanese activities, and
a month later, in June 1932, the Kuomintang Minister of Propaganda distributed
an order to all film companies:

Now that the military situation has been settled, our government needs peace
with the rest of the world. A treaty has been signed, a conference will be held,
and the atmosphere is calm. If provocative films should suddenly appear, this
could hinder the peacemaking actions of the government. . . .

All films about war or with a revolutionary character will be placed on the forbidden list. . . .[28]

Censor power was taken from the Ministries of Interior and Education and delegated instead to more reliable Kuomintang committees. Films hitherto forbidden
only in the foreign concessions were now proscribed in Kuomintang areas as
well. As the Japanese advanced through Jehol and Chahar, approaching Peking
and Tientsin, the Kuomintang grew more conciliatory to them, and more harsh
to the "troublemakers" at home. When Japanese troops were shown in a Chinese
film they could not be identified as Japanese. Any use of the term "anti-
Japanese" was categorically forbidden. In *Children of Storm* a schoolroom
blackboard showed a map of China emphasizing the provinces now occupied by
the Japanese — that shot had to be cut. Lien Hua's *Share the Burden of the
National Crisis* was withdrawn, and another scenario, *Red Blood Spurts*, was
stopped before production. But Japanese productions displaying a different
rationale on the actions of September and January and showing admiration for
the power of the imperial troops were shown without hindrance in the foreign
concessions. Not even sidewalk demonstrations, which a few months before
would have given some slight annoyance to cinema managers, ticket buyers, and
concession police, were in evidence now. The only and indirect protest appeared
in a series of nine articles entitled "May We Ask?", in *Film Art*, asking rhetor-
ically (for everyone knew) why patriotic films were forbidden.

In addition to violence, reaction now brought out its whole arsenal of more
subtle weapons and methods, for the authorities gave more of their attention to
films than to any other art. The basic technique, control, began earlier, in the
spring of 1933, when there was an attempt to enforce controls over scripts,*
advertising, and cinema programs, and it may have been the obvious ineffec-
tuality of these controls that helped to produce the extreme solution of Yi Hua's
destruction. Another form of control was espionage, employed in the most
suspected studios, but the staffs were too tightly knit to provide outsiders with
much information, and the agents' efforts to learn the methods of the film team
for use in productions of their own choice were equally feeble. In only one field
did the authorities get what they wanted: all the film supplements (of the daily
and weekly newspapers) were stopped.

It was, of course, the studio owners and heads that were pressed most directly
and in their most vulnerable spot — finance. In the winter of 1933–1934 the

---

* The Kuomintang did not release statistics on this period, but on a later, more "successful"
period: from November 1934 to March 1935 they forbade the production of eighty-three
film scripts.

Ming Hsing Company found their usual loan apparatus working less smoothly: banks were polite, but the money was not coming through as before. When the censors delayed the release of several finished films, the studio's difficulties became clear to all, and one creditor brought the studio to court. At this point the company was approached by the American Commercial and Exchange Bank: would they sell out for 300,000 yuan? It was only the success and foreign sales of *Twin Sisters* that brought the company past this crisis. Then the Kuomintang tried kindness and persuasion, offering to lend money to Ming Hsing. This form of control may have worked, for soon several undisguised Kuomintang people were brought into the administration offices. Two Ming Hsing productions of 1934 were obviously made to appease the authorities, *Morals of Women* and *Second Marriage.* The first shows the suffering and increasing virtues of a daughter-in-law whose husband is a wastrel student, neglectful of parents, family, and tradition. The second, equally moralizing, also concerns a student son who leaves his first wife and father in a village; they pay painfully for his useless education, his new wife, and his high-living debts in Shanghai. The main aim of the second film appears to have been to counter the effect of left-wing films of class struggle in the countryside.* The appearance of the two films coincided (surely it was not wholly coincidental) with the Kuomintang campaign for the New Life Movement, to which the Generalissimo and Madame Chiang gave their personal support. The main purpose of this movement must have been to throw together elements of Christianity and Confucianism and Moral Rearmament to make something that could compete with the positive and moral program offered to China by the Communist Party. *Morals of Women* was especially praised by the highest Kuomintang officials — and the left-wingers at Ming Hsing now had even firmer protection for their activities!

Nineteen thirty-four was the last year of an *open* struggle between left and right in Shanghai's film studios, with the right using the weapons of authority and annihilation and the left defending its ideology and life with the weapons of ingenuity and persistence. When the right-wingers of the Ming Hsing administration and staff used this opportunity to increase the quantity and importance of the studio's "soft" or low films (*Three Sisters,* from a Japanese story, "The Green Pearl," *The Heart of a Beauty, Madame Mo, Enemy of Women, Orchid in the Ravine*), even resubmitting scripts that the leftists had rejected, Hsia Yen's

---

* Its scenarist, Wan Pi-lin (member of the Kuomintang Central Propaganda Bureau and leading spirit of the China Educational Film Association), made this clear in a statement: "Some people think that Chinese villages are full of high ideals and that peasants' heads are stuffed with progressive notions — that's all a dream . . . the left-wing films that show village life aren't true — they're even laughable. That's why I felt obliged to write this little story." — *Contemporary Cinema*, Nov 1934.

cleverness used this opportunity, too. His next scenario after the Yi Hua destruction (though officially credited to the "editorial committee") was calculated to
exploit this "soft" tendency. *The Common Enemy*, even in its title, is crammed
with ambiguities, pretending, on the one hand, to tell a story of domestic
intrigue (suffering wife, philandering officer-husband, luscious and deceitful
courtesan), while actually giving its audiences a message of class solidarity and
anti-Japanese struggle (see Plate 7). Next, the studio wanted a 100% dialogue
film; Hsia Yen proposed that many writers work on a sequence of short episodes
that he would supervise and pull together.

Each of the eight short stories of *A Bible for Daughters* (even the New Life Movement might have been fooled by this title) is a suffering episode of upper-
middle-class life told by the seven guests (all ladies, played by the studio's stars)
and their hostess (played by Miss Butterfly Wu) at a chic evening gathering without a hint of class struggle — I don't remember seeing even a serving maid. The
whole first of its sixteen reels is taken up with the loved minutiae of high
society: cards, trays, announcements, gowns, overstuffed sofas. Hsia Yen may
have held his tongue in his cheek, but the device worked, for the whole wet film
(one of the wettest I've seen, with either rain or tears falling in each episode,
sometimes together) was passed with only one change. To the hostess's final
story (set in the Northern March) the authorities insisted on adding a lantern
parade for the New Life Movement. The film's form, a cluster of short films
bound by a thin thread of continuity, is one of the first experiments of the
inventive underground period of Chinese films. It is an effective instrument
devised for a particular necessity, and its triumph cannot be dimmed by the
possibility that Hsia Yen may have seen one of the several tentative short-story
films in the twenties or the good-humored *If I Had a Million* (shown in Shanghai
the year before *A Bible*). The more famous French and American "episode-
films," *Carnet de Bal* (1938) and *Tales of Manhattan* (1942), were still in the
future when *A Bible for Daughters* was made. One resemblance that must be
noted, though closer to Hsia Yen's later "cross-section" film, *New Year Coin*, is
Die Abenteuer eines Zehnmarkscheins (1928). Its author, Béla Balázs, described
its form and purpose in a way that would certainly have caught the attention of
Hsia Yen, even if he had no opportunity to see this film: according to Balázs, it
is as if the plot "followed a thread that, connecting the dramatic junctions of the
ways of Fate, leads across the texture of life."[29]

A Bible was finished and shown in October 1934, and in that month both Hsia
Yen and Ah Ying were dismissed, on instructions from above, and in November
the efficiently dangerous editorial committee was dissolved. It was a blow, but,
while Hsia Yen helped T'ien Han form a new company and himself moved to a

less conspicuous position at the Lien Hua second studio, the party team altered
its methods and tactics. All left-wing and party workers changed their professional names. Group contacts were replaced by personal contacts with individual
filmmakers. Producers had grown dependent on left-wing writing talents, and, as
the newly emerging agents turned out to be incapable of writing scenarios, there
was a script crisis: it was then decided to allow directors to prepare their own
scripts, and the most important films of 1935 were the result of quiet collabora-
tions between directors and party writers. Hsia Yen later recalled this first
"severe" period of underground film history:

This is how it usually worked out: the studio would decide on a film story and
begin preparations to produce it, while the director would come to talk with us,
or we would go to him. We would suggest that he should change these scenes or
those words of the dialogue — we made the most of this opportunity to get our
ideas into the film, and make it as useful as possible. So in this way, too, we
entered capitalist films, getting progressive ideas into them and making them
work for our policy.[30]

The destruction of the Yi Hua studio marks a turning point in Chinese film
history, artistically as well as politically. We can see that this was by no means
the end of progressive or revolutionary films in pre-1949 China, but, forced into
underground channels by government oppression, the left-wing filmmakers were
also forced to abandon the bald, easy, superficial portrayals of social evils and
revolutionary solutions that had been acceptable for too long. This acceptable
superficiality was not to reappear until after 1949; now it was replaced by
deeper treatments, more seriously developed characters, new methods and
forms, all evolved through the necessity to evade censorship and the total repression that was always threatened, but never quite achieved, by the Kuomintang.
Cheng Chi-hua's chapter on this period is accurately entitled: "An Indirect
Method for Anti-Japanese and Anti-Imperialist Propaganda, and a Concealed
Method for Revealing the Dark Side of Society."

This new method of combating the Kuomintang's propaganda and ruthlessness
resulted in films that were more effective, both as films and as communications,
than anything produced in the previous "open" period. Though Hsia Yen continued "personal consultations" with those directors at Ming Hsing who had not
been too scared by the post Yi Hua developments, his real victories in 1935 all
came from the Lien Hua studio, where he now occupied a much humbler position than at Ming Hsing. He arrived at Lien Hua just as its ambitious head, Lo
Ming-yü, was involved in a struggle to maintain domination of his three scattered
studios; he may not even have been aware of his new employee.

As at Ming Hsing the destruction of Yi Hua was the signal for right forces at Lien

Hua to take charge, and Lo's aim, at the beginning of 1934, was to show the Kuomintang that he was their man. He produced a film about military planes and fearless pilots (but without an enemy!), *Iron Birds*. His more entertaining films were "wholesome": *Princess of Sport* was an amusing, even somewhat useful idea for a film, showing an inflated ego brought under control by rather incredible circumstances; *A Man's Life* was serious enough to win the government's prize for the year's best silent film. Both of these were directed by Fei Mu, who was to show his real talent in collaboration with the underground writers a year later. Lo himself was sent by the government to the United States and Europe to study film technique, but on his return the situation at his studio was so tangled that if he learned anything abroad, there was little opportunity to apply it at home.

Lo's first move, a fusion of his three studios, was nearly his last move, for his chief backer, Wu, then in personal charge of the Second Studio, saw this as a scheme to eliminate his control there and fought back with all the money and credits and power at his disposal. When the dust settled Wu was the de facto chief of Lien Hua, and the Second Studio was the new base of the party's film team: Wu had brought them in to strengthen the quality of his productions, and Lo's Kuomintang connections lessened the authorities' anxiety about Lien Hua. The interesting result of this contradiction was that for two years Shanghai's most "reactionary" films and most "progressive" films were coming from the same studio. Such a situation, in which Japan was being both mollified and resisted by the same Chinese organization, is typical for these years.

The first famous product of this contradiction was *Song of the Fishermen*. Its scenario and direction were credited to Tsai Chu-sheng, whose *Dawn Over the Metropolis* a year earlier had tempered its traditional situations and performances with an occasional surprising use of real places, a good direction for Tsai's future. His *Song of the Fishermen* was released 14 June 1934, at the height of the worst heat wave that Shanghai had experienced in sixty years; though the Chin Shen Cinema was not air-conditioned, the film established a new record of eighty-four days. Its popularity throughout China and the overseas Chinese settlements was overwhelming, and its theme song has by now achieved the status of folk art. It left an extraordinary impression on the audience at Moscow's first International Film Festival at the beginning of 1935. I recall such simplicity and directness that I am quite astonished to read a synopsis of its loosely ranging plot:*

---

* Only parts of the film have survived in the Film Archive of China. There is hope that a complete copy may be recovered from abroad.

A fisherman's family on the East China Sea is left helpless by the death of the father in a storm. The mother is forced to turn over her orphaned twin children to others and go to work for the family of a rich boat-owner, Ho. Ho's son plays with the twins (an attractive girl and a dim-witted brother) until he is sent overseas to learn industrial fishing techniques. The twins join the fishing fleet but after two years of struggles by warlords and bandits for their coast they leave the village with their mother, now blind, and join her brother-in-law, a Shanghai street-singer. The twins can't find work so with their uncle they sing the songs of their childhood on the street, where they encounter the returned son of Ho (he is working in his father's company, now allied with foreign companies); he gives them money that is stolen from them, and somehow leads to their being jailed. They return to their uncle's home to find it burned and their mother and uncle dead. Ho's son takes them into his house, where they are exposed to another kind of unhappiness — one of his father's wives runs away with the family fortune, the company goes bankrupt and Ho commits suicide. The son sees how social conditions hamper his hopes for reconstructing the Chinese fishing industry and goes to work with the twins on a simple fishing-boat. The film ends on the injury and death of the superfluous brother to the music of the fishermen's song.[31]

The triumph of the film is that none of these overpointed situations interferes with the conviction that we are witnessing some direct expression of the Chinese people — a naive expression, certainly, but genuine. To its first foreign audience of 1935 it seemed a miracle, with an effect similar to that on later European audiences of *Rashomon* and *Pather Panchali*.

Compared with the similar subject of *Angry Tide of China's Sea, Song of the Fishermen* shows how swiftly — in less than two years — the left filmmakers had learned how to reach and touch their audience. Music, handled with dramatic and technical confidence, had become a natural element. The theme song was composed by Jen Kuang/Chen Guan* to a text by Ahn Wo which was as direct and simple as the film:

> We mend the nets,
> We find the fish —
> We labor under cloud and rain . . .
>
> Our hands are blistered,
> Our necks are stiff,
> The fish are caught —
> And our bellies are empty.

---

* Born 1909 in Shaohsing, worked in France as a piano repair man, returned to Shanghai in 1929 where, in his job at the Pathé Gramophone and Film Company, he wrote many popular songs. Died in 1941.

If one hears in this the voice of an intellectual who never hauled a net, one should also note that the makers of *Song* expected to have few fishermen in their audience: the aim was to establish and deepen sympathies among people who could afford to buy cinema tickets.

Even the improved quality of the sound recording had a political meaning. In September 1933 three well-to-do radio engineers, patriotically left wing and trained in American schools, had constructed their own sound camera (Three-Friend-Type Camera winning a $10,000 prize from General Chiang) and founded the Dien Tung Equipment Company, Ltd., to sell and rent film equipment. It was their link to Wu that helped to bring the party's film team into the Lien Hua Studio; their technical help increased the solid success of *Song of the Fishermen*, and eventually, when Lien Hua's welcome to the party team wore thin, the team transformed the equipment company into their own film-producing studio.

Before the team's influence weakened at Lien Hua it pushed a number of themes into production that I suppose reflected credit on party policy in 1934. There was *A Good Night*, fighting feudal prejudices against the remarriage of widows and the unarranged marriages of daughters. *The Goddess* (a term that meant prostitute) and *Goodbye, Shanghai* both wasted the fine Ruan Ling-yu in subjects that only she could rescue from worse than mediocrity: the "goddess" has to suffer not only direct persecution, but the humiliation of her son at school, as well; in *Goodbye, Shanghai* she plays a schoolteacher fallen among corrupt characters (a wicked doctor gives her a sedative in order to rape her) while a sailor sweetheart is prevented by the scenarists from returning to her. In *Perfumed Snowy Sea* (presumably white lilac in blossom) Ruan plays a twice-dedicated nun who finally returns to normal life. The team's next two films (after, note, Hsia Yen's move to Lien Hua) were successes from every point of view — one of them, *New Women*, fatally successful.

The Big Road enjoyed both an original subject and treatment (see Plate 9). The script, inspired by watching road workers in Shanghai, was written in one month, May 1934. The scenarist-director adjusted his final script to the actors who were to play in it, even to the point of using their family names for the roles.[32] Each of the eight prominent characters (all played by young or future "stars") is individually characterized and developed, and the film's camaraderie is unforced and convincing; the scenes in the workers' quarters have excellent touches of reality that made me more watchful for other work by its scenarist and director, Sun Yu, than had his previous films. A group of friends take jobs in a road construction gang, become involved with the community that is used as

their base, and defend their new friends from a traitorous landlord's evil plans:
he had been bribed to sabotage the construction of a military road. There is an
unusual sparseness in the sentimental interludes, but melodrama wins out in the
end, the concluding lurid action (decorated with lavish banquet and torture
dungeon) tending to drive away most of the interesting ideas of the film. In a
bloody final sequence all the leading characters are killed by Japanese planes
strafing the now symbolic road (built for defense). As with many other tragic
conclusions then and later, an epilogue is added, with the optimistic ghosts of
the slain marching onwards.

Both *Big Road* and *New Women* were actually silent films with music tracks
(nearing the end of his brief career Nieh Erh composed a memorable song for
each of them; for *Big Road* Sun Yu asked him for a tune and rhythm similar to
the Volga Boatmen's song), but the scenario of *New Women* presented insuperable difficulties for the director (Tsai Chu-sheng): more is said and thought by
the characters than could ever be conveyed by subtitles. The scenarist, Sun
Shih-yi, may have hoped until the last moment for the studio to award synchronized dialogue to his script. The heroine (played by Ruan Ling-yu; see
Plate 7) sees her frivolous past, complete with subtitles, through the window of a
motorcar. Yet no awkwardness could have prevented the sensational success of
this film. Its story was freely based on the recent suicide of the film actress, Ai
Hsia, in February 1934. No one was deceived by the transformation of Ai Hsia
into a novelist, Wei Ming, and no one appears to have objected to the thinness of
this disguise, for known actuality shows through the scenario, making Ruan
Ling-yu's performance so moving as to become, occasionally, a painful experience. Wei Ming is an educated wife whose husband has left her with an infant
daughter. She gets work as a music teacher in a girls' school and hesitates to
marry again, though she is offered pity and jewels by the school's principal.
Burdened with debts and the illness of her six-year-old daughter, she writes a
novel, which is accepted by a publishing friend, though no payment is possible
then. To get some immediate cash she finds a procuress, but the first customer is
the school principal. . . . In despair she takes her life; as she lies dying in the
hospital she hears the shouting newsboys under the window, "Famous woman
writer commits suicide." The last scene: "Many women-workers, after reading
this news of her, walk together to the morning sun!" This is still praised as a
device to remove the sting of hopelessness from a tragedy.

The film opened in February 1935, for the Chinese New Year festival. On 8
March Ruan Ling-yu herself committed suicide. She was twenty-five. Her farewell note said, "Gossip is a fearful thing," and Lu Hsun wrote a bitter essay with

this for title, blaming unscrupulous journalism, without mentioning Ruan's last film: *

. . . brilliant writers dash off big headlines: "More Concupiscent than Wu Tse-tien" . . . in the case of an educated woman, especially one who is a social figure, they do great damage, even more so, of course, when exaggerated, highly colored language is deliberately used. But in China such phrases flow unsought at the flourish of a pen. . . . No epithet whatever matters to those in power, for they have only to write a note and immediately an apology or correction will be printed. But a helpless woman like Ruan Ling-yu is made to suffer, smeared with mud she cannot wipe clean. Should she fight back? Not owning a newspaper, she cannot. There is no one with whom to argue, to whom to appeal. . . . And those who thought the newspapers had something to do with her suicide were telling the truth too.[33]

In Moscow the success of *Song of the Fishermen* at the International Film Festival was followed by another Chinese pleasure, the tour there of Mei Lan-fang and his theater. He came to Moscow with Miss Butterfly Wu, as the greatest

Г.Е.

---

* Lu Hsun saw few Chinese films in his last years; his diary records these films for the beginning of 1935: 2 Jan. — *Cleopatra*; 29 Jan. — *Resistance* [?] ; 16 Feb. — *Tarzan and His Mate* (for the second time); 11 Mar. — *The Private Life of Don Juan* and *Treasure Island*. He saw films, foreign films, about twice a month.

star the Chinese cinema could send abroad, but next to Mei's art and fame, little more than polite attention was paid to her. His visit and performances have a place in international film history because of their effect on Eisenstein, who had never before seen the Chinese classic theater. As a tribute to it and to Mei he tried to film one of the episodes in Mei's programs, but no one was happy with the results. (See Plate 8.) Nevertheless it was an encounter that left a positive impression on both artists. Before Mei's departure there was a discussion, at which Eisenstein spoke:

When I was young I heard that all Oriental theaters were alike. But now that I have seen both the Japanese and Chinese theaters, I see how distinctly different they are — as different as the Roman and Greek theaters, or the American and European theaters. In the Chinese theater, happiness, anger, sorrow are expressed in a certain conventional way — conventional yet not rigid. Many good aspects of realism, used in the Russian theater, can be found in the Chinese theater. The Chinese theater has many special qualities of its own, but why isn't the Chinese cinema inspired by these?[3 4]

With the spurt of left-wing opportunities it may not seem so miraculous that the destroyed Yi Hua studio resumed production. The studio was the only business of the Yens, father and son, and they could not accept its annihilation without a struggle. By June 1934 they decided to rebuild and make films again, and a big gangster was brought into the company, for money and defense: his only condition was that Yi Hua must make films that were "easy to like." For this reason Tan Tu-yu was invited in to direct musicals and romantic stories. The studio's good reputation, as well as a sense of responsibility for the studio's trouble, brought support from the party's film team: T'ien Han and Yang Han-sheng used pseudonyms to continue to work on scenarios, and Nieh Erh joined Yi Hua's music department.

Of the eleven films produced by Yi Hua in 1934 and 1935 Cheng Chi-hua claims nine as "progressive," but Kuomintang supervision and censorship stripped these victories down to neutralities. The studio's two boldest films of 1935 were *Refugees* and *Victory Song*, and the release of the latter was followed by the arrest of both T'ien Han and Yang Han-sheng. Between this signal of Kuomintang impatience with Yi Hua and the Yens' total capitulation only one film indicates any progress: Hung Shen's scenario of *A Hero of Our Time* has a protagonist so negative that this seems unique in Chinese film history, a film without a hero. Its time extends from the beginning of the First World War to "the present," with a small businessman climbing ruthlessly to wealth and finding himself subservient to greater powers. The "positive" finale, a classroom of workers' children singing, could not have made its bitter taste more palatable.

The last Shanghai base of the party's film team in the 1930s was the Dien Tung Studio, the transformed equipment company. They had time to make only four films before they were forcibly closed, but this small group of films, made in little more than a year, is as important as any other studio's production that was supported by the party's team.

Their first film marked the debut, as scenarist and as film actor, of Yuan Mu-jih, one of the greatest talents in Chinese cinema, though this first film work, *Plunder of Peach* [Blossom] *and Plum* [Blossom] (also known as *Fate of the College Graduates*), is too obviously an effort to follow what had been done before (an intellectual and his wife sink lower and lower to tragic conclusion) to be representative of his real capacity. He had worked in theater groups since the age of thirteen (at eighteen he was writing one-act plays, and filling the leading roles of *The Wild Duck* and *Uncle Vanya*) and finally left both family and university when they objected to his theater work. He immediately identified himself with the left theater, playing in the Shanghai production of *Roar China* and as Lu Hsun's *Ah Q* making his reputation as a comedian. With his actress wife, Chen Bo-erh, he joined the Dien Tung Studio in 1934, and they played together in most of the films he wrote and directed. Dien Tung continued to make useful technical advances, for *Plunder* was the first Chinese film to use sound-on-film to replace the awkward disk system.

Yuan also played the leading role in Dien Tung's second film, *Children of Troubled Times*, a film that was associated with much trouble. After *Plunder* the Kuomintang kept an eye on the new studio and sent a police agent to investigate. Thereupon the studio was identified in official circles as "the base camp of the rat," and both T'ien Han and Yang Han-sheng were arrested before they moved from Yi Hua to their new posts. However, T'ien Han had written a script for Dien Tung about the tribulations of a traveling theater troupe (resembling the Bright Moon Troupe where T'ien Han had met Nieh Erh), and this was now given to Hsia Yen, who managed to finish a shooting script for it just before he heard about *his* impending arrest and escaped to Japan in September 1934. The film was completed and shown in May 1935, and a month before this its composer Nieh Erh was also forced to leave China — his name had been seen on a blacklist of writers and artists to be arrested. His film score for *Children of Troubled Times*, his last, has had the longest life, for a "March of the Volunteers" in it was adopted by the Red Army and in 1949 became the national anthem of the People's Republic of China.* Japan had its own reasons then for

---

* Early in 1938 Auden and Isherwood, in their *Journey to a War* (London: Faber & Faber, 1939), report hearing Nieh Erh's song adapted as a Protestant hymn in a Canadian mission near Hankow.

accepting political refugees from China, but Nieh Erh seems to have wanted to use Japan only as a means of getting to France or the Soviet Union. While there, though, he joined a Japanese left-wing drama group and on a beach excursion with them on 17 July 1935 was drowned, at the age of twenty-three.

The third film, *Statue of Liberty*, was made with a depleted, nervous staff. It was the first film work by its cameraman, Yang Ji-ming, and its director, Ssutu Hui-min. Ssutu was cousin to one of the three founders of the equipment company and, fresh from overseas training at Tokyo's Arts Academy and the film institute at New York's Columbia University, he was made responsible for the organization of the new studio, but he had not expected to be directing his own films quite so soon. This first work is slow but careful, with an unusual attention to composition and photographic quality. With no particular relation to its title the story covers Chinese history from the May 4 movement of 1919 to the Japanese shelling of Chapei in 1932, and its re-creation of historical events is notable, especially the Shameen massacre of 1925, witnessed in Canton by Ssutu at the age of fifteen.

The studio's last production was a masterpiece. At least the first half of *Scenes of City Life** shows how much more Yuan Mu-jih could do with the film medium than any of his predecessors. As prologue a peep-showman (played and sung by Yuan) at a rural railway station shows people who are on their way to the Big City what life is *really* like there, how their lives will change there, and the film shows this to them and to us — with the instant communication of Yuan's enjoyment and playfulness (as scenarist and director), though always with a sharp cutting edge. Tricks are played with music and unreal sound. There are many visual jokes (the remarkable first half of the film keeps dialogue to a minimum) and a seasoning of stylized action. There is even some use of animation (by the Wan Brothers). To the spectator today,† it is clear that the artist who made *Scenes* must have been acquainted with the work of Clair and Cavalcanti, and there are echoes on the soundtrack of *City Lights* and *Dreigroschenoper* (such as the singing showman), but it is not so clear how Yuan was able to translate all that into Chinese humor, Chinese character, and Chinese invention. Few have even approached this level of accomplishment. The rarity of any degree of satire on the Chinese screen today makes us appreciate Yuan's art all the more.

---

* When played for foreign audiences in 1935 the title was *Quo Vadis?* — perhaps a joke of Yuan's.
† For the present, *Scenes*, though preserved, is not available to any audience, because a minor role in the second half of the film is played by Lan P'ing, the actress who is now married to Mao Tse-tung and has taken the name of Chiang Ching. She, however, screens her films of the thirties for her intimates.

Circumstances, or lack of enthusiasm, or possibly party frowns on the idea of Chinese making fun of Chinese (even Chinese villains) discouraged Yuan Mu-jih from pursuing this best phase of his talent.

Toward the end of 1935, while Dien Tung was preparing its fifth film, *Big and Little Streets*, the studio was ordered closed. Its personnel scattered to the Ming Hsing, Hsin Hua, and Lien Hua studios, and took with it other planned scripts, *Sad Song of the Swallows, New Year Coin, Heaven in the Desert,* and *Great Joy,* most of which were made, usually with changed names, by the other studios. Though the progressive film movement had received a staggering blow with the arrest or exile of its leading spirits, good and useful films continued to appear from Shanghai studios for the next crucial months, until the studios were taken over by the Japanese, and left-wing artists followed the government to Nanking. The closing of Dien Tung marked the end of the most exciting (occasionally *too* exciting) period of Chinese film history, the Shanghai underground:

The ingenious construction of a whole film just to embody one dangerous line of dialogue in a way to fool the censors;[*] the concealment of forbidden topics in songs, sometimes children's songs (and usually composed by the briefly prolific Nieh Erh); the constant dance around a censorship lulled by bribes and tangled in its own confusion, and all this with the threat of prison or execution hanging over the film-makers — this is a chapter of film history not to be equalled in the pre-revolutionary struggles of any other country's film art. Even the many brilliant leftists working in German films before Hitler cannot point to such a steady sequence of victories in communicating their ideas to such a large audience.[35]

The editor of *Scenes of City Life* summed up the atmosphere of Dien Tung: "Underground film-workers put on no airs — we all ate and rested together. But people sometimes disappeared. . . ."[36]

The first to show the effect of the government's film purge were the small studios, so reduced in number that by the beginning of 1935, after the "Control of Ghost Films" regulation had wiped out eight studios and six others (including Dien Tung) were forced out of business by the authorities and censor-mutilated films, only ten small studios were functioning. By the end of 1935 only two of these survived, and these were closed a year later.

The press was also forced to withdraw its support of left-wing film substance, and the tone of film criticism quickly reversed itself. Now one began to read that

---

[*] And yet another extreme method was described to me: With the aim of getting a vital film past the censors, another film would be made just to draw the censors' fire, and make them less attentive to the next submitted film — the vital one. But my informant did not identify any of these deliberately produced pigeon-films.

"films should make spectators happy," and that "the social value of a film is determined by its quality as a work of art." Thus began the campaign for "soft" films* that all the studios endorsed by producing films that studiously avoided any relevance to the rapidly worsening situation in the world, both abroad and at home.

Fascist aggression in Abyssinia, the larger-scale German and Italian military support of Franco's rebellion against Spanish democracy — these went almost unnoted by the Chinese public, so closely concerned were they in Asian counterparts of the same reactionary forces. (The ample newsreel coverage of European reaction probably moved them as little as we were moved in the 1920s by newsreels of Chinese disasters.) North China still fell, bit by bit, to Japanese arms, and Chiang committed the rest of China, not to resistance, but to a form of civil war. His repeated drives against the revolutionary bases in Kiangsi and Fukien provinces led to the epic event of modern Chinese history — apparently unrecorded by cameras — the Long March.

The only Chinese filmmaker to see much of the outside world in these years was Ouyang Yu-chien. After his last film experience in 1927 he stayed in the theater until 1932 when he went to Europe: he visited England and France, saw the UFA studio soon after Hitler's political victory, and managed two visits to the Soviet Union, where he met Pudovkin. In the winter of 1933 there was an attempt in Fukien province to unite all anti-Chiang forces behind the new 19th Army, and Ouyang returned to China to help this just before the old divisions among the left parties broke up the coalition. Looking for work in Shanghai after a political cooling-off period in Japan, he was offered the chance to write and direct for a small studio that was newly organized, with the support of the Blue Robe Society — less than two years after they wrecked Yi Hua! This new studio, Hsin Hua, was headed by Chang Shih-gun, formerly in the tobacco business, whose introduction to films was as manager of the Great Wall chain of cinemas, and whose chief source of income now was a chain of night clubs. As a member of the Blue Robes he could afford to make patriotic films as well as "soft" films, and his certificate of patriotism was the newsreel of a Chinese victory, retaking an Inner Mongolian town from its Japanese conquerors. This was enough for Ouyang, and later Shih Tung-shan, to risk working for him.

Ouyang chose an old play, *The Apricot Blossom Fan*, to modernize to 1926/1927, with a warlord villain versus a revolutionary playwright (a self-portrait?) and

---

* A term probably related to the phrase that films should be "ice cream for the eyes"!

his heroine actress. It was Ouyang's first sound film, and lack of confidence and equipment nearly defeated him:

I was afraid to jump from shot to shot, or even scene to scene — I couldn't imagine how they would connect. I wasn't able to recognize the difference between a good take and a bad take, or what should be reshot. We had a second-hand sound camera and one precious microphone, a foot long and heavy as a full thermos flask — we called it the "thermos."[37]

Synchronization was always a problem, and every move by the camera required someone's inventive genius. Each edited sequence had to be taken to a cinema for sound projection, for there was no adequate screening room in the studio. One of Hsin Hua's economies was to avoid long contracts, so after *The New Apricot Fan* struggled to completion and release Ouyang accepted Ming Hsing's offer to write and direct for their reorganized studio.

Considering the conditions described by Ouyang, it is amazing that responsible filmmakers continued to work for Chang Shih-gun, but Shih Tung-shan succeeded in making two films there in 1936, *Long Song of Hate* (a good film hampered by careless cutting) and *Mad Night*, a version of Gogol's *Revizor* that translates the action to a small town in South China in the 1920s.* Shih Tung-shan had produced *Revizor* in a Shanghai theater the year before and most of his cast played in the film, too. In 1937 Shih Tung-shan directed *Youth on the March*, an openly patriotic scenario by T'ien Han (the first to be acknowledged by him, possibly in celebration of his release from prison), which may have escaped trouble by being shown when patriotism was popular, three days after the clash near Peking at the Marco Polo Bridge. Shih Tung-shan's most valuable move at Hsin Hua may have been to excite Chin Shan with the idea of film work. This brilliant actor, in the left theater movement since 1932, was not proud of his first film role in *Mad Night,* the last film of the Bright Moon Studio in 1935. He worked in the theater with Shih Tung-shan, and went with him to the Hsin Hua Studio to play in two films, the comic manager of a radio station in *Long Song* and the Khlestakov role in the *Revizor* film. After a more obviously showy role in *Song at Midnight*, a Hsin Hua composite of various American successes, mostly *Phantom of the Opera*, his film career was well under way.

---

* "When I adapted this play I tried not to lose the spirit of the original: I did not alter the story and I tried to use most of the original dialogue whenever it did not clash with my change of the setting to China." — Shih Tung-shan, in a newspaper's film supplement.

The most explicitly patriotic film made at Hsin Hua was *Courage That Reaches above the Clouds* (about the defense of a community against the invaders), that appeared at the end of 1936, in time to be useful in the limited United Front that followed the Sian Incident (an ideal film episode that has never been used in a film). In mid-December, when Chiang Kai-shek was in Sian to lead another extermination drive against the new Shensi base of the Communists, the two local generals took him prisoner to convince him to fight Japanese rather than Chinese.

Meanwhile in Nanking . . . the family of Chiang were utterly opposed to measures against the rebels which would endanger his life; others were not so solicitous. . . .

In Sian, while this debate continued, and preparations for an attack both by land and air went forward, the Generalissimo had had to see a visitor, one most un-welcome to him: Chou En-lai, the Communist leader who had organized the Shanghai uprising, and narrowly escaped with his life when Chiang carried out his counter-revolutionary stroke. Chou had several talks with the leader of the Nationalist party. He at last convinced him of two things; firstly that only by accepting the terms which the rebels and Communists proffered could he save his life, for, unless he accepted, the rebels would put him to death. Secondly, that if he accepted these terms the Communists would acknowledge his authority as head of the state. The terms were amnesty for the rebels; an armistice and peace pact with the Communists, and a united front to oppose any further Japanese aggression. Chiang accepted.[38]

Though the Japanese in *Courage* had to be disguised as "bandits" (with all shots of recognizable uniforms cut), and the film's locale, Northeast China, had to be made more vague, as "near the border," the film had, clearly, a political effect and a popular success. Its timing, only partially an accident, was a left-wing triumph.

In careful retrospect, even after the Greater East Asia Co-Prosperity Sphere was set in motion by the Japanese, the imperialist villain in China was usually Ameri-can, and Cheng Chi-hua's history rarely mentions any nationals or influences harmful to Chinese cinema other than American ones. But a French journalist visiting Shanghai in 1934 introduces us to film companies with an international flavor more credibly typical of the city then:

The company head is named Marcus Avadjian. He was born in Mosul and travels with an American passport. His assistant is Greek, but holds Portuguese citizen-ship. Their distributor is a deserter from the Russian navy. The board of direc-tors of a rival firm is presided over by a Turk of Spanish nationality. Other members of this board: an Englishman expelled from England, a Filipino, a Russian, and an Armenian.[39]

American *films* may have been the most insidious influence on Chinese films, but Chinese film companies offered a financial gamble on a reduced scale that interested all the nationalities that made Shanghai their home. Chang Pei-hai mentions in 1936 that "about $4,000,000 has been attracted to this field of investment."[40]

In mid-1936 Ming Hsing's precarious financial situation (chiefly a debt to the Kodak Company) was rescued by a large credit from the Nanking Commercial Bank, and Chang organized his new security into two studios, concentrating the several refugees from Dien Tung in his Second Studio. There the imprisoned Yang Han-sheng's scenario, *Unchanged Heart in Life and Death*, was filmed with Yuan Mu-jih in two roles, a revolutionist and an overseas patriot. The action is supposed to take place in 1926, but spectators correctly recognized it as a summons to fight against Japanese aggression. Strange that the censors were not as perceptive, especially in view of the film's unusually direct description of a revolutionary hero — the underground's methods of evading the censors must have been still in use.

When Ouyang Yu-chien came to the Second Studio (where he found the equipment only a little less primitive than at Hsin Hua) the United Front was still in the future, and his three films in 1936 were all obliquely political, with a base of half-real romance: *Red Begonias, Little Bell, Time of Ching Ming.* I have seen none of these, but synopses and Ouyang's memoirs make the first of these sound the most interesting. *Red Begonias* is the name of a *pin-ju* opera, an opera form in which the singing is closer to folk singing than in Peking opera, and modern subjects could be used; it was a form that attracted left theater workers, who enlarged the *pin-ju* repertory with new plays. Ouyang had written *Red Begonias* for the Peking opera star, Bai Yu-suan, and the Ming Hsing studio asked him to build a film scenario around the idea of a *pin-ju* actress's life, in which scenes from the real actress's latest success would be used. Ouyang was always distressed by the haste with which this good idea was executed. He had to fill a mere outline with dialogue in two days, and as Bai Yu-suan was illiterate Ouyang had to help her memorize her lines. Shooting was begun before the script was ready: "Many films were then made carelessly, with the director rushing a film through to a swift release and then 'leaving responsibility for the bill.' "[41]

Hsia Yen returned from Japan early in 1936 to work in the Shanghai theater and to adapt his Dien Tung script of *New Year Coin* (borrowing Hung Shen's less suspect name) for Ming Hsing's production, directed by Chang Shih-chuan. We follow a silver coin from hand to hand (and from story to story), all adding up to a richly informative though somewhat stylized picture of Shanghai life then.

An obstacle to its continued enjoyment is its lack of artistic discipline: Chang threw in everything that seemed salable, even a seven-year-old tap-dancing cutie.* *Crossroads,* written and directed by Shen Hsi-ling, is a much more serious and lasting film. Four unemployed students (or ex-students) live one thin wall away from a girl who has just finished college and found a job as instructor in a textile mill. Without developing the *story* aspects of this situation, Shen made a credible film based on his own experiences and those of unemployed young friends whom he interviewed. *Crossroads* introduced to the public two actors who were to maintain their popularity for the next thirty years, Chao Tan (who plays the student who found a proofreading job) and the sixteen-year-old Pai Yang (the girl, just as lively after she loses her job, too). The only film written and directed by Yuan Mu-jih for Ming Hsing was effective though unoriginal: *Street Angel* was based on an American film (set in Italy) called *Street Angel*! Regardless of its source Yuan made a film in his own style, with sharply incised characters, sparse dialogue, an always alert use of sound, and story points indicated in gesture or camera movement; the film opens with a long camera movement, from the highest roofs of Shanghai to the cluttered surface of a canal.

On 1 August 1936, all film production at the Lien Hua studio was taken over by the Hua An Bank: Wu Hsin-tsai had finally won the long duel with Lo Ming-Yü. Various left-wingers joined the studio for a last year of activity before leaving Shanghai altogether. The first works were not distinguished. Tsai Chu-sheng had admired *Road to Life* when it was shown in Shanghai in 1933 and wanted to make a Chinese equivalent about the homeless children of Shanghai. In 1935 he planned such a film, using Lu Hsun's translation of Panteleyev's story, "The Watch,"† but as developed it turned into an ordinary film fiction, *Strayed Lambs*, with children made repulsive by being told to act, act, *act*! The film's one conspicuous value is its handsome photography (not always helpful to the drab surroundings) by Chou Ta-ming, who was to give greater assistance to later films. Tsai's next film, *Old Wang No. 5*, ran into censor trouble as it involved Chinese collaboration with the Japanese; the Kuomintang objected, "There are no traitors in China," and the film's release was delayed a year. Sun Yu's 1936 film was *Back to Nature*, a free adaptation of Barrie's *Admirable Crichton.*

The first film to show that life had returned to Lien Hua was *Blood on Wolf Mountain.* It was an echo from the best period of 1932–1934, when all the contributors to a film agreed on their goal. In this case the goal was the defense

---

* Si-lan and I had the pleasure of meeting her in 1964, then the Directress of the Shanghai Dance School.
† Lu Hsun said all he could to discourage a film adaptation of this story.

of China without the censors realizing it. Shen Fu had written a story called "Cold Moon and Wolf's Breath," and he and Fei Mu, who was to direct the film, enlarged the tale in scenario to a parable of wolves (the Japanese) threatening a community, killing its people individually until they learn to stand together against the beasts. This symbolism, filmed chiefly in dramatic landscapes, was a subject that Chou Ta-ming's talent for composition and light could help. *Blood on Wolf Mountain* was submitted to the censors under its milder foreign title of *Brave Hunters:*

When it was shown to the Shanghai Municipal Council censors, they suspected that the wolves in the story alluded to the Japanese, and insisted that they would not say "yes" before the Japanese gave their nods. But when the Japanese censors saw the pictures . . . , they refused to admit that wolves were symbolic of the Japanese people, and so let the picture go.[42]

In the early months of 1937 the Lien Hua writers and directors tried several short story films. The whole staff contributed to the eight stories of *Lien Hua Symphony*, each of the eight being made by a different director, and most of them with at least a patriotic or defense flavor: the eighth, "Five Little Moral Ones," written and directed by Tsai Chu-sheng, condensed *Emil und die Detektive* to Chinese patriotic use. There is a half-hearted effort to link the stories with a 20-cent note, which is sometimes forgotten, but the whole is a better film than the similar *New Year Coin*. *Vistas of Art* is a group of three stories about theater arts: "Film City," "Theater," "Variety Troupe." The first of these is told with some verve, an actress's device to obtain a film job; the source is said to be "a French story by Merrick [Meilhac?]." The best of all these short-story experiments is a single short film written by Fei Mu, made almost accidentally.

After the Hua An Bank took over Lien Hua, the bank's only proposal to the studio was to make a series of opera films with Chou Hsin-fan, whose last try at films was left unfinished in 1920, at the Commercial Press. The first of the 1937 series, *Tsai Jin-tang*, an Anhwei opera, was made with Fei Mu's artistic supervision. Some other commitment by the actors brought the production to a short halt, and Fei Mu had the idea of making a short story film *about* opera performers, using the settings and costumes that were waiting for the opera film to be resumed. The result is a spontaneous and sparkling five-reel film called *On Stage and Backstage*, possibly about the relation between Peking opera and money, but actually about everyone's enjoyment in making opera and this film. The play to be performed is *The Emperor's Farewell to His Favorite*, but the Favorite is angry about the manager's broken agreement, and hasn't arrived — a street-singer takes her place. After the interval *Tsai Jin-tang* was finished, but the war prevented the continuation of the bank's series. Another exceptional film

from Lien Hua was *The Freedom of Heaven and Earth*, written and directed by
Shen Fu in a surprisingly free manner, marred only by a quantity of heavily
"symbolic" shots. Shen Fu's associative scenario and cutting were helped by the
rich photography of Chen Chen.

Lien Hua ended its history with three comedies of unusually high quality, all
with a satirical tinge. *United by a Hyphen*, written and directed by Shen Fu, is a
realistic treatment of the black-market characters who surround a Chaplinesque
victim. *So Prosperous* was written and directed by Ouyang Yu-chien ("I can't
recall exactly how I got into Lien Hua. . . . "), with the "prestige set" of
Shanghai tripping up each other into a tangle of unwanted truths. Of the greatest
importance to the search for a realistic style of Chinese film comedy is *The
Money Tree*. Its script, by Hsia Yen, derives from a play written the year before,
Drunken Life and Dreaming Death, inspired by O'Casey's *Juno and the Paycock*.
But by the time Hsia Yen's script was completely rewritten by Chu Shih-ling
there's little to connect O'Casey with *The Money Tree* (See Plate 9). The only
hope of a quarreling, aimless family is the daughter — its "money tree" — and
the only hope she has turns out to be a snobbish adventurer-lawyer who doesn't
see how this noisy family fits into his plans. And just as one is congratulating all
concerned (including the director, Tan Yo-liu) for avoiding the plot formulas, an
end is tacked on that shows how all characters and problems can be solved by a
love for work. Up to that late point, however, the communication of this frustrated, shabby milieu is done with a humor that doesn't require farce or sentimentality. Its simple light-heartedness goes back to *Romance of a Fruit-Peddler*,
and its slashes of pain and violence anticipate the achievement of *Crows and
Sparrows* ten years later.

The chief of the once big Tien Yi Company had seen the signs in 1934 and had
begun to move equipment to Hong Kong, content to make films in the
Cantonese dialect for his Pacific markets. One of Tien Yi's last contributions to
Shanghai's film industry was *Mr. Wang*, based on a popular comic strip and
played by the Chinese Laurel and Hardy, Dong Chieh and Hsiao Chen. This
was so successful that its makers founded their own short-lived company to
manufacture sequels, *Mr. Wang's Secret, Mr. Wang's New Year, Mr. Wang Visits
His Native Village* — stopped only by the Japanese army. After the battles of
July and August 1937 all that was left of Tien Yi was hurried away to Hong
Kong where it vanished into commercial neutrality as the South Seas Studio.

The only other sizable film studio functioning before Shanghai was surrounded
by war was the Yi Hua, but how far it had moved from its heroic days of
ruin and resurrection! The small request by the protecting gangster, to make

"Mr. Wang throws the discus" from a continuing newspaper cartoon by Yeh Chen-yu.

"films that are easy to like," had swallowed up all other aims. Their great success
of 1936 — breeding sequels for the next two years, regardless of the Japanese —
was *Miss Change-Body*. The Shanghai father of a rich Singapore merchant
wants a grandson, so when the merchant's wife gives birth to a daughter, a
telegram announces the birth of a grandson. Eighteen years later the grandfather
demands that his grandson visit him in Shanghai; the girl is dressed in boy's
clothes, and *Twelfth Night* with all other antecedents to transvestite fun gets
pushed a little further. When a girl falls in love with this "boy," and this "boy"
falls in love with a real boy, all the homosexual implications in this situation
are made as explicit as possible, with no objections from the censors.[43] This and
numerous other super-soft films roused thirty-two critics to sign an open letter
of protest to the Yi Hua Company, warning it to refrain from producing further
"soft" films. This had no effect on Yi Hua's policy.

On 7 July 1937 Japanese soldiers (brought to the southwest of Peking by bribed
locomotive engineers and other Chinese railway employees) launched an attack
on the Chinese troops at Lukouchiao, known as the Marco Polo Bridge, that
turned their steady aggression in China into the beginning of the Second World
War in the Orient. On 13 August the Japanese attacked Shanghai.

The two films that gained the greatest support for China's defense against Japanese aggression were not made by Chinese.

In 1933 Irving Thalberg planned a filming of Pearl Buck's *The Good Earth* to be one of M-G-M's biggest productions.

When this reached the ears of the Chinese Vice Consul in Los Angeles, he immediately took up the matter with the studio officials asking that certain parts of the story which were considered derogatory to China and the Chinese people be omitted from the film version.

Later the M-G-M officials sought approval from the Chinese Embassy in Washington, D.C., which referred the matter to the Waichiaopu in Nanking. Subsequently the Ministries of Interior and Education gave their assent to its production adding, however, that the case would be handled in accordance with the Chinese regulations governing the making of films in China by foreigners.[44]

In December M-G-M sent a crew to China, headed by the director George Hill (chosen for his Chinese experience on *Tell It to the Marines*!), but approval for this move had not been granted and three months were spent waiting for the Kuomintang to allow them to work.* Charles Clarke, cameraman with this first crew, recalls[45] that Chiang Kai-shek finally gave this permission after a private screening of the "wrong" kind of American film about China, probably *The Mask of Fu Manchu* ("That's what decided His Excellency!"). He does not seem to have realized that this was also an M-G-M production.† in any case there was always to be a government representative present during the filming.

[Hill] spend several months shooting background‡ and collecting masses of costumes and props. Among the assorted stuff he brought back were two live

---

* There is a trace of a compromise project, dating from this time, in *The Chinese Year Book 1935–36:* "The picture [*The Good Earth*] will have Chinese dialogue in the Mandarin dialect with English titles superimposed. . . . The two principal roles of this picture will be acted by Chinese. . . . " (article on Motion Pictures, by Y. Kao).

† An awkward fact cleverly concealed from His Excellency by assistants who had accepted bribes from the desperately waiting M-G-M administrators?

‡ Little of this 100,000 feet of film was actually used in the finished film, but study of it helped "create in Hollywood an accurate portrayal of China. . . . In addition, some footage taken in China — for example, some of the striking scenes of refugees streaming over the mountains on foot on their way South to escape the famines in the North — was incorporated in the completed film." Dorothy B. Jones, *The Portrayal of China and India on the American Screen, 1896–1955* (Cambridge, Mass.: Massachusetts Institute of Technology, Center for International Studies, Communications Program, 1955), p. 26.

Chinese water buffalo.* which became prominent features of the landscape of a
complete Chinese village and farm that were built near Chatsworth, California.
Paul Muni was got to play the Chinese peasant and Luise Rainer was cast as his
wife. . . .

Then, one morning, just before they were ready to start shooting, Hill committed suicide. There was no indication that it was because of the film. However,
this meant a delay in starting. Victor Fleming [who accompanied Fairbanks to
China in 1931] was next assigned to direct. He became ill while making final
preparations, and Sidney Franklin [whose Oriental background was gained in
East Is West!] was hastily called. It was under his able direction that the film
was made.[46]

The government continued to be anxious about the delicate realities of the film's
subject, the Chinese peasant:

To allay these fears, Thalberg suggested the Chinese government assign its own
observer [in California]. It sent a young Nationalist army general, Tu Ting-hsui,
who arrived with his wife and two children and rapidly became a genial and
popular companion of the people working on the film. Tu was a devoted singer.
He had a fine repertory of Chinese songs, from which Herbert Stothart, the
musical director, selected themes for the picture's musical score.

Sometime before the picture was finished, Tu and his family suddenly disappeared. Attempts to find out what had happened, where he had gone, were to
no avail. Later the Chinese consul in San Francisco showed up and announced
solemnly that he had been instructed to take Tu's place. It seemed that poor Tu
had committed the error of entertaining a disfavored Chinese general in Los
Angeles and thus was suspected of having been corrupted into permitting a bad
picture about China to be made.[47]

Of course the Chinese audience (who knew the truth, anyway) could be protected from the most offensive moments in the finished film:

In China certain deletions were made by the Central Censorship Board in Nanking before the film was released there, and it is interesting to note that most of
these deletions had to do with portrayals of Chinese poverty and the violence on
the part of the new Republican Army toward poverty-stricken Chinese who
looted the palatial residences of urban centers. For example, in Reel 4, the
Chinese censor deleted the scene of a refugee lying by the side of the road and
another of an old woman lying on the ground while vultures are seen in the
barren trees. Likewise, a scene in which O-lan teaches her small children how to

---

* "The ultra patriots in China were ashamed that Americans should see the water-buffaloes
and hand plows. They tried to insist that only tractors and modern up-to-date farm
machinery should be shown with Wang Lung and his family, and this despite the fact that
tractors were even then — and today are — rare sights in China." — Pearl S. Buck, "Films
and People in China," *New Movies*, Nov. 1942, p. 5.

beg and the begging scenes themselves were deleted. Scenes of looting during the revolution and of the soldiers shooting at Chinese who had participated in looting the homes of wealthy Chinese were also cut. Two other minor omissions were made in connection with the portrayal on the screen of the affair between Wang's second wife and his son. [And one character almost completely eliminated, the feeble-minded daughter.][48]

The Chinese government's fight was as much against showing a real as against showing a fantasy China. Mrs. Jones draws a natural conclusion:

In general, China, like other countries, has not been concerned so much with the accuracy of a screen portrayal as with whether or not the portrayal is a favorable one. Thus, the Chinese government has always been very much against picturing on the screen the extreme poverty which is to be found among the Chinese people, the strife and political confusion which has characterized the China scene over a period of many years, and other topics which it regards as undesirable.[49]

The more realistic the intent, the more trouble for the filmmakers, especially if they were foreigners. No one who saw the film by Joris Ivens, *The Four Hundred Million*, could suspect that it emerged from constant struggles with Chinese authorities, censors, bureaucrats, military jealousies, and political intrigues. Ivens's aim "was to tell America about a China which they had never before been told about truthfully and completely,"[50] and the finished film brings this aim close to realization. (See Plate 10.)

The financing of the filming, in 1938, followed the plan used to make *The Spanish Earth* the year before, with a group of distinguished American artists (this time headed by Luise Rainer, fresh from her triumph in *The Good Earth*) helping to raise funds, and the makers themselves taking absolute minimum salaries. These minimum salaries ($50 weekly for Ivens and John Ferno) created the first conflict with the Chinese authorities, who decided that people who accept such a low salary "must be third-rank artists who cannot get work in the USA or in Europe . . . and therefore came to China to get it." Another of their obstacles was the same General Tu who had been recalled so abruptly from his advisory job on *The Good Earth*. He was now assigned as censor* to the Ivens group and still dreamed about a return to his popularity in Hollywood. They got

---

* One of the most irritating procedures of the censorship: "Every time I took a shot one of the Chinese took exactly the same shot with a 16 mm camera. All 16 mm film was sent to Hong Kong for development and flown back to Hankow where it was inspected by the censor who then could authorize the shipment of our undeveloped 35 mm negative to Hollywood."

rid of General Tu after he disgraced himself at the battle of Taierchwang, but
the new censor was just as bad.

One of the greatest crimes of that censorship, and a good lesson for us happened
in Sian. I was standing on those rocks up in the hills where Chiang Kai-shek was
kidnapped. A thousand feet below you could see a typical Chinese walled town.
In a square in the middle something was happening. When John and I saw people
go from little stores and houses to the market square, we tried to get down
there — it looked much more interesting than the rocks of Chiang Kai-shek.
When we were allowed to go down we saw a tremendous thing. There were
about four students in front of a little Buddhist temple. They had a primitive
sound system and soap boxes for a self-built loudspeaker. They were singing
songs agitating the people in the fight against Japan. The audience were men,
women, soldiers, children, chickens, pigs. The whole market was alive. You felt
that elementary latent force that one finds everywhere in China in the people
and those students made it active. It was a great demonstration. We were not
allowed to film it because it would give the impression that the Chinese mass was
dirty and not very well organized! We argued with the censor. . . . The censor put
his hand over the lens. A very conclusive argument.

The next morning the Chinese advisors hurried the filming group out to the great
square of Sian where they had lined up about 10,000 people, "four shiny loudspeakers and not four, but forty students," a thoroughly organized filming so
dear to the heart of a censor. "China's governmental ways are complicated as
Chinese writing, but less beautiful."

4

War: The Film Industry
Moves Up River
1938—1945

Literature for national resistance — it is not easy!

What a stupendous phenomenon is war! Where should the writers start? They don't know about the mechanics of war, the military life, the tactics and weapons used for attack and defense, for transportation and control; probably they don't even have a too clear idea about the state of preparedness, the regulations and rules in the interior. What should they write? How can they write?

— Lao Shê

Between the Japanese attacks at Peking and at Shanghai the left filmworkers were full of projects for films to help fight against the aggression, but an understandable inertia seems to have struck both film financiers and government film officials. When "topical" films were most needed, only one got made and released in 1937: *Martyrs of the Northern Front,* written and directed by Fei Mu. Defense organizations were formed, scenarios were written, but in these last Shanghai months the only finished defense achievement of the film leftists was the staging of an opera, *Defend the Marco Polo Bridge. Dawn in North China,* on a similar idea, was one of many film scenarios submitted for approval, but a final response came only in December, when the film industry was somewhere between Nanking and Hankow: "The Marco Polo Bridge battle was six months ago — out of date now."

By 22 September both Peking and Tientsin were in Japanese hands, and the defense of Shanghai looked hopeless, even before the army withdrew to Nanking. At Shanghai the Japanese seized the Ming Hsing studio, outside the protected concessions, and all studios had second thoughts about anti-Japanese subjects they may have considered. Film and theater workers who had joined anti-Japanese defense organizations followed the army to Nanking. There an official film studio, the Central Film Company, made little effort to absorb and employ any of this personnel, for this company's function was not so much production as approval (or disapproval) of finished Chinese films. In this time of crisis some newsreels were attempted, but these had to be sent for processing to film laboratories in besieged Shanghai! Release machinery was so slow that the Kuomintang newsreels gained a reputation for containing no news.

In November Shanghai and Taiyuan fell. The "Doomed Battalion" that fought a rearguard action in Shanghai from the vaults of the Chinese Mint Godown was finally persuaded to withdraw — not by Madame Chiang, whose ringing words were, "No, they must die that China may live," but by the British General, Telfer-Smollett, whose negotiations with the Japanese command made it possible for the entire battalion, with its weapons and remaining ammunition, to escape into the International Concession with minimum loss.[1] One of the few Chinese victories of 1937 was won in Shansi Province by the main body of the

Red Army that the Kuomintang had been forced to join in defense, vividly described as follows:

On a rainy night on 24 September, the Eighth Route Army decided to ambush the enemy east of Pinghsingkuan. It took positions on the mountains flanking a gully through which ran a motor road. At dawn, units of the Japanese army came along the road. They were thrown into utter confusion when the soldiers of the Eighth Route Army sprang to the attack. Their trucks crashed against each other. Under the rain of grenades and the hand-to-hand attacks, the Japanese were demoralized. The fierce fighting lasted almost a whole day and ended in the annihilation of the Japanese.[2]

One is inclined to believe that the chronicler was acquainted with "westerns" of before 1937 and many Chinese films since then. This could be a scenario sketch for dozens of scenes filmed since 1949.

In Cheng Chi-hua's list of actuality and newsreel films there is a title, *Eighth Route Army Attacks at Pinghsing Pass*, an eight-reel film released in 1938 by a Hong Kong company, but without having seen this I'm inclined to doubt that it contained much pictorial information.* There are, indeed, some vivid and exceptional documents of this war's later phases, but I have been so unfortunate as to have seen two supposedly actuality wartime films with titles as exciting as this Pinghsingkuan film: the few images (explosions and fictional trench warfare) came from a stock-shot library, and the body of the film was made up of title after title after title, in the most exhortatory language, seasoned with vaguely drawn maps that were also not intended to give much information. The verbal rhetoric was splendid, but the screen was empty.

The government's Nanking film company produced nothing before the government withdrew further up the Yangtze to Chungking, which remained the capital until the war's end. By the time Nanking fell to the Japanese on 13 December (its sacking was one of the most savage episodes of the war), all the filmworkers who had paused there were now in or on their way to Hankow, and this city became the first wartime film production center. To the usual governmental delays and bureaucracy a new dilemma was added: even the officials could somewhat imagine the kind of rousing films that should be circulated in this emergency, but the only filmmakers trained and able to make such films were the very leftists who frightened the officials as much as did the enemy. Association with them was "dangerous," encouragement or technical cooperation was "dangerous," but as the first months of defeat tapered off into an

---

* The stills from this film reproduced in Cheng Chi-hua's history (in Vol. II, after p. 24) show the army either before or after the battle.

accepted condition, the left filmmakers were allowed a certain isolated independence of action. With the government deep inland in Chungking (though still within range of Japanese bombers) the important Political Section of the National Military Council,* in which Chou En-lai was a Vice-Minister, representing the Eighth Route Army and New Fourth Army, stayed in more vulnerable Hankow, and got several films made. Before its end the dilatory Hankow Film Studio was changed to the China Film Studio, directly responsible to the Political Section; Yang Han-sheng headed the new studio and its scenario department. Nearly of equal importance were the trials at this time of sending film exhibition teams out to the countryside in trucks and breaking the old dependence on city cinemas and city audiences. Later, in Chungking, Robert Payne attended such a projection, probably of *Courage as High as Heaven*, with the audience actively assisting the screening:

. . . half the University has flocked over the river to see a film of Chinese soldiers fighting against the Japanese in the north. . . .

It was shown in the open air with a travelling projector, benches have mysteriously appeared, and we can see it on either side of the screen. When galloping horses cross the screen, the sound of their footprints is made by small boys; when the hero attacks the Japanese bandits unarmed, the machine-guns decimate the enemy soldiers, the sound of machine-guns is faithfully reproduced; and when, at the very end, the hero advances towards the camera, waving his blood-stained sword at the end of which waves his blood-stained shirt, their joy knows no bounds, and they refuse to go home until it is played all over again.[3]

A magazine was published: *Anti-Enemy Cinema*. But government officials were always careful to keep these activities at arm's length; when Joris Ivens, finally in Hankow with official permission to make his film, asked to meet his Chinese film colleagues, his government advisor "thought this was not such a good idea."[4] But the Ivens group performed a more tangible service to Chinese films: his Dutch persistence got them to the front in time to film the only victory in 1938 of the Chinese armies, now united under a National Military Council: the battle of Taierhchuang (their hard-won footage became the climactic sequence of *Four Hundred Million*). They pressed their luck, tried to get to Yenan, were refused; as a substitute Ivens sent the small Yenan film group a badly needed hand camera.

W. H. Auden and Christopher Isherwood, unattached to a delicate film production (such as the Ivens film), had better luck in Hankow. At the end of April

---

* This propaganda office, headed by Kuo Mo-jo, was established 1 April 1938; T'ien Han and other leftists worked here.

1938 they were taken to Hankow's suburbs to see the largest film studio in wartime China:

There were two buildings: a big shabby villa, once the property of a Chinese general, now used for dark-rooms and the accommodation of the actors; and the more recently built studio itself. In the garden half a dozen young actors and technicians were playing netball beside a dismantled set representing a shell-wrecked village. Dresses were hung out to dry on a clothes-line. The whole place looked very domestic and untidy and cheerful. Our hosts explained that no work was done during the daytime, because of air-raids. After dark the shooting in the studio would begin.

Mr. Lo, the sound-engineer, showed us round. Neither he nor any of his colleagues had studied abroad, nor had they ever imported foreign advisers. He had learnt everything out of books, constructing his own sound-recording apparatus . . . This home-made equipment was excellent. Technical problems had been solved with astonishing economy and ingenuity. We particularly admired the Interior set itself. It was the living-room of a farm-house, prepared for a wedding, with an eye for detail which would put most western art-directors to shame. . . . Mr. Lo showed us a whole arsenal of machine-guns, rifles and uniforms, most of which had been actually captured by the Eighth Route Army from the Japanese.

At present the studio was producing only war-films. Just now they were at work on the story of Shanghai's "Doomed Battalion". It would be called *Fight to the Last*. We were shown some of the rushes. The war-scenes were brilliant. The producer [Ying Yun-wei] had an astonishingly subtle feeling for grouping; his weakness lay in the direction of the actors themselves — he had indulged too often the Chinese talent for making faces. All these grimaces of passion, anger, or sorrow, seemed a mere mimicry of the West. One day a director of genius will evolve a style of acting which is more truly national — a style based upon the beauty and dignity of the Chinese face in repose.[5]

In Hankow's short film history three films were made and a series (continued in Chungking) of modest single reels, *Songs of the Anti-Japanese War*. The first Hankow film was completed in January 1938, *Protect Our Land*, by Shih Tung-shan. It was a first attempt to make a film for a specifically peasant audience — all dialogue was slow and clear, situations were kept simple, and there was no embarrassing love element. Though few peasants saw *Protect Our Land* it is important in the series of hard lessons still being learned by the Chinese cinema in how to reach the basic Chinese audience.

The least useful of the Hankow films was the one written and directed by a Kuomintang man, Yuan Tsun-mei, *Hot Blood and Faithful Soul*.* His solution of the

* At its first French showing in 1938, under the title of *La Grande Muraille*, it was introduced by Professor Langevin and sympathetically reviewed by Georges Sadoul: "This work is far from having the technical perfection of Russian, American, or French films. But it has the great merit of being completely without 'exotic gimmicks,' and being truly and deeply indigenous." *Regards*, 3 Nov. 1938, reprinted in Sadoul, *Le Cinéma pendant la Guerre* (Paris, 1954).

peasant spectator problem was to show everyone in the film as stupid and requiring explanations for each key word ("What does 'anti-Japanese' mean?"). The only unquestioned success from Hankow was Yang Han-sheng's scenario on the "Doomed Battalion." The end of this famous episode was made more thrilling and self-sufficiently patriotic than in actuality, but no one protested, for the effectiveness of the film, released in China as *Eight Hundred Brave Soldiers* (see Plate 11) and abroad as *Fight to the Last*, was vital to the Chinese war effort. Overseas Chinese settlements brought the film to France, Switzerland, Burma, Hong Kong, and the Philippines, and collected funds to support China's defense.

On the impetus of this international success the Hankow group began at least three more films: Yuan Mu-jih (who played the heroic commander in *Eight Hundred Brave Soldiers*) wrote *China Roars* (though I am unable to learn if this related in any way to Tretyakov's play), T'ien Han wrote *Go Back to the Front* (for which the wedding set admired by Isherwood may have been prepared), and Hung Shen wrote *Last Drop of Blood.* Yang Han-sheng resumed his prewar project, *Storm on the Border.* As the Japanese approached Hankow (they captured both Hankow and Canton in October) all film personnel were ordered to Chungking by the end of September. Yuan Mu-jih and his wife Chen Bo-erh (who joined the Communist Party while in Hankow) decided to risk, instead, the long and devious journey to the Red base at Yenan.

In Chungking the film industry's dependence on imported materials made this far-inland city a problematic production center. A Canadian journalist's report, from later in the war, tells us about both problems and solutions:

Movie-making in Chungking is a laborious, heartbreaking, even dangerous business. First, because of the tightening blockade and terrific expense when measured in depreciated Chinese currency,* the Chinese have been obliged to rely heavily upon native substitutes for necessary materials. Lacking celotex, the big stages are sound-proofed with hard-packed straw. Moreover, many of the more important scenes are shot after midnight, when the neighbourhood has gone to bed.

Laboratories are equipped with many home-made devices and gadgets — some copied from illustrations appearing in American technical magazines, which found their way here, others wholly improvised wherein Chinese ingenuity is amply expressed. A cardinal principle in all installations, especially valuable, unreplaceable machines and such, is that they be easily and quickly removable to

---

* "A drop in foreign exchange during production boosted costs so high that production would have to be stopped to wait for more money."

safety in nearby dugouts. . . . At the sound of the first alarm everything is pulled up and packed in special boxes always at hand.[6]

Combining supply trouble with other wartime problems, such as installing film laboratories and storerooms in chambers carved long ago from the rock of Chungking's hills, brought the production of the transferred China Film Studio almost to a halt: after starting work in November 1938 only two fictional films were completed in the next fourteen months, and these two were so crammed with compromises that they satisfied no one — neither the makers, nor the government supervisors, nor the audience. So long as *any* supply lines were open, American films kept Chungking's swollen film public entertained, undiscouraged by the occasional air-raid alarm that sent them into nearby shelters in the rock foundations. Not many considered it their patriotic duty to pay to see either *Defend Family and Country* or *Good Husbands* (two young peasants who are paid to be substitute recruits); Chungking preferred Betty Grable and Jeanette Macdonald.*

In all the cities furnished with cinemas the film audience changed during the war. The city populations of unoccupied China were crammed with refugees, usually with too much time on their hands, and many from the countryside, if they could afford the few cash for a ticket, saw their first films. The northern cities were the first to feel the inexorable movement of refugees from the Japanese bombs and brutality in North China, where guerilla warfare had become the only defense. Agnes Smedley tells of the first exposure of some country boys to films, American films. In September 1937 she was brought, her back injury needing city treatment, to Sian. Her guards and carriers from Yenan had never been in a big city before, and its many splendors and novelties excited them.

But one wonder of wonders they could never get over — the moving pictures! Coming down from Yenan, I tried to explain what a moving picture was. They did not know what I was talking about. So, on the night of our arrival, they went to the movies. Such was their wonder that they waited impatiently the next morning for the theater to open. They saw a jungle film, returned with

---

* An American report from the following year: "Prior to 1937 the whole of China was open to business and the American distributors had a clear field...."
"Due to hostilities, however, there are today only five key cities that can be served regularly by the American distributors. These are Shanghai, Tsingtao, Tientsin, Peiping and Hong Kong. Of course, films are still being sent to some cities in the interior such as Yunnanfu, Chungking and Chengtu, but with the risk of losing the prints on account of the continual bombardment of these cities...."—B.W. Palmertz, in *Motion Picture Herald*, 3 Aug. 1940, p. 29.

wonder still in their eyes, and told me they had seen lions, tigers, elephants, and a huge hairy animal that looked something like a man. . . .

They became movie fans. On the third day they said they were going to see a foreign movie and they asked me to go along. I went. They led me to a theater with gaudy advertising posters outside. The film was called *Diamond Jim.* Though my heart sank at the title, the film itself was even more depressing. . . . All the women in the film were dressed in elaborate, gaudy gowns and the boys decided that all women in America dressed like that. . . .

There were four shots in the film that had some meaning for them. One was a horse race, which interested them. One was when Diamond Jim and three of his friends, back in the early nineties, went out riding on a bicycle built for four. . . .

Another scene . . . showed an engine and train of ancient vintage. They had not at that time seen the trains in Sian. . . . Still another scene was the inevitable Hollywood love scene. One of the actors pressed the leading lady to his manly bosom and held her in a passionate kiss. Just as this started, my guard was searching for his lost ticket stub on the floor. But the Kiangsi lad, his eyes starting from his head, gave a loud exclamation, punched him violently and cried, "Look!" My guard, still bending, lifted his head and sat transfixed. His mouth hung open and he did not even straighten his back until the scene before him was finished.

The Kiangsi guard had more presence of mind. He shot a startled glance at me to see how I was taking such a shameless sight. As I was looking at him and at my guard, he quickly turned his guilty head away. . . . For such scenes as that happen only in the bedrooms of husband and wife in China.[7]

In 1938, when the cities of the south began to feel the pressure of refugees, a traveling English lady attended an American film in Yunnan-fu (Kunming) and reacted traditionally, telling us nothing of the *audience's* reaction:

The hall was packed, and . . . space had been economised by using wooden forms. When those in command decided not an inch of space was wasted, the show commenced. Everyone ate something . . . loud speakers from front and back alternately translated the English captions into Chinese . . . It was the most horrible thriller I have ever seen. . . .[8]

In the same period the other government-controlled film company, the Central Film Studio, also managed to produce two fictional films; the first, about Shanghai, was released in April 1939, *Blood Runs through the Orphan City*. In September *Children of China* appeared, a group of three stories, "A Peasant Awakes," "Love in the Anti-Japanese War," and "Woman Partisan." I have not seen this, but it sounds the most promising production of Chungking. *Children of China* was written and directed by Shen Hsi-ling, and his next months were occupied in preparing two films, both repeatedly delayed: *Miraculous Eagles* and *Big Epoch — Little Person*. A promising career ended with his death in an air raid in December 1940.

Another factor impeding any regularity of film production in 1939 was the confusion in sales prospects abroad. This had become an anxiety not only in Chungking but also in semi-occupied Shanghai, where the following report originated. Chinese defense propaganda and the Chinese economy were becoming identical; the contraditions of one were reflected in the other.

For years British Malaya and the Netherlands East Indies constituted a good market for Chinese films. With war waging at home it is only natural that the people overseas should want to see Chinese pictures depicting the war. In these war pictures they expect to see, of course, the atrocities and brutalities committed by the Imperial Japanese Army portrayed. To maintain neutrality in the Sino-Japanese Conflict, however, the British and Netherlands authorities are forbidding the showing of such pictures in Malaya and in the East Indies. Chinese producers are, therefore, faced with a double standard: one for home consumption, and one for overseas. . . .

To overcome such censorship difficulties overseas, Chinese cinema producers have to resort to either of these alternatives: the production of historical or "costume" pictures, or the production of modern pictures of a light and romantic nature, which, however, must not call into question the patriotic spirit of the Chinese people.[9]

While the "costume" and "light" films continued to come from cautious Shanghai, Chungking tried in 1940 to make the less neutral films that said something about the war. But increasing tensions and conflicts in those offices made them less clear about what this "something" should be. "Compromise" could be the title of any film made in Chungking that year.

Light of Asia had the advantage of a sincerely felt amateur film. Its central action takes place in a prison camp where most of the thirty Japanese prisoners were really Japanese prisoners willing to play their first film roles in the interest of peace. Victory March was a more professional film written by T'ien Han and directed by Shih Tung-shan (see Plates 16 and 17). Unfortunately its episodic form* made it ideal material for manipulation and revision — one general insisted on a place in the film, and each office asked for changes. The released film had little effect, except for the episode of a Buddhist priest who breaks his vows by killing Japanese. Discouraged, T'ien Han gave up film work until after the war.

At the Central Studio Sun Yu began Ten Thousand Li of Empty Sky, a panorama of the war from the Mukden Incident of 1931 to Shanghai and Hangchow in 1937, all through the experiences of two student pilots and a girl. The

---

* All the sketches were related to the war in North Hunan province, and exteriors were filmed in Changsha (T'ien Han's home town) just before the Japanese took the city.

production problems of this film temporarily defeated Central and Sun Yu, and he moved to the China Studio to make *Baptism of Fire*, a physically simpler film, being set entirely in Chungking. Its story was simpler, too:

A Chinese woman is employed by the Japanese to spy in Chungking, where the workers at an ammunition factory help her to get a job, and she begins to be ashamed of her spying assignment. She falls in love with a man at the factory, and almost adopts a little girl in the workers' tenement where she lives. The little girl is killed in a Japanese raid and the spy confesses the truth to her lover. He takes her to the police, where she tells all she knows about the enemy's espionage apparatus just before she is killed by another spy.[10]

The release of this unobjectionable film was delayed until May 1941, by which time Sun Yu had returned to Central and completed *Ten Thousand Li*.

Three scenarios by Yang Han-sheng were completed in 1940: his Mongolian story, *Storm on the Border*, was finally finished after adventures and revisions (see Plate 15). To make this drama of Han and Mongol youths uniting against an ingenious Japanese spy who tries to divide the two nationalities, the film crew (of thirty persons) spent nine months working north of the Great Wall, and they managed to stop in blockaded Yenan before returning to Chungking. *Young China* was a direct, unpretentious (and intelligently photographed) patriotic comedy about a young propaganda troupe (resembling Boy Scouts and Girl Guides) that lures back the scared population of a village with bags of salt and songs. The most sensational of Yang's scenarios resulted in the most extravagant film made in Chungking, *Secret Agent of Japan*. It is based on the biography of Amleto Vespa, whose memoirs, *Spiritual Son of China*, had been recently translated and published in Chungking.[11] Somehow linked to the Italian consulate at Harbin (according to the film),* Vespa's thirty-six years' residence there were made extra comfortable for him and his family by the information he procured, first, for the warlord Chang Tso-lin, and, finally, for the Japanese, but the film remains vague on the nature of this information or the use to which it was put. The whole of *Secret Agent of Japan* looks as inept as Vespa's espionage, though apparently the film enjoyed a great popular success, partially explained by the international flavor of its Harbin orgies. These orgies and other obviously expensive scenes indicate large amounts of money flowing through the easily corrupted bureaucracy of Chungking. The officials' other function, delay, was also successful, for Kuomintang censorship and other obstacles held up the film's release until April 1943! Its final obstacle was the Generalissimo himself:

---

* Actually Vespa was general manager and part owner of a Harbin film theater, the Atlantic, where he had cover for his main activities of spying and gun-running.

. . . Chiang's curiosity and whims reached down to the lowest [!] levels. . . .
When he saw the preview of the only big motion picture produced in Chungking
during the war, . . . *Secret Agent of Japan*, he sent it back to the studio with
personal instructions to insert more footage on the work of the Kuomintang.[12]*

Both government studios made a low bow to the non-Han nationalities in the
interior. *Long Live the National Minorities* (nine reels, China Studio) and *Visit
to Tibet* (ten reels, Central) sound like important documentary records, no
matter what their bias or purpose. The former had been in production for nearly
three years before its release in 1940.

Military collaboration between the old antagonists, Kuomintang and Communists, was a delicate balance that had to be maintained with the greatest
patience, even in the presence of the common enemy, Japan. Film collaboration
in Chungking presented similar difficulties and the left filmmakers sought other
ways to make films with less compromise and more fighting spirit. An unusual
situation in Chengtu, farther inland, offered such a possibility.

It was first in Taiyuan that the Northwest Film Company was established in May
1935 by a warlord, General Yen Hsi-shan, who provided the funds and protection. Vanity was one of his motives, for the first films were "documents" of
himself and his army. It would be instructive to know what arguments were used
by his filmmakers to permit them to move into more ambitious productions,
though we should remember that no really large sums of money were at stake. In
any case the money ran out in April 1936 and the company seemed about to
recede into the same historical oblivion that welcomed so many Chinese film
companies. But in November 1936 enough forces were brought together to make
a battle document, *The Suiyuan-Mongol Front*, and the company found itself
back in business. General Yen sent to Peking and Shanghai to recruit young
technicians. The wider outbreak of war forced the revived company to move
from Taiyuan to Sian — just as the money gave out again! In May 1938 Yang
Han-sheng and other film leftists foresaw the need for a studio partially independent of government support, and brought the Northwest Film Company back to
life, now in Chengtu, where it was to stay as long as money, General Yen, and
the Kuomintang would permit.

Chengtu's first work, completed at the end of 1939, was an actuality film of
great value, both in its circulation then and as a historical document now: the

---

* The final scenes of Chinese partisans capturing Vespa to use him against the Japanese had
to be reshot, with all Chinese wearing Kuomintang uniforms.

six reels of *North China Is Ours* still exist (under its later, more realistic title of *Storm in North China*). It provides a detailed picture of the progress of the anti-Japanese war in the Northwest, with the United Front shown by Chu Teh and officers of the Eighth Route Army amidst their erstwhile Kuomintang opponents, and the picture of training and civilian life behind the Japanese lines was the first glimpse the Chinese film public had of what became known as the Yenan way of life. The film also shows the hand-to-mouth method of production in the Chengtu group: Chen Chen's camera was hand-held, the developing and printing appear to have been done by hand, and the editing presented so many physical difficulties that often a series of shots were left in as filmed. Despite the obvious lack of experience this is a valuable example of the extended propaganda actuality film.

To the film refugees from Shanghai, Hankow had resembled home, somewhat reduced in scale, but Chungking and Chengtu were so far inland that they must have looked exotic to the filmmakers: the sharp hills on which the river city of Chungking was built, and the walled, feudal aspect of Chengtu, farther west — farther west than Chinese filmmakers had ever worked before. They were now surrounded by the peasants and once-remote people that they had pretended to make films about, two thousand miles away in Shanghai. Nevertheless there was a mistaken though comprehensible tendency to cling to the forms and attitudes developed in Shanghai. I have not seen the one fictional film completed in Chengtu, *Wind and Snow* [Struggle?] *in Taihan Mountains*, written and directed by Ho Men-fu, but its synopsis sounds familiar:

The Japanese come to establish a coal mine near a village. They capture many of the peasants to work the mine. To buy the freedom of his son one old man offers himself as a guide through the mountains for the Japanese, who pay for his service by blinding him. Then the miners and peasants unite to fight the Japanese.[13]

Shen Fu worked on a more original second film, *Long Life to the People!* * (based on a story in the Chungking *Hsinhua Daily*); he had made 80% of it in six months of production when General Yen ordered the film stopped and the Northwest Film Company disbanded, probably a reflection of the disintegrating united front in the summer of 1940.

In Chungking in October 1940, almost simultaneously with the Nationalist massacre of the Communist-led New Fourth Army as it crossed the Yangtze under Nationalist orders, the Kuomintang propaganda department stopped the

---

* The published stills show the new and useful influence of *Four Hundred Million*.

production of *Women's Army* (scenario by Sun Shih-yi, directed by Ssutu
Hui-min), Sun Yu's *Young Peony*, Shih Tung-shan's *Long Live China!*, Ying
Yun-wei's *Three Brave Men*, Shen Hsi-ling's posthumous scenario of *Big Epoch –
Little Person*, and a cartoon about Wang Ching-wei* — all presumably touchy
subjects. It was clear that the most militant and dedicated filmmakers would
have to find a new base, if they wished to continue making films worth sending
abroad or worth being shown in the remaining cinemas of China. Hong Kong
seemed the only hope.

Until war scattered Shanghai's film industry to all corners of China, its filmmakers and critics looked down on the productions of the South. In a serious
article of 1937 there is a contemptuous footnote:

In the present discussion the films produced in South China are not referred to,
because their artistic standard is much lower and they are only shown in South
China, being made in the Cantonese dialect.[14]

Despite this attitude Hong Kong production and the Cantonese dialect played
an increasingly vital role after 1932 in Chinese films, both patriotic and commercial. Though the Kuomintang never approved the production of films in the
Cantonese dialect, most of the spectators in overseas settlements could understand Chinese sound films only when they were spoken in Cantonese.

When the left filmmakers had to leave Shanghai in 1937 the two leading
Cantonese among them, Tsai Chu-sheng and Ssutu Hui-min, chose to retreat to
the South rather than to the West up the Yangtze. In Hong Kong they found an
already active defense film organization, formed by five small companies,
making a quantity of propaganda films cheaply, quickly, and in Cantonese dialect.
These methods and results were obviously to be preferred to the cumbersome
official production plans in Hankow and Chungking, even if it meant defying the
Kuomintang on questions of language and policy, and the Shanghai refugees
joined in wholeheartedly. Tsai and Ssutu began by writing *Blood Splashes on
Paoshan* (a city near Shanghai where five hundred Chinese soldiers stood against
the invaders before all were killed) and Ssutu directed the film. Cheng Chi-hua
writes that it is equal in quality with Hankow's first film, *Protect Our Land*. In
their next film, *March of the Partisans*, the most striking story element is that
Japanese soldiers help and join the partisan fighters. Even the obligatory finale,
the heroine's death, is more genuinely emotional than the usual tableau. It is one

---

* In March 1940 this important Kuomintang personage defected to the Japanese to head a
puppet government in Nanking.

of China's best wartime films, and the Hong Kong government endorsed this judgment by promptly banning it when it was completed in 1938.*

All this activity and quality impressed the Chungking authorities in spite of their reservations, and at the end of 1938 it was decided to set up a Hong Kong branch of the China Film Studio — the Ta Ti, or Great Earth Company — which would use only the approved Peking dialect. Their first film in 1939 was written and directed by Tsai Chu-sheng, *Orphan Island Paradise*, a rambling and incredible picture of espionage and underground heroism in Shanghai (see Plate 12): even Cheng Chi-hua considers it "too heroic." Ta Ti's next (and last) film appears to have been another of the infrequent wartime film triumphs: *White Cloud Village* was not completed in Hong Kong, for at the end of 1939 the Kuomintang closed Ta Ti† (moving too far left, out of Chungking control?) and the director, Ssutu Hui-min, took the group to Chungking where the film was finished and shown in April 1940. The story, partly set in Hong Kong, was written by Hsia Yen, who had reappeared just when Chinese films needed his talents again. He had been writing editorials for a patriotic newspaper in Kweilin until the Kuomintang stopped the paper. Then Hsia Yen moved to Hong Kong where he worked on the *Chinese Merchants' Daily* and wrote operas, *Microbes of Fascism* and one based on Tolstoy's *Resurrection*, changed to a Chinese setting. His scenario for *White Cloud Village* employed elements that had been misused in *Baptism of Fire* and *Orphan Island Paradise* (such as ammunition secrets and dancing girl spies), now shaped by his superior dramatic and political talents into one of the best-remembered films of these years.‡

After the withdrawal of the Kuomintang's trust and money from Hong Kong films Tsai Chu-sheng's next film, *Ten Thousand Li Ahead* (or, *Glorious on Parade*), had real difficulties getting made: having no studio of its own the little company had to rent studio space by the day — in these circumstances working days of fourteen to sixteen hours produced eight hours of actual work, taking six months to finish the film.

Glorious on Parade was about two labourer friends in Hong Kong who refused to load a ship destined for an enemy port. A fight ensued with the foreman, and one of them was sent to jail. On his release he discovered his friend working as a

---

* This ban was not lifted until June 1941 when the film was shown in Hong Kong with a changed title, *Song of Justice.*
† "In pursuance of the policy of national reconstruction as enunciated by Generalissimo Chiang Kai-shek, the Tati Motion Picture Corp. will shortly move from Hong Kong to Yunnan." *T'ien Hsia Monthly*, November 1939.
‡ A copy of *White Cloud Village* has not yet (1964) been located by the Film Archive of China.

sandwich-board man. One night the two men rescued a servant girl who was being beaten by her mistress and gave her shelter in their home. To help with her upkeep and unknown to her benefactors, she became a strip-tease dancer, but they discovered her secret and persuaded her to resign. The cabaret manager proved difficult, but under threats from the two men was forced to comply with their demands. Then, realizing the uselessness of their lives in the city, the two men and the girl set off for free China to work for their country's good.[15]

Before this production Tsai lived in a fishing village where he heard stories of the boat-people that he used in a scenario, *Storm in the Pacific*, but twenty-five years passed before his scenario was filmed.

A new difficulty appeared in Hong Kong films of 1940: *all* productions, no matter how lewd or feudal, called themselves "patriotic." Horror films (*She-Devil Takes Another's Soul, Body Floats Along, Madame Eat-Man*), swordsman-adventurer films (*Seven Swords and Thirteen Adventurers*), and quasi-pornography (*Playing Three Times with White Chrysanthemum, Song of Rapture*) — all competing with the less inhibited product then exported from Shanghai studios — attached a patriotic label that Shanghai was in no position to use. Hsia Yen in the *Chinese Merchants' Daily* and Mao Tun in *Modern Culture* discussed this dangerous trend ("Why do people not welcome films dealing with the beginning of the anti-Japanese war?") and prominent Chinese citizens of Hong Kong led a "Clean Film Campaign."

The question of Cantonese dialect seemed settled. This and a core of a few genuinely patriotic films that encouraged the more conscious filmmakers to do better, made the 1941 prospects for Hong Kong production look splendid,* especially as the government studios in Chungking attempted less and less. The collected small studios within the Ta Kuan Company became the new center for left hopes and Cantonese dialect. The company's leading director, Tang Hsiao-tan, had come in 1934 to Hong Kong with considerable experience in Shanghai studios. For Ta Kuan he directed *Behind the Shanghai Lines* (1938) and *Roar of Our Nationalities* (1941). Spirits were so high in 1941 that when the Japanese film industry sent Ichikawa in April to explore the possibilities of financing production in Hong Kong the united front against his offers was formidable. The *Chinese Merchants' Daily* gave this attention to his welcoming banquet: "He who attends this banquet will be eating the soul of the Chinese people and selling himself to the enemy." Failure for the moment, but Mr. Ichikawa's opportunity was to come later.

---

* In December 1940 Joseph Sunn opened a San Francisco cinema to show his Hong Kong productions exclusively.

Ta Kuan's plans grew bolder. They invited Hsia Yen to write *Fifty Years of China*, from the Opium War to the anti-Japanese war of 1894. Tsai Chu-sheng was asked to prepare *New Life*, or *Ten Thousand Years' Perfume*. Before work began on either of these projects the Japanese bombed the U.S. fleet at Pearl Harbor, and before the end of December the two key British bases in the Pacific area, Hong Kong and Singapore, had fallen to the Japanese. Some filmmakers stayed on in Hong Kong to make Cantonese films for Japanese export, but all those who were identified with defense film production fled into unoccupied parts of South China. It took months to get from there to Chungking.

Kuomintang film production was its own worst enemy. From the beginning of 1941 to the end of 1943 the government film studios in Chungking were unable to produce a single fictional film.* Apparently endless budgets drifted, just as apparently, into convenient sleeves. One film begun in 1939 on the Chinese Air Force became a standing but expensive joke; I'm not sure if it was ever completed. The prices of raw materials for film production fluctuated wildly; speculators and their friends in government offices made profits, but few films of any sort. Filmmakers shifted their careers to the usual alternative, opera.

The Japanese attacks in the Pacific brought China new allies in her struggle with Japan; one of these continued to dominate Chungking's film tastes. American films filled the theaters, even after the cutting of the Burma Road made Chungking dependent on the airlift. Yet the war had made subtle changes in the film diet. By November 1942 *The Great Dictator*, forbidden for two years, was now enjoyed publicly. The older censorship of *Four Hundred Million* still held; the U.S. Army's *Battle of China* in their "Why We Fight" series was shown but with more equivocations than in the original version, already a tangle of compromises, explaining little to the spectator. There were private showings of many Soviet films, but only one, the actuality record of *Stalingrad*, had a public Chungking showing, in October 1943.

Three years without a single new Chinese fictional film in the cinemas of China's capital — an amazing situation (that had not occurred since 1920) though it seemed to amaze nobody. In 1942—1943 some progressive filmworkers (under pseudonyms) found employment in the Chinese Educational Film Studio and Chinese Village Education Company, concealed in the Education and Agricul-

---

* A reflection of the political and military stalemate: "From 1941 to 1944 China's war against Japan was largely in suspense as far as Chungking was concerned. But a strong military cordon was set up around the Chinese communist base in Northwest China." O. Edmund Clubb, *Twentieth Century China* (New York: Columbia University Press, 1964), p. 234.

ture Ministries and supervised by a former police officer, Tsai Chin-jung. After resumption of studio production there was a dampening episode that probably added to the opera staffs: a film crew sent to Kweichow and Kiangsi provinces to make a film had nearly completed their work when, at Liaochow, they ran into a roving Japanese regiment, and the film was destroyed in the clash. The title of the never finished film: *A Way to Consolidate the Country*!

From the end of 1934 to the end of 1945 four films were completed at the China Film Studio. *A Brave Man Can Make Mountains and Rivers Brave* (completed April 1944) tells the story of a young army officer, on the trail of Japanese spies; the chase leads to Burma, where he falls in love with an overseas Chinese girl. *Splash of Blood on Cherry-Blossom* (completed February 1945) sounds a more original film, though other work of Ho Fei-guan, its scenarist and director, does not lead to very high expectations. *Splash of Blood* shows the life of an air-force officer and his wife in China, parallel with the life of a Japanese air-force officer and his wife. The scenes in Japan were an ambitious effort to show foreign life in a wartime Chinese film. *Give Me Back My Country* (completed October 1945) was the only film of this time to be written and directed by an important filmmaker, Shih Tung-shan:

The inhabitants of a little town in North China flee to the hills when the Japanese occupation troops move in. The clever Japanese police chief brings them back by a ruse — he offers some of the stolen food to the town's gentry, and most of the people return, too. The next marketing day has a prosperous, good look — until the Japanese seize everything and everybody. From this revelation of the enemy's real character develops an active anti-Japanese movement in and around the town. . . .[16]

The last wartime production was *The Warning Song of the Soul*. Its original title was *Road to Togetherness,* written by Li Tsung-hsin, director of the Kuomintang's Central Police College; with such a source and such an uplifting title, it is not surprising that Chiang himself found time to read the script, approve it, and order China Film Productions to film it. Even before the war's end there was a campaign to make the police popular, to give them more than deserved credit for destroying spy organizations, and a whole police literature was deliberately created to further this aim. *Road to Togetherness*, with its heroic police officers on the trail of Japanese spies and its artificial conflict between the old-style police and a new far-seeing police ideal, was easily fitted into the campaign. By December 1945, when it was finally completed and shown in Chungking (with a last-minute change of title to *Courageous Police*), the war against Japan had been won five months before, and a new war was beginning in which the police were as important to the government as its army.

The official control of China's cinema during the war makes this the least effectual period in its history. These twenty or so films released show what the whole Chinese film, before and after the war, might have been without revolution as a theme (even concealed) or without revolutionaries to make the films. Each wartime film, no matter how many good people worked on it, presented a wavering choice between the half-hearted and the half-suppressed. The country's defense, as controlled by Kuomintang terms, and compromised by indecision and corruption, made too thin a theme for any kind of artistic life. The Kuomintang's larger, social weakness was to be finally demonstrated within four years.

———————————————

In the first year of the war, as they came down from the movieless mountain resort of Kuling, Isherwood and Auden spent their evening at the cinema in Kiukiang, a considerable town on the shore of the Yangtze (I have not identified the film they saw):

The big picture was about a Chinese weakling who turned traitor to his country and agreed to make signals to Japanese aircraft in exchange for cocaine injections given him by a fiendish Jap doctor. He was shot, of course, and the audience clapped. And then the avenging Chinese troops captured the town — and everybody clapped still louder. We both wondered how long it would be before we were applauding similar trash, only a shade more sophisticated, at all the London cinemas.[17]

As Auden was then writing his sonnet sequence, "In Time of War," I sense a connection between the depressing experience at the Kiukiang cinema and his lines:

But ideas can be true although men die,
For we have seen a thousand faces
Ecstatic from one lie. . . .

5

Fictions and Realities
1932–1945

A film can be re-edited, an author can be persuaded to rewrite a novel, but an epoch cannot be repainted: it is great, but not rose-coloured.
— Ilya Ehrenburg

1. Changchun

In 1927 a Japanese gendarmerie officer, Masahiko Amakasu, traveled to Europe to learn about filmmaking. After a rather extended stay in Paris and at Berlin's UFA studio Amakasu returned to Japan as a film expert but stayed with the gendarmerie. After the successful attack at Mukden on 18 September 1931, Amakasu was put in charge of the police organization of Japanese-occupied Manchuria. "His artistic interests were not, however, to be frustrated, and in a few years he was to assume control of the Manchurian film industry."[1]

The first politico-dramatic mission of Amakasu, in collaboration with Colonel Doihara, was to smuggle Henry P'u Yi, last emperor of China, from Tientsin to Port Arthur, in a series of moves that were to culminate in P'u Yi's installation as the puppet emperor of Japan's new vassal state.

The Republic of Manchukuo came into being in February 1932 [a few weeks after the attack on Shanghai], and P'u Yi was formally installed as Chief Executive on March 9th in the city of Ch'angch'un, now renamed Hsinking or 'New Capital'. He had been taken there by special train the day before and as the arrangements were in the charge of Amakasu it is not surprising that occasional touches revealed the influence of the UFA studios. . . .

In 1934, the Republic was transformed into an Empire, with P'u Yi as Emperor, but apart from an increase in stipend the promotion made little perceptible difference in his position, and none at all in his duties.[2]

In the Hsinking palace P'u Yi ordered one room to be equipped as a cinema, but if he hoped that he could continue to see the American comedies that he had enjoyed in his Peking palace, the limits of his powers were soon made clear to him: his private programs were made up exclusively of Japanese and Manchurian films.[3]

The Emperor might have done worse. The Manchurian and Japanese films that I've seen of this period, though unknown in Europe, had considerable style and spirit. The only difficulty then was to distinguish one country's product from the other's. The Anderson-Richie history of Japanese films records that Japanese audiences rejected Manchurian films (except those that starred Shirley Yamaguchi), because "the quality was poor and . . . the pace was too slow,"[4] but I find the differentiation too subtle to be remarked, possibly because the same Japanese filmmakers were working at home and in the new colony. It is true that their Manchurian subjects sound more obviously like political duties, and this may have reduced their interest for the Japanese public: in 1932, the year that the Republic of Manchukuo was brought out of the Japanese hat — and a Japanese-sponsored Mongolia was intended to arrive soon afterwards — Mizoguchi filmed *The Dawn of the Foundation of Manchukuo and Mongolia*, and in 1933 Uchida's duty was to produce a rousing proof of Japanese-Manchurian solidarity, *Asia Calling*. Mizoguchi and Uchida could not have felt much personal enthusiasm for either of these films. And they were neither the first nor the last Japanese to be given Manchurian assignments; films were used surprisingly early in Japan's calculated conquest of North China:

. . . The Japanese-controlled South Manchuria Railway Company set up a film unit in 1923 to make publicity films to attract settlers and tourists to the country. Thereafter, Japan used Manchuria for location work. In the early 1920s Yasujiro Shimazu made both *Firm Handshake* (Kataki Akushu) and *The Cry of Blood* (Chi no Sakebi) in Manchuria. Both were thrillers based on foreign sources requiring wide-open spaces not found in Japan. In 1928, Hotei Nomura made [in Manchuria] *The Cry of a Nation* (Minzoku no Sakebi). . . .[5]

It is the involvement of Chinese filmmakers that makes the Manchukuo episode relevant to later Chinese film development, and they were not drawn, in quantity, into production here until the Japanese went more deeply into war and into China:

After the war in China had begun, the Japanese felt the need for stronger propaganda in Manchuria and other parts of China. In 1938, under the sponsorship of the army, Manei, the Manchurian Motion Picture Association, was established with a [capital] of two million dollars.* Financed by the Manchurian government and the South Manchuria Railway and staffed by both Manchurians and Japanese, the company built studios in Hsinking . . . .

Despite the enormous population of Manchuria, there were only around eighty permanent theaters in 1938, though traveling exhibition units were rather highly organized. By 1942, however, the Japanese influence had been such that there were two hundred theaters and the Manchurian company was helping to fill them with seventeen to twenty-four features a year.[6]

In the eight years of Manchukuo cinema it produced about two hundred films; about one hundred twenty of these were fictional "entertainment" films. At least three hundred short and news films were issued in this time. It was an important and new Manchurian industry, but it was doomed (no doubt wisely) to a little-publicized existence, partly because of its propaganda function and

---

* Negishi, responsible for the high quality of films made at Japan's Nikkatsu Studio, was placed in charge of production at the Manei Studio.

because of the large number of Japanese staff who could not all be given Manchurian disguises. One does not find the film industry among those industries officially designated as "important to Manchukuo," nor is it mentioned in the proud statistics of new education there. Nevertheless, each step in Japan's plan to broaden its new industrial base was given remarkably swift support by the new film studio at Changchun. An area that was first opened to industry by a Russian railroad and then forcibly modernized by Japanese ambition was a long way from the Manchuria previously famous for only two products, soya beans and bandits, and the film studio helped it maintain its new status.

The purpose of the films made in Manchukuo was to have, or to display, *no* purpose. They were intended to show the world (or the Asian world) a stable, self-confident, unworried regime. Of the several I've seen few have had an openly propagandist point, and often such points vanished as abruptly as they came into view. Even a fantasy using giant furniture to diminish the actors' figures had less "theme" than a similar film by Laurel and Hardy, *Brats*. The last three Manchukuo films that I happened to see, after leaving China, had been captured in Manchuria as enemy property and were certainly made while war went on nearby, though no one would guess it from watching the screen alone. One, a comedy, *General Happiness*, observes (with quite good humor) an old lady who comes to the big city (Harbin) to visit her children and conquers all with her directness and innocence. *Blossoms in Late Spring*,* the most serious of the three, could be an entirely Japanese film set in Manchukuo. It shows us local customs with a rather aloof air of tourism (*peculiar* streets, *peculiar* food), perhaps logical, since the protagonist is a Japanese clerk come to work in Harbin. His virtues are clear. He is an unorthodox hero, fat, awkward, and slow to understand, and he is pursued by *two* attractive heroines! The third film, *The Aromatic Jasper Has Lost Its Odor*, employed my favorite subject: life behind the scenes (any scenes!) with aging actor-manager, heartless financial support, the training of a maid who will assume the leading role at a moment's notice. If there was propaganda in any of these (aside from rocks shied at Roosevelt and Churchill figures in the fair scene of *General Happiness*), I failed to detect it.

The Changchun or Hsinking studio (to become a vital center of postrevolutionary Chinese films) was headed by Captain Amakasu, placed there by the Japanese army in Manchukuo. The speedy recruitment of Chinese filmmakers from Shanghai, where there was not yet a fully controlled Japanese studio, was

---

* This may be an alternative title for *Song of the White Orchid*, mentioned below. The two heroines are played by Shirley Yamaguchi and Setsuko Hara.

clearly a propaganda duty of Amakasu, not merely a personnel emergency. It was especially necessary for non-Japanese faces to appear on the screen, but "the new Asian spirit" also had to be transmitted to the Chinese behind the camera. The earliest Manchukuo film that I know had an almost equal number of Japanese and Chinese (known as Manchurian) names among the credits. This was *Girl of the Frontier,* based on Japanese hopes to win domination of Mongolia, too. Its climactic sequence was a reconstruction of the battle of Tsitsihar, a Japanese victory in Manchuria intended to impress any Mongolian spectator. Fear of Soviet influence was expressed in a scene of Mongol priests laughing at a caricature of Joseph Stalin.

The studio also made a more open attack on Bolshevism, *Sing-Song Girl of Harbin,* about (and possibly aimed at) the large Russian population of the second industrial center of Manchukuo. Most of its dialogue is in Russian, but the speakers (under the Japanese director, Shimazu) are a sadly mixed crew, ranging from two or three with some professional skill down to those from backgrounds of nightclubs and amateur theatricals. The film's confused ideas, including both self-pity and adventurism, may be traced to an effort to please all the bickering political parties in Harbin's Russian colony.

This film gave me my first look at the only star of Manchurian films who interested paying audiences in both Manchukuo and Japan, Li Hsiang-lan, whose Japanese name is Yoshiko Yamaguchi, and who is known internationally as Shirley Yamaguchi.

It is difficult, and possibly unnecessary, to establish now for which studios in China and Japan the successful Shirley Yamaguchi was employed on which films. Throughout the war years each studio that wanted the credit for one of her successes would submit ideas to her and their government controls, and the struggle for her would sometimes be resolved only by coproduction, Changchun and Peking, or Shanghai and Tokyo. Her first real triumph was *Song of the White Orchid,* directed for Changchun by Kunio Watanabe in 1939. The résumé given by Anderson and Richie sounds more realistic than its "national policy" purpose:

The story was about the love between a beautiful Manchurian girl and a Japanese immigrant. The boy must marry a Japanese in the interest of his country, but despite the rather expected plot, the characters were lifelike and the stereotypes which the story would seem to suggest were avoided.[7]

Shirley Yamaguchi and the Japanese actor, Kazuo Hasegawa, made a starring team that lasted through the war and worked in all the Japanese-run studios of

China. *China Night* (1940) was set in Shanghai, the love story of a Chinese war
orphan and a Japanese naval officer. *Suchow Night* (1942) was a film about
Japanese doctors in Shanghai, all kind, heroic, selfless. (The only European
shown was a German restaurant manager.) Other Yamaguchi films mentioned by
Anderson and Richie: *Peking Night, Vow in the Desert** (1941), *Fighting Street*
(1942), *Sayon's Bell* (1943), the last "aimed at introducing the customs of
Formosa into Japan," with Yamaguchi playing another non-Japanese exotic,
Formosan this time.

No matter in which Chinese studio these Japanese propaganda films were made,
it would be absurd to deny that the Chinese filmmakers associated with them
were immune to their obvious technical skill. The Japanese (or even "Manchurian") way of telling a story is quite different from Chinese film narrative,
that is, as it was before the war. Japanese films depend more on implication, and
their whole approach to a theme or to a sequence is more oblique than the
frontal simplicity of pre-1945 Chinese films. The experience in Changchun and
other Japanese studios employing Chinese filmmakers gave them, willy-nilly, a
new string to their cinema bow, and, I am certain, altered the character of the
best Chinese films made after 1945. Yasujiro Shimazu was a director particularly
noted in Japan for the large number of young directors that he trained and
fostered; it is unlikely that he changed this good habit while in Changchun.
Besides the few experienced Chinese who were exposed to this unfamiliar way of
making films, there were many Chinese (or Manchurians) working with film for
the first time and even more susceptible to Japanese influence — and some of
these, too, are making today's Chinese films. I am prepared to have these connections passionately rejected, especially by those Chinese filmmakers who
worked for the Japanese, but that will not change a fact that, in my opinion,
is a positive and visible advantage. Nor can I believe that the influence went only
in one direction. Tokyo filmmakers, working outside their island, could not
return to it unchanged, for Chinese artists were also solving the problems of
Manchukuo's films.

Before the formation of Manei and its modern film studio, Changchun was a
base for the systematic newsreel and actuality films of Japanese military might
on the continent. Between 1934, when a Yokohama company made the feature-

---

* " . . . a Japanese civil engineer, [played by] Kazuo Hasegawa, falls in love with a Chinese
girl, but their idyll is interrupted by a Communist attack. Hasegawa, on his death bed, con-
verts several of the Communists to 'pan-Asianism'." Joseph L. Anderson and Donald Richie,
The Japanese Film (Tokyo: Charles E. Tuttle, 1959; New York: Grove Press, Evergreen,
1960), p. 155.

length actuality film, *Japan Advancing to the North*, and 1936, when a Manchukuo company, Mantetsu, produced *Forbidden Jehol* (directed by Mitsuzo
Akutagawa), Manchukuo was recognized as stable enough for Japan to transfer
at least the legal foundations of its continental Asian film enterprises to the new
"Empire." And the puppet empire needed each drop of finance and prestige that
the mother country could spare. Thenceforward Japan's films about China came
from its Chinese studios. The only exception I know is the extraordinarily
detailed series of "conquest films," *Hammer Blows Against China*, begun in
1937 and continuing until the stalemate of 1939, an efficient coverage by a
corps of newsreel cameramen comparable, at least in quantity and organization,
to the German camera coverage of the invasions of Poland and France. I am not
aware of any Chinese cameramen participating in these aggression records.

In August 1945, as the Soviet army approached Hsinking, many Japanese fled
but Amakasu stayed on to oversee the affairs of the Manchukuoan film studio:

Wages were paid in full, with as handsome a bonus as there was money for, and
testimonials were written for those who wanted them. The Chinese were urged
to stay at their posts and keep the studios ready to continue production under
the new authorities, whether these should be from Moscow or Chungking.. . .
Only when he was satisfied to the last detail did he shut himself in his office and
swallow his cyanide.[8]

2. Peking

Very soon after the war began [in 1937], the Towa Company, main distributor of European pictures in Japan, formed a production unit under Shigeyoshi
Suzuki to go to Peking to shoot *The Road to Peace in the Orient* (Toyo Heiwa
no Michi). The interiors were shot in a rented studio and the Chinese actors
featured in the film were recruited by newspaper advertisements. . . .[9]

There was, however, a surer source of information on film personnel for the
Towa Company; after the fall of Peking the new Japanese head of the local
military intelligence bureau found himself being courted energetically by
Chinese ladies:

In particular, some film actresses had been hearing with admiration of the
chances of professional advancement in P'u Yi's empire, and thought it would do
them no harm to be civil to the most influential of the conquerors. Colonel
Yamaga was naturally deemed to be in this category. . . .[10]

From the beginning of Chinese film production Peking hoped to become an
industrial and artistic center for Chinese films. After the remarkable 1905 initiative of the Feng Tai Photography Shop there, the French attempt in 1920, and
later halfhearted enterprises, the Old Capital and nearby Tientsin came to some

brief film life only when an upswing in the nation's film business encouraged the gambling of Peking money. Some Shanghai companies attempted to establish branch studios in Peking, but these usually melted into mere distribution offices. Mei Lan-fang's third hope to record his performances took place on the roof of Peking's Gaumont Cinema, and in an ancient Peking garden. In 1926 there was a flurry of Robin Hood films, and even a mild attempt to tell the unmild story of the last Dowager Empress. It must have been frustrating for Peking's smaller financiers to watch Shanghai and foreign film companies — from Universal's *The Dragon's Net* in 1919 to the North China Company's *Spring Dream in the Old Capital* in 1930 — use the handsome and famous locations and Ming architecture of Peking without exploiting them themselves; but the comings and goings of various warlords made the immediate future too uncertain for continuous production. Even the sound film, which placed a premium on every pure Peking accent in the Shanghai studios, did not help Peking's film hopes.

The enemy, finally, did bring a film industry to Peking, lasting enough for most of the Peking film studios of today to reveal foundations built by the Japanese. Only ruthless enterprise and persistence could dent the lethargy of Peking. From the Japanese point of view Peking was a far more attractive film setting than Changchun; ancient Chinese culture and arts had determined Japanese modes for centuries, and the real thing was now in Japanese hands, to use as they wished.

The combination of postwar Chinese hate and American policies in occupied Japan have left almost no trace of the films made by Japanese companies in Peking, but an occasional hint of their quality can be heard in the number of Chinese film actors who curse their training in that period — if they mention it at all.

Another energetic film country preferred Peking to Manchuria, in spite of its longer accessibility. Even before the military alliance of fascist powers, which called itself the Axis, made it simple for Japan's most formidable partner to take such a step, Germany moved its film cameras into Peking. Germans had also arrived early in Japanese Manchuria: in 1931 *Kampf um die Mandschurei* (also shown as *Die Welt der gelben Rasse*). Tibet and roads to Tibet were also a constant source of film interest, with or without scientific support, from the 1931 *Himatschal, der Thron der Götter*, through *Der Dämon des Himalaya* (1935), *Kampf um den Himalaya* (1938) and *Geheimnis Tibet* (1942) — all feature-length actuality films. Following the Japanese army into Peking, German cameramen kept Peking's architecture and exotica on German screens, in a quantity of shorts and *Kulturfilme*. The most ambitious German statement of Japanese policy is *Das neue Asien,* filmed in 1938 by Dr. Colin Ross and released in 1940. German filmmakers also traveled, under Japanese protection, down the Yangtze, to show the most primitive aspects of Chinese life (to prove the value of Japan's mission there), in *China zwischen Gestern und Heute.*

German memories of their secure authority in Peking and Tientsin, after as well as before the Boxer Uprising, were easily awakened. The flood of detailed films sent from Peking and other familiar Chinese scenes was the climax of a renewed paternal interest in China that appeared in Nazi studio films, too. The earliest of this group of films appeared at the end of Hitler's first year: *Flüchtlinge,* directed by Ucicky with such expert camerawork by Fritz Arno Wagner that one can't be sure whether it was filmed in Harbin or in the UFA studio. The *Flüchtlinge* are a group of Volga Germans trying to escape capture by the Soviet mission in Harbin. The hero — an echo of earlier German films about China — is not German, however: Hans Albers plays a resourceful Englishman in sympathy with the Germans' plight. *Moskau-Shanghai* (1936) is a more sensational picture of White Russians in China than Manchukuo would ever have dared to make. Pola Negri is the suffering heroine.* In 1937 the Boxer Uprising was economically reconstructed for *Alarm in Peking* by Herbert Selpin, a dress rehearsal for his bigger film about a group of brave victims, *Titanic.* Gustav Fröhlich here plays a German officer who outwits the Chinese attackers, led by Bernhard Minetti in the best Wu-Fu-Manchu tradition. Helmut Käutner's *Auf Wiedersehen, Franziska* (1941) follows the adventures of a newsreel cameraman through various battlefronts, notably China versus Japan, although the Shanghai scenes, except for real newsreel material, show no Chinese! In only the earliest of these films does a camera unit appear to have been sent to China.

Japanese organizational talents in Peking produced more offices and studios than in Changchun, but fewer films. In February 1938 a Peking branch of the Manchurian Motion Picture Association was set up (in the Japanese headquarters of the New People's Association), to control all film production in their new territory and to produce short films. A year later the Japanese North China Film Factory was opened, also for short propaganda films (*To Establish a New Order in East Asia, March on, East Asia!,* and more of the same). Ichikawa, chairman of the Japanese newsreel association, called a meeting in Peking that resulted in the formulation of the Japanese Mainland Film Policy. Thereafter the Japanese

---

* Paul Wegener (brought to Moscow for the soon abandoned German version of *Revolt of the Fishermen*) directed this after his return from the Soviet Union. Its anti-Bolshevism came in handy later: it was reissued in 1949 as a cold-war instrument (renamed *Der Weg nach Shanghai*).

film authorities in Peking adopted a new method that was later to be applied to the captured Shanghai film industry: avoid an open Japanese label. In November 1939 all film organizations in Peking were united to make the North China Film Company, Limited, with capital supplied by Japanese producers and equipment manufacturers, and a new studio was built whose actual task was the production of propaganda for the Japanese army and policy: *Reconstructed China* and *Co-operation* were two of the titles from the new studio. In February 1941 a next step was taken, further from outright propaganda: a *very* Chinese studio was established, the Yian Ching Film Company, to make opera films and other "unpolitical" subjects. This subtle program lasted less than a year. When the Japanese widened their war in the Pacific, *all* organizations were given tasks in the total war effort of Nippon, and the productions of Yian Ching changed their character accordingly. The widened war also cut down the hopes of selling "innocent" films abroad: these markets were now either held by the Japanese army or by the countries allied against Japan.

3. Shanghai

Each film-producing country has a veiled or unwritten chapter in its history, for various reasons. France Is ashamed of the dependence of some of its most honored filmmakers, *before* the German occupation, on Nazi money and Berlin studios. For some reason German film histories skirt the years of the First World War. No one mentions the American films made in the two years between *The Jazz Singer* and the general adoption of the sound film. The years between the end of the Second War and the Twentieth Congress of the Communist Party are a period that Soviet film historians would rather not discuss. A more impenetrable silence is maintained by Cheng Chi-hua and all other Chinese commentators on film history, making it difficult to establish even the chronology and output of the large film industry in Shanghai and Peking during the three and a half years of Japanese occupation, and in Changchun for a longer period. One of their reasons is similar to the reason for the present French silence about German alliances of the thirties:[*] the names of filmmakers now respected and active would seem sullied by too close an attention to their work then, though this is not the explanation that Cheng Chi-hua gave to me:

On the views in your article about the films made by the Japanese puppets after 1941 in North China and Shanghai. I consider that such puppet films were only the product of Japanese imperialist aggression with a small group of traitors who

---

[*] Notably the Alliance Cinématographique Européenne — A.C.E., supported by German banks and "advised" by the Propaganda Ministry. Georges Sadoul's report (dated August 1939) on this *guerre blanche* and the various camouflages adopted by German control in the French film industry appeared in *Films* (New York), Nov. 1939.

had gone over to the enemy. Such films are absolutely contrary to the consistently patriotic spirit of our people. They were the opposite of the Chinese national film, an object to be condemned in a history of Chinese films, and can not occupy a place in that history. This is a matter of principle.[11]

I could understand the condemnation, but not the silence. If it is humiliation that is being veiled, the same veil obscures the development of the many Chinese artists who worked under the Japanese in those years. Their survival should be recognized.

This unwritten chapter does not begin until December 1941, when the Japanese declared war on the democratic powers and seized the enemies' concessions in Shanghai. The Chinese filmmakers who, from then to the end of the war, worked for the Japanese (though some effort was made to "save their faces" then and to make their productions more salable in the occupied Chinese cities by calling the film companies "Chinese") had not left Shanghai in 1937, when they were able to.

Between 1937 and 1941 the Shanghai film industry, confined to the concessions, regarded itself as in an "orphan island." The tone of self-pity in this term is not unjustified, unless we find ourselves unsympathetic to their choice, in 1937, when most of the "commercial" filmmakers ignored the commands flung over the shoulder of the fleeing government to leave with them. In this period Japanese pressure was constantly felt by the film studios in the enclosed city, but semi-independent production continued. Bluster was tried in December 1937, when the Japanese command summoned the managers of all film companies, distributors as well as producers, to announce that all films must be submitted to them for examination and approval. This had little effect on the already scared filmmakers, and the Japanese tried a new tactic in 1938: money was offered to persons in key positions to make them more cooperative; for example, the Guang Min Company's production of *La dame aux camélias* (1938) was ostentatiously purchased for Japan at a price far beyond the film's worth. Some of the money scattered by the Japanese must have remained in Chinese hands, but this is not a matter of public record.* At this time uncooperative newspaper proprietors would receive the heads of minor employees in the mail, but I have not heard of this kind of pressure applied to film companies.

The element of "patriotism" in Shanghai films was soon so reduced that only the smallest gestures of opposition were visible. Nevertheless, open sale of one-

---

* Cheng Chi-hua mentions only two people as taking the Japanese money; these were both company managers (the more important being Chang Shan-kun, head of Hsin Hua) who adopted strong anti-communist positions before 1949.

self to the Japanese still bore a stigma. For the time the Shanghai film industry tried to be as neutral as possible. And when a whole film industry is trying to
make films about nothing, it takes very little substance to draw attention to
itself. Against a background of deliberately harmless adaptations of Peking opera
subjects, borrowings from safe episodes in *Water Margin, Romance of Three
Kingdoms,** *Western Pilgrimage* (all Chinese classics equally popular in Japan and
also used there for film plots), and vague spectacles suffocated in costumes and
extras, *Mu-lan* looked like a miracle to the audiences of Shanghai: an English-
woman living there then told me that she couldn't believe her eyes when she saw
what was on the screen. How had this escaped the Japan-oriented censors? And
as late as February 1939!

It was the persistence of Ouyang Yu-chien, again. He had reached Hong Kong,
and friends founding a new Shanghai film company appealed to him to write
"something for classical costumes." Within a month he sent them the scenario of
Mu-lan Joins the Army: he changed the emphasis of the familiar story (a loyal
daughter replaces her feeble father as a soldier) from a tragedy about the unorthodox behavior of a feudal woman to a lively patriotic romance with a titil-
lating element of transvestism. The barbarians that she goes off to fight (alongside a slightly confused future husband) were so clearly the Japanese that both
the studio and the literary journal that published the scenario† carefully altered
its patriotism, though Ouyang, in his memoirs, bitterly remarks that neither
journal nor studio was yet fully controlled by the Japanese. *Mu-lan*'s popularity
was enormous: it put the new company (Hua Chun) in business, it established
the career of Chen Yun-san, who played and sang the role of Mu-lan, and
Ouyang's songs for the film were heard all over China. Stimulated by this success
he at once wrote the scenario for another pseudohistorical film, this time an
allegory of the Sian kidnapping of Chiang, *Creation of the World*:

As I recall this now, I must confess I was really too stupid. If no one could
detect the parallel, then the film would be useless; but if everyone can see the
parallel, then it was impossible for the studio to produce a film with such
content.[12]

He wrote no more film scenarios until after the war.

Beyond survival there are few causes for pride in the "orphan island" period.
Mu-lan had many imitations but no equally brave successors. There was a technical victory: the clever animators, the Wan brothers, returned from Hankow

---

* *Diao Chan* (1938) was based on a neatly cinematic episode in *Three Kingdoms*. With
English titles, and named *Sable Cicada*, it is one of the few Chinese films to be offered,
though unsuccessfully, to the American public (see *Variety*, 18 Jan. 1939, 25 Feb. 1942).
† *Wen Hsian*, 10 March 1939.

and Hong Kong to Shanghai in 1940 to attempt the first feature-length Chinese cartoon, *Princess Iron-Fan* (another episode from *Western Pilgrimage*). Its year of production and the organization of seventy apprentices to execute the thousands of drawings still amaze Chinese journalists. Its faintly Chinese reflection of Disney prettiness (adapted here to black and white) gives it now mainly a curiosity value; it comes to life only in those moments where no Disney models were available for imitation, forcing something to be invented. Into the 1960s the Wan brothers continue their work on its subject of the Monkey King. A less publicized source of pride is that the Shanghai film industry made it possible for at least one film to be made by émigrés from the German film industry: Jakob and Luise Fleck never made a masterpiece, but their one Shanghai film (very probably, their last work*) was a decent, human film with none of the frantically sensational appeal of other "modern dress" films in Shanghai at this time. *Children of the World* (1941) was written and directed by the Flecks in collaboration with Fei Mu: it touches the politically delicate periods of 1927 and 1937, ending on an almost realistic picture of Shanghai life in 1940.

Though the "orphan island" period meant freedom from the Kuomintang censors, the Japanese threatened a worse suppression of both art and life. But those who could best use the new freedom or who could best evade the new threat were already far from Shanghai. Without these hardy characters the four years of the orphan island displayed, in microcosm, all that was worst about the world of films. The safety of the costume film gave it domination of the whole period. But laziness and haste show up in a costume film more disagreeably than in any other form, chiefly because the makers often believe that the costumes are a substitute for drama and imagination. I've never seen such poor reconstructions of the past on the screen — they make the works of Film d'Art look lively and scholarly. A typical one was *Go Nun-nian* (1939, by the company that was founded on *Mu-lan*), a "costume film" in every wrong sense of the term. What we see amidst the bric-a-brac are actors standing about in glued beards and gaudy costumes, so obviously afraid of these glittering draperies that they feel safe only when not moving. Military costumes are given special authority with a lavish use of presumably brass bosses, though one suspects every material employed. The result has neither the virtues of stylized Peking opera nor of credible modern theater. If anyone had some historical parallel in mind, it's been forgotten in the haste of turning out this product. The opulent effect of *Empress Wu Tze-tien* (1939) is somewhat more related to the film's violent action, but it was more important to show the spectator how much money had been spent:

---

* The Flecks somehow survived to return, after the war, not to Berlin, but to their birthplace, Vienna.

The "Super-Production" film "Empress Wu" was said to have cost approximately Chinese $100,000.00 and according to the company, the throne alone of the "Empress," a very beautiful work, did not cost less than $10,000.00. In comparison to the sums we know with reference to Western productions these amounts seem more than modest![13]

Each studio stole from others, hoping to show its theft first: Yi Hua's *Three Smiles* appeared on 3 June 1940, a week before Guo Hua's *Three Smiles*; Hsin Hua's *Jade Hairpin* appeared on 4 July 1940, beating Guo Hua, again, by four days. Yi Hua made its *Three Smiles* in seven days and nights, not allowing the actors to sleep or change their clothes. In these races to the screen rival companies conducted uninhibited slander campaigns against each other in willing newspapers. It was open season for remakes and unabashed plagiarism. Remakes of and sequels to old Chinese successes, like *Singsong Girl Red Peony* (1941) and *Song at Midnight* (Part II, 1941),* were sold on little more than their familiar titles. *Street Angel* was remade as *Rouge and Tears* (1938) with the ever popular Butterfly Wu. *Miss Change-Body* and *Mr. Wang* went on and on. The series of *Red Lotus Temple* thrillers was revived after ten years. One studio (Hua Hsin) appears to have specialized in borrowing from foreign films, chiefly American: Marcel Pagnol's *Topaze* became *Gold and Silver World* (1939); *Club des Femmes* was transferred to a Shanghai apartment house; *Snow White and the Seven Dwarfs* (laced with *Dr. Jekyll and Mr. Hyde*) became an acutely embarrassing *Chinese Princess White Snow* (1940);† Tarzan, the Invisible Man, and even Charlie Chan and the Three Musketeers all appeared in Shanghai carbons. *Resurrection* came from Tolstoy via Hollywood. The Garbo successes, *Camille* and *Grand Hotel*, were tediously copied, and no one knows what other originals sit behind the extravagant titles of this period; a film that I have not seen, entitled *The Soul Flies to Blue Bridge* (1941), is said to have had an American model (*Waterloo Bridge?*). American films themselves enjoyed a pre-Pearl Harbor boom, as if Shanghai knew that its favorite cultural aggressor was about to vanish for four years. *The Film Daily* (New York) of 20 March 1941 reported "Inflation Sends Shanghai Grosses to Dizzy Figures": at the Cathay *Tin Pan Alley* brought in 132,000 Shanghai dollars in two weeks; at the Nanking *Northwest Mounted Police*, 138,000 in fifteen days; at the Grand and Metropole, *The Mark of Zorro*, 70,000 in four days; and *Gone with the Wind*, of course, won over all others. These grosses should not intoxicate the reader, however, for inflation had forced the Shanghai dollar down to six cents, and the top admission charge was four Shanghai dollars, or twenty-four cents. Yet the figures do

---

* Chin Shan's role continued, even though he was then in Yenan, by using a similar voice and a horrible mask or black veil for all the "appearances" of his character.
† Made and released so hastily that some clapper boards were left in!

testify to full houses. It is the permanent cultural damage of such admirations (*Tin Pan Alley*!) that can never be fully estimated in any accounting of the modern Chinese film.

Long before Pearl Harbor and their total occupation of Shanghai, the Japanese had repeatedly probed there, looking for the same foothold in the film industry that they already had gained in other Shanghai industries:

As early as 1923, Yasujiro Shimazu had made one of his innumerable thrillers, *Market of Human Flesh* (Jinniku no Ichi) there, and in 1925 Nikkatsu's *Day of Rough Waves* (Namiaraki Hi) had a two-month location in Shanghai. A year later Minoru Murata went to Shanghai to make the first Chinese-Japanese coproduction, *The Spirit of the Man from Kyushu* . . . , and in 1926 Genjiro Mie's *O-Ryo from Siberia* . . . was released. From 1937 onward the Japanese filmed a great deal in China.[14]

In 1938 a cutter at the Japanese company, Toho, was employed by the army to make his first actuality film, about occupied Shanghai. Fumio Kamei had studied at the Leningrad Film and Theater Institute, and as his decision to make films had been determined by Bliokh's *Shanghai Document*, it is not surprising to find a general similarity of attitude; Anderson and Richie describe Kamei's *Shanghai* as contrasting "the lives of rich [white] foreigners and poor Chinese, much to the detriment of the former."[15] In the same year Kamei made *Peking*, not as a victorious song but as an elegy. His next film, *Fighting Soldiers*, on the capture of Hankow, was banned by the army censor and Kamei's career as an army propagandist was finished.

In 1939 Toho reconstructed the Japanese victory at Shanghai, using the actual ruins as their exterior settings, in *Landing Party at Shanghai* (Shanghai Rikusen Tai), with their future star Setsuko Hara in the role of a frightened Chinese girl tenderly cared for by the Japanese soldiers!

The greatest success of Japanese money in 1939 was in its support of a group of "soft" filmmakers in setting up the Chung Hua Film Company to make *Kulturfilme* supervised by the enemy. With Chung Hua as base, and precious raw film as purchasing power, the Japanese added several small companies to their unit: their prize capture was Chang Shan-kun and his Hsin Hua Company.

We have an unexpected document* from the official who was appointed to head the Japanese-controlled studios and cinemas. This is Nagamasa Kawakita, still (1970) a leading film producer of Japan. In 1939, not yet able to enter the foreign concessions, Kawakita's first thought was: "What sort of films would this audience want?" His decision was to make them on former Chinese lines with established stars. "But I was criticized: these were not sufficiently political." When Manchurian films were brought to the Shanghai cinemas, the audience "did not welcome them." Kawakita was so nervous about his dilemma that he feared for his life. When open war on the concessionaries was declared in December 1941, Kawakita's position changed for the better. During the full occupation of Shanghai, however, he learned that "decisions could not be acted upon if pressed in a hurry." He was careful to use only one good cinema, the Roxy, for Japanese films (dubbed in Chinese): "not popular at first, but after six months, 90% of the audience for these films were Chinese." He also testifies to the great aid given the box office by Shirley Yamaguchi. The only production under his supervision that satisfied both civil and military authorities was *Raising the Signal-Fires Over Shanghai* (1944), codirected by Hiroshi Inagaki and Yueh Feng.

---

* Nagamasa Kawakita, "Film Making in Southeast Asia and China," *Kinema Jumpo* (Tokyo), 25 July 1961, pp. 26—28.

Though all Shanghai newspapers changed their ownership on 9 December 1941, no drastic change came to the film industry; but in April 1942 the twelve leading film companies of Shanghai found themselves amalgamated into the Chung Hua United Film Company, Ltd., a Chinese company with Japanese policies.

Georges Sadoul's observation on Nazi film plans for occupied Paris shows an exact parallel to Japanese film plans for occupied Shanghai:

Since Hitler wanted to turn Paris into the Luna Park of National Socialist Europe, wouldn't it be best to have the French cinema specialize in comic and dramatic entertainment?[16]

In reality neither capital became a Luna Park, but the films that came from both occupied Paris and Shanghai did their damndest to look jolly and confident, with an emphasis on farce that rings hollow as soon as one considers the circumstances under which it was manufactured. Yet neither victor could resist the temptation to press the occupied cinema into what he imagined was subtle propaganda.

All the propaganda lines determined by the Japanese in Shanghai are easily detected. After Pearl Harbor the main aim seems to have been to convince the Chinese spectator that the European (meaning the Englishman and American) was and is his worst enemy. The Miki-Kamei actuality film of 1938, *Shanghai*, was a preliminary gesture in this direction. The first film made under Japanese supervision would have made David Belasco proud — *Madame Butterfly!* I wish I had seen this Pinkerton. When the Japanese took full control of Shanghai films, they spared no expense in dramatizing the most embarrassing episodes in the history of European evils in China. There were plenty to choose from. The First Opium War was obviously perfect for this purpose. *A Perfume to Last Ten Centuries* [*Eternal Fame*] , filmed in the winter of 1942–1943, employed six Chinese directors and the pick of Chinese actors. The first half of the film (before political pressure and anxieties grew heavy on the production) is a fine demonstration of what a Shanghai studio could do with maximum resources. Lin Tse-hsü is played in a manner heroic enough to please any Chinese patriot. As usual, in both Chinese and Japanese films of the time, local actors are transformed into anti-English caricatures with long wax noses and curly blond wigs. The British Ambassador is extremely decayed and shifty. The last big Japanese film made in Shanghai was an even more pointed historical spectacle: *Sorrows Left at Spring River* showed the Taiping Rebellion as supported by a wise Japanese antiforeign movement, and as betrayed by the British (see Plates 18 and 19). A Japanese (Hiroshi Inagaki) and a Chinese (Yueh Feng) codirected this Japanese-Chinese production, and the camera-team was also divided. Popular

Chinese actors again played the main roles and the Europeans here are played by Europeans, probably Russian émigrés. All Japanese dialogue scenes are translated into Chinese subtitles.*

A propaganda line running parallel with this was cooperation — all Asian peoples living together harmoniously and happily. An unconscious caricature of this idea can be seen in the variations on *Love for Everyone* (1942), that employed *all* the popular actors, climaxed by the Chinese Laurel-Hardy team, of Shanghai (with a different director for each short story) to show us eleven examples of selfishness overcome by love. (It must have been this film that helped make "humanity" a dirty word in China today.) *Man and Woman* is a musical comedy with the same theme. One song, in the manner of *Sous les toits de Paris*, spreads through a whole neighborhood. Another song extends this by continuing over several places and changing seasons — love and happiness without limit.

A more desperate and dangerous propaganda line was to place Chinese in humiliating situations, even in relation to each other. The most lurid trial of this tactic was *Chu Hai-tang* (1943, in two parts; see Plate 18). The first part is based on a real incident in the 1920s, but one that Chinese would never have filmed in this way.† Chu Hai-tang is a famous and handsome actor of female roles in Peking opera. He attracts the attention of a general who "makes advances" to him that are at first rejected. A beautiful heroine, fresh out of normal school, is introduced as a candidate for the general's third wife. To save her from such a fate Chu Hai-tang sacrifices himself to the general's clearly expressed wishes. The whole film puts unusual stress on sensuality and no one, least of all Chinese society, comes off with much dignity. All contribute to the Japanese aim for this film: the general, a Chinese Bogart, shows us the corrupt state of the Chinese army and government; the hero's sacrifice, not especially noble, is only another symptom of softness and weakness; even the heroine is used to show us marriage customs from an antiquated world. The film is guaranteed to disgust and discourage its audience. And a non-Chinese audience, if any saw it, would be convinced that China had a decadent and outworn social system.

An undercurrent of self-pity that ran beneath even the most revolutionary of the films of the 1930s, and that one finds, more openly, in the literature of the period, was finally being exploited as an anti-Chinese weapon. Considering this, it may not be so strange that the conscious films of the thirties drew upon so

---

* Cheng Chi-hua notes that extra efforts were made to popularize this film in China, but that "this film followed the Japanese to their tomb in 1945."
† Possibly to counteract the effect of this film, the Chinese remade it in 1948 as a story of martyrdom under Japanese occupation, omitting the sexual element.

little of the distinguished literature that was published in those years. We know of Lu Hsun's refusals when film adaptations were suggested to him, but why were left novelists (with the exception of Ting Ling) so unconnected with left films then? It is revealing that Pa Chin's sentimental novels should be the only modern literature of standing that fitted occupation policies for film production. His *Family* (in two weepy parts) was made just before the Japanese took over, and they had no objection to his *Spring* and *Autumn* being filmed by Chung Hua United Films.

In the year following May 1942 the forcibly combined studios of Shanghai made about fifty films. In May 1943 the Japanese instructed Wang Ching-wei to issue a law that took over *all* the film studios and offices of occupied China (outside Manchukuo) as the Chinese Film Company, Ltd. To increase production there were more coproductions with Japanese studios. Neither quantity[*] nor quality was helped by these moves. Perhaps Shanghai filmworkers were inventing better ways to impede and evade cooperation, though none could have been more ingenious than Mei Lan-fang's simple device of growing a moustache, enabling him to decline all Japanese invitations to perform as a lovely young girl. Cheng Chi-hua mentions only two filmmakers who "refused to cooperate," Ko Ling and Fei Mu, but without details. Some Chinese were brave enough to attend screenings at the Soviet Club, but we are not told if these included filmworkers. Anderson and Richie provide such encouraging detail on the various evasions by some Japanese filmmakers during the war that I wish we had as much infor-mation on individual Chinese methods to compare with that.

The end of Japanese rule in China was abrupt and bloody. The removal of the hundred thousand Japanese from Shanghai seems to have been less violent than their annihilation at Harbin, where the only Japanese left alive was a doctor with a Chinese wife. The events of August 1945 must be added to the dramas in China that will never be filmed there.

One war was over, and the Chinese film industry faced new battles.

4. Yenan

Another center during the occupation produced few films, but it was here that the people and ideals were formed that were to decide the nature of Chinese films after 1949. At our distance, in time and space, from the now legendary Red base of Yenan, the film problem would seem a simple one: whenever we

---

[*] 1943, twenty-four films; 1944, thirty-two films; 1945 (before August), twenty-four films. Statistics in Cheng Chi-hua, Vol. II.

get the means we'll make films to help fight imperialism and build socialism. Yet such a simple formulation sounds wonderfully naïve beside the complexity of the actual political and cultural situation there, reflecting an inner party struggle that neither then nor now was fully resolved after the catastrophe of 1927.

To add to Chiang's victorious coup d'état in 1927 the new dictator was blessed by a split in the Chinese Communist Party. Even in defeat the party centers, in Shanghai and Canton, clung to the "unalterable" principle that only the proletarian class could lead China to a successful revolution. Mao Tse-tung, no less an intellectual than the Shanghai party leaders, was more realistic in his estimate of China's revolutionary future: in his generation and his century Mao saw no prospect of a Chinese proletariat gaining sufficient quantitative weight to determine the course of China's revolution, and in this he had the support of Lenin's similar doubts.[17] Only the Chinese peasant had the strength and a centuries-old tradition of revolt. When Mao could not convince the party leadership that a basic Marxist tenet had to be revised for China, he proceeded to demonstrate the correctness of his heterodoxy. With the fighters who stayed with him he built in the Chingkangshan range of Kiangsi province a Red stronghold sustained and protected by the peasants there. By 1931 the party leaders in Shanghai removed Mao from the Central Committee and made official the separation between the wings of the party. From Kiangsi and later from Shensi Mao watched the tactics and behavior of Shanghai's "intellectual" Communists with increasing distrust.

Chiang's "antibandit" campaigns against the revolutionary base in Kiangsi eventually forced the Red Army to abandon it in October 1934.* Mao led the main force of the army west and north on the twentieth-century epic known as the Long March. Isolated from direct government control a communist and anti-Japanese base had been developed in the northern province of Shensi, where Mao and half of the army that started with him (including thirty women) arrived after a year of battles and hardships. A year later, in November 1936, Chu Teh and other troops, coming by a different route and with other obstacles, arrived in Shensi, and joined the local center in Pao-an. The first political victory was immediate — in December Chiang was kidnapped at Sian and the Kuomintang was compelled to join the communists in resisting the Japanese.

As early as 1936 the world outside China was more aware of the new revolutionary base than was the rest of China. An American journalist, Edgar Snow,

---

* In Fukien province anti-Kuomintang groups had formed a "government." It had no army and proposed coalition with the Kiangsi Communists, who rejected the offer. Mao later considered this a mistake.

got through to Pao-an that year, and his account, *Red Star Over China*, published in New York and London in 1937, was the first information that most of Shanghai's left-wing intellectuals, already on their "orphan island," had about the Long March, about life at the new base, and about the life histories and views of those leaders. By now the base had been moved from Pao-an to Yenan, and to get to Yenan became the goal of thousands of young intellectuals all over China: hundreds of them managed to pass both Japanese and Kuomintang barriers throughout the years of war. The film people who arrived could bring little equipment, and almost all were trained in studio work rather than in the documentary improvisation that would be the sole film method of the guerrilla fighters. Chin Shan, the clever actor who had not yet worked in film direction, chose Yenan rather than sitting out the war in Chungking. Among the other film actors who came, one relinquished her film career completely:

Mao Tze-tung met me at the entrance of the little compound . . . where he lives with his family and immediate aides. His comely, youngish wife was with him — the former Lan Ping, well-known Shanghai movie actress, an extremely intelligent woman, a member of the Communist Party since 1933. In 1937 she gave up her movie career and went to Yenan to work in the Lu Hsun Art Academy. Here Mao's interest in the drama brought them together, and they were married quietly in the spring of 1939.[18]

Even photographs were rare in the first months of Pao-an and Yenan. It was an American and a Russian who brought out the first detailed film records of the Shensi Communists.*

Just as the film underground of Shanghai was scattering to Yenan and Hankow and Hong Kong, a group of us in New York, in unconscious imitation of Shanghai, adopted pseudonyms to work on "dangerous" films. Early in 1937 an enthusiastic amateur cameraman named Harry Dunham brought us several hundred feet of film that he had just brought from China — this was the first filming of the Red Army in Shensi. With some additional newsreel footage to show the war and the new united front we edited it as *China Strikes Back*.† Its unique material and the adventure of its cameraman gained it more circulation and attention than any other film we made. It even achieved some foreign sales and was shown in the Soviet Union.

---

* Snow had previously taken a few shots of Pao-an on 16 mm that he used in his American lectures.
† Another unconscious echo of Shanghai: twenty-five years later I discovered that the "folk song" we used for the sound track was actually Jen Kuang's theme song for *Song of the Fishermen*.

No official Soviet attitude to the Shensi Communists was yet known. Contact
with the Chinese Communist Party, through students who usually traveled via
Shanghai-Japan-Vladivostok, tended to bypass the "agrarian reformers" who
were technically, in any case, outside the party. Mountains and the Gobi Desert
barred any direct link, except by air, between the Soviet Union and the new Red
areas. As the Japanese war went deeper into China, and as the Soviet Red Army
itself fought the Japanese at Lake Hassan (near the junction of the Chinese,
Mongolian, and Soviet borders), no Soviet air route crossed Japanese lines, and
no one at either end had decided what purpose would be served by such contact.
Arms and supplies were neither asked for nor offered. In Moscow alongside
openly expressed skepticism ("margarine Communists" was Stalin's phrase)
there was considerable public curiosity about the new breed of Communists in
the Shensi mountains. When *China Strikes Back* showed that a foreign cameraman could get through and would find something worth filming, the Soviet
cameraman Roman Karmen decided in the autumn of 1938 to take his Eyemo
to China rather than back to Spain. It was the defense of China against an
aggressor that was to be recorded (in a series called *China in Battle*, 1938–1939,
later compiled in a full-length actuality film entitled *In China*, 1941), and
Karmen wanted to see more than the well-covered front. He was more successful
than Joris Ivens in evading the Kuomintang bureaucracy that tried to keep
foreigners (and Chinese!) away from the guerrilla fighters; in May 1939 he made a
detailed filming of Yenan life and Shensi guerrillas. His diary records his meetings
with Mao Tse-tung and Chu Teh; the only foreigner mentioned is the Indian Dr.
Dwarkanath Kotnis, whom Karmen had known in Spain, and who later died on
duty in Yenan.[19]

Nine months before Karmen's visit, the several filmmakers who had found
their way to Yenan organized the Yenan Film Group, with Yuan Mu-jih in
oharge. It was not, however, until 1939 that their supply and equipment problems (aided by a hand camera sent in by Ivens, and film apparatus captured from
the Japanese*) were sufficiently solved to make and show their first films, all
actuality records. The first production, *Yenan and the Eighth Route Army*, was
the most ambitious of the twenty-one films made between 1939 and 1945.[20] It
was directed by Yuan and photographed by an experienced still photographer
and cameraman Wu Yin-hsien (at Ming Hsing he photographed *Unchanged Heart*
and *Street Angel*), who also filmed *Dr. Bethune* in 1939 (see Plate 14). The
Canadian doctor, Norman Bethune, spent the last nine months of his life with the
guerrilla fighters of the Border Region, and Wu followed this brave, determined

---

* In the counteroffensive against the Japanese of 1941–1942, among the captured supplies:
"112 cameras [possibly projectors] with films." Smedley, *The Great Road* (New York:
Monthly Review Press, 1956), pp. 387–388.

surgeon, to make the only film of this period to give a sense of real fighting; the victories of these years had to be won without cameras. The material of *Dr. Bethune* is sparse and fragmentary, but it served in 1961 to be re-edited with sound, as *In Memory of Bethune*, a tribute to the only foreigner whose help to the Chinese revolution is acknowledged. The other films of the Yenan Film Group show the speakers and delegates at meetings and conferences (*Shansi, Chahar and Hopei Mobilization Meeting*, 1939; *International Youth Festival*, 1941; *Yenan Celebrates the Thirtieth Anniversary of the 1911 Revolution*, 1941; *Comrade Mao Tse-tung at the Arts Forum in Yenan*, 1942, on 16 mm) or communal industries and activities of the area (*Newspaper Behind Enemy Lines — "New Great Wall,"* 1939; *Cloth-Weaving Behind Enemy Lines*, 1939; *Tang County Youth Cooperative*, 1939; *Production and Struggle Unite* [or *Nan-i-wan*], 1942*). Traveling projection teams, equipped with improvised or captured Japanese apparatus, distributed these films (and only these films) throughout the region.

Though only one fictional film, so far as I know, was attempted in this period, a policy for their future was laid down in the Yenan Forum of Art and Literature in 1942. These discussions, initiated and led by Mao Tse-tung, were the result of the large number of writers and other artists who came "from the garrets of Shanghai" to the Red base during the war.

The writers and artists who had chosen Yenan when they were seeking a refuge from the Japanese invasion were making a happy decision. In fact, it was more than a refuge that they sought. They wanted to play their parts in the war against Japan, and the Communist leadership based in Yenan looked more likely to bring about victory. Many of them had accepted Communist leadership without question. For the hardships in the barren hills and on the loess plains in the north-west, they were psychologically, if not physically, prepared when they bade farewell to Shanghai or Peking (then Peiping). . . . Obviously, an illusion of personal heroism helped them to make up their minds to share their fate with the Communist Party. But there was also a common ground of faith between them and Mao.[21]

Yenan welcomed them, but they altered the unanimity of method that Mao and the army had brought with them from the south. Though agreed on aims, many of the artists believed that their contribution to the revolution should be through a fuller use of their skills and arts than had been possible in the old society, even in the underground. For the present, the painters of Yenan were

---

* These last two films were shown to K. S. Karol in Yenan in 1965: "These old films shot by amateurs had the rhythm and dimension of the classic cinema; they were the best films I saw in China. . . . It is a kind of *cinéma-verité* which has no room for the stereotyped images of propaganda." *China: The Other Communism* (New York: Hill and Wang, 1967), p. 109.

glad to make posters, musicians were glad to train choral groups, and writers were glad to write the newspapers and pamphlets that were urgently needed, yet they continued to dream and discuss the larger and more creative tasks that they felt necessary. This, in Mao's words, produced "controversies, divergences, conflicts and discord among some of our comrades."[22] The distinction between the "cultural front" and the "military front" polarized in the two new institutions founded in Yenan, the Lu Hsun Art Academy and the Anti-Japanese College. By May 1942, coincidentally with his first "rectification" or purifying movement, Mao decided to show the intellectuals their duty in a discussion that could lead in only one direction:

The fundamental task of all revolutionary artists and writers is to expose all dark forces which endanger the people and to extol all the revolutionary struggles of the people.

In the talks (as published) the artists are addressed as recent arrivals, temporary visitors, tolerated outsiders who will probably find cause to leave:

. . . to arrive at these base areas is not the same as to identify oneself completely with the people here. In pushing forward the revolutionary work, it is necessary to identify oneself completely with the people. The express purpose of our meeting today is to make art and literature a component part of the whole revolutionary machine, to make them a powerful weapon for uniting and educating the people and for attacking and destroying the enemy, and to help the people to fight with one heart and one mind.

In pre-war Shanghai the public for revolutionary art and literature consisted mainly of a section of the students, office workers and shop assistants. . . . Here in our base. . . . The public for our art and literature consists of cadres* of all kinds, soldiers in the armed forces, workers in the factories and peasants in the villages. . . .

. . . writers and artists who cling to their individualist petty-bourgeois standpoint cannot truly serve the mass of revolutionary workers, peasants and soldiers. . . .

. . . there may of course be some opportunists who will not remain with us long. . . .

An intellectual himself, Mao could illustrate his most cutting points with memories of his own "remolding":

I came to feel that the unremolded intellectuals were unclean as compared with the workers and peasants who are the cleanest people, cleaner than the bourgeois and petty-bourgeois intellectuals, even though their hands are blackened by work and their feet smeared with cow dung.

---

* The Chinese term for which this has become the standard translation (via French and Russian) covers a wide range of politically responsible citizens, chiefly party administrators on all levels — functionaries.

Even after modest actuality films were being made, film people who heard this must have felt particularly superfluous. Mao's summing up speech mentions that "scores of Party and non-Party comrades have spoken" in the three meetings, but I do not know that any contribution other than his has been published. Today these talks are still intended to produce an effect of unanimity, but Mao's phrases make it clear that opposition was voiced there:

Many comrades have by no means arrived at a clear understanding of this problem [for whom are our art and literature intended?].

. . . they do not appreciate their [the workers, peasants, and soldiers] emotions, their manners, their budding art and literature such as wall newspapers, murals, folk songs, and folk tales.

. . . we need a thoroughgoing and serious campaign to correct . . . such defects as idealism, doctrinarism, utopianism, empty talk, contempt of practice and aloofness from the people which are still found among our comrades.

. . . corrupters in the revolutionary ranks . . .

Discussion on the subject is closed:

It is wrong to deviate from this principle, and anything at variance with it must be duly corrected.

No mention of films, though after 1949 the cinema (never an art admired by Mao*) was the most conspicuous target for supervision and attacks determined by this policy. In later years the question would be often, privately, asked: Should principles valid for guerrilla fighting communities of 1942 be applied unchanged to the whole of China — after a revolutionary victory and a visibly altered economy?

Once declared, the Yenan or "folk-arts line" was pressed on all, even visitors. Harrison Forman, a journalist who came to Yenan for some months at the end of 1944, was told — and believed:

Under war conditions, away from Shanghai, the literati resembled fish out of water. It was almost impossible for them not to look down upon the ignorant peasants, the workers and soldiers, who retorted by rejecting them. Without a

---

* Aside from his marriage to a film actress, Mao's known interest in films, up to this point, is limited to his laughter at Edgar Snow's recollection, in Pao-an, of the action of Chaplin's *Modern Times* (see Snow, *Journey to the Beginning* [New York; Random House, 1958]), and this highly apocryphal comment by Maurice Bessy (in his *Histoire du cinéma en 1000 images,* Paris 1962) on *The Good Earth:* "Mao Tse-tung must have forged his doctrines on the several occasions he attended this film."

public, they wrote, painted, and made music for themselves, ignoring the common folk below their cultural and intellectual level. . . .

Far-seeing Mao Tze-tung observed this and decided that it was no good. Calling a meeting of all cultural workers, he flayed them for their high and mighty airs, warned them of retrogression and decay if they persisted. They must adjust themselves to new conditions, a new society — a society unlike the feudal Shanghai aristocracy of intellectuals, students, and wealthy patrons, but a new democratic society created by and for the peasant, the worker, and the soldier. . . .[23]

One would think, from this highly colored accusation, that its author had observed examples of the corrected arts, but his only evidence for the correctness of the "folk" policy are several variations on the *yang-ko*, derived from an ancient fertility rite. Forman would not be the last foreigner in China to try to be more Chinese than the Chinese.

With few hesitations the teachers and students at the Lu Hsun Art Academy adapted all the familiar arts to the newly fixed cultural line. Cinema, of course, with minimum equipment and minimum encouragement, had to wait longer for full conformity. It was theater that claimed attention now. Peasants of the Border Region preferred to see any play rather than hear any musical work or look at any form of painting. Observers and journalists reported seeing effective propaganda "shows" (not always plays or opera), and the eagerly responsive audiences were noted. Edgar Snow fully describes a play, *Invasion*, that he saw in Pao-an in 1936,[24] six years before Mao's "talks," and close to their demands. In August 1937 Agnes Smedley traveled with a Front Service Group of thirty persons, organized by Ting Ling. Ting Ling and other members of the group wrote for performances that they gave wherever the Eighth Route Army halted:

Those ready for production are *Lay Down Your Whip, Fight Back to Your Native Home*, both plays about Manchuria; *The Whistle in the Forest*, a play about the Manchurian Volunteers; *The Woman Spy*, the story of a woman patriot who acts as a spy and kills a leading traitor; *The Last Smile*, a pantomime without words about peasants arising against the Japanese; the theme of Gorki's *Mother* adapted to the Lukuochiao struggle near Peiping.

Tonight [9 November] the Front Service Group gave a performance in the streets of the village. One of the gates leading into the city was transformed into a theater by the group. About six feet up from the ground they built a platform across the gateway, strung their red curtain across the stage, and announced a play. The street leading to the gate and the street running across it became filled with the townspeople and our men. The roofs of the houses were black with men. The light on the stage consisted of two ancient hanging lamps of iron. . . . They have combined the old Chinese storyteller methods with modern theatrical ideas. They have developed singers of news, much like the minstrels of the Middle Ages.[25]

The Catholic priest, Raymond de Jaegher,[26] mentioned two Communist plays
he saw during the anti-Japanese war. And during Harrison Forman's stay at
Nan-i-wan in 1944 he saw a simple, stylized propaganda play using music, song,
dance, and speech.[27] Another journalist on this same trip, Gunther Stein, enjoyed
yang-ko evenings with their one-act plays, "written by the best among Yenan's
authors* who have been made to understand in recent years that realism is not
achieved by exaggeration."

The villains are either Japanese soldiers and Chinese traitors or witch doctors,
loafers, and other anti-social elements who hamper the war effort, the increase
of production, or the march of political and social progress. The heroes and
heroines are Eighth Route Army soldiers, militia men, or simple pioneers of
class unity and mutual aid; fighters against superstition, illiteracy, dirt, and
disease; or model workers in villages, factories, cooperatives and government
offices whose individual action has aroused the initiative of the masses. . . . The
play always ends on a cheerful note of success. . . .[28]

After his visit to Yenan and Kalgan in June 1946 Robert Payne published full
descriptions of the several performances he witnessed there.[29]

The single theatrical achievement of this policy and period that pleased policy-
makers and audiences equally was an opera (in the Chinese sense, of course), *The
White-Haired Girl*. The genesis of this work has itself become familiar; it is told
quite circumstantially:

In 1940, in northwest Hopei, which was part of the Border Region, there spread
a story about a "white-haired goddess". . . . Nine years earlier (before the War of
Resistance to Japanese Aggression broke out and before the Eighth Route Army
reached this district), there had been a wicked landlord in the village, who
oppressed the peasants cruelly. One of his old tenants had a daughter of
seventeen. . . .[30]

On the other hand, the writer (one of the authors of the play) speaks of the
story as one of Mao's recommended forms, the folk tale:

This story was told and retold. It was amended, amplified, and polished by the
people. From the first day of telling, it spread rapidly, and soon enjoyed
immense popularity . . . by 1944 it had reached Yenan. As with all stories
handed down orally, there were different versions, and ours is only one of
many. . . . When we hear this story we are deeply moved by it, for it is a superb
folk tale.[31]

---

* One of these playwrights, Chou Erh-fu, gave details of some *yang-ko* plays of the period in
China Digest (Hong Kong), 11 Feb. 1947, pp. 17—18.

One explanation of this and other discrepancies in describing the play's source[*]
is the demand of the new line to subordinate invention to real sources, to "life."
This may account for the author's own insistence that they invented nothing;
and the composer of the opera (whose name is omitted in the printed 1949
version) later went into more emotional detail than necessary.in claiming to have
added nothing to the folk music he found in and near Yenan.[32]

The play, nevertheless, is carefully dramatized. It is so neat that this reinforces
the probability of a more ancient source or a more deliberate modern hand than
is acknowledged. (The resemblance to *Way Down East* may not be accidental.)
Whatever faults the carping critic may note nowadays were, in Yenan in April
1945 when *The White-Haired Girl* was first performed, either virtues or neces-
sities. Subtlety or reality would have blurred its purpose. To round or develop its
characters might have weakened their clear positive or negative functions. This
leaves us with a lyrical element, expressed directly in song, and with the reason
for the play: to give "concentrated expression to the sufferings of the peasants
under the dark feudal rule of old China, at the same time revealing the splendor
of new China and the new democracy led by the Communist Party in which the
peasants have become their own masters."[33] Exposition is the political lifeblood
of the play; constant exposition is, artistically, its poison. The opening solo by
the girl, Hsi-erh,

   . . . Dad's been hiding a week because of his debt,
Though it's New Year's Eve, he's still not back. . . .[34]

is repeated in her following soliloquy, in case the sung words were not understood by each spectator:

Dad has been away for a week, and still isn't back. We've nothing in the house
for the New Year. There are only Dad and I at home: my mother died when I
was three. My father cultivates one acre of land belonging to rich Landlord
Huang. . . . Every year we're behind with our rent, so just before New Year he
always leaves home to escape being dunned.

In the next scene Landlord Huang characterizes himself in full incriminating
detail:

Well, I haven't lived in vain! I have nearly a hundred hectares of good land, and
every year I collect at least a thousand piculs in rent. All my life I've known how
to weight the scales in my own favour. . . .

---

[*] If the wronged girl was real she could not have vanished after her dramatic reappearance,
for Ma Ko, the composer of the opera, writes: "The story ended happily, the woman was
avenged. Her hair turned black again and she finally married the man who had brought her
'back to life'." (*Peking Review*, 25 May 1962, p. 22.) This heroine has never been named or
located.

Later in the play, after Hsi-erh has been forced into his household, Huang sings his self-portrait:

Fate's been kind to me, I'm rich and respected,
My barns are stuffed with grain and my chests with gold.
The poor, of course, must go cold and hungry,
Because that's their destiny, fixed by Fate!
. . . if the poor set themselves against me,
They'll find out to their cost what fools they've been!

One reason that the exposition seems so packed is that repeated revisions reflected every change of policy in the Region between 1945 and 1949. Underlying all is a thickly dangerous vein of sentimentality and self-pity that we have seen before, in Shanghai's semirevolutionary films of the thirties. Here it is modified by gestures of rebellion whose most active phase is to escape now and return, later, with an army. For me the most positive character in the play is a sympathetic woman servant in the landlord's household who befriends the persecuted girl and helps her with ingenuity and good advice (which, if followed, would have prevented both crisis and play).

At the same time that *The White-Haired Girl,* a confirmation of Mao's cultural demands, had its first performances, the boldest critic of those demands was receiving the first of what was to be an endless series of reprimands. The standpoint of Ting Ling was that a war had been declared against "intellectuals" (representing the Shanghai intellectual party members who expelled Mao from the party), and she would be the last to capitulate. Ting Ling had been welcomed in Yenan as the most distinguished of left Chinese artists, and Mao had greeted her arrival with a poem; but before Mao's "talks," where she seems to have led the challengers of approved policy, she demonstrated her vision of a communist Chinese literature with three short stories[35] that were unusually stripped of all ornament and sentimentality to embody a harshly realistic attitude to life in the Border Region — taking a direction diametrically opposite to that officially wanted. In a short-lived literary journal in liberated Harbin Ting Ling made her position clearer: to be useful to new China its artists must be encouraged to develop their arts, experimenting in themes and methods. She was relieved of her editorial duties, though her continuing stubbornness later led to more punishments, the "long and even painful process of remolding" that Mao promised in 1942. In Harbin she was still able to write and publish (her next and possibly last novel, *The Sun Shines Over the Sangkan River*, appeared in 1948 and won a Stalin Prize in 1951), but her brief career as a filmwriter was quite ended, just when her boldness and sharp-eyed attitudes were most needed by the Chinese cinema.

6   Between Victories
1945–1949

If peasant doesn't cheat field
Field won't cheat peasant.

                       — Farmer's Almanac

The most obvious change in Chinese films after the war's end was visible not in Shanghai or Chungking, but in the studios of the former Republic of Manchukuo. In the confusing military and political ups and downs of Changchun its film studio, left by Amakasu in such meticulous order, was well used by the Yenan film group. This was their first studio facility since they had left Shanghai and Chungking, and they made the most of their opportunity. Few films were made, but because they were so significant it is worthwhile to look into the larger historical issues that made them possible, though it is hard to reconcile the puzzling contradictions in the various chronicles. Here, for example, is a Chinese film journalist:

As early as 1945, after the People's Liberation Army had coordinated its actions with those of the Soviet forces which drove the Japanese from [Changchun], its cultural department took over and began to operate the former quisling "Manchukuo" [film] studios there. A few months later Chiang Kai-shek launched his all-out civil war against the liberated areas, and the studios were obliged to move to safer quarters in the small town of Hsinshan far to the north. Setting up in the buildings of a primary school and a cinema, the staff immediately began shooting documentaries about the liberation war. In April 1949, the studio moved back to Changchun. . . . [1]

and, from an American diplomat who has specialized in the history of this period:

On April 14 [1946] the Soviet garrison evacuated Changchun, leaving it in the hands of four thousand Nationalist troops, who had been recently air-lifted into the area, and some two thousand Manchoukuo Peace Preservation forces enlisted by the Nationalists. A Communist force under Chou Pao-chung attacked Changchun the same night and captured the city on April 18.[2]

Apparently there are issues here that are opened only with reluctance by all interested parties.

The Chinese account is particularly unhelpful for it conceals any explanation for the most important film that came from Changchun before 1949. Instead of the whole Yenan film group being moved to Hsinshan and waiting until 1949 to move back into the Changchun studio, they divided forces: a small group of Yenan Communists, who had established reputations in theater and cinema in Shanghai and Chungking before going to Yenan, were delegated to work in the Kuomintang-controlled Changchun studio at least two years before the Communists took Changchun and its studios for good. Those connected with this maneuver are as unwilling to discuss it as the chronicles are to reveal all the political motives behind the military history of these years. No one likes to admit either deception or laxness.

It may astonish us that the Changchun studio (named "Chang Tseh" by the Kuomintang near-monopoly, Chung Dien, that controlled it then) would employ filmmakers whose political background and Yenan years could not have been kept secret. Both the actor Chin Shan and the actress Chang Jui-fang had been members of the Communist Party since the thirties. However, since the "Chang Tseh" studio was the most remote branch of the powerful Chung Dien combine — and these two actors were two of the best (who had not worked for the Japanese) and most liked — the studio head may have needed them and felt he could watch over and remove any subversive tendencies in their work. Whatever his motives we should be particularly grateful to that unnamed studio head, for he gave Chin Shan the chance to write and direct his first film.

Along the Sungari River, completed in autumn 1947 and shown in Shanghai and elsewhere by November, contains some of the finest filmmaking in China. I say "contains" because its whole cannot be thought of as unified except as it stays with one group of characters from beginning to end. It was, indeed, with this film that I learned, to paraphrase a more modern film title, not to worry about such contradictions, and to love them. In Chinese films, from their beginning to their present, conflicting factors have entered each film, more than in any other film-producing country that I know. Commerce and art make only one of the conflicts, drama and sermon another. More serious and a more Chinese condition is the headlong clash of an ancient native culture with a modern alien one, a clash that I think can be seen more clearly in cinema than in any other cultural area. Also present, perhaps, is a certain Chinese thriving on conflict, not altogether unrelated to an artist's need and use of conflict. One effect of this is to erect new critical procedures for Chinese films. If you look only for unified wholes you may miss the most exciting indications of China's future cinema, for the conflicts occasionally bring a film to an extraordinary, *new* cinematic life.*
If unity had been Chin Shan's aim we could not have had the perfect and realistically original film poetry of the first thirty minutes of *Sungari River*. (See Plate 21). The jingling gaiety of drivers and horses along the road, the human warmth of the inn scenes, the loveliness and *belief* in such simple shots as the waiting horses in the courtyard at dawn — all make a passage that must be reckoned among the high points of international film history. In resolving the approaches

---

* Such moments can occur in the most single-mindedly commercial films, but I have rarely, if ever, encountered such instances in the purely commercial productions of, say, Bombay.

of this total absence of film clichés with the subsequent two hours of nearly unrelieved clichés (probably the studio's victory) the beautiful opening would certainly have been sacrificed, and we should not have guessed the quality of Chin Shan as a filmmaker.

The film is packed with the miseries and anxieties of the Japanese occupation years, and it may have been thought dramatically necessary to contrast these with a prologue of peace and comradeship and good feeling. (Yet this alone does not explain the enormous difference in style between the opening and the rest of the film.) The story begins in a village by the river where the inn is used as a regular stop by carters. The parents and daughter who manage the inn are good friends of the carters, and there is some sadness when they part the next morning. That day is 18 September 1931, when the Japanese army occupied the whole district, beginning with the railroad and the river. In our village their first acts are to push the heroine's mother into the river and to frighten the father. The carter-sweetheart of the heroine returns to propose resistance to the invaders, but when this encourages the soldiers to kill the father and threaten the daughter, she and the carter escape. A long and wearing journey by foot only delivers them into the slavery of a Japanese-run coal mine where they meet fresh blows and hardships. The approach of the war's end finds them ready to lead a miner's rebellion and overthrow their Japanese masters. From the point when deaths and dangers proliferate, logic has to be suspended to accept the dramatic formulas. The only element that can be compared with the opening is the music, which remains surprisingly helpful throughout the film.[*]

For once all levels praised a film. When Lo Tsin-yu (of the film-financing family, and now executive director of the Chung Dien monopoly) went abroad in 1948, he always managed to mention *Along the Sungari River* in interviews.[†] It was a popular film, but it was more than ten years before Chin Shan made a second film. He did some film acting, but these years (not completely empty for posterity) were spent directing and acting in a Peking theater.

Weather is like fire,
Time will not wait for you.

— Farmer's Almanac

When the Second World War ended, the challenges confronting the National Government loomed large. There were some two million Japanese military and

---

[*] There are some details on this exceptional score in *China Digest* (Hong Kong), 15 June 1948, pp. 17—18.
[†] Though I can find no record of its having been shown abroad.

civilians to be repatriated. . . . The United States and Britain had relinquished their extraterritorial rights in China during the war, thus creating new problems for Chinese law and administration. The capital had to be moved back from Chungking to Nanking, which the government had left seven years before. Manchuria, lost fourteen years earlier, beckoned to the resources and energies of the Chinese governmental apparatus. A new administration had to be set up for Formosa, ruled by Japan since 1895. . . . And finally, there was the task of settling differences with the Communists. . . .[3]

This could be a list of themes taboo in the postwar Chinese film industry, for none of the films that I've seen from this period did any more than hint at these "challenges" to the Nationalist government. And for a good reason. For the first time the industry was not merely controlled by the government, it was now more identified with government than during the war. In "one of the biggest carpetbagging operations in history" the Four Great Families,* in control of government as well as the Kuomintang party, seized industries in the formerly Japanese-occupied areas. Mines, mills, public services were all grabbed as indisputable loot. The old film studios of Shanghai and the Japanese-built studios in Changchun and Peking, though not regarded as a potential fortune for the Big Four, offered the possibility of a propaganda medium to serve their purposes, and claims by former Chinese owners were evaded. On 20 September 1945 the Kuomintang issued a law that closed all communication media in the recovered areas and ordered their equipment to be turned over to the Propaganda Ministry.† The film industry was divided into four "take-over areas," and rival government offices fought for the richest one, Shanghai. New wealth and power made the four ramified families greedy for more, even at the expense of each other. It was natural that no "national" issue, except the anticommunist drive, would be touched by the increasingly corrupt nation.

This is not to say that the monopoly always won. Filmmakers had been toughened by war and bureaucracy. As individuals and as groups they found ways to cope with these new pressures. Of two films ordered by the Defense Ministry, one, *Terrorist Activities of Communist Bandits*, never overcame a series of postponements; the other, *Communist Bandits Destroy the Nation*, was made but somehow didn't get shown.

Anti-Communist pictures were sabotaged by their makers. The Nationalist government attempted to force them to make two feature films . . . but its

---

* The families of Chiang Kai-shek, T. V. Soong, H. H. K'ung, and the Ch'en brothers "had grown rich beyond the wildest fables of a fairy tale." C. P. Fitzgerald, *The Birth of Communist China* (New York: Praeger, 1964), p. 105.
† To show the scale of the campaign, from January to August 1946, 263 publications were ordered closed.

efforts were in vain. Producers, directors, actors, technicians, and all other studio personnel refused to cooperate in the releasing of the films. [The latter film] proved on studio preview to be so full of finger-marks and over- and under-exposed shots that it was shelved, never to be exhibited.[4] *

Another anticommunist scenario, *Iron*, was revised to death. The new Kuomintang slogan for the film industry, "Fight for quality with quantity," got off to a slow start.

In spite of presumably total control the old censorship problem delayed the "quantity," too. Of the 162 films produced between October 1945 and September 1948, 48 were delayed for revision, were cut, or were shelved.[5] Considering this official watchfulness it is amazing how much reality found its way into the films of this period. Filmmakers bypassed the areas where the government felt greatest sensitivity − the "challenges" listed by O. E. Clubb − but other aspects of those years, in retrospect equally sensitive and significant, soon provided the basic dramatic material of Shanghai's film studios. The underground of the thirties was coming to the surface, braver and more ingenious than before. To show how close films were to the bone of the period, here are descriptions of Chinese society then by two noncommunist witnesses and chroniclers, Mr. Clubb and Emily Hahn:

Corruption infected the political administration, and from there the rot was transmitted to the military machine. Political and economic forces weighed as heavily in the civil war scales as men under arms. When Kuomintang rule was confined to a half-dozen poor provinces in West China, the growth of Nationalist venality and maladministration was restrained by geographical factors. But with the triumphal Nationalist return to East China such restraints were left behind. The restoration of Nationalist rule over Japanese-occupied territory was accompanied by one of the biggest carpet-bagging operations in history.[6]

The government duly moved to Nanking, where everything was supposed to be all right and people could live happily ever after. It did not work out like that. Inflation was worse than ever, and brought much suffering. Officials who had held authority through the war years had grown chronically overbearing. Financial corruption spread rapidly. . . . The dishonest plundered, the humble suffered, the bullies swaggered, and the ordinary people, who had waited so long for freedom from the Japanese, found it all a great disillusionment. More and more Chinese, especially the poorest, began to listen to the Communists.[7]

Without intending to, Miss Hahn has stated the four major story ideas in the films after the war. "The dishonest plundered. . . ." Two concessions were made

---

* The memoirs of Ouyang Yu-chien also mention this "resistance": "Many progressive filmmakers refused to make such films . . . but if forced to, they would try to postpone production. Not *one* of these films was finished before liberation!"

here — the top plunderers were neither shown nor named, and Nanking itself was
not used as a setting — but not one spectator, even among the children, missed
the point. "The humble suffered. . . ." Here was a theme for which the Shanghai
filmmakers, even the least conscious of them, had had the longest training.
"The bullies swaggered. . . ." Ready-made villains, easily fitting into their new
uniforms of fedoras and long robes, clothes that became forever as much a
theater and film symbol of paid Kuomintang bullies as the pince-nez indicated
Mensheviks in post-1917 Russian films. "A great disillusionment." Disillusion is
one sensation that must be fully felt by an artist, whether a Céline or a
Stroheim, before he can convey it to an audience, and no Chinese film artist now
had been left untouched by either wartime or postwar disillusion.

From the end of the war until 16 April 1947 (when a change was forced) the
major Shanghai and Peking film studios were in the hands of the Propaganda
Ministry's creature, the Chung Dien (China Film Studio) which had, in its eight
years of wartime power, produced only three films that were anti-Japanese in
effect. The only other film producer permitted production was another government agency, the Chung Tse, formed to occupy the Nanking studio; it was
responsible to the rival Ministry of the Interior. The only filmmakers they could
completely trust were those who had worked for the Japanese, such as Hsu
Guan-chi who had remained steadily employed throughout the occupation in
Shanghai's Hua Yin studio. The Chung Tse felt safe, too, in inviting U.S. advisors
to work in Nanking — who better would know how to achieve success without
involvement? Aside from the anticommunist fiascos the first productions coming
from "the dual monopoly" carefully avoided *all* themes in favor of pure box-
office attraction. Carrying the banner of "quantity" Hsu Guan-chi displayed his
efficiency by producing two films simultaneously, using the same actors and
crew: *From Night to Dawn* featured an engineering student whose frustrations in
the reconstruction of villages were eliminated by the Kuomintang's secret
service; *Code No. 1* (adapted from a play, *Wild Rose*) was set in occupied Peking
where the Chinese wife of the Japanese general is actually the head (No. 1) of
the Kuomintang agents in the city — she is in love with someone else who is in
love with someone else — all end beautifully in death. These were produced at
the Third Studio (Peking) of Chung Dien and were completed in April 1947.
Other films at this time were even worse. About half of the productions from
the three studios of Chung Dien were mechanical transfers of recent American
film stories to Chinese settings.* The first postwar musical film, *Songbird Flies
over the World* (1946), was made by a successful director of occupation films,

---

* While screening *Doubt in the Boudoir*, made in 1948 by the Peking Studio of Chung Dien,
I felt I had seen it before. It was an imitation of Hitchcock's *Suspicion*.

Fan Pei-lin, with "the Deanna Durbin of Shanghai"; its ostentatious luxury is clearly intended neither as criticism nor parody.

Yet the first positive film to come from the government-run studios also used a foreign source, at least for its start; this may even have made the unusual character of *Far Away Love*, as it later developed, seem less dangerous to the authorities. It is a lighthearted variation on an older literary convention, the conflict between romantic love and revolutionary duty. The film begins in Shanghai in the winter of 1927 (understood, though, as 1947), with an authority on "the woman question" demonstrating the correctness of his theories by educating the country girl who works as maid in his house. From here the resemblance to *Pygmalion* is dropped and Chao Tan's satirical portrait of a professional reformer goes beyond the frame of Professor Higgins. He marries his Galatea (a child or children later appear and disappear according to the exigencies of the scenario), and his decay and worthlessness increase as she grows more independent and conscious. The finest part of the film shows his half-voluntary wandering from place to place during the war, pushed as much by inertia as by danger. Most of their rare meetings are unexpected as when, in the incongruously smart setting of a hotel lobby he, in his intellectual's cloak and airs, meets his wife, now in the humble uniform of a soldier (see Plate 24). Other parts of the film are less pointed, and perhaps it covers too much ground and tries to say everything related to its central satire, but the good detail and characterization are remarkable in a film culture habitually opposed to satire. The film ends with the ineffectual reformer established as a Kuomintang official!

Far Away Love appeared in January 1947 from the Second Studio of Chung Dien, the first fictional film of Chen Li-ting, who had previously made actuality films for the government. The scenario was his own. Before the end of the year his second film was shown, *The Crazy Fantastic Melody of Luck*, written by Chen Pai-chen, *his* first film work. This takes a tragic situation, the desperate measures employed by little city people to stay alive, and translates it, successfully, into comedy, a means used before in Ouyang's *Money Tree*, and to be used two years later in one of the best of Chinese films, *Crows and Sparrows*. Chung Dien made the film's end less critical (with the capture by the police of the troublemaking rascal), and Chen-Li-ting left the organization. This was made possible by a group established outside direct government control.

While the government still operated its film monopoly, the "take-over" that it represented found its way, as a theme, into several films. It was, apparently, so conspicuous an element of postwar life that it was accepted as natural to the Chinese milieu. It was an element that, once allowed in, was shown with an increasing color of corruption. *Heaven Spring Dream* (March 1947) shows, circumstantially, the suffering of an architect whose last commission, an airport, is stopped by the war's end. He returns to Shanghai, to his wife, and tries to design new housing, though they can't find housing for themselves. He becomes a victim of black marketeers and take-over experts (one wartime traitor, now rich, has *bought* the honorable status of an "underground fighter"). The hero's tragic end was changed to a happy one by Chung Dien. In *The Dress Returns in Glory* (May 1947) a high-school teacher buys the position of a take-over official and returns to Shanghai with a gorgeous new wardrobe. Yuan Jin's first two films were critical comedies, resembling Chen Li-ting's first films, and both dealt with take-overs. *Diary on Returning Home* (July 1947), based on his own experiences on coming back to Shanghai, also develops the housing theme; and in *Quick Son-in-Law on Dragon* (January 1948) a family imagines a poor journalist, just back from Chungking, to be an ascending take-over official, and tries to hurry one of their daughters into this secure marriage, but it is the "wrong" daughter who learns who he really is and falls in love with him; he resists bribes and the destruction of his newspaper office in order to continue his exposures of such officials. Altogether not a bad record for a government film agency, even though Chung Dien's cleanup of the conclusion of *Quick Son-in-Law* angered its director so that he left for Hong Kong. The filmmakers had to go further than Chung Dien permitted.

The first serious attempt to break the government's hold on filmmakers came in 1946 when a group of militants, headed by Yang Han-sheng, Tsai Chu-sheng, and Shih Tung-shan, returned to their old Lien Hua studio (used during occupation as the Fourth Studio of Hua Yin) and opened it for production. They were ordered to turn over the studio and its equipment to Chung Dien, but they made a strong case for their former ownership and Chung Dien was forced to let them keep the studio. With Kuomintang encouragement Lo Ming-yü tried to reorganize a Lien Hua studio of his own, but his former employees made the most of their independence and kept what they had won. Their first film was begun on 21 September 1946, *Eight Thousand Li of Cloud and Moon*.

Shih Tung-shan filled this film (originally entitled *Before and After Victory*) with his own experiences and observations in working with a theater troupe during the war, and what he saw happening to them when the Four Families replaced the Japanese:

The eight years of war were hard for us, but we can find reason and justification for this hardness. It is more difficult for us to understand why in the months after victory we felt defeated — this is the theme of *Eight Thousand Li*.[8]

The film's importance lies in its wish to touch this fundamental contradiction, but the story found for its embodiment is burdened by too many traditional "sufferings" from past films: two young theater people (an actress and a musician) are parted by the war, tested by the war, and then, reunited after the war, meet new and insuperable obstacles. However, against a background of the sugary and soft films that dominated this first postwar year, *Eight Thousand Li*, released in February 1947, looked like a remarkably honest film. Hsia Yen, then working as a journalist in Singapore, wrote an open letter to the makers of the film:

After the eight years of anti-Japanese struggle you deserved time to recover yourselves. Instead, in the darkness of the postwar months you took the heavy cross on your own shoulders. You became the strongest fighters of this period. I am embarrassed to see you carrying these heaviest burdens, but otherwise I am proud and happy. This first battle is *your* victory.[9]

Development of a subsidiary element in *Eight Thousand Li* made the group's next scenario more critical and more original. In the first film a brother-in-law of the young actress (rejected by her) comes to Chungking, where he grows powerful in a government job, and then becomes one of the enriched take-over officials in Shanghai. In *Spring River Flows East* this character and situation is made central and startling. The structure of the two films is similar, and several actors play similar roles in both casts. Pai Yang plays the poor wife separated from her liberal and rather carefree revolutionist husband by the war. Little that happens to the waiting, suffering wife, with her ailing mother-in-law and young child, surprised the filmgoer then, but the detailed portrayal of the husband's moral disintegration among the office-sitters gazing at the clock and the temptations of Chungking is a genuinely original piece of filmmaking. The upward climb of the "hero" in the barber-shop sequence was worthy of Preston Sturges or the Ealing Studio at its best. Tao Chin plays the husband's role with equal portions of sharpness and smoothness. It is a level hard to maintain, either realistically or dramatically, and the husband's acquisition of a new and ambitious wife, their return to take over more power in Shanghai, and the climatic confrontation of changed husband with former wife (employed for the day to serve at a cocktail party in the new, grand house) are all effective situations, but with less artistic adventure. The long film was issued in two parts (I, "Wartime Separation"; II, "Darkness and Dawn") in October 1947, and attendance was the largest since *Song of the Fishermen*. It was a personal triumph for Tsai Chusheng and Cheng Chun-li, who wrote and directed the film together, and for the bold group at Lien Hua. Most left critics had praised the film and no one seems to have worried or remarked that the loyal, unchanging wife is as feudal a

character as her disgraceful husband. Hsia Yen's Hong Kong review,[10] quoting
the poem that explains the film's title,

Asked the volume of tears you have to shed,
Alas, it was like a river of spring water running eastwards!

indicates his reservations:

. . . this film resembles an unyielding tuft of grass jutting through a mass of
rubble in its struggle for life. We know that the author could not fully speak his
mind, and we know his difficulties, but his purpose is finally made clear
although in a somewhat devious manner.

Before the completion of this all-round success the Lien Hua group had joined
another nongovernment company, organized after the war but without a base of
its own: they rented studio space to make decent but undistinguished films
such as *Spring Welcome Song*. This group, calling itself Kun Lun,* had one
trump card, a "progressive national capitalist" named Hsia Yin-hu, who had
begun discussions on amalgamation with the Lien Hua group after observing the
success of *Eight Thousand Li*. In June 1947 the two companies joined forces as
the Kun Lun Studio, and so many dissatisfied artists deserted the Kuomintang
studios that government film officials could no longer maintain any pretense of
authority. The Kuomintang censors did, of course, make life difficult for every
Kun Lun scenario, but the new studio remained the artistic leader of Chinese
films until a completely new government took charge of Shanghai's studios in
May 1949.

Hsia Yin-hu headed Kun Lun, and the head of its important scenario committee
was Yang Han-sheng (later, Chen Pai-chen). In addition to its struggles with the
Kuomintang censors the scenario committee had a clash with one of the group's
charter members, Shih Tung-shan. Shih wrote a scenario about the piteous state
of Chinese married women, *Sorrow after Honeymoon*, that did not fit the
militant program of the group. The scenario committee pointed out his mistakes,
and Shih changed some things without changing the "basically negative" attitude
of the film. He made the film, but it was added to his dossier of errors, along
with his prewar film, *Women* (1934). In 1952 he confessed his nonconformism
and explained his stubbornness with *Sorrow after Honeymoon*:

At that time I turned away from the good suggestions of my friends and pressed
my incorrect views into this film. At that time I thought abstractly that wives
should get away from their family ties, but under certain conditions they cannot

---

* A neutral name, that of a mountain north of the Himalaya Range.

leave the family without a definite principle and choice. That's how my film
came to promote the capitalist idea that women should not leave home.[11]

After the success of *Spring River* the authorities paid closer attention to the
activities of Kun Lun. When Tsai Chu-sheng wrote the scenario for *Spring Awakes
by West Lake*, planning to direct it with Chen Pai-chen, "Tsai and others were
forced by the terror to go to Hong Kong."[12] Just after the merger of the two
groups Yang Han-sheng and Shen Fu wrote what was planned as the new studio's
first production, *Fortune is Awarded by the Heavenly Officer*, a satirical film
that the Kuomintang stopped immediately. Another scenario, *Hope among
Mankind*, was also forbidden production. Yang Han-sheng and Shen Fu tried
again, with *New Lucky Family*, and this was permitted production as *Lights of
Ten Thousand Homes*.

This film is clearly an important achievement. I consider it a better and more
coherent work, as scenario and as direction, than the famous *Spring River Flows
East*. Even its photography, by Chu Chin-min, is quite out of the ordinary —
both realistic and effective (see Plate 20). Obviously the people who worked on
Lights felt, perhaps as a result of their scenario frustrations, that they had a great
deal at stake. Here is Yang Han-sheng's reason for the film:

We all know that the worsened life of our citizens is caused by high prices and
growing unemployment, but who made the prices climb? who produces unemployment? Of course this is done by money and sword [*chien jen* — capitalist
and military]. In such a society who can have warm feelings for whom? I believe
that only the people who have a hard life can feel warm towards others who
have a hard life. The only thing for us to do is expressed by the protagonist of
our film, "Let us all move nearer together."[13]

As is customary, the film's virtues are mixed with a sentimentality that was considered a necessary ingredient of any modern film story.* There is no humor,
but in its situation of a harassed and poor clerk's increasing troubles, there is
little room for humor. The acting staff worked with care, though more emotion
might have been evoked with less "acting," especially in the role of the hero,
played by Lan Ma, who still employs his extremely sympathetic personality
in new Chinese films.

With Lan Ma in the chief role Shen Fu managed to rescue the earlier scenario of
Hope Among Mankind, and made enough concessions to the censors (such as

---

* And popular Chinese dramas had "the same elements that make moving pictures like *Way
Down East* and *Over the Hill* great popular hits in China." Lin Yu-tang, *My Country and My
People* (New York: Reynal & Hitchcock, 1935), p. 255.

transforming two Chinese traitors into Japanese) to be allowed to start the film.
With its story involving professors, students, and assassinations (I have not seen
this film) it still bore too close a resemblance to the Kunming clash between
students and Kuomintang in December 1945, and the censors continued their
watch over the production until its release in March 1949.

The Kun Lun victories inspired the formation of other independent companies
in Shanghai, and during 1948–1949 there were as many films of substance as
films of trash available to the increasingly conscious audience. The Fu Ming
Company adapted Lu Hsun's famous story, "New Year Offering," as *Hsiang
Lin's Wife* (I am unable to compare this with Hsia Yen's film adaptation of
1956). Ta Tung also depended on literary sources: Anatole France's comedy,
The Man Who Married a Dumb Wife, and a Labiche farce were made into
Chinese films. Wen Hua was another "literary" studio: *Mother and Son* may have
been based as much on the 1945 Soviet film of Ostrovsky's *Guilty Though Guiltless* (a film that Mei Lan-fang admired) as on the play itself, though the whole
effort was worth little; *Night Lodging*, Tso Lin's filming of Gorky's *Lower
Depths,* was a more responsible and more cinematic effort.* *The Lower Depths*
also influenced *Gang of Demons*, set in the Japanese occupation; the talents of
its makers were wasted on a shapeless fable of dog-eat-dog. Tsao Yu, after seeing
his plays picked at by so many scenarists, decided to write and direct his own
film for Wen Hua. *Bright Day* makes me regret that Tsao Yu did not pursue a
film career, for it makes good use of the toadies and bullies of the period; it has
a realistically humorous portrait of a gentle and unselfish lawyer (played charmingly by Shih Hui) and a situation that maintains a credible tone until the plot
begins. As in many films of this and an earlier period *Bright Day* has a brilliant
opening *minute*:† a pedicab, seemingly on its own, rolls along a street, creating a
strong atmosphere of violence and threat in the offing.

For the Wen Hua company Mei Lan-fang made an experiment at this time that,
as usual, discouraged him. He and Fei Mu agreed to make a color film of one of
Mei's plays, *Happiness Neither in Life nor in Death* (its English title: *Wedding in
a Dream*):

The film was to be made on 16 mm Kodachrome, but the plan was to enlarge it
for theater exhibition. Another innovation: the soundtrack was to be recorded
before the filming in order to increase the flexibility of the camera work.[14]

---

* Based on the adaptation made of Gorky's play in 1946 by Shih T'o and Ko Ling.
† John Huston, speaking through the mask of the director in Peter Viertel's *White Hunter,
Black Heart*: "Almost every movie you see has a wonderful beginning. And then they die.
I'd rather have a lousy beginning and a wonderful end."

The color and recording innovations added new difficulties to Mei's old problems, but it was chiefly the old contradiction that broke the effect of the film according to Mei's biographer, A. C. Scott:

Its conventional, almost hackneyed pathos, required the severity of Peking stage technique to bring out its dramatic quality; translated into screen terms, with realistic settings and wide vistas, it lost its point.[15]

One can understand its creator's wish: "I sometimes wanted to throw it into the Whangpoo River."

The most carefree of China's filmmakers, Ouyang Yu-chien, spent the postwar years in a characteristic hand-to-mouth existence with his filmmaking covering a lot of territory. After an attempt in the winter of 1945 to organize a theater in Kweilin was thwarted by suspicious Kuomintang authorities, Ouyang moved to Shanghai.

Housing was a difficult problem. I needed two or three little rooms for my family of four or five mouths, but you had to turn over fifteen ounces of gold to a landlord just for the privilege of renting a place. So I wrote a scenario for Kun Lun, to get a roof over our heads.[16]

Impossible to Imprison the Light of Spring takes place during and after the war. The main figure is a woman singer, weak and a little stupid, who is used by reactionaries. Ouyang's tendency toward parable surrounded her with three symbolic figures; a black marketeer who uses women (representing the Kuomintang), his hypocritical mother (the United States), and a patriotic agronomist. Before the scenario could be filmed a New China Theater Club was formed to tour Formosa and Ouyang joined them as writer and director.

After the February 28 [1947] events in Taiwan our situation became precarious and we returned to Shanghai. Many of the artists went away to the Liberated Areas. The Kuomintang asked me to write film scenarios, but I wriggled out of it, though this made it difficult for me to remain in Shanghai. Furthermore, I was Secretary of the Democratic League at the time of the National Congress in Nanking [Chiang Kai-shek was hounding the Democratic League in 1947], and that made it impossible for me to stay. Just before leaving Shanghai [and probably to pay his passage] I wrote a scenario for the Ta Tung Studio. I've forgotten what I called it or what was in it, but later someone pointed to a poster for *Frailty, Thy Name is Woman!* and said that was my scenario — but I never saw it.

I went to Hong Kong, to talk with Hsia Yen. There the Yung Hua Studio was being founded and I joined it. Li Tsu-yun, chief of the new studio, had made 3 million HK dollars through gold speculation in Chungking, and brothels and opium in Hong Kong, though this was strictly forbidden in the Colony. He invested one of his 3 millions in the film studio that he said "would never be used by the communists" — everything was new and American, but much of it was never touched. I wrote two stories for Yung Hua, but they weren't filmed, so I asked to leave. . . .

Another Hong Kong studio, the Ta Guan Min, did not have much capital, but it was determined not to be a one-film studio* — for many Cantonese opera groups would scrape together enough capital for one Hong Kong film. That is why I was invited to direct the scenario of *Wild Fire and Spring Wind*, about a theater troupe in a small town. . . . This was absolutely the worst film I ever made. The scenario was a hopeless distortion and whenever I think of the publicity for this film I break out in a cold sweat.

The last film made by Ouyang Yu-chien was *The Way to Love*, begun in November 1948 and released in May 1949 from the Nan Chun Studio. He was credited with both the scenario and the direction, though actually Hsia Yen wrote the script. It is a competent film that does not capitulate to Hong Kong filmmaking habits, and it occupies an honorable place in the Colony's film history. It opens on a Christmas Eve in Shanghai, the twentieth wedding anniversary of a couple who are waiting for their daughter to come home. She comes and announces her engagement. Her parents recall their past twenty years together and the scenario gets down to its political task of reminding the audience of the people's victories in those years. Not too persistently, however, for the revolution is dropped whenever the story doesn't demand it, possibly to placate the censors here and elsewhere. Ouyang writes that it was made with the Liberated Areas in mind, "independent of the Hong Kong, Macao, and Southeast Asia markets," and Shanghai was part of the Liberated Area of China by the time the film was ready. He concludes: "I greet New China with this film."

Snatch your harvest,
If not snatched,
You lose all

— Farmer's Almanac

After the Normandy landings had altered the balance of war in 1944 the U.S. Army Air Force established a temporary post in Yenan, making it possible for direct flights between Chungking and Yenan, enabling the Communist mission in Chungking to keep in regular contact with its home base, enabling U.S. officials (Ambassador Hurley did not leave a very good impression) and journalists (including Anna Louise Strong), all determined to talk with Mao, to visit Yenan,

---

* The studio made *two* films.

and getting the first American films to the Border Region. Regardless of ideology these left fragrant memories after the passing of this brief idyllic period: many years later certain generals continued to give hard wear to the Technicolor prints of various "kicking legs" films that they had first seen outside a Yenan cave; Chu Teh, characteristically, adopted a warm, stubborn fondness for the films of Abbot and Costello.

The postwar atmosphere grew tense with an increasingly hostile demeanor between the forces of the officially victorious Chinese government (supported by U.S. money and arms) and the forces of the Border Region where the war had been won the hard way. The air connection was used by General Marshall in 1946 "to induce the two Chinese parties to form a coalition government and thus avert civil war."[17] Such efforts were doomed before they began; soon after Marshall's last visit to Yenan the Kuomintang army bombed and occupied Yenan, though not until after the withdrawal of its army and government. The only fictional film attempted in Yenan was left unfinished: *Labor Hero of the Border*, scenario by Chen Bo-erh and Yu Ming, directed by Yu Ming, Chai Chiang, and Fen Pai-lu and photographed by Chen Mo.[18] It was also in the interval between wars that a Canadian cameraman made a more systematic recording of Yenan life than had yet been seen:

A newsreel scoop has been scored by A. Grant McLean, cameraman for the National Film Board of Canada, who has brought back to Canada the first [sic] films shot in the Chinese Communist Capital of Yenan. . . . The material will be used for a full length Canadian documentary film on China. Three reels have been turned over to the United Nations Relief and Rehabilitation Administration, Mr. McLean said. While in China he also arranged for a monthly exchange of newsreel film between Canada and the Central Film Studios of China.[19]

I have not seen the film as edited in Canada, but on the strength of some of the censor's 16 mm duplicate reels (the same bureaucratic method that was inflicted on Ivens in 1938) I can say that McLean's film deserves to be better known. Perhaps it was the spread of China's civil war soon after he returned to Canada that prevented more interest abroad in such a small place as Yenan.

Without admitting it to themselves the Central Government had lost the war in 1947 by trying to take Shantung and Manchuria at the same time, and the "victory" over Yenan was a mere face-saving gesture. By the summer of 1948 the People's Liberation Army had started its drive towards the Yangtze, and by the end of October the Kuomintang army, now in total confusion, had lost all of Manchuria. The fall of Tientsin on 15 January 1949 was followed at the end of the month by the surrender of Peking, assisted by left and discouraged elements in the Kuomintang army. Lin Piao's army marched into the city on 31 January.[20] The rapid succession of these blows was so demoralizing to the government officials that it was generally assumed that the diminished area of their control, the south and west, would soon be lost, too. The assumption was right — Nanking fell in April 1949, and Shanghai was liberated on 2 May.

This was a day awaited with excitement by most of Shanghai's millions. During the past twelve years it must have seemed to many the day that would never come. To the oldest revolutionaries of the city there was always the tragic memory of a liberation that almost arrived in 1927. The betrayal of 1927 prepared Shanghai's underground workers for 1949 — that was not going to happen again. Intellectuals in general were so disgusted by Kuomintang corruption that this increased the expectation of change.

The increasingly left intellectuals who were making Shanghai's films were also prepared. There were many films in production in May 1949, and some that were completed after the great change had looked forward to liberation before it arrived. The five major Shanghai studios that were "nationalized" in May as the New Shanghai Film Production Company must have discarded some productions after this change of status, but we know only those films that were completed. The films that Ta Tung initiated early in 1949 and finished with the approval of the new administration were:

T'ien Han's scenario, *Martyr of the Pear Orchard*, the Chu Hai-tang story (see p. 147), cleaned up for Chinese production
Tso Lin's *The Watch* (for Lu Hsun was no longer alive to discourage this adaptation of Panteleyev's story)
Good Scenes of Shaohsing Opera

The Guo Tai studio finished *Love Already Lost*, directed by Tang Hsiao-tan, played by the Korean actor, Kim Yen (King Shan).

The best and furthest left of the studios, Kun Lun, completed two important films after liberation. One of these, *The Winter of the Three-Hairs*, challenged the taboos on satire and stylization. The other, *Crows and Sparrows*, I consider a milestone in Chinese film history, worthy to be shown alongside the best of international cinema produced in the postwar years.

After *Lights of Ten Thousand Homes* Yang Han-sheng wrote *Three-Hairs* (the adventures of a vagabond waif), based on a popular newspaper strip cartoon by Chang Lo-pin, and the style of the finished film gives the impression that real miseries are being cleverly shown through unreal characters, extending even

to make-up that reproduces the cartooned faces (see Plate 21). The sets and camera compositions also look deliberately flattened or exaggerated. The film was, apparently, effective in its aim, for the makers received threatening letters. The shooting was completed in August 1949 and the film was released in December, with a new ending: Three-Hairs cheering the arrival of the People's Liberation Army.*

The shooting of *Crows and Sparrows* was finished a few days before the People's Liberation Army entered Shanghai on 2 May, but it was cut and synchronized after the new administration was established in Shanghai and in the film studios (see Plate 24). Much of its passion and boldness and sharpness can be attached to its makers' exultation in this victory and the expectation of victory in the months when it was being written and filmed. The scenario is signed by Chen Pai-chen, but it was actually the work of six writers: Chen, the director Cheng Chun-li, one of the actors, Chao Tan, plus Shen, Fu, Hsu Tao, and Wang Ling-gu. This time everything that the censors removed from the dialogue was replaced with a vengeance in the final recording: for the first time the audience

---

* This ending has been removed from the copy deposited at the Pacific Film Archive.

heard from a screen the antigovernment slang that was familiar on the streets in 1948 and 1949. The following extract of the scenario[21] is the opening of reel 2 as the aging newspaper worker (played by Wei Ho-ling) returns from his night shift:

In the early morning light we see Kung Yu-wen leave the street on his way home. Kung knocks at the door of his courtyard, and is surprised when the Little Broadcaster [Chao Tan] opens it at once. The Broadcaster still looks sleepy and his clothes are rumpled.

"Ai-ya, Old Kung, pretty late for you! I've been expecting you for some time."

As Kung lifts his foot to enter, he notices that the courtyard drain is full and calmly steps around it; he speaks with a quiet smile: "What makes you so excited this morning?"

The Broadcaster follows him, answering: "There's big news for you. . . ."

"More news from the Central News Agency – more lies!"

At the house-door Mrs. Broadcaster [Wu Yin] holds a washbasin: "Early morning – nothing but nonsense – watch out!" She is about to throw the water into the courtyard.

Little Broadcaster avoids her stream of water and pushes Kung into the kitchen: "Listen – this house is about to be sold!"

Kung laughs: "I know – you've broadcast this before."

The Broadcaster leans towards him, confidentially: "Can't you guess why it's to be sold now? Monkey's going to make a run for it, before trouble comes. Here's your opportunity – you can get your house back."

Kung starts. Mrs. Broadcaster is fanning the oven, dark smoke comes from it. When she hears her husband's last remark, she takes over the discussion: "This time his talk is useful, Old Kung. Yesterday she brought someone here to inspect the house, and she shouted at our little Mao-mao, crazy words – telling us to move, move. You see, they're forcing us, step by step, into a corner. You better make up your mind, Old Kung, before it's too late."

Mrs. Hua is making her fire: "That's right, Mr. Kung – you should be in charge here."

Kung shakes his head: "Forget it."

The Broadcaster objects: "Forget!? How can you give up so easily? This was *your* house - before he used force and the take-over people helped him grab it. But why let him frighten you now?"

The smoke makes Kung sneeze. He goes toward the door, saying, "Yes, everything you say is reasonable. But who's going to listen to my reason? There's no justice in this world – none at all, my friend!"

The Broadcaster realizes he has chosen the wrong moment for discussion: "All right, all right – but you're not the only tenant here. I'll ask Mr. Hua to come downstairs, and then we'll all discuss this." He leaves.

Mr. Hua, the teacher [Sun Tao-ling], toothbrush in hand, is just poised before his washbasin; he likes order and cleanliness — all his toilet articles are arranged in perfect order.

"Mr. Hua!" It is the voice of the Little Broadcaster, shouting through the door. Without waiting for a reply, he opens the door and comes in. Mr. Hua's welcome is not very warm, but his rude visitor, his chest bursting with emotion, says: "Come on down! We all have to talk over this house business, Mr. Hua, you're an educated man — you must raise your head above the rest of us, you must represent us."

With a belly full of unexpressed displeasure Mr. Hua answers: "Just a minute, please — I haven't even washed my face yet."

But the Broadcaster doesn't care whether three times seven makes twenty-one: "Everyone expects you — we have to talk it over!"

He takes the toothbrush from Mr. Hua, lays it on the table, and pulls Mr. Hua out of the room — dead or alive, it doesn't matter to him.

This casual naturalism determined the approach to every element in the film, its acting most evidently, its direction and camerawork most subtly. It is a new tone in Chinese films; it was new in European films, too, when Rosselini and De Sica established a style, gathered from many *tentatifs* in that direction from the cinema's beginning, that critics happily labeled neorealism. But the Shanghai filmmakers had not seen the Italian films that were pointing the way to the rest of the film world. With or without models to follow, *Crows and Sparrows* is a significant film, and it was an Italian critic, Ugo Casiraghi, who was the first foreign writer to draw attention to it:

The film is serious and well constructed, with the psychology of many characters in continuous and interesting development. Readers may have noticed that the film directors of old China, with much care and persistence, were preoccupied with subjects about intellectuals. That is a natural fact in Shanghai, where most of the students and many teachers learned to know and to despise the Four Big Families that kept the country in servitude. In *Crows and Sparrows*, side by side with its subtle description of greed and abuse of authority, and of children in need of food and medicine, there is a very remarkable sequence showing the student crowd being beaten by the police in front of the National Bank. Though its montage, which contributes so much to the conviction of the film, was accomplished after the liberation, one feels that the director was a man of vigor and clairvoyance.[22]

The last important American film about China, while China and the United States were still, officially, allies, was made without Chinese supervision or approval. The lessons learned by M-G-M during the troubles of *The Good Earth* had been attended to by other studios.

A. J. Cronin's novel, *The Keys of the Kingdom*, about a Catholic missionary in the Chinese interior, was quietly purchased by Twentieth-Century-Fox in the summer of 1941. Tentative inquiries by the studio received disheartening replies from everyone, first from the Production Code Administration:

It is our impression that the present governmental regime in China is likely to protest rather vigorously against the picturization of these kinds of incidents [warlords, famine, pestilence] in a film, which is to be distributed throughout the world. . . .[23]

A year later the Office of War Information stated its warning in harsher terms:

The story is replete with matters which modern China prefers to have buried in the dead past . . . on the question of our relations with the Chinese there are almost certain to be questions raised as to this film's suitability for export.

Both reports advised the studio to work with the Chinese consul in Los Angeles, who exploded when, in February 1944, he heard that the book was to be filmed:

[In Cronin's book] the character of the Chinese people is described with serious distortion, totally oblivious of their good virtues, such as honesty, politeness and tolerance. The presentation of a picture seething with civil war, bandits, flood, famine, epidemic, torturing and murdering of foreign friends can but create misunderstanding and resentment in our relationship . . . we are anxious that this picture should be produced in the light of our modern development.

This only confirmed the studio's decision to work without official Chinese help, and to find a technical advisor who would "confine his efforts to telling us how to build sets and design clothes and not be involved in the politics of the situation." A young Jesuit priest was found for this job; Father Albert O'Hara had worked for eight years at a mission in the Chinese interior, and his advice was supplemented by other unofficial persons, including the few Chinese who acted in the film. Official Chinese agencies continued to exert pressure on the studio, but neither was a script submitted to them nor were they asked for help. The sympathy and accuracy of the result surprised all — the film's Chinese distribution was hindered by only a few minor cuts.*

The gently ironic tone in the depiction of Chinese character makes *The Keys of the Kingdom* the only foreign film about China to bear a resemblance to the

---

* In the period of many imitations of American films even *The Keys of the Kingdom* was copied, in *The Holy Town* (directed by Shen Fu, released in November 1946).

unusual truthfulness of *Crows and Sparrows.* The Chinese film is a greater artistic victory; even an approximation of it is an achievement for an American film.

What surely would have been an important Chinese film, from any point of view, was attempted in 1948. One of the great experimental cameramen, the Chinese-American, James Wong Howe, went to Peking to film Lao Shê's novel, *Rickshaw Boy.* * Twice before, in 1924 and 1930, Howe had planned productions in China that could not be realized. In 1948 his sponsors thought conditions for a Chinese-American coproduction could not be better. Actually, conditions could not have been worse.

The old problem of official Chinese sensitivity about Chinese reality was the first obstacle. Howe's group thought that a famous modern Chinese novel would guarantee approval of their film project but even in the diluted, "happy" version of Lao Shê's novel that had become a best seller in America, there was too much unpleasant reality for the Kuomintang authorities. What an unfortunate image of China to show abroad, especially in these difficult days of open warfare with the Reds! Then the Red Army's drive towards Peking gave Kuomintang officials other preoccupations, and Howe's film was canceled a few months before the taking of Peking.

All of *Rickshaw Boy* that James Wong Howe took back to Hollywood were some magnificent color tests filmed on the streets of Peking. The Kodachrome color was simple and real, all glamour washed away by a clear artistic aim. For the first and only time the extraordinary buildings of the old capital were shown as part of an ordinary life, from the viewpoint of a Peking worker.

A much needed UNESCO project was also lost. An experiment in speedy, simplified animations, with minimum apparatus and materials, to assist in peasant education[24] was set up in the province of Szechuan, far enough from Chungking to be independent, and some unusual official had the inspiration to appoint Norman McLaren to be in charge. Such a sensible start was made that one can only regret, from a social as well as an artistic viewpoint, that in 1949 this came to an end along with all other "foreign teaching."

---

* At this time Lao Shê was in Hollywood, a guest of the State Department.

The minimum animation experiment devised by Norman McLaren for his Szechuan
UNESCO job, 1948.

A scissor-cut animation of 1964, *Red Army
Bridge*

7

The Chinese revolution is like a train that starts out on a long journey. Some men get off at side stations, others get on, but the vast majority will remain on until the train reaches its destination.

— Chu Teh

On the first of October, 1949, from the guards' portico of Tien An Men, Mao Tse-tung, with visible tension, proclaimed the new government of the Chinese People's Republic. The recording of this historic event is one of the few film documents from the beginning of the republic that the public is still shown. Of Mao's speech then, as of his speech a week earlier to the Political Consultative Council, a reviewer could safely say, "His voice is powerful, and the sound recording is excellent."[1]

Though all persons in positions of authority, then and now, consider the approval or rejection of a film their rightful province, those who were directly responsible for what appeared on the cinema screens were in the Ministry of Culture and the special Department of Propaganda. Fortunately for these first years of a new Chinese cinema the Minister of Culture appointed was experienced in filmmaking and film problems, as scenarist and actress. This was Chen Bo-erh, wife of Yuan Mu-jih, and Yuan was made vice-minister in direct charge of the Ministry's Film Bureau. Both had spent the years of civil war in Yenan. Both appointments were regarded as exceedingly auspicious for the cinema's future, as Chen Bo-erh also continued her filmwriting. Disaster soon struck these fortunate circumstances: in 1951 Chen Bo-erh died suddenly and Yuan Mu-jih withdrew altogether from administrative and creative work. Today this original artist remains a recluse, presumably engaged on some undefined research project.

The direction of propaganda was outside the ministries, and the powers and authority of this department were as strong (on occasion stronger) than those of any ministry. It was headed by two reliables from Yenan days, Lu Ting-yi and Chou Yang, who seemed (until 1966) the permanent occupants of these posts. In 1949 the propaganda task was simpler than at any later time. The majority of Chinese and the majority of other people rejoiced at the success of the revolution. Enemies inside and out were a conspicuous minority.

In all eyes China was the hero who had defeated Giant America (standing behind Chiang Kai-shek) and had won over the greatest odds. Each necessary tightening and economy by the hero was pointed to with pride and satisfaction. The poor paper on which its first publications went abroad became another evidence of frugal virtue. The bare simplicities of the first films that emerged from there

were a source of critical delight: the less they resembled the films we were used
to, the more praise they merited. At first Chinese audiences enjoyed the change:
the townspeople who had seen films before experienced the novelty of characters (no matter how stylized) that bore more resemblance to themselves, and the
new films won appreciation and attendance. Later, as it became apparent that
there was to be little else, the narrowed choice brought irritation and complaint
to these more sophisticated spectators. The films imported from the Soviet
Union and other socialist countries quieted this muttering. For the new audiences
in the depths of the country who had never seen films before this new entertainment was "almost as good as theater." This was the audience that the filmmakers tried hardest to present on the screen.

A film industry must be created for China that fully serves the interests of all its
people and that speaks out clearly and truthfully on the burning questions of the
day.[2]

The film studio that came closest to realizing this commendable aim was the
newly named Northeast Studio of Changchun. Abroad we only read about the
first films that came from there. Though I was later able to see almost all the first
productions, either in the Peking Archive or in copies distributed to friendly
countries, I have never managed to see the very first film that appeared, *Bridge*,
directed by Wang Pin. The Northeast Studio was the earliest in the hands of the
victorious Communists, and this first film, begun in 1948, was released in April
1949:

The first film of New China . . . showed the reconstruction of a bridge destroyed
in the war, portrayed by the actual workers who had rebuilt this bridge across
the Sungari River. It was received with great enthusiasm by the Chinese people.[3]

The same journalist writes that in the next film from Northeast, *Light Spreads
Everywhere*, "workers are also the main actors." But as all the actors in *Light* are
clearly actors, it's difficult to accept this one piece of interesting information
about *Bridge*.

It was a year before her appointment to the Ministry of Culture that Chen
Bo-erh was assigned to prepare the scenario for *Light Spreads Everywhere*. She
went to live with her subject, the Harbin Power Company,[4] an "immersion in
real life" that Yenan principles required of any artist. The finished film is effectively simple, with a minimum of rhetoric, and the usual result of such "immersion," a quantity of naturalistic detail (as in *Women Locomotive Drivers*), is
missing in *Light*. Chen Bo-erh could have worked out its main structure without
leaving her desk, wherever it was at the beginning of 1949. The film depended
more on her earlier film experience than on her visit to Harbin.

The film opens "now," at an industrial exhibition in some northeastern city. A proud citizen (the hero, played by Chang Ping) takes his son to the exhibition, and in a gallery of labor heroes sees his own portrait, reminding him of 1947 when he peddled old clothes through the slums of this city. A newly authoritative workers' organization (more precise identification is held for later) offers him a job, helping to bring the power plant back into operation. A Kuomintang agent tests his sympathies (unsatisfactorily) and, as the plant is nearly ready, tries to destroy it. He is caught and reveals all. The hero joins the party and heroically saves a furnace. We are brought back to "today" and the exhibition, a framing device that became obligatory for most films about the recent past.

Light has a certain stiffness, but not from the habits that came later. Here it is some new thing creaking, whose makers are not sure whether it will work. The plant itself is well photographed, with its machinery used for pictorial and dramatic effect (recalling the factory scenes, scaled down and drastically simplified, of the Ermler-Yutkevich *Counterplan*), though the *sounds* of the place are left unexploited (possibly because of technical inadequacies). The flaming scene of sabotage is filmed and edited as efficiently as a Peking opera battle scene. "Typecasting," whose social implications were to worry me increasingly, is already apparent here. Actors with nasty faces are condemned, for their entire careers, to play nasty roles, heroic roles are filled only by heroic faces, and so on, ad infinitum.

Daughters of China was filmed at the same time and released in November 1949, the first new film to appear after the People's Republic was proclaimed (see Plate 25). It is even simpler than *Light*, and stronger, a story of women in 1936 fighting in the Anti-Japanese Army of the Northeast, ending with their choice to drown rather than be captured by the surrounding enemy. (The eight young women striding into the Mutan River are also the subject of a familiar painting, after the film.) The filming of *Daughters of China* is unusually expressive, and the tragic climax is as cathartic as it should be. It is the earliest film still to be publicly shown (especially when, as in 1966, the public must be reminded of the necessity for struggle and martyrdom), and it continues to be offered for sale abroad. It is a film whose "revolutionary purity" has never been questioned.

The next film from the Northeast Studio is, internationally, the best known of Chinese films, *The White-Haired Girl*. Adaptation to the film medium, even so limited in its film freedoms as here, has put some life into the mechanical rigidity of the opera, and elements other than exposition are given play. It is a good mixture of the real and the stylized, real enough for film, stylized enough for fable. The finale is purely theatrical, a tableau of confrontation, but the scenes added for the film's sake are so adventitious (river rapids and a fire not attached to the drama) that it might have been wiser *not* to pretend to make a genuine film. The chief beauty of the film is the actress chosen to play Hsi-erh: Tien Hua was the daughter of a peasant family in the liberated area who joined a dramatic troupe of the Eighth Route Army in 1940. Her fresh loveliness could not have been bettered, and the camera brings this freshness and sweetness so tangibly near (and makes it so permanent), that this seems reason enough to film *The White-Haired Girl*. Tien Hua reminds me of Ruan Ling-yu: she makes incredible actions credible so long as you are watching her.

In the several times I have seen the film I have grown more conscious of patterns and attitudes that were on their way to becoming fixtures in the Chinese cinema. A contradiction new in this film, and one that was to haunt the films of the next fifteen years, is the need to show cruel oppressors without showing Chinese cruelty as a trait (the Japanese army could not always be the villain). The contradiction is not so serious on a stage, where cruelty as well as cruel characters are so exaggerated as not to involve one in the action, but in films a cruel act, no matter how obliquely shown,* strikes at each spectator, and we are persuaded to believe that even the evil characters are real people, no matter how unreal their behavior. More obviously, the general passivity of the play has not been corrected for the adaptation: tearful responses were still thought useful to evoke. Superstition as a dramatic element is, compared with later films, astonishingly emphasized here. Typecasting is so firmly defined that in the introductory cast list, which would always be divided in Chinese film credits between good characters and bad characters, the music actually changes at the division from good to evil: the audience is being guided before the film begins. Some permanent taboos can be glimpsed: the bound feet of the older generation of women (and in the landlord's house) have been made normal; and though the heroine is allowed to indicate symptoms of her pregnancy, her figure does not change. The film decides that the child must die unseen — it was probably judged unwise for the audience of 1950 to sympathize with the offspring of a rapist landlord.

In 1954, the fifth anniversary celebrations were attended by, among others, the French resistance novelist, Vercors, and his wife, Rita Barisse. They were shown several films and Rita Barisse decided that *The White-Haired Girl* "is the most Chinese film of all those I have seen."[5] "Many of their other films could have been made in almost any 'people's democracy,' " but this film, "with its blend of

---

* The most extreme avoidance of film violence is not in a Chinese film but in Buñuel's first Mexican film, *Gran Casino*: whenever a shot is to be fired or a blow to be struck, the *camera* turns away as if disgusted.

realism and stylization, of melodrama and poetry, of visual beauty and strident
but haunting music . . . could only have been made in China." She continues:

[*The White-Haired Girl*] was not meant to be "artistic," it was meant to be
useful: useful in the fight against bad conditions and ignorance. It was made as a
deliberate piece of propaganda and turned out, only incidentally, a work of art
. . . this film shows the way, to my mind at least, to what may one day be
China's major contribution to the art of the cinema.

The logic of this may be faulty but the enthusiasm is valuable, as is the hope.
The Dean of Canterbury's enthusiasm went beyond usefulness; in a Peking
speech he said:

The magnificent film, *The White-Haired Girl*, is a masterly piece of art, utterly
unknown in Hollywood, a masterly and passionate expression of the spirit. It
explains so much. . . .[6]

The next two films from Changchun also gave women the central roles (respect
for women was still a "burning question of the day"), but the two films have
almost nothing in common. *Chao Yi-man* is an excellent biographical film of an
actual revolutionary heroine who served as political commissar in the Northeast
Anti-Japanese Army until her capture and death in 1937 at the age of thirty-
two;[*] her short, intense life determined the driving pace of the film, as well as its
serious tone, as of a discussion vital to all concerned. To add to the film's
strength the matters discussed are all made clear through what we *see* on the
screen. There is an enthusiasm for filmmaking and communication apparent
throughout *Chao Yi-man*; the lessons available here for subsequent films are
more central and mature, as politics and as art, than in any other film made in
the first two years of China's new cinema. As shown in films guerrilla leaders are
often either too wise or too mawkish, but Shih Lien-hsing in this role tells us
something of what such a life was like; Chao Yi-man was luckier in her actress,
in her scenarist (Yu Ming) and director (Sha Meng) than most revolutionary
heroines.

At the other extreme *Women Locomotive Drivers*† is ludicrous. The scenarist
has used most of the stock characteristics of stage and film ladies — caprices,
quarrels, coy playfulness, easy tears — to undercut its point of women winning

---

* Amleto Vespa, in his *Secret Agent of Japan* [(Boston: Little, Brown, 1938), p. 292]
describes her betrayal and arrest.
† "Art of Mass Character," a letter from A. Doak Barnett, dated 12 May 1954 (published by
American Universities Field Staff), gives a detailed synopsis of this film as shown in Hong
Kong.

their rightful place in industry. The aim of this tale of female trainees may have been real, but the effect is artificial and decorative; the end is so childish as to be quite endearing: the bouqueted ladies' team drives three decorated engines abreast in punctilious parade formation, to the accompaniment of a Soviet march. The trains of the film are fictional objects; one is never shown the "un-dramatic" business of real railway work — no loading or unloading (only freight trains are shown, so as not to scare prospective passengers with the nightmare of one of these ladies in control) — only fearless driving through space. There are so many familiar Shanghai actors' faces in this Changchun film that it's tempting to speculate that someone thought the politics of the Northeast Studio could be made more attractive dressed in stars, but the actress of *Empress Wu Tze-tien* (Ku Kang or Violet Koo) as the eager heroine here lends little conviction. Sun Tao-lin, an actor who was to play in Shanghai's best films of the fifties, here plays the girls' priggish but patient instructor.

One important film of 1950 I haven't seen, nor did anyone mention it to me while I was in China. I can only give the testimony of two deeply impressed visitors to China, Wilfred Burchett and Claude Roy.

Another impressive film made by the state studios* was "Stand Up Sisters," a full length feature, excellently and sensitively produced and filmed. It is a simple and factual account of one of the prostitutes from the Peking brothels, a peasant girl who came with her mother to live with city relatives when the father died, and left them penniless. The mother finger-printed a document which both thought was a labor contract for work in a textile factory. The girl was taken instead to a brothel, where she had the customary initiation by being raped by the proprietor. The film faithfully follows the case history of one brothel where abortions were carried out by the "madame" with scissors and no anaesthetic; where a girl dying from haemorrhage is dumped into a coffin which is nailed down while she is still alive; where girls who tried to escape were branded on the shoulders with red-hot irons; an accurate record of the inhuman life of girls sold into prostitution, and the way they have been set on their feet since Liberation. There is not a hint of moralising in the film as far as the attitude to the girls is concerned. . . . There is no hint that it was disgraceful for the girls to have been prostitutes; emphasis is on the brutal social system which put the girls into brothels and the fact that the girls can now have a good start in life. . . . It was a film which left many people in the audience weeping on the occasion on which I saw it. . . .[7]

Roy's further detail on the audience's reaction to the film is of exceptional value. He also describes a degree of cinéma vérité that was ahead of its time (the director was Shih Hui).

---

* It was probably made by one of the last private studios in Shanghai. The title is sometimes given as *Peking Prostitutes Liberated*.

In China I saw an amazing film whose beauty seemed to challenge all the esthetic rules of the game between film stock and light. For the first quarter hour in this long documentary on prostitution and its suppression, the camera did not move away from the ordinary and very distressing face of a young woman who only told her life story. A French audience probably would have been annoyed by this fifteen-minute-long passage in which the camera remains immobile and where *nothing happens* — except the reflection on one face of a whole destiny of humiliation and servility. I can imagine how a French audience would have sought release either in laughter, no matter how tense and nervous, or in flight from the theater. What was most moving for me in this film showing was not merely the nakedness and authenticity of the woman's testimony, it was the attitude of the audience. The hundreds of spectators in this Chinese cinema did not give the usual impression of being spectators, of being on the other side of a mirror that stretched across this great space of a face and a life. An almost concrete link was established between them and the screen — nor was this merely uneasy curiosity or pharisaical hostility. No fear of ridicule, no enjoyment of indiscretion, no contemptuous withdrawal broke the equality between the woman who laid her burden before all of us and the "spectators" who received it without irony and without scorn — I might even say, without pity. At least without that pity which is already a judgment in its condescension. Each one felt that it could have happened to him. That is all. That is enormous.[8]

By the first anniversary in 1950 the particular functions and distinguishing attitudes of the several studios were already distinct. The Northeast Studio remained the most political and trusted studio, but this leading position was soon to be taken by the new studios of Peking, closer to the government: the first productions of the Japanese-built Peking Studio were actuality records of the military victories of 1948–1949, *The Huaihai Campaign* and *Victorious Crossing of the Yangtze*, but as the studio had been equipped for the production of fictional films these began to appear in the winter of 1950–1951. There was a plan for a new army film studio in Peking, the August First,* but its building and equipment were not ready until after the armistice in Korea. China's original film base, Shanghai, remained the largest producer, but it was also a constant source of political anxiety: "Were the influence of the past and of America still too strong?" Both state-owned and private studios made Shanghai's films; both were carefully supervised yet neither was quite trusted. The most popular Shanghai film of 1950 was *Life of a Peking Policeman*, written by Lao Shê, directed and acted by Shih Hui; its popularity did not protect it, and it did not stay long in distribution. I did not see it at the Karlovy Vary festival in 1950; Sadoul describes it as "a sort of *Cavalcade* that shows a half-century of China's history, through one family, from the Boxer war . . . to the Japanese occupation."[9]

---

* The date in 1928 when the guerrilla armies under Mao and Chu Teh joined forces, a date celebrated as Army Day.

Tsai Chu-sheng gives the statistics for 1950:

At present over 3,000 people are directly engaged in the making of new pictures in the three state-owned studios in the Northeast, Peking, and Shanghai. They will produce this year 26 full-length features, 17 documentary films, one colour feature film, 48 newsreels, 40 Chinese dubbed versions of Soviet films, and Chinese versions of 36 Soviet educational films. In addition, it is estimated that private companies in Hongkong and Shanghai will be able to produce about 50 new films as well as a number of Chinese versions of Soviet films. This year the state-owned enterprises plan to organize more mobile exhibition units for the rural areas and to establish film-laboratories and factories to provide the growing industry with equipment.[10]

In another report[11] of 1950 Kuo Mo-jo gave a more generalized picture:

In the film industry, the basic principle is to eliminate the poisonous imperialist films gradually and strengthen the educational nature of the people's film industry, orientating our films towards the masses of workers, peasants and soldiers.... Before the liberation, seventy-five percent of all the movie-goers in Shanghai went to see American films, but the percentage was reduced to 28.3 by June 1950. This is a great victory on the cinema front.*

He presents this against a background of the chief task for all cultural and educational work: "to liquidate the feudal, comprador, and fascist ideologies and develop the ideology of serving the people."

The link between the new Chinese film industry and the long-established Soviet film industry was working from the day of Mao's proclamation. The Soviet delegation that came for this occasion included two film directors, Sergei Gerasimov and Leonid Varlamov (whose *Stalingrad* was shown in Chungking in 1943), with a group of cameramen. Their plan was to produce two large actuality films about China as coproductions with Chinese filmmakers, and they went to work at once:

Our group of producers and cameramen arrived in China in the historic days when the People's Republic was proclaimed. Obviously, these festivities had to be included in the film, and so at first we had to work without any definite plan, simply filming everything that seemed important and interesting. And actually, everything we saw came in that category.[12]

---

* Within another year, partly due to the Korean War, American films had been completely eliminated: by then there were enough "correctly orientated" films to keep the cinemas in operation.

These festivities, an important sequence of the finished film, *Liberated China*, lasted until mid-October, when the Soviet team had to get down to the more difficult job of establishing a scenario and a shooting plan:

In our efforts . . . we received very valuable assistance from the Communist Party of China, whose Central Committee appointed a number of its officials to act as consultants to our group. . . . Most of our consultants were military men who had just given up their battle-dress for the traditional [?] blue garments of the Chinese workingman. . . .

They collaborated in drawing up our scenario plan. The chief difficulty at this stage was the tremendous mass of material that we had to deal with. There was far too much of it to go into one documentary, even a very long one.* Yet our task was to depict clearly and with historical accuracy in one documentary the basic stages of the Chinese people's liberation struggle in the last hundred years.

Four drafts of the scenario plan were written before we succeeded in solving this difficult problem.

After that the work entered the next stage, the actual shooting of the film. . . . The core of the filming group was made up of seven Soviet cameramen expert in documentary and fictional films and in color photography. . . . The Peking State Film Studios appointed Comrades Chou Li-po [the writer], Ho Shih-teh [composer] and Hsu Hsiao-ping [cameraman] to work with our group.

The shooting was done according to a detailed plan . . . The scenes of land reform, partly spontaneous, partly staged, are the most reliable extant film record of this short but exciting chapter in Chinese history.

In spite of all the natural obstacles of a first coproduction, the enthusiasm of the time speeded the work, and the film was actually ready a year after it was begun:

. . . the reception we were accorded on 1 October 1950, the anniversary of the Chinese People's Republic, when we brought *Liberated China* to Peking for its first showing to the leaders of the Chinese government and the general public, was the reception accorded to brothers.

The second coproduction, *Victory of the Chinese People*, supervised by Leonid Varlamov, was ready on schedule (see Plate 30).

Also in October 1950 the first Soviet film crew to ask for Chinese assistance, locations and actors, arrived in Peking. Sergei Yutkevich was directing a film

---

* Several short films, also released as coproductions, were made from the immense amount of color footage shot for *Liberated China: New Peking, In New Shanghai, Hangchow — Pearl of China*, and *Along the Yangtze.*

about the nineteenth-century Russian scholar and explorer, Nikolai Przhevalsky, and was naturally eager to use real Chinese places to represent the China that Przhevalsky knew. He received maximum cooperation, though *Przhevalsky*, when finished in 1951, was not distributed in China. No official reason was offered, but it was clear that the discovery by a European of China's art and antiquity was not a fit subject for China's modern audience and national feelings.

Yutkevich's visit to Peking was not only as a film director, but also as a connoisseur of theater arts, and his account of the experience[13] is a record of the plays, operas, films, dancing, and drama schools that he saw in 1950; his opinions of the films then and his conversations with their makers are a valuable source for a period that seems more remote than it is in reality.

At the Peking Studio, where he was to get the personnel and help he needed, Yutkevich was shown a rough-cut of *Defenders of Peace* by its director, Hsi Liang, and its cameraman, Hsu Chih-tsin (who had studied at the film school in Moscow). This "patriotic, agitational film" did not make a deep impression on the Soviet director. A less heroic Peking film, showing more of Chinese life, *New Marriage*, written and directed by Tu Hsin-hua (his second film, the first being an actuality film on the remolding of beggars and wild children), was more interesting. The new Marriage Law had been enacted on May Day, and the film was quickly made to illustrate its new blessings to Chinese girls. Yutkevich found the film "poetic and at the same time instructive and stirring." Another film from the Peking Studio was *March of Democratic Youth*, an adaptation of the play about Peking students in 1947 — a film directly influenced by Gerasimov's *Young Guard*.

I was happy to read that Yutkevich found more pleasure and alertness in the productions of the Northeast Studio. *The White-Haired Girl* won him, of course. The only other Changchun films he saw were two about the wars against Japan and the Kuomintang, *Heroes of Liuliang Mountain* and *Steeled Fighter*. The latter was the first fictional film made by Cheng Yin (see Plate 26). He and the leading player of *Steeled Fighter*, Chang Ping, obliged Yutkevich with autobiographical sketches. Each had taken an active part in the war years, both as fighting soldiers and as members of army theaters. Both had been assigned by the Communist Party in 1948 to the newly freed studio in Changchun. Chang Ping had more film experience — as spectator, that is — than Cheng Yin, who had not seen films since his childhood (he was 33 in 1950); he had somehow missed all the film shows in Yenan, and the actuality films that he first made in 1948 grew directly from their subjects, without benefit of traditions. The Soviet cinema was the only stylistic influence on *Steeled Fighter*.

Soviet films were the first foreign films to be introduced into China on a massive scale. Between 1945 and 1949 some less political Soviet films (notably *The Stone Flower*) had limited showings in the larger cities,* but after 1949 no limits were apparent, and Soviet films were distributed as intensively as the new Chinese films. The language barrier was removed: the first Chinese dubbed versions were prepared at the Changchun Studio and these were among the 38 Soviet films displayed ceremonially between 10 February and 5 March 1950 (the Sino-Soviet Treaty was signed in Moscow on 14 February, witnessed by Stalin and Mao Tse-tung), at two Peking cinemas, in Tientsin, Mukden, and Shanghai. Gerasimov's films occupied the foreground of this Soviet film festival and his *Young Guard* "inspired many young people to join the China New Democratic Youth League" (according to Tsai Chu-sheng). In an educational conference of this year Li Li-san cited Varvara, in Donskoy's *Village Schoolteacher*, as a model to be studied by Chinese teachers. Two years later Ivor Montagu was told, "In Soviet films we see our future; in the films of the People's Democracies [that arrived later], our past and present struggles."[14]

Inevitably this flood of Soviet films, with the assurance and weight of their postwar style, presented a model also to be followed by Chinese films. There were imitations to all degrees, depending on the purpose and intelligence of the filmmakers, and the sensitivity and common sense of the Soviet technicians and advisors (whose names never figured among the credits) working at each studio. At the lowest level of mechanical imitation, or travesty, was *Women Locomotive Drivers*. More sensible but also superficial, *Steeled Fighter* borrowed as much of its heroic manner from *Young Guard* as from Peking opera. *Young Guard* was also a source for *New Heroes and Heroines*, one of the first and strongest films from the new Peking Studio, but the tone of this new film was determined by the new war.

Although this time Chinese were fighting outside Chinese territory, all of China was to be seriously affected by the Korean War. The beginnings of most wars are hard to define, but there are unusually thick shrouds of unreliability and propaganda over the clashes between North and South Korea in the last week of June 1950, and over the background and exact purposes and aims of the large-scale intervention of Chinese "volunteers" in October, after a mere year of technical peace in China. The American support of South Korea and the American pressure to conduct its campaign under the flag of the United Nations were more closely related to American shock and humiliation in China the year before than

---

* There were also occasional showings before 1938 of Soviet films, some of which have been mentioned earlier.

Washington's pronouncements would suggest. The United States and China were at war again, now on Korean soil.

Though the "allies" knew at once of China's entrance into the Korean War, it was a month before the Chinese public was officially informed about their new war. However, everyone in China knew without being officially told. Even before Chinese participation in the war was publicly acknowledged there were camera teams sent from China's studios to record the life and fighting of the volunteers there — to be held for later use. There was time for the Chinese commander in Korea, Peng Teh-huai, to be replaced by Lin Piao before the radio and press at home said that a Chinese army had crossed the Yalu River boundary. It may have been the return of wounded soldiers that was the first clear sign — before any announcement — that China was fighting in a foreign war.

No one in China was to be left in any doubt as to America's role in the Korean War. All propaganda channels were put to intense use, and each film initiated in the latter half of 1950 and completed in 1951 either referred specifically to the fighting in Korea, or its theme was one that could be related to the war — defense against an aggressor, heroism in the face of brutality, individual sacrifice for the revolutionary cause. *New Heroes and Heroines* (an adaptation of a popular novel of 1949) absorbed all these themes and, despite the group of protagonists implied by its title, its tensions were those of a classic drama. The shift of dramatic emphasis from one character to another was not only interestingly managed, but it assisted the film to get a great deal said, penetratingly. The final battle, which was often to be an exercise in cinema rhetoric, is vividly handled here. Though not the first film from the Peking Studio (in its new management), its technical directness compares well with the flamboyance and theatrical postures of many other films made during and about the Korean War. Telling a good, meaningful story well was rarely considered the correct propaganda method.

The climax of the film was based on a real victory:

Seven years ago the people's militia of Paiyang Lake in South Hopei attacked and captured an armed Japanese steamboat and the ammunition on it. When the film group brought their steamboat to Paiyang Lake to reenact the incident, old memories were stirred. Guerrillas reconstructed the events, brought out their original boats and arms and participated in the scenes.[15]

This was the earliest film in which I noticed an experiment in visual simplicity. The camera compositions are kept *central* or *frontal*: when two persons are on the screen they face each other in the same plane; a group of three has the commanding personality (and his speech) centered (see Plate 26). Compositions using diagonals and depth are very rare. Was this a conscious exploitation of Chinese *theater* compositions? An effort to embody the film's story in images that would give the minimum difficulty to new filmgoers? The effect in *New Heroes and Heroines* was neither stilted nor theatrical, as my description may imply; the film's feeling of ease made this method look like a most valuable one to pursue, esthetically and dramatically. Yet after a few films in the early fifties, mostly from the Peking Studio, I notice that this approach appears to have been discarded, at least in its most visible form.

In *North Shensi Shepherd's Song*, which came from the Peking Studio in January 1951, there is also simple imagery and composition, but so attached to one-dimensional characters and time-honored, international "movie logic" (the rescue of a kidnapped heroine precipitates a massed battle) as to give a different color to the virtues of simplicity. The final sequence may have been added after Chinese troops entered the Korean War: some time has elapsed since the couple's wedding (possibly the original conclusion) for both are now in uniform and are being sung on their victorious way by their young son. It is difficult to determine whether the childlike manner of *People's Fighters* (from the Northeast Studio, early in 1951) was deliberate or involuntary; it may have been prepared hastily to stiffen public morale during the Korean War (though its events happen between 1946 and 1949), for its only clear purpose is to bolster faith in the personnel and decisions of the People's Liberation Army. Even more than in *Steeled Fighter* all the soldiers are shown as magnificent, joyous, wise, and polite creatures. The regiment's political commissar is a courteously cast double of Malenkov. The scenarist (a poet, Liu Pai-yu) went so far as to eliminate all negative characters, even making the Kuomintang army a remote abstraction. This is the way the technical advisors of any army would like to arrange screen battles: abstract enemy, unerring strategy, splendid heroism, and the right kinds of wounds. (A usually unemphasized dramatization of wounds and hospitals was permitted here.) From the start there is a display of Changchun's equipment (a camera crane, obtrusively), but groups are arranged as on a stage, with the camera often sitting in the auditorium. Any real film effort is centered on the night attack on a Kuomintang-occupied town, an effort that comes too late to rescue our interest.

People's Fighters is one of the films that I came to classify as "behavior lessons," though all new Chinese films contained some pointed models to replace the condemned old manners and habits linked with the past and the bourgeoisie. In this film, in addition to being shown in full detail the precisely correct behavior for communist soldiers, the audience learned how a husband and wife should greet each other after being parted for many suffering years: when they meet they do not embrace — they do not even touch each other! The audience, though, may have been distracted from its lesson by the baby, who has aged only slightly with the passing of years.

The Shanghai studios released two films of political importance in the early months of 1951, *The Shangjao Concentration Camp* and *Red Banner on Green Rock*. When Jerzy Toeplitz saw them at Karlovy Vary in 1952, he made some general comments on Chinese cinema. Noting the dependence on theater traditions, the leisurely development and the simplified plots, he sums up:

Together these causes reduce the attraction of Chinese films for a European public, but the chief reason for this is that the spiritual development of human beings is almost untouched. In general, the characters are fixed from the beginning of a film, and as the film progresses we see only the hero struggling against some evil, without ever failing, not even in the most difficult situations.[16]

He has put his finger on the most striking characteristic of Chinese films since 1949, the strangely non-Marxian changelessness of the film characters, and this is particularly evident in these two Shanghai films of 1951, where the most violent action has no effect on the characters. Good characters grow only firmer in their resolve, bad characters only become more violent and desperate.

Its cinema cannot be expected to mobilize millions of people for struggle with the use of psychological sensitivity or intellectual experiments. The behavioral direction is clear — the audience must know from the beginning which side holds truth and heroism.

In spite of this clarity and their technical Shanghai polish both these films have a basic carelessness that places them on a lower plane than the more frankly struggling films from the Changchun and Peking studios. *Shangjao* is the most artificial and crudely sadistic concentration camp film that I've seen from any country, including B-films made in the outskirts of Hollywood. It's all here, wailing violins, creaking torture-chamber doors, and minimum respect for the spectator. The horrors did not move the filmmakers to find ways to move the audience, leaving the film as hard and inhuman as the conditions that it shows. Of all the Chinese films he saw in 1952 this one quite floored Toeplitz:

. . . it is the greatest puzzle for a European spectator. Nearly the whole plot of the film is conveyed in "interior monologues" with images held on the screen for several minutes at a time without changing the camera. Only the inner concentration shown on the faces of the young actresses is memorable. . . .

It is hard to say what produced such stylized behavior and presentation coming from a naturalistic Shanghai studio. It could have been either incompetence or a dutiful wish to adhere to formulas. Other arts may also have had their influence: *Shangjao's* source was a novel and its cast (unfamiliar faces then) was drawn from the theater of the Shanghai People's Art Society.

The pastoral, idyllic opening of *Red Banner on Green Rock* (see Plate 31) signals that horrors will have to be endured before the red banner can wave over Green Rock (Mt. Tsuikang, the fortress where the Kuomintang has herded everyone for a last stand). Most of the tragedies are arranged by the scenarist, Tu Tan, as well as by the Kuomintang; he has hastily pulled together a scenario out of various real and theatrical situations, and the execution and editing have been equally hasty. The director, Chang Chun-hsiang, has done his best, helped only by the effective exteriors of the cameraman, Fen Tsi-chi, and by the only moving per-formance, that of Yu Lan in the central role of the wife whose husband goes on the Long March. With anyone else in this role, the film could be called *How to Be a Heroine in Sixty Clichés,* but Yu Lan is one of the most convincing actresses in Chinese films. When she is not on the screen, the film has the drama of a well-arranged parade. In a rare statement of 1953 on his directorial method Chang Chun-hsiang enunciates a principle that can be only partially applied to his work:

Directors, like scenario writers and actors, now have a new conception of their work. One of their chief responsibilities is to see that people depicted on the screen are not only true to life but show real development in response to the problems they face. . . .

We have also found that sharp images emerge only when writer, actor, and direc-tor have strong likes and dislikes for the characters they create.[17]

The two films have several similarities — there are plenty of tortures and execu-tions in both, and another vital behavior lesson: "When all else fails, show defi-ance to the enemy, especially if he is about to shoot or hang you."* The actor and cameraman always get the most out of such moments, and I have been in young audiences that responded enthusiastically to the hero's defiance of a contemptible executioner, but I cannot imagine that this lesson means much after its twentieth repetition, and the cheering filmgoer is growing up. It is curi-ous that the best filming and cutting in both films is a brief sequence of panic in the army and citizens, in the former film as the Japanese occupy Chinghua in 1942, near the Shangjao camp, and in the latter as the returning Red Army nears the Kiangsi region. A member of each film crew could have seen such moments, without knowing an actual concentration camp or the Kiangsi mountains.

---

* One whole film of this time was built upon the defiance formula, *Heroine Liu Chu-lan,* from the Northeast Studio.

Though the Shanghai filmmakers looked down on the films of the Northeast
Studio as "emergency" productions, it was just this that made Changchun's films
superior in these first years (and for many years, in my opinion) to Shanghai's
films, at least in their willingness to wrestle with a mass of urgent themes, some
of them matters that safer filmmakers preferred to avoid. During 1951 *The
Victorious People of Inner Mongolia* treated the delicate subject of a national
minority's revolutionary movement in relation to China's whole struggle; *Song
of the Red Flag* (based on a play of 1949) touched changes in industry and
administration; *Leap Ahead* was a light treatment of gentle conflicts between
two generations of Communists; and the subject of *Invisible Front* was espionage
in Mukden in 1948. *Heroine Liu Chu-lan*, of the anti-Japanese war, and *People's
Fighters* were the only films that you could imagine coming from any Chinese
studio in 1951. The greatest surprise from the Northeast Studio in 1951, certainly from today's standpoint (and the possibility of comparing it with other
modern Chinese films about peasant life and problems) was *Remote Village*. It
is difficult enough to make believable films about the life of Chinese peasants
before the revolution; to have made a half-credible film in 1951 about conditions in the countryside *after* the liberation of Manchuria is a feat that cannot
be ignored. Its theme resembles *Rio Escondido*: a politically educated couple is
sent from the cities where the revolution has been won, to bring its light to the
darkness and ignorance and prejudice of the remote hinterland. But where the
Mexican film toyed with this theme ornamentally, the Chinese film approaches
reality. The lesson of the film is the need for persuasion, and we listen to the
arguments in such detail as might be thought tedious; but the film's unusual sincerity gradually won me to prefer this to the jolly, house-cleaned, smoother pictures of peasant life. There is a minimum of the grinning that became obligatory
in later films of any contemporary subject, and the glimpses of real poverty and
resentment speak volumes. It is as brave, in its way and its time, as Part 1 of the
recent Soviet film on peasant life, *Chairman*. Though efficient, it is technically
and artistically an awkward film, with a rooted, inflexible relation between
characters and camera; and the soundtrack and music give the film no help. It
ends in formula, the new irrigation brings a rich harvest, the *yang-ko*, firecrackers,
and speeches. But China and Changchun can be proud of this modest film.

All these films were displayed in a proud film festival in March 1951, as reported
in *People's China*:

On every one of 26 nights from 8 March to 2 April this year, a different new
film was shown at 60 cinemas in 20 major cities. . . . The 26 full-length features,
60 documentaries and 47 newsreels and 43 Soviet films dubbed into Chinese,
produced last year, together with rereleases, the 24 films from private studios
and good progressive films from abroad. . . .[18]

Despite the confusing statistics, the article makes it clear that there were plenty
of new films to see. A large two-part film that was probably shown on this occasion became a disaster for the old filmmaking hands of Shanghai. Publicized as
"the story of a worker's struggle for self-education," *The Life of Wu Hsün* appeared in December 1950, was distributed widely and generally praised by
critics.* It was a few months before some high official† happened to see it — and
did not see its value as a weapon against Western-educated intelligentsia. Not
only was the film withdrawn, but all writers (especially those who had praised it)
and filmmakers were obliged to denounce it, its writer-director Sun Yu (who had
made the popular *Big Road*), and all that Wu Hsün represented:

Within six months, *Wen Yi Pao* [edited by Ting Ling] carried a dozen articles
which submitted the dubious ideas spread by this film to a close scrutiny. Wu
Hsün was thereby seen to be one of the ugliest, most hypocritical lackeys of the
reactionary feudal class in the latter part of the nineteenth century. In the hair
shirt of a penitent and ascetic, he lent money to the peasants at exorbitant interest, while groveling to big landlords, begging for money to establish schools
which propagated feudal ideas and virtues, so that the resurgent peasant revolts
of that time might be crushed and the tottering feudal regime saved. But the film
made about Wu Hsün in 1951, and many articles written about the film, praised
him as a revolutionary hero![19]

The suggestion that Wu Hsün helped to crush peasant revolts and save the Manchu regime is an obvious exaggeration that only weakens the attack. It is the
"feudal" rather than the "foreign" ideas propagated by Wu Hsün that are mentioned here, but the foreign base of his school system, displayed on public
screens in this period of a bitter war against foreigners in Korea, may have been
the primary cause of the film's condemnation; it may even explain why the film
seemed harmless early in 1951, and a menace a few months later. A Chinese
historian abroad sums up the case:

The heinous fault of the movie *The Life of Wu Hsün* . . . is that the makers of
the film have misconstrued Wu Hsün to be a proletarian hero whereas from the
Marxist point of view he was but an abject knave. Granted that this legendary
beggar, this founder of charity schools for the poor, did have all the accessory
proletarian virtues of courage, zeal, and self-denial, did he not beg all his life
from the rich rather than start a revolution against them?[20]

---

* The release of a Chinese film automatically indicates that it has been approved on all
levels, but there have been a few instances when Chinese film reviewers have been scorched
by this belief.
† At the time it was assumed that this was the highest official, Mao Tse-tung. This assumption could be supported by the fact that the attack on *The Life of Wu Hsün* continued to be
cited as a landmark in the cultural revolution. By now (1969) any criticism of Wu Hsün
quotes Mao's attack. There is a predenunciation opinion of Wu Hsün in A. Doak Barnett,
pp. 4—5.

In China the final word came from Chou Yang, in an article in *Wen Yi Pao* entitled "Ideas that Offend against the People and History, Art that Offends against Realism." He saw the central problem raised by the controversy as "whether the path followed by the Chinese people has been the path of revolution or that of reformism and capitulationism."[21] The fear of reformism and surrender was a real one, but the heat of the attacks on *Wu Hsün* indicate that more was at stake, possibly the control of Shanghai's cultural institutions. Dependent as I am on angled descriptions of the film, I can only speculate about these more important targets. *Wu Hsün* was the first post-1949 film to be publicly attacked, but each wave of the cultural revolution was to bring more denounced films, with similarly veiled motives. In greater quantity were the films completed and silently shelved.

The final, *final* word on *Wu Hsün* came from the Film Bureau: before the end of 1951 the condemned film's production company, Kun Lun, was merged with another private company to become the government's Shanghai studio of the Film Bureau.

It is difficult for me to look at the films shown between 1949 and 1951 only as social documents, though that now appears to be their greatest potential. For me they are more important as first steps toward an art that may not emerge fully until after the present sociologists finish their work.

Each of the greatest Soviet film artists was drawn to Asia — as subject, place, tone. Vertov's most emotional film was set in Soviet Asia, *Three Songs About Lenin*. Pudovkin's most sensuous film, *Storm Over Asia*, was filmed in Mongolia. Dovzhenko went to the Far East, to the site he chose for a city on the Siberian coast, *Aerograd*, where the saboteurs were Japanese samurai. Eisenstein set two unrealized projects in Asia — Tretyakov's scenario for *Zhung-guo*, and Pavlenko's for *Ferghana Canal*.

In 1951, at a time when Dovzhenko considered a return to filmmaking (though he never made another film), he sketched ideas for a film about China. Two plans survive in his notebooks, each a group of five plotless glimpses of Chinese life in varied aspects. An introductory note[22] outlines his intention and, unintentionally, shows us why this film was left unmade, then and later:

The whole film must be blazingly graven by the grandeur of history. But not in a mash of churning thousands as a mass deprived of individuality, but in individualized images, in deeds, ideas, and the highest of intentions. How is a person to be measured? By the height of his aims and deeds, and not by the height of his buildings.

8

Open Door — See Mountain
1952–1957

A hand raised was caught in a net, a foot advanced was taken in an entanglement.

— *Romance of Three Kingdoms*

A theater of masks, as most ancient theaters were, is a theater where instant recognition is essential. The mask enables such a theater to perform its function more precisely than does the too ambiguous human face. The audience at the commedia dell' arte, as well as its repertoire, would have been thrown into confusion if its masks were discarded, and the platform showed only faces like the audience's own. The masks of Peking opera are created with colored paints in traditional patterns that, in the same way, prevent the confusion and ambiguities of reality. The instant a character appears before the audience they know its whole personality and dramatic purpose, and can rest content that there will be no surprising wandering outside this set frame during the course of the play. In Peking opera this instant recognition has its own phrase, "open door — see mountain." Even without the identifying masks and costumes, the several forcible attempts to give Peking opera "modern," revolutionary subjects have been partially successful, for the adaptors have clung to most of the other means of identification — gesture, voice, pose, music — to suit the habits of the Chinese audience: here, still, are the consoling patterns that threaten stimulation only in matters of style and execution.

The first years of world film history saw many adaptations of the theater of masks, via the most popular theater forms of the nineteenth century — the music hall, the variety show, the circus — but as film technique moved closer and more analytically to its subjects the cruder masks were replaced, except among the comedians, with figures that were less predictable and more like life. The evolution of Chaplin's tramp figure shows this development. He won his fame as a mask among other masks; as he gained more economic and artistic independence he gave more subtlety and surprise to his persona, but surrounded it with the old masks (Eric Campbell and Henry Bergman, for example) probably to emphasize the new human complication and interest of the central tramp.

The struggle in filmmaking between formula and the disturbing art of stimulation continued in every country and in every decade; and the salable formula is too often in control. The formula needs the old masks, or "types," as the film industry has classified them. Here is a Hollywood news item of 1923:

In order to obtain a real medical "type," Marshall Neilan photographed fifty noted physicians who were here at a recent convention. A composite picture will be made from the photographs and thus, a representative M.D. type obtained.[1]

It's the "scientific" tone of this silliness that brings to mind other scientific approaches to the business of making and selling films, even in socialist countries.

The audience's demands for the cinema's closer resemblance to reality grew along with the growth of the technique and art that made it possible. Some audiences, however, especially among primitive societies, showed a distaste for any deviation from established patterns. African spectators, for example, were interested only in those films where good and evil, menace and retribution were clearly labeled and unchanged. I do not consider the Chinese audience as primitive, but habit has attached them to those dramas and films that are furthest removed from the surprises and changes of the real. The immutability of a beloved screen figure has been more important in China than elsewhere. If "Small Moustache" (Chaplin's first label in China) had altered his makeup along with his tramp's character, he would have lost his Chinese audience. When a Canton exhibitor showed Mary Pickford in *Suds,* the insulted audience left and smashed the windows of his building — *this* actress did not have the curls of the beautiful Mei-li, and must be a cheap imitator.[2] Apparently, as art and life separate, the autonomous life of art can arouse as much passion as if it were real. A story is told of Mao Tse-tung at the age of fifteen that shows him defending the reality of a novel, *Romance of Three Kingdoms*:

The tale had assumed such importance in [Mao's] life that any doubts cast on its veracity assumed the proportions of accusations against his own personal truthfulness. . . .
"But, Mao, hasn't the Headmaster told you that the *San Kuo Chih Yen I* is only a romantic novel? . . ."
"But it is history, I tell you. History! It's just nonsense for you to say it's not true. Of course it's true!" he shouted.[3]

Once art claims its own kingdom, all that it does within its autonomous sphere becomes justified, bad as well as good. A story has been handed down of the fourteenth-century recluse painter Ni Tsan who, when someone remarked that his paintings of bamboo did not look like bamboo, replied, "Ah, but a total lack of resemblance is even harder to achieve; not everyone can manage it."[4]

After two years of trying to adjust various conditions of the world's cinema to the new China, the decision makers found their guide in tradition, with almost "a total lack of resemblance" to Chinese life, taking as much pride, with less justification than Ni Tsan, in the difficulties of achieving this. For the unchanging masks offered a convenience and conformity that more modern film attitudes, even those developed in China before 1951, did not. Exceptions to this rule continued to appear, fortunately, over the next five years, before the second public attack on filmmakers.

In Korea, the period between the cease-fire arranged for 10 July 1951 and the armistice signed two years later, on 27 July 1953, placed the war ahead of all other subjects in Chinese film studios. The two parts of *Resist American Aggression and Aid Korea* were distributed very thoroughly throughout China in 1952. Hsu Hsiao-ping, the Chinese cameraman on Gerasimov's *Liberated China*, headed a crew of twelve other news cameramen,* and the poet, Ai Ching, wrote the narration.

In December, 1951, . . . the Peking Film Studio of the Ministry of Cultural Affairs released the first part of a documentary film called *Resist-America Aid-Korea*. It was obvious that the Communists were eager to have a huge audience for this film, but they did not go about winning it simply by placing attractive advertisements in newspapers or on colorful posters on streets. Instead, a special committee was formed in every major city to see to it that the film was shown to the largest number of people.[5]

The Canton committee was set the goal of an audience of 450,000, and it issued the following directive:

This film is to be shown in all theaters in the city beginning the 28th of this month. It is expected that all related organizations, immediately after receiving this directive, will start informing the masses of people of their jurisdiction to organize and mobilize group audiences. It is also expected that all organizations will report the size of audiences to be mobilized and other related comments to this office and keep in touch with this office by phone every day so as to guarantee that this task of propaganda and donation will be achieved.

The campaign was not to end with seeing the film. "After seeing the movie, the people were to participate in discussion groups, in order to shake off their 'Respect-America, Worship-America, and Love-America' mentality and to establish their 'Despise-America, Condemn-America and Hate-America' viewpoint." At the same time they were to join other activities, demonstration parades, volunteering for the Korean front, or contributing money to the war effort.

Released at the beginning of 1953, *Oppose Bacteriological Warfare*, a coproduction with Korea, was edited by Tsai Chu-sheng and Shih Tung-shan. Even so pastoral a film as *Bumper Harvest* (1953), whose main and original aim was to persuade a peasant audience to accept the idea of socially cooperative work (and

---

* One of the cameramen, Yang Hsu-chung, was killed during the film's production.

to criticize individualist pride), was obliged from the start of the film to tie the successful harvest to "our volunteers in Korea." One of the farmers' sons is in the army there, and in reel 8 (nearing the film's end) a letter is read from him, "Have a good harvest — help us to defeat the Americans." As part of the finale (in reel 10) a newsreel from Korea is shown, encouraging the most backward and individualist thinkers to reform. *Cutting the Devil's Talons* (1953) is a film overflowing with propaganda purpose (American spies are linked to the Bishop of Shanghai's espionage organization), but there is still room to step up the tension by keeping the audience also aware of the Korean War and the threat of the American enemy sabotaging or bombing Shanghai's industries.

The Chinese troops in the field probably saw films; their prisoners certainly did. By mid-1952 the showings had a certain routine; Frank Noel, in a North Korean prisoner-of-war camp, reported, "A mobile movie projection team usually manages to show Chinese-produced movies every two weeks."[6] The political education of the prisoners was a matter of prime importance, and it would be instructive for us to know more about these showings. Another prisoner cautiously broadcast to his parents, "We have seen movies, although not produced in the States, I enjoyed seeing them."[7] Another wrote to his family in Muncie, Indiana, about the 1953 New Year's celebration: "Last night I went to a movie, it was a musical, something like a [Ziegfeld Follies Revue*], everybody's talking about the movie this morning."[8] The few scraps of information on these showings do not indicate a "hard sell" propaganda function.

Next in importance to Korea, the studios kept the victorious war with Chiang Kai-shek in the foreground, but one now perceives a commendable effort to find fresh means of showing and understanding it. The flat statement of virtue and victory no longer suffices. Now there was more concentration on a single action or person (closer, note, to stage dimensions) to represent the wider areas embraced by earlier films about the civil war. The large-scale, diffuse panoramas of entire campaigns were put aside for several years (there was to be significance in their return); the last of that sort for the time was *From Victory to Victory* (literally, *Conquer South, Victory North*), a Shanghai film of 1952. This deals with the winter campaign of 1947:

In our counter-offensive, after winning all the seven battles we withdrew our troops rapidly in order to wipe out the enemy more effectively in mobile war-

* This is the writer's meaning, regardless of his spelling. The only Chinese film of that time to fit his description is *Great Union of China's Nationalities* (1950), which includes the dancers and singers who performed at the October conference of minority representatives in Peking. Or was this a Soviet "concert-film"?

fare. And the reactionaries, thinking we were retreating in defeat, sent two armies by two different routes to attack us. Thereupon we massed a large force which swiftly surrounded and annihilated [one] enemy army. . . . At the same time we sent one battalion to attack the other Kuomintang army and lure it on, then wiped it out in mobile warfare.[9]

The strategy of planned mobility, while eating away at the enemy's forces, is difficult to dramatize clearly, but the film succeeds in this. While its central battle scenes have neither the factuality of *Westfront 1918* nor the expressiveness of *Chapayev*, it is a tribute that any comparison with such films is possible. The fighting itself is too decorative and deliberately designed, and there is a tendency to increase the odds, making each victory greater, to respond to the scenario's needs and the audience's wishes. The nonfighting scenes, on the other hand, are so credible and lacking in affectation that I believe the better of the two direc-tors (Cheng Yin or Tang Hsiao-tan? probably the latter) must have concentrated on these sequences. Even the enemy is not shown as silly (until the traditional finale of disintegration) and the Kuomintang war conferences are as believable as if supervised by someone who had been present at real ones.

The two war films of 1953 that have survived, politically and artistically, are more concentrated. After *Red Banner on Green Rock* Chang Chun-hsiang wrote and directed *Letter with Feather*, a lively, simple, and well-made children's film — up to its last quarter, when dramatic discipline is shattered altogether by incredibility and "audience appeal" (see Plate 27). Why do the Japanese always have to behave so stupidly for the sake of the Chinese audience? No hint that propaganda could change a Japanese soldier, and class alliances are never men-tioned. The last Chinese film to show individual Japanese soldiers as allies was the 1940 *Light of Asia*.

Capture by Stratagem of Mount Hua, from the Peking Studio, has an excessive neatness of development and style that is built upon characters whose masks rarely melt into a human resemblance. (The film's stratagem will surely become the subject of a "modern Peking opera" some day.) One reviewer claimed that "None of the action in this film was made up,"[10] but its total effect is one of the most artificial that I've experienced in Chinese films. In addition to stylizing its characters, it also uses the device of composing within the screen's center. When there is camera movement, this "centralizing" of the action compels the camera to move *with* the central figure. Visual exhaustion can be sensed very soon. It does *point* everything inescapably, but there is no visual pull into the center, and no mental or dramatic stimulus from the repeated hammering at one area of the screen. The sharp stony peak of Mount Hua (the real place in south

Shensi Province was used), always present, might justify the consistent employment of this device, but my expectations for its development, after *New Heroes and Heroines,* were silenced by *Mount Hua.*

The first of the postwar, civilian, mass construction projects was undertaken in late 1950, and the actuality film of it was completed in 1952. The valley of the Huai River, running east through central China, was devastated in July 1950 by the regular flood that had devastated it every two years for seventy generations. In September a government plan for flood control in that area was made a national cause through Mao Tse-tung's slogan, "Harness the Huai River!" And this became the title of the film that recorded the excavation work by 2,200,000 peasants and the building of a system of dams and hydroelectric stations. Directed by Shih Mei *Harness the Huai River* is too leisurely and rambling for so serious a subject, and there is a strange neglect of the people concerned: actual suffering caused by the 1950 flood is reduced (for politico-emotional reasons) to a mere glimpse, though that suffering presumably provides the impetus for the whole construction; even the reception of the volunteer young workers from other parts of China (a key sequence thematically) is left undeveloped and anonymous.* Cutting and sound are, understandably, rather primitive, but less understandable is the dependence on a lyricism that derives more from the cameramen's wishes than from the film's theme. Yet the film communicates its theme. Nicolas Guillen, the Cuban poet, saw it in 1953 and, praising it as "a splendid documentary . . . a really first-class film," tells about it in images:

. . . there was started against [the Huai River] a hard, personal and implacable fight. The Huai was no longer a geographical accident, but took on the shape, figure, bones and bulk of a living, monstrous creature which had to be tamed, like the marauding tiger which nightly decimates the horses on the farm.[11]

To have been guided by such imagery could have made it a more powerful film. Regardless of reservations, this is a film that shows more of China in 1951 than does any fictional film of that year.

The other major actuality films of 1952 reverted to the military theme, now with the extra color of deserts, jungles, and the remote edges of the Central Kingdom. In October 1950 the ambiguous relation of Tibet and China was tentatively but officially clarified by the army's arrival there, and by 1952 this clarification reached the film audience as *March of the People's Liberation Army into Tibet,* a film that I have not seen. But I have seen so many fictional films

---

* On the other hand, a Soviet engineering advisor (Bukhov?) is shown with a prominence surprising to see today.

whose climax of liberating entry of the People's Liberation Army into Tibet is so pat — *Gold and Silver Sandbank* (1953), *Dawn Over Meng River* (1955),* *Daughter of Tibet* (1957), *By the Kinsha River* (1960), and *Serfs* (1964), the best of them — that it's hard to believe anything resembling this did happen. Earlier in 1952 *Fighters on the Border* showed the role of the People's Liberation Army in the reconstruction of Sinkiang, and the Moslem and Mongolian areas of Northwest China were also to be embroidered fictionally, though without much variety: *People of the Grasslands* (1953; see Plate 32) was a less believable treatment of the Mongolian people's modern history than the 1951 film, *Victorious People of Inner Mongolia; Hassan and Djamileh* (1955) features the same horses and simplified class struggle that were felt necessary for any film about Sinkiang.

Dramas of the exotic southern borders and peoples were apparently always in some stage of production in the studios of Shanghai and Changchun: in 1955 alone the Miao people were allies of the People's Liberation Army against Chiang Kai-shek's bandits in *Caravan* (Shanghai; see Plate 32) and the Yao people were similarly shown in *Mysterious Companions* (Changchun). Both these films were infected by the condescension and masquerade atmosphere that seem unavoidable when Han filmmakers observe any people of the southern border. Later years did not mature this view of the southern minorities — the Chingpo people in *Flames on the Border* (1957, Changchun), the Pai people in *Five Golden Flowers* (1959, Changchun), the Li people of Hainan Island in *Red Clouds* (1959, August First), the last a dance drama that makes the stereotypes more conspicuous. Though these films are made to show and even to promote equality and comradeship between Hans and "the others," the true attitude of the superior Han people creeps into view in a slavish flick of the eyes (I have seen only Han actors play leading Miao and Yao roles), or a carefully childlike gesture, or the obligatory dance where the headdresses and footwear show us which minority (the key word) is furnishing the backdrop this time. In all these superficial films about southern minority peoples I cannot recall one in which the "minority problem" escaped the traditional Han attitudes that Lu Hsun cruelly exposed in 1932, in commenting on *Romance in the Yao Mountains*: "Nowadays one rarely hears big talk about Chinese civilization controlling the whole world. So when we have the urge to enlighten others, we have to resort to Yaos and Miaos."[12] By 1955 the "big talk" had returned, but the condescension to Yaos and Miaos was unchanged.

---

* *Dazhong Dianying* (No. 2, 1956) published extracts from a discussion, after a showing of this film, with Tibetan students at the Central Academy of Nationalities. They were very critical of the (Han) actors who did not know how to wear or to move in Tibetan clothes, and especially of the women actors who could not speak or walk "like our working people."

As the Huai River film appeared in 1952, another reclamation project was being
filmed; though on a much tinier scale, its film possibilities were equally great. In
May 1950 the cleanup began of Peking's most squalid slum area, known as
Dragon-Beard Ditch, and five months later the place had been transformed from
eyesore (or worse) to decent living quarters. Lao Shê, always in search of ways
to express his love of Peking and its people, saw this as ideal material for a play.
The success of *Dragon-Beard Ditch* as a play depended more on Lao Shê's enjoyment of the district's characters and idiom than on dramatic structure, but the
new Peking Studio was eager to film it (with Lao Shê as scenarist) and overlooked such niceties. The contrast between dirty past and clean present was
enough, and it was this contrast that impressed Simone de Beauvoir when she
was shown the film:

[It] presents, I am told, an accurate image of what Peking used to be like. The
main characters [a rickshaw puller's family and neighbors] live in mud kennels
grouped about a court whose door opens onto an alleyway; the latter is almost
entirely taken up by [a gutter]; a narrow ledge on either side overlooks semi-
stagnant water in which household garbage and every variety of carrion rot; it is
bridged every now and then by a plank. When it rains the ditch overflows, muck
invades the courtyard, penetrates into where people are living; the walls crack or
melt, threaten to or do collapse; a week later the inhabitants are still wallowing
in a mire. The little incident that serves as a pretext for the film has happened
more than once: crossing the ditch one stormy day, a little girl slips on a rotten
plank, falls into the stew underneath and drowns.[13]

She describes another scene, "showing one of these racketeers tearing through
the terrified crowd with the arrogance of an Al Capone . . . in a pedicab and his
strong-arm boys escort him on bicycles."[14] Her visit to the place itself verified
its improvement. A more professional foreign eye looking at the film was that of
Vladimir Petrov, in China with a large delegation for a Soviet film festival in
November 1952. The Peking Studio showed him *Dragon-Beard Ditch* just as it
was finished, and he was less satisfied with the simple contrast:

. . . the scenarist was not able to repair the inadequacies of the play. The second
half of the film shows the new, freed life of the Chinese people in a posterish
and schematic way. The first half is too static: the images do not move or grow,
and show no conflict. Nevertheless, the film glows with a mature directorial
craftsmanship (even though this is only Hsiang Tzu's [?] second film), using excellently chosen and harmonious details, well developed characters and interesting
mise-en-scene.[15]

Petrov probably spoke as frankly to the filmmakers at the time, too. He had
himself just completed work on a film based on one of the world's most perfect
plays, Gogol's *Revizor*, and may have been more harsh than was useful under the

circumstances. He was more pleased with the "direct and unusually truthful" acting, particularly praising the always fine Yu Lan, as the elder daughter of the rickshaw puller, and Yu Shih-chih (in his first film performance) as the "madman."

Gate No. 6 is another past-and-present film of 1952, also based on a play.[*] Here the present is wisely reduced to a speedy epilogue of the liberation of Tientsin. The body of the film, circling about the desperate schemes of a Tientsin gang boss, is the most realistic picture of rich life immediately before 1949 that I've seen in a Chinese film. It uses an ingenious method of overlapping action that makes one forget its theater source: an especially good sequence is the festive occasion honoring the birthday of the family patriarch, while in an inner room the hard realities of economics and Kuomintang politics are discussed. The action, a strike of dockers, is touched off by the senseless killing of a docker's child, but even this is given a more real dramatic weight by its concluding shot, one of the best in the film: the gang boss coolly wheeling away from the unpleasantness in his private rickshaw. The whole film is simplified but effective in this manner. The middle-aged boss is an original and understanding (almost sympathetic) characterization, with a stiff, bent figure, by Hsieh Tien, an always responsible actor who later moved into direction. Liu Pan directed *Gate No. 6*, with the Northeast Studio helped by the old Tientsin studio.

A Hsinhua news release of 5 September 1951:

A Monaco imperialist element named Antonius Riberi was deported from China yesterday.

This "element" was Archbishop Riberi, Inter Nuncio at Peking. The government had assembled a formidable case against him:

1. Taking part in the war against the people in league with the American and Chiang Kai-shek circles.

2. Giving cover to the spies of American espionage organizations to carry out subversive activities.

3. Plotting and organizing the illegal, reactionary and secret organization, the "Legion de Marie."

---

[*] "Two young Tientsin writers [Wang and Chia] worked on the wharves during the final stages of the war against the gang bosses. After the victory was won, together with the dockers they wrote a play. . . . The dockers themselves wrote most of the dialogue and the production I saw [in Peking in 1951] was acted almost entirely by dockers with a few of the leading roles played by professionals." — Wilfred G. Burchett, *China's Feet Unbound* (Melbourne: World Unity Publications, 1952), p. 65.

4. Stirring up Chinese Catholics against the people's revolutionary movement
and the People's Government of China. . . .[16]

The need to present this case to the Chinese public in the most dramatic form is
obvious; even in the bare statement of the case one can discern the shape of a
film scenario. Not only did the Shanghai studio go to work immediately on a
film about the Archbishop's link to American spies, but the scenarist Chia Min
and the director Shen Fu succeeded in making the most effective anti-Catholic
film produced in China.

A plot to kill Chairman Mao during the first anniversary celebration (for which
an Italian and Japanese were executed) and the Korean War (during which an
occasional threatening bomb was dropped on Shanghai) combined to make
China extra spy-conscious. "Watch U.S. Spies" became a national slogan; they or
their influence often appeared in films about border regions and minority
nationalities. But *Cutting the Devil's Talons* hits at concealed hostility and
Catholicism where they were thought to be strongest — in Shanghai and Tientsin.
I doubt that the film worried the easygoing people of Shanghai, except the
western-trained intellectuals who are the film's real target. Its neat dramatic
structure made it popular in Shanghai and in Europe's socialist countries (where
the church's power was also a problem).

A westernized engineer is employed on the construction of a vital Shanghai
factory. He recommends a colleague (whom he has never met) then in Hong
Kong, but before this man leaves for Shanghai, he is kidnapped by U.S. authorities, who replace him with one of their Chinese agents. The agent arrives, is
accepted by the gullible engineer, but is watched by internal security forces as he
makes contact with the Archbishop, who heads and shelters the spy ring, trans-
mitting information to the Americans through a secret radio (operated by a
formidable nun). Innocent Chinese Catholics are involved in a conspiracy to
sabotage the factory, but they eventually help the police expose and expel the
church foreigners. In the last few minutes of the film we see the ammunition,
the sexy photos, and precious Chinese objects hidden in the Archbishop's desk
and the repentant engineer, now dressed in proper Chinese uniform, is forgiven
his carelessness.

Shen Fu has made the most of this juicy material. Notwithstanding the unprofes-
sional gaffes of a trained spy, and the long noses that have been added to all
European faces (it took a long time for Chinese filmmakers to trust spectators
not to expect all Europeans to be equipped with long, pointed noses — for
identification's sake), the film holds one's attention. Scenes that would ordinarily adhere to formula are here developed freshly: an interrogation scene

makes you believe in the veracity of both sides of the questioning. Though the conclusion is conventional, some of the dialogue is more subtle than one would expect in such a drama. The makers had seen Hitchcock's films, and his help is certainly detectable in a most original idea (for a Chinese film) — the casting of a charmer for the spy's role. Han Fei, a skillful comedian, is cast counter to type and tradition. It is the main help to the film's suspense, but possibly not to the long-conditioned audience. Later spy films return to the familiar masks.*

A group of directors and technicians went to the Soviet Union in 1950 to study the problems and practice of color film, and their first results were on Chinese screens by 1953. The army sports meet of 1 August 1952 was actually the first Chinese color film to be made (except for the unhappy 16 mm experiment of Mei Lan-fang in 1948), but by the time of its release, on the following Army Day, several others had reached the screen. The first to make a real stir, in and out of China, was the Shanghai Studio's film of a Chekiang opera, *Liang Shan-po and Chu Ying-tai.* At home the film was explained as "a folk story of the struggle of two lovers against feudal oppression in ancient China"[17] while the emphasis abroad was on its delicacy and sentiment. Simone de Beauvoir saw it in France under the title of *Les Amoureux*:

. . . despotic father forbids his daughter to marry the boy she has been in love with for years, he [pledges] her to a stranger; the boy dies of grief and on her wedding day she follows him into the grave.[18]

Over their tomb the two spirits appear as "a pair of beautiful butterflies." The self-conscious sweetness of all this becomes dangerously apparent as performed by an all-girl opera troupe; and as the heroine also adopts a male disguise to study (for three years!) with the "hero" (also in travesty), one can imagine that this had an effect on its Chinese audience similar to that of *Miss Change-Body* of 1936. When the film was first shown in London, *The Observer*'s critic saw it as an introduction to the "mysteriously pure and delicate world of the classical Chinese theatre," but found himself faintly worried, too:

One might think, with a girl playing a girl who impersonates a boy and falls in love with another boy played by a girl, that a disconcerting amount of sexual confusion would result. But a highly formalised art takes this extra refinement in its stride, and finds an innocent piquant humour in it.[19]

I was just as disturbed by the color. It was the Sovcolor process (derived from

---

* The Swedish authors of *Politics and Film* quote the Nazi filmmaker, Fritz Hippler, "In the cinema the audience must know with greater certainty than in the theater whom to love and whom to hate." *Betrachtungen zum Filmschaffen* (1942).

Agfa), but a uniform, one-dimensional pastel range was chosen to enhance the delicate story's charms. This was neither the color of life nor of the Chinese theater. Perhaps it harmonized with this wishy-washy material, but excessive admiration for it as China's first color film,* with too many compliments from Europe, resulted later in these boudoir pastels being applied to quite inappropriate subjects.

The national prestige and finances of the film industry were well settled by 1951–1953. Films were now energetically exported, still an exotic novelty for foreign audiences, especially in socialist countries, and each year new ones were entered in the international competition at Karlovy Vary (western competitions were closed by the diplomatic precedence of Taiwan). In July 1949 the All-China Association of Cinema Workers had been formed in Peking (with an executive committee of forty-one that reads like a list of Shanghai's filmmakers of the thirties), and in 1951 the Cinema School of Peking was expanded into a Cinema College, with much Soviet help: the veteran filmmaker Yuri Zhelyabuzhsky was the chief pedagogue-advisor (he died there in 1955). The political necessity for films was demonstrated by their several functions in the Korean War. The security of filmworkers was established by regulations, though these went by the board in the emotional atmosphere of a political crisis.

At the end of 1952 Ivor Montagu was in China for the World Peace Council and took the opportunity to gather information on working conditions in the Chinese film industry, which he passed on to the British film trades:

There is as yet no national trade union of film workers; preparatory work is in progress at the All-China Federation of Trade Unions for the foundation of a unified trade union of film workers, and it is hoped this may be realised next year. At present the technicians in each studio are organised under their own Trades Council. . . .

The trade union organisation defines its duties as basically twofold:

To educate its members to adopt a new attitude to productivity;
To see to it that the administration acts in conformity with the Trade Union regulations and Social Welfare provisions. . . .

---

* In August 1954, on the occasion of the British Labour Party delegation's visit to China, the Chinese cinema acquired a new function. On their first evening in Peking they were formally shown *Liang Shan-po and Chu Ying-tai*, much as state visitors to Moscow are taken to *Swan Lake* before the official conversations start. This function for Chinese films became standard diplomatic practice, in Chinese embassies abroad as well as in Peking: a film was more portable than *Swan Lake* and required less explanation than any Peking opera. The simplifications and undisturbing prettiness of *Liang Shan-po* made it an ideal display piece for such occasions. It was, indeed, the film that opened several capitalist countries, notably England, to more systematic film imports from China.

The standards of remuneration are set by the Government in consultation with the Unions. There are three grades . . .

Grade One includes Art Directors, Actors, Directors, Scenarists, Musicians.
Grade Two includes Camera, Laboratory Workers, Sound, Editing.
Grade Three includes Administrative Staffs. . . .

"Standard" depends on three factors: "ability and good character," "past experience," "relations with the masses."

Salaries, like all Chinese salaries, are tied to the Cost of Living and vary with an index that is pegged, particularly to the price of rice. . . . With present rice index 115, minimum wages for film technicians amount to 300,000 [Chinese] dollars a month. . . .

The week is 48 hours — 6 days of 8 hours. Overtime is paid double time, but no overtime may be worked without approval of the chairman of the studio trade union organization.

. . . Bonuses are obtainable for finishing on schedule; for rationalisation proposals leading to improved working methods, or for economising in materials. . . . as In other Industries and in villages, there is public discussion and election, within the union, of "model workers," who also receive bonuses.[20]

Four years later another British trade unionist made a similarly detailed report[21] (translating the money into British amounts) that shows little change in conditions:

The average minimum earnings in that country, taking industry as a whole, and including the earnings of the agricultural workers, is about £2 a week. . . . At the studios the bottom wage for artists was £2.10s. a week. The top grade performers get £7 to £8 a week. The technicians start higher and rise higher.

Nor had studio conditions made any great change by 1956. Here is Changchun:

I was told that the average time for making a feature film is from six to eight months, for studio shooting alone. They are aware that this is inordinately long and are trying to cut down on time. "We are making twelve films this year, which will give us an average of six months apiece on the six stages. We are aiming to double this and eventually to step the figure up to thirty films a year — before very long," they told me. . . .

All the cameras are old Mitchells, some of them tied up with bits of string. We went through that ourselves during the war and our films were none the worse for it. Here, too they seem to make-do extremely efficiently. All the gantries are made of wooden scaffolding, with wooden steps and galleries. The dolly rails are of wood too . . . the studio floor was very uneven and the rails had to be laid with pads here and there to get them straight[22]

Another glimpse of the Changchun studio in 1956 comes from Jean Painlevé,
then touring China with a program of his scientific films:

As at Peking and Shanghai, the [Changchun] stages are decrepit and dangerous —
no French technicians would wish to work in such conditions. Only acrobats, as
these Chinese workers really are, could man-handle 2,000 watt lampions, without losing their balance or running very serious risks.[23]

But Painlevé also noted the new studios, then under construction alongside the
outdated Japanese studio.

All the new studios under construction were part of a long-term plan to build
the Chinese film industry with help from European socialist countries, and
chiefly from the Soviet Union:

East Germany is building a factory to manufacture raw film as well as an optic
industry to make cameras and other accessories. . . .

Poland is aiding the Peiping Government to build a large studio to synchronize
Russian and East European movies in Chinese and other regional languages. . . .

Czechoslovakia is aiding the Red Chinese Government build new studios and
modernize the existing four studios. . . . Chinese technicians now are undergoing
training in the Czech movie industry.[24]

Every film school in East Europe had Chinese students; every socialist film
industry contributed to China's film industry.*

I have seen three good films of 1954. *Marriage* was a credit to the youngest
studio, the Peking. A comedy of marriage arrangements repeatedly frustrated by
social duties, it had excellent spirit, without the usual pace of a film comedy,
but its own maintained satisfactorily. Almost the only flaw that would prevent
its appreciation today outside China is an unthinking and unnecessary reliance
on studio "exteriors": the real exteriors are so well used that one regrets the
studio was ever entered during production. The film was based on a short story
by Ma Feng. Liu Ching's novel, *Wall of Bronze*,† was also the base for a film, but
its adaptors wisely chose to use only a part of the novel rather than to condense
the whole, the usual film practice everywhere. As *Granary of the Sa Family* the
first half of the film is fine, but its last half commonplace, similar to the division
within *Letter with Feather.* In its first half Gan Shih-wei showed ingenuity in

---

* By 1958 the Czechs built a new film processing plant in Peking with Czechoslovak
technical help and fitted with Czechoslovak equipment. It was designed to develop and print
60 million meters of film a year.

† An English translation (of a part) appeared in *Chinese Literature*, No. 2, 1954.

finding fresh natural movement and in keeping all surroundings vividly convincing. One can believe that these families and guerrillas (the time is 1947) are
based on real ones; there is a nonsentimental mother and a credible weak character who is *not* a villain. The image of *granary* is carefully developed without
becoming a literary symbol. But then the familiar silly enemy mask pops up, to
be pushed over easily, the guerrillas become fixed, heroic figures, and the film
turns into a moral tale told in wood.

As reseen today the most lasting film of 1954 came from the Shanghai Studio.
Cross River, Establish Base, known abroad as *Reconnaissance across the
Yangtze*, is entirely concerned with the preparations of the People's Liberation
Army to move across the Yangtze in April 1949, in order to advance to Nanking
and Shanghai. The central figures of the film are the small group of scouts who
cross the river unobserved and pass through the Kuomintang's fortifications to
establish contact with the local guerrilla underground on the south shore, from
where they radio information to their base. It is an adventure film, and a good
one, full of suspense. It is the best and most continuously interesting of the
guerrilla films of China, the heir of all that Shanghai studios developed in the
thirties. It dares to dilute the formulas that were already hardening and
dehumanizing the films of the fifties: there is even the hint of a love story, and
the film's lyrical passages are integrated in the dramatic structure rather than
inserted as decorative interludes. The girl (Li Ling-chun) looks charmingly and
solidly real, unlike the usual Shanghai heroines. The commander of the scouts is
played by Sun Tao-lin — the role gave him a following unknown since the
"star" days of Shanghai. In addition to the director, Tang Hsiao-tan (the leading
director of the anti-Japanese films made in Hong Kong during the war), and the
scenarist, Shen Mo-chun, the cameraman, Li Shen-wei, deserves particular praise
for an effectiveness that is always controlled by the action.

By comparison with 1954 the films of 1955 seem more superficial and uniformly warlike. Besides the exotic skirmishes that represent the liberation of
Sinkiang and Yunnan, there was the first of several purely model behavior films
on army heroes who were to be singled out as public examples for all to
follow. *Tung Tsun-jui* told the story of the soldier who held "a package of
dynamite in his hands to blow up the enemy fortifications [a pillbox] so that the
vanguard could advance unimpeded, ensuring the victory of the entire battle [of
Lunghua, in May 1948]." The navy's war was represented in *Naval Cutter in
Stormy Seas*, directed for Changchun by Wang Pin and Tang Hsiao-tan (a step
backward for the latter after the progress of *Reconnaissance*). The fighting past
was shown in *Sung Chin-shih* (or, *Black Banners*), about a complex nineteenth-
century rebel leader cleansed and simplified into the mythical hero of a comic

book (more politely known as "serial picture book"). The authorities were beginning to appreciate the film as a major means of rerouting the already fluid history of China. The last two films introduced to film work the bold presence of the actor Tsui Wei. The films of 1956 that continued the chesty bravado of 1955, which was to grow regrettably over the next ten years, were *The Battle of Sangkumryung Ridge* (known by the enemy soldiers as "Heartbreak Ridge"), the only Chinese fictional film I know to be entirely about an action of the Korean War,* though others were planned or started; and *Guerrillas on the Railroad*, almost uninterrupted derring-do for the benefit of the youngest members of the audience.

The most significant films of 1956 and 1957 took another but short-lived direction, reflecting the preparatory gestures, the short life, and dire consequences of the Hundred Flowers campaign. "Let a hundred flowers bloom, let a hundred schools of thought contend" was one of the slogans gleaned periodically by Mao from his classical studies that produced many of the pithy sayings now taught as Mao's "thought."†

Mao first pronounced the Hundred Flowers slogan and principle in an unpublished address of 2 May 1956. This may account for the number of unusual film ideas that appeared this year, two of the most imaginative Peking opera

---

* This ridge was defended only by Chinese; a degree of Korean partnership may have discouraged the other projects. A translated excerpt of a short novel by Lu Chu-kao, *The Battle of Sangkumryung* (published in 1953), appeared in *Chinese Literature*, No. 9, 1960: the novel may have served as one source for the film.
† The "hundred flowers" phrase derives from a poem of the Warring Kingdoms period; the "paper tiger" comes from *Water Margin* and related opera.

films, for example (*Fifteen Strings of Cash* and *Sung Shih-chieh*), and the first
(and last) openly satirical film in Communist Chinese film history. In September
1956 the Communist Party of China held its Eighth National Congress (it was
eleven years since the Seventh, in 1945) and what was said on this occasion
often sounded like an implementation of the new liberalizing principle. In
"Proposals for the Second Five-Year Plan for Development of the National
Economy, 1958–1962" (supposedly written by Chou En-lai) there was clear
encouragement: •

We should carry through the Party's policy of uniting with, educating and
remolding the intellectuals and the principle of "letting diverse schools of
thought contend," and encourage them to cultivate independent thinking and
engage in free discussion. We should make more suitable use of the services of
intellectuals, and pay attention to improving their working conditions and give
full play to their enthusiasm and creative ability so as to meet the needs of
development of scientific research and economic and cultural development.[25]

And Teng Hsiao-ping was critical of present apparatus, party bureaucrats,
"commandism," etc.

. . . our Party abhors the deification of the individual . . . it has been against
exaggerating the role of leaders in works of art and literature.[26]

But throughout 1956 came a series of shocks to the world communist movement
that made Chinese party leaders, and especially Mao, doubt a policy that might
grant a too risky degree of freedom — of speech and action. In February
Khrushchov denounced Stalin and the cult of personality. The attack was hard
to follow in China, but Teng Hsiao-ping's remark about deification shows a wish
to adapt to this new attitude, a wish that had fatal results for himself ten years
later. Those who argued *against* the new liberalism were supported by the disturbing news from Budapest and Warsaw later in 1956, where open revolts
against local authorities and Soviet support of these authorities had bloody
results. Then the joint attack on Egypt showed the Chinese that the powers
(diminished but still aggressive) of imperialism could not yet be written off by
the world communist movement. Twentieth Congress, Petofi Society, Warsaw,
Suez — the accumulation must have staggered the leaders in Peking, but on the
surface Chinese declarations continued their benevolent tone, with Mao's speech
of 27 February 1957, "On the Correct Handling of Contradictions among the
People,"* and a general invitation to all in April and May to criticize and correct

---

* This speech was not, however, published until June, when the benevolent period had
passed.

party methods and party mistakes. At this distance, and in the light of sub-sequent events, this whole year's program has the snap of a trap. Or was there a sudden fright or an abrupt change of policy that had the effect of a sprung trap?

The amount of criticism that was thrown at the Communist Party of China went beyond anyone's imagination, in violence, degree, and affected circles. In May 1957 big-character posters attacking party policy appeared in the corridors and compound walls of colleges and universities, but by June the terrible "rectifica-tion" or antirightist movement was under way and "independent thinking" was shunned as a sin. No one was spared the tests or the punishments. The formal education of every student who had taken part in the criticism was stopped, and rectification was conducted in distant villages where the student had no further communication with home or studies. Criticism plus a past misdemeanor justi-fied arrest. Not only criticism but any compassion shown to a critic or "rightist" was enough to cost you your job in any school or organization. Under pain of being denounced yourself *you* had to be quick to denounce.

The drama producer and film director Wu Tsu-kuang was a 'rightist', and his wife stood up at an 'anti-rightist' meeting and denounced her own husband, and actually separated from him, but rang him up later to say that her personal feelings for him remained the same. The telephone conversation was overheard and exposed by her servant at the next meeting, and she was convicted of 'pro-rightist' sympathies and political hypocrisy.[27]

Another Chinese drama that may never be seen on a Chinese screen.

One relatively small cultural area that gained a respite from the Hundred Flowers campaign was Peking opera, and other Chinese opera forms, happily postponing for ten years the demise of classical opera on the Chinese mainland. The first shots in the long battle against the "feudal" opera came after the 1942 Yenan Talks of Mao Tse-tung: the Chinese were to return to the people for their theater, but not necessarily to what the people enjoy. Even before the liberation of Peking and Shanghai a program to alter the nature and repertoire of Peking opera was announced in an anonymous article sent from the Liberated Area: "Old Dramas To Be Reformed," published in *China Digest*, 28 December 1948. By 1951, when Wilfred Burchett reported from Peking, the reform had begun, vigorously:

A highly skilled panel of writers and dramatists is entrusted with this delicate piece of theatrical surgery. Often with a few deft strokes of their scalpels, they can change the entire ideology of an opera.[28]

The two great veterans of Peking opera, Mei Lan-fang and Chou Hsin-fang, made personal appeals to those leaders (including Mao and Chou En-lai) who admired classical opera to protect it from the cleansers. Hundred Flowers brought an official reprieve, and Chinese and foreign readers were now treated to sarcastic comments on the "lack of understanding in applying the policy of theater reform." Noting the significance of "dwindling box-office receipts," one writer explained:

Drama workers, critics, and the cultural committees of local [!] governments all had the praiseworthy idea that the theatre must be a place of education for the people. But their standard of what was educational was often too narrow. Many tended to measure plays solely by political standards, ignoring both historical context and aesthetic considerations, and sometimes substituting personal likes and dislikes for objective critical judgment.

Present-day social morality, for instance, was used as a yardstick for changing or shelving historical plots or characters. Plays that showed a man with two wives (a common thing for centuries) were condemned as "not in accordance with the new Marriage Law." Some even suggested that tragedy should not be played "because it does not reflect the people's optimistic spirit." . . . An extreme of absurdity was reached in one case where local authorities decided that the fine old *Fisherman's Revenge* should not be played during the collection of rural taxes. They thought that to see the ancient fisherman's revolt against unjust taxes was not conducive to the "right spirit" needed at that particular moment.[29]

Gestures were made to the two actors who helped to save their art. The long-delayed filming of *The Stage Art of Mei Lan-fang* was pushed through in spite of the displeased film administration, and Chou Hsin-fang's favorite role, in *Sung Shih-chieh* (or, *The Four Scholars*), was filmed faithfully. Though a valuable record of Chou's intensity and command, the latter film suffered from the prettiness that Sang Hu, director of *Liang Shan-po*, applied to all his opera films, but Mei Lan-fang took Chaplin's advice[*] to simplify the filming of opera, with good results. If the film is preserved, it will keep alive the memory of Peking opera as well as of Mei, through the five scenes from the best-known plays of Mei's long career.

Yet another step was taken, important to Chinese cinema as well as to theater. The high and popular point in a festival of traditional opera held at Peking (an early demonstration of Hundred Flowers policy) was a new production of *Fifteen Strings of Cash*, a Kunchu opera staged by the Soochow company.[†] It

---

* "Comrade Hsia Yen mentioned that Chaplin had seen *Liang Shan-po and Chu Ying-tai* and had criticized the Chinese paintings used as settings for being distracting to the audience." — Mei Lan-fang, *The Filming of a Tradition*, translated in *Eastern Horizon*, August 1965.
† "The recent performance of the Kunchu opera *Fifteen Strings of Cash* shows how wrong it was to say there was nothing good in Kunchu opera." — Lu Ting-yi's speech of 26 May 1956.

combines the righting of a wrong (using the familiar conventions) with the detection of a criminal (in a more modern, naturalistic style); the money of the title provides the motive for the murder and the evidence against the innocent. The Shanghai Studio immediately made a color film of the Soochow performance that welds its two styles together beautifully. Tao Chin (the clever actor of *Spring River Flows East*) was the director responsible for this best of all Chinese opera films. He too put aside the charms of *Liang Shan-po*, employing instead a darker, harsher palette for this macabre comedy: no shining surfaces and plenty of shadow. He gave a frank interview, early in 1957, as the film was finished:

Some say that opera films should be as stylized as possible. But what is stylization? In the theater it usually means no more than the application of exaggeration or an extra emphasis on a vivid romantic imagination. In directing *Fifteen Strings of Cash* I wanted its means to be more realistic. I thought this would bring its 300-year-old story closer to the film audience. I consider that its background and characters demand a realistic method. And we tried to give its designs a maximum simplicity.

In spite of our hard discussions I enjoyed working with the cameraman Huang Shao-fen — and we finally resolved all disagreements. We experimented with light and used stronger colors than usual.[30]

His most remarkable achievement was little followed, however: this was to draw ideas for camera viewpoints and *cutting* from the old opera conventions. To base the film rhythms of a sequence entirely on its music was an important innovation for China, and the film is full of striking moments that could only be accomplished with film — based on an imaginative study of opera traditions. I hope that Tao Chin's step will one day be followed by another.[*]

The Hundred Flowers granted a shorter and more ignominious life to satire. The authorities seem to sense that, no matter what its apparent target, satire dissolves the illusions and false fronts which all authority needs to maintain itself. If a variety of theme or treatment is ever sought in Chinese films, satire will be the least welcome. Nor is satire healthy for the satirist. Even as applied to negative characters or "poisonous weeds" it is a two-edged weapon that can easily cut the writer who uses it. It is only the merest seasoning of this dangerous humor that can be found in Chinese films before 1956 and after 1957.

The manners of bourgeoisie and gentry are too reprehensible to deserve comic attention. . . . There are, of course, a few still permissible subjects for comedy —

---

[*] Tao Chin did not take this next step. His next film, a modern comedy, *Diary of a Nurse*, was withdrawn after many objections (see reviews in *Zhungguo Dianying*, March 1958).

the old-style peasant fearful of change but basically good enough to merit improvement [as in *Bumper Harvest*] , or the haughty or fumbling cadre who has
not committed serious errors. . . .[31]

C. T. Hsia is here speaking of the taboos on satire in modern Chinese literature.
He goes on to give an example that shows how much more vulnerable to censorship the film is.

Even in a short story there should be no faintest suspicion of satire against the
positive characters. Thus Hsiao Yeh-mu was severely censured for "Between Us
Husband and Wife" and his other fiction — *after the film based upon the story
had attracted party attention* in 1952 [my italics] — on the ground of his
supposed bourgeois levity. The story tells of a city intellectual and his peasant
wife. . . . Upon their transfer [in 1949, from northwest Communist areas] to
Peking . . . they begin to experience an estranged relationship. The wife's rustic
manners and her eagerness to find fault with the wicked ways of the capital
shock her husband, and she, in turn, resents his easy resumption of city manners.
The wife's excessive zeal finally brings upon her head the displeasure of party
superiors, who ask her to exercise self-criticism. Later, as she confesses her error
to her husband, he re-experiences the emotions of love and discerns more clearly
her good qualities behind her boorishness . . . the party critics were taken aback
by the story's disclosure of conflict and tension between a Communist couple
and by its supposed malicious caricature of the [peasant] wife.

It is hard to imagine the filming of such conflicts in 1952, but it is clear that
even a hint of them in a film would draw more attention than on the printed
page. Some effort is involved in buying and reading a novel or story, but the
minimum effort and expense of seeing a film multiplies its Chinese audience by
many millions. It is this enormous (and inflammable) audience that draws the
extra and minute attention of all film censors, professional and self-appointed.

Before the New Director Arrives began as a one-act play, and the film runs less
than an hour — large trouble in a small package. Before the trouble, the film was
actually offered for sale abroad;* this is the synopsis published for foreign consumption:

Section Chief Niu, who heads the general affairs section of a certain bureau, is an
irresponsible bluffer. On learning that a new director will soon be arriving to take
charge, he mobilises all the men in his section for the "top priority" task of
making a big splash to welcome him. He squanders a big sum of money on furnishing a new office, buying a sofa, a spring bed and all sorts of luxuries for the
new director. But he pays no attention to the fact that a lot of cement has been

---

* This is one of a growing number of Chinese films that are easier to find abroad than to see
in China.

left lying in the open, exposed to the rain; or that the roof of the [dormitory] where the workers and office staff are living is leaking.

The new director, arriving sooner than expected, is mistaken for a contractor of the same name, Chang, and thus finds out what is going on. Section Chief Niu starts boasting to him that he and the new director were comrades-in-arms in the guerrilla fighting in the old days. He discovers his mistake too late to save himself. His conduct utterly exposed, Niu is sacked from his job.[32]

Despite the commercial acceptance of his film, and the encouragement of the Hundred Flowers in 1956, the film's director, Liu Pan, had qualms about going "too far," according to this interview with him:

Press notices and audiences alike applauded the long-overdue arrival, on our screen, of a satirical film. . . . The director of the film himself confessed that he had pulled his punches in the production. "The satire had been more penetrating on the stage," he said, but he had been afraid of over-stepping what some might think were the bounds "between satire and slander" at the undesirable aspects of life.[33]

Liu Pan was right to worry about what he had done. The unaccustomed deluge of satirical portraits in his film — bureaucrats, toadies, time-wasters, amateur art authorities (discussing the painted ornamentation for the new director's walls), big planners, and (perhaps worst of all) the large number of underlings habitually saying Yes to anything the boss wants — was too much for those people in the film and culture administrations who had sat for these portraits. In spite of Liu Pan's softening touches, everything was spelled out, unmistakably: the rift between people at the top and the people who do the work; the cultivation of words as a substitute for work. This is as cruel a picture of bureaucracy as Eisenstein's in *Old and New*, and the efforts to balance it with "positive" elements — modest good-hearted new director, conscientious young people, and a moral epilogue spoken directly to the audience (as at the end of the similarly dangerous satire, *Don Giovanni*) — do not remove the deeply embedded sting. Liu Pan executed the whole with a sharp style; some of the ideas have the tone of vaudeville — but how refreshing!

Liu Pan's next subject was even more risky. *The Man Careless of Details* was an absent-minded famous writer of satirical short stories (Zoshchenko?) whose encounters with the authorities (Zhdanov?) show them as blind and stupid, if not worse. Liu Pan's last film — a later attack said "fortunately not shown" — was called *Unfinished Comedy*, and for the authorities and the antirightist movement at the Changchun Studio it made an ideal weapon. It ended Liu Pan's film-making career (no one seems to know how he has earned his rice since 1957) and always heads the list of 1957's "weeds," as in this report by Hsia Yen:

In 1957 some of the films we produced were "poisonous weeds" or embodied ideological mistakes, such as *Unfinished Comedy, Who Is the Forsaken One?, Steps of Youth** and so forth [!]. As a matter of fact, most of these scenarios were written at the same time as "Gongs and Drums in the Film Industry" [an anonymously published attack by Chung Tien-fei] and filmed in the last quarter of 1956 and the first half of 1957. In 1957 we carried out a strong antirightist campaign. . . .[34]

The antirightist meetings in each studio were fully reported by *Dazhong Dianying* (Masses' Cinema); they concentrated on one scapegoat, linking him or her to the already condemned "rightist leaders," and combing through the nominated victim's past films and utterances. In the Changchun Studio the target was Liu Pan, and the article on his crimes and evil ideas was called "Liu Pan's 'Comedy.' "[35] Illustrated with a caricature labeled "Poison Spread by the Liu Company," it analyzed only his last three films — no reference to his

"呂記" 毒片   米 谷

---

* *Who Is the Forsaken One?* used the familiar story of peasant going to city, while the wife he leaves behind makes a *greater* contribution to society. I don't know the subject of *Steps of Youth.*

previous noncomedies: it was his "mask of humor and his appeal to the superficial laughter of the audience" that concealed his true antiparty and antisocialist ideology. Evidence was thoroughly collected: At some point he had said
"Let them laugh — it's good for their health" (and he "had dared to say we
have no comedies"), and even his start in the theater as a comic actor was used
against him.

After the introduction of the Hundred Flowers policy Liu Pan, in common with
other rightists, felt that now was his opportunity to start his personal attack on
the leaders of culture and literature. This was the chief task of his *Unfinished
Comedy*. . . . We now know that the script [of *Man Careless of Details*] was
originally written by Chung Tien-fei, who advised Liu Pan that in order to make
satirical films he must begin with everyday situations, and by no means to touch
the social system. Liu Pan followed this advice, but then felt confident enough
to go beyond everyday situations in *Unfinished Comedy*.

All that I know of *Unfinished Comedy* comes from this attack on it, but if its
use in the case against Liu Pan can be removed from the facts, the comedy
appears to have been made in three sections, the first about wasteful methods in
a factory, the next a factory social attended by rowdy teenagers, and the last
about cadres and workers who hide their cruelty to their mothers (!) under
positive political slogans. Each section was commented upon by an "authorized
critic" whose name was a homonym for "wooden club," and who ended the
film with a piece of wood falling on him from above.

We need satiric comedies, *but* . . . Liu Pan looks on our new society as if it were
exactly the same as the old society before Liberation. . . . He has rejected the
idea of using typical characters of our society and uses instead common behavior
"that could be enjoyed by all." [His characterization of the head of the writers'
union and his comic scene of the regular morning exercises of the union's staff
were examples of this love for "foolish slapstick."]

He even proposed that his third comedy be shown publicly, "and that we should
listen to the audience's opinion." This shows his arrogance and self-confidence,
because he was sure the audience would laugh.

This was also the doom of the Chinese satirical film. Seven years later another
was attempted, and it, too, got into trouble.

In other countries a play or novel or story continues its public life long after its
film adaptation has been condemned, preached against, or shelved,[*] but in China

---

* Every country can provide examples of this, from Maugham's "Sadie Thompson" (and the
play *Rain*) to Erik Neutsch's *Spur der Steine*, which is still available as a novel in the German
Democratic Republic after the film (which followed the novel closely) was condemned and
shelved. But neither Maugham nor Neutsch was punished for his association with films.

official adverse criticism affects, retroactively, everyone and everything attached
to the quarantined film. An attack on a director or a filmwriter results in the
withdrawal of *all* films and books signed by the offenders, from circulation and
from history. No way now of knowing *what* films the "rightist" Wu Tsu-kuang
made. Not only is there no record of Sun Yu working again after the mistakes of
Wu Hsün, but the references to his once-admired work before 1949 are all now
darkened in Cheng Chi-hua's history by his post-1949 misdeed. Other pre-1949
writers and directors have been "disciplined" with altered credits: Shih
Tung-shan, the director responsible for the quality of *New Heroes and Heroines*,
was replaced among its credits* (*after* the film was finished) by Liu Pan. Liu
Pan's turn came soon. And most of Liu Pan's actors disappeared with him. Fat
and jolly Tien Ji-ling, "China's Oliver Hardy," whom he had brought back from
disgrace to work, vanished for another seven years.

One of the hopeful signs that "Hundred Flowers" might have some meaning for
the future was the appearance in 1956 of an ambitious new monthly, *Zhungguo
Dianying* (Chinese Cinema). Until it appeared the leading film journal was the
popularizing biweekly, *Dazhong Dianying*, and there was a need for a more
professional film magazine. In a rich first 96-page number of *Zhungguo
Dianying*, published on 28 October 1956, were Hsia Yen's scenario for *New Year
Offering* (with an article on Lu Hsun's interest in films), Chang Chun-hsiang's
recent speech at the Shanghai Filmmakers' Club on "Specifics of Film Expression," the first installment (1899–1921) of Cheng Chi-hua's history, reports,
reviews, criticisms; most of the contents were useful and interesting. There were
even some delicate subjects touched, an essay by Yuan Wen-chu on "Harmful
Regulations in Film Creation," others on "Let's Develop the Spirit of Individual
Creativity," "Why the Scenarist Has a Feeling of Inferiority," and an article on
the two wrong extremes, "All Winds from One Source or Striving for Originality." The most openly critical piece was a quotation from the *Liaoling Daily*
of 4 August 1956. It is signed "Ni" (You):

At the first showing here of *Inextinguishable Flame* the two sitting next to me
began to chatter. I felt annoyed and then I listened more carefully.

on screen (without words):
Yu-mei, newly arrived wife of the guerrilla fighter Chang San, enters the cave
where he lives and looks about emotionally at its simple furnishing. She sees the
sack where food is kept and puts her hand in it. . . .

---

* Someone had revived the matter of Shih Tung-shan's disobedience in 1948 over the
making of *Sorrow after Honeymoon*, and he was put through the self-criticism wringer after
his return from Karlovy Vary in 1951. He did no more film work (except to help edit
Oppose Bacteriological Warfare in 1952) before his death in 1955. (Extracts from his notebooks were published in *Zhungguo Dianying*, No. 2, 1959.) It was fifteen years before *all*
pre-1949 directors became suspect.

Neighbor A:
Now she'll pull out an old bun!

on screen:
Yu-mei brings out an old, blackened object, puts it back, and her eyes continue to look around the cave.

Neighbor A:
Now she'll talk about poor living conditions.

on screen:
spider webs in the corner, dirty straw on floor and bed, a threadbare cover over the bed — the eyes of Yu-mei look down.

Neighbor A:
Now she'll see the brick-pillow.

on screen:
the eyes of Yu-mei fall on two bricks under the bed-straw.

Neighbor A:
Now she'll start to cry!

Neighbor B:
Yes, she'll cry, but absolutely silently. . . .

on screen:
a big close-up of her face, eyes full of tears — she finds it hard to control herself and clenches her lips.

Neighbor B:
That's the expression of a strong woman!

Neighbor A:
Watch — Chang San should come home soon.

on screen:
he enters the cave.

Neighbor B:
Now she can cry, and there'll have to be a political lecture, too.

on screen:
Yu-mei collapses on him, sobbing, while Chang San strokes her hair.

Neighbor A:
Oh, my Yu-mei-ah!

on screen:
(echoing) Oh, my Yu-mei-ah! . . .

You can see why my annoyance changed to attention, But should I praise the exactness of their predictions, or should I admire the simple directness of the film?

Quotations from ancient critics of literature occurred to me: "One should try to say only what cannot be easily expressed" — "There at the end of all mountains, at the end of all ocean, there seemed no way out — and suddenly: another beautiful village, with shady trees and lovely blossoms." The reader expects the imagination of the author to be more rich and more clever than his own, but if every reader can predict the next page, shouldn't the author be embarrassed? . . .

The film audience understands all, but the director and actors understood nothing. This is a true indication of the illness of our time.

———————————

No one who sees on the screen a coproduction with China, no one who has not participated in the struggles to achieve a coproduction with China, can guess the height of the visible wall or the depth of the invisible, usually unmentioned problems involved in such an enterprise. Some hopeful producers leave Peking without meeting any representative of the Film Bureau and without ever knowing why their proposal was not discussed: this happened to Raoul Lévy who expected to film *Marco Polo* against genuine Chinese backgrounds. No one told him that Marco Polo is something less than a hero of modern China.

In 1957 Carlo Lizzani, an aware and responsible artist, came to China to make a large-scale and friendly actuality film that was finally released as *Behind the Chinese Wall*. His journal (extracts from which were published five years later[36]) is a valuable document, not for the benefit of future coproduction schemes and struggles, but because it tries to analyze the nonmeeting of minds, even on a filmmaking level. Soon after the arrival of the Italian crew the Chinese advisors expended their efforts not on suggestions but on objections. They were against showing any bound feet (which stopped the use of a hidden camera on the streets, which the advisors didn't consider such a good idea, anyway). They were against the inclusion of Lu Hsun's bitter little story, "Medicine." Chenghis Khan was not to be mentioned in any way. And similarities that Lizzani had noticed between Chinese cooking and their pharmacopoeia were not to be referred to. In his entry for 15 March 1957:

What are we dealing with? the personal opinion of the men we're working with directly? some larger group? or — this is what we think it is — the official attitude of the authorities? . . . But actually we already understood pretty clearly that many Chinese are Chinese first and Marxists second and that they prefer, if possible, not to expose any serious or shameful defects to the critical Western eye, even if they existed in the past or were typical of feudalism. In other words, they do not want to be criticized as *Chinese*.

I think this is the lack of a sense of history, a strange feeling of being jointly responsible with the past, tied to the Middle Ages by a double bond. Too, it is a way of feeling separated from the West, for their centuries-old guilt also means that we are excluded, lets us know that not just today, or yesterday, but *always* we have belonged and still belong to another family, and cannot be allowed to criticize.

A few days later:

We're still on the questions of bound feet and Lu Hsun. The distinction they make between cinema and literature is interesting. China's greatest friends (Western) have written terrible things about China's past, but the Chinese still consider them friends. . . . Besides, I don't think the Chinese react as violently to something written as they do to seeing it on the screen.

In a later crisis (23 September 1957) Lizzani tried to force an issue (of a bath!) into the open. He failed but he recorded the failure:

I know I'm overstepping the line, but because I'm more a friend of the Chinese than of Bonzi [the producer] I think it's better to get right to the bottom of things. . . . My duty is to look the Chinese reality in the eye, pave the way for those who'll follow me and make other films in China. And also to give the Chinese, without formalism or hypocrisy, the documentation, the concrete proofs of the inevitable difficulties involved in a work undertaken in collaboration with Westerners. . . . And then, on their side, how much is it a question of principle — moral principles or even hypocrisies, but nevertheless manifestations of customs that should be respected — and how much is it just bureaucracy?

9

Leap
1957—1958

Apart from their other characteristics, China's six hundred million people are, first of all, poor, and secondly, "blank." That may seem like a bad thing, but it is really a good thing. Poor people want change, want to do things, want revolution. A clean sheet of paper has no blotches and so the newest and most beautiful words can be written on it, the newest and most beautiful pictures can be painted on it.

— Mao Tse-tung

多, 快, 好, 省
Greater, faster, better, more economical . . .

— slogan for 1958

The Chinese cinema enjoyed a year of comparative relaxation before the Hundred Flowers campaign was halted and then reversed in June 1957. In that year with two significant films and a new director, we were again granted a glimpse of the potential abilities of Chinese filmmakers.

Within that year, too, the voices that demanded tighter harnessing and more control of arts and artists were by no means silenced. Chou Yang attacked film critics who had momentarily imagined that their duties had been altered by the Hundred Flowers. At the beginning of 1957 an anonymous article, "Discussions on the Cinema," had pointed to decreased cinema attendance as a symptom of something wrong, and Chou Yang was furious:

. . . there is no doubt that the article "Discussions on the Cinema" is an expression of rightist opportunism. The commentator who wrote this article in *Wen Yi Pao* is the same who, under the pen name Chu Chu-chu, wrote "For Progress," the article in *Wen Wei Pao* of January 4. This comrade* has kept in pretty close touch with the film industry and it would have been a great help if he had stuck to sound reasoning. . . . As it is, his criticism is a sweeping negation, a complete denial of all achievement in the Chinese cinema since the liberation.

According to him, our film art has nothing good to offer, starting from methods of production and ending with the content of our films. It seems that the more we stress the principle of serving the working people, the smaller the audience we get; the stronger the leadership we give, the more chaotic our work . . . although we naturally want our films to be popular we aren't engaged in an unprincipled chase after box-office takings. We always attach more attention to the educational value of films.

By emphasizing the "take" and defending the old "traditions" of Chinese films (which should, there is no question, be respected), our author simply erases, at a stroke, the principle of serving the working people. If this erroneous view goes

---

* Chung Tien-fei, who had recently been responsible for film affairs in the Ministry of Propaganda attached to the Central Committee of the Chinese Communist Party.

unchecked, there is the danger that our cinema will be led back to the road of capitalism.[1]

In other words, there was no critical service that could be rendered constructively by a film critic: the film had *no* obligations beyond those pronounced by the Propaganda Office, nor was the critic to recognize standards other than those needed to convey these obligations to the public. Another symptomatic casualty of this period was the first detailed history of Chinese films. It was prepared and translated into English in 1957 for the Foreign Languages Press, but the nerves of the period preferred not to present *any* opinion on the traditions "respected" by Chou Yang, and its publication was canceled.

I have mentioned only those films of 1956 and 1957 that took advantage of the Hundred Flowers atmosphere to try to advance Chinese cinema. There were, of course, others that marked time, carefully confining themselves to the accepted (and acceptable) norm. Some of these are interesting works in their own light, no matter how dimly this may shine today.

After the Hundred Flowers policy had vanished, leaving behind only its shell of slogan, Yang Yu, a writer for *People's China*, introduced an article on "New Films" thus:

One of the effects of the policy of "letting a hundred flowers blossom, letting a hundred schools of thought contend" which the Communist Party announced in 1956 has been a further enlivening of activities in the Chinese cinematographic world. The crop of films in 1956 and this year has been gratifying.[2]

As if to point to the gap between slogan and truth, the two bravest films of 1956 were not mentioned in the article: by September 1957, when the article was published, the *New Director* had been withdrawn from circulation, and *Fifteen Strings of Cash* had to wait two years after its production before being removed from the "poisonous weed" category (it was not released until 1958).

Two historical films were praised in the article, though it is only the process of research that is emphasized for *Sung Chin-shih.* * *Li Shih-chen*, about the sixteenth-century pharmacologist (played by Chao Tan), is a film I have not seen:

---

* "In 1951 a group of writers, visiting the province of Shantung, picked up enough during their conversations with local people to convince them that there was a wealth of oral tradition about the hitherto little known activities of the nineteenth-century peasant general. . . . The next year ten writers returned to the province, visited 163 villages and talked to 719 of the oldest inhabitants . . . quantities of material were collected and from them two playwrights, Chen Pai-chen and Chia Chi, spent two years distilling a scenario. It was not until the spring of this year [1957] that *Sung Chin-shih* was finally finished. . . ."

Once returning with a friend and pupil after a mountain expedition where speci-
mens of medical plants were collected, Li was attacked by a band of alchemists
and his friend lost his life trying to save his notebooks. But Li Shih-chen pushed
his field work to completion, then spent the rest of his life writing his *magnum
opus* [*Pen Tsao Kang Mu*] which remained for many years in manuscript form
for lack of a publisher.[3]

But nothing more critical than Chao Tan's "happy combination of skilful acting
and use of his rich voice" helps us to judge the film. In the autumn of 1957
neither critics nor journals courted danger by referring to the *quality* of a film.

The article then notes the films of 1956 and 1957 that touch our century. The
best of those mentioned is *Mother*, a free adaptation of Gorky's novel (and the
films of Pudovkin and Donskoy), transferred to China before 1949. Ling Tze-
feng had, in this film, a more complex subject than in his *Daughters of China*,
but the solid, emotional performance of Chang Jui-fang as the mother helped
him to hold the film together. The article gives a less vivid description of the film
than does the comment of Ugo Casiraghi, which I quote here:

The opening, for example, has a rare strength. The exterior setting was entirely
constructed in the studio, but this is one of the few occasions in which this has
been achieved with some poetical vision. . . . Through a land laid bare by storm
and wind, under a sky heavy with shadow, the mother walks with her husband
and two sons. By a leafless shrub an abandoned little girl is crying. The group
gazes at her and then moves on — but the mother is unable to forget the helpless
child: she turns back to take the girl-child with them.[4]

The power of this opening slackens as the film encounters more familiar dramatic situations, and in no case does the film show any "enlivening" of Chinese
cinema. Even less enlivening is the effect of *For Peace*, about the tribulations of
a Shanghai history professor and his family, under the heels of the Japanese, the
Americans, and the Kuomintang, all of whom give more interesting film performances than do the hero and his wife, played dully by the most experienced
Shanghai actors, Chao Tan and Pai Yang. The actors' publicized study of life at
Futan University did not help their performance. Casiraghi explains their failure:

The film is rigid, without nuances, and the director seems to consider his characters as rigidly structured and formed from the beginning instead of using the
film to reveal the development of their ideas and maturing of character.[5]

Pai Yang has the impossible task of delivering *three* heroic addresses to us, and
Chao Tan has *two* death scenes, the second, in the hospital, giving him time for
parting words of advice (also to us) to follow the Party's leadership.*

---

* "Films of previous years about intellectuals were few and far between, and not very
successful. *For Peace* is a change for the better." — Yang Yu, "New Films," *People's China,*
September 1957.

Basketball Player No. 5, a colour film, is about the problems of a woman athlete
who thinks she, not the whole team, is the decisive factor in winning a game.
Thanks to her coach . . . the wayward girl begins to understand the new meaning
of athletics in New China.[6] [See Plate 37.]

Aside from its praise of teamwork,* the film is distinguished by a sense of ease
unusual in Chinese films about teenagers or sportsmen. The two older actors, Liu
Chiung and Chin Yi, do their simple tasks well.

Girl from Shanghai has a similar leisurely pace and teenage group, in this case
working on a Hankow construction project (the subject resembles *Spring on
Zarechnaya Street*, a Soviet film of 1956), but there is a persistent atmosphere
of waste about it: it is in color, though there is no need for color; film time is
squandered as if the audience had no place else to go. Its greatest interest for me
is as a behavior document: I have never seen such involved scenario devices to
prevent the hero and heroine from touching each other. You may wonder how
so much ingenuity could be spent on so small (and unnatural) a lesson, until you
note that the film appeared near the end of one of the sporadic birth-control
campaigns.†

The last modern film mentioned by Yang Yu is *Loyal Partners*, described only as
"the story of how two scientists, after hard research, invent a new medicine." As
the article was being prepared for *People's China*, suspicions of this film reduced
the space planned for it. By March 1958, when the following appeared in *China
Reconstructs*, the film was no longer shown (though copies had already been
sent abroad):

Loyal Partners, the story of two friends who work in a research institute on
antibiotics, came under fire. . . . The more conservative of the two friends is dissatisfied with his position and wants to resign. But he changes his mind — throwing himself wholeheartedly into a new scientific quest — when his friend's life is
in danger due to an unknown disease contracted in his work. Innumerable
letters, written by spectators to newspapers and film magazines, criticized that
script for endorsing personal friendship as a stronger motive than the duty of a
scientist to serve the public interest.[7]

The film (directed by Hsu Chang-lin) is a poor one, on any count - another
product of factory methods and worn suspense devices. Its "Institute of Micro-

---

* An incident during the film's making contradicts its theme: the girl first chosen for the
central role was replaced when it became known that she was only half Chinese.
† This campaign was discarded when the authorities decided that "the larger the population,
the more it is possible to achieve greater, faster, better, and more economical results in
building socialism. . . . " editorial in *Hong Qi*, 1 Oct. 1958.

biology" is peopled with stereotypes of "scientists," in the full ideological war paint of grayed-hair wisdom and much play with white hygienic smocks. The conflict between conservative "old attitudes" (the returned overseas scientist is played by a villain-type actor) and the gentle, patient new life is announced in the first few minutes, and the film does not develop any other thought, notwithstanding the "innumerable letters" mentioned in *China Reconstructs*. What may have pleased audiences more, and the authorities less, were the quasi love scenes of students, who were shown in as undisciplined a mood as the returned scientist. This film, too, had a lesson for young spectators: how to one-step with dignity if not much joy, where to put your hands and arms while you scrape about in time to music, and what conversational subjects are recommended for a dance floor.

Yang Yu's article concludes with praise for two films based on well-known literary works, Lu Hsun's story, "Hsiang Lin's Wife" (or "New Year Offering"), and Pa Chin's novel, *Family*. *New Year Offering* (see Plate 33) was produced for the twentieth anniversary of the death of Lu Hsun — who had not wanted his works filmed. The mixture in *Family*, of course, began with Pa Chin's sentimental novel; if it is difficult to decide whether the novel is a revolt against tradition or a disgracefully disguised exploitation of it, it is even more difficult to clarify the motives of the film. With a token bow to the "revolt" premise the filmmakers show a more sincere wish for unrestrained and ostentatious display. Pa Chin's epic of self-pity has been given the most luxurious treatment possible. "See what I suffered!" the voice of Pa Chin wails through the novel, and it is this that the cameraman and actors (apparently in charge of the whole enterprise) use as their excuse to milk all of the commercial cinema's possibilities for vicarious, safe suffering by the spectators. None of the obligatory scenes for a good Chinese sob are missing: the tears fall copiously and steadily on and in front of the screen. By the end of the film no character has been denied the chance for at least one closely observed cry: everybody's quivering lips and running eyes are photographed with all the silky polish of an overtrained and uncontrolled cameraman (see Plate 34). The film dissolves in the very decadence that it pretends to analyze. But what else could have been done with this maudlin novel?

On the other hand Lu Hsun's story is ideal for film — hard, spare, pointed — but these are not the qualities of the 1956 film. Hsia Yen's adaptation is workmanlike and unexceptionable, though it is to be regretted that he simplified Lu Hsun's story and reduced its interwoven levels to a single easily comprehensible tale. If he understood the story as a tragedy, this was not the aim of the film's executants, for the whole action of the film has been smoothed into a uniform prettiness quite unresponsive to the film's subject and theme. For example, here is the episode in the story where the family of Hsiang Lin's runaway wife abducts her; she has been working for the narrator's uncle:

Some people [by the river] told him that a boat with a white awning had moored there in the morning . . . when Hsiang Lin's Wife came out to wash rice, two men looking like country people jumped off the boat just as she was kneeling down and seizing hold of her carried her on board. After several shouts and cries, Hsiang Lin's Wife became silent: they had probably stopped her mouth.[8]

I grant that it may have been difficult to achieve this particular fusion of direct action and indirect narration (one of the aims of the modern film!), but aside from that Lu Hsun has told the filmmaker in his bare lines exactly how it should be filmed — even to the sound track. I was shocked to see that the abduction was filmed through a banal frame of pink blossoming trees, against the most charmingly quaint arched bridge. Nor could the director leave the poor woman's stifled shouts unornamented — these were muffled not by the "stop" in her mouth, but by the instruments of an unwanted, unneeded orchestra.[*] The effect was *Liang Shan-po* all over again, and indeed, it was that decorative film's director, Sang Hu, who softened Lu Hsun's masterpiece of objectivity into a pretty fable. The actors tried hard to give substance to the film, and Pai Yang, as Hsiang Lin's wife, gave her best post-1949 characterization. People who remember *New Year Offering* usually recall only her role.

The first number of an English-language weekly, *Peking Review*, 4 March 1958, gave a grand picture of the film industry's plans for that year:

China's film workers, at a conference last week, decided to produce 75 feature films this year, 23 more than originally planned, in the spirit of socialist emulation now sweeping the country. . . .

Reflecting present trends in Chinese art, a good proportion of the new films deal with the life of the workers, peasants and soldiers. At least two will be wide-screen; *The Long March* deals with the epic march of the Chinese Red Army from Kiangsi to Yenan; *New Story of an Old Soldier* tells a typical story of today about a demobilized verteran who gets a tough assignment as director of a new state farm in China's north-east. . . .

---

* An insight is given by Wilfred Burchett into the usually unoriginal and unhelpful scores for Chinese films: "The research teams dig the tunes out; sometimes from local village actors and musicians, more often from the peasants themselves. Tunes are committed to manuscript and carefully filed away. . . . When a writer is working on a new opera or film, he can go to the research libraries and have the tunes played or sung until he finds the ones which most nearly express the emotions and atmosphere he wants. Those he selects are then worked up . . . by the composers." (*China's Feet Unbound* [Melbourne: World Unity Publications, 1952], pp. 102-103).

. . . there will be historical films, such as *The Opium War*; films adapted from Chinese legends and folk tales . . . ; and films adapted from modern Chinese stories, such as *The Shop of the Lin Family* based on Mao Tun's short story. . . .

Stories of the revolutionary struggle inspire some of the best scenarios. *Daughters of the Communist Party*, based on the background of the Second Revolutionary Civil War of 1927—36, is one of these. . . . *Wang Hsiao-ho* is the story of the workers in a Shanghai power plant. . . . It is based on the actual life story of Wang Hsiao-ho, a trade union leader executed by Chiang Kai-shek's police. There will also be a film about the building of the spectacular Sikang-Tibet Highway and one about the creation of China's modern air force.[9]

Most of these, however, did not appear until the next year, 1959, in honor of the tenth anniversary. Of those named here only the almost credible *Daughters of the Party* (thanks to Tien Hua and the Changchun Studio; see Plate 36), *Sentinels of the High Sky*, on the air force,* and *Crossing the Natural Barrier*, the August First Studio's drama of the army's construction of the disputed highway, were released before the end of 1958. I don't know *Wang Hsiao-ho* — it may have been lost in the confusion of the new "movement."

Before the film industry could recover from the ups and downs of the Hundred Flowers, a Great Leap was demanded of it. In November 1957 Mao Tse-tung had defied circumstances and Soviet advice in proposing to double and triple production efforts in industry and agriculture, enabling China to leap across all transitional phases to communism without further delay; in May 1958 the Second Session of the Party's Eighth Congress officially endorsed the plan, and everyone in China was strained by the Great Leap Forward for the next two years, before all but the slogan was thrown back on the heap of discarded projects.

Essential to the film industry's place in the campaign, fresh, dizzying quantities had to be announced: among the *decisions* of a June meeting called in Peking by the Ministry of Culture's Cinema Bureau were these comforting figures:

Within the next decade hundreds of features will be produced annually with tens of thousands of supplementary shorts, newsreels and documentaries. Attendance at film shows will rise from the estimated figure of about three thousand million this year to tens of thousands of millions. . . . By the time the Second Five-Year Plan 1958—1962 gets well into its stride the film industry will have 160,000 employees, a good 100,000 more than at present.[10]

The masses were to participate in the writing of these films:

The ranks of professional film workers and scenario writers are also being reinforced by a growing body of informed amateurs. Government employees,

---

* There is a detailed review-synopsis of *Sentinels* (August First) in *Peking Review*, 5 Aug. 1958, p. 21.

workers, teachers and housewives in Liaoning, Kirin and Heilungkiang are among
those currently writing scenarios for the Changchun Film Studio and 90 scripts
are expected to be ready before the end of the year.[11]

With the enthusiastic help of the Communist Party committee of the Changs-
intien Locomotive and [Railway Carriage] Works, the film director Hsieh Tien,
two amateur worker-writers and a lathe-turner are collaborating on a scenario
entitled "Eighty-eight Days" which tells how China's first locomotive was
made.[12]

As with the iron-furnaces erected and tended with a staggering waste of time by
every organization, and the thousands of amateur "poems" bundled in from
every province, there was little to show for these efforts except the figures.
Architecture and cinema were two industrial arts offering little room to amateurs,
and their gestures of participation, insisted upon by the Propaganda Office, were
quietly buried.

However, the particular projects of the Leap *could* be dramatized in films, even
by professionals. The building of the Ming Tombs Reservoir went beyond the
Huai River project in recruiting volunteer builders: most of Peking's population
(including government heads and friendly diplomats, accompanied by a small
army of photographers) hauled dirt and dug smilingly.* The first fictional film
about this effort came, in a hurry, from the Changchun Studio, *The Reservoir
Builders* (the Ming Tombs Reservoir was also to furnish an example for hundreds
of smaller, *amateur* reservoirs begun that year):

A young couple, Second Lieutenant Ku Chih-chiang and Lan-hsiang, a peasant
girl, are going to be married during the Spring Festival, but the wedding has to
be put off when Ku and his unit get orders to go and help build a reservoir at the
Ming Tombs. . . . As luck has it, however, the agricultural cooperative to which
Lan-hsiang belongs decides to build a small reservoir to irrigate its fields, and
she is sent along with her prospective father-in-law to the construction site of the
Ming Tombs Reservoir to get some experience. . . . The story ends happily. . . .[13]

T'ien Han's new play, *Ballad of the Thirteen Hills* [Ming Tombs] *Reservoir*, was
filmed in time to be shown during the October celebration, past epochs in black
and white, the present and future in color. As we have to thank this forgotten
quickie for making possible (soon afterwards) the production of one of the best
and most important Chinese films, it deserves some attention. The play was
produced in July, after only seven or eight days and nights of rehearsal; the

---

* See Joseph Peterson (pseud.), *The Great Leap — China* (B.I. Publications, Bombay, 1966),
for a uniquely realistic analysis of the Ming Tomb Reservoir (in Chap. II, The Great Leap in
Irrigation).

China Youth Art Theater and the play's director, Chin Shan, were much praised for their effort in reflecting such a current event so swiftly on the stage.

Then the Peking Film Studio discussed with me their wish to make a color film of this play, using the same shock tactics with which we had prepared the play, to finish the film by October First, and distribute it to all the villages of the country to propagandize the urgency of building irrigation schemes throughout China. We studied how such a film could be made, writing the script, doing set construction, location work, editing, sound, and all, knowing that we could not exceed 45 days altogether. We knew it would be difficult but we knew that such a vital task must be accomplished. The party organization asked me to have the script ready in three or four days. It was, and I then showed this to all responsible comrades, including the playwright T'ien Han. Between August 4 and 12 I listened to their opinions and made alterations. I changed some scenes entirely, and then showed it again to T'ien Han and the responsible comrades. The script took its final form on August 20, and we started shooting.[14]

They chose Kunming Lake at the Summer Palace to build the reservoir as it would look twenty years in the future, and then the rain began! Yet after only 29 days of shooting, with the composer Yao Mu working alongside the editor (all sound was postsynchronized), they had a finished film of 2,700 meters ready by October First. It gained Chin Shan the reputation of an efficient and responsible film director. Without it he could not have started *Storm* (*Feng Bao*) later in the year.

Through no fault of its own the *Reservoir* film did not stay long in circulation, due to a great change in policy while it was being made. In the same article, written soon after the October screenings, Chin Shan explained and apologized:

The great leap of the people's communes was made while our film was in production, and this made my vision of communism in the future look superficial. I only wanted to show how good life would be in the future, but I should have shown how people would be working then, too. I didn't realize that advanced and progressive people would never ask for rewards.

Leaping occurred in all fields. A news item in *Peking Review* of 8 July was headed "God of Death Foiled":

When Chiu Tsai-kang was admitted to hospital, the doctors gave him three days to live. This Shanghai steelworker had had a bad accident and was suffering from second degree burns. . . . It was a hopeless case, the doctor pronounced.

Should we stick blindly to the medical texts, or should we forget about these books for once and try every conceivable way to save the worker's life? The matter was put bluntly before the doctors by the Communist Party secretary, who is also vice-director of the hospital. . . .

The "bad accident" did not lead to a film about industrial precautions, but to *several* plays* and a film about the Party's victory over "old shibboleths." *Spring Warmth Among the People* (1959) is a hastily made color film with a high proportion of talk (the bandaged hero is the only character who does not deliver orations) and a minimum of action — another collaboration of Sang Hu and Pai Yang after their *New Year Offering.* The moral of the film, applied everywhere, was that there are no limits to the human body, so long as it has the correct revolutionary directives, nor to any piece of machinery, no matter what the conservative European socialist advisors tell you.

The four most substantial films of 1958† had little connection with the policies of the Great Leap, neither in material nor in method; the bureaucratic slowness of production was not to be prodded into more speed until the next year, after which it slid back into its old ways. Three of these best films came from Shanghai studios: *Red Shoots*, on prerevolutionary organization among the peasants of Kiangsu province; *By the March 8 Canal* (see Plate 36), based on the real conflicts of the real woman chairman of an Anhuei commune (though played by Chang Jui-fang);‡ and *Ordeal by Iron and Fire*, about a hero-martyr (in the person of an impossibly angelic "star") in Shanghai in 1948 — the last being the most popular of these. In my opinion the best film of the year was a modest, almost unexploited film, *The Constant Beam*, with underground Shanghai heroes that one could believe. It was produced at the army's August First Studio by Wang Ping, a consistently able director who had begun her film career as an actress (one can see her in a small role in *Spring River Flows East*), and has always kept her films, since she began directing in 1952, credible and intimate; it is hard to understand how she has been able to maintain in her films a clear character — her own. The protagonists of *The Constant Beam* are a man-and-wife team operating a secret radio contact between Shanghai and Yenan, but Wang Ping tempers the heroics and builds her suspense with the ordinary details of their lives.

The Constant Beam touched an area that constantly tempted — and often scorched — Chinese filmmakers: the subject of spies, enemy agents, saboteurs, and detection of criminals. So long as the saboteurs and underground agents

---

* At least three of the plays were shown in Peking during September and October: at the Peking Experimental Theater, *The Party Saved My Life*; at the Peking People's Art Theater, *The Red Flag Unfurled*; at the Central Drama School, *The Victory of Communism*. These nearly identical plays must also have been seen in Shanghai where the film was made.
† The Chinese entry at the Karlovy Vary film festival of 1958, *Flames on the Border*, had been completed by the Changchun Studio in 1957.
‡ A valuable experiment was made this year, in having a real heroine play her own role, in *Huang Pao-mei*.

were on *our* side, as in *The Constant Beam*, they could be cheered; but in the eyes of the dutiful critics, the suspense of watching the *enemy's* forbidden activities and filling the foreground with these negative characters usually outweighed these films' function of warning the public. Two typical "exciting and dangerous" films (a term intended to replace the bourgeois "thriller") were made in 1958 by the Changchun Studio, *Sound of the Old Temple Bell* and *The Case of Chu Chou-lin*. Both were well made, both were popular, but this sort of film can't win ideologically, so both were subjected to a remarkable kind of criticism. The very qualities that made them exciting and popular had to be attacked in the press. *Temple Bell* told of an enemy group that took over an old temple as their base, conducting sabotage (including the destruction of a munitions factory) over a period of four years. It is clear that this story describes modern enemy activity, but it was considered wiser to shift the period back to the anti-Japanese war, with the agents "a knife in the heart of the Eighth Route Army." The shift was made convincing enough, but the attacking critic[15] was outraged by the film's vagueness of place and time, the very thing that permitted its audience to link it with the present, and turn it into a modern warning film. Chu Chou-lin was a former Kuomintang agent who, in 1951, was pursued by her former employers to resume her espionage; when she refused, they murdered her and pinned suspicion on an ex-sweetheart.* The suspense is managed so well that *this* becomes the ideological flaw! The critic testified that the atmosphere of fear was so strong that it chilled his spine and made his hairs stand on end. *But,*

Showing such dark and fearful things to young people is not the way to build class hatred for the enemy; on the contrary, they will be overwhelmed by fear and become discouraged — leading to bad effects.[16]

He concluded that it was a poisonous and antiparty film, but neither *Chu Chou-lin* nor the *Temple Bell* was immediately withdrawn from distribution. Pointing to their dangers was a necessary gesture.

By the end of the year the main *negative* targets of the Leap were being touched by films. These targets had been defined in May[17] as the *san feng*, three bad styles — bureaucracy, sectarianism, and subjectivism — and the *wu ch'i*, five airs — bureaucratic airs, lifeless airs, spendthrift airs, haughty airs, squeamish airs. It is not difficult to see these as more promising film subjects than the heroics that were to speed us all toward a fully communist society, and during the last month of 1958 two films were shown that attacked "haughty and

---

* The scenario was based on a supposedly factual article in *Renmin Ribao* in 1955, "Why Was She Killed?"

squeamish airs." In *An Ordinary Job* (the Haiyen Studio of Shanghai) Lin Pei-
ming graduates from college, expecting to receive a teaching job, but is assigned
to a kindergarten; she is most disappointed, feels humiliated, but then. . . . In
Our Land So Dear (Changchun) a young girl schooled in the city is returned to
work in her village; she is deeply disappointed at the low level of village life, but
then. . . .

The August First Studio and other studios were also busy on the military aspect
of the Great Leap (with the bombardment of Quemoy and Matsu islands begun
in August), but these films were not completed until well into the anniversary
year.

An acute reader of *Zhungguo Dianying* noticed certain changes in the Chinese
films of the previous year and asked some rhetorical but pointed questions; his
letter to the journal is entitled, "Leaning East, Falling West":

I read an article in *Renmin Ribao* with this title. It brought many questions to
my mind, especially about visible changes in the films of 1957 and 1958.

In 1957 we had several "muches" — much love, much kissing, much giddiness,
much praise for intellectuals. . . . But in 1958 all these "muches" went into
reverse. Suddenly there is no more love in our films, and any scene where love is
just about to walk in — a cut! Even when love is *necessary* for the story, it's
missing. Suddenly all heroes are bachelors, planning to marry only after we have
surpassed England industrially. Actually, I believe such heroes do exist, but this
can't be the only way to show a man being a hero in a work of art.

In 1957 you rarely saw factories and workshops on the screen. But in 1958 you
rarely see the homes where the characters live. You see the hero *only* in factories,
on dams, in fields. If you show the life of a Hero of Labor as so monotonous,
no one will want to be a Hero of Labor.

In 1957 there was much praise for intellectuals, but in the films of 1958 I
haven't seen one single, positive intellectual. When an intellectual appears on the
screen, it is only as an object for criticism and reform.

In 1957 many controversies among people were dramatized as controversies
between the people and their enemies. In 1958 — no controversies.

How could such an extreme change take place in one year? I believe that film
writers cannot synthesize the opinions of the audience with their own thinking.
When such people feel the wind blow they lean wherever the wind points, and
often from one extreme to another. The films we see now are *lowered* from
those of a year ago. Present films reflect gray opinions. We even feel embarrassed
to see the posters of films made last year.

In recent years we were always afraid — of the wolf in front and the tiger
behind — always looking for a safe path. We need more courage.[18]

In 1958 the Documentary Studio of the German Democratic Republic sent Joop Huisken, a Dutch filmmaker, to China. The plan was for a film to be made in many parts of China, some places not yet shown on any screen, and these were the locations that the Chinese authorities wished removed from the film's plan. They restricted Huisken to the familiar scenes and even carefully supervised his filming of these. When Huisken tried to recover parts of the original plan, the Chinese would complain to his superiors: he was creating obstacles between two friendly countries. The unsatisfactory miscellany was brought back to Berlin and was somehow put together as *China — Land zwischen Gestern und Morgen.*

10

Anniversary Year
1959

"Real" is at the service of all schools of thought.

— E. M. Forster

While my wife and I were in Europe in the autumn of 1958 she received an invitation to come to Peking, to the newly established Ballet School, to work as a choreographer, and we went to the Chinese Mission in London to discuss it. It seemed an excellent idea, especially after several years of working for me, to return her to her profession. And too, the prospect of returning to her father's country, and contributing something to its new culture, was too exciting to be denied. There was one awkwardness — my American passport. It specifically forbade its bearer to travel in "Communist controlled portions of China," but I had no intention of letting Si-lan take this long, hazardous, and fascinating trip by herself. I had never been in China, though she had, twice before. So in the spring of 1959 we crept eastward. With a certain juggling of papers and a conspiratorial manner that everyone enjoyed I shed my identity as we approached the Chinese border.

15 May. The "friendship corner" in the border station — and a meeting of the Soviet-Chinese Friendship Society in progress. Probably hard work. Seen words and heard words — will we ever learn them? Jazz in the restaurant car — for *our* benefit.

16 May. First morning glimpse of China, a brown round hill stubby with — are those trees? A pheasant flies up beside train. Farm with every inch and muscle at work. Finish Emily's proofs in Manchuria! How I enjoy being where I'm not supposed to be. . . .

17 May. We'll be in Peking this morning — three more hours. They must have a great film problem: respect for tradition and established forms, with no premium on originality in either theater or film. And another theater problem: emphasis on actor with neglect of all other elements. Trouble if this is translated literally into film.

The first sight of the city brought a quite inarticulate excitement. We were well met, by family and future colleagues. We drove from the old station through the torn-up center of the city — the square before Tien An Men was being enlarged for the Tenth Anniversary celebrations in October — to a small hotel, the Pei-fang (Northern), the most modest of the new hotels, the first to have been built after Liberation. It used to house correspondents, but now we were to be the only foreigners there. That and the experienced, very accommodating staff were the reasons for choosing the Pei-fang for us. We were told about a huge place northwest of the city where foreign advisors were housed but as we were, for my security, to be kept away from Peking's foreign colony — at least for a while — we were allowed to live in the city, a privilege much to be preferred.

How long were we to stay? In London we had talked about a year, and that seemed settled.

The chief subjects of our first discussion, in a sitting room of the Pei-fang, were Si-lan's work and our living conditions, how much we wanted to be on our own, financially, transport to the ballet school, etc., etc. I had expected some delay in deciding what to do with "the husband," but it was taken for granted that I was to join the staff of the new Film Archive of China as an "advisor." Our salaries would probably be the same, and ample. Details to emerge later. That evening we were taken to a program of the Chinese folk dance and song troupe (obviously Moiseyev's company had had a successful tour here) and I saw my first Peking audience.

Next day I ventured out by myself and returned to find a magenta invitation to a dinner, to be followed by a concert. My attempts at dinner to introduce the subject of my work were politely parried with more helpings of Peking duck, and I assumed that my job had not yet been defined. We hoped there would be new Chinese music on the concert program, and there were *two* new symphonies, both effective; the second, by Lo Tsung-rung, inspired by Mao's poem, "A Thousand Years," was impressive and original. Both composers were in the audience. Great impression made on us by the late arrival of the Mayor of Peking, Peng Chen, with son, whereupon the program was begun again.

19 May. Pleasant walk through Imperial Palace with Niu-tsung [my newly met sister-in-law] as interpreter and Comrade Gao of the Archive — animated crowd with us all the while. Terraces and ornaments that might have inspired Mayan and Aztec buildings, a sundial that Brancusi could have claimed — and a whole garden of abstract rock formations. Into a nearby park (portrait of Sun Yat-sen) for tea and a first talk on archive problems and future — apparently *much* done in its first year of existence. Later, alone, first intoxicated shopping in big bazaar near the Pei-fang, and first soothing haircut in elegant Peace Hotel [another foreign center to be avoided]. How I wish Emily could have come with us — far enough from Amherst.

And there were films to be seen, for I knew only *The White-Haired Girl* from a Paris screening, and in London we saw the basketball film, and some short films. Within our first Peking week I saw samples of most kinds of film and of film programs. My first and last high-level screening at the Ministry of Culture included Joris Ivens' new film, *Early Spring* (which I asked for the day we arrived), a pretty landscape film of the Kwei-lin rocks, and a cartoon against complacency (*The Conceited General*, 1956). This screening concluded with a long but gentle controversy with the Archive director on art for the masses. A vice-director of the Film Bureau (whose English was learned at Columbia University) had wisely escaped earlier. An evening at the Newsreel Theater: a poor film on the Tibetan crisis (made by graduates of the film school!), a bright film about the May Day demonstrations, good spot news, and a few foreign items; the theater (formerly attached to the next-door YMCA) was packed — the balcony especially vocal in their response.

Three recent films had been offered to me, and I chose *New Year Offering* (1956) because of my admiration for Lu Hsun (this screening had a curious sequel — a new job!), and from a list of archive films I chose the two earliest I noticed, *Daughters of China* and *Chao Yi-man* (both 1950). Two foreign films (dubbed into Chinese) were shown at the People's Consultative Assembly — rather like a screening in the House of Representatives, with a capacious desk before each spectator: a Czech *Svejk* and an Armenian tearjerker, *The Heart Sings*, the dignified audience being slightly more concerned with the latter. A visit to the Film School (*not* a hive of activity) where I was shown a group of very inhibited student films and experienced an unstimulating discussion: typical was Cheng Chi-hua's explanation for the absence of most of Eisenstein's films. The two sound stages there that I was shown were occupied by settings, but not for student films; one of the studios had taken them over.

My greatest drama excitement ended our first week — a performance by Mei Lan-fang, whom I had not seen since his Moscow tour. *Full* enjoyment by the audience of everything he gave them, as playwright and actor — every sorrow, every gaiety, every breath of poetry. Their enjoyment seemed doubled by their feeling for Mei himself (this was my first experience of the Chinese audience's recognition and pleasure in the theater's artificiality): the two children of the heroine (Mei) were played by Mei's actual son and daughter, so that when they addressed him as *Mama* — uproar in the auditorium! One modern idea may have been distracting: the text of the arias, line by line, was projected on a space beside the proscenium; if the audience was visible from the stage, the singing actor would see most of them looking away from him, like the audience at a television show watching the monitor image.* Afterwards, backstage, we saw

---

* "When *Way Down East* was shown in Peking [in 1921], an interpreter was engaged to narrate the story scene by scene to the audience. This device was, however, soon dropped. . . . Instead, a glass panel, on which simple sentences were written in Chinese to tell the audience something about the story, was provided at one or both sides of the stage. This is still practiced up till today. . . ." — Lau Shaw [Lao Shê], "Hollywood Films in China," *The Screen Writer*, Nov. 1946. The general employment of dubbing for foreign films after 1949 did away with this support for films. Between 1946 and 1949 the larger American film companies prepared (in America) superimposed translations into Chinese of the English dialogue, which helped urban audiences.

Mei, to give him a souvenir from Tretyakov's widow, and we planned to meet again.

23 May. After screening [of *Daughters of China*] a hasty introduction to archive quarters, in a wing of the film distribution offices, and to some of the staff. . . .

By the time the staff and I parted, exactly five years later, its personnel had completely changed. On this first visit I saw the progress made by the first staff on their biggest project, cataloging the collection of Chinese films: it was already workable. Some hints about the non-Chinese films showed that this part of the collection had been left for later and would probably be my job.

From now on I was seeing at least one film each working day, from the Chinese collection, the foreign collection, or recent productions and imports. The showing of *New Year Offering*, with translator, seemed routine, but I was not yet used to making notes with a translation going full tilt into one ear, and the notes I took back to the hotel were *very* vague as to the makers and actors of the film, so I was not ideally prepared for a request from the Film Bureau to please write a report on *New Year Offering.* The exhilaration of our arrival had not yet worn off and I wrote a brash account of what I really thought of the film, its relation to Lu Hsun's story, where the adaptation had been less filmic than Lu Hsun, etc., ending on a sweeping generalization (based, you'll note, on very few Chinese films):

One of my aims, while I am in China, is to find out *what* it is that prevents Chinese film production from using the full power of the film. Is it because the audience is being patronized and protected — and is being given *less* than it is able to comprehend? Or is it because the influence of the Chinese theater is so strong that the film cannot develop its own methods?

One of the names, unclear in my notes, was the name of the scenarist and adapter of the story. Only a week later I was told that this was Hsia Yen (whom we had not yet met), Vice-Minister of Culture and head of the Film Bureau. I expected some unpleasantness or, worse, *silence.* Instead Hsia Yen sent word to me and to the archive that I was to see every new film of importance and submit comments on them, which he would first read in English and Chinese, and then distribute. Since I had mistakenly made such an honest beginning, I decided to continue that way.

28 May. To the Central Documentary and Newsreel Studio where Joris had made *Early Spring.* Polite conversation with Deputy Director on color problems. Tour of lab and cutting rooms — French developing machines, Soviet printers, German projectors, Belgian stock (Gaevert).

A briefer, more necessary visit to the suburban vaults of the Archive. Good temperature control and constant inspection. A large staff — offices — dormitory! — garden — one vault full of problems (*my* meat). . . . [later told that total staff numbers 40 and there are about 60,000 reels in collection]

Eve. — with Ai-lin to "By the Kinsha River" — on Tibetan crisis (a boon to the theaters, so this will certainly spread to movies). This was a pleasingly primitive musical, related to Peking opera much as Hammerstein relates to Gluck, and with other resemblances. Surprising encounter in "green room" (with green tea): Emi Siao! looking not much older than in *International Literature* days. Also Ouyang Yu-chien, much quieter and much older than I remember him in Moscow. As we left at end of Act I, there was some understandable coolness from playwright and director.

1 June. International Children's Day, so after an opening, blistering assembly, the school outside our window went somewhere else for the day . . .

A dull film of *Yevgeni Onegin* all afternoon — but the day ended with a magnificently concrete conversation with the Archive's director. I start work tomorrow morning — na konets! I'm to be allowed to begin on the non-Chinese catalog of archive holdings. As Niu-tsung's office will not release her to translate for me, some other person will be found. Salary 500 yuan a month, starting from the moment I stepped off the train. [Very comforting to learn this is the amount of Mao's salary.]

From June through September the anniversary films came in increasing numbers; at the end of the year it was proudly announced that more than 170 feature-length films had been produced in 1958 and the first nine months of 1959 — more than in the whole period from 1949 through 1957.* Those that I saw at the distribution office, the Filmworkers' Club, and the Writers' Union looked very encouraging.

The first new film made me an immediate partisan of the Changchun Studio, especially as I later grew aware that its young staff and inexpensive films were being looked down upon by the more experienced and traditional hands of Shanghai's and Peking's studios. The film was *Young People of the Village*, and its subject was one of the hundreds (or thousands) of small reservoirs that Chinese villagers were building that year. The scenarist, Ma Feng, and the director, Su Li, had the right idea of casting this needed instructional film in the form of an entertaining comedy, and I found the result to be as genuinely entertaining as I imagined it useful, as well. The color of the photography was as bright and lively as its young actors; its photography, indeed, spoiled me for the misuses of color that were more often encountered in Chinese films. Best of all,

---

* Probably an understandable exaggeration, for a later Hsinhua release (dated 30 July 1960) said that 480 feature-length films had been produced since Liberation.

actuality had provided its characters and situations. Alongside the usual quibbles of my report on it, I praised this victory more than any other accomplishment:

No death-bed scenes to pull tears from our eyes. No foolish villains to be neatly disposed of in the last five minutes. No fortunate coincidences to solve a desperate scenarist's confusion. A film without a cliché! True, there is one theatrical "misunderstanding" that might have drifted in from an operetta, but it comes so close to the conclusion that for his responsible work up to that point one is willing to forgive the scenarist.

The verses I find in my diary of these first months are amazingly hopeful, read in a later light. After seeing the demolition of the huge old city wall near the central square:

4 June.
  New scars on its antique earth,
  The wall of Peking opens
  To a flood of optimists
  Cycling to a certain glory,
  Undeterred by the dust
  Of bricks falling from the past
  To reinforce tomorrow.

9 June. At last! another European bus rider, the first I've seen in all my weeks of bus between hotel and archive — a vaguely churchy character, accepted by all. I suspect that Europeans aren't *supposed* to use public transportation, but I don't see why not.

11 June. Reached office in time for emotional farewell to the truckload of office workers on their way to the harvest.

  Underneath the new straw hats,
  The smiles of the departing
  Make the deserted sad
  And a little ashamed
  To be too old or tired
  For this great leap.

Big surprise of afternoon: a mountain of precious bound volumes of U.S. movie trade papers, from a Shanghai theater. I'll enjoy these (they begin in 1919) whenever I'm idle.

12 June. An agreeable surprise: without announcement my frail (pregnant?) assistant took me to the Liulichang shop that makes reproductions of Chi Pai-shih's paintings. They also had a few originals for sale — one (75 yuan) extremely handsome that I wanted — and maybe I could prove something with it at the Shanghai Animation Studio. An early work — at the age of 60! Bought it, though warned I couldn't take it out of China.

Afternoon at Peking Library, ordering Olga's microfilm of Chinese translations of *Roar China*, presenting my extra Meridian copy [of the two Eisenstein books] ,[*] and other accumulated errands. Colonel and corporal jostled together on bus — both trying to avoid a breach of army discipline.

Evening, an Army ballet — better than the mechanized pretty revues. X made fun of me for buying a painting. He hasn't seen it yet.

17 June. Visited, with S. and Ai-lin, the Tien Ma dance group, an elegant establishment unexpected in this dusty alley. The Heavenly Horse himself is a very smooth talker — we'll see tonight what sort of choreographer he is. New device for disconcerting visitors: serve them green tea with a Sargasso sea floating on top, and wait for them to try to drink it. Raisins (from Sinkiang) are easier.

First beggar — stump of arm.

21 June. Sunday passed placidly, until evening, when X and X took us off to their "dance." Overseas Chinese collectively are a strange and somewhat sad sight: how many tortuous decisions before they were pulled back to China and Peking — from U.S. colleges, from Hong Kong luxuries (a Chiang general was chairman of the occasion!)? Dancing was timid and desperate — supposedly good for their morale? Music was an effort. Females at any male's disposition. Lots of "sparkling conversation" at tables. Story of the cramming Chinese language course for the returnees — 100 characters a day — and the breakdowns.

27 June. A good, big day at the vaults. Tough getting through the preliminaries of politeness and initial confusion, but we finally did get our hands on film — and what film! —an original Griffith fragment (1912?), two Max Linders, some hand-colored Pathé fantasies, an early wartime film with Pola Negri (neutral English titles made in Germany), and various second-rate U.S. features — *Calcutta, Heidi*, etc. We must pick at this at least one day a week. What a joke — to be handling *here*, and with such care, Betty Grable and ilk.

Later at office saw part of a sloppy Iraqi film about the revolt — chiefly on the trial. The uninterrupted commentary was accompanied by a single record over and over — The Stars and Stripes Forever!

First sexy inspection by truck-driver of some passing hips. And first street fight over the dust-bins — a discussion?

5 July (Sunday). A splendid morning symphony concert. After Ma Sitson's suite, Voices of the Forest, the Beethoven Ninth, sharply and excitingly played. Hearing the Ode to Joy in Chinese made me weep buckets. An inquisitive little girl, investigating the full stage, made everything more poignant.

The next new film was less of a pleasure than *Young People*. It was one of the big films for the anniversary, big materially, big politically. *Song of Youth* was an enormously successful novel, recommended for every young Chinese to read

---

* Years later, in the Peitaiho bookshop where I bought most of my "comics," I found a copy of a *Chinese* translation (from the English, of course) of *The Film Sense*, published in 1953 — no one had mentioned this to me, possibly because the period was a criticized one.

for its treatment of the student movement of the thirties, but I did not know this when I saw the film:

I have not read this novel, and I hope it is more truthful than the long [almost three hours], expensive film that has been made of it. But I'm sure this will be a successful film, due more to the novel than to the filmmakers. In the audience among whom I saw it, I was apparently the only one who did not look at it as an illustration of a beloved literary work — so that a familiarity with its source may lend to the film a credibility that it has not earned itself.

My first shock was to see its heroine treated as the starring actress of a typical American film. No Hollywood star has been more isolated and artificially illuminated than this unreal central figure. I found some of the close-ups actually revolting in their super-sweetness. (Whatever the rationale for such photographic treatment, it's poison for films.) How could the cameraman have been content with such unconnected, meaningless prettiness? Even the police scenes are lovely! While looking at the film I imagined that it must have been directed by an old director who had seen too many American films, but I have since learned that it is a first film by the actor Tsui Wei.* Where did he learn to transform the realities of his subject into such familiar affectations? Is the cameraman to blame — or was there a dangerous seed of sentimentality embedded in the novel that the scenarist did not guard against? Even the film score drips with glycerine tears.

The only passage in the film that moved me was the monologue by Chin Yi in the prison scene. Was it a determined, talented actress who overcame a misled director and a showy cameraman?

The influence of Hollywood, and in one of its worst aspects, was a shock. First, it contradicted everything that I heard and read here about the poisons and falsehoods of Hollywood being discarded by a revolutionary, bold, new Chinese cinema. The Soviet cinema had been occasionally tempted in the same way, but never so unblushingly as here. And I was shocked to find here a part of the past revived that was long since judged as a sham and embarrassment, while a new important Chinese film turned away deliberately from the progress being made in world cinema, even so near as Moscow and Warsaw.

I was slow to realize that *anything* that now came from the Soviet Union was regarded, not only with suspicion, but as fuel for a quarrel already outlined. When we went through Moscow on the way to Peking in the spring of 1959 we heard nothing of the rift that had opened two years earlier, connected with much older suspicions, and the serious accusations and counteraccusations made at the Moscow conference of November 1957. Nor did anything we heard and saw in Peking during our first month indicate what was beneath the surface of

---

* Actually a collaboration: Tsui Wei and Chen Huai-ai.

energetic Friendship Societies, the banners, the speeches, and songs in praise of
the Soviet Union. But from June on, when there were screenings of A Man's
Destiny, the reactions to it which I heard should have warned me, but I was
used to the idea that one socialist country did not always admire or endorse
another socialist country's best films. The best Polish films I had seen in Paris
and London were not the ones shown in the Soviet Union, and there were even
fewer shown to the Chinese public. Yet to hear, here, a Soviet film (and one that
I admired) used as a small but sharp anti-Soviet weapon was so peculiar that I
could not believe I had understood (though repeated to us) correctly. "This film
shows the dangerous loosening of Soviet ideology in all spheres of life there." I
don't recall yet hearing the term "revisionist," though it must have been used
then for Yugoslavia. Sholokhov was not mentioned as the author of A Man's
Destiny (the attacks on him were to come later); it sometimes sounded as
though Khrushchov had written and directed this film. Opinions of a film were
easy to dismiss; besides, we had a joyous farewell dinner with the delegates going
to the Moscow Film Festival in August — how could anything here be fundamentally wrong?

At Moscow the Chinese entry that year was New Story of an Old Soldier.* My
preparations for seeing it were too complete. In a recently translated volume of
Chinese short stories of the fifties the only one that remained vividly in my
memory was "Not That Road" by Li Chun, so I was particularly interested to
hear that Li Chun was the scenarist of New Story. I had an opportunity to read a
translation of his scenario before seeing the film, and this too whetted my
anticipation. Early in 1958 Li Chun had seen an actuality film by the August First
Studio, Conquering the Great North Wastelands, about the soldiers of the
People's Liberation Army reclaiming the northeast swamps with drainage and
irrigation, to establish large state farms in this neglected part of China. He
immediately grasped this as an idea for a scenario and went there to see for
himself and to talk with the veteran soldiers doing the work.

One tradition of the Chinese cinema that was reinforced after 1949 was that the
scenario was the really important, creative element in filmmaking: it could be

---

* New Story won a prize (for High Technical Level) at the Moscow Festival. The many
prizes collected by Chinese films at friendly film festivals do not necessarily reflect the
quality of the film work awarded or the judgment of the jury. Often a category was
invented, in the line of keeping all important contestants happy: Karlovy Vary's invention
of the category of "Struggle for World Peace" had the specific purpose of satisfying China at
each Czech festival. In most cases the prizes were gestures of encouragement to or fraternity
with the People's Republic of China. For this reason I have not felt obliged to point to all
such awards. Since 1961 these comforting pats have been transferred to films entered in
festivals by the People's Republic of Vietnam.

discussed and revised, but once given to the director, his job was to transfer the
scenario from paper to celluloid efficiently, without adding any new elements.
Even in my short time in Peking I may have been infected by this attitude, for I
didn't foresee that anything could go wrong with Li Chun's excellent script.
Growing up in this traditional respect for the written word, the director, Shen
Fu, applied his long directorial experience and training* to adding nothing to the
script. And a film that cannot be as bold as its script inevitably moves backward.
My disappointment became almost lyrical in my report:

the script soared, the film plodded along.
the script was advanced, the film reached back into the past.

How ironic for this contradiction to appear in the first Chinese film to be
offered the opportunities of the wide screen! Yet I should have remembered that
most of the cinema's technical innovations, wherever they appeared, were
encased in the past. New Story was also, of course, in color. The final damage to
my appreciation of it came from my screening, shortly before seeing it, of the
extraordinarily real and poetic introduction to Along the Sungari River, where
the integration of action and northeast landscape made New Story's combination of action and a more beautifully photographed Northeast look cinemati-
cally primitive and feeble. The scenarist and cameraman had won this time,
but the film had lost.

Only the central role (played by Tsui Wei almost simultaneously with his codirection of Song of Youth) had enough fire to communicate the passion of the
scenario, but to the neglect of all other elements. The strength of his performance helped to injure the film's theme, according to one overseas Chinese reaction to its first London showing:

. . . we learn that [the hero] was able to overcome all difficulties only because
he "mobilised and relied on the masses of the people, under the leadership of the
Party." It may be because of the forceful personality of our hero, but the
impression we get from the film is that the Party's leadership seems to be not at
all strong here. We have in this old soldier a simple, honest character who defies
all hardship and devotes himself wholeheartedly to his work, while the Party's
Political Commissar seems to be rather a weak and useless man, though kind-
looking and reasonable. True, all the help came from the masses of the people,
but we never see the Political Commissar doing any actual work. All he did was
to telephone to say that the tractors promised earlier had now been cancelled!
But all the way through the film the makers have tried hard to stress the role of

---

* Just before directing this first Chinese wide-screen film Shen Fu served for six months as
an apprentice (at the age of fifty!) to Grigori Roshal during the Moscow production of
Roshal's wide-screen trilogy, based on Alexei Tolstoy's Road to Calvary (or, Ordeal).

the Party in everybody's life with lines like: "Don't thank me, thank the Party," "If I can't trust the Communists, who can I trust then?" or "Do you think I am good enough to join the Party?"[1]

A film that Shen Fu can be prouder of is *Huang Pao-mei* (1958), whose scenario he worked on (with Yeh Ming?) just after returning from Moscow. The idea for this film was excellent and original. Huang Pao-mei, a spinner in Shanghai's Cotton Mill No. 17, was to play *herself* in a film about her inventions (she devised a system of eliminating knots in thread joins) and initiative. This was helped by the truly vivacious and attractive figure of this real "heroine." She gave an interview after the film's production:

When the director told me I was to play this role I was frightened . . . if there was failure the state would lose a few thousand yuan. I also thought it somewhat shameful to draw attention to oneself — to emphasize an individual might reduce the influence of the Party. . . . But the factory director quoted Chairman Mao, "We must dare to think, dare to speak, dare to act." . . . On the day of the test my heart started to thump. The director kept looking at me so strangely that I couldn't help giggling. And then this was not the place I was used to working in and the light was peculiar. He said "Relax and don't be nervous." I started off by doing only what the director told me, without understanding what I was doing. But I gradually got used to the factory built in the Tien Ma studio and I took more initiative.[2]

If the makers of the film had had her initiative, we would have had a memorable Chinese film. I reported:

With such exceptional real people and places to work with, I should think this would have inspired everyone to reflect that reality as excitingly as is possible in a film. Instead, the real people were lit artificially, the sound engineer preferred to substitute manageable studio voices for the rich real voices (which didn't come up to his standards!) of the Shanghai textile workers,* and, to make it easier for everyone, much of the filming was taken from the factory to studio reproductions of factory rooms. At what a sacrifice of conviction and intimacy! The total effect was very much that of a wholesome loaf of bread covered with the icing of a cake.†

I was to learn that the icing was not only normal but necessary. After later experiences and viewing many more "documentary" films, my criticism now sounds naive. The only realistic sentence in this report was, "Many documentary

---

* There was another consideration I didn't realize at the time: most Shanghai workers do not speak the authorized national (Mandarin) dialect easily, so dubbing was "educationally necessary."

† This and subsequent quotations without identified source are from the author's diary or his reports to the Film Bureau; this quotation is from the latter.

films are planned to look like *plans*." Joris Ivens' *Early Spring* was the only Chinese actuality film that seemed to grow as you watched it. Would they, could they learn from him?

The supposedly *real* films were in a deeper rut than the frankly fictional films; the cameramen for both are given the same training, in which all humans and objects must be *arranged*. This is why the graduate cameramen on the spot during the uprising in Tibet were helpless in filming the real events in front of them. In general the Chinese film does not want spontaneity, does not trust it, and struggles resolutely against even an appearance of spontaneity. An unstaged shot in a newsreel was so rare that it stood out like a jewel. The only Chinese news film that I saw in 1959 that caught an unprepared event was an extra-ordinary record of a serious flood in the Pearl River valley in Kwantung province. The title had a cinematic as well as political significance: *Man Can Conquer Nature*. Eventually the conquest of natural behavior and speech and emotions exacted too great a price. In the next years I saw how the cameramen were losing the joy of real life in their pursuit of a *correct* view of the Chinese world. When I once suggested that camera students be allowed to use hidden cameras, to study how people really behave and walk and argue, the suggestion was received with horror, "We cannot invade the privacy of Chinese citizens." But I now realize that something more delicate than privacy was at stake: the *control* of everything seen on the film screen, as part of a total control that was the aim, the desire, the dream of most of the authorities.

As it turned out, *Huang Pao-mei*, with all its icing, had too much reality to survive. It was not sold abroad, and its domestic circulation was surprisingly brief.

Purely instructional (called "scientific") films were happier experiences than the more glorious "documentaries," partly because they required plans that were visible from beginning to end, wasted less time on decorative elements, and their aim was always clearer, to filmmakers as well as to audience. But such films never went outside China. I made an unsuccessful effort to break this barrier, recommending for export a local subject that bore an even more local title, *The Eight-Character Charter Assures a Greater Harvest.* Mao had compressed his eight pieces of advice for improved planting to eight characters. Some of his advice was later recognized (without acknowledgment) as having harmed the harvest, but the film was made in the first excitement of a discovered law, embodied in eight miraculous characters. It was produced at the August First Studio.

It is not only the best Chinese educational film I know, but it is also one of the best modern instructional films made anywhere. Here is one film that was *not* made in a hurry, and worth all the time and care expended on it. One of the most valuable filmmaking aspects of it is the care taken to vary the structures and treatments of each of the eight parts of the film. The "Water Conservation" section is built on a method completely different from the "Close Planting" section. Compare this care with the repetitious pattern of the ordinary popular-scientific film, to see how much more surely this well-planned variety captures and holds the audience's attention.

At this time I was bitten by the bug of ambition: I persistently submitted scripts and ideas to the Film Bureau. Nothing, of course, happened to any of these (though one unexplained echo turned up in a later film), but I went on being tempted, trying to find an actual filmmaking job there. I should have realized that foreigners couldn't do this. Even such totally(?) accepted foreigners as Rewi Alley and Gerry Tannebaum told me of film ideas they had submitted without result. But a Canadian friend in Peking had been brought to China for the express purpose of writing a scenario on Norman Bethune, and this kept my hope alive (the film was made but never shown). The first suggestion I made was my most ill advised. In Warsaw I had seen the powerful "Black Series" of critical actuality films, and thought this might indicate a way, with a fresh range of subjects, to break away from the tightening Chinese actuality-film orthodoxy. I proposed a series called "Bound Feet," on the remnants of feudal attitudes that were holding back China's progress. In my naïveté I had not yet learned Lizzani's lesson that no one here speaks of bound feet, or the more serious lesson that feudalism was still so much a part of Chinese society that no mere film could change it. I was even so foolish as to list "Han superiority" among the traits to be fought! If I had any friends at the Film Bureau, they must have quietly destroyed this project. Next, "Bouquet for Lu Hsun" was to touch some of the several sides of his writing, with different studios contributing to the miscellany. Idea liked, but no result. The next was worked out as a full treatment — *Actress*, which would view modern Chinese history seen through the ups and downs of a Szechuan opera company: I started this after reading in *China Reconstructs* a detailed account of a real actress's life before 1949. I still think this a good idea; the Film Bureau must have too, because the Changchun studio later made a film with much the same plan (and *two* sister actresses) — it was bitterly attacked and discarded soon after its release. My last two suggestions were a comedy about an itinerant film projection team (I've not heard of a film made on this subject yet) and a drama whose protagonist would be a night-soil collector, to show change on his level, too.

Watching the preparations for our first October celebration was more entertaining than the final parade. As early as 11 September one could see at Tien An Men and elsewhere the rehearsing militia, great floats parked on side streets, and

（下图：《舞台姊妹》拍摄外景速写 ）

During the production of *Sisters on the Stage;* drawing by Yu Yen.

the electric bulb outlines for big buildings, making the humorous shapes of the
Edwardian Post Office more so. The huge portraits were in place, but still
veiled — strange to see Stalin again. Solid streets of latrines were dug for the
October First crush.

18 Sept. S. and I visited Imperial Palace, to look for newly opened museum halls
[some paintings on view only at this time each year]. Saw one, but a bigger
surprise was to see that these enormous marble-paved, grass-grown courtyards
are used for mass rehearsals — the pieces of the coming parade that require props,
music, costume. Regiments of dancers look tired but willing. The rifles, etc. are
out on the square.

19 Sept. Jets rehearsed again this AM and tonight full-scale rehearsals of everything, search-lights, tanks, sportsmen. There are now paper flowers in the
trolley-bus.

Days and *nights* (a search-light platoon was under our hotel window) were spent
on polishing formations and timings, and there were few who got any other
work done through the holiday. Made another unthinking suggestion: to film the
preparation for the big holiday. I didn't realize it was all intended to look
spontaneous. When the Day finally came, every effect worked, and the rehearsals

paid off. Camera positions were built into the decorations, just as at the Berlin Olympiad of 1936.

8 Oct. Such Japanese riches at FAC [Film Archive of China] — and unsuspected works (wartime and before) by every important Japanese director. Possibly many of these are unique copies, after the film seizure and/or destruction by occupation authorities in Japan — what a gesture could be made of returning some to Japan! I sense little wish to see them here.

Evening's entertainment: reading this year's Guggenheim list.

17 Oct. Szechuan opera, *Tale of the White Snake*, seen for the sake of "Actress" and the pregnancy scene [that had startled me on a Peking opera program]. If Peking opera is a combination of the very sophisticated and the very childish, perhaps local opera styles stick to the latter. [I had not yet seen *Fifteen Strings of Cash*.] Lots of hints for "Actress" — mostly for pre-Liberation scenes.

I often smelled a certain snobbism in attitudes to films coming from the Changchun studio. Its staff was the youngest. Whatever old hands were still around worked in the Shanghai and Peking studios, and it was *their* old friends who sat in the Film Bureau and the distribution office. I felt that Changchun films always got the thinnest chance, critically and commercially; naturally this made me defensive about each worthy film that came from the Northeast. On more than one occasion both entrenched and younger studios would finish films on a similar subject, and I sensed that the "young" film (which invariably tried harder) was helped less. I noticed this for the first time when two comedies on the new life of urban women came from the Changchun and Haiyen (Shanghai) studios. The sales synopsis for the Shanghai version, *Everywhere Is Spring*, could fit both films:

. . . the story of a group of housewives in a lane in Shanghai [or new flats in Changchun] who leave their kitchens during the big leap forward to plunge into social production. They are bubbling over with eagerness to play their part in building up socialism. Undaunted by the disapproval of mothers-in-law with feudal ideas or the opposition of husbands, they overcome all manner of diffi-culties and take the road to happiness pointed out by the Party, organising them-selves to join in productive labour.[3]

Everywhere Is Spring could have been one of those big leap productions made in four weeks, no structure and all situations predictable. The characters were as cut and dried as the synopsis hints, but they were played by familiar and popular actors — the names of Chang Jui-fang and Sun Tao-lin were a partial guarantee to filmgoers that their evening would not be wasted.

Using less popular actors the competing film from Changchun was revised so
often I'm not sure that it was ever publicly shown. Even its title was harried by
the administration, each change for the worse: I first heard of it as *Women's
Army*, then as *The Flowers Meet the Rain* (or *Rain Upon the Flowers*), and the
last time I saw it it was called *A Smile on Every Face.* In my futile effort to have
it sent abroad I suggested *Woman's Place* as an English title that might indicate
the humorous tone of the film. As a "homely comedy" (perhaps the most
original form developed in new Chinese films) it was a prize, regardless of
an occasional carelessness (a scene that begins with an aching back should
remember that aching back to the end of the scene) and an unhelpfully rigid
photographic style. Both films were in color, but the Shanghai color was as
"safe" as if supervised by Mrs. Nathalie Kalmus. More seriously, the Shanghai
film was superficial, while the Changchun film showed more genuine concern for
the changing situation of its characters.

A film about the Long March was in preparation for several years. The magni-
tude of the subject was only one of the difficulties, but it was, in my opinion,
the one that wrecked the film. Another difficulty, though less fatal, was the
necessity to dissociate (at least on the surface) this proud historical moment
from the real persons associated with it in every mind. Soon after the victory of
1949, when it was clear that theater and films would treat the recent past, Mao
decreed that no government leader could be represented on stage or screen.
Paintings, prints, sculpture, tapestry — any medium without breath, indeed —
could show us the features and figure of Mao (always paired with Chu Teh in
those days), but no actor could pretend to be Mao. There were several reasons
for this, all worth analysis, yet I prefer to think that Stalin's "negative example"
was foremost among Mao's considerations. Gelovani's idealized duplicate of
Stalin in numerous Soviet films had become a joke for everyone but Stalin, and
Mao wanted no one to suspect a duplicate, and no jokes. The Long March film
shows an interesting solution: to divide the characteristics and known actions of
Mao between *two* fictional roles, so that no single actor could be thought the
embodiment of the leader. Every new Chinese film showing China after 1927
had, of course, other ways to keep Mao's name and face in the spectator's
consciousness: through quotation and praise in dialogue or commentary, and
through the ubiquitous Face; some modern domestic films have this hanging in
every room shown.

The first step toward the film was to find a dramatic form that would be an
adequate substitute for the real events, though drawing upon them in details and
geography. Chen Chi-tung's play, *Across Ten Thousand Rivers and a Thousand
Mountains*, was first seen in 1954, and the filmed Long March was under way at

last. Few of the play's scenes were omitted in the final film adaptation by Sun Chien and Cheng Yin, and little was added beyond the interest of seeing the real places. The next step was to rehearse the real places, and the August First studio sent out a crew to explore them and, so as not to waste their time, the footage they brought back was edited into an actuality film, *Along the Route of the Long March* (1957). Finally in production, the large-scale film (in wide screen and color, of course) was to be a joint enterprise of the August First and Peking Studios; its first title was *Long Live the Red Army!*, but when released it assumed the play's title *Across Ten Thousand Rivers and a Thousand Mountains* (a quotation from a Mao poem).

The film begins with its strongest and most effective episode (not the first of the play's scenes — it could have meant little in the theater): the crossing of the Tatu River over the Luting Bridge, from which the Kuomintang enemy had removed everything but the swinging iron chains: it was over these that the Red Army crawled to victory.* For the rest of the film, heroic small figures of marchers through great forbidding spaces are resorted to for continuing tension, but such a single, repeated effect becomes exhausting rather than dramatic for the spectator. Though obvious, my report had to point this out: "The usual danger in such big imagery is that it tempts cameramen to build static tableaux rather than the coordinated fragments that are necessary for coherent editing." I was more interested in the split representation of Mao (not mentioned in the report). The more significant of the two was the "political director" Li Yu-kuo, played by Lan Ma with a precariously close resemblance to the real thing. A wound and fatal illness are added to cut the identification and to increase our sympathy. His exaggerated modesty, which makes him a burden to everyone else (no matter how attentive their raised, glowing faces), is an especially telling "character note":

The horse which Li Yu-kuo is riding — a gift of a Tibetan family — drops dead under him. To avoid burdening his comrades and to cheer them up, he not only refuses to be given special attention but, making light of his wound and illness, challenges his orderly to see which of them can walk faster. Despite his festering wound, a stomach bloated from the indigestible food he has been eating, and dizzy spells from exhaustion, he still shows himself as cheerful as ever, and imparts this optimism to all his comrades [who finally have to carry him!] .[4]

This, the biggest film for the anniversary, was possibly the least successful. The occasional humor misfired, the prolonged illness of unmistakable actor-heroes

---

* A satisfactorily dramatic account of this crossing, "the most famous legend of Red China," can be read in Malraux's *Antimémoires* (just before his conversation with Chen Yi); translated by Terence Kilmartin as *Anti-Memoirs* (New York: Harcourt, Brace and World, 1968).

was fatiguing, and as the huge landscapes were more depended upon, they grew heavier and less interesting.

Despite the care in shaping its dramatic form *Across Ten Thousand Rivers* suffered from a familiar disease of modern Chinese films: it ended several times. And each time "The End" did not appear you felt a little more cheated — a disaster for either film enjoyment or film belief. That year a critic, Hsu Chi-wu, published an article in *Zhungguo Dianying* entitled "How to End a Fictional Film." One suggestion is that the spectator pays more attention to the last scene than to any other part of a film and, among other warnings, he told filmwriters to beware the false ending. For his example he used a film less venerated than the Long March film, a manufactured product of 1957, *Soul of the Sea*. His point is that an audience knows better than a filmmaker: "When the revolutionary mutiny looked successful, all the spectators got up to go, but then fighting broke out, and they had to sit down again."[5]

Anyone who opens a history of Anglo-Chinese relations can find material for films. From a British viewpoint this is material for a comedy — the casualties have been forgotten.* Chinese see this as a shameful tragedy, but their films about it try to eliminate both shame and tragedy. It is unlikely that either side will ever film the Opium Wars without adopting a distortedly defensive position. It is clear that the Chinese have the better case (it is the baldest instance of economic aggression in modern history), and it was inevitable that the Republic would make its film about the 1840 Opium War and its true hero, Imperial Commissioner Lin Tse-hsu. In one respect the 1959 film of *Lin Tse-hsu* does not differ from the film about him made under Japanese occupation: they both showed undiluted hate and contempt for all foreigners. In 1942 it was enough to make the Sassoon family ridiculous in appearance, but in 1959 the foreigner had to be a *comic* villain, to make the audience forget the old humiliation: not only was the Chinese disguise that a foreign devil (played by Gerry Tannebaum) had assumed pierced by Cantonese boat people, but he had to fall in a puddle, and his hat into the river. In the filming this episode went further than the published script; the sequence ends with the capture of the cowardly Dent — by a mere female:

Dent is trapped as if in a cage with no way out. He shrinks into one corner, his face twitching with fear.

Mai Kuan's wife catches hold of him and throws him out on to the deok.

---

* In one history, full of humorous touches, the causes of the first Opium War are summed up in this priceless statement: "The British government adopted a very correct attitude." G. B. Endacott, *A History of Hong Kong* (New York: Oxford University Press, 1958).

Dent in desperation tries using the threat so effective with Ching government officials. He protests indignantly, "I . . . I'm a foreigner."

But the common people are not impressed by this, Mai Kuan's wife deals him a resounding slap on the face. "We know you're a foreigner." Dent shamelessly changes his tune. "No . . . I'm Chinese."

Mai Kuan's wife hits him again. He claps a hand to his cheek and says no more. Liang San and others tie Dent up.[6] [applause from audience]

As a historical reconstruction *Lin Tse-hsu* is remarkably rich (see Plate 41) but suddenly, halfway through, you can see its collapse into shoddiness and hasty solutions. Explanation: the Big Leap. While in production drastic economies of both time and money were demanded of all enterprises, and this film's deliberate progress was reformed disastrously. In his report on the film industry's celebration of the anniversary year Hsia Yen boasted, " . . . of the 18 fictional films produced as a gift for National Day last year, most were filmed in four or five months, some in as little as three."[7] Chao Tan's characterization of Lin also changed from careful to hasty well before the end of the film. Great things were expected of this association of the makers of *Crows and Sparrows*, Chao Tan and the director Cheng Chun-li, but the hopes were only half realized, thanks to the Leap.

29 Oct. Rewards for the morning's search: a Marx Bros. film with Japanese titles [*Monkey Business*] , *Swamp Water, Scarlet Street, Die ewige Maske.* Most of morning devoted to putting *Les Miserables* in order.

Interrupted for excursion to August First studio to see stereokino tests. In icy projection room couldn't work up much enthusiasm for any of the tests (with divided spectacles — an already shelved idea abroad). Introduced *in whisper* to all as "from Hollywood"! No shooting to be seen — "another time."

This excursion turned out to be an introduction to another, which gave me one of my most pleasant experiences this year. Would I meet the studio's group of amateur scenarists? A lecture was suggested, and I bargained for a discussion instead, with film extracts. At the Archive we decided on the extracts and the next day all that I needed were found and readied except *The Flowers Meet the Rain* — suddenly unavailable, possibly returned to Changchun for revision.

31 Oct. Taken to the studio in the afternoon where I met a large, filled auditorium — this was surely more than a small group of "amateur scenarists." It turned out to be most of the studio staff, and I was glad I had prepared the program carefully. Glad, too, for such an alert interpreter.

I began by explaining my choice of extracts and the main subject for discussion; here are my notes, didactic tone and all:

These fragments were selected from films that you know, so that you would be reminded of the whole of each of these films. Each has a vital and important subject, but in each case I sense some contradiction between the content and its treatment — and that is what I hope we can talk about today. For it is one thing to have good content in a film — but your job is to *convey* that content to its audience in the most fully expressive way. It doesn't matter whether you will be working in instructional films, or animated cartoons, or historical films, or newsreels — so long as you are working in films, for a film audience, you have the task of using film to speak to that audience. To give them the right *words* is only part of your job. Those words have to be supported — and sometimes transformed — with all the arts and sciences that make the film medium. If this is neglected, your content will touch no one's heart or brain. If you learn to use film, you can change the people as they sit in the theater — they will not be the same people who entered the theater before they saw your film.

The first extract was the beginning (the first two reels) of *Huang Pao-mei*, to show a contradiction between its reality of cotton mill and the artificiality of treatment and photography. Without being able to show a sample of *The Flowers Meet the Rain* (several raised hands showed that some had seen it), I mentioned that its scenario was the work of a collective team of writers and that "one of the great assets of the film is the spontaneity of its dialogue — you can easily believe that real people are saying these words." But the director and cameraman had not worked out together "the right way to photograph the action, to accent this spontaneity and humor." Reel 2 of *Lin Tse-hsu* provoked the main part of the later discussion.

I felt very bold with my next extract, the first reels of *Across Ten Thousand Rivers*, the chief effort of *this* studio for the anniversary year!

Test it for some of the factors we have been talking about:
Do you participate in every moment of its action?
Where are you conscious of merely watching a performance from outside?
Does the photography express, in the best possible way, the content of the scene and its action?
Are the actions and pictures as strong as the words?

Taking a further chance, I spoke about the difference between the film's theme and the film's effect:

As a play the theme of selfless heroism remained in the foreground constantly, while the big actions of the Long March could be only indicated or talked about on the stage — the battles, the crossing of the Great Snow Mountains or the swamps. But in a film all these actions jump into the foreground, with all the power of real places and circumstances. The statement of the theme has to be newly measured against these powerful new conditions.

I believe that this would have been a stronger film if it had altered the play's structure completely, and shown us the theme through *one* incident of the Long March — even a small incident can express the spirit of the whole march better than crowding the film with everything that happened. Please look at this sequence of crossing the Tatu River with the idea that it could have been the material for the entire film. Perhaps someone in this group will some day write the great film about the Long March that still waits to be made.

For the last extract I chose what I considered a completely successful piece of Chinese filmmaking, a perfect fusion of content and style — the first two reels of Chin Shan's *Along the Sungari River.* Judging from what was said later, it was unfamiliar to most of those present.

The discussion was fine, as open as any I heard in China. I was startled but pleased to hear my reports to Hsia Yen being quoted and challenged, along with what I said that afternoon. They did not actually *say* that my objections to *Lin Tse-hsu* were those of a foreigner, but I was criticized for commenting on the absence of opium in a film about the Opium War. The Long March film was not defended, but I thought then this was because it was untouchable. In general the occasion was so lively and good that I was sure it would have a sequel, but this was my last visit to the August First Studio. I was told there would be more sessions, but this was the end. Should I have been more diplomatic about the Long March film, or was I altogether offensive? Did someone remember the regulations against foreign teachers (except for languages), and stop further meetings at this studio or the film school? Or had I miscalculated everything?

To add to the stimulating (for me) afternoon I met the director whose work I admired most at the August First studio. Coming out into the chilly dusk I was introduced to Wang Ping, and her warmth and charm changed the temperature of the air. She was about 45 and managed to be both brisk and soft in her movements and voice. You could see at once that this solidly plump woman could be determined and persuasive with the people working around her. I had recently seen her *Constant Beam* and she deflected my compliments like an experienced duelist. I hoped to hear about her new film, or even to be invited to see her at work, but we all moved along just then.

Lin Tse-hsu had alerted me to some of the dilemmas of Chinese biographical films, but I was quite unprepared for the nonsense and uselessness of *Nieh Erh*. This went further from the composer's life and further into fiction than any of the forgotten "biographies" produced in either the United States or the Soviet Union when this form was a substitute for making real films. People who knew

Nieh Erh told me that the figure on the screen was wholly fictional. Yet most of the people working on this film — scenarists, cameraman, the director Cheng Chun-li (leaping from one anniversary film to another) — had been acquainted with the real Nieh Erh. The only conclusion I could draw from this was that there had been a deliberate decision to make a "stronger" film story than could be made from Nieh Erh's real life. Then and now I think it would have been more satisfactory, as well as more honest, to make a frank synthesis of several revolutionary composers' lives, possibly with the guidance of Rolland's synthetic composer.

Nor did the things one saw on the screen give much comfort or stimulation. The color was "like needles in the eyes" (as one viewer expressed it to me) and the performance of Chao Tan was a constant embarrassment. To the bouncing youngster he had played in *Crossroads* he added the furrowed brow, open mouth and poised pen required of any composer shown in a film, and the combination was as unreal as the film's story. How often he must have prayed during the production that he would never again have to pretend to be twenty!

The Lin Family's Shop was a film heard about long before it was seen. Its scenario by Hsia Yen from a famous story by Mao Tun (then Minister of Culture, and Hsia Yen's superior) was enough to whet all expectations. Its director was the surviving member of the team that made *The White-Haired Girl.* When we finally saw the film it was clear that it had been made with the greatest of care, greater than in the case of *New Year Offering* or *Lin Tse-hsu,* and its period was more precisely evoked: the reconstruction of a provincial town in the early thirties was managed with extra attention to each costume, each background. The camerawork was rich, though timid:

The absence of leading characters from some scenes appears to have freed the cameraman to take more chances and get finer results; an example of this: the scene outside Kuomintang headquarters (with Shou-sheng and Mr. Yu — at the end of reel 7) showed a bold use of giant characters written on the background wall (and I should like to think that these characters for "salt" and "vinegar" were placed with intention behind this bitter conversation).* What a pity that a similar boldness could not have heightened the more important dramatic moment at the beginning of reel 9 when Shou-sheng writes the character for "Go!" on the table — this is a moment that almost passes unnoticed, so weakly

---

* Such an intention was denied to me so vehemently that I felt more sure that it had motivated this sequence. The idea of filming for such reasons was too taboo to be admitted. The pale filming of the money scenes was another reflection of this taboo on idea emphasis.

is it filmed.* And money — the very subject of the film — is filmed as an
incidental object, with one or two ordinary close-ups. Rarely does a camera
position or composition place money in its proper relationship to the characters — this could have determined and strengthened the whole pictorial element
of the film.

I detected a far more serious flaw in this handsome film that I had to mention.
In the light of the later bitterness around this film and its scenarist, I quote the
doubts of my report fully:

I read Mao Tun's story [of 1933] just before I heard that it was adapted as a
film. I thought then that it would have to be an extraordinary film to be as
objective and as uncompromising as this story. I tried to imagine how this
nightmare about money could be conveyed with film, and though film seemed
an ideal medium for it, I wondered if a Chinese film would want to be this harsh.
Brecht also is a writer whose work demands a resistance to all the concessions
that films normally make.

So it is easy to understand that as much as I admire many aspects of this film,
there is a basic worry in it for me. The tradition that demands that a screen
family must all be sweet, though sometimes mistaken and often victimized, is a
tradition that is at war throughout the film with the meaning and aim of Mao
Tun's story. When we are shown glimpses of these lovable people doing mean or
cruel things, the spectator is bound to feel confused and torn between opposing
concepts. The people he watches look like normal film heroes and heroines —
self-sacrificing, fearless, etc. — but their acts are the acts of villains, selfish and
regardless of the fate of others. When we see Lin, at the end, sailing sadly away
(in a melancholy twilight!) over the screams of Widow Chang and the crowd,
though this is an excellent film moment, it is the climax of the film's contradictions. I should have preferred a colder, more realistic film (*without* music) in
which the appeal to my sympathy would have grown from watching believable
people in a hopeless predicament. But this film made a dangerous concession to
"tradition." Pleasant film characters who do unpleasant things deprive the film
of emotion as well as logic. I must confess to having been more touched, in the

---

* Even the picture-book version of this moment was stronger, though similarly cluttered.

restaurant scene (reel 7) by an old man in the background picking his teeth than
by the foreground sufferings of Lin himself.

The ambivalence forced on Hsia Yen by the soft traditions of Chinese films
shows clearly in a letter written to Hsieh Tien (playing Lin), on 16 April 1958.[8]
From the crew's first days on location in the small town of Lin Hu, near
Hangchow, Hsieh Tien had inquired, with the approval of Shui Hua, the director,
how to resolve certain contradictions in the scenario's character of Lin, and Hsia
Yen replied:

[Such people] could still exploit others weaker than themselves (i.e., smaller
merchants, peasants, salesclerks, widows, and orphans). But generally speaking,
in the conditions of that time, the pressure on them was heavier, and the
pressure they could exert on others was lighter. Imperialism and feudal force
then still exerted the greatest pressure on such people; that is why they, within a
certain period and within certain limits, can be seen as having a little resistance
character. . . .

In acting Lin the problem is to control these proportions. One cannot show Lin
as a 100% negative figure, nor can one allow the audience to sympathize with
him. Faced by wolves he is a sheep, but in front of a rabbit he becomes a wlld
dog. . . . In moments of the latter tendency the *interior* acting should be intensi-
fied, so that the audience senses this element without your resorting to overheated,
exterior acting. — What I say is merely for reference.[*]

Yet my conclusions may be mistaken — Hsia Yen may have been aiming only at
a subtler style of acting, especially as Hsieh Tien was known as an actor of
"negative roles."

By now I was aware that this film's scenarist (and probably its personal super-
visor) was the same official who ordered my reports. We were at a dinner
with Hsia Yen soon after he recieved my report on his film, and though he made
no reference to it or to the *Lin Family*, he urged me to continue the reports. It
was an extremely moving moment.

As the anniversary year approached its end, Hsia Yen prepared a public report[9]
on the current position of the film industry. He begins with an account of its

---

[*] The same letter shows care for the atmosphere of the period:
"Today Minister Chen and I saw the test. We were quite satisfied, though there's still one
matter to be watched: in showing those hard tImes in such a small, backwater town, a feeling of prosperity should be avoided in the settings and clothing. Minister Chen noticed that
the things on the teahouse tables were too well arranged, and the fruits and sweets looked
too rich. If you've already shot this scene, there's no need to redo it, but for future scenes
please keep in mind the atmosphere of the time, and the beat of the political pulse. — But
this also is merely a point for reference."

physical growth in the ten years of the Republic, including the increased film audience, and a marked decrease in production costs. Some necessary self-criticism (in speaking of the *quality* of recent film productions) is followed by references to victories through earlier criticism (of *The Life of Wu Hsün* and the "poisonous weeds" of 1957). The Big Leap of the film industry in 1958 is identified with Chou Yang's indoctrination speech of 11 March 1958 (quoted at length). A present obstacle is "undue reverence for the West" and for bourgeois art (Stendhal and *Jean Christophe* were still tempting young people). This may be the reason why "many films made in the past were unacceptable to peasants,* who could not understand or enjoy them."

The main problem is that many of those who are dealing with this art and producing films are extremely westernized and cut off from the masses. The modern play is also an art form which came from abroad, but we film workers have not succeeded in making the cinema as popular and national as the modern theater. We seldom pay attention to the problem of national form which Chairman Mao raised long ago; instead we usually imitate the West, not daring to liberate ourselves from the form of foreign films. Premier Chou En-lai has told us time and again that a film must be intelligible to the masses; the story must have a beginning and an end, must develop clearly instead of jumping from one thing to another, the character should talk like a Chinese and every sentence must be clear to the audience. To my mind, some of us still ignore these important instructions completely. As I said at one conference, it is puzzling to me why certain film workers should show so little interest in the Party's instructions and put such difficulties in the way of carrying out Party directives, while they are so quick and eager to accept the so-called new techniques and forms of expression of foreign films. Some time ago, when we learned of a new mode of expression called "poetic montage," some of us seized on it as if it were a treasure, regardless of whether this was necessary or not, whether the people wanted it or not. Film workers of this sort are adept at taking over other people's methods. . . . What they lack entirely is a mass viewpoint, a sense of responsibility towards our five hundred million peasants.

Hsia Yen took a cautious view: "In the film world the task of 'demolishing the old base' has not yet been completed."

Though my filmgoing had become rather systematic, it was by chance that I first saw the film I yearned for, a new Chinese film that needed no apology or explanation, a fine film. No one had prepared me for this experience: the screening was not for me — I passed a door, saw that a film was beginning, and walked in. It was so wonderful to see emotional, imaginative filmmaking that I was afraid of my own satisfaction — maybe the surprise had unbalanced my

---

* The Communist Party told the film industry to produce at least eight films for the peasants in 1960.

judgment — what was I drinking just before this screening? — so I asked to see *Storm* again. A week later it was just as good — no, better. I wish I could see it again.

The subject of *Storm* is the second great strike in China in which the recently founded Communist Party played a role: the general strike called by the workers of the Peking-Hankow Railroad in 1923. (See Plates 38 and 39). The scenario and direction are by Chin Shan, an adaptation of his play[10] which he had directed and in which he played a central role, Shih Yang, the Hankow lawyer, the same role he plays in the film. When it was clear to me that this was the same Chin Shan who made that pearly opening of *Along the Sungari River*, I felt the pleasure of watching a sure artist's growth. Only later and gradually did I learn why he had waited ten years to make his first creative work in film since 1949.

The play had gone into the repertory of Peking's China Youth Art Theater in June 1958 and had remained there, a notable success, until the film's production began for the anniversary (an unusually swift decision, based on the success of the *Reservoir* film's production scheme), when Chin Shan with some others of the original cast were freed for work in the film. Chin Shan had been the leading director and actor of the Theater (I heard particular praise for his *Uncle Vanya*) but his work was out of the repertory during and after the film's production (though he remained on the theater's staff). It was the unquestioned success of *Storm* as a play that determined its film adaptation for the anniversary. As its author and player one might have expected Chin Shan to cling to the form and effects of his play (or its production), but a comparison of the play with the film shows us that he took the opportunity to reshape and point the film's action beyond what was possible in its play form. Every shot counts — and mounts — with a film purpose.

Into a film subject area, the recent past, which was threatened by a reduction of situations and characters to unreal patterns and symbols, Chin Shan moved with dignity and originality, whether showing the miserable life of Hankow's workers (without sentimentality) or the intrigues and traps and smooth talk of their masters (whose cleverness you can almost admire). To have so much imagination fused with so much reality was the greatest film accomplishment, for me, of the anniversary year. I completely believed that this was Hankow in the early 1920s.* The same fusion in the acting, of stylization from Peking opera (note the unreal but powerful pauses just before a gesture or larger movement) and

---

* "For the scene in which lawyer Shih Yang walked through the streets of Hankow, whole blocks closed shop and were transformed into what they looked like thirty years ago. . . ."
— Liu Yi-fang, in *China Reconstructs*, Nov. 1959.

credibility from the Moscow Art Theater, may also have increased the popularity of the play.

Another dangerous element, color, was also challenged by this boldest Chinese film artist. His film's color is a living argument to any cameraman and director that color can be made a dramatic support rather than a pretty ornament; here you feel its care adding to the intensity of each speech, each moral lesson. Both interiors and exteriors show the same command and restraint of this difficult and usually defeating element. Each sequence is given its own limited color range — it helps you taste the opium smoke in the room of Wu Pei-fu's political adviser or conveys the bright buoyancy of the opening of the union hall. Chin Shan must have had the most understanding and harmonious working relation with cameraman and designer.

Another quality that sets it apart from the Chinese plays and films of the period (and most of the films of previous years) is that its characters grow and change and *have character*. Even the "negative" characters seem unmanipulated: the warlord Wu Pei-fu on his tiger-skin chair is a powerful figure whose next move you cannot predict. Even more remarkable (and for this Chin Shan's contact with the modern theater, especially with Chekhov, may be thanked) is that characters in his work are *involved* with each other. These are not separate chess pieces being moved about in traditional or novelettish relationships that customarily provide the links within a Chinese film. Here are true involvements of love and of hate that eventually touch the audience and, further, each spectator's imagination. This, incidentally, lifts all *performances* in the film: good actors, such as Shih Yu in the role of Wu's advisor, look better than ever; untrained actors, such as Gerry Tannebaum in the role of the British Consul, look confident and experienced.

Both of these qualities, change and involvement, so fundamental (one would think) in passionate revolutionary art, excited criticism and suspicion of *Storm*. My praise was met with sour looks. All felt, along with the film's effectiveness, that there was something wrong here, even though it was hard to identify the sin. In any case no further film jobs were considered for Chin Shan. He returned to his theater work and soon suffered a heart attack that continues, till this writing, to immobilize him.

After my two viewings of *Storm*, and well before its public release, I noticed that Chin Shan often dined near his theater at the Peking Hotel, where we were also eating that month, and once as we were leaving together (I must have contrived this), I thanked him effusively, and probably a little frighteningly, for

his great film. He was no longer the dashing dandy that I knew from his first
Shanghai films; now his presence was imposing, even towering. I noticed that his
hair was still in the style of Shih Yang — just in case retakes were required.

I knew a friend of his, and counted on this to meet Chin Shan, but his heart
condition and hospitalization (and some other factors, no doubt) ruled this out
for the time. Two years later, though, he was well enough for a talk. He spoke
some English, and his wife, who was directing productions at the Drama School,
understood Russian, so we didn't have much trouble.

Sunday, 28 May [1961]. Extraordinary hours with Ch. — very direct and
enthusiastic about everything. No reluctance to make more films — on the
contrary, eager. But his contract is with a theater [by choice, I learned later].
More fundamental difficulty: a difference of opinion as to the necessity for
simplicity. Too much of the old stressing of the "novelty" of films holding back
their progress. But not sure whether he agreed with me on the industry's *under-*
estimation of the Chinese film audience. Has lots of ideas he wants to try (said
rather sadly). Does not need his own play or his own performance. Would prefer
other's scripts, but he must do the shooting-script himself. Glad to act for other
directors, but always is tempted to direct his own performance. Does not object
to *not* playing in films of his direction, so he may not have the Welles disease.
(He had not wanted to play his old role himself [in *Storm*], but time was getting
short and no one else had been found.) Very good on casting [of *Storm*] — and
how to work with unskilled actors, cast for their appearance (the man who
played Wu Pei-fu).

Could not understand his explanation for difference between beginning of the
Sungari film and the subsequent story part — but he was happy I liked the
beginning more.

Wanted to ask him if he knew the Southern Sung painting, "Departure at
Dawn," when he made the courtyard scene of *Sungari* — but it suddenly
seemed irrelevant.

Roar of laughter when I said I had seen *Song at Midnight*. Roar of appreciation
when I told him my instructions to the National Film Theater projectionist to
stop *Storm* as soon as he saw the shot of the sun obscured by the smoke of the
burning workers' quarter. That's where he wanted to end his film — the rest was
obligatory.*

Physically not at all well — has had six months of rest — not back in theater until
autumn.

---

* This postscript is embarrassing: to prevent the film ending tragically, the ghosts of all the
heroes gather with the living (the time is left vague) to march on to victory. This unsatisfactory optimism was first tried for the ending of *Big Road* (1934). The play of *Storm* also
had an epilogue, less objectionable.

But I have not heard that he ever went back. Theater work may have been less strenuous, politically, than films, but it still meant more struggle than he could stand.

Before leaving China I learned more about the ten filmless years. Soon after 1949 he resigned from the party, itself an unforgivable act (Kuo Mo-jo was the only Chinese party member whose career was not broken by resignation). Then, as a reduced actor, he joined a troupe that entertained Chinese troops in Korea, and it was there he made an even bigger mistake — being found in the wrong bed. It was not "just" adultery — the lady's husband was important, and Chin Shan's friends thought he would never be seen on a stage again. Films were out of the question. His two sins help to explain the negative reactions I heard in official quarters to China's best film. It seems a miracle that he was allowed to make it. It is one of China's many tragedies that their best filmmaker is not making films.

In September 1959 I was offered a job in London for a few months at the beginning of 1960. As my passport was due to expire then this seemed too opportune to decline; I asked for and was granted a leave of absence. After seeing *Storm* I thought it possible to arrange an attractive Chinese film season in London. One such film could justify a whole display of this sort, and no city west of Berlin had seen a group of new Chinese films since 1949. The film export office in Peking was less than enthusiastic, and we did not agree on the selection of films to be shown. *Nieh Erh* had been dubbed in English and could not be dismissed. Needless to say, by the following August, when the season was shown, the export office *and* the Chinese Mission in London had the final say on selection. By that time I had been back in China for some time and was too concerned by Si-lan's serious illness, which attacked her while I was in London, to struggle over such trifles as whether *Two Generation of Swimmers* was a better choice than *Sisters on Ice*. But *Storm* was shown.

The tenth anniversary also marked the end of foreign coproduction with the Chinese film industry.* Just before the October celebration I attended a screening of *Wind from the East*, a rather thin story that added up to little more than an "adventure film" about Soviet and Chinese engineers working together to build a dam and then to protect it with a linked chain of their bodies, when a storm threatened the unfinished structure. But this was made to look more

---

* Since then only television films made in China by Japanese, English, French, and Italian companies have received Chinese cooperation.

important and significant than it actually was by the expert direction of Yefim Dzigan (famous for his *We Are from Kronstadt*) and the photography of Arkadi Kaltsati. The modest interiors contributed as much to the visual power of the film as did the magnificent scenes at the dam. The total effect was conspicuously bolder than in "normal" Chinese films — more chances were taken, and more rules were broken.

At the final program on 3 October in the Congress Hall we found ourselves sitting between Burmese guests (a monk and his sister) on one side and some of the Soviet delegation on the other. The man sitting next to me was Dzigan, and beyond him was Surin, the head of Mosfilm and coproducer with the Changchun studio of *Wind from the East*. Dzigan felt so miserable about his film that he was relieved to have someone new to tell his troubles to. His "adventure film" had started out two years before as heroic tragedy, but the Chinese fear of any modern tragedy on the screen had brought all their delaying tactics into play: they made so many demands for changes and deletions on each script that was submitted to them that the only way to get the film made was to make it their way. It was the last Chinese-Soviet coproduction.

11 Hong Kong

Before 1949 Hong Kong was a refuge (not always wholly happy) for filmmakers running from threats to their work or their lives, whether the threats came from Japan, or the Kuomintang, or the bureaucracy that discouraged Benjamin Polaski in 1913.

In 1923 Polaski's Hong Kong partner, Li Ming-wei, gave up trying to establish a profitable film production center and Hong Kong's film business resumed its primary function as a showplace, rather than as an industrial base, until a political and commercial crisis drove theater people there. The bloody end of Canton's commune made that city an uncomfortable place for any kind of entertainment. The show people who fled to Hong Kong in 1927 were too numerous to be supported by paying Chinese customers; one desperate alternative was for a group of unemployed actors to pool enough savings to start a film (often left unfinished), and these improvised, hopeful gestures toward filmmaking became the base for Hong Kong's film industry, always a little precarious and groping.

In the early thirties, sound and dialogue brought some independence from Shanghai's industry and also made Hong Kong film production a less risky matter, for most films made there were in Cantonese dialect, a boon to the overseas Chinese colonies, especially through the Pacific, where the emigrants from South China could not understand the spoken northern (or Mandarin) dialect. used in all Shanghai talkies.

Japan's aggression in the North was also a factor. The first Shanghai producer to move his studio to Hong Kong away from the Japanese advance was Lo Ming-yü, early in 1932. In 1934 the Tien Yi Company also began to move its equipment from Shanghai, and after the Japanese attacks in July and August 1937 this studio was transformed into Hong Kong's South Seas Studio. After Shanghai was left in Japanese hands Hong Kong, rather than Hankow or Chungking, was made by film refugees into the most active source for political, anti-Japanese films, and the British colony was for the first time the center of the Chinese cinema. By 1940 the Japanese occupation of Canton swelled the number of film émigrés available for studio work in Hong Kong.

But by the end of December 1941 Hong Kong was also in Japanese hands.

. . . when they moved into Hongkong, the Japanese took over the seventy small producing companies which formed the center of anti-Japanese movie production and organized them into the Hongkong Motion Picture Association.[1]

I have learned nothing about the Chinese films made for the Japanese in Hong Kong: the Chinese who worked on them are not eager to draw attention to their wartime histories.

Between the end of the war and the capture of Shanghai by the People's Liberation Army, a new wave of film refugees arrived in Hong Kong, escaping from the
new repressions by the Kuomintang of Shanghai's left intellectuals. Hsia Yen
reappeared in Hong Kong, Ouyang Yu-chien made a "quickie" for a new company there, Chu Shih-ling, one of the scenarists of *The Money Tree*, Li Pin-chian
(who became P. T. "Jack" Li) arrived, and the veteran directors Tan Du-yu and
Cheng Bu-kao came to stay. As usual in Hong Kong the best and the worst films
were made side by side. Early in 1946 the first film of the Great China (Ta
Zhung Hua) Film Company touched themes that were still untouchable in
Shanghai:

The picture describes the degeneration of a young man after the victory in contrast to his successes during the hard days of the anti-Japanese war. It also
ridicules the "Chungking Guests" [the take-over officials] and traitors claiming
to be underground agents of the Government.[2]

This film, *Gone Are the Swallows When the Reeds Turn White*, was shown
successfully in Shanghai as well as in Hong Kong, and may have assisted such
bold criticism to squeeze through the Kuomintang production censors a year
later. But the same studio was capable of such "yellow" films as *She's Old
Enough to Marry, Heavenly Night, Oriole Outside the Blossom.*[*] In a satirical
short play of the time, *Miss Hong Kong*, a film official introduced himself: "We
represent the Patriotic Film Company. We specialize in pictures with a love
interest."[3]

While Ouyang Yu-chien was briefly in Hong Kong he was also employed as
scenarist by the Yunghua Studio, founded on brothel and opium profits; his
scripts were not produced.[†] The studio's second film, *The Secret History of the
Ching Court* (1948), was written by Yao Ke, editor of the *Tien Hsia Monthly*,
and directed by Chu Shih-ling (see Plate 23). It was an expensive historical spectacle, ancestor to Hong Kong's later spectacles, and had a political viewpoint
that was to cause trouble in Peking.

After the liberation of Peking and Shanghai a new and more complicated relationship was worked out between the film studios of "Mainland China" and of
Hong Kong. The Crown Colony now functioned as a refuge for the artists and
merchants of Shanghai's film industry who decided that there was no future for

---

[*] A news item in *China Digest* (25 Feb. 1947) on the breakup of the Great China Co., when
they were unable to pay salaries, suggests that a new management may have been responsible for those later films.
[†] See pages 171—172.

them with the communists. Yet there also flourished, alongside these émigré
enterprises, the film projects of Chinese (largely Cantonese) filmmakers who
were so sympathetic with the new regime in Peking that their operation was
eventually placed on a firm basis of companies and studios aided by mainland
finance and occasional mainland distribution. These opposing film factions of
Hong Kong do not seem to have clashed openly, any more than as rival companies. Their main markets were the same overseas Chinese settlements through
the Pacific area and in Latin America, and it is likely that cutthroat sales
methods, using politics as a weapon, were until recently more openly practiced
far from Hong Kong.

The first step toward stabilizing film commerce between communist mainland
and imperial island came in 1950 when a commission was appointed by the
Ministry of Culture in Peking to decide which Chinese films (including those
produced in Hong Kong) should remain in circulation. This was a vital activity
for the Propaganda Department, and Lu Ting-yi and Chou Yang worked on the
commission (probably Chung Tien-fei also served on it), voting for or against
each film under consideration. Another important member of this commission
was Chiang Ching, the former film actress Lan P'ing and present wife of Mao
Tse-tung, whose personal delegate she was on this commission. She never forgot
an argument that she lost on this occasion; seventeen years later, when the Mao
forces sought evidence to use against Liu Shao-ch'i, she told her story about the
commission's disagreement on *Secret History of the Ch'ing Court*, still current in
mainland cities in 1950. As in other evidence against Liu, he played no part in
this discussion or disagreement, but the sins of the Propaganda Department and
of the film are inseparably identified with him. The film is represented as being
not enthusiastic enough or patriotic enough on the subject of the Boxer Rebellion, and this is automatically shaped into an accusation against Liu Shao-ch'i.
This is the way the old argument came to light in 1967:

Comrade Chiang Ching, then a member of a committee for guiding the work of
the cinema under the Ministry of Culture, upheld the proletarian revolutionary
line of Chairman Mao and at a number of meetings proposed that the film
[*Secret History of the Ch'ing Court*] should be firmly criticized and repudiated.
However, Lu Ting-yi, Chou Yang, Hu* and others vigorously opposed this proposal and did their best to advertise the "patriotic progressiveness" of this reactionary film. When Comrade Chiang Ch'ing wanted to act according to Chairman
Mao's directive, they threw at her the reactionary talk of their boss behind the

---

* Elsewhere in the article he is identified only as "a certain Hu, a standing vice-director of
the Propaganda Department of the Party's Central Committee at that time [1950]." This
may be only a way to avoid printing the full name of Hu Feng.

scenes, the top Party person in authority taking the capitalist road [Liu Shao-ch'i], and said: "Comrade so and so holds that it is a patriotic film." Firmly upholding the truth, Comrade Chiang Ch'ing stood her ground and in no uncertain terms refuting their reactionary and ludicrous statements insisted that the film should be criticized and repudiated. They had to give way, but perfunctorily appointed an historian of reactionary views to write a short fake criticism which was really aimed at shielding the film. They considered even such an article "too sharp," and held up publication, thus smothering a major [!] struggle between the proletariat and the bourgeoisie on the cultural and ideological fronts.[4]

I am fascinated by the variety of possible motives for reviving this attack on a forgotten film. Beating Liu over the head is the most visible motive. Beating the already prone heads of Propaganda is always a help to the cause, too. Establishing an intellectual's attitude to the Boxer Rebellion (and the role of the Empress Dowager) as a test of his patriotism is another motive. Recording Chiang Ching's early courage in defying the enemy is another. The divided feelings within the Peking governing circles to the left intellectuals of Hong Kong play some part here, too. The Yenan group would see no advantage in encouraging Hong Kong leftists (by not beating them); the "Shanghai group" — the "realists" — would do everything possible to win more support for the Peking authorities. I have not seen *The Secret History of the Ch'ing Court*, but the Italian comments of 1950 and the quotations in the 1967 attack show little deviation from the familiar "patriotic" position in regard to the Boxer Rebellion, and the makers of the film would have been shocked to be told that a "little deviation" was too much for Peking in 1950. So nothing was said at the time (the quarrel waited, like so many others, seventeen years until the revelations of the Cultural Revolution), and the Mao family kept their silence, too. An angry letter from Mao Tse-tung of 16 October 1954 to the Political Bureau, whipping up the storm around *The Dream of the Red Chamber*, mentioned *The Secret History*, but his letter, too, waited until 1967 to be revealed:

At no time since it was shown all over the country has the film [*Secret History of the Ch'ing Court*] — described as patriotic though in fact a film of national betrayal — yet been criticized and repudiated. *The Life of Wu Hsün* has been criticized, but the lessons have not yet been drawn. . . .[5]

A minor but distinctly curious aspect of this case is that the published attacks in the present quarrel never mention that *Secret History* was made in 1948 and in Hong Kong.*

---

* A Hong Kong journal did reveal this much at the time of the film's "discussion-screenings" in Canton (*Eastern Horizon*, June 1967, pp. 3—4).

Secret History was the first postwar Hong Kong film to reach Europe, through the Locarno festival of 1950, where it was seen as the hopeful sign of a new source for vital films.[6] Chu Shih-ling's Dividing Wall (1951), a realistic film of living conditions in Hong Kong, does not appear to have been sent abroad; it may be the bravest of his many films for the Feng Huang Studio. Cheng Bu-kao maintained his Shanghai reputation with a great success of 1954, Merry-Go-Round, and a steady output that ceased in about 1960 with his unannounced retirement. Jack Li has been a support to Great Wall since its start: Casiraghi praises the satirical elements in his Terrible Truth (1949) and Blood Will Tell.

On 10 January 1952 Hong Kong authorities deported eight Chinese filmworkers on suspicion of too much activity on behalf of the Peking government. The best known of the eight was the scenarist, Ssuma Wen-sen. A second group of deportations — also including some filmworkers — occurred later in the month. This was a setback for the left-inclined studio of Hong Kong, though Shanghai studios must have benefited from the experience of the deportees. The unaligned film companies of Hong Kong, especially that of the Shaw Brothers, from Singapore,* "the tycoons of the Southeast Asian film world" (in the phrase of A. C. Scott), now had the island's film industry to themselves; to make themselves less dependent on Chinese personnel, they brought some technicians from India in 1952, probably adding to the already ornate tendencies of their films. Old favorites, under new titles and with more money (such as A Torn Lily, shown at the 1953 Edinburgh Festival, and Pa Chin's predictably weepy Spring and Autumn), became the fundament for the Shaw and other Hong Kong commercial film enterprises.

Hong Kong's films at this period seemed an uninterrupted continuation of the films made in Shanghai's "orphan island" period. Now that it is difficult to see Shanghai films of that time, it may be useful to know that Hong Kong films of after the war can be examined for their close resemblance to them in every way. They had more lavish budgets, but here were the same historical spectacles, the same tearful dramas, the same faces, indeed (for Hu Tieh and Li Li-li now starred there), that had held on to Shanghai's film business after its radicals moved west and south in the war. In 1954 there was an attempt, not to break these profitable patterns, but to make them more attractive (and with color), by arranging a coproduction with a Japanese studio: Mizoguchi was brought there to direct Yang Kuei-fei, about the emperor's concubine who helped to end his reign and

---

* There were two studios in Singapore, the Cathay and the Malay, and one in Kuala Lumpur; most of their films are in Chinese and made for Chinese audiences.

dynasty. Sumptuously handsome and deliberate, it may have improved the Shaw
fortunes and prestige. For by 1958, when the critic Ezra Goodman visited Singapore, the Shaw Brothers had become the undisputed leaders of Southeast Asian
film production:

Runme and Run Run Shaw are a couple of cagey Chinese peasant boys who run
the largest entertainment empire in southeast Asia. They control everything from
movie studios and theaters to night clubs, restaurants and amusement parks. . . .
[In his Singapore office] Runme spoke of everything but movies. He talked
about yachting, horse racing, automobiles, even television. . . . Whenever I tried
to engage him in a discussion of movies, he would dismiss it with a remark like
"I don't really know much about it. I have people and pay them well to look
after my movie interests for me." . . . The closest competitor to the Shaw
brothers, Loke Wan Tho, head of the giant Cathay organization, who has a mere
fifty or sixty million dollars, also was loath to talk about the movies. When I saw
him in Singapore, the British-educated Loke discoursed at length about his
hobbies of ornithology and racing Lancias and looked at me as if I had committed a social error when I mentioned motion pictures.

Carol Reed, the British director, told me how the Shaw brothers conduct business. If you want to buy something from them or sell them something, they
receive you in their dignified, wood-paneled office . . . where they sit at opposite
sides of a gigantic desk. They listen to your sales talk without uttering a word.
You are then ushered outside to wait while they confer. Presently, you are again
summoned into the presence of the brothers. They simply inform you "yes,"
they will, or "no," they will not. That is all.[8]

A casual Indian journalist placed the Shaws in the whole Hong Kong picture:

There are three studios in Hong Kong of which two are in the hands of big business Chinese with their chain of cinema houses all over South East Asia and the
other is controlled by a group which has leanings towards Mainland China.
Amongst these three studios, there is an average of 300 films produced annually.
Hong Kong films do not reflect any political trends but keep to a middle road
policy because the situation in the countries of South East Asia is very shaky.[9]

The "hands of big business Chinese" can actually be detected in all four leading
studios of Hong Kong: the Shaws' enormous enterprise, the Feng Huang
(Phoenix) Studio, the Cathay (run by MP & GI, Motion Picture and General
Investment), and the Great Wall; the last being the "group which has leanings
towards Mainland China" — meaning that Great Wall is supported by the Bank of
China and, until recently, enjoyed favored treatment in films chosen for main-
land distribution. All four major companies, plus smaller Chinese studios in
Hong Kong and other cities of Southeast Asia, sell their films effectively to the
Chinese communities of the world, governed only by the political tendency of
each "overseas colony" and the spoken language of each film.

These easy sales attracted eager investors, as they often had in Shanghai. A pessimistic report on the "one-picture companies" was given to Hong Kong's Rotary Club in 1955:

. . . so many people got their fingers burnt so badly in producing motion pictures that there is now a common saying here that when you want to wreck a man, the best way to do it is to persuade him to be a producer. . . .[10]

On the lowest level of security and income were Hong Kong's "refugee film studios." In 1957 two reporters, William Stevenson and Leonard Lyons, visited one of these desperate places:

The studio worked twenty-four hours daily on a shift system. We arrived at midnight as one producer ended his film and another began a new one. Ng Chor-fan, a famous Cantonese actor, told us it was necessary to shoot films like machine-gun bullets to stay alive.
"After a month's circulation," said Ng, "the film is useless. It won't make another cent. Our takings barely cover expenses. Standards are necessarily low. Yet we have some of the best actors in Asia working here. . . ."[11]

Outside the formulas and extravaganzas that were becoming characteristic for Hong Kong, an adaptation was made in 1957 of Lu Hsun's *Ah Q*. Without the author here to object Yuen Yang-an made a good film that does no harm to Lu Hsun's spirit, though there is little connection with his firm, bare style. In this respect it may have been influenced by the Peking adaptation, the year before, of *New Year Offering*. Morando Morandini, president of the Locarno jury in 1958, wrote an enthusiastic appreciation of *Ah Q*, partly in apology for the lack of official recognition it received at Locarno:

The film moves, without losing its equilibrium, from comic to pathetic moods, and develops from a peasant farce to a political satire, from a grotesque to a drama, up to the final scene — the death of Ah Q, condemned without being guilty — almost truly epic in tone.[12]

Sadoul was also an admirer of Yuen's *Ah Q*: "Perfect black humor and social polemic stand out in an honestly made and very well acted [by Kuan Hsiang] film."*

The circumstances of the film's production were not auspicious. The Great Wall Company, then in some sort of crisis, gave *Ah Q* too small a budget, forcing

---

* *Dictionnaire des Films* (1965), p. 9; the other Hong Kong films noticed here by Sadoul are Chu Shih-ling's *Dividing Wall* (1951, as *Chambre à la cloison de bois*), *Pendaison de la crémaillère* (possibly *My Lonely Heart* of 1955) and Mizoguchi's *Yang Kuei-fei* (1955).

Yuen to find most of the needed money himself — possibly the cause of his subsequent departure from Great Wall, to set up his own company, the Sun Sun. According to Casiraghi[13] Yuen was Shanghai-born, but his whole film career was developed in Hong Kong: his first film was *The Torn Lily* of 1952; *Ah Q* was his fifth film. It established his artistic and commercial reputation.

In Peking, from 1959 to 1964, I saw a steady sampling of Hong Kong films, chiefly from Great Wall and the other "left" studio. The first two that I saw, in June 1959, were almost exactly alike, in plot, stock characters, and surface gloss imitated from American films: most of the same cast could be seen in both *Who Is the Murderer?* and *Shadow of a Murderer*. Not an encouraging beginning, and nothing from Hong Kong that I saw later in 1959 gave me greater hopes — *Wilderness*, based on a play by Tsao Yu (reinforcing my doubts about his reputation), and a film pretending to be about the slum dwellers who live on rooftops (with typhoon for artificial climax). Chu Shih-ling's *Little Moon* (from Feng Huang) and Hu Hsiao-feng's *Spring Comes to the Seashore* (from Great Wall) were also distributed on the mainland that year. Everything that I saw from Hong Kong, including these products of "progressive studios," had an extraordinarily emptying effect, with any moment of emotion canceled before the end. In a letter of correction to *Sight & Sound*,[14] one Hong Kong filmmaker (George C. Shen) defended the popularity of the left studios' productions, naming a later film that I did not see:

Last year [1963] a black and white small screen comedy produced by Great Wall Movies Enterprise Ltd. grossed nearly half a million dollars, breaking box-office records of all local productions and out-grossing all Western films except two, all local productions except one, all in color and widescreen. The title of the film was *The Gentleman Steals*, directed by Hu Hsiao-feng, a young man in his thirties.

The Shaw Brothers sent their *Kingdom and the Beauty* to the Asian Film Festival in Frankfurt in the Spring of 1960, but I could not see more in it than the prettiest sort of musical comedy; even its Peking opera base was lost in a maze of capitulations. The Shaw Spectacle was established as a formula with another *Yang Kuei-fei* in 1961, and the 1963 version of *Empress Wu*, both directed by Li Han-hsiang. Ian Jarvie comments:

Li's method [in *Empress Wu*] is to select key scenes and string them together, relying purely on the development of the Empress's character to give any drama to the overall structure. His personality as a director is rather buried among all the historical trappings, but clearly he has ideas, knows how to execute them (as in the throne room sequence in which the Empress confronts her rebellious son), and shows a certain command of the medium. He has many pupils and has recently [1963] left the Shaw organisation to set up an independent company under the MP and GI. This could mean either increasing caution in order to ensure financial success, or increased freedom to get out of the traditional historical-picture rut.[15]

Yet the thirty expensive films annually produced by Shaw Brothers seem quite content to remain in this rut. While Li Li-hua was repeating her Shanghai performance of Empress Wu, Ivy Ling Po starred in the 1963 version of Hua Mu-lan's legend, *The Lady General*.[16] I have detected no possibility or wish to transform these familiar materials into better films: sometimes an outsider will be engaged, as was Pearl Buck to write *Imperial Woman* (about Tzu Hsi, the Dowager Empress), but such talents become mere ornaments on the sales campaign — and the formula reigns.

Chang Ai-ling, who as Eileen Chang moved from filmwriting in Shanghai in the 1940s to a successful international career as novelist, was added to the formula of one of the earlier spectacles, with more discouraging results:

In 1960 Hong Kong finally decided to make an ambitious picture that has some chance on the international market, a faithful version of our famous 18th century novel, *Dream in the Red Chamber*. I specially went back to Hong Kong to write the script. . . .[17]

But Shanghai's Haiyen Studio and the Great Wall Studio saw an opportunity to beat the bigger company: the all-female Yuehchu Opera Company of Shanghai (the same group who had played in *Liang Shan-po and Chu Ying-tai*) had staged an operatic version of the classic novel, and a sumptuous filming of this ready-made material came to the screen so suddenly as to cancel the other production, echoing the cutthroat production races in "orphan island" Shanghai. The Haiyen *Dream* had an unrealistic fragility that looked refreshing after so many ponderous opera-films — even the rods for beating were lacquered an exquisite vermillion; and the women of the opera troupe, having played the *Dream* for so long, brought to the performance the effect of infinite labor without ostentation.

Into the sixties, Hong Kong's quantity of film production could compete with the staggering annual quantities from India and Japan. The United States Commerce Department announced that Hong Kong produced 303 full-length fictional films in the year ending March 1962.[18] In the previous years this number had not gone beyond 230–250 annually. Of the 303 reported in 1962, 224 films were in Cantonese dialect, 42 in Mandarin, and 37 in "other Chinese dialects." Quality and substance were matters more open to question.

Raymond Durgnat appears to be the only English critic to have given Hong
Kong's industrial successes a careful examination as films. His report of 1954 is
still valid:

Two main types of films are produced. The stories drawn from the vast repertoire of opera, usually set in the past with love or patriotism in conflict with the
rigid Confucian family system, or with corruption and intrigue, move in the
world of Emperors and high officials. The present-day films, usually humorous
and tolerant, deal with family problems, matrimonial misunderstandings, young
love, the cost of living (themes of ambition are conspicuously absent). . . .

[In the old stories] the women are custodians of integrity and idealism; the
theme of self-sacrifice is common. These period films are usually tragedies, pregnant with a sense of downfall and suffering, in contrast to the films of present-
day family life, which are imbued with tolerance and cheerfulness.[19]

It should be pointed out, however, that since 1954 the female protagonists have
grown less uniformly positive (the Empress Wu, for example), and that the left
studios' attitude to present-day life (in Hong Kong or elsewhere in the capitalist
world) is much less uniformly cheerful. The Great Wall Company even shows an
occasional modern tragedy, where blame can be clearly (or superficially) placed
on the oppressions of society; Peking and Shanghai filmmakers have to tread
much more delicately on approaching any degree of tragedy.

In 1965 the Hong Kong journal, *Eastern Horizon*, listed some of the Chinese
films banned by the Hong Kong Government Film Censorship Panel.[20] As
selected by the journal and the distributor, the Southern Film Corporation, the
list makes the censorship regulations look as ridiculous as possible: "a newsreel
showing the consecration of Catholic bishops in a Peking cathedral" must surely
give the effect of injured apolitical innocence, but behind the joyous title of an
actuality film, *The Road of Happiness to Lhasa*, is the highway built across the
disputed territory that led to war with India! The only three fictional films listed
seem too uncontroversial to be banned — *Withered Tree Revives* (1962, on the
fight against schistosomiasis*), *Muslim Detachment* (1959), and *Sung Ching-
shih* (1955) — though anyone who has seen these can easily imagine at which
sequences there could be audience demonstrations, apparently the greatest fear of
the Censorship Panel; and one can also imagine the dozens of more openly
inflammatory titles that do not appear on this discreet list. No matter how selec-
tive, the list gives an accurate impression of government nervousness. Three
broad taboos are mentioned: any reference to Chairman Mao, any appearance of
the People's Liberation Army, any comparison of preliberation life in China with

---

* Not yet "wiped out"; in March 1970 Hsinhua announced a new drive against "snail fever"
in eleven provinces.

life there after liberation. It's difficult to see how any film not based on classical literature or opera could enter freely.

The cultural revolution of 1966 had as much effect on the left studios of Hong Kong as in Peking or Shanghai. The first response was to hesitate, and then to stop production. One confused executive of a Peking-supported studio of Hong Kong gave an interview to an Associated Press correspondent:

"We just don't know," one studio executive said privately, "what kind of pictures we are supposed to make now. Many of our best-selling pictures were based on stories written by those now considered by the Communists as subversive."

There are two main Communist-controlled studios in Hong Kong producing about 12 pictures annually. The Chinese Communists subsidize the studios with $50,000 annually.

The official reason given by the studios for the low production [in 1966] is that their top stars are inside Communist China at present celebrating the cultural revolution, but many fear that the revolution might spell death for the studios. . . .

Period pictures, according to one Communist studio executive, are now out. "The cultural revolution," he said, "has completely uprooted Chinese operas. It would be highly embarrassing for us to revive them."[21]

By the end of 1967 industry and cultural revolution had learned to endure each other and the Peking-controlled studios of Hong Kong resumed partial production. This year the "right" studios of the Crown Colony also suffered a setback. The widespread and increasingly violent anti-British rioting* scared some of the island's rich inhabitants into finding other bases. Film people, too, began to leave: the actress Li Li-hua took her daughter to Taiwan (where films in the Hong Kong manner are now being produced) and said goodbye forever to Hong Kong.[22] The rioting also frightened some of the European and American firms that used Hong Kong for their "Chinese" location shooting. A reduction in their rental of Hong Kong crews and studio space was a serious loss, even to the entertainment tycoons who had seemed so invulnerable.

This may have been the reason that the Shaw Brothers, who have always done well without the American and European film public, finally attempted to enter the American market in the summer of 1967 with their new spectacles, *Beyond the Great Wall*, which the *Time* critic[23] unkindly but accurately labeled "a

---

* One of the women arrested was Yam Yim-chi (according to Cantonese pronunciation), a left-wing playwright and film director. She was released a year and a half later.

hysterical hybrid of cinema and opera." The cultural revolution's taboos against classic operas and tragedy meant nothing to the Shaws. Emperor Yuan Ti of the Han Dynasty finally meets the star of his harem (Lin Dai), whose beauty has been hidden from him by the villainous court painter:

At that point, this Chinese film becomes suddenly and inscrutably Oriental. Gongs ring! Girls sing! Emperor excited! Girl delighted!

Is it the end? Not quite.

The perfidious painter escapes to the Huns on the other side of the Great Wall. There he shows the Khan a lifelike picture of the girl, persuades him to assemble his army and demand her hand. To save her country, the girl nobly leaves her Emperor, journeys to the Huns and presents herself to the Khan.

Chorus weeps! Music leaps! Khan glad! Emperor sad!

End? Not quite.

First, the painter has to be caught and executed. Then the girl takes one look at the Hun's ugly head and horde, decides that she can never share his bed and board, and throws herself into the ocean.

Cymbals clang! Drums bang! Orientals confused! Audience bemused!

End.

12

A Chinese People's Cinema?
1960–1967

The [film] story must have a beginning and an end . . .

— Chou En-lai

There were a few agonized days in 1960 when the Chinese Mission in London would not help me get back to Peking — until they heard how seriously ill Si-lan was. As her crisis passed soon after my arrival, it was of first importance to work on her convalescence, and make it possible to continue her work on a program of new ballets. She asked to be sent to the resort of Lu-Shan where (then Ku-ling) she was enjoying the mountain air in 1927 when news came of Chiang Kai-shek's coup. In the summer of 1960, from the same mountains, we witnessed an event of equal significance in modern Chinese history — the departure of foreign socialist advisors. One day the resort was crowded, chiefly by Soviet engineers and experts working in nearby Hankow's factories and on the new bridge across the Yangtze, and the next day we were almost alone in the dining room. No explanation, and the stray Italian and French families were as much in the dark as we were. The previously nightly cinema was canceled — the audience was too reduced to justify the effort. In the park a few days later we encountered a strolling kindergarten.* As all foreigners were thought to be Russians the infants and their teachers addressed us as "our Russian friends" in a happy chant that had no hint of irony.

It was a year before any public reference was made in China to this technical break with the European socialist community, but the year was busily spent in continuing the underground campaign (promoted by party organizations since 1956) against the Soviet Union — before the accusations and adjectives exploded distinctly. During this time press and speech references to Yugoslavia and revisionists were an accepted code to mean the Soviet Union and Khrushchov, just as Soviet newspaper references to "Albanian dogmatists" were to be read as "Chinese leaders." Even after the open declaration of ideological war (surely based on more material factors than ideology) it was long before any of us in Peking's "foreign colony" — or, for that matter, among unprepared Chinese — could adjust to this disaster.

Thus the first noises were all strange and nightmarish to us. One trial explosion was a manipulated, disproportionate attack on a Soviet film maker. Grigori Chukhrai gave an interview to *Films and Filming*, an English monthly with the deplorable habit of turning interviews into signed articles by omitting the interviewer's questions. In this "article" Chukhrai, obviously agreeing with leading questions, said:

---

* The most startling encounter at Lu-Shan, on another walk, was to meet a striking double of Mao, surrounded by entourage. We were told it was his nephew.

We still have to fight for new conceptions of cinema because there are so many
people in the studios and cinemas who still think about films as they did in
Stalin's time. They will die thinking the same things in the same way. This is not
progress.

I have been asked if the Soviet new wave is likely to influence other Socialist
countries. This is a complex problem. For instance, there is a great difference
between Chinese and Czechoslovak films. The Chinese films are an example of
the dogmatic and anti-artistic way of thinking. The Czechs, on the other hand,
are looking for real cinema art. On the whole I think Czechoslovak films are very
good. . . . In Czech films there are emotions.

The Chinese people themselves are not without emotions. They have as many as
any man. But their films do not express this. Dogmatism and the process of logic
are not essentials of art and with dogmatism and logic alone the Chinese artist
cannot make good films. I know from my own experience what dogmatism
means and I understand very well the nature of present day Chinese pictures.[1]

If he had seen this before publication I doubt that he would have permitted it,
even in this mild form. But it was enough to be turned by zealous Chinese journalists into a weapon, not only against Chukhrai and his films (all dissected in
scathing detail) but as well against all Soviet films and beyond — against Soviet
policy, culture, government. If they noticed that his unforgivable comment had
actually appeared in a casual *interview*, they never told the Chinese reader so: it
was presented not only as an anti-Chinese article but as a major policy statement, a proof of something rotten in Moscow.

Starting even earlier the Chinese propaganda office used films vigorously in the
battle of words with the Soviet Union — printed words, broadcast words, filmed
words. To supplement the portraits of Stalin on sale in every art shop, we were
also offered his self-portraits: *The Fall of Berlin* and *Unforgettable Year 1919*
were brought out of the archives and shown on television and in cinemas during
the November anniversary of 1961 — and for later holidays. The year before,
when all new Soviet films became suspect, the Chinese made their own Soviet
film. *In the Name of the Revolution* was the hurried recording of a play at the
Children's Theater that showed Lenin and Dzierzynski supported by the purity
and high purpose of Soviet children. It was based on a Soviet children's play, and
its costumes and details were tediously faithful, but the inevitable curly blond
wigs, always associated with the cursed foreigner, must have confused large sections of the Chinese film audience. This was one of the compulsory films: *everyone* — not only children — was mobilized to see it in the autumn of 1960.

The films of 1960 were good enough to make *In the Name of the Revolution*
look like the sad and empty gesture that it was. *Battle for Shanghai*, produced

by the August First studio on a scale comparable to that of their Long March film, was better made but equally forgettable. The same studio's *Tracks in the Forest Snow* was an "ornamental" film in all the worst senses possible in cinema: its handsome camera work displayed only the cameraman's schooling, and its acting was operatic in its poses and tableaux. The novel on which it was based, about a hero's invasion (in disguise) of the bandits' lair (a reversion to the "knight errant" and Robin Hood films of the late twenties), was labeled "revolutionary romanticism," and I was not surprised, later, to see it used for a "modern" Peking opera. The Peking Studio's *Red Flag Chronicle* was also based on a recent, successful novel, with a more dangerous effect on its adaptation: apparently in an effort to keep his preliberation peasant portraits from seeming too passive, the novelist Liang Pin so exaggerated them as active and positive (usually in some phase of a family feud) as to lean repeatedly towards unreasoning violence to give some substance to his episodes. This is so much a part of the novel that the film also is forced to have a violent, impulsive tone. *Chin Yu-chi*, from the Changchun studio, was a more responsible piece of work; it was actually better than my schoolteacherish report makes it sound:

There was a highly commendable attention to economy of image, never showing more than was needed to convey the idea or the event, and this seems to me one of the most expressive ways in which the cinema medium can be used — and one that makes a powerful effect on its audience. For example, how much stronger was the torture scene that was *not* seen (*between* shots 385 and 386!) than the customary scene of the heroine's torture. Here, because the audience was shown everything it needed to feel what Chin Yu-chi was suffering, intelligence and emotion were appealed to in the right way — through imagination. It may be significant that Pai Yang gives her best film performance (that I have seen) as Chin Yu-chi — could the atmosphere of work in Changchun have inspired her more than in Shanghai studios?

Shanghai's *Three Generations of Steelworkers* and *Story of Whangpoo River* were almost alike in their contrasts of Shanghai workers' lives before and after 1949 — and in their willingness to be distracted by any excuse for prettiness or ritual: in the former film the scene of a new furnace's first trial is treated with the majesty of a Manchu coronation; and each sentimental scene is signaled by a sunset or some equally routine lyricism.

Shanghai's best film of the year — for me — was an unpromising-sounding comedy about a policeman, *My Day Off*. It made me doubt my suspicion of some negative Shanghai influence on modern Chinese films. A previous attempt to escape from the Shanghai formula, *Huang Pao-mei*, had spoiled its original idea with traditional methods. In *My Day Off* a traditional story idea was transformed by a fresh filmmaking attitude into the best film comedy I had seen

from Shanghai since 1959. (See Plate 37.) A Shanghai policeman finds that his
free day, which he had planned to fill with recreation and a visit to his fiancée's
family, is instead filled by unexpected emergencies that finally involve his
fiancée's family. And it is a film that one can't imagine having been made anywhere but in China, no matter how familiar its situation. The scenarist did not
always play fair: the strain to invent comedy-breeding obstacles moved too
often, as the film progressed, into farce. But the actual spirit of the film's production was exhilarating:

One of the obvious values to be treasured (and learned from) in this film is the
facility shown for filming in real places without seeming to interfere with the
natural life of these places (a lesson for actuality crews, also!) — whether streets
by day or by night, the interior of a bus or a steelplant. Working together, the
director and cameraman (and their assistants), with the actors, performed small
but vital miracles of reconstructing reality on the screen. These miracles were all
the finer for being almost invisible — as they should be.

Taoism may be officially discouraged as a way of life in China today, but there is
one aspect of Taoism that is privately practiced by all but a few socially conscious artists — passivity. Particularly conspicuous is the passivity of Chinese
filmmakers, who wait so long to be told what to do and delay so long in finding
ways, safe ways, to do it, that the film is the last art to promote any movement
or to reflect any urgent measure. For certain campaigns, such as the Great Leap,
the political heads of the studios manage to speed up this leisurely tempo with
threats against the whole personnel. But the personnel find guidance in an old
saying, "Outward conformity and inward alienation," and retreat into mental
caves where they cannot be followed. In the later record of an intellectual defec-
tor[2] I was surprised to read this advice from an older student, given in the
summer of 1960; this can be read as the private program of the Chinese film
industry, and of intellectuals in general, no matter how much self-criticism or
how many big-character posters they produce:

. . . we should always make the effort to contribute to the discussion in these
[political] meetings, but we should not be the first to speak. We should not be
the last either [though it usually worked out this way for films]; a place in the
middle was best. Also, we should not speak for too long a time, or for too short
a time. [In films, be careful not to be too long-winded or too abrupt.] Again a
median approach was best. Above all, we should never, under any circumstances,
introduce a new idea. We should only repeat the ideas that had been expressed
by those who had spoken first. We should not be original even in our phrase-
ology; we should express the same ideas in the same words that had been used
before.

I observed too often a behavior based on some unwritten law: "Nobody should
take a chance, nobody should sign anything, nobody should take responsibility

for any act." The film artist who struggled against this current of passivity and careful mediocrity grew increasingly rarer in the face of the worsened living conditions of the early sixties, but it was only this rare artist who showed a spark of what the Chinese film was capable.

Passivity among the people was countered by a perpetual series of "movements," campaigns to make evasion or retreat ignominious and punished. Aside from its leisurely reflection of such campaigns the film industry would occasionally sweep aside its habitual excuses and normal bureaucracy to push through an efficient, emergency production, such as *For Sixty-One Class Brothers*. Its subject was recurrent:

In 1958, a great to-do was raised by the Chinese press when thirty or forty roadbuilders came down with food poisoning. The newspapers wrote about medicines being flown to the sick men, about the virtues Mao and the Communist Party had shown in their paternal concern for the poisoned workers. And finally, to make the happy ending complete, persons "responsible" for the poisoning were unmasked, and, as might be expected, they turned out to be "members of families of the hostile classes." No one in his senses, of course, had any doubt that the poisoning was simply due to unsanitary food; nor were there any medical-legal documents produced specifying the poison used.[3]

On 2 February 1960 there was a similar case, also road builders, also food poisoning, also given the widest publicity, but the emphasis of the drama was transferred from the class enemies of 1958 to the heroic saviors of 1960. When a film was immediately ordered, to broaden the campaign and fix the "Pinglu Incident" more surely in everyone's memory, it was the urgency of conveying the medicine from Peking to the sick workmen waiting near the Sanmen Gorge on the Yellow River that became the subject of the film. Urgency was the keynote of the production, as well: the scenario was finished in twenty-two hours, filming was completed in fifteen days (with some additional shooting a few days later, after a first cutting).

While the film was being made, the Peking Film Laboratory and the China Film Distribution and Exhibition Corporation completed preparations so that as soon as the finished product reached them, prints could be sent out one after another to distribution centers all over the country for general release. The first print of all was naturally sent to the actual site of the film — Pinglu in Shansi.[4]

At the Peking Studio all filmworkers and actors who took part were unnamed on the screen (so there was a wave of satisfied murmurs through the audience when a familiar face appeared), but Hsieh Tien seems to have been chiefly responsible for the actual direction. He had wanted to move away from acting and this emergency, coming soon after his performance in *The Lin Family's Shop*, was an opportunity that he used to change his film career to directing. The action of *For Sixty-One Class Brothers* covered the thirty-six hours of the operation so precisely that whenever a large amount of time was unaccounted for, spectators tended to feel that someone's laziness or bureaucracy was being covered up.

The winter of 1960—1961 was the second of the three bad years. We heard only rumors, usually via Hong Kong, of troubles in the interior, but we were so well protected and so well fed in our comfortable hotel — we had been moved to the more elegant Peace (Ho-ping) Hotel — that we couldn't believe anything serious or tragic was happening beyond the city walls. The occasional banquet had a few less courses, but there were still banquets for any official excuse. Chauffeured Buicks and Cadillacs continued to carry the children of big shots to and from school (the wives were more cautious, visiting their shops and hairdressers in less conspicuous vehicles). I heard about the stripping of leaves from trees for food, even within Peking, but it was still a shock to see (at a filmworkers' union screening where I was not supposed to be) an instructional film on which leaves to use and how to prepare them tastily.

The main films produced, however, were careful not to hint at any disaster, either natural or political; and my duties remained within the walled-off enclosure of the Chinese film industry. That winter I tried to pass on to the next stage of the archive's task: now that we knew what we had, let's use it. I arranged three series of foreign films, mostly American, because that was what we had the most of. One series was to show the work of filmmakers now exiled from Hollywood studios — we had one or more films from each of the "Hollywood Ten" and plenty by others now working abroad or behind pseudonyms. This series was planned for filmmakers in Peking, Shanghai, and Changchun (I hoped to be sent there with the films). Then Shanghai filmmakers wanted a series of good comedies, and I think this series helped. A season of "skillful film jobs" that Peking filmmakers had not seen was planned for the following autumn. The Chinese section prepared a series of "May Fourth" films — Shanghai films of the thirties with a progressive tendency.

10 Feb. [1961]. Visit to British Consulate [for Si-lan's new passport] gloomy. Saw *Crossroads* for second time. Gosfilmofond should love *Sheherezade*, a fanciful episode in Rimsky Korsakov's naval life.

Another New Year party at FAC. This turned out to be the enjoyable way to hear Chinese music — not professionally, from a stage, but intimately, among friends. It becomes warm and emotional. Could not stay for new film, *Blossoms Face the Sun*. The first few minutes convinced me.

Mao Tse-tung's love of the classical Chinese arts produced some curious and perverse effects on the modern regulation of arts. The use by young poets of classical meters and forms was actively discouraged, while the Chairman calmly continued his poems in the forbidden forms. The only theater he enjoyed was the classical opera, but he was determined to keep this poison from the Chinese audience and to replace it with modern revolutionary themes.* The only art of the past that was permitted open respect was the classical novel, especially Mao's favorite, *Shuei Hu Chuan,* which also served as source and model for other arts. The first attempt to film a modern opera was almost a direct transcription of that admired novel. *Red Guards at Lake Hung* took the stage-bound opera out into the open air and filmed it with plenty of action and color, resulting in a film that I thought would be a new experience for foreign audiences, especially in India where most films already employed songs for dramatic purposes, but the distribution office was too timid to try the untried; no push from above was yet felt. Five years later the *only* Chinese fictional films were such "modern operas." The film of *Red Guards at Lake Hung* helped to make it possible for Kuo Mo-jo, in an address of July 1966, to claim that, "The old Peking opera of China, this most stubborn stronghold, has been taken by storm with the emergence of Peking operas on contemporary revolutionary themes. . . ."[5] In the same address films are mentioned only as among the enemies' cultural weapons.

The next film that I saw in 1961 to promote "modern opera" was a successful compromise. Changchun adapted the Kwangsi "folk opera," *Third Sister Liu,*[6] into a careful and witty film. No classic base was claimed for this opera when it was shown in Peking in the summer of 1960 — only that it was based on a "popular folk legend" of the Chuang people of Kwangsi province, and that it used Chuang folk songs. Though the "real" Third Sister Liu was said to have lived and sung during the T'ang dynasty, this did not inhibit the filmmakers. They gave the singer a more passionate love story than was customary in Chinese opera; they found bright means for even such wordy scenes as Third Sister Liu's song contest with the three despicable scholars; and they filmed the whole with as much action and open air as in *Red Guards at Lake Hung.* The costumes came from the classic stage, but there was a freshness of movement and enough reality (caricature was less depended on than in the stage version) to separate this film from tradition.

---

* On his visit in June 1946 to Yenan and Kalgan, Robert Payne attended several performances of these "modern" plays and operas, but the only performance that Mao also attended was a classical opera based on *Shuei Hu Chuan* (*Journey to Red China* [London: William Heinemann, 1947] , pp. 44—49).

Third Sister Liu outwits her three examiners. Sketch by Li Ke-yu.

My diary entries for the spring of 1961 show a small book being born:

27 March. Japanese newsreels of the invasion of Manchuria and a propaganda film for Greater Asia (had not realized they aimed at Australia, too). A spy film, very confusing and lurid, *Spy Not Dead Yet* — Chinese student spies working for the United States in Tokyo.

6 April. *Monkey Battles the White-Bone Ghost*, a dully filmed Shaohsing opera, and *The Keeper of the Flame*, that deserves a place (for Don S.) in the Exiles series. Fascist threat too subtle for here?

7 April. Remarkable Soviet film about the Congo — and a Medvedkin (back to life!) film using Gosfilmofond footage — *Reason vs. Insanity*. Made me want to do a big article or a small book on archive films, from Schub to Thorndike. Look more carefully at Japanese propaganda. Hurry home to Chinese lesson.

From then on I looked more carefully at every scrap of compilation, even embedded in fictional films. By summer,* now on the beach at Peitaiho (in a rest home no longer housing vacationing Soviet experts), I had enough notes to draft the first two chapters of *Films Beget Films*. A new push had been given it by seeing the first Chinese films, this year, that used archive materials; I asked the Film Bureau if they thought such a review of compilation uses and methods and

---

* Summer holidays were usually used for translation: worked on Nizhny's book in the floods of 1959, and even the painful summer at Lu-Shan was used for pieces of Eisenstein's memoirs.

problems would help these first steps. I received informal approval, but the finished book never saw Chinese print.

9 April. We saw the team finals of bing-bong tonight — glorious stadium, unruly audience: patriotism stronger than all appeals to politeness over the loud-speaker. Ivor, the father of ping-pong, in pleased authority.

15 April. A low this A.M. with a disappointing Laurel & Hárdy, but a great high this afternoon: Defa's film of Brecht's *Mother*. A big stimulus — rare in movies — Bergman closest in fullness and directness?

4 May. *A Friendship Ever Green* — big wheels' visit to Burma. The ceremonial film form seems hopeless. Something like home movies — never see kitchen or reality, only the parlor and smiles and surfaces. But who enjoys home movies except filming family and filmed family? But they have to be made, and will go on forever, without change. I hope the ones I have to see will always have Chen Yi — he likes to cut loose and play the fool before any camera, especially when visiting outside China. Does Liu Shao-ch'i's handsome wife come from theater?

18 May. Passed the evening (the correct phrase) at Mei Lan-fang's home. Very polite, very delicate and observant, and very impatient with his staff. Seemed satisfied with progress on translation.* Was shown his daughter rehearsing a man's role, the watching family backed by a frigidaire.

20 May. My first Chinese wedding — fascinating mixture of present and past. Shy but firm bridegroom from vault staff (just from People's Liberation Army in November) and much shyer bride, a nurse (or maybe nursery!). Our director gave long, solemn sermon, then groom's brother and bride's organizer spoke — finally groom said a few words, she, nothing. Active master-of-ceremonies from the other vault, but he couldn't budge the bride. Candy and wine passed round, with profuse bows in all directions. After tortured couple left, we saw *Tenth Degree Typhoon* — standard heroics.

Within two days I saw the worst and best that the Changchun Studio could show. The poor quality of *Tenth Degree Typhoon* must have been disconcerting for both Studio and Ministry, for this film had followed all the rules for a Chinese people's film, beginning with its collective scenario, written by sailors of the Tunghai Fleet.

It does not always follow that people who do one kind of work are the best qualified to express that work dramatically. Too often they defeat themselves and their purposes by trying to conform to familiar or cheap dramatic patterns, or by using theatrical types rather than the rich and original characteristics that they can observe around them.

---

* Of his film memoirs, later published in condensed form in *Eastern Horizon*, as "The Filming of a Tradition."

One interesting result of a scenario written by the sailors themselves is that remarkably little normal work was shown on board this presumably busy ship. Heroics and speeches occupied all, and the heroics were so baseless, and "left adventurist," that a spectator could say at the film's end, "If they had obeyed the storm warnings at Shanghai, they would have saved themselves needless risk and many other busy people unnecessary anxiety and trouble." But this would have frustrated the sailor-scenarists.

Changchun's *We Are the Same Generation*, without resorting to flashy and empty effectiveness, had an emotional effect completely lacking in *Typhoon*. This modest film about apprentice workers outshone, even photographically, the "bigger" picture. Direction and acting were fine, and the portrait of the master-craftsman Tsao by Kuo Chun-chin belongs among the best film acting I saw in China.

23 May. The most enjoyable puppet theater I've ever attended — from Hunan, playing "The Golden Hook" (same story as *The Scholar and the Fairy Carp*) preceded by "Difficulty at the Inn." The figures weren't merely realistic — they did things that only puppets could do, strikingly and with great effect on the packed audience in the tiny theater (in the "Chinese city"). Groucho Marx eyes — bright red drunken tongue — vigorous fish — right music. All so good I didn't even mind being accompanied by X's active ego. Secretly I was glad for his brass when he pushed backstage and we saw *that* wonderful spectacle. . . .

I could never understand why Chinese animation or stop-motion films, chiefly those employing any sort of doll or puppet, could be so uninteresting, with such a lively puppet tradition as in China. The films with flexible figures, no matter what new materials they learned from the work of Trnka, remained dully uniform. Flat or cartoon animation showed more spirit, though it was a long time before they employed any Chinese style, so completely had the factory techniques and draftsmanship of Fleischer been taken over, via Moscow. Without being told one could not know that *Why the Crow Is Black* (1955) or *The Red Flower* (1956) was a Chinese film. The Wan brothers, best known and longest experienced of Shanghai animators, also feared to venture far from Fleischer-Disney orthodoxy (*Snow White's* success in Shanghai was now a legend) in making *Disturbance in Heaven* (1961), a sequel to their gamble, the first full-length Chinese cartoon of 1941, *Princess Iron-Fan*.

The "flat" animators were more open to experiment, and even to Chinese tradition, trying such things as cut-paper figures and sets (an old folk art) and folded paper, but the fear of looking "primitive" forced such unfamiliar techniques into familiar-looking channels and had little effect on the subjects — bold hunter, evil tiger or more evil landlord, honorable maiden, and decadent princeling, with a

From a scissor-cut animation, *When We Work Together We Have More Than Enough* (1963), by Ho Yu-men.

D 大王

鸡蛋总统

炮筒
将軍

蚊子先生

E 大王

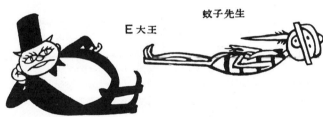

A Dream of Gold (Shanghai Animation
Studio), designed by Tzu Ching-ta.

bird or an insect glimpsed to tantalize us with unexplored possibilities. The fairy tales were presented in cleansed versions (I enjoyed imagining these story conferences), but the contradiction would often show through.

Before its demise the experimental collective formed at the Shanghai Animation Studio to develop new methods produced one outstanding, lasting experimental cartoon. One of their tasks was to animate contemporary Chinese paintings that used traditional techniques: the first trials were to be based on the work of Chi Pai-shih and Hsu Pei-hung. The trial film on Chi Pai-shih motifs was a complete success. Each motif, whether crabs or chicks or fish, worked perfectly. The trial film was followed by *Where Is Mama?*, the watery adventures of newly born tadpoles — it made both children and adults laugh. It was wonderful to see a kind of *Chinese* animation on the screen that had its own fluidity, wit, and charm. The making of this apparently simple thing must have cost much more labor and struggle than we could guess, because the animators had discarded the usual hard-edge, enclosed forms of the animated cartoon to animate the much more difficult, almost diffuse forms of Chi Pai-shih's ink and watercolor. They also used his white backgrounds, minimal color, and open compositions — it was a completely new film experience and deserved international attention (see Plate 40). In spite of this extraordinary achievement we heard of no successor to *Where Is Mama?* and the animation of Hsu Pei-hung's famous horses must have fallen short of expectations.*

30 May. Evening: dress rehearsal of *Fury of a Black Slave*, Ouyang's dramatization (with recent revisions) of *Uncle Tom's Cabin*. Sat next to political revizor, a nice squat old lady. Production highly, overly colored. Theme music was that Famous Negro Folk Song (by Jerome Kern and Oscar Hammerstein), Ol' Man River! X tried to save us from green-room exposure, but we were captured, and I was closely questioned by Chou Yang! Then I asked my usual question,† without much answer. Had to wriggle out of a back-stage group photo.

Five weeks of June and July were spent in Moscow (mostly the Film Festival), and this time we went together. No more lonely disasters for this family if we could help it.

Just before leaving Peking I saw a film that reinforced my hopes in the Shanghai studios as the right place for new Chinese comedies. It was even possible that they could manage "the past" better than Peking, for *Master Chiao Mounts the*

---

* A possible successor in 1965: *The Cowboy's Flute*, an animation based on the paintings of Li Ko-ren.
† About his reaction to Si-lan's first trial concert — I had heard he attended it.

Sedan was almost as funny as *My Day Off*, and the first three open-air reels of *Master Chiao* fused a casual but sure period feeling with its gently comic pace.

But once the night scenes began, and the filming entered the studio, everything took a more ordinary and pedestrian tone; just when the comedy should be building, with all characters taking a more active part in the comedy's action, the cameraman (and director) used methods that might have applied to a melodrama or an advertising film. The last reels offered few surprises, and what is a comedy without surprises? With a cast including many of the actors who were in *My Day Off*, I waited for something as satisfying as that film's memorable character — the hotel resident who doesn't want to be alone — but I waited in vain.

Three reels, though, were enough for optimism — that was enough of *Along the Sungari River* to give me intense pleasure — and the makers of *Master Chiao* were on their way to an equally important discovery: the period film comedy unattached in style to Chinese opera.

Moscow and the Moscow Film Festival threw us back into a world that was easy to forget or to pine for in Peking — old friends, new films, fewer taboos on speech and behavior. One old friend, when I leaned across a restaurant table to mutter something, almost shouted, "No! no whispering! I'm never going to whisper again!" The Chinese entry was *A Revolutionary Family*; here it looked less interesting as a film, though Yu Lan was still a moving actress and deserved the award she received (see Plate 43). This was China's last entry at a Moscow Film Festival.

The really experimental *Where Is Mama?* was shown, though not in competition; few saw it as few could imagine anything unorthodox from China always doubts about this film were probably reinforced by this lack of interest. This didn't worry me, for my three-pronged persuasion plan to get this surprise entered at the Annecy Festival of Animated Films — aimed at the organizers, at the export office in Peking, and at the distribution office in Paris — looked hopeful.

Every sensible effort, whether commercially or politically motivated, to introduce films to the great masses of peasants in the interior of China always depended on some form of traveling cinema. The enterprising Munich operator of 1910, the advertising boats of the early twenties, the wartime plan of 1938 to send out film trucks from Hankow — all recognized the necessity to take films to the audience. The work of the Yenan Film-Projection Team in 1939, equipped with a projector and a group of Soviet films* brought from Moscow by one of

---

* Including *Lenin in October, Lenin in 1918, We from Kronstadt, Chapayev.*

the team, was a model for making the most out of little. With open-air audiences of two or three thousand for every showing, the team was still dependent on needle and thread whenever the film broke. Yet that did not discourage the team later from compiling their own film, *The Red Army Cannot Be Defeated*, from portions of these films that still hung together.[7] Included in the first film equipment received from the Soviet Union in 1950 was a large number of mobile projection units.* Within the next ten years the itinerant film service grew into an extensive organization that accounted for a large percentage of each film's distribution. The activity and conditions of the traveling film teams were so difficult *and* colorful that I submitted a script outline for a film about these necessary film people. By 1965 there were 25,000 young men and women in 8,800 projection teams.† The service already has its heroes; one team of four young men celebrated its tenth anniversary in 1964. Their circuit in Kirin province was rough:

The team serves two people's communes with 39 hamlets perched [in the mountains]. It takes the team a month to make one round of the cinema-showing centres there. On the way they cross three mountains, 3,000 metres above sea-level, many smaller hills, and 18 rivers and streams. The most out-of-the-way centre — the team makes a point of visiting it every month — is up a stiff 80-degree gradient, on the top of which is a bridge of two pine logs, thrown across a precipice with a sheer drop of 100 metres to the river below. The team has conquered these difficulties cheerily. . . .[8]

The service has its heroines, too; one team, of three country girls who had nine years of schooling, has become famous as the "Three Sisters." In *China's Screen* (No. 1, 1965) there is a detailed account of their bravery and determination, climbing wintry peaks and wading icy streams to get the films to the audience. Chang Tzu-cheng, a young veteran of the Korean War working in a team whose circuit was through the villages of eastern Hopei province, invented a presentation that has been widely imitated:

He kept up a "running commentary" as the film was shown. At opportune moments during the opening sequences, he introduced the story shortly, its main characters, setting and background. As the film went along, he slipped in a few words of explanation wherever he felt it might be hard for some peasant audience to grasp.[9]

Another report on the projection teams stressed this "grasping" problem:

---

* This aid continued, for Chinese manufacture of projectors remained in the handicraft category for some years.

† This may not include those projection teams employed to tour the sometimes very large area of a single commune.

Making ready in the village for a film showing; woodcut by Li Ming-yuen.

The country people are very quick to love or hate during a motion picture. The minute a character appears on the screen they want to know who it is, whether he is good or bad [!] . So the projection teams have to give some explanation as the story develops.[10]

Considering the many years that these peasant audiences have now being seeing films, I'm inclined to be somewhat skeptical about their "difficulty" in understanding films that have already been so simplified in production. I often wonder if such talk is merely another form of peasant caution or resistance to the continuous campaigns pressed on them, in which films now take a leading part. I never had an opportunity to question a peasant group myself — and I doubt that I would have learned anything if I did — but one objective interviewer has made the most of this privilege.

In 1961 Jan Myrdal, the Swedish sociologist, forced past diplomatic barriers to live for a month in a North China village near Yenan and to question the villagers intensely on their lives, work, tastes, pasts. Perhaps because his wife, Gun Kessle, helping with the interviews, is an excellent photographer, the villagers were often asked about films. One bookkeeper, aged thirty-three, made a natural link between "picture books" and films:

. . . I can also read simpler books of fiction. I stick most to serial stories in parts with lots of pictures and a few simple characters on each page. The pictures make it possible to understand the characters I don't know.

I am very fond of films. Opera and that sort of thing doesn't appeal to me so much. Opera is a bit old-fashioned. Films have much more variety, more themes, more reality, and much more that is funny and makes you laugh. I usually go to the cinema or opera once every ten days. We often have films in Liu Ling; but mostly I take myself into the town [Yenan]. Sometimes I go in with my wife and my eight-year-old son, my other children are far too small to appreciate going to the cinema. But, sometimes, when we have finished work for the day, someone will say: "Come on, let's ride into town and go to the cinema." Then we jump on our bicycles and ride off.[11]

A housewife, aged twenty-nine, was less enthusiastic about films:

Sometimes films come to the village. Then I see them. We have a film show every month or six weeks. But I don't like films all that much. Opera is much better. When we have a film show, it is in the collective dining-hall.

Another theater fan, aged thirty-five, was tolerant of *other* people's enjoyment of films:

I bicycle into Yenan twice a month. Then I go to the opera. If there's a good opera in Yenan, we stop work at half past five. . . . The older children like films best . . . when there's a film in the village, even Granny goes to it.

Introducing the story before the film starts.

A militia-man, aged thirty-three:

Of the films I remember, I can mention *Monkey Battles the White Bone Ghost Three Times*, that is a filmed opera, and [*Capture of Mount Hua*]. I like films. My ten-year-old son can't get on with opera, but he likes films, he wants to see films like [*Steeled Fighter*]. He wants adventure and excitement and war and that sort of thing.

A schoolmistress observes the effect of each new film on her pupils:

. . . I often wonder what this one or that will make of life. . . . They don't even know themselves yet. They are so young. If they have seen a film about the People's Liberation Army, they all want to be soldiers; and, if they have seen a film about tractor drivers, they all want to be tractor drivers.

Another reason to make a full claim on control over films: It is not unusual to find in Chinese publications of the first years after 1949 that some real exploit was inspired by the hero's or heroine's impression of a fictional, filmed hero. Before his death a publicized hero of the Korean War, Huang Chi-kuang, testified that his heroic (and fatal) action at the Battle of Sangkumryung Ridge (Heartbreak Ridge) was modeled on an exploit in *Private Alexander Matrosov*, a film made by the Soviet Children's Studio in 1948.[12] China's first woman tractor driver, Liang Chun, was given moral support by a Czechoslovak film of 1951, *Road to Happiness*:

It is almost unthinkable for a woman to become a tractor driver in a village that has just been liberated. . . . Although village life in Czechoslovakia is different from that in China, the struggle between old and new ideas as we move towards collective farming is the same. I remember in the spring of 1948, when I first wanted to learn to drive a tractor, I also met with opposition. I was the only girl in a class of 70. The instructor did not want me in his class in the beginning and sarcastically said to me, "You had better go home, you'll never learn to drive a tractor, it's too dirty." Some of the other trainees made unpleasant remarks. But, fortunately the director of the school supported me. . . .[13]

More recently the film of Lei Feng is often cited as inspiration to soldiers, workers, and children in leading self-sacrificing lives. But Lei Feng himself looked at films as models for his model behavior. Here is his diary entry[14] after admiring the heroine of *Red Guards at Lake Hung*:

Her words were so heroic that they are engraved deeply in my mind. She will always be my example. For the Party I'll not be afraid to climb knife-edge mountains, or to enter oceans of fire, and even if my body is crushed to powder and my bones smashed – if it's for the Party I'll never change my path.

Inevitably, film models are sometimes followed by the filmmakers themselves.
Here is the story of an army cameraman, Wang Ching-an, in the last campaign
against Chiang's armies:

During the assault on Chinchow, south of Mukden, a people's army platoon
commander fell with a wound in his shoulder. But Wang Ching-an immediately
leaped forward and, with camera ready in hand, calmly shouted, "Forward,
comrades! Let me take pictures of you." This was a great encouragement to the
assault party.[15]

Seeing a steady quantity of Chinese films I found myself imagining, too easily,
that if there had been films in the Middle Ages, this is what they would look
like. Here are the conformity, the self-satisfied and defensive insularity, the
almost scientific reduction of personal interpretation to its minimum, the rigid
stratification of social groups (classes?!), the fixed place for each individual and
the molding of people to types that we find in medieval arts, with rare exceptions. There are the same rare exceptions in Chinese cinema, I'm glad to see, for
it's only from such brave exceptions, recognizing the values of humanity and art,
that we can expect any progress to grow — or a socialist cinema to tear itself
away from feudalism. These exceptions make me hopeful for China's future and
film future; without this hope there would be little point in this book.

The exception of 1961 was as encouraging in its way as *Storm*; it was an adaptation of the novel, *Hurricane*, by Chou Li-po; the scenario was prepared by Lin
Lan, and it was directed by Hsieh Tieh-li — his first film.

In studying Chinese films a European or American observer has to be prepared
for a situation not so evident outside China: that most Chinese films, especially
those of particular importance, are based on works already developed in literature or the theater.* Few films there are born as film ideas, directly. Even quite
modest films can usually be traced to a literary source: a pleasant comedy of this
year, *Sowing the Clouds* (about a girl weather forecaster), is an almost line-for-
line transcription of a new story by Li Chun.[16] For more significant films this
test in another medium's fire seems essential: *Storm*, for example, could not
have reached the screen without its success in the theater. Though *A Revolutionary Family* carries on its credits the authorship of Hsia Yen, it is actually his
adaptation of popular memoirs by Tao Cheng — *My Family*, also adapted for the

---

* A dependence on literary sources does not appear to have tied down *titles,* especially of
foreign films. Three made-in-England Dickens films appeared in China as *Bleeding Tears of
Lonely Star* (*Great Expectations*), *Lost Child in Foggy City* (*Oliver Twist*), and *Hell on
Earth* (*Nicholas Nickleby*). Under the title of *The Prince's Revenge* Olivier's *Hamlet* has an
echo of Peking opera.

theater — but the film adaptation was considered too free to be officially
attached to her life. The Chinese cinema might move along faster without such
literary ballast, but one has to get used to this situation and watch directors
developing within these limits.

Another attachment to the written word: in China a director films the script as
approved by his studio. Little is improvised during actual shooting. All the more
credit, then, to Hsieh Tieh-li, for giving so much life (in his shooting-script and
direction) to what is not a particularly distinguished scenario, by Hsieh's wife. It
was Hsieh, working with a young cameraman, Wu Sheng-han (also *his* first film),
who found a cinematic means to communicate the best qualities of Chou Li-po's
novel. The studio was nervous about his new methods and his wish to go beyond
the usual job of putting the script and dialogue onto film, but the audience's
enjoyment of the completed film was clear to all.

The film experience of Hsieh, then about forty years old, was swiftly formed:
assistant director on *The Lin Family's Shop*, codirector of *The Nameless Island*
(an adaptation of a schematic play), and then the opportunity to direct a film of
his own. I reported his triumph in the last article on Chinese cinema to appear in
Iskusstvo Kino:

Though the action of the *Hurricane* novel (which won a Stalin Prize in 1951) is
involved, its structure is very simple: After the defeat of the Japanese in 1945
the Eighth Route Army sent land-reform teams to villages in Northeast China. In
convincing the peasants of the necessity for change, the teams encountered
difficulties among the peasants, the powerful influence and armed threats of the
landlords, and even divisions of opinion and method among themselves. [See
Plate 43.] Through crisis and revelation the peasants unite against the landlords
and their Kuomintang support — land reform is effected and the Kuomintang
forces are defeated. The film's scenario has made the usual heroic effort to condense a 400-page novel into an hour-and-a-half film, but Hsieh's shooting-script
deserves particular praise, for the execution of the film has been done forcefully
and pictorially, in *film* terms, without depending on dialogue alone to communicate the drama of the subject. That is why the characters, for the most part,
seem closer to being real people; their actions have been as carefully considered
as their words. The fresh elements in the acting may have come from Hsieh's
direction of the studio's acting group. The feeling of a tense race with time in
accomplishing the land reform work could not have been conveyed so vividly
with traditional or conservative methods of film writing or direction. The screen
is dramatically and imaginatively filled all the time, giving a satisfaction to the
spectator that he may not be able to analyze, but is nevertheless within the
film's plan. It is an inconspicuous but true victory for director and cameraman.
Among the actors there are some oversimplifications of characterization, but old
habits of typecasting are hard to overcome. In general, the belief engendered by
the film is very high, indeed, and everyone contributes something to this.

Hurricane may not be so original a work as *Storm*, but it serves a very useful purpose: it takes the characters and situations that long have been identified with the land-reform period and removes the accumulation of crust and pattern that has obscured both their reality and drama on the Chinese screen. Without the former polite and formal method of presentation it is again possible to believe in the actuality of those people, in the possibility of their change and development of character, in the bitterness of their struggle, and in the fullness of their triumph. Without such belief the spectator cannot be expected to relate the events on the screen to his own life.[17]

Seen also at the end of summer: a film destined for a lengthy and even international career. After reading my report on *Red Detachment of Women* the Film Bureau must have lost any trust they may have had in my judgment:

By itself this would have seemed a quite effective and commendable film, but seen in comparison with *Hurricane*, it looked like a film from the past, while *Hurricane* gives one a hint of Chinese films of tomorrow. Despite its novelty of subject, the handsomeness of its treatment, and the luxury of its production, *Red Detachment of Women* seemed (again alongside the maturity of *Hurricane*) a film for children — an adventure story with abstract time, abstract place, stereotyped characters and illogical action. I read a magazine account of the laborious research done on this film's subject, but what a waste if all this was used only to manufacture one more superficial film. I hope the good young actress will get a film worthy of her talent one day.

A clear case of wasted sympathy: I don't know if the young actress, Chu Hsi-chuan, has since had a film worthy of her talent, but this one film brought her enough rewards for a lifetime — medals, honorary posts, the best actress award for 1961, and travel to some of the countries that still showed Chinese films. The film's story (*not* an adaptation, so far as I could learn)* was itself adapted to a "modern opera" and, a greater novelty for China, a "modern ballet." †

24 Sept. (Moon Festival). Holiday season opened with street loudspeakers put to work — startled one morning last week to hear "My Old Kentucky Home" followed by Gershwin's "The Man I Love"! Carelessness or sabotage at radio station?

Ideal name for a socialist realist painter — Foto Stampo — a real person, really, an Albanian painter here for the celebration. Funny if he turned out to be a good artist!

---

* When *Chinese Literature* published Liang Hsin's "It Happened in Hainan" (No. 4, 1963), it was subtitled "The Story of the Film 'Red Women's Detachment' "; it reads like an early literary treatment for the film.
† Attended and approved by Chairman Mao. The ballet adaptation has also been filmed.

Our last meeting with Ouyang Yu-chien was during the October First parade. In one of the occasional voluntary intermissions that one must make to continue standing and watching a parade that changes little from year to year, I wandered off behind the stands while Si-lan spoke to the Russian advisors who were still working at the Ballet School. I was shocked to see Ouyang approaching in a wheelchair that he propelled himself. Seeing me, and then Si-lan, who joined us, did not have a good effect on him — it reminded him of our first meeting, long ago, in Moscow, and all the (unmentioned) contradictions of today, which probably gave him as much trouble as they did us. We all hoped we'd meet soon, but he was dead before the end of the year.

4 Oct. Last night the 3-day holiday ended with a surprising conversation — with David Young, of Newcastle and the *Amethyst*, lately of a Kwangtung sugar factory. Enviable undefeatableness and clear sight.

7 Nov. Undignified doings at 44th anniversary of October Revolution. Tonight we watched our hosts refute the national tradition for "a good face." During the Soviet ambassador's speech noses were picked, heads were stroked and ceiling was studied — even before our little [Albanian] champions huffed out, followed by well-prepared "spear-carrier" students, brought in for the staging. Rewi a hulk of theatrical indignation during the same speech (he gets his cues fast). X more Chinese than the Chinese in intermission. There were only two who sounded as sad as we felt.

Found the source of Chen Yi's gruesome quotation (used in all films and speeches nowadays about Southeast Asia): "We are to you as are the lips to the teeth. When the lips are gone, the teeth will feel the cold." It's from the last Kin Emperor's appeal to the Sung for a military alliance against the Mongols of Chenghis Khan.

It was the fortieth anniversary in 1961 of the founding of the Chinese Communist Party that brought out the first historical actuality films to make full use of archive materials. There were at least three short films about Yenan (and that "Region") in the thirties, but only one of these, about Norman Bethune, using Wu Yin-hsien's good footage, was carefully executed — *In Memory of Bethune*. The two big anniversary compilations, *A Spark Can Start a Prairie Fire* and *Decisive Struggle between Two Destinies*, hurried my manual on compilation because the former film was full of avoidable mistakes and the latter, a superior film, showed how rich the waiting materials were, and how its makers were learning their own lessons from the newly explored riches. I had the first draft of *Films Beget Films* done before Christmas.

21 Dec. Through the Indian cultural attaché Harry generously helped me see Ray's *Tagore* — useful for FBF. Compare with the Lu Hsun film.

A crowd around spilt milk on Wan Fu Ching — sadder than if someone had been hurt. A general reduced to a plastic shopping basket. A perfect Japanese scene at dusk — black crows restlessly nestled in an arc over silver branches, and a pale orange rising moon (was this the YMCA garden?).

If you wonder where all the dead violin pieces went, come to Peking.

By the end of 1961 we were beginning to feel the relaxing effect of a speech that Chou En-lai made to the June national filmmakers' conference: ". . . barely mentioning the class struggle, [Chou] demanded more variety, better quality, and use of themes of yesteryear on the screen."[18] For about a year this relaxing of subject matter and treatment brought us better films. No one was bold enough to produce a masterpiece, but the pleasure of filmgoing perceptibly increased. It was even encouragingly possible to argue about finished films. One film, *People of the Great Northern Wasteland*, appeared, disappeared, and re-appeared — one could almost hear the arguments also taking place on higher levels. (Only gradually did I realize how against "unanimity" China had made me.) In this film the most delicate issue was the "placing" of the older, more experienced, better-trained intellectual engineer. That he was allowed to indicate these qualities at all was a signal of something new, and that his methods should be shown as more correct than those of the amateur engineers of the People's Liberation Army and Party was — revolutionary! When the film disappeared for some months, we all assumed (and I think rightly) that this unorthodoxy was the cause. However, this became, for a while, orthodoxy ("red *and* expert"), and when the film reappeared, I noticed only slight wounds after its battle exper-ience. It was eventually shelved for good. In looking again at my report on *People of the Great Northern Wasteland* I am not surprised that it contains no hint of all this, though I was fully aware of it — I was learning to be "diplo-matic." Most of the report is filled with comments on the cameramen and the actors — Tsui Wei, for example, was behaving as much like a star as he had made his heroine look in *Song of Youth*. The deterioration of Chang Ping as an actor was, somehow, more disturbing:

How interesting he is when he is *not* showing the audience what a good actor he is! His acting should be entirely concentrated now on the avoidance of "acting" — this will be more difficult but more rewarding, both for him and the audience. Though he may have had the reputation on the stage of a restrained actor, this is not yet enough restraint for film purposes. He has one scene of "recognition" that is as theatrical and as stylized as Peking opera — and not the best of Peking opera at that. That one scene, with its carefully polished starts and poses, could be used as an example of what *not* to do before the merciless camera. His "non-acting" moments show how skillful and cinematic he *can* be when he is encour-aged in the right direction. The actors (and directors) of the film should be aware, by now, that it takes more than a weeping actor to make an audience weep. And, why, by the way, so much weeping? I have not observed this as a national trait, except on the stage and screen. I suspect these tears of being a substitute for convincing, emotional acting.

My only positive comment touching the content of the film stuck to technique, too:

This may be a weaker story than *New Story of an Old Soldier*, but the scenarist here achieved something for which he deserves special commendation: the source of the scenario — the play on which it is based — is not allowed to burden the film, as so often happens (as in, for example, *The Long March* film, where everyone tried to open up the play onto a large scale, but the limitations of the play continued to hang on the film's neck, and held it down to stage proportions).

Shelved scripts must have outnumbered shelved films, but only occasionally did someone commit the gaffe of publishing a work before its condemnation. In 1958 the Changchun journal, *Film Literature*, published a script by Wu Hung-yi, *The First Year.* Late in 1960 this script was analyzed and condemned in the leading theoretical journal, *Dianying Yishu.* In the two passing years something must have justified the reopening of this negative example: it may have been filmed and found wanting, or evidence may have been needed against Wu Hung-yi, or *Film Literature* may have had to be reprimanded. The introduction to the analysis states a dilemma sharply:

How shall literature and the arts be applied to the reflection of internal contradictions among the people or, more precisely, the internal contradictions among the people of a socialist society? This is an important problem for works of literature and the arts. In this respect our films have achieved certain successes that satisfy us. But there are also a few bad works. For example, *The First Year*, a script by Wu Hung-yi. . . .

The synopsis that follows shows a subject area (namely, *any* hint of dissatisfaction) that Chinese studios had long since learned to avoid; the story (possibly true) is set in "the first year of our country's first five-year-plan," when

. . . a great number of workers, in a factory making brushes of bristles, responded to the Party's call and changed their work to a state construction site. Because of a bureaucratic management that did not organize the proper training and education of those who changed their jobs, and because the political consciousness of some workers was not high, and also because of the demagogy of some concealed counterrevolutionaries, this resulted in trouble and confusion. Things even went so far that the workers of the collective boarded trains in order to present their demands at Peking. Fortunately one old worker happened to discover that the most active demagogues were actually counterrevolutionaries who had thus lured the workers into making trouble. The troublemaking workers suddenly came to their senses, and the cloud of confusion over the town cleared away.

On the surface, and looked at formally, this scenario raises the banner of anti-bureaucracy and reflects the so-called internal contradictions of the people, but in reality it mixes up right and wrong, reverses black and white, makes something out of nothing and, as for its political and ideological tendency, it is anti-party, antisocialist — a poisonous weed.[19]

Another scenario attacked was *Good Flowers, Round Moon*, an adaptation of Chao Shu-li's novel, *San Li Wan*. The scenarist, Go Wei-gun, after being labeled a rightist, was accused of modifying the novel dangerously, by transforming a "struggle story" into a love story.[20]

My diary for 1962 records street impressions, leaving implications to be chiseled out later:

16 Jan. Imagine a pavement filled with a hundred low-powered driverless bull-dozers chugging head on against each other.
Man in tiger-hat and basketball sneakers. Two soldiers, each with business-like accordion wrapped in pink silk.
Lynch justice in the hutung [an unpaved side street] : one stubborn six-year-old being repeatedly tried and punished by several of his peers, led by an older (10 years?) judge.
A poor fellow at the music shop buying expensive pocket scores (a Beethoven piano concerto and others I couldn't see) to *study*, not to play!

19 Jan. For more than a week an All-China (?) collection of Catholic dignitaries (all Chinese, of course) have been staying at the Peace Hotel. Last night they blossomed out (for a convocation?) in full regalia — crimson and magenta robes and tremendous sashes, massive gold and jeweled crucifixes, tiny ceremonial red silk embroidered skull-caps — the works. The lobby and lifts were startling. To-day we watched the group being photographed in the courtyard — as much pro-tocol as at Versailles.

20 Jan. No more tragedy? Tonight *A Night to Remember*, dubbed in Chinese, moved me as much as any tragedy could — parable, consciousness, and all. Felt lost and emptied after.

I imagine that the distribution office chose this English film about the *Titanic* disaster to show a collapse of western technology and morale to Chinese audiences, but the one conversation I had on leaving the cinema where we saw it offered an opposite (and less neat) interpretation: an old lady who spoke English was astonished that western civilization had reached by 1912 such a peak as we saw on that great ship — only a year after the overthrow of the Ching dynasty.

10 Feb. A heavy snowfall, the heaviest I've seen here, and the streets are left fatalistically (Taoism?) to take care of themselves.

We see *Kennedy in His True Colors* at the Red Star — not a good job, but it seems to animate the audience. A fight on the stairs, with a baby used as weapon and shield. We hurry out without knowing the end. Are these small clashes — on streets, on buses — considered as "safe" clashes, that won't be held against you, or trip you up later?

Violence *was* in the air, and all propaganda media appeared to promote it. There was an instructional-cum-drama film about the use and laying of homemade land mines that was particularly offensive in its fun-and-games attitude to mutilation and human life. The children in the audience when I saw it were delighted with every explosion. Another film enjoyed by the children was *The Knife-Thrower*, a drama built around a circus act. When schoolchildren took up knife throwing as a national hobby, using sharpened slivers of scrap metal, it worried no one until a couple of eyes were put out — and the film was quietly shelved at home (though offered for distribution abroad!).

21 Feb. At work 1961's "work" is still being reviewed, a perfect way to postpone the work of 1962.

Glenn orbitted — ignored here. If an American found a cure for cancer, it would not be considered news. No — it might appear in the form of cartoons warning Chinese not to allow themselves to be used as guinea pigs by American doctors.

1 March. Surprised to see Chinese translations of condemned Soviet books — in *very* limited editions. Not exactly *published*, as you have to flash the right card in the bookshop to be allowed to buy and taste such translated poisons as Yevtushenko's poems and Ehrenburg's memoirs.

If a newly purchased article holds together or works properly — "Ai! This was made before the Great Leap!" *Not* a public exclamation.

The problems of *Nieh Erh* versus the real Nieh Erh were tiny compared to the conflicts and questions raised by a proposed film about Lu Hsun, first announced early in 1961 for his eightieth anniversary in September. There were more people who knew Lu Hsun's difficult actuality, and more who would dare to object to a conveniently neat film frame fitted around him. The problem of a Lu Hsun film had a precedent in the Soviet film about Pavlov. The Pavlov shown in the 1949 film (written by Papava and directed by Roshal) was merely a prickly character with a sharp tongue. To show him in such a manner was a necessary dilution of his reality, which was a continuously open antagonism to the Soviet government, no matter how dependent he was on it for the maintenance of his staff and the large laboratory of his physiological institute. There were ironies (and extra problems) in showing Lu Hsun in a Chinese communist film as a revolutionary hero: revolutionist and hero he certainly was — and wonderful artist, too — but his running war with the Shanghai dogmatists of the Chinese Communist Party was too well known to be wiped out by the optimistic heroics of *Nieh Erh.* The same people were involved in the new project which one heard was moving, being revised, going again, stopped for a while, going now — over several months. It was Chao Tan who was, of course, to play the role of Lu Hsun, and he was my barometer for this changing weather. Though some exteriors were to be made in Peking, the production was in Shanghai, so that when Chao Tan appeared in Peking restaurants one could be pretty sure that the *Lu Hsun* group had come to the capital for more discussions, more arguments. I knew that the project was totally shelved when Chao Tan appeared in the dining room of the Peace Hotel without the long Lu Hsun moustache he had cultivated for many months. The shaving of Chao Tan was as clear a signal as the mous-tache grown by Mei Lan-fang during the Japanese occupation. Though I then warned the staff of *China's Screen* (the export office's journal) that it would be embarrassing to send reports abroad about the progress of a film already halted, they had no choice in the matter: the publicity continued, perhaps hopefully. When we later visited in Shanghai the last home of Lu Hsun and the museum devoted to his life and work, no one could admit that the film would not be made (the costume designs, in a showcase, already looked dead). This was a project whose contradictions could not be resolved enough to make even a neutral film.

19 June. At the Peking University Medical College hospital [formerly Rocke-feller!] I listen to two patients in physiotherapy discussing the merits of *Red Shoes.*

A woman wailing, keening in the hospital corridor. Was it her husband who died? I was struck by the poetic regularity of her cries — that surely could not have been a rote or ritual. Sobs of a little daughter punctuated her cries. Many onlookers collected — *one* tried to be comforting.

27 June. Today it was a corpse, covered by a sheet — unwept.

4 July. When will these enemies pass — defeat, humiliation, hunger?

5 July. Before midnight last night a suitable explosion for the Glorious Fourth — two power lines outside the hotel banged and flashed frighteningly. When I went out this morning a crowd standing by the hostel (which also faced the flash) indicated a jump last night — fatal?

8 July. The Chaikovsky laureate showed his piano equipment this afternoon. A taste for the worst side of Liszt could be blamed on his Leningrad teacher, I suppose. A talent for extreme contrasts (thunder and whipped cream), the skill of a machine and the mannerisms of a ham, or an abbé. Are there courses in stage comportment in conservatories? Yin Cheng-tsung looks like someone who listens to no one any longer — soon no one will try saying anything to him.

Wang Ping, the good woman directing at the August First Studio, showed her annual film at the Film Workers' Union. *Locust Tree Village* had little help from

its writer and all of Wang Ping's talent and craftsmanship were required to hold
this professional audience's attention. (This film won her the national award for
the best direction of 1962.) In the report that I submitted to the Film Bureau I
concentrated on her obvious troubles with the script and production:

Usually, Wang Ping tries to break up her groupings to prevent a sequence from
looking static, and she is not extravagant with camera movement. But photographically, she had one large, unnecessary obstacle here — *color.* I could not
understand why this simple subject was burdened with the expense and problems of color — the greatest problem, of course, being that it usually makes a
film look *less* real (until much more restraint is learned in the use of color for
interior scenes).

By now, of course, I was aware that Chinese films were awarded the added expense of color less for appropriateness, and more for the importance of their
subjects; color was a prestige signal.

Analysts of modern Chinese culture regard Chou En-lai's speech to the film
conference of June 1961 as the announcement of a year's comparative relaxation in the arts, and not only in the film industry. It is in films, however, that
this respite shows most clearly, though with the slowness of decision and manufacture the good films that seized the opportunity often appeared only after the
respite had passed — and suffered hard knocks then. The good realistic comedy
with unexpected satirical touches, *Li Shuang-shuang*, came out before the tide
turned, but the even better satirical comedy, *Better and Better*, appearing at the
end of 1962, ran into trouble, and was withdrawn from circulation in six
months. Another comedy that appeared at this time was accused of flippancy
and vanished for technical reasons that were, for once, really technical: *Wondrous Encounters of a Magician* was made as a three-dimensional experiment
(that required two-color glasses) and showings were limited (see Plate 42). More
serious films, or films on a larger scale, were delayed into 1963, and their tribulations will be mentioned later.

Li Chun seems to be the only writer in China who is continuously associated with
filmmaking. His "Story of Li Shuang-shuang" was published in 1959[21] as a
believably humorous reflection of the Great Leap of 1958, but by the time it
was filmed in 1962, as adapted for the screen by the author, changes had to be
made: no more communal kitchen (where Shuang-shuang of the story had won
her battles), and a considerable softening of the sharp portraits of the story,
especially that of Sun Hsi-wang, the heroine's negative husband. Li Chun's adaptation, probably through no fault of his, lowered the dramatic level of his idea
and the political effectiveness of his story, but there was still plenty of life left in

The official seal for the film *Li Shuang-shuang*

the finished film of *Li Shuang-shuang* to be enjoyed.* Both Chang Jui-fang and Chung Hsing-hua, as activist wife and passive husband, here showed their best film work. My report's only real gripe was directed at the artificial picture of village life, in spite of the exteriors filmed in a Hunan village:

The exteriors are too clearly separated from the studio photography of all interior scenes. Work details look like "stage business" given to actors — "Carry this bunch of tools past the window" — "Sharpen this scythe during the dialogue" — and so on. This was not the case with *Young People of Our Village.* The inserted song sequence, with its unrealistic orchestra, its polished choral singing and studio moonlight, unjustly surrendered the film to artifice. Shanghai actresses have such a hard task pretending to be peasants that nothing should add to their burden — but the costume designer has given them all uniformly brightly patterned jackets, etc., that the most conscientious of actors would have difficulty making into a part of this village's streets. But in general I believe that the Haiyen Studio has here made its greatest effort in rural realism.

The other two successful comedies of this period turned further away from realism than I thought possible in China. It was possibly the three-dimensional experiment of *Wondrous Encounters of a Magician* that excused its agreeably casual story of a vaudeville performer returning to Shanghai after years abroad; in any case there was laughter throughout (his adventure in a film studio was fully slapstick) in addition to wonder at what was seen through the two-color spectacles. This lighthearted film made me forgive the director, Sang Hu, all his past prettiness. But *Better and Better* was remarkably brave *and* funny. Its Chinese title is a quotation from Mao's Yenan talks — a familiar saying about adding flowers to embroidered silk, the equivalent of "gilding the lily." I never found the direct relevance of this title to the series of genuinely amusing incidents around a tiny railroad station; possibly a Mao quotation was thought protection enough for its unorthodoxies, but the film followed the relaxed period into

---

* There is a full précis of the conflicts in Li Shuang-shuang's village, as revised for the film, in K. S. Karol's *China: The Other Communism* (New York: Hill and Wang, 1967), pp. 176–178. His discussion with the filmmakers at the Haiyen Studio, following the screening, is also telling: "Ever since we first met, the Chinese film-makers and I had disagreed on practically everything."

oblivion. The person most responsible, so far as I can judge, for the film's unusual quality was its director, Hsieh Tien, but there was obviously enthusiastic teamwork. The fine jazzy scene of the timber-hauling song could only have come from a group of film inventors — writer, director, composer, cameramen, actors, all! The whole film used film ideas instead of clinging to literature, and the effect was of a sparkling piece of music that you regret must end. I was so delighted with the film that I had to be carefully solemn in my report: ''. . . a great but modest contribution to the development of a specifically *Chinese* comedy film.''

Advertising for *Better and Better*

The warm summer of 1963 has a somber look in my diary, beginning with the meditations of a sleepless midnight:

28 May. To take a shortcut in Chinese society is as impossible as to take a shortcut through the ever right-angled intersections of Peking's streets. Parks turn out to be long-cuts — longer cuts. The best you can do is to slant across a sidewalk or cross a street at a long diagonal. As in your social behavior you must stick to the east-west and the north-south streets — a pattern that you can vary slightly but never shorten.

22 June. At 6:30 A.M. this neighborhood — the whole city, too, I suppose — explodes into life: radios, shouts, children's unwillingness (except for breakfast), slammed doors — all beautifully clear through the summer's opened windows.

And it is already fiercely summer — can we hold out in 709 for another month before the grand move to Peitaiho? The other (north) side of the corridor is cool and tempting.

30 June. (Sunday) A day at the Summer Palace, with complete family. Can't do this often, too loud and wearing, in spite of intermittent pleasures (rowing back in moonlight). The little island is probably as artificial as the lake, but it is relatively free of loudspeakers, has good food and pleasant service.

4 July. The Mongolians across the hall left for the evening happily and came back roaring drunk and quarrelsome — just like the swift transition of Marceau in his ''Going to a Party'' sketch.

10 July. X's situation tragic. Returning defeated and alone. We may see the sad trio having a last fling at Peitaiho.

Japanese paintings at that architectural bargain counter, the *former* Soviet exhibition center. Most were chosen to please here, but there are a few surprises —
perhaps deliberately included as horrible examples. [A later Japanese industrial
fair at the center became so popular that you couldn't attend without permission from your street committee.]

On 7 February 1931, when the Kuomintang government considered anti-
Japanese propaganda dangerous to its own safety, twenty-four young writers,
artists, and actors who were active in the left-wing leagues were arrested by the
British police in Shanghai and delivered to the Kuomintang commander. He
ordered their execution that night, shot all but six of the best known, forced
these to dig their own graves, and then buried them alive, an old Chinese punishment for subversives.[22] The best known of the writers was the thirty-year-old
Jou Shih; his 1929 novel, *Second Lunar Month*, was republished as a memorial,
with an introduction by Lu Hsun. This and Jou Shih's martyrdom gave novel
and author a seemingly permanent place in China's modern history. The novel
remained in print through all changes of policy; it was translated into English
(by Sidney Shapiro, as *Threshold of Spring*, in *Chinese Literature*, Nos. 6 and 7,
1963) and in 1962 a film adaptation was begun.

The film's trouble began before it was made. On all levels where discussion was
possible there was a division of opinion on the wisdom of filming Jou Shih's
novel. When some officials of the Film Bureau joined literary critics in speaking
of the novel's weakness and sentimentality, its defenders raised the shield of Lu
Hsun's praise — to be answered: "But Lu Hsun did *not* say one word in praise of
the novel — he was too scrupulous a critic for that — he praised only Jou Shih's
revolutionary activity and condemned his murder." Not a very sound basis for
the film adaptation of a melancholy literary work (and one that employed an
endless coy exchange of written messages), yet production went on, and *Second
Lunar Month* (in color) came out in 1964. It was unusually popular — such
continuous weeping on and off the screen had not been so enjoyed since the last
film of Pa Chin's *Family* — but the press was persistently hostile. The relaxation
of 1961—1962 was clearly over. A foreign visitor obtained a seat "with the
utmost difficulty," found it "the most interesting film" that he saw in China,[*]
and inquired about the contradiction between its popularity and the unanimous
attacks:

The Chinese Press, from the day the film was shown, embarked on a witch-hunt
against all those connected with it. By the time I left China, over 100 newspaper

---

* "... here was a film which dared to show a pre-revolutionary China in adult terms, giving
a glimpse of a courtly, civilised, spacious and vanished age. No wonder most of the older
people watching the film were in tears."

articles had been published, attacking it for "escapism" and "bourgeois humanitarianism."

I asked an official what would happen to the director [Hsieh Tieh-li]. . . . I was told, "It is not likely that he will make such a film again."

I asked my interpreter why the film showed to packed audiences. He replied: "Chairman Mao wants us to see for ourselves what is good and what is bad so we can differentiate between the two."[2] [3]

What they saw may have been too startling for the audience to judge whether it was "good" or "bad" for them:

. . . in one scene, three schoolteachers, including the hero, are gathered round a table after dinner. One of them talks about the possibility of revolutionary uprisings in the area. "Enough of socialism, communism and all the other isms," he says. "Let us drink." The audience gasped with shocked, incredulous surprise. But there was snickering among the younger spectators during the love scenes, as though they were watching something obscene.

20 Sept. One of the dailies has published an advance synopsis for a film, *The Proletarian*, an allegory that I doubt can be made. The hero proletarian is threatened by lions from the East, tigers from the West, leopards from the South, and *bears from the North* — and defeats them all.

8 Oct. Departures accumulate swiftly — the Morrises left for a power station job in Moscow — Ted goes next week (his reluctance is a refreshing variant) — the Whytes are recalled to Toronto, leaving next month, even Sally leaves the catalog department to its own ancient devices, for Indonesia and love. The whole group of Iranians tomorrow. The Xs will be left high and dry — dry with our meager sociability. I wish we could be better company. . . . Only exchanged magazines seem to hold us together now.

Only variations at banquet were a new, pleasantly naïve interpreter and the search for newly arrived Andrea G. She was nearly overwhelmed by my ill-timed appearance (in the midst of the stately entrance ceremonies). . . .

Holiday instructions: be polite to Them [foreigners] but don't talk.

Nothing really doing at FAC and I just putter around . . . I've sent off some piteous job-hunting inquiries.

20 Oct. Episode in university dormitory: two postcards and a movie still fastened over a top bunk, caused a Big Inquiry.

No dancing since New Year, except on square for holiday night, by smooth slips away from orthodox circlings. Youngsters equally ingenious and surreptitious about clothes. They wear what they like *inside* the conformist shabbiness. Dilemma of FLP's blood pressure: got his doctor to prescribe dancing (but not for his wife) — and then *all* dancing was stopped.

The fish infected by a "Japanese" disease — those who didn't get it one day got it the next when the same pots were used.

Almost got caught at hospital by Felix Greene and his BBC cameras working outside my doctor's room — now wish I'd stayed to watch (at a safe distance) his methods of management and selection. The lights and smocks impressive. Greene concentrated first on Long White Beard, the distinguished theatrical property in that institution — he was still combing it lovingly when I sneaked out.

7 Nov. We weren't invited to celebration (?) last night — meaning — ?

Prices up: sugar from 76 to 82, soap 31 — 37 — 48. The meat table trick on buyers.

Someone could write a dissertation on the function of rumor here today. Starting with the deliberately planted rumor of a monster at the zoo.

D.D.R. consulate very helpful about our Leipzig invitation, but no tickets yet.

The only nibble to my job-hunting letters: the Staatliches Filmarchiv of the DDR replied with a suggestion that I come to the Leipzig documentary film festival. No job was mentioned, but obviously this was to be discussed and I was to be inspected in person. After our last mistake I couldn't leave Si-lan behind in Peking so we both applied for visas. The sympathetic people at the DDR consulate helped with that and our tickets and we prepared ourselves for a winter crossing — and return — through Siberia.

19 Dec. [after Leipzig] In general status quo: S. tinkering with classes and I watch all the office jobs left undone for several months being crowded into the last days before the magic date of January 1 -- the crazy custom.

Feeling against foreigners (us, anyway) seems deeper. Yesterday, someone asked me a direction and when I turned to answer and he saw he had spoken to a foreigner, he had such a fright that he literally ran away. My sanitary mask conceals nothing. It only makes me feel a little more secure about the (superstitious?) increase of spitting as I approach.

Christmas. X's editorial job at the Marx-Lenin Institute has just evaporated, along with the Institute. The name may remain a while longer, but only Mao's works are to be published.

29 Dec. Too many gruesome stories lately, though not intended that way. Aging, desperate Dorothy dodging the stoning. African diplomats house-hunting in an undiplomatic district — and openly jeered at. The police who returned four of the nine confiscated tapes — "Yellow music — not good for you." Protection of Chairman from anything too technical — his irritation and commands.

Another biographical film that went on the rocks of contradiction was intended to be a life of Norman Bethune. They had a good script but for some years every foreigner interested in films who passed through Peking was invited to resolve its contradictions; production was finally launched in 1963 with Gerry Tannebaum in the role of Bethune* and Chang Chun-hsiang as director of the ill-fated project. Dr. Bethune was the only foreigner praised by Mao for his help to the Chinese revolution, but by 1963 and even more by 1964 (when production stopped) the "white world" was depicted as China's antagonist. Even China's one European ally, Albania, was mystically linked to the Asian and African and Latin American worlds where China still had hopes of influence. Writing about Bethune could always be armored by citations from Mao, but to make Bethune's Canadian-American face and character the positive center of a Chinese film, even as one who was learning at the fount of socialist theory, must have become less and less thinkable to the Propaganda Bureau. Xenophobia finally won — the film did not appear.

A biographical film purified of *all* contradictions appeared in 1964. *Lei Feng* is a film so crammed with lessons, sermons, and virtuous examples that there is no room for anything else. I can imagine a film made just after the death of St. Francis that would look like this. Only three main characters are needed for this morality play: the righteous little soldier-driver, his easily tempted and back-sliding comrade (Wang), and a priestlike political instructor.

Reel 1.   Introduction of Lei Feng (from Hunan, Mao's province) and Wang Ta-li (*What's the hurry? You can fix it tomorrow*). Opening of thrift and anti-luxury themes (another soldier, Wu Kuei, relies on his parents' money). Lei Feng dances with children and tells them of his miserable childhood.

Reel 2.   Lei Feng reacts to threat of invasion by Chiang and the United States by insisting on volunteering for a combat assignment (Instructor: *You didn't forget the class bitterness and applied for permission to fight, that is a good thing. But it is a bad thing if you complain when you are not satisfied . . .*). Lei Feng studies Mao's lesson in "Serve the People" and the instructor gives him the four volumes of Mao's works.

Reel 3.   He studies the four volumes. He prefers cooled boiled water to soda water. When Wang is headstrong and wasteful, Lei Feng persuades him to criticize himself.

---

* Gerald Tannebaum, "Impressions Collected Over 40,000 Li," *Eastern Horizon*, May 1965, is a record of a year's location-shooting for the abandoned *Dr. Bethune* through 1963—1964, though little is mentioned of the actual filming. He tantalizingly writes that some rural teachers met by the film unit had "valuable suggestions about the films they saw," but no more.

Reel 4.   Wang boasts of his knowledge (mechanical) of Mao's works and is gently reprimanded by Lei Feng (*It may take us a lifetime to study the essay, "Serve the People." If we study it well, it will be enough for us to use it for a lifetime*). Lei Feng buys pamphlets by Mao for his whole squad. He declines to take care of a cold, runs errands for his comrades instead of playing basketball. On his free day he helps workers complete their construction, inspires them "to launch an enthusiastic emulation drive," and modestly refuses to give his name.

Reel 5.   Wang falsely reports Lei Feng's interest in a girl teacher and is anwered by the instructor (*It's good that you are taking such a keen interest in your comrades and the collective. But you should have a basic trust in our comrade*). In a rainstorm Lei Feng helps an old woman and her grandchild to get home — but refuses even a bowl of drinking water.

Reel 6.   He returns to barracks, exhausted (*You mustn't get up, Wu Kuei — be careful, or you'll catch cold*). Instructor tells him that a primary school has asked him to be their spare-time trainer (*No, I don't think I am good enough*), but he accepts — at a grandiose ceremony. Wang (learning from Lei Feng) washes the squad's clothes.

Reel 7.   Lessons in thrift. (Wang: *Don't you feel awful with this old pair of socks on your feet? Lei Feng: Awful? The socks of our revolutionary army men are for wearing and not for showing. They may continue to serve me as long as they don't affect my training and driving*). He helps pioneers plant trees, and tells them a story about a screw he once found.

Reel 8.   He is determined to help the people's communes and the people of the flooded areas of Liaoyang, so he and Wang leave in a truck with relief supplies. He halts for a stalled bus that needs a spare tire, and some passengers on the bus recall his face as someone who had helped them before. Once the truck stalls and as Lei Feng gets out to fix it Wang tries again to throw away the old socks.

Reel 9.   Lei Feng leaves 100 yuan ("from a Liberation Army fighter") for the flood victims, and refuses to take it back (*The Party and Chairman Mao are my parents who have given me my new life. . . . My home is everywhere, all over the country. Now my home here is flooded, so I have the right as well as the obligation to help my own home*). His socks are found and the director of flood relief is amazed. Wang's mother is sent 20 yuan by Lei Feng, posing as Wang, and Wang goes to fight the flood, inspired by Lei Feng.

Reel 10.   With improved behavior Wang takes a bus, where he reads a news-paper item about Lei Feng's death (though death is not mentioned). There is a ceremony of the (dead) soldier's relics, Wang is given Lei Feng's four volumes, and the film ends with Mao's inscription: "Learn from Comrade Lei Feng."

A friend of K. S. Karol told him that a cinema audience in the suburbs of Sian rose at the end of the film, chanting in unison for a full five minutes, "All honor to Lei Feng!"[24]

Lei Feng was only the first of a new series of soldier-heroes sainted and drama-tized as models for the behavior of all. Earlier soldier-heroes had not been used to such an intense degree of propaganda, employing every medium. Ouyang Hai was another of the new series of army models: his purity and discipline were first celebrated in 1965 in a novel, *The Song of Ouyang Hai.* The novel increases our difficulty in believing that Ouyang Hai was a real soldier, but for the millions of Chinese readers (needless to say, it was *the* popular book of the year) the novel heightened his reality. "What he did we must do." He too shows "us" the way to be inspired by films:

Towards evening, Hai climbed the slope with his book [*The Story of Tung Tsun-jui,* also a novelized and filmed soldier-hero]. Before he could open it, he heard the squad leader calling him. Chen shouted that there was a film show that night. . . .

As usual, two pictures were to be presented. The first was a documentary about how a million serfs are rising to their feet. The second, *The Battle of Sangkumr-yung,* dealt with fighting the U.S. imperialists in Korea. Hai's interest was aroused. [If] He couldn't fight the imperialists and the reactionaries himself, at least he could see it in a motion picture.

The screen was a sheet between two bamboo poles. As they sat on the ground waiting for the show to begin, the soldiers sang song after song.

Finally it started. On the screen appeared white snowy mountains, turbulent streams, dark primeval forests and endless grasslands. The narrator, in a low resonant voice almost in Hai's ear, was saying:

"On the southwestern border of our motherland stands the Tibetan high plateau, known as 'the Roof of the World.' It forms a defensive screen for our great country. . . ."

A big lama temple glittering with gold and jade was seen next, and well-fed lamas. From a dark squat stone building, ordinary Tibetan people, thin as sticks, emerged.

The narrator's voice grew somber. "They have lived here for generations, in conditions worse than animals!"

Talk and laughter among the soldiers were stilled. Some of them swore angrily.

At previous films, Hai had laughed from beginning to end. This was different. He was uncomfortable from the start. As he watched, the images on the screen became blurred. The narrator's voice became inaudible. He rubbed his eyes, but to no avail. What he was seeing was not the high plateau, not his Tibetan brothers, but his dear ones in snow-blanketed Ravens Nest. Hai saw his mother setting her jaw, her mouth twitching painfully, as she trudged the streets of Lienchi. . . .

He couldn't see, and he didn't want to. In this world there were still monsters who ate human flesh and drank human blood. Those reactionaries were torturing people who were oppressed as he had been. . . . Why was it there were still places [in China?!*] where the poor were being tormented?

The voice of the narrator grew strong and excited: "People who were slaves for thousands of years have broken their shackles. A million serfs are rising to their feet."

On the screen our border troops pursued the fleeing rebels through the snow. Our soldiers crossed icy rivers, scaled precipitous heights. It seemed to Hai that a fighter in their ranks was looking right at him and shouting:

"Hurry, Ouyang Hai. What are you waiting for? Join us, quickly, good brother."[2 5]

15 Jan. [1964] Third day of mise-en-rallies to "support Panama." 19 cameras recorded first day. Easy to encourage or applaud someone else's adventurism.

17 Jan. Much activity, banqueting and whispering. Will we ever know what was going on tonight?

26 Jan. A curious program at the Hung Hsing [the Red Star newsreel theater] this afternoon: the Panama pageant plus (Hungarian?) *Wild Swan Island*, plus a Soviet (1960?) cartoon of a vegetable revolt, plus a Yugoslav (!!) short about the mongoose's enmity for snakes — is this Snake Island shown as allegory? Definitely not a tourism film.

8 Feb. The new *Optimistic Tragedy* made me want to do a piece on Photographic Rhetoric — what a *pretty* mess they made of Vishnevsky's noble play! The age and control of the production designer should be declared Finished.

A pleasant children's film, *Little Ding-dong*. [See Plate 44.] Hsieh Tien one of its codirectors — condemned for good, I suppose, to turn away from genuine comedy. *Better and Better* was not a beginning — but an end.

It was not a favorable year for comedy. There was an embarrassingly unfunny film, *Woman Barber*, about a wife's efforts to learn a useful profession without

---

* In the ten years between the People's Republic of China's declaration (that Tibet was an integral part of the country) and 1959, year of the Tibetan uprising and the full occupation of Tibet by the Chinese army, the words "serf" and "slave" were never mentioned in any contemporary account of Tibet. The descriptions of that country in the 1950s by quasi foreigners, such as Israel Epstein, gave no indication that a slave society was still in existence there. This may seem an insuperably contradictory propaganda problem, but it was soon solved, as here, by ignoring social fact and exploiting its political value.

disturbing her sensitive husband.* A traveler got some amusement from a more political comedy, *Satisfied or Not Satisfied?*:

Time: the present. Place: a restaurant in Suchow. . . . Main character: Waiter No. 5, an utterly impossible man. All the other waiters, and the customers, too, are blissfully happy, but he is surly, slams the plates on the table, brings the wrong dishes, barks at the guests, and snarls at them if they show displeasure. . . . His colleagues vainly try to make him see the right way. He regards waiting on others as beneath his dignity and refuses to recognize that serving the people is man's highest vocation . . . his co-workers give him another lecture, citing the example of Lei Feng, the epitome of Communist virtue [and reminding him of the capitalist past and a waiter's life *then*]. His conversion is complete.[26]

A more analytical traveler through China later in 1964, K. S. Karol, found the attitudes of *Sentinels Under the Neon Lights* rich in implication. A comparison of the play I saw with the film he describes (directed by Wang Ping and Ko Hsin at the August First Studio) shows little change in adaptation. The period is the entry of the Red Army into Shanghai in May 1949, to cope with the intrigues of the reactionaries, who declare, "The Communists came here red, but they will leave here black." Karol was struck, not by the artistry of the film, but by its "realism mixed with frankness." There are constant threats to the high morale of the victorious peasant company given the responsibility of patroling the notorious Nanking Road. "Like devils, [the conspirators] watch for the slightest personal weaknesses in order to trap lost souls." Karol's chief surprise was that

. . . the policing of the Nanking Lu was entrusted to young peasant soldiers completely dazzled by the big city, not to the workers' militia, recruited in the Chapei district and noted for their revolutionary spirit. It is as if, after the victory of a new Paris commune, the Champs Elysées were guarded by peasants from the heart of France, and not by the workers of the city's Red belt.[27]

He found the film an illustration of Mao's tactical principle, "surround the towns by way of the countryside, then take the towns," intended, in 1964, to be read in a worldwide application:

The Western countries, industrialized but firmly held by the capitalists, are the "towns." The underdeveloped countries . . . are the "countryside."[28]

Another urgent function of *Sentinels* or *Lei Feng* or of any other film touching the pre-1949 past was, again, the Lesson — this time the memory-sharpener, *hui-i-tui-pi* (recollect the past and contrast it with present happiness) — a

---

* Similar in theme, but in nothing else, to Satyajit Ray's *Mahanagar* (or, "The Big City"), made the year before.

campaign in which films played a leading role. A Peking newspaper praised a properly class-oriented mother, Wu Ju-ji:

By recollecting her own personal sufferings in the past when she was a child apprentice-worker, by comparing her past misery with her present happy life, and by taking her children to see films depicting class oppression and class struggle, for example, she gives her children class education . . . so that her children will hate the old society and warmly love the new.[29]

A further step in this campaign was recorded by a young teacher of English in Shanghai, writing home in November 1965:

. . . of course the Chinese always shed tears when they see films depicting life before Liberation, which happens about once every three weeks. One of the most frequent slogans here is: "Never forget the past or you'll betray the world revolution."[30]

10 Feb. Only bad news today — the winter's epidemic of pneumonia is still packing and overpacking the children's wards. And we read that Marc was killed in Martinique.

13 Feb. The Year of the Dragon begins today. At yesterday's banquet I tried to entertain the table with a Sillitoe story: "You see, his father was a veteran of the International Brigade that fought in Spain." My ministerial neighbor: "That means he was a bad man, doesn't it?"

17 Feb. At last I've seen the New Year fair — and it was worth the effort: packed streets (no vehicles here for eleven days) from the city wall south to the next boulevard, stalls mostly of store goods but jolly withal — long rods of crabapples, topped with a white cornball or blue banner, are the fair's insignia. Some wear ropes of crabapples, like cartridge belts — lots of other foods nibbled and priced. The clacketting pinwheels make the fair's music. There are big hawk kites for sale but the Monkey King is more popular. At the bus stop an amateur Solomon takes charge of an argument over a goldfish bowl broken in a pushing queue.

No other "European" face in sight. There must be fewer of us moving about Peking these days than during the reign of the Empress Dowager.

5 March. Another "command" film — this time one I couldn't see. Birth control is having another try, and all Chinese citizens, carefully divided into male audiences and female audiences, are being shown a film too frank for mixed reactions — or for foreigners.*

---

* The film seen by K. S. Karol in Sian this year was apparently a later and more persuasive step in the campaign — building a little drama on contraceptive methods, and a little comedy on sterilization. (*China: The Other Communism*, p. 296)

Ever since we arrived five years before we were periodically urged to take one Grand Tour or another. Now, with the prospect of a move to Berlin that might make this a farewell tour, we said yes, and started out on 28 March, by train toward Shanghai and Canton, where we were to meet the Hong Kong branch of the family.

The trip south gave me my first glimpses in China of actual film production moments — aside from watching the behavior of cameramen recording such rituals as parades, demonstrations, arriving notables. Permission for these glimpses in Shanghai and Canton came, of course, from the Film Bureau in Peking; they must have preferred such observations to be made at some distance from the home office.

In Shanghai the Tien Ma Studio was being used for only one film, *Family Problem*. The construction of the interior set, the model room of a worker's family, looked more fragile than similar sets in other countries, and there was a pleasantly casual working atmosphere between shots. Actors, director (Fu Chao-wu), camera crew, all joked with each other (with minimum consultation between actors and director), but actual filming brought a certain rigidity to all present. I was inclined to blame this on the controlling script, but a day's visit to any studio might have given the same impression. Shots were fully rehearsed, using dry runs without film, and while I was there, there were no retakes.

At the Pearl River Studio outside Canton work and conversation were even further relaxed, perhaps partly because all staff lived in buildings within the studio compound — the excitement of the new organization had not yet worn off. A Canton opera was being filmed by an extremely enthusiastic young group determined to explore new territory, and they were eager to explain and discuss all their purely technical problems with an outsider. I was shown two films, a modest new children's film, and the first work of the studio, *Waves on the Southern Shore* (1960), written and directed by Tsai Chu-sheng, the most prominent left director of the thirties.* I left with the feeling that this and the Changchun studios, with their young personnel, contained the greatest promise for China's film future, no matter how little proof I saw on this visit.

More than any studio visit in Shanghai, I looked forward to the prospect of seeing Ta Shih Chieh, The Great World, a unique complex of more than a dozen theaters, gathered together in a structure built before the First World War in the French concession. This buzzing, sprawling building at the intersection of Tibet Road and (the former) Avenue Eduard VII is best described (as it was in 1936, at the height of its fame) in Josef von Sternberg's memoirs:

The establishment had six floors to provide distraction for the milling crowd, six floors . . . studded with every variety of entertainment Chinese ingenuity had contrived. . . . On the first floor were gambling tables, singsong girls, magicians, pick-pockets, slot machines, fireworks, bird cages, fans, stick incense, acrobats, and ginger. One flight up were the restaurants, a dozen different groups of actors, crickets in cages, pimps, midwives, barbers, and earwax extractors.[31]

And so on, up through the multiple joys of the sixth and top floor. By the time we made our visit the pimps and pickpockets had taken up other professions, but the place still buzzed. In no other place in the world could you see such an ample cross section of a country's theater life — all for one admission, with the special privilege of entering any of the many theaters or leaving at any time without giving offense. In all but one of the theaters you could see that the campaign for "revolutionary opera," no matter what the dialect, had won the stages but not the audiences. Their benches always had a few (dutiful?) spectators. The only theater where we couldn't get a good view of the stage, and where the overpacked audience was clearly enjoying itself, was in the single theater allowed to play good old uninhibited Peking opera† — about humane Pao Kung and an imperial concubine. That was a real treat. The only other

---

* This turned out to be his last film.
† Whose entire classical repertoire was discarded throughout the People's Republic (at the insistence of Madame Mao) in the following summer.

auditoriums there to compare with this one's popularity, though not quite so
packed (and more passive), were the improvising ballad singers (from Soochow)
and the cinemas (one was showing *Mine Warfare*). A possibility: the earliest
Chinese films got not only their actors, but also their stories from The Great
World.

The theater at the Hot Springs resort (a long drive from Canton and the scene of
our family reunion) also gave us a taste of "modern opera":

A pretense of folk-opera built over the arias, gestures and situations of classic
opera. Another pretense: its theme — young people in relation to work in the
country — was all quickly wiped away (and forgotten) by antique plot — lost
child, rival fathers, etc.

The last two poems I wrote in China, both on weekend excursions to the
Western Hills, show a disillusionment that is a long way from the optimistic
verses of 1959.

The Pheasant Shrine

> Through the lace of young pines,
> Past a black mouth — the hill's entrance,
> The pheasant pairs flick onward,
> In and out of the bright-edged shadow,
> Up stairs of path to a goal —
> Stone upon stone of meditation,
> Housing the flaked paint of great dolls
> Deserted in their shrine.
> Under a torn flutter of bannered prayer
> The sun dims on a myriad fuzz.

Foundation

> Two dried pools and a single stalk of corn
> Nourish this broken house.
> The stripped trunks lean over,
> The rocks fall against
> The bashed up upright skull
> Receptive to the sun.
>
> The tea once taken upon this terrace
> Held that generation
> Fixed and content:
> Weed heirs and wasp children
> Now build here
> Their afternoon's end.

We received word that the Berlin job was set, we asked for a year's leave from our respective Peking organizations, and prepared to meet my new employers at a Moscow conference.

Happily, the last film of 1964 that I saw had a character of its own and a minimum of traditional self-censorship. For its film about Tibet the August First Studio took an adventurous step: not only was the story to be drawn from the scenarist's trips to Tibet, not only was some of the photography to be done in Tibet, but the cast was to be made up of Tibetan actors! The absence of Hans from most of the scenes, combined with the usual relaxation of inhibitions about the brutal past when showing areas around the perimeter of Han China, gave a fresh tone to *Serfs*. One could believe the raging passions and violent movements of these people, playing in a story of oppression and brutality that *they* knew to be at least partly true — and they made it truer. Much of a spectator's belief is based on the remarkably convincing performance of the chief character, Jamba, an orphaned serf and house slave:

Wangdui, who acts this role, had a life that paralleled this in many ways. He became an orphan at fifteen and was a house slave. He ran away to become a lama in a temple to end his life of misery. But when it was discovered that he was a fugitive serf, he was forced to kneel on the temple steps and received one hundred lashes. . . .[32]

After the tortures of Jamba (the character) he deliberately becomes a mute, determined to speak no more until he can be free. With Wangdui's expressive face and intense movement this device, the unspeaking center of a violent film, helps to hold our attention on him whenever he is on the screen. In a published report of his work on the film Wangdui describes the scene in which he prevents his owner from escaping the arriving People's Liberation Army troops:

We shot this scene out on the mountains, so that it seemed very real. I completely forgot I was acting and was carried away by my anger until the director shouted to me to stop. But not until we took off our costumes and make-up to have dinner did I realize that I had mistaken the actor playing Namchal for a real serf-owner and had kicked him too hard. I felt very bad and told him how sorry I was. Still rubbing the small of his back, he said that was all right — he could understand how I had felt at the time.[33]

The people who made *Serfs* (director: Li Chung; cameraman: Wei Lin-yueh) took so much advantage of the unprecedented circumstances of its production that they showed, in one of the rare but occasional miracles of Chinese cinema, what Chinese filmmakers could do if their government would trust them.[34]

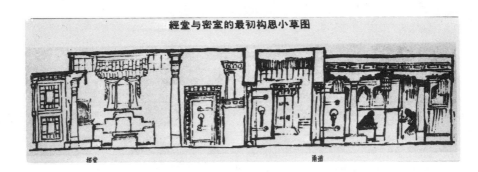

經堂与密室的最初构思小草图

The images in *Serfs* are unusually vivid for China in the sixties. Imagery in *film*
terms is one of the taboos of Chinese cinema — it is one signal that can lead to
denunciation for crimes that have nothing to do with imagery — and the delay
between the completion of *Serfs* and its release may indicate administrative
anxieties. But in the most normal production *literary* imagery is encouraged in
the scenario stage, so long as it does not run over onto film. This sort of imagery,
with a distinctly rhetorical tone and possibly deriving from the classics, can be
found in any script — the more dramatic the more frequently employed. Here
are some random passages from the script for *Lin Tse-hsu:*[35]

A host of smaller craft skim like dragon-flies over the water, tacking this way
and that. A gay sampan approaches Shamien. Sturdy Mai Kuan is pulling on two
oars at the prow. The boat shoots forward through the foam like an arrow.

Great Tiger Hill rises from the river like a great crouching tiger, ready to leap up
with bared fangs to guard the way. Near Shakok, a precipice plunges into the
sea.

Word flies from one to another, from one hill-top to another. At once on all the
hill-sides far and near and along the shore, heads are turned and raised. It seems
as if mountains are rising up or oceans spilling over.

The giant banyan trees with their twisted branches are like an army camp. Now
the fighters crouching there drop down like winged warriors from heaven and
hotly pursue the British troops.

And the script of *Serfs* begins:

The towering Himalayas. Like some huge dragon they soar through the sea of
clouds. Snow-drifts crumbling seem like falling dragon scales. . . .

The fields on both sides of the river are a rolling sea of barley.

A harvest procession sweeps along like a swirling wind. . . .[36]

What I found inexplicable, as I read more widely in the published translations of
ancient and recent Chinese literature (and having other translations read to me),
was that Chinese filmmakers had learned so little from their arts of the past. Mei
Lan-fang was one of the few connected with films who is known to have sought
applications, in the occasional film that he made, of older Chinese arts. The
simple tropes and similes used above are small gleanings from the riches of *film*
ideas waiting at every turn in the past for any Chinese filmmaker who is eager or
willing to broaden and deepen his medium. Eisenstein wrote in 1929 about
Japanese cinema, as "the cinema of a country that has, in its culture, an infinite
number of cinematographic traits, strewn everywhere with the sole exception
of — its cinema"[37]; as much, or more, cinema is waiting in Chinese art to be
discovered by Chinese cinema.

I can suggest one general explanation for this neglect. In the constant struggle to remove all ambiguities from the film, it is absurd to demand that traditional Chinese painting and theater should be regarded as models for the filmmaker. Those old arts thrive on the very subtlety and ambiguity that would blur the clear aims required of each film. "Open door — see mountain" may be the only theatrical rule applicable to Chinese films.

The links to some arts and often the arts themselves were lost to the Chinese cinema. Even so relevant and recent an art as the performances in the court theater of the Summer Palace was unknown to Chinese filmmakers. It was quite unlike the public Chinese theater, possibly because the Empress Dowager laid down rigid restrictions for public performances in order to make her productions a novelty for the court. Her theater was the only one to use a curtain between scenes, as well as wings and backdrops — all to promote the illusions that were taboo in Peking opera. She "was very fond of reading religious books and fairy tales, and wrote them into plays and staged them herself."[38] On the twelfth day of the second moon the court attended a theatrical performance:

This represented all the tree fairies and flower fairies celebrating their birthday. . . . The final scene was a very fitting ending to the performance. It represented a small rainbow which gradually descended until it rested on the rocks; then each fairy in turn would sit upon the rainbow which rose again and conveyed them through the clouds into Heaven.[39]

If this brings to the reader's mind the name of Georges Méliès (rather than the customary appearance of Peking opera), think how envious he would have been to see the performance on 2 March 1903 (third day of third moon); at both his Théâtre Robert-Houdin and his film studio at Montreuil he dreamed and strove for such effects as the Empress Dowager (and the court treasury) made possible for "The Empress of Heaven's Party, or Feast to All the Buddhist Priests to Eat Her Famous Peaches and Drink Her Best Wine" (later familiar as the Monkey King story, *Uproar in Heaven*):

The first act opens with a Buddhist Priest, dressed in a yellow coat robe with a red scarf draped over his shoulder, descending in a cloud from Heaven to invite all the priests to this party. I was very much surprised to see this actor apparently suspended in the air and actually floating on this cloud, which was made of cotton. . . .

As this Buddhist Priest was descending, a large pagoda began to slowly rise from the center of the stage in which was a buddha singing and holding an incense burner in front of him. Then four other smaller pagodas slowly rose from the four corners of the stage, each containing a buddha the same as the first. When the first Buddhist Priest had descended, the five buddhas came out of the pagodas, which immediately disappeared, and walked about the stage, still singing. Gradually from the wings came numbers of buddhas singing until the stage was full, and they all formed into a ring. Then I saw a large lotus flower, made of pink silk, and two large green leaves appearing from the bottom of the stage, and as it rose the petals and leaves gradually opened and I saw a beautiful lady buddha (Goddess of Mercy) dressed all in white silk, with a white hood on her head, standing in the center of this flower. As the leaves opened I saw a girl and a boy in the center of them. When the petals of the lotus flower were wide open this lady buddha began to gradually ascend, and as she ascended, the petals closed until she seemed to be standing on a lotus bud.

[After a scene of the Monkey stealing the peaches and causing trouble] the Empress of Heaven called a little god about fifteen years old by the name of Neur Cha. . . . When Neur Cha got to the monkey's place and the monkey saw him, he said: "What! A little boy like you come to fight me? Well, if you think you can beat me, come on," and the boy transformed himself into an immense man with three heads and six arms. When the monkey saw this, he transformed himself into the same thing. When the little god saw that this would not do, he transformed himself into a very big man and started to take the monkey, but the monkey transformed himself into a very large sword and cut this man into two pieces. The little god again transformed himself into fire to burn the monkey, but the monkey transformed himself into water and put the fire out. [etc.][40]

The well-known traditions of Peking opera were as little exploited for film principles as were these unknown Chinese theatrical illusions.* Peking opera was constantly filmed (before its transformation in the 1960s to the propaganda machinery of "modern" opera) but not used as a working source for film art. The rare exception, such as Tao Chin's *Fifteen Strings of Cash*, makes this neglect even more remarkable.

There is some consciousness of the unexplored wealth in classical literature, but so far as I could hear, it was confined to lessons from the antique in how to build dramatic conflicts. "How to Study the Cultural Heritage," an article that appeared in the first issue of the Peking Studio's journal, *Film Production*, points to such lessons in *Romance of Three Kingdoms*, with this promising opening:

Cinema is a young art, a synthetic art that must learn from its sister arts. Our country has a long history of art traditions and skills — film art can learn much from these.[41]

But his example (the chapters on the burning of the Red Wall) does not go beyond its "good arrangement of dramatic conflict." It is possible that no writer

---

* Yet it's tempting to imagine a Chinese cinema springing, like the French cinema, from *both* reality (Lumière) and fantasy (Méliès).

in China today could suggest *other* filmmaking lessons to be found in classical
Chinese literature. But this was not the only case where I observed that no
distinction was made between the way to tell a story and the way to tell a film.

Chunks of *Three Kingdoms* have found their way, via theater, into films. The
most filmic chunk, though not yet the base of a good film, is the early episode
known as *Sable Cicada* (or *Diao Chan*). The film suggestion in the following
passage[42] could have dictated a new kind of Chinese film. The country is
threatened by destructive division and in Governor Wang Yün's distress at this
prospect, one of his handmaidens offers to do *anything* to lessen his pain:

A sudden idea came to Wang and he struck the ground with his staff. "Who
would think that the fate of the Hans lay on your palm?"

and Wang Yün outlines his scheme (a scenario for the next two chapters):

"The people are on the brink of destruction, the prince and his officers are in
jeopardy, and you, you are the only saviour. That wretch Tung Cho wants to
depose the Emperor and not a man among us can find means to stop him. Now
he has a son [Lü Pu], a bold warrior it is true, but both father and son have a
weakness for beauty and I am going to use what I may call the 'chain' plan. I
shall first propose you in marriage to Lü Pu and then, after you are betrothed, I
shall present you to Tung Cho and you will take every opportunity to force
them asunder and turn away their countenances from each other., cause the son
to kill his adopted father and so put an end of the great evil. . . ."

In other words, Wang proposes destructive division against the dividers! We have
been shown previously horrifying glimpses of the brutality of both father and
son, so we are aware of Sable Cicada's risk in placing herself as the bait in this
trap. Her ingenious attraction of Lü Pu and Tung Cho is dramatically developed
in scenes of increasing sensuality:

[Lü Pu] made his way into the private quarters and questioned the maids.
Presently one told him that the Minister [Tung Cho] had brought home a new
bedfellow the night before and was not up yet. Pu was very angry. Next he crept
round behind his master's sleeping apartment.

By this time Cicada had risen and was dressing her hair at the window. Looking
out she saw a long shadow fall across the pond. She recognised the headdress and
peeping around she saw it was indeed no other than Lü Pu. Thereupon she contracted her eyebrows, simulating the deepest grief, and with her dainty handkerchief she wiped her eyes again and again. Lü Pu stood watching her a long time.

The purposeful montage of the whole scheme, a compound of intrigue, uncontrolled violence, and manipulated beauty, makes a perfect model for a film's use

of both silence and sound. An original film could be made without departing from the fourteenth-century text.

A similarly stark and sensual suggestiveness waits in this scene:

Now that woman knew already that he had made accusation at the court and that the magistrate would not hear him and she let her heart rest and feared him no more and with a brazen face she watched what he did. He called out, "Sister-in-law, come down! I have a few words to speak to you." That woman came slowly down the stairs and she asked, saying, "What have you to say to me?"

What a full moment of filmwriting! The silent, half-smiling woman looking down confidently into the courtyard, the calculated slow descent of the stairs, the tone of voice so clearly indicated by the words, "What have you to say to me?" This could be Phyllis (Barbara Stanwyck) in Double Indemnity; it is actually Golden Lotus, Wu Sung's sister-in-law, in Shui Hu (Water Margin).[43] The few actions and words are so carefully selected that they seem the only natural details; they even look ordinary at first glance. Yet on second thought it seems impossible to find equally correct details to express the same tension. A possible explanation for the significant, involving details of Three Kingdoms and Shui Hu: the storytellers who recited them (before someone wrote them down) captured and held the audience's attention by making them feel the experiences of the stories' characters. Nothing could be a firmer base for film technique.

And listen to this simple but perfect and original idea for sound-and-image combination in "The Painted Wall," a story by P'u Sung-ling:

Mr. Chu in his concealment [under the bed] hardly dared to draw his breath; and in a little while he heard the boots tramp into the room and out again, the sound of the voices getting gradually fainter and fainter in the distance.[44]

Even without watching Mr. Chu at this moment, one can sense his held breath. Here is another fragment of P'u Sung-ling, where everything seems visible, but is equally suggestive of more than we see, especially as we've never seen this on a screen:

At the door of the temple they sat down to rest, the powder and paint on the young lady's face having all mixed with the perspiration trickling down.[45]

But for Chinese filmmakers Chinese literature has functioned as little more than a storehouse of stories and plots waiting for transfer to the screen. Even modern (twentieth-century) Chinese literature made little impact on the expressive means used in films. Note, for example, this passage from a story ("Leaving the Pass") by Lu Hsun, written and published in 1935:

Having bid farewell, he turned the ox's head and it plodded slowly down the sloping highway. Soon the ox was making rapidly off with big strides. The others watched from the pass. When Lao Tzu was seven or eight yards away they could still see his white hair and yellow gown, the dark ox and the white sack. Then dust rose covering both man and beast, turning everything grey. Presently they could see nothing but yellow dust — all else was lost to sight.[46]

The beautiful conveyance of a dramatic moment through visual means makes us sorry, all over again, that Lu Hsun was not pulled into filmmaking. Filmmakers concerned with evoking all the senses should look at his stories, "The White Light" (1922) and "Remorse" (1925). In the generation that followed him there are at least two writers who can convey the whole range of senses, offering lessons to a word-bound cinema. Lu Hsun's protégée, Hsiao Hung, had too short and hard a life to make much impression on readers, but each small work by her brings us a world — for example, "Spring in a Small Town."[47] Shen Tsung-wen is also a master of the small, sharp form; in his masterpiece, "The Border Town,"[48] the reader can feel nothing forced or arranged in the action or behavior of its people — another lesson waiting for Chinese filmmakers. How much the studios that make the artificial gestures to the minority peoples could learn from his stories of the Miao people, in which he uses their folk forms and ballads, with their abruptness and directness, to govern his style.

If Chinese cinema learns too little from Chinese literature, it is equally unfortunate that modern Chinese literature learns too much from cinema or, more probably, from a combination of cinema and "serial picture books" (comic books). What it learned was not to its improvement. Many stories, long and short, of the past fifteen years sound like superficial scenarios — dialogue and description of action; the faces of actors are indicated, but nothing behind their faces. This is from a story of 1953, about the Korean War:

Ch'in Ming lowered his eyes, cigarette in hand and asked, after a long thoughtful pause: "How are the workmen? Can they adapt themselves to this type of fighting?"

Wu Cheng said: "Genuine gold fears no beating. After all, they are of the proletarian class, so there is no problem; only some of them seem a little below par in feeling."

Ch'in Ming asked thoughtfully: "Have you stirred up their zeal?" Wu Cheng said: "Haven't I! Every Party member is in the front, producing the effect of leadership."

Ch'in Ming sat up, extinguished his cigarette on the edge of the brazier and said: "This is correct. There is something more. You should universally stir up the new heroism of the people under the leadership of the Party members. Have you been able to do that?"

Wu Cheng said nothing.

Ch'in Ming glanced at him and said: "You should know, heroes are not born, they are cultivated. In every man's chest is buried a seed of fire, with something noble hidden in it. All that you have to do is to give it a stir," and, as he said this, he took up the fire tongs and gave the fire a shove, at which crackling spots sputtered brilliantly from the fire, and he continued: "Every man can shine, every man can be a hero. Why don't you launch an over-all movement for merit establishment? It is only through the movement of merit establishment that workers may get the honour that is their due."[49]

Such immobile sermonizing is typical of films made in the early fifties, and later, and becomes increasingly characteristic of fictional works published in this period. When I read a translation of *Red Crag*, the best seller of 1962, about the Sino-American prison camp near Chungking, I was sure it would have little difficulty in becoming a scenario — it was already written as a superior scenario; see how easy it is to break up the following passage into separate shots:

[Sister Chiang] strolled towards the town gate. There was still a large crowd around it. This disturbed her. She walked faster. As she drew nearer, she saw that the crowd contained bare-footed porters and peasants in conical straw hats as well as town dwellers and merchants holding umbrellas. Some of them looked up at the guard atop the gate, then dropped their eyes and walked away. Others kept staring upwards and whispering among themselves. Sister Chiang was puzzled. Through the hazy rain she seemed to see a number of objects hanging from the guard tower above the gate.

She walked a few paces nearer. She could see more clearly now. High on the gate tower were several wooden cages. Those things inside — could they be heads? Shocked, Sister Chiang hurried forward for a closer look. Sure enough, each cage contained a human head, smeared with blood and gore!

. . . Her roving eyes spotted a large announcement pasted on the town wall. The rain had already blurred many of its words. It contained a list of names, marked roughly in red. Soaked by the rain water, they were trickling down like blood.
. . . Sister Chiang pushed her way forward until she was standing directly in front

of the announcement. The first name on the list suddenly caught her eye. She stood staring at it, petrified.*[50]

The whole novel is built from such scenariolike descriptions of action plus dialogue, always conscious of camera viewpoint, with one added advantage learned from films: contrasting and parallel scenes were cleverly juxtaposed. There is a wide artistic gap between a literature which is no more than an imitation of current film continuity methods, and a literature that leads, or could lead, its country's cinema into new expressive territory.

The clearest lessons taught by films to another medium (and vice versa!) appeared in the picture-story books — a child of ancient illustrated literature and the comic books introduced to China by American soldiers. Chinese picture-story books of the 1960s still show stylistic traces of Harold Foster's *Tarzan* and *Prince Valiant* and (even!) Milton Caniff's *Terry and the Pirates.* Since their introduction in 1935, they had moved beyond the children for whom they were first intended. By the 1960s it was not unusual to see adults depending on the pictorial supports of this dubious literature that seemed to increase the dangers of simplification. And children read little else. Filmgoing in China is very inexpensive — comic books are even cheaper and have the added powers of possession and personal circulation: much like the dream of everyone owning his own film library. Roughly half the comic books to be found (before *Quotations from Chairman Mao Tse-tung* took over most printing facilities) were reproductions of popular and required films; here, from *Nieh Erh*, are the scenes of the composition of "March of the Volunteers," on the eve of his departure:

---

* I have not yet seen *Red Crag*, but a Japanese friend who saw it in January 1966 tells me that little was altered in this scene, except the note of color (Shui Hua, its director, had apparently insisted on black-and-white for this film) and a substitution of a photograph of Sister Chiang's executed husband for his name on the list: a wet portrait that suddenly filled

It was eventually thought necessary for the true-life moralities in newspapers and magazines to be dramatized in film shots as well as verse:

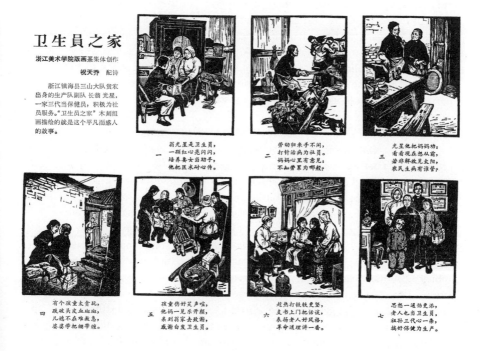

卫生員之家

浙江美术学院版画系集体创作

祝天乔　配诗

浙江镇海县三山大队贫农
出身的生产队副队长翁光星，
一家三代当保健员，积极为社
员服务。"卫生員之家"木刻组
画描绘的就是这个平凡而感人
的故事。

一　翁光星是卫生員，/一颗红心亮闪闪，/培养妻女当助手，/他把医术耐心传。

二　劳劲归来手不闲，/打针治病为社員。/妈妈心里有意见，/不知劳累为哪般？

三　光星他把妈妈劝：/看看现在想从前，/谁非胖救见太阳，/农民生病有谁管？

四　有个孩童太贪玩，/跌破头皮血斑斑，/儿媳不在唯救急，/婆婆学把绷带缠。

五　孩童伤好笑声喧，/他妈妈一见乐开颜，/来到翁家去致谢，/感谢白发卫生員。

六　趁热打铁铁更坚，/支书上门把话谈，/表扬老人好风格，/革命道理讲一番。

七　思想一通劲更添，/老人也当卫生員，/祖孙三代心一条，/搞好保健为生产。

Again and again as we go through the country, I am deeply, irrevocably convinced that the principles embodied in the heart of the Eighth Route Army are the principles that will guide and save China, that will give the greatest of impulses to the liberation of all subjected Asiatic nations, and bring to life a new human society. This conviction in my own mind and heart gives me the greatest peace that I have ever known.[51]

the screen startled both Sister Chiang and the audience with more effect than the novel. There is enthusiasm for the film in Hans Koningsberger, *Love and Hate in China* (New York: McGraw-Hill, 1966), Chap. 10.
When a Japanese delegation to China, headed by Iwasaki, saw the film in May 1965, *Red Crag* ended with a general execution. By the time it arrived in Japan, Shui Hua had criticized himself, reduced the casualties in the prison escape, and emphasized the final victory of the People's Liberation Army. Yet the synopsis published in *China's Screen*, No. 4, 1964, appears to fit this final version. Perhaps the director deviated from his own approved script, and had to be brought back to it.

That is the voice of Agnes Smedley, speaking from the depth of her love for China and its hope, as she travels with the Red Army in November 1937. All over the world then and since her conviction has found an echo in other minds and hearts, so fortified against disappointment that they can believe nothing heard of China that does not correspond with their wish. Mao Tse-tung a dictator? Nonsense! Those charming and sincere young people a howling lynch mob? I won't listen to you any more. All those suicides or "suicides"? Weak intellectuals or malicious rumors, obviously! All right, if the shock of the autumn of 1966 isn't the national insanity that U Thant foresaw, what was the plan behind the violence, and who was its author?

Before we left China, in May 1964, we heard the first mild preliminary noises of the explosion that was to come two years later. When we returned from London a few months before, we found army personnel firmly in both our organizations. They were not in charge but decisions were not made without consulting them. In the Film Archive an early rumbling could be heard in the halt of all planned screenings; more than a year before, these had been limited to film studio staffs,* and now these people, too, were to see neither foreign films nor Chinese films made before 1949. Who had decided China's past cinema was poison, and why? At that time I thought the explanation was to be found somewhere in an unheard (by us) struggle between the revolutionary leaders trained in Yenan and those — "the Shanghai group" — who had unwisely spent the war years some-where else, Chungking, Hong Kong, abroad.† This was visible in film circles: an obvious instance occurred during my visit to the Animation Studio of Shanghai in 1964, where I was briefed by the Yenan-trained studio head, who complained about the unreliability of "these Shanghai people," especially the studio's artists (he refused even to give me the names [learned otherwise] of the artists respon-sible for the most original animation made in his organization). His attitude was anti-art and anti-intellectual as well as "anti-Shanghai": "it's better to live in poverty — to enjoy the comforts of the twentieth century only weakens you." Smiling Wall (that is not his name!) said openly, and with smiling irritation, what we had heard repeatedly hinted in Peking. Even my invulnerable Shanghai interpreter looked a little staggered by such talk to a visitor.

The abrupt shelving of all the pre-1949 Shanghai films that had been generally admired and claimed as revolutionary works was another confirmation of my interpretation. The Yenan group appeared to have won its campaign for 100%

---

* After a severely criticized archive screening of Billy Wilder's *Double Indemnity*.
† A regular department in *Chinese Literature*, "Writings of the Last Generation," did not again appear after the issue of December 1964.

purity, in films, at least. Total confirmation seemed at hand, a year later, in Berlin, when I was shown the full-scale attack on Hsia Yen in three articles in *Renmin Ribao*[52] and in the following year, the equally destructive denunciation in *Renmin Ribao* of Cheng Chi-hua's history and all its formerly approved praise of the left films of the thirties. Both attacks so startled me with their sweeping disposal of huge quantities of Chinese films both before and after 1949 (the articles against Hsia Yen, though triggered by a bitter analysis of his scenario for *The Lin Family's Shop*, struck out at all his work as Vice-Minister of Culture, in charge of film production, as well as his prerevolutionary work in Shanghai and Hong Kong), that I looked for no other interpretation beyond Yenan versus Shanghai. In actuality it turned out to be a Yenan versus Yenan war, already engaged beneath the surface unity in May and June of 1966; by August the disarray in the Chinese government and party was so clear that in following the news of upheaval I lost sight of the cinema's small role.

The three articles that had attacked Hsia Yen and *The Lin Family's Shop* coincided with a deliberately timed (but limited) rerelease of this 1959 film — to aid discussion and denunciation. The first article (signed "Su Nan-yuan") was entitled "*The Lin Family's Shop* Is a Film that Beautifies the Capitalist Class," leaving the issue in no doubt. Hsia Yen's superior, Mao Tun, as author of the 1932 story on which the film was based, also came under attack (making it known to the reader that he was no longer Minister of Culture*):

Mao Tun's original story did not describe the principal exploitation of the proletariat by the capitalists of that time. This was a great mistake, but it was an even greater mistake to film it in 1958.[53]

In response to Hsia Yen's defense that he believed this film could tell young people something about the past and help in remolding the capitalists still in China, "Su Nan-yuan" blamed this film for "the present confusion of the young people" and for the revived hopes of the capitalists in China, "like the capitalists in Yugoslavia and Khrushchov's revisionism," to regain their power. "It showed so much sympathy for capitalists that some of them now believe that they are good men."

The fact that this was made for the tenth anniversary, just after the disruption of the rightists, shows that the struggle between the two systems was continuing.

---

* Mrs. Merle Goldman reports that his place was taken by Lt.-General Hsiao Wang-tung and that another high army officer, T'ao Chu, filled the propaganda posts vacated by the denounced Lu Ting-yi and Chou Yang (*China Quarterly*, July–Sept 1966), but there has been further shaking up of all cultural and propaganda appointments since then.

Comrade Hsia Yen liked the story so much that he wanted it filmed in 1933.*
This shows that Comrade Hsia Yen always felt sympathy with the capitalist
class — their pain was his pain. He cannot feel the oppression suffered by the
people, and this shows clearly the class tendency of Comrade Hsia Yen. Like
many other cultural comrades he was born in a capitalist intellectual family
[according to Cheng Chi-hua, it was "a poor family"] . . . and has strongly clung
to his capitalist viewpoint. Such people have the kingdom of capitalism deeply
embedded in their hearts, and whenever they get a chance they will reveal their
capitalist ideas and leanings. They will try to change not only the youth, but all
society, as well. Comrade Hsia Yen is one of those writers who have not changed
their viewpoint. We can see this not only in this film, but in many articles
written by him before and after the revolution.

The second attack (signed "Chou Shan"), on another full page of *Renmin Ribao*,
went through Hsia Yen's writings with a fine-tooth comb in search of each hint
of his wrong viewpoint, then and during the anti-Japanese war. His film's presentation of that period was wrong, for it was "a high point in China's revolutionary
struggle."

Comrade Hsia Yen saw the thirties as a time without light, without life. For him
China was a broken old boat in a dirty canal. His film is a pail of dirty water
emptied into that canal, rather than a spark to start a prairie fire.[54]

This description of the opening of the film, with its stagnant water and passive
community in the path of the Japanese advance, reminds one that the *direction*
of the film and the *director*, Shui Hua, are regarded as unconnected with the
content or quality of the film; though I doubt that Shui Hua has been given any
film work since 1965.

The third article (signed "Hu Ko") continued the investigation of Hsia Yen's
other writings in the light of this reactionary film, and quoted (ironically) an
article that he published in 1963, "Life, Themes, Creation":

Of course a writer must write about good persons and bad, but how can a writer
test the inner life of a bad person? Or of a person from the past?[55]

The implication being that only an evil writer would consider such problems.
Hsia Yen was exiled not only from the cinema industry and the Ministry of
Culture: he was moved out of Peking to the province of Szechuan, where we
next heard of his appointment as Vice-Mayor of Chengtu.

---

* The Mao Tun story that Hsia Yen *did* adapt in 1933, "Spring Silkworms," is not
mentioned here.

Soon after the publication in 1963 of the first two volumes of Cheng Chi-hua's *History of Chinese Films* he was told that its third volume (1949—1959) would have to be postponed until a thorough revision and correction of Volumes I and II had been made and published. Though he probably saw this as a storm signal, he could not have been prepared for the end of his historical work and of his career, made public in 1966 by *Renmin Ribao*. A full page is devoted to "Tien Hsin's" article, "Let Us Destroy the Mystic Belief in the Films of the Thirties." Cheng Chi-hua's history is called "a poisonous weed" in the campaign to revive the petit bourgeois ideas in the Shanghai films of the thirties. This is the "black line" that must be countered vigorously. His book was written under the influence of Hsia Yen's wrong thinking. (We are incidentally told that Lu Hsun was also "half-mistaken" in the thirties — an advance notice of more violent attacks on Lu Hsun.) The bad films recently made — *Second Lunar Month, The Lin Family's Shop, City Without Night, From South of the Yangtze to the North* — are all attempts to bring the mistaken ideas of the thirties into films today.* Now Cheng Chi-hua must be doing his remolding penance weeding the fields of some distant village — but perhaps glad to have left Peking before the greater storm.

By the autumn of 1966 a Soviet observer,[56] reporting on the Chinese film situation within the Great Cultural Revolution, wrote that *all* productions of the Changchun and Tien Ma Studios had been halted or shelved. He found the central cinemas occupied by three new "documentary" films: *Great Revolutionary Friendship* (on the Albanian delegation to China), *Chairman Mao Joins the Millions of the Cultural Revolution's Army*,† and *Great Victory of the Ideas of Mao Tse-tung*. This last, celebrating China's three nuclear tests, giving film "proof" that with certain precautions one need not fear being harmed by a nuclear explosion (I have learned that Vietnamese audiences received this film with disappointing coolness), is of genuine historical interest. A young English teacher in Shanghai wrote home about its reception by Chinese audiences:

Of course we are getting all the films about Chairman Mao in Tien An Men with the Red Guards . . . when Mao comes on the screen there's a wild burst of applause and shouts of Mao Xushi Wan Sui! . . . Last week we saw the film of the experiments with the three atomic tests . . . the comrades in the cinema

---

* An unsigned later attack on Cheng Chi-hua's history was translated in *Chinese Literature*, June 1968; the full text is reproduced in Appendix 3 of this book.
† To those unable to see this extreme example of the personality cult, showing the Chairman at the first Red Guards meeting on Tien An Men, its adulatory commentary can be consulted, as published in *Renmin Ribao*, and translated in *Chinese Literature*, November 1966.

were cheering and clapping — 'China's got the bomb — she can stand up to anybody!'[57]

Zhelakhovtsev mentioned only one recent fictional film "accepted" in the first months of the cultural revolution: *The Red Pack*, the story of an enterprising peddler who learns to build his sales talk on the thoughts of Mao. Showings of Stalin-cult films (*The Fall of Berlin* again!) were also reported, as well as more restricted discussion-showings of criticized films of the recent past, such as *Red Sun* and *The Lin Family's Shop*. Chief blame was given to "the revisionist responsible for directing the black line" — Chou Yang! By the following summer these tried-out lessons-by-negative-example were expanded to general distribution — a political and economic victory that could not have displeased the film-starved audience.

The Red Guards of the Peking Film Institute published a twenty-eight-page brochure commenting on 400 poisonous weeds — 300 Chinese films and 100 foreign,* including forty Soviet films.[58] Early in the cultural revolution (20 July 1966) *Renmin Ribao* attacked "the strange habits of the Film Institute":

These days certain monsters there create a lot of trouble. They actually organized an "art committee" that is nothing more than a miserable antirevolutionary club.

The newspaper accused the students (under Chou Yang's influence) of preferring Russian revisionist films such as Dovzhenko's *Poem of a Sea*, as well as Fellini's *Nights of Cabiria* and an American film whose Chinese title (ts'ui ti ch'un hsiao) I do not recognize. (A friend suggests that this may be *Blackboard Jungle*.) The Film Institute's brochure on poisonous films is its penance for the student sins of 1966.

Another measure to keep Chinese cinemas running *and* pure: a few films from the first years after 1949 were approved for rerelease. Schools and organizations looked at *Daughters of China* and *The White-Haired Girl*;† from the films of the fifties only *Guerrillas Sweep the Plains* (1955)[59] passed the purity test. But the stable cinema fare through the summer of 1967 was the growing repertoire of films that could be used as evidence against Liu Shao-ch'i. A particularly handy

---

* The disease of Olivier's (and Shakespeare's) *Hamlet*: "strives only for personal revenge, serves king and military commanders, rehabilitating them."
† The export office was also reduced to these pure, early films to keep itself alive, as there were no new films to fill contracts; when the six-day war of 1967 removed American programs from Cairo television, Egyptian viewers were treated to such pure films as *Women Locomotive Drivers*!

film for this purpose was *Land Aflame*, on the strike of Anyuan coal miners in
Kiangsi province in 1922. Unluckily for their place in history at present, the
miners were led by Liu Shao-chi, a year after the founding of the Chinese
Communist Party — a fact much publicized at the time of the film's release in
1962. Though the figure representing Liu in the film was disguised, according to
the policy of not showing leaders in fictional films, *Land Aflame* clearly offered
itself for a raking over the coals.

There were plenty of new films, also, to feel the bludgeon of the Cultural Revolution. Soon after the formation of the Red Guards several announcements
appeared in the press, condemning new films and organizing their condemnation
by the "people":

Under the guiding influence of this black line, some bad writings and bad films
have been turned out. To thoroughly eliminate this black anti-Party and antisocialist line and eradicate its pernicious effect, various bad films such as *The
Siege*, *Sisters on the Stage*, *The Press-gang* and *Red Sun*, were recently released
so that the people could discuss and criticize them.[60]

Recently, another batch of bad films has been released for the revolutionary
masses to criticize. . . . These newly released films are *A Thousand Li Against the
Wind, Big Li, Young Li and Old Li*, and *The Peach-Blossom Fan.*[61]

Among the films attacked was *City Without Night*. In 1957, when its scenario by
Ko Ling was published in the first number of *Shou Hu* (Harvest), a reviewer's
synopsis makes it sound like a film difficult to fault ideologically:

It shows the ups and downs of a textile mill in Shanghai over a period of twenty
years, how the Chinese national capitalists made their fortune by exploitation,
and how China's national industry was squeezed by imperialist and bureaucrat-
comprador capital under Kuomintang rule. After the liberation, production is
stabilized and grows, but the bourgeoisie, true to form, still makes mischief: the
mill-owner breaks laws and government regulations and resorts to speculation
and sharp practices, till ultimately, guided by the correct policy laid down by
the People's Government, educated by stubborn facts and helped by his wife and
daughter, he sees his mistake and willingly steps out on the road of socialist
transformation.[62]

Looking at it more closely, you will note that it touches several delicate matters
that suffered sudden changes of policy (on the sincerity and capacity for
political education of the national capitalists, on the wisdom of production
dominating political decisions, on the ever-ticklish and rarely resolved question
of class background, etc.), and when a film cannot respond to *these* "ups and
downs," it is convenient to condemn it — and the people who made it.

There was, of course, only one side to the "discussion-screenings" of 1967. The mass audience was given the proper line for its mass criticism before entering the cinema.

A conspiracy led by "the top capitalist roader within the party" (Liu Shao-ch'i) was shown as behind all the criticized films. Compare the following with the 1957 synopsis:

City Without Night spun a tale about a "red capitalist." Running counter to Marxism-Leninism, Mao Tse-tung's thought, it presented its leading character as a capitalist hero of "national salvation through industry." It showed this capitalist family as diligent, thrifty and hard working. . . . It deliberately obscured the nature of the class struggle by portraying this capitalist as voluntarily accepting socialist transformation because of his good conscience and intentions. When the script of the film was first published in 1957, many people took objection to it. But the revisionists suppressed the correct criticisms and went on with production as planned. When the country met with temporary difficulties in 1960—62, the handful of revisionists released this film in an attempt to exacerbate the situation. [63]

A figure that had remained in obscurity for many years emerged in this new movement and noise to assume a leading role in determining China's cultural future, with a special emphasis on its films — for this was the former film actress Lan P'ing, now Chiang Ching. As the wife of Chairman Mao she was given a position of command and decision that had not been touched by any Chinese woman since the death of the Dowager Empress — with the possible exception of Madame Chiang Kai-shek. Foreign journalists, describing Chiang Ching as a former "film star" and beautiful, have shown unconcealed relish in her new status (at one time second "in succession" to her husband, preceded only by Lin Piao), her public appearances and speeches, and the posters for and against her on Peking's streets. It was she who proclaimed in December 1966 a cleansing of all Chinese arts, now to be placed in the (then) reliable hands of the army. It was easily imagined that her campaign and new power would soon challenge the Chinese cinema, and her first known confrontation with it was at the army's August First Studio. She halted production there and denounced the studio's party leadership, causing their removal: they had prevented the production of a film vital to the cultural revolution and the teaching of Mao's thought. Now that this (along with all other film studios) is under her watchful eye, the disputed film may be made and we shall then know on what theme the pro-Maoists and anti-Maoists parted film company. We can expect further, possibly less publicized film activity from Madame Mao.*

---

* "It is seldom that individual women in China rise to power, but when they do it is with a vengeance." Nym Wales, *Inside Red China* (New York: Doubleday, Doran, 1939), p. 170.

Neither Madame Mao nor the Red Guards could bring an end to the Chinese cinema, but they have brought it to a standstill that will change its character whenever production and creation are resumed. The two generations of film-makers responsible for the Chinese films of the last twenty years will no longer be part of the next (whenever resumed) period of filmmaking; they have all been contaminated by criticized films and doctrines and associations. Younger film-makers of the Red Guard generation? I believe they will be too intimidated by the often witnessed process of condemnation and banishment to risk anything beyond a lower, more rigid form of what has been. Looking at the old Hollywood devices that hold together 1966's *Great Victory of the Ideas of Mao Tse-tung* and listening to the piano accompaniment to *Scenes from Revolutionary Operas*, the only attempt at a fictional film in 1967, does not rouse much faith in the film revolution of Madame Mao and the Red Guards. We may have to wait much longer for Chinese films of meaning and expressiveness.

One of many enigmas: after the elevation of cinema to an acknowledged leading role in Chinese domestic propaganda, how can the manufacture of fictional films be halted altogether for four — five — six years? Is it possible that the Chinese acted film has been relegated to the same oblivion that is intended to make Peking opera a forgotten art? Or has the recognized political importance of films paralyzed their Chinese masters?

A poem on this conflict was translated in *Chinese Literature*, No. 2, 1970:

New Scenes on the Screen
by Liu Hsi-tao

Golden rays shine on the screen,
A crimson morning sun rises
From beyond the vast blue waves;
Chairman Mao waves his mighty hand,
Our great motherland turns
Into a surging sea of rolling red billows.
A series of pictures, colourful and splendid,
Unfold before the audience, and stir my heart.

Behold! Beautiful rainbows flow round the loom,
Molten steel flows, its sparks smiling to the sun,
A golden bridge flies over the Yangtse River,
Red mushroom-clouds curl against the blue sky,
S.S. Morning Sun churns through the eastern sea,
In the people's communes, golden wheat dances,
Paddy ears spread fragrance far and wide,
Mountains of cotton pierce the blue sky. . . .

The people rejoice at these exciting scenes,
Happy tears well up in their eyes;
They want to brush them away, but fear
To miss a single precious moment.
A storm of applause resounds in my chest,
To the accompaniment of the projector my heart sings.
Solemn memories, like a heaving tide,
Rush in upon my mind. . . .

When the revisionist line ruled the screen,
Turbid billows rose, miasmal mists raged,
Ancient corpses were embellished as human beings,
Demons were dressed up like charming beauties,
Traitors pretended to be heroes,
Prostitutes assumed to be pure and virtuous,
Monsters howled wildly, sharpening their swords,
Emperors and kings, generals and ministers,
Scholars and beauties. . . .
All blatantly swept in a swirling dance.

Once only halfway through a film,
A veteran worker left in wrath,
At the theatre exit frankly he said:
"Those ghostly faces nauseate me!"

Cultural revolution blusters like the heavenly wind,
Sunlight breaks forth upon the screen,
Showing the heroic images of workers, peasants and soldiers,
These glorious films fill me with happiness and pride.

Contributors to the Art and History of Chinese Films

Reference at end of an entry indicates the chief source or sources of information. Some abbreviations are used:

BD
Biographical Dictionary of Republican China, ed. by Howard L. Boorman (New York: Columbia University Press, 1967, 1968), Vols. 1–3.

CH
Cheng Chi-hua, *History of the Development of Chinese Cinema* (Peking, 1963), Vols. I and II.

GCR
The Great Cultural Revolution in China, documents compiled by the Asia Research Centre (Rutland, Vermont, and Tokyo: Charles E. Tuttle, 1968).

MB
Ming Bao (Hong Kong), April, June 1970, "Film Makers on the Black List," by Kang Li.

Ouyang
Ouyang Yu-chien, *In the Midst of Life Comes the Vocation of Cinema* (Peking, 1962).

RB
Régis Bergeron, "Le Cinéma Chinois," *Cinéma 64* (Paris), May 1964.

Scott
A. C. Scott, *Literature and the Arts in Twentieth Century China* (London: Allen & Unwin, 1965).

Talk
film memoirs in *Talk of the Past* (Peking, 1962).

WW
Who's Who in Communist China (Hong Kong: Union Research Institute, 1966).

Yutkevich
Sergei Yutkevich, *V teatrakh i kino svobodnovo Kitai* (Moscow, 1953).

AH Ying   阿   英
(A Ying)*
real: Qian Xing-cun
scenarist

Enters Chinese film history as the link between the Ming Hsing Company (in its financial difficulties of January 1932) and Hsia Yen, who then came to the company as scenarist and led the Communist Party's team in the Shanghai studios. Ah Ying entered the studio with the team, working on the scenarios of *Salty Tide, Children of Our Time, Years of Plenty, Three Sisters, A Bible for Girls.* Though a reliable and steadily employed writer in the quasi-underground period, he does not reappear in Cheng Chi-hua's history after the beginning of full-scale war in 1937. A recent script, however: for the memorial film to Mei Lan-fang (1962).

CH

CHANG Chun-hsiang   張   駿   祥
(Zhāng Jun-xiang)
(also used name of YUAN Jin)
scenarist, director

Born 1911, in Chinkiang, Kiangsu Province. From 1928 to 1931 at Tsinghua University, Peking, studying western literature. From 1936 to 1939 in George Pierce Baker's theater class at Yale. Returned to China in 1940, organized a theater in Chungking and wrote plays for it. At the end of war was invited to work in a government film studio (Chung Dien) where he wrote and directed his first films in 1947, *Diary on Returning Home* and *Quick Son-in-Law on Dragon.* Since 1949 he has been the artistic leader of the Shanghai studio (officially he is Director of the Shanghai Film Bureau) where he directed *Red Banner Over Green Cliff* (1950) and wrote the script for *Letter with Feather* (1953), two widely acclaimed successes. Since 1963 worked on the unfinished *Dr. Bethune.* In 1958 he published a definitive work, *Specifics of Cinema Expression*, and in 1963 (possibly revising the earlier book), *Artistic Expression in Films.*

CH

CHANG Jui-fang   張   瑞   芳
(Zhāng Ruì-fāng)
actress (see Plates 21, 36)

Born in 1918 in Peking. Before the war an art student at a Peking college, but after the Japanese attack of 1937 she joined a students' mobile agit-prop group

---

* Strict approved transliterations are given when they differ significantly from familiar spellings of names.

that showed anti-Japanese plays through the streets (Tsui Wei was another
member of this group). With a more professional theater group she toured
Shantung and Honan before the Japanese reached those provinces. In 1938 she
arrived in Chungking and in December joined the Communist Party of China.
While continuing her theater work (notably in Tsao Yu's plays) she played her
first film role in *Baptism of Fire* (1940). After the capture of Changchun and its
new Japanese studio, *Along the Sungari River* was produced with Chang Jui-fang
in its leading role. After the liberation of Peking she joined its Youth Theater,
and then moved to Shanghai, where her film work grew regular: *Mother* (1956),
By the March 8 Canal (1958), *It's Always Spring* (1960), *Li Shuang-shuang*
(1962) — the last her most popular role.

CH; *Dazhong Dianying*, No. 4, 1960.

CHANG Ping   張   平
(Zhāng Pìng)
actor (see Plate 26)

As a child loved theater and acted in school plays. In 1936 organized his friends
into an acting troupe. In 1937, when war began, his party organization delegated
him to agitational work and in March 1938 he began his studies in Yenan. In
1939 was sent to Southeastern front as theatrical director of an army group. In
1940 returned to Yenan, studied Stanislavsky's works and dramatic theory. Next
military mission was underground work behind the Japanese lines. In August
1945 organized the Northeastern Ensemble and with it took part in fighting
through Manchuria. In 1948 he and his ensemble were transferred to the Northeast Studio at Changchun. There he played the heroes of *Light Spreads Everywhere, Chou Yi-man, Fighters in White, Invisible Front, Steeled Fighter, Victory
of the People of Inner Mongolia, Remote Village, Granary of the Sa Family.* In
1956 was sent to study acting at the Central Theater College. Thereafter worked
at the Peking Studio: *Visiting the Relatives, Storm, Food, Nameless Island,
Revolutionary Family, After the Cease-fire, Red Crag.*

Yutkevich; *Dazhong Dianying*, No. 3, 1960

CHANG Shih-chuan   張 石 川
(Zhāng Shí-chuan)
director, producer

An uncle of Chang brought him into the film business by overhearing, at his
Shanghai hotel, two foreigners trying to find Chinese actors to try out their film
equipment (just acquired by their insurance company). The uncle introduced
them to Chang Shih-chuan who bossed an amateur Peking opera troupe. The
result for the troupe was work by day as well as by night. These were the Asia

Company's first substantial films, in 1913. Chang's various film companies were short-lived, but he was resilient enough to find fresh financing each time and somehow managed to produce and direct most of the early popular successes: *Wronged Ghosts in Opium Den* (1916), *Romance of a Fruit Peddler* (1922), *Orphan Rescues Grandfather* (1923), three key films of this first decade, on which the Ming Hsing (Star) Company was founded. Chang directed most of Ming Hsing's films, including the nearly endless serial, *Burning of Red Lotus Temple* (1928–1931). He also directed some of the scenarios written by the Party team at Ming Hsing.

CH; Talk

CHAO Ming   趙   明
(Zhao Ming)
director

First training was in acting in Shanghai theaters, from 1937 to 1946. Entered films in 1947 as an assistant director, codirected *Winter of Three-Hairs* (1949). Best known films, *United for Tomorrow* (1951), *Guerrillas on the Railway* (1956).

Dazhong Dianying, No. 24, 1959

CHAO Tan   趙   丹
(Zhào Dān)
real: Zhào Fèng-áo
actor (see Plates 24, 41)

Born 1914 in Yangchow and grew up in Nantung. When he was thirteen a modern theater group visited Nantung and so impressed Chao that at once he organized his friends into a Little Theater. He soon moved to Shanghai and its theater life, joining the Left-Wing Theater Union. Besides acting in anti-Japanese roles Chao played in *Romeo* and Ostrovsky's *Thunderstorm*, while in 1932 he began work, in an unusual variety of roles, at the Ming Hsing Studio: his first film was *Spring Sorrow of the Pi-pa*. He appeared in nearly thirty films before the production of *Crossroads* (1937) established Pai Yang and him as "stars." Ever since he has remained at the center of the Chinese film industry, associated with films of the greatest interest: *Far Away Love* (1947), *Crows and Sparrows* (1949), *Lin Tse-hsu* (1959), and the unrealized film about Lu Hsun. His prestige has also brought him roles in miserable films, forgotten a year after they seemed of vital importance to the Film Bureau. He has had at least three tries at film direction, *The Dress Returns in Glory* (1947), *Bless the Children* and *Precious Green Mountains* (1964). He joined the Chinese Communist Party in 1958. His daughter, Chao Ching, is a dancer who appeared in *Magic Lotus Lantern* (1959; see Plate 42).

The Red Guards ended Chao Tan's career on four counts:

1. He is condemned for resisting Chiang Ching's (Mme. Mao's) commands.
2. In Japan he was too intimate with the Soviet Ambassador there.
3. He played in a low-class Czech film with a low-class Mexican actress.
4. The films that he played in between 1946 and 1949 were "worthless."

CH; MB

CHEN Bo-erh   陳　波　兒
(1910-1951)
actress, scenarist

Born 1910 in San-to, Kwantung Province. To Shanghai in 1929 to study at the Arts University where she was introduced to Marxism. She joined the left-wing theater movement, played leading roles in four plays before her first trouble with the Kuomintang police in 1931. She escaped to Hong Kong but returned in 1934 to Shanghai where she began her film work at the Ming Hsing Studio. Her first film with Yuan Mu-jih was *Plunder of Peach and Plum*, and thereafter they acted together. Their last film roles were in *800 Brave Soldiers* (1938, in Hankow), and they left together for Yenan after she joined the Communist Party. She spent the next ten years working with theater groups at the Red Army base, and in 1946 worked on the scenario of the unrealized *Labor Hero of the Border Area*. In the first government of the People's Republic in 1949 she was appointed Minister of Culture. Her last film work, as scenarist of *Light Spreads Everywhere*, was completed a year before her appointment. She died suddenly on 10 November 1951.

CH

CHEN Huang-mei   陳　荒　煤
administrator, producer

A politically committed citizen since his boyhood in Hankow, where he witnessed the return to China of the British concession in 1927. After 1949 attached to Ministry of Culture in various capacities, the last being as a director of the Film Bureau under Hsia Yen.

"Ch'en Huang-mei was attacked in the *Chung-kuo Ch'ing-nien Pao* [*China Youth Daily*] of Peking on June 9, 1966 for disseminating revisionist, bourgeois theories of film making, reviving nearly one hundred films of the thirties, and catering to bourgeois tastes in films under the pretext of making films for export." Also accused of setting up, in these same years, "a collective group for handling fairy tales, to propagate the poisonous ingredients of feudal superstition." Aside from the released films used as evidence against him (*The Lin Family's Shop,* * *Second Lunar Month*, etc.), he was held responsible for "films which had not been finished or had been abandoned — such as *Rapids on Red River, Rolling Waves, Happy Is the Whole Family* and *Ulan O-te*." A dozen other "revisionist" projects are also attached to his accusation.

GCR

CHEN Pai-chen　　　　　　　　　陳　白　塵
(Chen Bái-chen)
real: Chén Zhēng-hóng
scenarist

Born 1908 in Huai-yin, Kiangsu Province. In 1928 joined T'ien Han's Southern Arts Academy, playing in *The Returned Father.* Later worked as salesman, teacher, clerk, before losing work in a strike. In 1932 was jailed for anti-Japanese activity. In jail he wrote three plays and when released in 1935 he wrote a play on the Taiping Rebellion. At the beginning of the war he left with other Shanghai theater people for Szechuan. In Chengtu he continued his play writing and edited the film supplement of a newspaper. In October 1945 he wrote three performed comedies; his best-known play is *Wedding March.* At the beginning of 1947 he joined the Kun Lun Studio. He headed the collective of writers responsible for the scenario of *Crows and Sparrows.* After the dispersal of the Kun Lun Studio his best known scenario work was his collaboration on *Sung Ching-shih* (1957). In 1958 he was one of four playwrights who signed an agit-prop play on the smallness of U.S. satellites: *Ah, Ya, Ya, Small American Moon.*

CH; BD

CHENG Bu-kao　　　　　　　　　程　步　高
(Chen Bu-gao)
(Hong Kong name: P. K. Cheng)
director

5 March 1933 is the accepted date for the beginning of socially conscious Chinese cinema — it was the opening of *Wild Torrent*, directed by Cheng Bu-kao.

Cheng was educated in Paris. His directorial career began at the Ming Hsing Company, making the inexhaustible knight-errant films popular in 1928, with an occasional more realistic subject (sometimes written by Hung Shen). After 1932,

---

* See Hsia Yen's letter of 16 April 1958, page 263, footnote

with the increase of revolutionary or patriotic themes brought to Ming Hsing by Hsia Yen and the Party team, Cheng Bu-kao became one of their most reliable directors, with *Wild Torrent, Spring Silkworms, Twin Sisters* (1933), *The Common Enemy* (1934), *New and Old Shanghai* (1936, with a scenario by Hung Shen), *Little Ling-tze* (1936, with a scenario by Ouyang Yu-chien). No record of wartime film work. After the war Cheng Bu-kao moved to Hong Kong, where he made the successful *Merry Go-Round* (1954) and many other films. In 1960 he abruptly retired from the film industry.

CH; Robert Florey, in *Pour Vous* (1934)

CHENG Chen-chin   鄭　正　秋
(Zhèng Zhèng-qiū)
(1888—1935)
writer, director, actor

Brought into the Asia Film Company in 1913 by his friend, Chang Shih-chuan, Cheng's love of theater and his critical taste did not sustain more than his first experience in *The Difficult Couple*, as writer, codirector, and actor. He left film-making to the more enterprising Chang, coming back only in 1922 to work as scenarist and actor. The success of his scenario for *Orphan Rescues Grandfather* (1923) kept Cheng with the Ming Hsing Company through the three-year serial, *Burning of Red Lotus Temple*, which was started on his initiative.

CH

CHENG Chi-hua   程　季　華
(Chén Jì-huā)
critic, historian

Born 1921, Kiangling County, Hupeh Province. After the war worked in Peking theaters as writer and critic. In 1949 turned to film work, also as writer and critic, finally heading a committee to prepare a history of Chinese films; two of the proposed three volumes appeared in 1963. He and the history were unequivo-cally condemned in 1966.

Chinese Literature, No. 6, 1963

CHENG Chun-li   鄭　君　里
(Zheng Jūn-lǐ)
actor, scenarist, director

Born Shanghai, 1911, of a Cantonese family. In 1928 left after two years of high school to join T'ien Han's Southern Arts Academy, where he began to work as an actor in left-wing theaters. In 1932 he entered the Lien Hua studio as an actor

(*Wild Rose, Big Road, New Women, Money Tree,* and other films). During the war he worked for the government's China Motion Picture Company, producing the actuality film *Long Live the National Minorities,* and in 1943 left film work for theater direction in Chungking. At the end of war he returned to Shanghai and the Lien Hua Studio, where he collaborated with Tsai Chu-sheng on the scenario and direction of *Spring River Flows East.* His first solo direction was a great success, *Crows and Sparrows* (1949). His next years are obscure (administration? remolding?) but he returned to prominence in 1955 with the direction of *Sung Chin-shih,* and then in 1959 he codirected *Lin Tse-hsu* and directed *Nieh Erh.* His unrealized project to film *Lu Hsun* returned him to obscurity.

CH; *Dazhong Dianying,* No. 21, 1959

CHENG Yin   成   蔭
scenarist, director

Born 1918. Arrived in Yenan in 1938; worked there as student and as director of an Eighth Route Army theater team. First film work in 1946. In 1948 made two actuality films, *Kindergarten* and *Return to His Platoon.* First scenario and direction: *Steeled Fighter* (1950). Collaborated with Tang Hsiao-tan on the direction of *Conquer South, Victory North* (1952). Studied film-production methods in the Soviet Union until his return to China in December 1955. Collaborated on the scenario and on the direction (with Hua Tsun) of *Across Ten Thousand Rivers and Thousand Mountains* (1959) — to date the most ambitious film of the army's August First Studio. For the Peking Studio directed *After the Ceasefire* (1962) and *Rolling Waves* (1964).

Yutkevich; *Dazhong Dianying,* No. 2, 1963; *China's Screen,* No. 2, 1963

CHIANG Ching   江   青
(born Li Yun-ho; acting pseudonym, Lan P'ing)
actress, politician

Born in 1913 in Shantung Province, she completed her elementary education in Tsinan; then sent to Taian, to the government-supported Provincial Vocational School for the Performing Arts. Here she met her first husband, T'ang Na (born Ma Chi-liang), who wrote film criticism for Shanghai newspapers. "She married T'ang in the spring of 1934, with three other couples, all connected with the film industry." Until their separation in 1937, she worked as actress in Shanghai film studios, using the pseudonym of Lan P'ing. She had small roles in two important films, *Scenes of City Life* (1935) and *Blood on Wolf Mountain* (1936). "Her colleagues knew well that she resented the insignificance of her parts," and her poor pay. Accompanied by Huang Ching, a communist and

former lover, she went to Yenan in 1938. She enrolled in the Lu Hsun Art
Institute, where she met Mao Tse-tung; in less than a year she had agreed to
marry him.

This was not easy. While Huang was unexpectedly cooperative, apparently in
dedication to the Communist cause, Mao's wife, Ho Tze-chen, was not. She
appealed personally to the senior members of the Party, including . . . Mao's
former teacher Hsu Teh-lih. The elders listened sympathetically and almost
unanimously took her side, especially in view of her sufferings during the Long
March and the difficult years on Chingkang Mountain. But Mao insisted, and
finally a compromise was reached on the understanding that Chiang should
remain in the background as a housewife and not involve herself in political
affairs.

She has had two daughters by Mao. After the establishment of the People's
Republic the "understanding" was broken by her appointment early in 1950 to
the Central Steering Committee for the film industry, under the Ministry of
Culture. It was here that her attack on *Secret History of the Ching Court* was as
Mao's spokeswoman. Here she began the systematic elimination of her antagonists and colleagues that culminated in her closing of China's film studios in
1966. She was in Mao's original "Group of Five" that led the Cultural Revolution.
          "Mao's Wife — Chiang Ching," by Chu Hao-jan, in *China Quarterly*,
                                                          July–Sept 1967.

CHIN Shan   金   山
(Jin Shān)
(pseudonym)
actor, director, writer

Born 1911 in Yuenlin, Hunan Province. After a hobo youth and the influence of
left ideas somewhere along the way, he joined a left-wing theater group in 1932.
Organized the Blue Robe Theater Group in Shanghai and in 1936 the Forties
Theater Group. After outbreak of war joined the Rescue-Country Theater
Group, based in Chungking, traveling (in December 1939) as far as Singapore
and Malaya. After some theater work in Hong Kong he returned to Chungking.
By this time he had directed over forty plays. His film work, as actor, began in
1935 with a role in *Mad Night*, the last film of the Bright Moon Studio. His
theater work with Shih Tung-shan led him to the Hsin Hua Studio for work in
Long Song of Hate, Song at Midnight, and *Tsao San*. The war and the traveling
theater group halted his film career. By 1941 he had escaped from Chungking to
Yenan, and his film work was resumed with his first film direction, *Along the
Sungari River* (1947). Another theater interval of ten years elapsed before his
return to film direction in 1958 with *Ballad of the Ming Tombs Reservoir* — that
made possible his last and best film, *Storm* (1959), based on his play, *Red Storm*.
Subsequent ill health has prevented any work other than intermittent theater
consultation.

                                                                    CH

CHIN Yi   秦   怡
(Qín Yí)
actress (see Plates 24, 44)

Born 1922, Shanghai, and first acted in a school play. From work in a propaganda troupe she entered wartime films in Chungking — *Long Live China* (1938)
and *Good Husband* (1939). But more notice was taken of her after her appearance in 1941 in a Tsao Yu play and when she returned to Shanghai in 1945 film
work became her chief occupation. Her most important role before 1949 was
in *Far Away Love* (1947). Since 1949 her best work has been in *Guerrillas on
the Railway* (1956). *Girl Basketball Player No. 5* (1957, as the heroine's
mother), *Red Shoots* (1958), and a brief role (but the best) in *Song of Youth*
(1959). In the Cultural Revolution she was condemned for three "harmful
films" and "for far too much travel." Chiang Ching (Mme. Mao) describes Chin
Yi as "one of the most infamous ones."

CH; *Dazhong Dianying*, No. 12, 1956; MB

CHOU Hsin-fang   周 信 芳
actor (of "wise-man" roles in Peking opera)

His early attempts to transfer his performances in Peking opera to the screen
were even less successful than Mei Lan-fang's. After the 1920 trial at the Commercial Press, Chou's best and last film was made in 1956 — *Sung Shih-chieh,*
based on the opera, *Four Scholars*. His possibly innocent act of collaborating on
the writing of an opera with a good role for himself precipitated him into the
violence of the Cultural Revolution. The opera, *Hai Jui's Memorial to the Emperor*, was one of the several works interpreted as an attack on Mao and the
Party. His suicide was reported but never confirmed.

CH; GCR

CHOU Shih   周   石
(19??–1957)
actress, singer

Remembered for her striking performance in Yuan Mu-jih's *Street Angel* (1937).
First appearance in films, in 1933, as a dancer in *Night of the Flower Candle*.
Among other films: *Unquiet Life, Memories South of Yangtze, Night Lodging*.
An unhappy marriage in 1937 — husband treated her cruelly, and his Kuomintang friends threatened her with accusations. Her first commitment to a mental
hospital was in 1940, and her life after 1949 was spent in the hospital where she
died in 1957.

Dazhong Dianying, No. 18, 1957

CHU Shih-ling   朱　石　麟
(Zhū Shí-líng)
(Hong Kong name: Chusheck Lane)
director

Distinguished for the direction of an exceptional comedy, *Money Tree* (1937)
and a Hong Kong production of 1948, *Secret History of the Ching Court*, still
under political attack in Peking. During the period of Japanese-Chinese coproduction in Shanghai Chu Shih-ling was one of the directors of *Perfume to
Last Ten Centuries* (1943), a film about Commissioner Lin Tse-hsu and the first
Opium War. His last films were made in Hong Kong. *The Dividing Wall* (1951)
is one of his best.

FEI Mu   費　　　穆
(1906–1951)
director

Born in Shanghai, of a Soochow family. In 1916 they moved to Peking where
Fei Mu entered a high school for foreign languages. He found work in 1924, but
used his spare time to meet other film enthusiasts and to write articles about
films and then film scenarios. His first film job was the translation into Chinese
(for projection alongside the screen) of the subtitles and later the dialogue of
American films. In 1932 he joined the First Shanghai Studio of Lien Hua. His
first direction, *Night in the City* (1933) made him the favorite director of Lien
Hua's owner, Lo Ming-yü, but his sympathies were shown to be anti-Lo with
Blood on Wolf Mountain (1936) and *Martyrs of the Northern Front* (1937).
During the "orphan island" period Fei Mu wrote and directed *Confucius* (1940)
and collaborated with the German exiles, Jakob and Luise Fleck, on *Children of
the World* (1941). After the war he encouraged Mei Lan-fang to use color film
for the first time, though neither was satisfied with the result, *Happiness Neither
in Life Nor in Death* (or, *Wedding in a Dream*) in 1947.

CH

HSIA Pei-tsun   夏　佩　珍
actress

Born 1912 in a poor Shanghai family. At age of ten worked in a textile mill. In
1926, when when she was fourteen, her parents found employment for her at
the Ta Tun Film Company. For this company and for Ming Hsing she acted in
about twenty films (including *Wild Torrent* and *Bible for Girls*) before disappear-
ing from public life when she was twenty-three. In 1963 a reporter for *Dazhong
Dianying* found her working as a librarian in Wuhan (and published his article in
No. 4, 1963).

HSIA Yen   夏　　衍
(Xià Yen)
real: Shěn Duān-xiān
scenarist, administrator, producer (see photograph on Plate 35)

Born 1900 in Hangchow, Chekiang Province. (According to Cheng Chi-hua the
Hangchow family was poor; Hsia Yen's attackers in the Cultural Revolution
claim it was well-to-do.) While still in a vocational school he joined the staff of
the first Marxist journals in his province. Graduated from the Engineering
Department, Imperial University, Kyushu, though he preferred philosophy and
literature. After the failure of the 1927 revolution he felt obliged to return to
China. That year he joined the Chinese Communist Party in Shanghai, and
worked as a trade-unionist in the Chapei District of the city. In the autumn of
1929 the underground organization transferred him to prepare the Chinese
Left-Wing Writers' League, and out of this activity his own career as playwright
began. After the January 1932 Japanese attack on Shanghai the Communist
Party took more interest in the film industry and Hsia Yen headed the Party
team that worked in various studios between 1932 and 1937. In this first period
of his film career Hsia Yen was responsible for the scenarios and handling of
*Wild Torrent, Spring Silkworms, 24 Hours of Shanghai, Bible for Girls, New
Year Coin, Money Tree.*

When filmmakers left Shanghai as the Japanese entered in 1937, Hsia Yen moved
south, where his chief duty was the publication and editing of patriotic papers:
Salvation Daily in the Southwest, and *Chinese Merchants' Daily* in Hong Kong.
He also wrote a number of plays: *Within One Year, Fascist Bacteria, Under the
Roofs of Shanghai* (this last may have been the basis for the 1948 film, *Light of
Ten Thousand Homes*). After the war he remained in the south until the revolu-
tion was firmly established in the north, when the second period of his film
career began with his appointment to head the Film Bureau of the Ministry of
Culture (after Chen Bo-erh's death and Yuan Mu-jih's retirement from that post).
His scenario writing continued, with *New Year Offering* (1956), *The Lin
Family's Shop* (1959), *Revolutionary Family* (1960, with the director Shui
Hua). In addition to his administrative and creative roles, his interest in film
theory (begun in the thirties with criticism and the translation of Soviet theoretical essays) produced a quantity of theoretical and practical writing: "Problems
of Writing Scenarios" appeared in installments in *Zhungguo Dianying* through
1958—1959. This second phase of his film (and public) career ended with a
large-scale condemnation of his film work and viewpoint, in 1965. Throughout
1966 the accusations accumulated, even though allegations and interpretations
of his heroic career had to be resorted to. At the time of denunciation Hsia Yen
was exiled to Chengtu (as vice-mayor), but the latest report returns him to
Peking and total retirement.   CH; WW; GCR

HSIEH Chin   謝   晋
(Xiè Jin)
director

Director of *Spring Days in Water Village* (1955), *Girl Basketball Player No. 5*
(1957), *Huang Pao-mei* (1959), *Red Women's Detachment* (1961), and *Sisters
on the Stage* (1964), a condemned film. His most "poisonous" film, however,
was *Senior Li, Junior Li, and Old Li* (1962), about mass sports activities in a
meat-processing factory — with "jokes that aroused the general anger of the
working masses."

RB; GCR

HSIEH Tieh-li   謝   鐵   驪
(Xiè Tiě-lí)
director

Earliest job at Peking Studio: directing the studio's theater group. First film
work as assistant director on *The Lin Family's Shop*. Then codirector of *The
Nameless Island*, before his first solo direction, *Hurricane* (1961), his wife's
adaptation of Chou Li-po's novel. His unfortunate second film, *Second Lunar
Month* (1963), was attacked so immediately and so bitterly that it may have
ended his filmmaking career.

謝　添

HSIEH Tien   謝　　添
(Xiè Tiān)
actor, director

Career as actor began in 1933. First film acting in 1936 (*Unchanged Heart in Life and Death*). After 1949 acted in *March of Democratic Youth* (1951) and *Gate No. 6* (1952). In his New Year wish for 1954 he hoped "that I can stop playing villains for a change." In 1955—1956 while studying in the Peking Actors' School he was also employed in dubbing foreign films. (He also spoke the commentary for *Early Spring*). Played an eccentric role in the Franco-Chinese coproduction, *The Kite*, and a naturalistic role in *The Lin Family's Shop*. Then transferred all his energies to direction, beginning with two pleasant films in 1959, *Two Generations of Swimmers* and *A Feast of Fun* (his circus film). He organized the collectively produced film, *For 61 Class Brothers* (1960), and was one of three directors on *Red Guards at Lake Hung* (1961). His most remarkable film, a collaboration with Cheng Fang-chien, was the comedy, *Better and Better* (1963). In the same year he directed *Little Ding-dong,* a children's film, collaborating again with Cheng Fang-chien.

Dazhong Dianying, No. 6, 1960

HSIEN Hsing-hai   洗　星　海
(Xiǎn Xīng-hǎi)
(1905—1945)
composer

Son of a newly widowed Macao fisherman, Hsing-hai was born in a small boat at
sea. In 1911 he emigrated with his mother to Malaya. From 1918 to 1926
studied in Canton where he joined a student orchestra, then entered the music
school of Peking University. The Cantonese violinist, Ma Sitson, sponsored
Hsien's next stage of musical education in Paris, from 1930 to 1935, where he
studied with d'Indy and Dukas. In a reminiscence of the composer (*Chinese
Literature*, No. 12, 1965) Ma Ko wrote how Hsien Hsing-hai composed the work
that gained his admission to Dukas's class:

One day he went to the Overseas Chinese Trade Union office to see a documentary film recording the sufferings of the Chinese people since September 18,
1931, the date when the Japanese imperialists started invading northeast China.
The Chinese residents in France were moved to tears by this film. On his return
to the sixth-floor attic where he lived, Hsien Hsing-hai was too upset by the
misery of his motherland and his own misfortunes to sleep. The cold winter
wind blowing through the ill-fitting window made him shiver. . . . That night he
finished *The Wind* [for orchestra with soprano solo].

On returning to Shanghai Hsien worked in the music departments of the Bai Dai
and Hsin Hua studios. At the latter he composed the songs for *Courage That
Reaches Above the Clouds* (1936), *Song at Midnight* and *Youth on the March*
(1937) to texts by T'ien Han. His remaining years were spent in Yenan and
Moscow where he died of tuberculosis. His three Yenan vocal works and two
Moscow symphonies are still performed. His Yellow River Cantata was filmed by
Liu Pan in 1955.

                                                                CH; BD

HU Tieh   胡　　　蝶
(or, Miss Butterfly Wu)
(Hú Dié) real: Hú Rui-huá
actress (see Plate 7)

Born 1907 in Shanghai, daughter of a railroad worker, whose work took the
family to Tientsin, Peking, and Northeast China. When the daughter was twelve,
the family lived in Canton — when sixteen, in Shanghai. Hung Shen's film school
closed soon after she began to attend it, but her film career began without it, at
the age of eighteen, in the first production of the Yo Lien Company, *Hate of
Autumn Fan* (1925). In 1926 she joined the Tien Yi Company, for whom she
made twelve films. In 1928 she moved to the Ming Hsing studio, where she made
thirty films and lasting fame. Her Mandarin accent assisted her transition to

sound films (with *Singsong Girl Red Peony*, 1930). Her most successful film was *Twin Sisters* (1933), in which she played a dual role. Her rise at Ming Hsing coincided with the influence in that studio of the Party's film team. At the outbreak of war in 1937 she left for Hong Kong with her husband. When the colony was occupied they escaped to Chungking and returned to Shanghai after the war, though she does not appear to have resumed film work until 1958 in Hong Kong, for the Shaw Brothers.

CH; Scott

HUANG Shao-fen   黃　紹　芬
cameraman

Photographed *Three Modern Girls* (1933), Ouyang's *So Prosperous* (1937), and Pa Chin's *Family* (1941). After training in the Soviet Union he became a specialist in color photography: *Liang Shan-po and Chu Ying-tai* (1953), *Fifteen Strings of Cash* (1956), *Lin Tse-hsu* (1959), *A Withered Tree Revives* (1961), *Sentinels Under the Neon Lights* (1964).

HUNG Shen   洪　　深
(Hóng Shēn)
(1894–1955)
scenarist, director, actor

Born 31 December 1894 in a gentry family of Changchow, Kiangsu Province.

Began his play-writing career in 1915 with an opera. In 1916 finished Tsinghua University in Peking and left for Ohio State University to study the manufacture of ceramics. In 1919 joined George Pierce Baker's drama school, then at Harvard. He received an M.A. degree in 1922 and returned to China. For the next thirty years supported himself as an English teacher at various schools, while constantly writing plays and film scenarios. His first script, *Woman Named Shentu* (1924), was written for a company that failed before the film could be produced. He directed his next script, *Young Master Feng* (1925), and thereafter until the war wrote at least one or two scenarios each year, often directing them himself. He adapted *Lady Windermere's Fan* to a modern Chinese setting as *The Young Lady's Fan*, both as play and film. He played the leading role in T'ien Han's play, *Death of a Famous Actor*. His *Singsong Girl Red Peony* (1930) was the first Chinese sound film, and extremely successful (has been remade twice since then). This was followed by his *Old Prosperous Peking* (1931), less successful but more ambitious thematically. He joined forces with the Party team that began work in the film studios and wrote some of the scripts they endorsed: *Downtrodden Peach Blossom* (1933), *Flowering Grass* (1935). In 1937 Hung Shen left with the committed theater and film people for Hankow and Chungking. In 1940 he had a serious conflict with his left colleagues. The Kuomintang Cultural Commission announced that poor writers would be given subsidies on acceptable work in progress. "Only one literary figure of repute applied for a subsidy – the liberal playwright, stage director and dramatic teacher, Hung Shen. . . . [He] took the subsidy for a piece of work that had no political implications. Nevertheless he was so severely criticized by his students and by other writers, and felt their criticism to be so just, that he attempted to kill himself and his family by taking poison." (Israel Epstein, *The Unfinished Revolution in China* [Boston, 1947], p 138). Frustrated in his wartime scenarios, he concentrated on plays then and after. In 1948 he circled China to reach the Liberated Area. After 1949 elected to Consultative Conference and was often sent abroad in delegations. He died of lung cancer on 29 August 1955. Four volumes of his collected works were published in 1963.

Collected Works; BD

Joris IVENS
director, teacher (see photograph on Plate 35)

Born 1898, in Nijmegen, Netherlands. Though he made only two films in China, *The Four Hundred Million* (1938) and *Early Spring* (1958), he has been one of the most positive influences on Chinese actuality filmmakers, not only showing them, in his own work, the political and expressive advantages of realism, but also helping them as teacher and critic. The influence of *The Four Hundred*

Million can be found not only in Chinese actuality films, but also in fictional films from the time of its first showings in China. A third film, *600 Million People Are With You* (1958), was a concrete exercise-demonstration in filming and editing an actual event.

Fumio KAMEI
director, cameraman

The Japanese filmmaker who used his work in China to show his resistance to his country's policy there. His punishments were severe and lasting.

Born 1908, his first training was as a painter. In 1928 he planned to continue his studies in Moscow, but just after his arrival there he happened to see *Shanghai Document*, deciding his change of profession to filmmaker. He entered the Leningrad Institute for Film and Theater, where he stayed two years. After returning to Japan he found work in 1933 as a cutter in Toho's culture-film department. His editing of newsreels for *Battle of China* (1937) brought him the opportunity to work in the occupied portions of China: *Shanghai* and *Peking* (both 1938) showed contradictions between his wishes and those of his sponsors, the Japanese army and navy. His next film, *Fighting Soldiers* (1940), on the capture of Hankow, was overtly pessimistic; it was banned and Kamei was dismissed. In 1941 he made a biographical documentary about the poet Kobayashi, but later in the year he was arrested for his antimilitarist views. After two years in jail he was released but forbidden to work in films.

Kamei's first film after the war, a compilation entitled *Tragedy of Japan* (1946), was banned by U.S. occupation authorities. His next film, in 1947, a fictional film codirected with Yamamoto, *War and Peace*, has not been followed by any other film work.

Roman KARMEN
cameraman, director

Born 1906. Came to China in November 1938 as a news cameraman. Stayed in Wuhan until its fall on 25 November. Then through Hupeh, Hunan, Kwangsi, and Kwantung Provinces and, at the end of December, to Chungking. In May 1939 he managed to reach the Northwest liberated areas and Yenan. After sending back to Moscow regular news footage from this wartime journey (*Embattled China* was the series title), he edited all that he had filmed as *In China* (1941). There is a published diary of his stay in China, *Year in China* (Moscow 1941).

KO Ling   柯   靈
real: Gao Chi-ling
scenarist

Born 1909 in a poor Shaohsing family. Worked his way through high school and
normal school to become a teacher in a primary school and the editor of a
journal for children. In 1931 he began to write film criticism and joined a progressive group of writers. Earliest noticed film work was for the spectacle,
Empress Wu Tze-tien (1939). He "refused to cooperate" with the Japanese film
plans for Shanghai. The synopsis of another early scenario, *Flowery Landscape*
(1941), reads like a rough sketch for the postwar success, *Spring River Flows
East.* He adapted Gorky's play, *The Lower Depths*, as *Night Lodging* (1948). His
scenario, *For Peace*, was produced in 1956. Ko Ling has remained active as a
scenarist until recently. He wrote the script for *City Without Night* (1958), one
of the films attacked in the 1967 campaign.

CH

LAN Ma   藍   馬
real: Dǒng Shì-xióng
actor (see Plate 20)

Born 1916, Peking. As a child he associated with Peking opera actors and was
determined to live in the theater. Joined a left-wing theater group in Peking. In
1937 Lan Ma went to Wuhan to join the anti-Japanese touring theater (he played
the role of Ah Q), then traveled with the group to Hong Kong, joined the
defense movement there, and toured Southeast Asia. After occupation of Hong
Kong the group came to Chungking. His first film roles were small: one in 1935
for the Northwest Film Company and, while in Hong Kong, he played a patriotic
small merchant in Tsai Chu-sheng's *Orphan Island Paradise* (1939). No more film
acting until after the war. Became prominent in the productions at Kun Lun:
Lights of Ten Thousand Homes (1948), *Hope Among Mankind* (1949). His most
important role since 1949 was the semiportrait of Mao Tse-tung in the Long
March film, *Across Ten Thousand Rivers and Thousand Mountains* (1959).

CH; *Dazhong Dianying*, No. 19, 1959

LI Chun   李   准
(Lǐ Zhǔn)
scenarist

Born 1927 in village near Loyang, where in 1948 he taught Chinese language and
literature. In 1952 began to write short stories; "Not that Road" was published in
October 1953, and his first scenario was an adaptation of this story. *New Story
of an Old Soldier* (1959) was written as a scenario. His "Sowing the Clouds" was

adapted as a film in 1961. *Li Shuang-shuang* (1962) was his adaptation of a story written in 1959.

Dazhong Dianying, No. 13, 1959

LI Li-li   黎　莉　莉
(Hong Kong name: Lily Lee)
actress (see Plate 15)

Born 1915 in a revolutionary Anhwei family — her father later joined the Chinese Communist Party. From five to twelve Li-li had the status of a girl-slave, with the advantage that she was taught something of the Chinese classic theater. In 1927 her parents took her with them from Peking to Shanghai where she was placed in a singing and dancing school. In 1928 she joined the group later known as the Bright Moon and when, in 1931, this group was absorbed by the Lien Hua Film Studio, Li-li worked at once as an actress. Her first leading roles were in *Volcano in the Blood* (1932), *Daybreak* and *Little Toys* (1933). Now living in Hong Kong.

CH

LI Ming-wei   黎　民　偉
(Lí Mǐn-wěi)
actor, director, producer

First film experience in Hong Kong, 1913, in collaboration with Benjamin Polaski — *Chuang-tze Tests His Wife*, presumably shown by Polaski in the United States as well as in China. In this film Li directed his acting company and played the wife's role. His interest in films was resumed in 1921 when he attempted to open studios, first in Hong Kong, then in Canton. But his success finally came through his newsreels of 1924. Ouyang Yu-chien explained that "Li's political and artistic capital was his filming of Sun Yat-sen's inauguration as president." Following Sun to Peking, Li photographed five scenes played by Mei Lan-fang which he showed in the South before he and his brother, Li Yin-sun, made another attempt at a film plant — this time in Shanghai, and, joined by a third Li brother, the Min Hsin Company enjoyed a few years of comparative stability before being absorbed in the North China Film Company.

Ouyang; CH

LI Pin-chian   李　萍　倩
(Hong Kong: P. T. "Jack" Li)
actor, director

Film career began at the Shen Chou and Tien Yi companies. Directed twenty-three films in his five years at Tien Yi, including such potboilers as *Tales of*

Sherlock Holmes and *Arsène Lupin* (both in 1931). The Japanese attack on Shanghai in January 1932 affected his political and artistic ideals, and his work thereafter (chiefly at Ming Hsing) was in collaboration with Hsia Yen and the Party's film team — *Modern Women, Children of Our Times, Years of Plenty* (1933), part of *Bible for Girls* (1934), *Human Being* (1935), among others. During the "orphan island" period Li made necessarily more neutral films, such as his adaptation of Marcel Pagnol's *Topaze*. Eventually settled in Hong Kong, to work with the Great Wall Company.

CH

LING Tze-feng　　　　　　凌 子 風
director

Directed *Daughters of China* (1949, with Tsai Chiang), *Mother* (1956), *Red Flag Chronicle* (1960), and began a biographical film about Chan T'ien-yu, the pioneering Chinese railroad engineer at the beginning of this century.

RB

LIU Chiung　　　　　　劉 　 琼
(Liú Quióng)
actor (see Plate 9)

His first role in *Big Road* (1934), established his popular success. After many roles (*Blood on Wolf Mountain*, 1936; *Gold and Silver World*, 1939) he left Shanghai and did not return until 1952. One of his last roles was the coach in *Girl Basketball Player No. 5.* Thereafter he directed films; one of the best was *Master Chiao Mounts the Sedan Chair*, 1960. Directed Shanghai films of "minority" stories, such as *Ashma* (1963). The Red Guards labeled him "a hippy director."

MB

LIU Pan　　　　　　呂 　 班
(pseudonym)
actor, scenarist, director

He told Georges Sadoul that he borrowed this pseudonym from the Rue Lupin in Shanghai's French concession, but he did not mention his real name.

In his New Year's greeting to the journal *Dazhong Dianying* for 1957, as he was cutting *A Man Careless of Details*, he wrote: "Twenty years ago I was a comedian. I love comedies and always wanted to make them." His career, as well as Pai Yang's and Chao Tan's, was launched in *Crossroads* (1937) as an effectively humorous actor. The facts of his early years are missing, but it does not

appear that he directed films until after 1949. He may have assisted Shih Tung-
shan in the direction of *New Heroes and Heroines* (1951). *Gate No. 6* (1952),
Heroes of Liulian Mountains, and *The Yellow River Cantata* (1955) and other
"serious films" preceded the chance to realize his fatal wish to make comedies.
The first troubles came with *Before the New Director Arrives* (1956); the public
showings of *A Man Careless of Details* and *Unfinished Comedy* (both in 1957)
were brief and the unanimous condemnation of Liu Pan ended his film career.

MEI Lan-fang   梅　蘭　芳
(1894—1961)
actor, director

Before his death on 8 August 1961, Mei completed what he considered a first
version of his film memoirs, published serially in *Dianying Yishu* (and translated
in *Eastern Horizon*, Nos. 7 & 8, 1965, as *The Filming of a Tradition*). These
memoirs scrupulously chronicle Mei's continual and usually frustrated efforts to
make films based on his theatrical genius: in 1921, Shanghai, for the Commercial
Press; in 1923, for an American company (probably Pathé); in 1924, Peking, for
Li Ming-wei (and the North China Film Company); in 1924, in Japan; in 1930,
New York, for Paramount; in 1935, Moscow, a recording directed by Eisenstein;
in 1947, Shanghai, directed by Fei Mu; in 1955, Peking, the two parts of *The
Stage Art of Mei Lan-fang*; in 1957 (but not released until 1960), his last film,
Surprising Dream in Pavilion (combining two scenes from *Peony Pavilion*). He
joined the Communist Party of China in 1959.

Soon after Mei's death the campaign to use in opera only "modern revolutionary
themes" eliminated the traditions of Peking opera that Mei nurtured and revived.

                                                                    WW

NIEH Erh   聶   耳
real: Niè Shǒu-xìn
(1911—1935)
composer

Born in Kunming, his father a practitioner of traditional Chinese medicine. At
the age of twenty left home for Shanghai, where he joined the Bright Moon Song
and Dance Group. Here he met other musicians and T'ien Han, always on the
lookout for composers who could set his song texts. In 1932 T'ien Han found
him a clerk's job at the Lien Hua Studio, introduced him to revolutionary
activity, and recruited him into the Communist Party in 1933. He also gave him
two songs to compose for a film in production, *Light of Motherhood*, and Nieh
Erh's brief but prolific career as a film composer was begun auspiciously. His
songs for *Big Road* and *New Women* contributed to the success of those films.
His last song, "March of the Volunteers," for *Children of Troubled Times*
(1935), was first adopted by the Eighth Route Army and later made the official
anthem of the People's Republic. Avoiding arrest by the Kuomintang police he
escaped to Japan where he joined a left-wing drama group. On a beach excursion
with them Nieh Erh was drowned 17 July 1935.

Nieh Erh, a semibiographical film using much of his music (with Chao Tan in the
role of the composer), was made in 1959.

CH; T'ien Han, in *Chinese Literature*, No. 11, 1959

OUYANG Yu-chien   歐 陽 豫 倩
(Ōuyáng Yú-qiàn)
real: Ōuyáng Lì-yuán
(1889—1962)
writer, director

The only Chinese filmmaker to have left a full account of his film career (*In the
Midst of Life Comes the Vocation of Cinema*) was not, primarily, a filmmaker.
His fame in China was as an actor and a writer of operas, but fortunately he was
intrigued by cinema and returned to it repeatedly from his introduction in 1926
until 1948. The People's Republic appears to have made no use of Ouyang's
interest in films.

He was born in Liuyang County, Hunan Province, son of a Kwangsi mayor of the
Manchu Dynasty. His maternal grandfather was a Tuchun, the military governor of
Hunan. His education (from the age of fifteen) and his concern for revolution and
theater all matured in Japan. His assistance in 1907 in staging a modern drama
(a dramatization of *Uncle Tom's Cabin*) for the Chinese "Spring Willow Society"

of Tokyo determined his career as a man of the theater. "His decision grieved his family." After his return to China in 1913 he began the incessant activity of an itinerant succession of theater troupes, music schools, opera experiments — with an occasional film script or a few weeks of film direction to whet his film appetite or pay some bills. Though he retired in 1928 from a popular career as Peking opera performer of female roles (said to have equaled Mei), he continued to write operas and serve the revolution; any future investigation of the Peking opera's influence on films will have to study his contributions carefully. His first film scenario, *Pure as Jade, Clear as Ice* (1926) was directed by Pu Wan-chang for the Min Hsin Company. The first scenario that he directed himself was *After Three Years* (1926). He directed his first sound film in 1934, *New Apricot Fan.* His best known scenarios were *So Prosperous* (1937) and *Mu-lan Joins the Army* (1938).

CH; Ouyang; *China Digest*, 1 June 1948; WW

PAI Yang   白　　楊
(Bái Yáng)
real: Yáng Chén-fāng
actress (see Plates 23, 33)

Born 1920, in Peking. When her mother died in 1931, the eleven-year-old girl stopped her schooling and was accepted by the Acting School of Lien Hua's Peking studio; her first film role was in *New Sorrow in Old Palace* (1932). After Lien Hua closed this studio she joined a touring theater troupe (one of her roles was the always popular *Dame aux camélias*), and then a Chinese Dance Ensemble in Nanking. Since her first important film role in *Crossroads* (1937) Pai Yang remained popular in Chinese cinema (including her work in Hong Kong), and she was its senior leading actress. Her best-known film roles: *Spring River Flows East* (1947), *New Year Offering* (1956), *Chin Yu-chi* (1960). With a cast of young actors she directed *All You Need Say Is the Word Necessary.* There is a book by her, *Random Notes on Film Acting Technique.* But the Cultural Revolution may have ended her public career, for a Canton newspaper of 1966 condemned her, and applying the logic of "guilt by association," most of the male stars who played opposite her were also doomed. "This group of devils were condemned in 1966 because they were wrong in 1962, and presented poor stage performances in Shantung Province." A Red Guards poster also informed the public that "Pai Yang was once the mistress of the Nationalist Secret Service chief, Tai Li. In Chungking during the war she was involved in anti-Communist activities." Such public condemnations required no evidence. Rehabilitations of the accused are unlikely. Even Pai Yang's sister, Yang Mou, author of the best-selling novel and film, *Song of Youth* (1959), had to be accused — as the novel's positive portrayals of Peng Chen and Liu Shao-ch'i could not be left unchallenged, and — the last straw — Chou Yang and Hsia Yen admired the actress and her work.

CH, MB

Benjamin POLASKI
producer

I have found no information on the origin (presumed American) or background of this pioneer in Chinese film production, working in Hong Kong in 1909, Shanghai in 1913, and again in Hong Kong in 1913. He showed his last Hong Kong film (*Chuang-tze Tests His Wife*) in the United States, but I have seen no document on this distribution. Even his name is unsure, as I've seen it transcribed from the Chinese also as Brodsky, Brasky, Bratushki. Only "Benjamin" seems certain. We know a photograph of him (Plate 2 in Vol. I of Cheng Chi-hua's history), but which of the two Europeans is he?

CH

PU Wan-chang   卜 萬 蒼
(Bu Wan-cāng)
scenarist, director

First wrote and directed in 1926 for both the Ming Hsing and Min Hsin companies. In this year directed Ouyang Yu-chien's first scenario, *Pure as Jade, Clear as Ice.* Directed T'ien Han's scenario, *Spring Dream by the Lake* (1927). Made knight-errant films for other companies in 1928–1931. At Lien Hua directed *A Branch of Plum Blossoms* (1931, an adaptation of Shakespeare's *Two Gentlemen of Verona*), *Peach Blossom Weeps Tears of Blood* (1931, with Ruan Ling-yu), and, working with T'ien Han and the Party team, *Three Modern Girls* (1933). This year he also directed Nieh Erh's first musical assignment, *Light of Motherhood.* Greatest successes in "orphan island" period: *Mu-lan Joins the Army* (with Ouyang's script) and *Sable Cicada* (both 1938). Pu was one of the Chinese directors of the Japanese coproduction about Lin Tse-hsu, *Eternal Fame* (1943).

James RICALTON
(1844–1929)
cameraman

Born in Waddington, N.Y., moved to Maplewood, N.J. in 1871, and for the next twenty years alternated school teaching with photographic excursions abroad. First employed by Thomas Edison in 1888. In 1891 Ricalton gave up teaching to become a professional photographer and war correspondent for Underwood &

Underwood, covering the Boxer Uprising and the Russo-Japanese War. In 1897 he showed Edison films in Shanghai, and photographed "views" for the Edison catalog.

Life, 26 Dec. 1966

RUAN Ling-yu   阮　玲　玉
(1910—1935)
actress (see Plate 6)

Born in Shanghai, her father a Cantonese machinist who died when she was an infant. At the age of five went out with her mother to work. Her mother paid for her education at a girls' high school. In 1926 Ruan joined the Ming Hsing studio, and moved to the Lien Hua studio where her performances in scenarios by the underground film team there brought her attention as the most original actress in Chinese films. Her last film was possibly her best, *New Women* (1934). She committed suicide in March 1935. Lu Hsun's essay, "Gossip Is a Fearful Thing," is based on her suicide note.

CH

SANG Hu   桑　　張
director (see photograph on Plate 42)

His filmwriting appears to date from the "orphan island" period. After the war ended, directed many films, including *Long Live the Missus* (1947), from a script by Chang Ai-lin. After 1949, within the program of Soviet aid to the Chinese film industry, Sang Hu was a member of a group trained in Moscow in the technique of filming in color. First results: *Liang Shan-po and Chu Ying-tai* (1953, with Huang Cha). Any plan to continue a series of sweet opera and fairy-tale films was discouraged by attacks on *The Fairy Couple* (1955). (However, a poll in 1959 revealed this as one of the three Chinese films with largest attendance, along with *White-Haired Girl* and *Capture of Mount Hua*.) Thereafter Sang Hu applied his color training to other genres, the most successful being *New Year Offering* (1956) and *Wondrous Encounters of a Magician* (1962, a stereoscopic film).

Vladimir SCHNEIDEROV
director

Born 1900, in St. Petersburg. In 1917 left school to volunteer in the Red Army. By 1924 he was assigned to film work, but soon moved from an administrative post at Proletkino to the flight in 1925 of a group of airplanes opening a new route: from the U.S.S.R. to Mongolia to China. He and his cameraman Georgi

Blum made a full recording of the various stops, and, after arriving in China, they made a special film about the conflicts there after Sun's death, traveling from Peking to Tientsin to Nanking to Shanghai to Canton. Their two films were *The Great Flight* and *Civil War in China.*

Schneiderov's last film in China was made in Sinkiang in 1958, *Under the Sky of Ancient Deserts.*

SHEN Fu   沈　　浮
scenarist, director

Born 1905 in a Tientsin docker's family. Self-educated, he became an apprentice to a handicraft master and scrivener. From newspaper work he joined, in 1924, the Tientsin film company, Po Hai, where he wrote a comedy scenario, *Big Pocket.* In 1933 he joined the Lien Hua Studio, where he wrote *The Way Out* and *Unworried Gentleman* (1935), codirecting the latter. In 1936 he wrote the first draft of *Blood on Wolf Mountain*, in collaboration with Fei Mu, who directed it. (He played a small role in Fei Mu's *On Stage and Back-Stage.*) His most individual prewar film work was the scenarios and direction of *Freedom of Heaven and Earth* and the satirical comedy, *United by a Hyphen* (both in 1937). His most promising film during the war was left unfinished — *Long Life to the People!* (for the short-lived Northwest Film Company). After the war his progressive reputation was somewhat darkened by a religious film, *The Holy Town* (1946). Then Shen Fu had two scenarios rejected by the censors, but the third, *Lights of Ten Thousand Homes* (1948), collaborating with Yang Han-sheng on the script, was directed by Shen Fu with success. Also at Kun Lun he was on the large team that wrote *Crows and Sparrows.* After 1949 his career continued well. He made an effective espionage film, *Cutting the Devil's Talons* (1953), and prepared for the direction of the first wide-screen Chinese film, *New Story of an Old Soldier* (1959), by working as Roshal's apprentice in the Soviet Union. He also initiated the original semiactuality film, *Huang Pao-mei* (1958).

CH

SHEN Hsi-ling   沈　西　苓
real: Shen Hsi-chun?
(1904—1940)
designer, director

Born in Chekiang Province and studied in Japan, at the Tokyo Art School. Worked in the drama group of the Japanese Building Workers' Union. Returned to Shanghai in 1928, continuing his left-wing theater work (with a group that toured working-class districts and student organizations). In 1930 he joined the

Tien Yi studio as a designer. His first work as a filmwriter and director was on *Outcry of Women* (1933), based on material collected by Hsia Yen. His films grew progressively more interesting — *24 Hours of Shanghai* (1933), *Boatman's Daughter* (1935), *Crossroads* (1937), *Children of China* (1939). Wanted to film Lu Hsun's *Ah Q*, but when the writer saw a newspaper announcement of this in 1936, he wrote to Shen: "I don't want to forbid you, but I don't like the idea." Shen did not press him further. His death in a Chungking air raid in December 1940 was a great loss to Chinese cinema.

CH

SHIH Hui   石　　揮
actor, director

An observant colleague has distinguished Shih Hui's two professions: "Great actor — indifferent director," and his reputation depends more on his performances than on the several films he directed, beginning after the war. Two of the best performances in Chinese cinema are his roles in Tsao Yu's *Bright Day* (1948) and Lao Shê's *Life of a Peking Policeman* (1950, also directed by him). He directed *Stand Up, Sisters!* The better parts of *Letter with Feather* (1953) are probably to be credited more to Chang Chun-hsiang's scenario than to Shih Hui's direction. In the antirightist campaign of 1957 Shih Hui was labeled "a right-wing agent." May have continued his acting career in Hong Kong films.

石　　梅

SHIH Mei   石　　梅
director, editor

A guerrilla fighter near Peking during the anti-Japanese war. After liberation she
worked in the Documentary Studio; *Harness the Huai River* (1952) is her best-
known film. In 1960 was chief editor at the Newsreel Studio, where she collaborated on the compilation film, *Decisive Struggle between Two Destinies* (1961).

SHIH Tung-shan   史　東　山
(Shǐ Dōng-shān)
real: Kuāng Shǎo
(1902–1955)
director

Born in Hangchow. As a student studied painting and loved music. In 1921
joined the Shanghai Film Company as a designer, and also acted in three films.
Here he wrote and directed his first film, *Willow Fluff* (1925), before going to a
larger company where he joined the vogue in the late twenties for knight-errant
thrillers. Moving to a *larger* company, Lien Hua, Shih Tung-shan showed his
individual talents for unusually handsome films. His work at Lien Hua and Hsin

Hua brought him into contact with the realistic themes of the Party film team, but Shih Tung-shan maintained his own style. After the Japanese victory at Shanghai in 1937, Shih joined the government studios at Hankow and Chungking, where his only film was *Give Me Back My Country*. After the war he made *Eight Thousand Li of Cloud and Moon* (1947), about a touring wartime theater troupe, and then came into the newly formed Kun Lun Studio. In 1951 he directed one of the most effective early films of the Republic, *New Heroes and Heroines*, but he was disciplined (for a prerevolutionary recalcitrance) by having his name removed from it. Extracts from his notebooks were posthumously published (in *Zhungguo Dianying*, No. 2, 1959).

CH

SHIH Yu   史   瑜
actor (see Plates 16, 38)

His elegant performance in Chin Shan's *Storm*, as Pai Chien-wu, Wu Pei-fu's advisor, showed him as one of the most expert actors in Chinese films. Most of his previous film experience was before 1949; among his earlier films: *Young China* (1940), *Song of Wild Happiness* (1947), *Gang of Demons* (1948).

SHU Hsi-wen   舒 綉 文
(Shū Xiù-wén)
actress

Born 1915, in Anhwei Province. Her poor family moved to Peking and stopped Hsi-wen's schooling at thirteen. When she was sixteen the usurers from whom her father borrowed money asked for her as security, but she escaped alone to Shanghai, where her Peking accent got her a job at the Tien Yi Company. There she met T'ien Han, joined his theater group, and followed it through various clashes with the censors. Then she followed T'ien Han into the Yi Hua Company, where she worked in *Existence of the Nation* and *Angry Tide of China's Sea*. In 1933 she joined the Ming Hsing Studio where she played in *Downtrodden Peach Blossom*, *A Bible for Girls*, *Hot Blood and Faithful Heart*. During the war she played in *Protect Our Land* and *Storm on the Border*; an unpleasant and vigorous characterization in *Spring River Flows East*.

CH

SHUI Hua   水   華
real: Zhāng Shuí-huā
scenarist, director

Born 1916. Collaborated with Wang Pin on the best-known postrevolutionary Chinese film, *White-Haired Girl* (1950). Directed the controversial *The Lin*

Family's Shop (1959); the last Chinese film shown at the Moscow film festival, *Revolutionary Family* (1960); and *Red Crag* (1963).

RB

SSUTU Hui-min   司 徒 慧 敏
(Sī Tú Huì-mǐn)
director, producer (see photograph on Plate 35)

Born 1910, in Canton, to a family of well-known Cantonese restaurateurs. Grew up in Canton and Canada; after high school attended Tokyo's Art Academy and then Columbia University's theater arts department. Returned to China in 1931, joined left-wing theater movement in Shanghai — also joined Communist Party. He helped to construct the Three-Friend-Type sound camera in 1933, and the Party team put him in charge of a new studio, Dien Tung, where he directed its third production, *Statue of Liberty* (1935) — his first film. In 1938 during the anti-Japanese war he took the initiative in the production of patriotic films in Hong Kong, directing *Blood Splashes on Paoshan* and *March of the Partisans*. His last post was administrative, as deputy director of the Film Bureau of the Ministry of Culture, under Hsia Yen. One of his last duties in this post was the supervision of *The East Is Red*.

CH

SU Li   蘇   里
director

His first noticed direction, in collaboration with Wu Chao-ti, *Guerrillas Sweep the Plains* (1955). First solo direction, of children's films — *Brother and Sister, Little Heroes*. These led to the fresh and mature films, *Young People of Our Village* (1959) and *Third Sister Liu* (1962). All these films were produced at the Changchun Studio.

SUN Tao-lin   孫 道 臨
(Sūn Dào-lín)
actor

Since his appearance in *Crows and Sparrows* (1949) Sun has played continu-ously, sometimes in films as empty as *Women Locomotive Drivers*, but usually in films of greater interest: *Reconnaissance Across the Yangtze* (1954), *Family* and *City Without Night* (1957), *Constant Beam* (1959), *Revolutionary Family* (1960), *Second Lunar Month* (1963). He has developed a precise but under-stated style refreshing among the often exaggerated performances of Chinese film actors.

Dazhong Dianying, No. 1, 1963

SUN Yu   孫　　瑜
real: Sūn Chén-yú
scenarist, director

Born 1900 in Chungking, son of a scholar who taught in high school. Sun's
formal education began at Nankai University, Tientsin, continued at Tsinghua
University, Peking, and the University of Wisconsin, where he studied literature
and drama. In New York, where he joined the newly opened film department at
Columbia University, he also attended a theater class conducted by David
Belasco. In 1927 he returned to China and found work with the Great Wall and
Min Hsin companies. His first completely successful direction, for Lien Hua, was
Spring Dream in the Old Capital (1930), but his place in Chinese film history
was assured by his scenario and direction of *Big Road* (1934). During the war he
made *Ten Thousand Li of Empty Sky* (1940). There is some evidence that he
was the actual director of *Red Banner Over Green Cliff* (1950), but his responsibility in the same year for the bitterly attacked *Life of Wu Hsün* may have
made it necessary to alter the credits of *Red Banner* to keep it in distribution.
No film activity by Sun Yu has since been noticed. (A "Sun Yu" appears in the
cast of *Young People of Our Village*, 1959, but this may be an actor with a similar name.)

CH

TANG Hsiao-tan   湯　曉　丹
director

Born 1910, came to Shanghai in 1929. In 1932 entered films as a designer at the
Tien Yi studio, and in 1933 began to direct films: *Willow Fluff, Drifting, Woman
Star, White Gold Dragon* (all in his first year). His official biography (*Dazhong
Dianying*, No. 8, 1960) states that between 1945 and 1949 Tang went through
"ideological reform." His first films after 1949 were codirected with Cheng Yin:
Reunion after Victory and *Conquer South Victory North* (1952). He collabora-
ted with Wang Pin on *Reconnaissance Across the Yangtze* (1954) and *Naval
Cutters on Angry Sea* (1956). His latest film work was the direction of *Three
Generations of Iron and Steel* (1959), *Red Sun* (1963), and *Story of the Boat-
swain* (1964).

Gerald TANNEBAUM
actor (see Plate 39)

Born 1916 (?) in Baltimore. During World War II went from college into army.
Came to China after 1945 as an American army officer to supervise UNRRA
supplies, and stayed to work in Chinese Relief as Madame Sun's secretary.

Renamed the Chinese Welfare Association after 1949, one of its projects was the
Shanghai Children's Theater, where Tannebaum helped with direction and staging. Soon he was playing foreign roles in Chinese films, usually negative English
characters (in *Lin Tse-hsu* and *Storm*) as he declined to play similar American
characters — until his eagerness to play the role of Dr. Bethune induced him to
accept the role of the U.S. General Fielding in *After the Ceasefire* (1963). *Dr.
Bethune* was not completed.

TAO Chin   陶   金
actor, director (see Plate 23)

His acting career began at age of twenty, playing Romeo and about seventy
other roles before entering films. His first film role, at the Tien Yi Studio, is in
By the Whangpoo River (1936), but his reputation was established in films made
during and just after the war: *Young China* (1940), *Give Me Back My Country*
(1945), *Eight Thousand Li of Cloud and Moon* and *Spring River Flows East*
(both these exceptional successes in 1947). Employed with Pai Yang by a Hong
Kong firm, Yung Hua, to make *Child Husband* (1949). Best film roles after 1949:
in *Cutting the Devil's Talons* (1953) and *Sung Chin-shih* (1955). In 1956 directed
his first film, a brilliant exploitation of opera stylization, *Fifteen Strings of Cash.
Diary of a Nurse* (1957) and *The Miao Girl* (1958) followed, with little out of the
ordinary, and 1960 found Tao Chin in an administrative post, artistic director of
a newly finished studio in Wuhan. His 1962 film, *King of Ch'i Looks for a General,*
was condemned in the Cultural Revolution as a poisonous political allegory.

Dazhong Dianying, No. 6, 1957; GCR

T'IEN Han   田   漢
Tián Hàn
real: Shou Ch'ang
writer, director

Born 1898 in Changsha, Hunan Province. A "revolutionary-democratic" uncle,
Yi Mei-chun, guided him to progressive thoughts and actions, advising him to
become a teacher. After graduating from Changsha Normal School T'ien Han
entered an advanced normal school in Tokyo — all the while absorbing literature,
theater, and films. He returned to China in 1921 and found editorial work in a
publishing house. This led to an independent literary journal that published one
act of a play by him and brought him the companionship of other theater and
film enthusiasts. His film career began in 1926 when his group attempted to
produce his scenario, *To the People*, left unfinished. Then in 1927, backed by
his new post as head of the humanities department at Shanghai Fine Arts Univer-

sity, wrote and directed *Dying Strains from a Broken Reed*, on student life.
More regular film work did not begin until the Party's film team at Lien Hua
pushed T'ien Han's script for *Three Modern Girls*, a film so successful that he
was then put in charge of a small studio closely linked to the film team. The Yi
Hua studio's progressiveness was so outspoken that it was wrecked by a gang and
T'ien Han continued his film work underground and behind pseudonyms. Nevertheless the release of his *Victory Song* resulted in the arrest of T'ien Han and the
film's director, Yang Han-sheng.

By now T'ien Han had successfully combined his double training as teacher and
revolutionist with his work in theater and film. Everywhere he went amateur
theater or song groups sprang up. His most notable discovery was Nieh Erh, who
composed the lasting songs for *Children of Troubled Times* (1935), the scenario
T'ien left unfinished when he went to prison. Even in prison he worked on
the scenario of *Youth on the March* (1937), and offered it to the censors, for
his first time, as "T'ien Han's film." During the war he worked on propaganda
and scenarios, only one of which (*Victory March,* 1940) was realized. His best-
known work after the war was *Martyr of the Pear Orchard* (1949), but thereafter
he appears to have confined his writing to the theater. He has been a successful
playwright until recent years; he is not in the good, pure books of the Cultural
Revolution.

T'ien Han's film memoirs have appeared, so far as I know, only as scattered
chapters in film journals: *Dazhong Dianying*, 1957; *Zhungguo Dianying*,
1958–1959; *Dianying Yishu*, 1960.

CH; WW; GCR

TIEN Hua
(Tiàn Huā)
actress (see Plate 36)

Daughter of a peasant family in the liberated area near Yenan, Tien Hua joined
drama troupe of the Eighth Route Army in 1940. She probably played and sang
in one of the several productions of *The White-Haired Girl* in the area, though
there is little sign of routine or formula in her performance in the film adaptation of 1950. After this film debut Tien Hua did not obtain as interesting a role
until 1958, in *Daughters of the Party,* nor as significant a film until 1959, in Chin
Shan's *Storm*. Later roles, in *Green Seas and Loyal Hearts* (1962), *Seizing the
Seal* (1964).

Chang Chun-hsing, in *China Reconstructs*, Jan.—Feb. 1954

TING Ling   丁　　玲
real: Chiang Ping-tzu

Born 1906 in the wealthy Chiang clan of Hunan Province. In 1937, in Yenan,
she dictated a bold and honest autobiography to Mrs. Helen Snow (published in
Women in Modern China, The Hague, 1967), from whose record most of the
following sketch is quoted.

In 1925 Ting Ling "saw the first Chinese movies, brought to Peking by Hung
Shen, the well-known dramatist. And I developed a new fancy! I saw that these
movies were mechanical and had no emotion. I thought I could supply this emotion and that I could become an actress. I wrote letters and telephoned Hung
Shen many times. I wanted to become a film actress not only to express myself,
however, but also in order to earn money to live. I respected all forms of art very
much and saw the possibilities of the drama in the films.

I went to call on Hung Shen at Pei Hai in the Winter Palace. It was a cold windy
day but I wore only light clothes, so Hung Shen thought I was only a poor girl in
need of a job. He recounted all the various qualities needed for a movie actress
and I agreed with all he said. Then I told him that I was poor, but was not searching only for a job but to realize my talent for imaginative work. He finally promised to help if I should go to Shanghai, the production center.

Hu Yeh-p'ing [her lover] opposed my ambitions . . . so I told him he could stay
in Peking and write his poems while I became a famous star. Several of my

friends in Peking also dreamed of joining the movies but had not the courage to make the attempt. They collected money to send me to Shanghai to try my luck. I arrived in Shanghai jubilant at my success so far — and Hu Yeh-p'ing soon followed me.

At that time . . . the earliest Chinese movies were not only badly produced but the management was full of rascals. The Shanghai dialect was used too, which I understood, but thought stupid. I tried out twice and they said, "She is pretty enough," and appreciated me like a commodity, which infuriated me. They wanted me to sign the usual contract for three years but Hung Shen arranged that it should be for only one year. I refused to sign this because I was afraid. I had a good enough [offer] at first, but the life was hard and I felt that I could not bear the atmosphere of the place.

Then I went one day to visit T'ien Han, the leading dramatist in China, and head of the Nan Kuo Dramatic Society. At his house I saw his friends dancing with many "modern girls" and some of the men were dressed as women. This nauseated me and I ran out. T'ien Han followed me outside and asked why I was crying. I said to him:

I had thought to become an actress and had the high ideal and purpose of devoting my life to art, but when I came here and saw this type of people of the theatre, I knew I could never work on the stage nor in the movies, so I must go.

T'ien Han said "But you must be reasonable and patient."

Next day he came to see me and later wrote many kind letters to comfort me. He promised to write a [scenario] specially for me, which would express the new progressive Chinese woman. . . . At that time T'ien Han had a plan for a new type of [film] which he called *To the People!* a kind of folk drama. He wanted all actresses, famous or unknown, to try for the leading role. I put much makeup on my face and wore a long fashionable gown to try out for this. But I failed because I could not put my heart nor emotion into the role, for this painted character was not in harmony with my personality . . . .

And so this dream was broken, Although this was 1926, after the May 30th movement, I still retained the petty-bourgeois point of view . . . .

We had no money to continue to live in Shanghai so Hu Yeh-p'ing and I returned to Peking, where he continued his writing. . . . At this time the tide of the Great Revolution was very high in Wuhan and I wrote letters to many friends wanting to go there, but they replied that I should wait because the split between the Kuomintang and the Communist Party was beginning . . . so I began writing stories . . . I was then twenty-one years old. I used the pen-name "Ting Ling" for the first story. This was my movie-star name, which I had adopted when I went to see Hung Shen. It has no meaning. I didn't like the meaning of my real name, Ping-tzu — "Cold Dignity"!

The execution of Ting Ling's husband, her Nanking arrest and escape to Yenan in 1936, are well-known crises of her life. Her subsequent frictions with Communist authorities are documented in Mrs. Merle Goldman's *Literary Dissent in Communist China* (Cambridge, Mass.: Harvard University Press, 1967).

Though Ting Ling in 1926 gave up her ambition to be a film actress, it is possible that she has never totally relinquished her ideals as a filmmaker. Her connection with *Wild Torrent* (1933) can be only the first of her scenario ideas. Despite the suppression of her own writing career, she continued an encouragement of Chinese filmmakers that is clear in two of the documents used as evidence against her.

In 1952, for the tenth anniversary of Mao's Yenan Talks, Ting Ling wrote to the film director, Tsai Chu-sheng, asking for an essay on the Talks' influence on film production: "The 'wind has changed' before in literature and art, and perhaps it can happen again that in certain places certain comrades will follow one position, thinking that it is already art if it has been made for workers, peasants and soldiers — such people are always satisfied with beginnings, with bean-sprouts, with reducing life to terms, to formulas — this is frightening. Some of our comrades are afraid to speak about art and skill. When I came back [to Peking] this time, I was told that 'Guilty Though Guiltless' is a meaningless film. I went to see it, and it made me feel good to see how a great artist has the possibility of arranging complicated emotions and matters of deep emotions in such a concentrated way, and to see how strong were its characters.* It suddenly gripped the audience. We should look upon such films as a guide for our instruction. . . ." It is easy to see how Tsai could quote this bold statement against its author in the accusation meetings of 1957 ("A Poisoned Arrow from Ting Ling Against People's Cinema," *Zhungguo Dianying*, No. 8, 1957.) Mrs. Goldman (p. 210) refers to a statement with a similar purpose: "During this whole period of investigation [August 1955–March 1956?], Ting Ling wrote little that appeared in print. There was one speech of hers to a film study meeting, which, though it

---

* This Soviet film of 1945 was also admired by Mei Lan-fang (see "The Filming of a Tradition," *Eastern Horizon* (Hong Kong), August 1965, p. 48).

had gone through the hands of the censors, still spoke, albeit indirectly, against the party's insistence that everyone write in the literary form of socialist realism."

TSAI Chu-sheng   蔡　楚　生
(Cài Chǔ-shēng)
director

"Of all the film-makers of the 30s, Tsai was among the most realistic, the most clear-sighted. and the most conscientious." [Akira Iwasaki], *Thirty Years of Chinese Cinema* (Melbourne 1952).

Born in 1906 in Shanghai. Parents were Cantonese, and Tsai was schooled near Canton; from the age of twelve he was self-educated, with newspapers as his school books. In 1925, in a shop-clerks' union, he learned propaganda and journalism. He left home in 1927 (in the aftermath of the Canton Commune?) and found theater and film jobs in Shanghai. From 1929 to 1931 worked as assistant to Cheng Chen-hsiu at Ming Hsing, then joined the Second Studio of Lien Hua. In January 1932 he halted the conventional film he was then directing, *Pink Dream*, to make an anti-Japanese actuality film, *Share the Burden of the National Crisis*, before completing *Pink Dream*. Tsai became the leading left-wing director in Shanghai, with *Dawn Over the Metropolis* (1933), *Song of the Fishermen,* and *New Women* (1934). Between 1937 and 1942 he made patriotic films more freely in Hong Kong than in the government's Chungking studios. After the war his greatest success was his collaboration with Cheng Chun-li on *Spring River Flows East* (1947). After 1949 most of Tsia's energy went into administration and public tasks (until recently he was Chairman of the Chinese Film Workers' Association), but he accomplished one last film, *Waves on the Southern Shore* (1963), in collaboration with Wang Wei-yi, to inaugurate the new Pearl River Studio at Canton.

CH; *China's Screen*, No. 3, 1963; WW

TSAO Yu   曹　　禺
(Cao Yú)
real: Wàn Jiā-bǎo
playwright, director

Born 1910 in Tientsin. At high school joined the drama circle as an enthusiastic amateur actor, acting in plays by Ibsen and Molière. While still a student of medicine at Tsinghua University, Peking, he wrote his first play, *Thunderstorm*, and on the advice of more experienced writers abandoned his medical career.

Two years later he wrote *Sunrise*. His reputation is based on these two first plays, though he continued to write plays, prolifically and successfully. Most of his work was adapted, with or without credit to him, by the film companies. On only one occasion did Tsao Yu write and direct his own film, *Bright Day* (1948).

Interview by Yang Yu, in *Chinese Literature* No. 11, 1963; WW

TSUI Wei   崔   嵬
(Cuī Wéi)
actor, director

Born in 1912. Attracted to theater and political work at the time of Japanese aggression, joined a Peking troupe (Chang Jui-fang was also in this troupe) to play anti-Japanese sketches. Participated in the army theater of Yenan and after 1949 occupied a leading position in Peking's theatrical life. His first film roles were in *Sung Chin-shih* (1955) and *Soul of the Sea* (1957). From 1959 has played continuously in major films (*New Story of an Old Soldier, Red Flag Chronicle*, and others) while also working as a director, always with a younger collaborator, either Chen Huai-ai or Ouyang Heng-ying: *Song of Youth* (1959), *Women Generals of the Yang Family* (1960), *Young Soldier Chang Ka* (1963).

RB

Wan brothers
WAN Lai-min   萬   籟   鳴
WAN Gu-chan   萬   古   蟾
WAN Chao-chen   萬   超   塵
animators

The Wan brothers are the pioneers of the Chinese animated film. They made their first animations in 1926, their income dependent on short political and advertising films. In 1940 the two elder brothers, inspired by the success of Disney's full-length *Snow White*, gambled everything on the first full-length Chinese animation, *Princess Iron-Fan*. Wan Lai-ming joined the Shanghai Animation Studio in 1954, where his most important work was done on another full-length cartoon, *Disturbance in Heaven* (finished in 1959). Wan Gu-chan joined the studio in 1956 and in 1958–1959 made animations with scissor-cut paper figures and scenery (*Piggsy Eats Watermelon, The Fisher Boy*). The youngest brother, Chao-chen, worked in this studio since 1949, specializing in both painted cartoons (*Magic Paint-Brush*) and puppet figures: *Little Hero* and *The Carved Dragon* (1959).

Dazhong Dianying, No. 5, 1960

WANG Chia-yi   王　家　乙
actor, director

Arrived in Yenan in 1940, where he worked as actor, and joined the Communist
Party in 1945. In 1948 worked as actor (in *Bridge*) and director at the Northeast
Studio, Changchun. His best-known films are *When the Grapes Are Ripe* (1952),
Five Golden Flowers (1959), *Chin Yu-chi* (1960). Also codirected, with Roger
Pigaut, the Franco-Chinese coproduction, *The Kite* (1958).

RB; *Dazhong Dianying*, No. 7, 1960

WANG Chun-chuan   王　春　泉
cameraman

Began his film career in Shanghai in 1931, and before 1949 photographed forty
films. After 1949 returned from Hong Kong to Changchun, where he filmed
When the Grapes Are Ripe, People of the Grasslands (1954), *Five Golden
Flowers, Chin Yu-chi*.

Dazhong Dianying, No. 7, 1960

WANG H.-S.
(or "Newsreel" Wong)

His talents were first noticed in 1927 when he worked as assistant to Ariel
Varges, cameraman for Hearst's *International Newsreel*. Some of his most
memorable footage of the war against Japan was used in Ivens' *Four Hundred
Million*. During the civil war, and before the establishment of the People's Republic, Wang left China for Europe, where he hoped to sell the bulk of his newsreel work.

WANG Pin   王　　濱
(Wáng Bīng)
(19??–1960)
scenarist, director

Started film work in Peking, 1930, at the Lien Hua studio, then to Shanghai's
Tien Yi studio where he had various film jobs — actor, script clerk, literary
advisor — finally working as scenarist and director in 1935 (*Death at Sea*). Spent
the war years in Yenan, doing propaganda work after he joined the Communist
Party in 1938, and directing in the army theater: Tsao Yu's *Sunrise*, Korneichuk's
Front, Pogodin's *Man with the Gun*. It was here that he worked on the first
staging of *White-Haired Girl* in 1944. In films, directed *Bridge* (1949) and, in

collaboration with Shui Hua, wrote and directed their adaptation of *White-Haired Girl*. In 1956, *Naval Cutters on Angry Sea,* and the last work before his death on 17 January 1960 was *Person in the Painting* (1958).

Dazhong Dianying, No. 3, 1960

WANG Ping   王　　萃
actress, director

Can be seen playing small roles in various pre- and post-1949 films (such as *Spring River Flows East* and *Steeled Fighter*). When August First Studio was formed by the army, she joined as a director and since 1955 has regularly realized an annual film for that studio. Among the more important of these: *Story of Liupao Village* (1957), *Constant Beam* (1958), *Battle of Shanghai* (1959), *Meng Lung Sha* (1961), *Locust Tree Village* (1962), *Sentinels Under the Neon Lights* (1963, with Ko Hsin).

RB

WANG Ren-mei   王　人　美
actress

Born in Changsha, Hunan Province, where her father taught mathematics. Her mother died when Ren-mei was five, her father when she was eleven. After the crisis of 1927 her brother took her to Wusih where she joined the song and dance group that was later incorporated into the Lien Hua Film Company. Her first notable success was in her third film, *Dawn Over the Metropolis* (1933). She is best known for her work in *Song of the Fishermen* (1934). As her nickname ("Tiger Cat") indicates, she became identified with fiery, active roles. She is the only prominent actress of the thirties who is able to check her own films in the Film Archive of China.

CH

WANG Tan-feng   王　丹　鳳
actress (see Plates 19, 34)

A popular Shanghai film actress seemingly able to weather earlier storms of change; her work for the Japanese producers in occupied Shanghai (see Plate 19, top) did not prevent her continuing "stardom" (see Plate 34) in dramas and comedies. But the Cultural Revolution gathered enough gossip and accusations to end her film career: she had acted in the condemned *Fan* (possibly *The Peach-Blossom Fan*, 1965); "her private life is too dirty to be published"; when she worked as a waitress in Hong Kong she had affairs with Hong Kong merchants; in the theatrical troupe that toured North Vietnam she sang "yellow songs"; she played in Tao Chin's condemned film, *Diary of a Nurse* (1957) — "a film that advocates the capitalist way of life."

MB

WEI Ho-ling   魏 鶴 齡
(Wèi Hè-ling)
actor, scenarist, director (see Plates 33, 34)

Born 1906 in a poor Tientsin family. He left high school to become a dock laborer, and then tried to run a small shop. In 1929 he entered the Experimental Theater Academy of Shantung Province and after passing through T'ien Han's dramatic group he played his first film roles in *Victory* and Shih Tung-shan's *Beginning of Man* (1935), and it is as an actor that he has made his contribution to Chinese cinema. Before leaving Shanghai he played in *Diao Chan* (released in 1938), and in Hankow and Chungking played in *Protect Our Land* (1938), *Children of China* (1939), and *Young China* (1940). In 1950 appeared in *Life of a Peking Policeman*; in 1956, *New Year Offering*; in 1959, *Story of the Whangpoo River*.

CH

WU Wei-yun   呉 蔚 雲
cameraman

Born 1907 in Wuhsien, Kiangsu Province. Apprenticed to a Shanghai lithograph shop and in 1927 entered the Tien Yi Studio to learn camera work. Between 1930 and 1937 worked in various studios (*Plunder of Peach and Plum*, 1934). During the war first worked at the China M. P. Company (*Protect Our Land*, 1938), where he also began newsreel photography (for *War News*). In 1940 he filmed *White Cloud Village* in Hong Kong and *Secret Agent of Japan* in Chung-king. After the war Wu worked on *Far Away Love* and *Diary on Returning Home* before joining the Kun Lun Studio. Before 1949 Wu emigrated to Hong Kong, where he remained.

CH

WU Yin-hsien   呉 印 咸
(Wú Yin-xián)
cameraman

His best studio work was done with the director and actor, Yuan Mu-jih: *Scenes of City Life* (1935), *Unchanged Heart in Life and Death* (1936), *Street Angel* (1937). He was the most experienced and talented cameraman to go to Yenan. Though hampered by lack of equipment and materials he managed to film the three most important actuality films made there (*Yenan and the 8th Route Army*, 1939; *Dr. Bethune*, 1939; *Production and Struggle Unite*, 1942) as well as many newsreels of the liberated areas. After 1949 returned to studio work: *Red Flag Chronicle* (1960).

YANG Han-sheng   陽　翰　笙
real: Ouyang Chi-hsiu
scenarist

Born 1902 in Szechuan. Graduated from Shanghai University (sociology). First active in the Party film-team period – writing many scripts, including *Angry Tide of China's Sea* (1933), *Unchanged Heart in Life and Death* (1936). Followed the progressive filmmakers to Hankow (*Eight Hundred Brave Soldiers*, 1938), where he headed the emergency studio, and Chungking (*Storm on the Border* and *Young China*, 1940) before his dismissal. After the war collaborated with Shen Fu on the script of *Lights of Ten Thousand Homes* (1948). Alternated film scripts with plays: *Heavenly Kingdom* (on the Taiping Rebellion), *Three of Us Together* (1957, on intellectuals), and *Three Intellectuals* (1963). His last film work, *Chiangnan in the North,* directed by Shen Fu, was shown publicly in June 1964, but ten days later was withdrawn and attacked in the press.

One of the organizers in 1946 of the influential Kun Lun studio. In 1951, over a period of several months, Yang led a "land reform work group" of more than a hundred intellectuals in Kwangsi Province. In 1964 he was Vice-Chairman of the China Federation of Literary and Art Circles. In 1966 the Red Guards removed him from all posts, as "one of Chou Yang's right-hand men."

CH; *Hsinhua*, 14 Nov. 1963; WW; MB; GCR

YING Yun-wei   應　雲　衛
director

Born 1904, Shanghai. Enjoyed theater from boyhood and in 1921 left his job in a shipping company to join the Shanghai Theater Society, and then the Left-Wing Theater Union. In September 1933 he directed Tretyakov's *Roar China*, and in 1934 entered films, directing *Plunder of Peach and Plum* for Dien Tung and *A Hero of Our Time* (1935) for Yi Hua. He also continued his work in the theater. In 1936 he joined the Second Studio of Ming Hsing as manager and occasional director (*Unchanged Heart in Life and Death*, with Yuan Mu-jih). After the partial evacuation of the film industry from occupied Shanghai Ying directed *Eight Hundred Brave Soldiers* in Hankow and *Storm on the Border* (1940) in Chungking and in the Northwest. After 1949 his most notable film work was the codirection of *Sung Shih-chieh* (1956, based on the Peking opera, *Four Scholars*) and *The Scholar and the Fairy Carp* (1960).

CH

YU Lan   于   藍
actress (see Plate 43)

Born 1919, and grew up in Northeast China until occupation by the Japanese in 1931, when she moved to Peking. She joined the revolutionary movement, was arrested, and, when released from prison in 1938, left for Yenan. As an amateur actress she showed talent and entered the Lu Hsun Academy of Arts for theater training. After victory In 1945 Yu Lan returned to the Northeast in the No. 1 Cultural Troupe, and acted in many plays. Her first film role was in *Fighters in White* (1949), followed by *Red Banner on Green Rock* (1950), and *Dragon-Beard Ditch* (1953). Her most recent roles were in *The Lin Family's Shop* (in the small role of Widow Chang), *Revolutionary Family* (1960) and *Red Crag* (1964). During this production she gave an interview (*China's Screen*, No. 4, 1964), declaring that this was her last work as an actress — she now wanted to direct. She had worked once as assistant director, on *Peking Prostitutes Liberated* (1950).

YU Ling   于   伶
real: Rèn Xiàng-zhī
scenarist

Born 1907 in the city of I-hsing, Kiangsu Province. In 1927 studied in Moscow; on return studied commercial law and Russian law at Peking University. Joined the Communist Party in 1931 and in Shanghai began to write operas and film criticism. When Shanghai fell in 1937 Yu stayed on as a film scenarist. In the "orphan island" years adapted the French film *Club des Femmes* and one of his operas (as *Tears Splash on Blossom*) and wrote *Shanghai Night*. In 1941 he went to Hong Kong but before Japanese occupation reached Southwest China. Recent work: collaboration on film scenarios about Nieh Erh and Lu Hsun.

于　　敏

YU Ming   于　　敏
(Yú Mǐn)
scenarist

A co-author and codirector of the only fictional film made in Yenan, the unfinished *Labor Hero of the Border Area*; wrote the first fictional film to be
produced and distributed by agencies of the new central government: *Bridge*,
released in April 1949. Scenarist of *Chao Yi-man* (1950).

YUAN Mu-jih   袁　牧　之
(Yuán Mù-zhī)
actor, director (see Plate 11)

Born 1909 in Lin Po, Chekiang Province. His interest in theater began as a child,
acting and playwriting. Left home in 1930 to join left theater groups in Shanghai
and in 1934 entered the Dien Tung Studio where he became immediately
popular with audiences as "Man with Thousand Faces" (as an actor he enjoyed
strange and difficult makeup problems). He wrote the first film in which he
appeared, *Plunder of Peach and Plum* (1934), but played only a small role in the
first film that he wrote and directed, *Scenes of City Life* (1935), a film of the

first importance. Most of his film work after this and through the film industry's move to Hankow was as an actor. The last fictional film he directed was an imaginative variation on the American film *Street Angel* (1937). He married the actress Chen Bo-erh; together they left for the Red Army base in the Northwest. There, in the autumn of 1938, he organized the Yenan Film Group and directed its first actuality film, *Yenan and the Eighth Route Army* (1939). After October 1949 Yuan was made the first Vice-Minister of Culture in charge of films, but after the sudden death of his wife, who was Minister, he withdrew from all further film work. This retirement is, as yet, unbroken by any public appearance or duty. In 1957, before the end of the Hundred Flowers campaign, another attempt was made to bring him back to work, with the revival of *Plunder of Peach and Plum* and T'ien Han's memoir of their association (*Dazhong Dianying*, No. 19, 1957), but Yuan did not respond.

CH; WW

Important Chinese Films Made by Chinese and Foreign Groups from 1897 to 1966

(All film producers can be assumed to be in Shanghai unless otherwise located.) Any corrections and additions to this list will be welcomed.

1897
Views photographed by James Ricalton for the Edison Company:
Shanghai Police
Shanghai Street Scene
Chinese Procession
Canton River Scene
Canton Steamboat Landing Chinese Passengers
Landing Wharf at Canton
Parade of Chinese
Street Scene in Hong Kong
Sheik [Sikh] Artillery, Hong Kong
Hong Kong Regiment
Government House at Hong Kong
Hong Kong, Wharf-Scene
River Scene at Macao, China

1900
Nankin Road, Shanghai (74 ft)
photographed by Joseph Rosenthal for Warwick, London

1901
Views photographed for the American Mutoscope & Biograph Company, N.Y.
Filmed in January 1901, by Ackerman:
Assault on South Gate of Pekin, China
[Sixth U.S. Cavalry assaulting South Gate of Pekin. A thrilling picture. Copyright as *6th Cavalry Assaulting South Gate of Pekin*]
An Oriental Highway
[Street scene on the Taku Road, Tien Tsin, China. Copyright as *Street Scene, Tientsin*]
Li Hung Chang
[Taken at Palace of Roses, his summer home in Pekin. Copyright as *Forbidden City, Pekin*]

Filmed in September 1901, by Bonine:
Arrival of Tongkin Train
[Showing arrival of Chinese passenger train at station, Tien-Tsin. Copyright as *Arrival of Train, Tientsin*]
The Chien-Men Gate, Pekin, China
[Showing native vehicles, thoroughly characteristic of China. Copyright as *The Chien-Men Gate, Pekin*]

The above descriptions appear in *Biograph Bulletins*, reproduced by Kemp Niver (1971). In addition the following titles were registered for copyright by American Mutoscope & Biograph Company in 1902:
Bund, Shanghai
Sampans Racing Toward Liner

Returning to China
General Chaffee in Pekin

Views of Peking photographed by Oscar Depue

1904
[Execution of the Hung-hu]
photographed in Manchuria by P. Kobtzov for Pathé Frères, Paris

1905
[Russo-Japanese War]
photographed in Manchuria by Joseph Rosenthal for Charles Urban, London

1907
Homework and Street Scenes in China (392 ft)
In China — A Trip on the Imperial Canal (395 ft)
Naval Life in China (412 ft)
photographed by Félix Mesguich (?) for Pathé Frères, Paris

1908
Tingchun Mountain [Chinese characters] (1 reel)
photographed by Lin Ten-lun for the Feng Tai Photo Shop, Peking
3 scenes from the Peking opera, with Tan Hsin-pei (as General Huang Chung)

Shanghai's First Tramway
Imperial Funeral Procession, Peking
photographed by Enrico Lauro

1909
Films for the Asia Film Company (Benjamin Polaski), Hong Kong
Widowed Empress [*Hsi Tai Hou*]
Unlucky Fellow (or, *Unfilial Son?*)
Revealed by the Pot
Stealing the Cooked Ducks

Lovely Views in Shanghai Concessions
photographed by Enrico Lauro

Modern China (456 ft)
photographed by [?] for Charles Urban, London

Pekin et ses environs (304 ft)
photographed by [?] for Pathé Frères, Paris

1910
Films photographed by Roberto Omegna for Ambrosio, Rome:
Funerali cinesi
Shanghai
Usi e costumi dei cinesi

In China
photographed by [?] for Imperium Film (a branch of Pathé)

1911
War in Wuhan   Mei Li Co., Hankow
photographed by Chu Lian-kuei [see 1912]

Cutting Pigtails by Force
photographed by Enrico Lauro

1912
The Chinese Revolution   Asia Film Co., HK
dir.: Benjamin Polaski

1913
War in Shanghai   Asia Film Co.
photographed by Essler

The Difficult Couple (or, *Wedding Night*)   Asia Film Co.
scen.: Cheng Chen-chiu; dir.: Chang Shih-chuan,
Cheng Chen-chiu; ph.: Essler

Chuang-tze Tests His Wife (2 reels)   Hua Mei Co., HK
scen. & dir.: Li Ming-wei; ph.: Lou Yung-shan
with Li Ming-wei, Yen San-san

1916
Wronged Ghosts in Opium Den   Huei Hsi Co.
based on a new play;
dir.: Chang Shih-chuan, Kuan Hai-feng;
ph.: Enrico Lauro;
with Chia Tien-yin, Hsu Han-mei, Chang Shih-chuan

1917
Films photographed (probably in 1916) by Dr. Dorsey for Pat Powers;
distribution Universal (arranged in order of copyright registration):
Behind the Great Wall of China (13 Jan.)
In North China (18 Jan.)
Joys and Tears of China (20 Jan.)
Drama of the Orient (5 Feb.)
Foreign Legations in China (3 March)
Artistic China and Japan (9 March)
In the Heart of China (18 April)
Industrial China (28 April)
Navigation in China (14 May)
Perils of the Yangtze (19 May)
Superstitious China (26 May)
China at Work and at Play (2 June)
China's Wonderland (9 June)
In the Land of Many Temples (18 June)
Such Is Life in China (22 June, used as a Hy Mayer Travelaugh)
China Awakened (26 June, used as a Hy Mayer Travelaugh)

1919
Gambling to Death (1800 ft)   Commercial Press
scen.: Cheng Chun-tsun;
dir.: Ren Pun-yen; ph.: Liao Un-so;
with Bao Guei-yun, Chang Shun-wu

1920
Spring Fragrance Disturbs the Study (2 reels)   Commercial Press
Heavenly Maiden Strews Blossoms (1 reel)
based on plays;
dir.: Mei Lan-fang; ph.: Liao Un-so;
with Mei Lan-fang, Li Shou-san, Yao Yu-fu

Flight [*I Ko T'ao Tun Ti Jen*]   Martin?, Peking

1921
Yen Rei-sun (10 reels)   China Film Research Society
based on a new play by Yang Hsiao-chung;
dir.: Ren Pun-yen; ph.: Liao Un-so;
with Chun Tso-tze, Wang Tsai-yun

Sea Oath (6 reels)   Shanghai Film Co.
Dir. & ph.: Tan Du-yu;
with Yin Ming-chu, Tan Erh-chun, Cheng Bao-chi

1922
Beauties and Skeletons (12 reels)   New Asia Film Co.
[Eng. title: *Vampire's Prey*]
based on foreign film?;
scen. & dir.: Kuan Hai-feng; ph.: Liao Un-so;
with Ch'en Fen-yin, Wang Guei-lin, Hung Ching-lin

King of Comedy Visits China (3 reels)   Ming Hsing
scen.: Cheng Chen-chiu;
dir.: Chang Shih-chuan; ph.: (Brit.) Go-dai-ya;
with Richard Bell (as Chaplin), Cheng Chen-chiu

Romance of a Fruit Peddler (3 reels)   Ming Hsing
(or, *Love's Labor*)
scen.: Cheng Chen-chiu;
dir.: Chang Shih-chuan; ph.: Chang Wei-tao;
with Chung Jih-gu, Yu Yin, Cheng Chen-chiu

Fool   Great Wall
scen. & dir.: Harry Grogin (and others);
with Zeuling L. Loo, Margaret Yung

Story of an Ideal Woman (8) reels)   Commercial Press
scen. (based on "Coral" by P'u Sung-ling): Cheng Chun-tsung; dir.: Ren Pun-yen;
ph.: Liao Un-so; with Wang Fu-chin

1923
Orphan Rescues Grandfather (10 reels)   Ming Hsing
scen.: Cheng Chen-chiu;
dir.: Chang Shih-chuan; ph.: Chang Wei-tao;
with Wang Han-lun, Cheng Hsiao-chiu, Chung Jih-gu

1924
*Opening of the Yunnan Province School for Cadres; Speech by Sun
Yat-sen* (1 reel)   Min Hsin, Canton
ph.: Li Ming-wei

Five Scenes from Peking opera   North China, Peking
ph.: Li Ming-wei
with Mei Lan-fang

Divorcée   Great Wall
scen.: Hou Yao (from his play);
dir.: Li Tze-yuan, Hou Yao; ph.: Chung Pei-lin;
With Wang Han-lun

1925
Drunkard's Remorse (10 reels)   Commercial Press
scen., dir., & ph.: Yang Hsiao-tsun;
with Ch'en Hua-yin, Ma Ko-tin

Unbearable to Look Back (8 reels)   Shen Chou Co.
scen.: Chun Tsuei-yun; dir.: Chiu Tse-san; ph.: Wang Shü-ch'ang;
with Ting Tze-ming, Yen Gung-san

Rouge (8 reels)   Min Hsin, HK
scen.: (from story by P'u Sung-ling): Li Pei-hai
dir.: Li Pei-hai, Li Ming-wei;
with Li Ming-wei, Lin Tzu-tzu

May 30 Tide in Shanghai   Yu Lien Co.
ph.: Liu Lian-tsan; titles: Hsu Bi-ho

Willow Fluff (8 reels)   Shanghai Film Co.
scen. & dir.: Shih Tung-shan; ph.: Tan Guan-ting
with Han Yun-chen

Willow Tree and Butterfly Marriage   British-American Tobacco
[Eng. title: *Legend of the Willow Pattern Plate*]
dir.: William H. Jansen

Young Master Feng (9 reels)   Ming Hsing
scen., & dir.: Hung Shen; ph.: Dong Keh-i;
with Tseng Hsiao-chu, Chao Tan

Civil War in China   Proletkino, Moscow
dir.: Vladimir Schneiderov; ph.: Georgi Blum

1926
After Three Years (12 reels)   Min Hsin
scen. & dir.: Ouyang Yu-chien; ph.: Lian Lin-guan;
with Yang Yi-yi, Fan Hsin

Tragic History of Lian Shan-po and Chu Ying-tai (12 reels)   Tien Yi Co.
scen.: Tung Shuei-shuei (after play);
dir.: Hsiao Tsui-wun; ph.: Hsu Hsiao-yu;
with Hu Tieh, Ching Yu-ru

1927
Four Champions of the Wang Family (10 reels)   Ta Zhung Hua & Bai Ho
scen. & dir.: Shih Tung-shan; ph.: Chou Shih-mu;
with Wang Ren-lung, Wang Hsueh-tzang, Wang Ying-tze

To the People! (unfinished)   South China
scen. & dir.: T'ien Han;
with Chiang Guan-shih, I Su, Boris Pinyekev [?]

Western Chamber   Min Hsin
[European title: *La Rose de Pu-Shui*]
scen. & dir.: Hou Yao (based on *Tale of the Western Chamber*); ph.: Lian Lin-
guan; with Lin Tzu-tzu, Li Dan-dan, Ge Tze-kiang

Shanghai Document (1700 m)   Soyuzkino, Moscow
released in 1928
dir.: Yakov Bliokh; ph.: V. Stepanov

1928
Young Lady's Fan (9 reels)   Ming Hsing
scen. (from Wilde's *Lady Windermere's Fan*): Hung Shen; dir.: Chang Shih-chuan
and Hung Shen; ph.: Dong Keh-i;
with Hsuen Ching-ling, Yang Nai-mei

Burning of Red Lotus Temple (11 reels, the first of 18 parts)   Ming Hsing
scen. (from serial novel by Shang K'ai-jan): Cheng Chen-chiu; dir.: Chang Shih-
chuan; ph.: Dong Keh-i;
with Cheng Hsiao-chu, Hsia Pei-tsun

Strange Girl (9 reels)   Nai-mei
scen.: Chung Ing-shih; dir.: Shih Tung-shan; asst.: Tsai Chu-sheng; ph.: Shih
Shih-pan;
with Yang Nai-mei

1929
Papa Loves Mama (10 reels)   Ming Hsing
scen.: Hung Shen; dir.: Cheng Bu-kao; ph.: Chou Ko

1930
Spring Dream in the Old Capital (10 reels)   Lien Hua
scen.: Chu Shih-lin and Lo Ming-yü; dir.: Sun Yu; ph.: Huang Shao-fen;
with Lin Tzu-tzu, Ruan Ling-yu

Sing-Song Girl Red Peony (9 reels)   Ming Hsing
scen.: Hung Shen; dir.: Chang Shih-chuan; asst.: Cheng Bu-kao;
ph.: Dong Keh-i
with Hu Tieh (Butterfly Wu), Hsia Pei-tsun

1931
Peach Blossom Weeps Tears of Blood (10 reels)   Lien Hua
scen. & dir.: Pu Wan-chang; ph.: Huang Shao-fen;
with Ruan Ling-yu, Ching Yien

Old Prosperous Peking (12 reels)   Ming Hsing
scen.: Hung Shen; dir.: Chang Shih-chuan; asst.: Cheng Bu-kao; ph.: Dong Keh-i,
Jack Smith, Wei Lan-sun;
with Cheng Hsiao-tzun, Hung Shen

After Rain, Clear Sky (12 reels)   Hua Guan and Ji Nan
scen.: Hsieh Shih-guan; dir.: Hsia Shih-fen; ph.: K. Henry;
with Chen Chu-feng, Ling Ru-hsing, Huang Nai-sun, Liu I-hsing, Tsang Tze-tze

Heng Nian (7 reels)
scen. (from *Tale of West Chamber*): Chu Shih-ling; dir.: Shih Tung-shan;
ph.: Chou Ko;
with Tzu Fei, Tan Tien-hsu

Promenade en Chine
dir.: Titayna; ph.: Robert Lugeon

1932
Blood Debt (9 reels) [censored, unreleased]   Ming Hsing
scen.: ?; dir.: Hsu Hsin-fu; ph.: Chou Shih-mu;
with Hsia Pei-tsun, Wang Chen-hsin

Gorges of the Giants (2 reels, in series: Magic Carpet of Movietone)
Fox, NYC
ph.: Bonney Powell

War at Shanghai (9 reels)   Ming Hsing
scen. and dir.: Cheng Bu-kao; ph.: Dong Keh-i

Le Giornate di Fuoco a Shanghai   L.U.C.E., Rome
dir.: Alessandro Sardi; ph.: Mario Craveri

1933
Three Modern Girls (11 reels)   Lien Hua
scen.: T'ien Han; dir.: Pu Wan-chan; ph.: Huang Shao-fen
with Chen Yen-yen, King Shan (Kim Yen), Ruan Ling-yu

Wild Torrent (8 reels)   Ming Hsing
scen. (based on a novel by Ting Ling): Hsia Yen; dir.: Cheng Bu-kao;
ph.: Dong Keh-i;
with Hu Tieh (Butterfly Wu), Hsia Pei-tsun

Dawn Over the Metropolis   Lien Hua
scen. & dir.: Tsai Chu-sheng; ph.: Chou Ko;
with Wang Ren-mei, Wang Guei-lin

Outcry of Women (8 reels)   Ming Hsing
scen.: Hsia Yen and Shen Hsi-ling; dir.: Shen Hsi-ling; ph.: Wang Shih-jun;
with Wang Yin, Wang Jieh-ting

Spring Silkworms (11 reels)   Ming Hsing
scen.: Hsia Yen (from story by Mao Tun); dir.: Cheng Bu-kao;
ph.: Wang Shih-jun;
with Shao Yin, Cheng Hsiao-tzun

24 Hours of Shanghai (9 reels) [not released until Dec. 1934]   Ming Hsing
scen.: Hsia Yen; dir.: Shen Hsi-ling; ph.: Chou Shih-mu;
with Chao Tan, Gu Lan-chun

Existence of the Nation (11 reels)   Yi Hua
scen. & dir.: T'ien Han;
with Peng Fei, Shu Hsiu-wen

Angry Tide of China's Sea (10 reels) [not released until Feb. 1934]   Yi Hua
scen.: Yang Han-sheng; dir.: Yueh Feng; ph.: Chung Yung-shih;
with Hsia Rueh-leng, Wang Yin

Years of Plenty (9 reels) [not released until May 1934 *as Golden Valley*]
Ming Hsing
scen.: Ah Ying; dir.: Li Pin-chian; ph.: Yen Ping-hung;
with Ai Hsia, Mei Hsi

Twin Sisters (11 reels)   Ming Hsing
scen. (from opera by Cheng Chen-chin) and dir.: Cheng Bu-kao;
asst.: Shen Hsi-ling; ph.: Dong Keh-i;
with Hu Tieh (Butterfly Wu), Cheng Hsiao-tzun

1934

Song of the Fishermen   Lien Hua
scen. & dir.: Tsai Chu-sheng; ph.: Chou Ko; mus.: Jen Kuang (Chen Guan);
with Wang Ren-mei, Lou Peng, Yuen Tzung-mei

Big Road   Lien Hua
scen. & dir.: Sun Yu; ph.: Hung Wei-lieh; mus.: Nieh Erh;
with King Shan, Liu Chiung, Chung Yen-yen, Li Li-li, Lou Peng, Cheng Chun-li

Bible for Girls (16 reels)   Ming Hsing
scen.: Hsia Yen, Cheng Chen-chiu, Hung Shen, Ah Ying, Cheng Bo-chi,
Shen Hsi-ling; dir.: Chang Shih-chuan, Cheng Bu-kao, Shen Hsi-ling, Yao Su-fen,
Cheng Chen-chiu, Hsu Hsin-fu, Li Pin-chian, Chen Kun-ran, Wu Tsun;
ph.: Dong Keh-i, Wang Shih-jun, Yen Ping-hung, Chou Shih-mu, Chen Chen;
with Hu Tieh, Cheng Hsiao-tzun, Shao Ying, Yen Gun-san, Hsia Pei-tsun,
Chao Tan, Wang Chen-hsing, Shu Hsiu-wen

New Women   Lien Hua
scen.: Sun Shih-yi; dir.: Tsai Chu-sheng; ph.: Chou Ta-ming; mus.: Nieh Erh;
with Ruan Ling-yu, Cheng Chun-li, Wang Nai-tun

Plunder of Peach and Plum (or, *Fate of a Graduate*)   Dien Tung
scen.: Yuan Mu-jih; dir.: Ying Yun-wei; ph.: Wu Wei-yun;
with Yuan Mu-jih, Chen Bo-erh

1935
Boatman's Daughter (11 reels)   Ming Hsing
scen. & dir.: Shen Hsi-ling; ph.: Chou Shih-mu;
with Hsu Lai, Sueng Ming

A Hero of Our Time (12 reels)   Yi Hua
scen.: Hung Shen; dir.: Ying Yun-wei; ph.: Chou Ko;
with Hu Ping, Wang Lai-tung

Children of Troubled Times   Dien Tung
scen.: T'ien Han and Hsia Yen; dir.: Hsu Hsing-chih; ph.: Wu Yin-hsien;
mus.: Nieh Erh;
with Yuan Mu-jih, Ku Men-erh

Scenes of City Life (10 reels)   Dien Tung
(advertised in English as *Quo Vadis?*)
scen. & dir.: Yuan Mu-jih; ph.: Wu Yin-hsien;
with Chang Hsin-su, Tang Na, Wu Yin, Lan P'ing

Downtrodden Peach Blossom   Ming Hsing
scen.: Hung Shen; dir.: Chang Shih-chuan; ph.: Dong Keh-i;
with Hu Tieh, Shu Hsiu-wen

1936
Long Song of Hate   Hsin Hua
scen. & dir.: Shih Tung-shan; ph.: Hsueh Bo-ching;
with Mei Tsi, Wang Ren-mei, Chin Shan

Mad Night   Hsin Hua
scen. (from Gogol's *Revizor*) and dir.: Shih Tung-shan; ph.: Yu Hsing-san,
Hsueh Bo-chin;
with Chin Shan, Hu Ping, Shih Tsao

Unchanged Heart in Life and Death (9 reels)   Ming Hsing
scen.: Yang Han-sheng; dir.: Ying Yun-wei; ph.: Wu Yin-hsien; mus.: Ho Lu-ding;
with Yuan Mu-jih, Chen Bo-erh, Hsieh Tien

Courage That Reaches Above the Clouds   Hsin Hua
scen. & dir.: Wu Yung-gan; ph.: Yu Hsing-san and Hsueh Bo-ching; mus.: Hsien
Hsing-hai;
with King Shan (Kim Yen), Wang Ren-mei, Tien Fan

Ching Ming Festival (10 reels)   Ming Hsing
scen. (from story by Yao Sin-nung) and dir.: Ouyang Yu-chien; ph.: Yen Ping-
hung; mus.: Ho Lu-ding;
with Li Min-huei, Chao Tan

Blood on Wolf Mountain (or, *Brave Hunters*)   Lien Hua
scen.: Shen Fu and Fei Mu; dir.: Fei Mu; ph.: Chou Ta-ming;
with Li Li-li, Chang Yi, Liu Chiung, Lan P'ing

Red Begonias (10 reels)   Ming Hsing
scen.: Ouyang Yu-chien; dir.: Chang Shih-chuan; ph.: Dong Keh-i;
with Bai Yu-suan

On the Suiyan-Mongol Front (2 reels)   Northwest, Chengtu

The Birth of New China (6 reels)   Film & Photo League, NYC
a compilation film

1937
Lien Hua Symphony
1. Two Mao, scen.: Tsai Chu-sheng; dir.: Ssutu Hui-min; with Lan P'ing
2. Young Girl's Dream, scen. & dir.: Fei Mu; with Cheng Yen-yen
3. Unidentified Man, scen. & dir.: Tan Yo-liu; with Bai Lu
4. Ballad of Three Persons, scen. & dir.: Shen Fu; with Liu Chi-chung
5. Landscape Beneath the Moon, scen. & dir.: Ho Meng-fu; with Lu Peng
6. Devil, scen. & dir.: Chu Shih-ling; with Li Li-li
7. Music Dream of an Idiot, scen. & dir.: Sun Yu; with Wang Tze-lung
8. Five Little Moral Ones, scen. & dir.: Tsai Chu-sheng; ph.: Chou Ta-ming;
with Wang Tze-lung

New Year Coin (9 reels)   Ming Hsing
scen.: Hsia Yen; dir.: Chang Shih-chuan; ph.: Dong Keh-i; mus.: Ho Lu-ding;
with Wang Jieh-ting, Yen Gung-san, Sueng Ming, Li Ming-huei, Li Li-lien

Crossroads (11 reels)   Ming Hsing
scen. & dir.: Shen Hsi-ling; ph.: Wang U-ru; mus.: Ho Lu-ding;
with Pai Yang, Chao Tan, Sa Meng, Liu Pan, Wu Yin

On Stage and Back-Stage   Lien Hua
scen.: Fei Mu; dir.: Chou I-hua;
with Liu Ching, Shen Fu

Money Tree   Lien Hua
scen. (from Hsia Yen's adaptation of O'Casey's *Juno and the Paycock*): Hsia Yen
and Chu Shih-ling; dir.: Tan Yo-liu; ph.: Shen Yung-shih;
with Hsu Hsiu-wun, Li Ling, Cheng Chun-li

Freedom of Heaven and Earth   Lien Hua
scen. & dir.: Shen Fu; ph.: Chen Chen;
with Cheng Yen-yen, Li Ching

So Prosperous!   Lien Hua
scen. & dir.: Ouyang Yu-chien; ph.: Huang Shao-fen;
with Li Li-li, Mei Hsi

Youth on the March   Hsin Hua
scen.: T'ien Han; dir.: T'ien Han and Shih Tung-shan; ph.: Yu Hsing-san;
mus.: Hsien Hsing-hai;
with Shih Tsao, Hu Ping, Chang Ko

Street Angel (10 reels) Ming Hsing
scen. (from scen. for Street Angel [U.S., 1928], based on play by Monckton Hoffe) & dir.: Yuan Mu-jih; ph.: Wu Yin-hsien; mus.: Ho Lu-ding;
with Chao Tan, Chou Shih, Tsao Wei-gun, Huei Hu-lin

Martyrs of the Northern Front Dien Hua
scen. & dir.: Fei Mu; ph.: Chou Ta-ming;
with Liu Jin, Shao Guan-wu

China Strikes Back (2 reels) Frontier Films, NYC
ph.: Harry Dunham

1938

Diao Chan (or, *Sable Cicada*) Hsin Hua
scen. (from episode in *Three Kingdoms*) & dir.: Pu Wan-chang; ph.: Hung Wei-li;
with King Shan, Wei Ho-ling, Hsu Man-li

Protect Our Land (4 reels) China MP, Hankow
scen. & dir.: Shih Tung-shan; ph.: Wu Wei-yun;
with Shu Hsiu-wen, Wei Ho-ling

800 Brave Soldiers (or, *Fight to the Last*) (8 reels) China MP, Hankow
scen.: Yang Han-sheng; dir.: Ying Yun-wei; ph.: Wang Shih-chun;
with Yuan Mu-jih, Chen Bo-erh

Blood Splashes on Pao-shan [in Cantonese dialect] Hsin Shih Dai, HK
scen.: Tsai Chu-sheng and Ssutu Hui-min; dir.: Ssutu Hui-min;
with Cheng Yuen-shan, Li Ching

March of the Partisans [in Cantonese dialect] Chi Ming, HK
scen.: Tsai Chu-sheng and Ssutu Hui-min; dir.: Ssutu Hui-min; ph.: Bai Ying-tsai;
with Li Ching, Yung Shao-yi

Sunrise Hsin Hua
scen. (from play by Tsao Yu): Shen Hsi-ling; dir.: Yueh Feng; ph.: Dong Keh-i;
with Mei Hsi, Chang Chih-jih

Behind the Shanghai Lines [in Cantonese dialect] Ta Gwun, HK
dir.: Tang Hsiao-tan; ph.: Lo Yung-hsien;
with Pei Yen, Li Ching

Shanghai
dir. & ph.: Fumio Kamei

Four Hundred Million History Today, NYC
scen. & dir.: Joris Ivens; ph.: John Ferno and Robert Capa; ed.: Helen Van Dongen; mus.: Hanns Eisler

1939

Mu-lan Joins the Army Hua Chun
scen.: Ouyang Yu-chien; dir.: Pu Wan-chang; ph.: Yu Hsing-san
with Chen Yun-san

North China Is Ours (or, *Storm in North China*) (6 reels)   Northwest, Chengtu

Yenan and the Eighth Route Army   Yenan Group.
dir.: Yuan Mu-jih; ph.: Wu Yin-hsien

Empress Wu Tze-tien   Hsin Hua
scen.: Ko Ling; dir.: Fan Pei-lin; ph.: Yu Hsing-san;
with Ku Lan-jin, Han Lan-gin, Chang Chih-tze

Gold and Silver World   Hsin Hua
scen. (from *Topaze* by Marcel Pagnol): Gu Chung-yi; dir.: Li Pin-chian;
ph.: Hsueh Bo-chin;
with Liu Chiung, Ku Lan-jin

Children of China (11 reels)   Chungking
1. Peasant Awakes; 2. Love in Japanese War; 3. Woman Partisan
scen. & dir.: Shen Hsi-ling; ph.: Hung Wei-li; mus.: Ho Lu-ding;
with Chao Tan, Pai Yang, Wei Ho-ling

1940
Victory March (9 reels)   Central, Chungking
scen.: T'ien Han; dir.: Shih Tung-shan; ph.: Ho Lu-ying;
with Tao Chin, Yang Hua, Chen Li-do, Shih Yu

Storm on the Border (9 reels)   Central, Chungking
scen.: Yang Han-sheng; dir.: Ying Yun-wei; ph.: Wang Shih-chun
mus.: Sheng Jia-lun;
with Shu Hsiu-wen, Chen Tien-guo, Li Li-li

Ten Thousand Li of Empty Sky   Central, Chunking
scen. & dir.: Sun Yu; ph.: Hung Wei-li;
with Pai Yang, Tao Chin, Wei Ho-ling, Shih Yu

Struggle in Taihan Mountain (7 reels)   Northwest, Chengtu
scen. & dir.: Ho Meng-fu; ph.: Yang Ji-ming;
with Hsieh Tien, Ouyang Hung-yin

White Cloud Village (11 reels)   Ta Di, HK
scen.: Hsia Yen; dir.: Ssutu Hui-min; ph.: Wang Shih-chun
with Feng Dzi, Chang Tzun

Long Live the National Minorities (9 reels)   Chungking
dir.: Cheng Chun-li

Young China (9 reels)   China MP, Chungking
scen.: Yang Han-sheng; dir.: Su Yi; ph.: Wang Shih-chun;
with Pai Yang, Tao Chin, Wei Ho-ling, Shih Yu

Visit to Tibet (10 reels)   Chungking

Long Life to All People (unfinished)   Northwest, Chengtu
scen. & dir.: Shen Fu; ph.: Chen Chen;
with Wu Shih, Ching Chu-fa

Ten Thousand Li Ahead (or, *Glorious on Parade*)   Hsin Hsun, HK
scen. & dir.: Tsai Chu-sheng; ph.: Wang Shih-chun
with Liu Chiung, Yung Shao-yi

Confucius   Min Hua
scen. & dir.: Fei Mu; ph.: Chou Ta-ming;
with Tang Kwei-chu, Chang Yi

1941
Family   Hua Chun
scen. (from novel by Pa Chin): Chou I-bai; dir.: Pu Wan-chang, Hsu Hsin-fu, Yang
Hsiao-jun, Li Pin-chian, Wang Ssu-lun, Fan Pei-lin, Yueh Feng, Wu Yung-gan; ph.:
Huang Shao-fen, Chou Ta-ming, Yu Hsing-san, Hsueh Bo-chin

Children of the World   Min Hua & Ta Fun
scen. & dir.: Jakob & Luise Fleck, Fei Mu; ph.: Chou Ta-ming, Fei Jun-hsian;
with Ying Yin, Shih Hui, Chang Yi, Lan Lan

Princess Iron-Fan   Hua Chun
scen. (from *Western Pilgrimage*) & dir. & des.: Wan Lai-ming and his brothers;
ph.: Chung Chin-fa

Roar of Our Nationalities [in Cantonese]   Ta Gwun, HK
scen.: Li Fen; dir.: Tang Hsiao-tan; ph.: Tang Jien-ting;
with Chen Ten-jun, Wang Yin

In China   Central Doc., Moscow
scen., dir. & ph.: Roman Karmen

1942
Nan-i-wan (or, *Production and Struggle Unite*)   Yenan
dir.: Chien Hsiao-jung; ph.: Wu Yin-hsien

1943
Perfume to Last Ten Centuries (*Eternal Fame*)   China-Manchukuo
dir.: Pu Wan-chang, Chu Shih-ling

Chu Hai-tang (in 2 parts)
dir.: Mahsü Wei-fang (Japanese)

1944
Sorrows Left at Spring River
dir.: Hiroshi Inagaki, Yueh Feng;
with Tsumasaburo, Mei Hsih, Wang Dan-fong, Lü Yui-fang

1946
Labor Hero of the Border Area (unrealized)   Yenan
scen.: Chen Bo-erh, Yu Min; dir.: Yu Min, Chai Chiang, Feng Pai-lu; ph.: Chen
Mo;
with Chung Tze-fen, Ah Jia

1947

Far Away Love   Central
scen. & dir.: Chen Li-ting; ph.: Wu Wei-yun, Chu Chi-min;
with Chao Tan, Chin Yi

Eight Thousand Li of Cloud and Moon   Kun Lun
scen. & dir.: Shih Tung-shan; ph.: Hang Chung-lian;
with Pai Yang, Tao Chin

Spring River Flows East (or, *Tears of the Yangtse*) (in 2 parts)   Kun Lun
scen. & dir.: Tsai Chu-sheng, Cheng Chun-li; ph.: Wu Wei-yun, Chu Chin-min
with Pai Yang, Tao Chin, Shu Hsiu-wen, Wu Yin

Long Live the Missus!   Wen Hua
scen.: Chang Ai-ling; dir.: Sang Hu; ph.: Huang Shao-fen
with Chiang Tien-liu

Along the Sungari River   Central
scen. & dir.: Chin Shan; ph.: Yang Ji-ming and others;
with Chang Jui-fang, Wang Ren-lu, Pu Ko

Crazy Fantastic Melody of Luck
scen.: Chen Pai-chen; dir.: Chen Li-ting; ph.: Dong Keh-i

Happiness Neither in Life Nor in Death (or, *Wedding in a Dream*)   Wen Hua
dir.: Fei Mu; ph. (color): Hui He-ming;
with Mei Lan-fang

1948

Lights of Ten Thousand Homes   Kun Lun
scen.: Yang Han-sheng, Shen Fu; dir.: Shen Fu; ph.: Chu Chin-min;
with Lan Ma

Secret History of the Ching Court   Yunghua, HK
scen.: Yao Ke; dir.: Chu Shih-ling; ph.: Chuan Go-jun;
with Su Shih, Tang Guei-chin

Night Lodging
scen. (from Gorky's *Lower Depths*): Ko Ling; dir.: Tso Lin; ph.: Hsu Chi, Go
Wei-chin;
with Chang Fa, Shih Hui, Chung Tze, Wu Yin

Bright Day   Wen Hua
scen. & dir.: Tsao Yu; ph.: Hsu Chi, Go Wei-chin;
with Shih Hui, Han Fei

1949

Martyr of the Pear Orchard (or, *Story of "Half-Wit"*)   Ta Tung
scen.: T'ien Han; dir.: Chang Hsiao-jo; ph.: Lo Sung-jo;
with Liu Yu-kan, Chiang Hsu

Bridge   [April] Northeast
scen.: Yu Min; dir.: Wang Pin;
with Wang Chia-yi

Crows and Sparrows   Kun Lun
scen.: Chen Pai-chen, Cheng Chun-li, Chao Tan, Shen Fu, Hsu Tao, Wang Ling-gu; dir.: Cheng Chun-li; ph.: Miao Chun-hua, Hu Chun-hua, Wan Pei, Li Tien-ji;
with Chao Tan, Wei Ho-ling, Sun Tao-lin, Wu Yin

Light Spreads Everywhere (or, *Sparks*) (2818 m ?)   Northeast
scen.: Chen Bo-erh; dir.: Shui Keh; ph.: Fu Chung;
with Chang Ping, Wang Jen, Tsen Keh

Daughters of China (2548 m)   [November] Northeast
scen.: Yen Yi-yen; dir.: Ling Tzu-feng, Tsai Chiang; ph.: Chien Tiang;
with Chang Cheng, Yueh Shen, Po Li, Tsai Chiang

Winter of Three-Hairs   [December] Kun Lun
scen. (based on cartoon strip by Chang Lo-pin): Yang Han-sheng; dir.: Chao
Ming, Yang Gung;
with Wang Lung-gi, Wu Yin

1950
White-Haired Girl (3128 m)   [March] Northeast
scen. (from opera by Ho Ching-chih, Ting Yu): Shui Hua, Wang Pin, Yang Jun-shen; dir.: Wang Pin, Shui Hua; ph.: Yu Yuei-yun (Pao Tieh?); mus.: Ma Ko,
Chang Lu, Chu Wei;
with Tien Hua, Li Pai-wan, Chen Chiang

Chao Yi-man (2747 m)   [May] Northeast
scen.: Yu Min; dir.: Sha Meng; ph.: Yu Yuei-yun (Pao Tieh?);
with Shih Lien-hsing, Chang Ping

Life of a Peking Policeman   Shanghai
scen. (from novel by Lao Shê): Chang Liu-ching; dir.: Shih Hui;
with Shih Hui, Wei Ho-ling, Sun Chang

Victory of the Chinese People (2684 m)   [August] Mos. Dok.-Peking
scen. & dir.: Leonid Varlamov; ph.: 16 Soviet & Chinese cameramen

Steeled Fighter (2862 m)   [September] Northeast
scen. (from story by Wu Yao-ti, Su Li, Wu Yin) & dir.: Cheng Yin; ph.: Wang
Chiun-chien;
with Chang Ping, Tu Te-fu, Sun Yu, Wang Ping

Red Banner on Green Rock (*Red Banner on Mount Tsuikang*) (2875 m)
Shanghai
scen.: Tu Tan; dir.: Chang Chun-hsiang; ph.: Feng Ssu-chih;
with Yu Lan, Chang Fa, Sun Yu

New Marriage   Peking
scen. & dir.: Tu Hsin-hua; ph.: Han Kan-tzi;
with Shih Wei, Chuang Fei

Liberated China (2520 m)   [December] Moscow-Peking
scen. & dir.: Sergei Gerasimov; consultant: Chou Li-po; ph.: Mikhail Gindin,
V. Kiselev, Boris Makaseyev, Wulf Rapoport, Hsu Hsiao-ping; mus. consultant:
Ho Shih-teh

Life of Wu Hsün   [December] Kun Lun
scen. & dir.: Sun Yu
with Chao Tan

Stand Up, Sisters! (or, *Peking Prostitutes Liberated*)
dir.: Shih Hui; asst. dir.: Yu Lan

United for Tomorrow   Shanghai
scen.: Huang Kang; dir.: Chao Ming: ph.: Li Sheng-wei, Fang Shu-kao; mus.:
Wang Yun-chien;
with Chou Lai, Pai Yang, Sun Cheng

1951
North Shensi Shepherd's Song   [January] Peking
scen.: Shu Chien; dir.: Ling Che-feng;
with Liu Pin, Chang Ti-chuan

New Heroes and Heroines   [March] Peking
scen. (from novel by Kung Chueh & Yuan Ching) & dir.: Shih Tung-shan;
ph.: Kao Chung-tao;
with Ting Hsin, Jao Shiang-li

Shangjao Concentration Camp   Shanghai
scen.: Feng Shueh-feng; dir.: Sha Meng, Chang Ke; ph.: Chu Ting-ming:
with Chang Chua-ta, Tian Tun, Lu Min

Remote Village   Northeast
scen.: Chuan Wen-shu; dir.: Wu Chung-kang;
with Chang Ping, Su Fei

The Dividing Wall   Feng Huang, HK
dir.: Chu Shih-ling
with Han Fei

Resist American Aggression and Aid Korea (in 2 parts)   Northeast
ph.: Hsu Hsiao-ping & 12 news cameramen; narr.: Ai Ching

1952
Gate No. 6   Northeast & Tientsin
scen. (from play by Wang and Chia) & dir.: Liu Pan; ph.: Tu Yu
with Hsieh Tien, Kuo Chen-chiu, Li Tu-ping

Conquer South, Victory North (*From Victory to Victory*) (3722 m) [October]
Shanghai
scen.: Shen Hsi-meng, Shen Mo-chun, Ku Pao-chang; dir.: Cheng Yin, Tang
Hsiao-tan;
with Chen Ke, Fang Cheh

When the Grapes are Ripe   Northeast
scen.: Sun Chien; dir.: Wang Chia-yi; ph.: Wang Chun-chuan; mus.: Chang Kuo-
chang;
with Ouyang Ju-chui, Liu Yi, Liu Yen-chin

1953
Capture by Stratagem of Mount Hua (3476 m)   [August] Peking
scen. (based on story by Wang Tzung-yuan, Ren Ping): Kuo Wei, Chi Yeh, Tung
Fang; dir.: Kuo Wei;
with Kuo Yun-tai, Liu Liu

Cutting the Devil's Talons (2415 m ?)   Shanghai
scen.: Chia Min (Chao Ming?); dir.: Shen Fu; ph.: Yao Hsi-chuan (Shih-chuan?);
with Tao Chin, Lin Chi-hao, Hu Tu-chin, Han Fei

Letter with Feather (2224 m)   Shanghai
scen. (based on story by Hua Shan): Chang Chun-hsiang; dir.: Shih Hui;
ph.: La Tsung-chou;
with Tsai Yuan-yuan, Shu Shih

Liang Shan-po and Chu Ying-tai (3096 m)   Shanghai
scen. (based on a Shaohsing opera): Hsu Chin; dir.: Sang Hu, Huang Sha;
ph.: (color): Huang Shao-fen;
with Yuan Hsueh-fen, Fan Jui-chuan

1954
People of the Grasslands (10 reels)   Northeast
scen. (from story by Malasinfu): Hai Mo, Malasinfu, Ta Mu-lin; dir.: Hsu Tao;
ph.: Wang Chun-chuan, Li Kuang-hui;
with Wujihla, Enhosen

Granary of the Sa Family   Northeast
scen. from Liu Ching's novel, *Wall of Bronze*; dir.: Gan Hsuei-wei;
with Chang Ping

Merry-Go-Round   HK
dir.: Cheng Bu-kao

Reconnaissance Across the Yangtze (or, *Cross River, Establish Base*) (3127 m)
Shanghai
scen.: Shen Mo-chun; dir.: Tang Hsiao-tan & Wang Pin; ph.: Li Shen-wei;
with Sun Tao-lin, Li Ling-chun

Marriage   Peking
scen. from a story by Ma Feng

1955
Sung Chin-shih (or, *Black Banners*)   Shanghai
scen.: Chen Pai-chen, Chia Chi; dir.: Cheng Chun-li;
with Tsui Wei, Tao Chin

Stage Art of Mei Lan-fang (in two parts)
dir.: Mei Lan-fang; ph. (color): Vladimir Yakovlev;
with Mei Lan-fang

Guerrillas Sweep the Plains (2733 m)   [December] Changchun
scen.: Hsing Yeh, Yu Shan; dir.: Su Li, Wu Chao-ti; ph.: Li Kuang-hui;
with Kuo Chen-ching, Tu Te-fu

1956

New Year Offering (or, *Prayer for Luck*) (2757 m)　　　Peking
scen. (based on Lu Hsun's story, "Hsiang Lin's Wife"): Hsia Yen; dir.: Sang Hu;
ph. (color): Chien Chiang;
with Pai Yang, Wei Ho-ling

Before the New Director Arrives (5 reels) [December] Changchun
scen. (based on play by Ho Tin-yuan): Ju Jen-fu; dir.: Liu Pan;
ph.: Yuan Chiun-chiang;
with Li Chin-po, Pu Keh-chen, Kuan Ting, Pu Ko

Guerillas on the Railway (2464 m)　　　Shanghai
scen. (based on his novel): Liu Chih-hsia; dir.: Chao Ming; ph.: Feng Ssu-chih;
with Tsao Huei-chu, Chin Yi, Feng Cheh

Sung Shih-chieh (2822 m)　　　Shanghai
scen. (based on Peking opera, Four Scholars): Sang Hu; dir.: Ying Yun-wei, Liu
Chiung;
with Chou Hsin-fang, Li Yu-ju, Tung Chih-ling

Fifteen Strings of Cash (3389 m)　　　Shanghai
scen. & dir.: Tao Chin; ph. (color): Huang Shao-fen;
with stage group of Soochow Kunchu Opera of Chekiang; Chou Chuan-ying,
Chu Kuo-liang, Wang Chuan-sung

Mother (3600 m)　　　Shanghai
scen.: Hai Mo; dir.: Ling Tze-feng; ph.: Hsu Ching;
with Chang Jui-fang, Chang Tzu-liang

1957

Girl Basketball Player No. 5 (2526 m)　　　Tien Ma
scen. & dir.: Hsieh Chin;
with Liu Chiung, Chin Yi, Tsao Chi-wei

Flames on the Border (2475 m)　　　Changchun
scen.: Lin Yu, Yao Leng; dir.: Lin Nung; ph. (color): Nieh Ching,
with Wang Hsiao-tang, Ta Chi

Story of Liupao Village (2312 m)　　　August 1
scen.: Shih Yen, Huang Tsung-chiang; dir.: Wang Ping;
with Liao Yu-liang, Tao Yu-ling, Hsu Ling-go

Ah Q　　　Great Wall, HK
scen. (from Lu Hsun's story) & dir.: Yuen Yang-an;
with Kuan Hsiang

La Muraglia Cinese (Behind the Great Wall)　　　Astra-Bonzi, Rome
scen.: Ennio de Concini; dir.: Carlo Lizzani; ph. (color) Pierludovico Pavoni,
Allesandro d'Eva

1958

Red Shoots (2963 m)　　　Haiyen-Kiangsu
scen.: Hsia Yang; dir.: Lin Yang; ph. (color): Shih Chi?;
with Chin Yi, Sun Tao-lin, Gu Yeh-lu, Chung Yu-fang

By the March 8 Canal (2518 m)   Chiangnan
scen.: Lu Yen-chou; dir.: Huang Tsu-mo; ph.: Mu Yi;
with Chang Jui-fang, Chang Tze-lang, So Wei

Sound of the Old Temple Bell   Changchun
scen.: Liu Bao-do; dir.: Chu Wen-hsun

Case of Hsu Shou-lin (9 reels)   Changchun
scen.: Chung Shun, Li Chou; dir.: Yu Yün-fu; ph.: Yin Ji;
with Chin Ti, Li Chan-lin

Huang Pao-mei   Tien Ma
scen.: Shen Fu, Yeh Ming; dir.: Hsieh Chin; ph.: Shen Hsi-lin; mus.: Lu Chi-
ming;
with Huang Pao-mei

Constant Beam   August 1
scen.: Lin Chin; dir.: Wang Ping; ph.: Hsueh Pai-ching;
with Sun Tao-lin, Yuan Hsia, Wang Hsin-kang

Daughters of the Party (2691 m)   Changchun
scen.: Lin Shan; dir.: Lin Nung; ph. (color): Wang Chi-min;
mus.: Chang Ti-chang;
with Tien Hua, Chen Ko, Li Lin, Li Meng, Tu Feng-hsia

Early Spring   Doc & News, Peking
scen. & dir.: Joris Ivens; ph. (color): Wang Teh-cheng, Shih Yi-min, Chao Tse-lin

City Without Night
scen.: Ko Ling; dir.: Chang Chao-tan;
with Sun Tao-lin, Ling Chun

1959

Lin Tse-hsu (2903 m)   Haiyen
scen.: Yeh Yuan; dir.: Cheng Chun-li, Chen Fan; ph. (color): Huang Shao-fen,
Tsao Wei-yeh; des.: Han Shang-yi, Hu Teng-jen; mus.: Wang Yun-chieh;
with Chao Tan, Gerry Tannebaum

New Story of an Old Soldier (3158 m)   Haiyen
scen.: Li Chun; dir.: Shen Fu; ph. (color): Lo Tsung-chou; mus.: Ke Yen;
with Tsui Wei, Kao Po, Sun Yung-ping

The Lin Family's Shop (2284 m)   Peking
scen. (from story by Mao Tun): Hsia Yen; dir.: [Chang] Shui-hua;
ph. (color): Chien Chiang;
with Hsieh Tien, Yu Lan

Young People of Our Village (2794 m)   Changchun
scen.: Ma Feng; dir.: Su Li; ph. (color): Kuo Chen-chien; mus.: Chang Ti-chang;
with Li Ya-lin, Chin Ti, Liang Lin, Liu Cheng-ching

Five Golden Flowers (2859 m)   Changchun
scen.: Chi Kang, Kung Pu; dir.: Wang Chia-yi; ph. (color): Wang Chun-chuan;
mus.: Lei Chen-pang;
with Yang Li-kun, Mu Tse-chiang

Two Generations of Swimmers (2737 m)   Peking
scen.: Yueh Yeh, Chou Tseng, Hsieh Tien, Hsu Hsi-fan; dir.: Hsieh Tien;
ph. (color): Cheng Kuo-liang;
with Su Shih, Yu Yang

Magic Lotus Lantern (2334 m)   Tien Ma
from ballet choreographed by Li Chung-lin & Huang Po-shou; dir.: Yeh Ming;
ph. (color): Feng Tsu-chih, Lu Chun-fu;
with Chao Ching, Fu Chao-hsien

Three Generations of Iron and Steel   Tien Ma
scen.: Hu Wan-chun; dir.: Tang Hsiao-tan; ph. (color): Chung Hsi-lin;
with Chi Hun, Chang Yin

Storm (*Feng Bao*) (3009 m)   Peking
scen. (from his play) & dir.: Chin Shan;
with Chin Shan, Li Hsiang, Chang Ping, Tien Hua, Shih Yu, Gerry Tannebaum

Where Is Mama? (441 m)   Animation
des. (from paintings by Chi Pai-shih): Hsu Ching-ta, Teh Wei

Nieh Erh (3416 m)   Haiyen
scen.: Yu Ling, Meng Po, Cheng Chun-li; dir.: Cheng Chun-li;
with Chao Tan, Chang Jui-fang, Kao Po

Across Ten Thousand Rivers and Thousand Mountains (*On the Long March*)
(2814 m)   August 1 & Peking
scen. (from play by Chen Chi-tung): Sun Chien, Cheng Yin; dir.: Cheng Yin, Hua
Tsun; ph. (color): Kao Hung-tao, Wei Lin-yueh;
with Lan Ma, Li Meng, Liang Yu-ju

Wind from the East (Soviet Title: *In United Construction*) (2696 m)
Changchun & Mosfilm
scen.: V. Kozhevnikov, Yefim Dzigan, Lin Shan, Gan Hsuei-wei; dir.: Yefim
Dzigan and Gan Hsuei-wei; ph. (color): A. Kaltzati, Bao Tze; mus.: N. Kriukov,
Li Huan-tzi;
with Tien Fan, I. Dimitriev, Lin Tzi-hao

My Day Off
scen.: Li Tien-hso; dir.: Lu Han; ph.: Chang Kuei-fu;
with Chung Hsing-hua

Chin Yu-chi (2785 m)   Changchun
scen.: Wang Chia-yi, Chi Yeh; dir.: Wang Chia-yi; ph. (color): Wang Chun-chuan;
mus.: Pu Yu, Kao Tzu-hsing, Lei Chen-pang;
with Pai Yang, Chih Yen, Shih Ko-fu

Waves on the Southern Shore   Pearl River, Canton
scen.: Tsai Chu-sheng, Chen Tsang-ming, Wang Wei-yi; dir.: Tsai Chu-sheng,
Wang Wei-yi; ph. (color): Li Shen-wei;
with Wu Wen-hua, Chang Cheng

Revolutionary Family (2879 m)   Peking
scen. (based on memoirs by Tao Cheng): Hsia Yen, Shui Hua; dir.: Shui Hua;
ph. (color): Chien Chiang;
with Yu Lan, Sun Tao-lin, Chang Liang

Red Flag Chronicle ,   Peking
scen. (from novel by Liang Pin): Hu Su, Ling Tze-feng; dir.: Ling Tze-feng;
ph.: Wu Yin-hsien; mus.: Chu Hsi-hsien;
with Tsui Wei, Tsai Sung-ling

Red Detachment of Women   Tien Ma
scen.: Liang Hsin; dir.: Hsieh Chin; ph. (color): Shen Hsi-lin; mus.: Huang Chun;
with Chu Hsi-chuan, Wang Hsin-kang, Chen Chiang, Hsiang Mei

Eight Characters for Agriculture (2843 m)   August 1
scen & dir.: Chang Chin; ph.: Ho Chin-chan, Yang Yang-wei

Our World has Changed (2843 m)   Changchun
scen. (from play by Ko Fu): Hu Shu, Wang Ping, Wu Tien; dir.: Wu Tien; ph.
(color): Fang Wei-tse, Ke Wei-chin;
with Kuo Yi-wen, Kuo Chen-ching, Pai Te-chang

Master Chiao Mounts the Sedan   Haiyen
dir.: Liu Chiung;
with Han Fei

1961
Hurricane   Peking
scen. (based on novel by Chou Li-po): Lin Lan; dir.: Hsieh Tieh-li; ph.: Wu
Sheng-han mus.: Li Huan-chih;
with Yu Yang, Yu Ping, Li Bai-wan, Wu Su-chin, Liu Chi-yun

Red Guards of Lake Hung   Peking & Wuhan
scen. (from an opera): Mei Shao-shan, Chang Ching-an; dir.: Hsieh Tien, Chen
Fan-chien, Hsu Pei; ph. (color): Chien Chang, Chung Gou-liang; mus.: Chang
Ching-an, Ouyang Chien-shu

Land Aflame (2994 m)   Tien Ma
scen.: Peng Yung-hui, Li Hung-hsin; dir.: Chang Chun-hsiang, Ku Erh-yi; ph.:
Chou Ta-ming: with Wang Shang-hsin, Wang Hsi-yen, Wei Ho-ling

Naval Battle of 1894   Changchun
scen.: Hsi Nung, Yeh Nan, Cheng Yin "and others" (from play); dir.: Lin Nung;
ph.: Wang Chi-min;
with Li Mo-jan, Pu Ko, Wang Chiu-ying

Withered Tree Revives   Haiyen
scen. (from play by Wang Lien) & dir.: Cheng Chun-li;
ph. (color): Huang Shao-fen;
with Yu Chia, Hsu Chih-hua

Decisive Struggle between Two Destinies   Doc Studio
scen. & dir.: Shih Mei, Hao U-sun

1962
Third Sister Liu   Changchun & Nanning
dir.: Su Li

Wondrous Encounters of a Magician (stereoscopic)   Haiyen
dir.: Sang Hu;
with Han Fei, Chen Chiang

Li Shuang-shuang (2848 m)   Haiyen
scen. (from his story): Li Chun; dir.: Lu Jen; ph.: Chu Ching; mus.: Hsiang Yi;
with Chang Jui-fang, Chung Hsing-hua

Dream of the Red Chamber (4682 m)   Haiyen
scen. (from novel by Tsao Hsueh-chin): Hsu Chin; dir.: Chen Fan; ph.: Chen
Chen-hsiang; mus.: Ku Chen-hsia

1963
Locust Tree Village (2945 m)   August 1
scen. (from his play): Hu Ko; dir.: Wang Ping; ph.: Tsai Chi-wei;
with Hu Peng, Kung Jui, Ko Chen-pang

After the Ceasefire (3505 m)   Peking
scen.: Hsin Yi; dir.: Cheng Yin; ph.: Kao Hung-tao;
with Chang Ping, Hsiang Kun, Gerry Tannebaum

Better and Better (or, *Adding Flowers to Embroidery*)   Peking
scen.: Hsieh Tien, Cheng Fan-chien, Chung Chi-hsan, Lou Guo-yang; dir.: Hsieh
Tien, Cheng Fan-chien; ph.: Chang Ching-hua; mus.: Lu Yuan, Gao Erh;
with Tsao Tze-yueh, Chang Lo, Han Fei

Red Sun (3700 m)   Tien Ma
scen. (from novel by Wu Chiang): Chu Pai-yin; dir.: Tang Hsiao-tan; ph.: Ma
Lin-fa;
with Chang Fa, Li Po, Kao Po

Struggle in an Ancient City (2933 m)   August 1
scen. (from novel by Li Ying-ju): Li Ying-ju, Li Tien, Yen Chi-chou; dir.: Yen
Chi-chou; ph.: Tsao Ching-wen;
with Wang Hsiao-tang (in two roles), Wang Hsin-kang

Silkworm Flower Girl   Tien Ma
scen.: Gu Hsi-tung; dir.: Yeh Ming; ph.: Lou Chin-fu; mus.: Huang Huei;
with Lung Jia

Second Lunar Month (or, *Threshold of Spring*)   Peking
scen. (from novel by Jou Shih) & dir.: Hsieh Tieh-li; ph. (color): Li Wung-hu;
with Sun Tao-lin, Hsieh Fang

1964
Sentinels under the Neon Lights   Tien Ma
scen. (from his play): Shen Hsi-meng; dir.: Wang Ping, Ko Hsin; ph.: Huang
Shao-fen; mus.: Lu Chi-ming;
with Hsu Lin-keh, Ma Hsueh-shih, An Chia-hsiang

Red Crag (or, *A Life in Flames*)   Peking
scen. (from novel by Lo Kuang-pin and Yang Yi-yen) & dir.: [Chang] Shui-hua;
ph.: Chu Chin-ming;
with Chao Tan, Yu Lan, Hu Peng, Chang Ping

Serfs   August 1
scen.: Huang Tsung-chiang; dir.: Li Chung; ph. (color): Wei Lin-yueh;
with Wangdui, Beimayangchin

Lei Feng   August 1
scen.: Ting Hong, Lu Chu-kuo, Tsui Chia-tsiun, Feng Yi-fu; dir.: Tang Chao-ki;
ph.: Li Erh-chang; mus.: Fu Keng-chen;
with Hsu Lin-keh, Kung Tzu-pi, Ma Hsueh-shih

Struggle in North, Victory in South   Haiyen
scen.: Yang Han-sheng; dir.: Sun Fu;
with Chin Yi, Chiang Tien-liu, Sun Yung-ping

The East Is Red   Peking & August 1
recording of a Dance and Song Pageant

China!
scen. & dir.: Felix Greene; ph.: Felix Greene and Hsu Chih-ling

1965
Heroic Sons and Daughters   Changchun
scen. (from novel by Pa Chin): Mao Feng, Wu Chao-ti; dir.: Wu Chao-ti; ph.:
Chou Hsiao-yen;
with Tien Fang, Chiu Wen-pin, Liu Chang-hsian

Sow-thistle   August 1
scen. (from novel by) Feng Teh-ying; dir.: Li Ang; ph.: Wei Lin-yueh;
with Chu Yun, Yuan Hsia

Long Live the Victory of the People's War   Central Newsreel
ed.: Hao Yu-sheng, Hu Chung-hsin

Red Pack   Peking
scen. & dir.: Shih Ta-chien; ph.: Yu Tsun-yu;
with Cheng Han-kun, Huang Tsung, Li Yu-nung

1966
Victory of Chairman Mao's Thought †   Central Newsreel

Report from China (2470 m)   Iwanami, Tokyo
scen.: Junpei Yoshihara; dir.: Toshi Tokieda; ph. (color): Suehiko Fujise,
Shigeharu Watanabe

---

* Detailed scene-by-scene descriptions of *The East is Red* and of *The Red Pack* (or, *The New Peddler*) may be found in Maslyn Williams' *The East is Red: The View inside Red China* (New York: Morrow, 1967), pp. 30–36 and pp. 96–102.

† See *The China Cloud* by William L. Ryan and Sam Summerlin (Boston: Little, Brown and Company, 1968), pp. 205–207, for a thorough description of what one sees on the screen and what it is intended to prove.

Appendix 3

A Counter-Revolutionary Record Aimed at the Restoration of Capitalism

[This translation of an anonymous attack is reprinted from *Chinese Literature*, No. 6, 1968]

Our great leader Chairman Mao has taught us: "To overthrow a political power, it is always necessary first of all to create public opinion, to do work in the ideological sphere. This is true for the revolutionary class as well as for the counter-revolutionary class."

The hasty dishing up of the poisonous weed *History of the Chinese Film* by Chou Yang, Hsia Yen and their crew of counter-revolutionary revisionists, in February 1963, was done entirely to create public opinion for China's Khrushchov [Liu Shao-ch'i] to overthrow the dictatorship of the proletariat and restore capitalism.

This *History of the Chinese Film* edited by Cheng Chi-hua, a renegade and cultural spy who sneaked into the Party, brazenly fabricated history in order to sing the praises of Chou Yang, Hsia Yen and other counter-revolutionary revisionists, glorify the monsters in film circles, and frantically oppose Chairman Mao's revolutionary line on literature and art. It was a counter-revolutionary distortion of history aimed at the restoration of capitalism.

Its theme tune was first decided upon by the counter-revolutionary revisionist Lu Ting-yi, a scoundrel who strained every nerve to publicize the "achievements" of the films of the 1930s. At the meeting to inaugurate the Shanghai Film Studio in April 1957, he ranted: "Our post-liberation films have evolved from the pre-liberation Left-wing films. Who are the ancestors (of our present films)? Where are their roots? From what did they develop? The pre-liberation Left-wing films." He completely obscured the epoch-making significance of Chairman Mao's brilliant *Talks at the Yenan Forum on Literature and Art*, in a deliberate attempt to resuscitate Wang Ming's opportunist line.

Soon after this, his confederate Chou Yang assembled his accomplices Hsia Yen, Chen Huang-mei, Chou Li-po, Lin Mo-han and Shao Chuan-lin to launch a ludicrous and vicious attack on Lu Hsun, in the hope of reversing the verdict on "a literature of national defence," the slogan of Wang Ming's Right capitulationist line. Hsia Yen also lost no time in publishing his pernicious article *The History of China's Films and Party Leadership*, which presented their crew of opportunists as the personification of "Party Leadership" and shamelessly claimed that as far back as the thirties he himself had "waged an uncompromising struggle against all backward and reactionary ideas in the film world." He glorified the criminal service he rendered to landlords and capitalists as a "revolutionary tradition" of "serving politics," which should be "taken over" by film workers. It was at the time when this black wind was blowing, when fulsome praise was being heaped upon the literature and art of the thirties, that the reactionary scribbler Cheng Chi-hua enlisted help to compile his infamous *History*.

While this big poisonous weed was being cooked up, Hsia Yen not only read the outline, corrected the proofs and approved the final version, but kept encouraging Cheng Chi-hua by saying: "A history of the film is easier to write than an ordinary history of literature, because so much has already been achieved by men who are still alive." "You must get this book out as fast as possible." Chen Huang-mei, too, fell over himself in his eagerness to read and help revise the manuscript. Chou Yang, the chief of the black line on literature and art, showed even more enthusiasm. With a flourish of his pen he changed "on instructions from the Propaganda Department of the Central Committee" into "on instructions from the Central Committee." It is crystal clear that the dishing up of this *History* was planned by Chou Yang and Hsia Yen personally, as an organized counter-revolutionary action to reverse the verdict on Wang Ming's opportunist line.

The Summary of the Forum on the Work in Literature and Art in the Armed Forces with Which Comrade Lin Piao Entrusted Comrade Chiang Ching pointed out: "Wang Ming's line represented bourgeois thinking which was once rampant within our Party. In the rectification movement which started in 1942, Chairman Mao made a thorough theoretical refutation first of Wang Ming's political, military and organizational lines and then, immediately afterwards, of the cultural line he represented." In *On New Democracy, Talks at the Yenan Forum on Literature and Art* and other brilliant works, Chairman Mao had already made a thorough criticism of the black bourgeois line on literature and art headed by Chou Yang in the thirties. Yet the *History* concocted by Chou Yang, Hsia Yen and company described Wang Ming's line as "the Party's general line during the period of the democratic revolution." This was an outrageous counter-attack on Chairman Mao's correct criticism. On the one hand they wildly opposed Chairman Mao's revolutionary line, on the other they posed as the "correct Party leadership," claiming that they had already established a "Marxist world outlook" in the 1930s, when their orientation was already that of "serving the proletariat and the masses of workers and peasants." They claimed to have "paved the way ideologically, organizationally, technically and as regards cadres for the establishment and development of China's socialist films." They glamorized as fine proletarian films a host of films reeking of the decadent landlord class and bourgeoisie and "national defence films" preaching capitulation. As for the renegades, traitors, secret agents, capitalists and other monsters who had sneaked into film circles, they entitled them all "progressive film workers," the "forerunners" or "pioneering heroes" of revolutionary films, and recorded the names of each. They confounded men and monsters, mixed up black and white, and completely distorted history.

To make good publicity for Hsia Yen, Tien Han, Yang Han-sheng, Tsai Chu-sheng and other counter-revolutionary revisionists, the *History* devoted much space to whitewashing them, using every means to extol their "achievements" in spreading poison. Because Hsia Yen's big poisonous weed *Wild Torrent* idealized landlords, vilified peasants and praised the Kuomintang government, it was awarded the title of "best Chinese film" by the Kuomintang reactionary clique; but the *History* praised it as "the first red flag planted by the Party on the film position." *Three Modern Girls*, by the big renegade Tien Han, wildly advocated the decadent bourgeois view of life; yet it was lauded as "an excellent play, exerting a wide social influence." Yang Han-sheng's pernicious *Iron and Tears* presented a crime of passion in a landlord's militia as armed revolutionary struggle in the countryside, grossly slandering the peasants and land reform; yet it was cracked up as "a fine film powerfully opposed to feudalism and the local gentry." Tsai Chu-sheng's *Fisherman's Song*, preaching class conciliation and a slave mentality and glorifying bourgeois reformism, was also praised as an "overwhelming" indictment of bourgeois reformism; and the ridiculous claim was made that the author had "never faltered politically or gone astray in film-making." Many, many more fantastic encomiums could be quoted. The incredible thing, however, is that these passages were all touched up and expanded by the objects of praise themselves! They indulged in this shameless self-glorification solely to retain their positions as "veterans," to strengthen their bourgeois dictatorship over literary and art circles, and to drag the whole socialist film industry on to the capitalist road. This pipe dream of theirs will never be realized.

The concoction and dishing up of this *History* accorded completely with the needs of the counter-revolutionary revisionist political line promoted by the top Party person in authority taking the capitalist road. China's Khrushchov was a confirmed opportunist and counter-revolutionary, who consistently opposed Chairman Mao's teachings on literature and art. He preached a "literature and art of the whole people," and was against literature and art serving the workers, peasants and soldiers, serving proletarian dictatorship. He preached "seeing life in the country from a caravan," and was against literary and art workers going deep among the workers, peasants and soldiers, into the heat of class struggle. He preached bourgeois liberalization, was against the Party leading literature and art, and ranted that there should be "a more lenient censorship of publications,

plays and films." He said: "Films from all over the world can be shown, provided they are harmless, give a picture of different countries and help us to
understand conditions there. Even somewhat reformist ones can also be shown."
He was the No. 1 promoter of feudal, bourgeois and revisionist films, the main
root of the poisonous weeds which grew so rank in the film world, the chief boss
behind the scenes of the black line on literature and art opposed to the Party,
socialism and Mao Tse-tung's thought. Because they had such powerful backing,
Chou Yang, Hsia Yen and Chen Huang-mei, this gang of counter-revolutionary
revisionists, had the effrontery to concoct the *History* in a counter-revolutionary
attempt to reverse the verdict on Wang Ming's line; they actually dished it up
after the Tenth Plenary Session of the Eighth Central Committee of the Party in
1962. And Chen Huang-mei, making use of his position, lost no chance of boost-
ing and advertizing it. Even after Chairman Mao's two instructions concerning
literature and art exposed the question of the *History* to the bright light of day,
Chou Yang did his best to defend it, arguing that the book had "its merits. It is
no easy matter compiling such a wealth of material." "If I were asked to review
it, I would start by affirming its merits." Why did Chou Yang and company
spare no pains in the first place to concoct, and then by every means to defend,
this counter-revolutionary record aimed at the restoration of capitalism? Because
the *History* was the "capital" on which this gang of counter-revolutionary
revisionists relied for a living, and a weapon with which they attacked the Party,
they frantically obstructed a thoroughgoing criticism of it, in a vain attempt to
preserve this rotten filth and continue serving the top Party person in authority
taking the capitalist road.

Chairman Mao teaches us: **"It is up to us to organize the people. As for the
reactionaries in China, it is up to us to organize the people to overthrow them.
Everything reactionary is the same; if you don't hit it, it won't fall."** In the
present high tide of revolutionary mass criticism, we must raise still higher the
great red banner of Mao Tse-tung's thought and thoroughly repudiate all the
absurd reactionary views spread by the *History*, to reverse its reversal of history.

Plates

Plate 2

a. Probably the first staged film made in China, "Sixth U.S. Cavalry Assaulting South Gate of Pekin." Reconstruction of Boxer battle, by Ackerman in January 1901 for American Mutoscope & Biograph Company, New York.

b. Biograph cameraman Ackerman makes a formal presentation of a Mutoscope apparatus to statesman Li Hung-shang at his Palace of Roses (1901).

Plate 3

a. From the Charles Urban catalog of 1904:
"Execution of Li-Tang, the Chunchus chief
of Manchurian bandits: the only animated
picture of a Chinese execution ever taken.
Gruesome, but faithfully depicting the
actual scene." The newsreel that determined
the career of Lu Hsun (see page 13).

b. *The Chinese Revolution*, a staged reconstruction made in Hong Kong, registered for
U.S. copyright in 1912. This scene is introduced: "Rich Mandarin attacked by group
of Revolutionists."

Plate 4

a. Sun Yat-sen speaks at the opening of the Yunnan Province School for Cadres, 1924. (Frame enlargement by National Archives, Washington, from the Li Ming-wei newsreel.)

b. *Shanghai Document,* 1927, made by Yakov Bliokh for Soyuzkino, Moscow, before the coup d'état of Chiang Kai-shek.

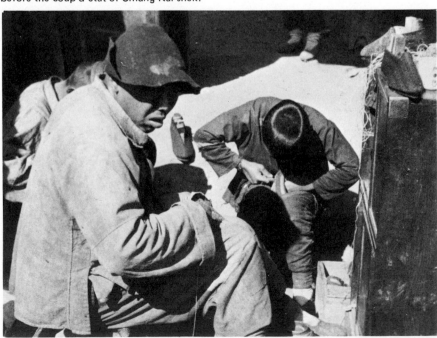

Plate 5

a. *Shattered Jade Fated to be Re-United,*
made in 1926 by the American-financed
American-Oriental Pictures Company.
b. *Wild Torrent,* 1933, the earliest of the
studio films to be initiated by the leftist
film group at the Star Studio; directed by
Cheng Bu-kao.

Plate 6

a. *Years of Plenty,* 1933, written by Ah Ying and directed by Li Pin-chian.
b. *Twin Sisters,* 1933, with Butterfly Wu in dual roles, her most successful film.

Plate 7

a. Ruan Ling-yu in her last film, *New Women,* 1934, written by Sun Shih-yi.
b. *The Common Enemy,* 1934, written by Hsia Yen and directed by Cheng Bu-kao.

Plate 8

a. During Mei Lan-fang's performances in Moscow in 1935, Sergei Eisenstein made a film (now lost?) of Mei's best scenes. Above: Mei, Tretyakov, Eisenstein. (Photo by author.)

b. This conclusion to *The Beginning of Man*, 1935, is typical for the period: it conveys the tone of revolution without being explicit — defiance without action.

Plate 9

a. *Big Road,* 1934, written and directed by Sun Yu, with a "collective hero."
b. *Money Tree,* 1937, based on O'Casey's *Juno and the Paycock;* the realistic humor of O'Casey was maintained by Hsia Yen and Chu Shih-ling.

Plate 10

Chou En-lai, on duty in Chungking during
the "united front" period, in *The Four
Hundred Million*, 1938, directed by Joris
Ivens, photographed by John Ferno and
Robert Capa. (Photo by Capa.)

Plate 11

Yuan Mu-jih in *Eight Hundred Brave Soldiers,* 1938, produced in Hankow, with scenario by Yang Han-sheng; shown widely in overseas Chinese settlements to collect funds to support China in the anti-Japanese war.

Plate 12

The first production by the Hong Kong branch of the Chungking government film company: *Orphan Island Paradise,* 1939, a melodrama of espionage in Shanghai, written and directed by Tsai Chu-sheng.

Plate 13

Fight to the Last, 1938. Japanese soldiers
violate a Chinese home while the head of
the family is at the front.

Plate 14

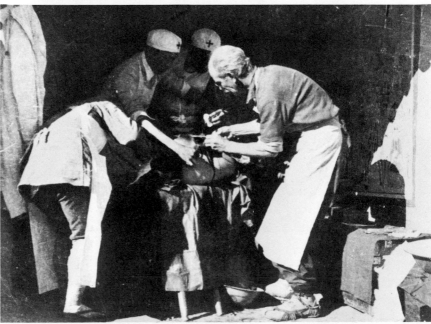

Plate 15

Yang Han-sheng's scenario, *Storm on the Border,* its direction completed by Ying Yun-wei in 1940. The heroine is played by Li Li-li.

Plate 16

Plate 17

Photographs from two episodes of *Victory
March,* 1940, written by T'ien Han,
directed by Shih Tung-shan.

Plate 18
Japanese Productions in Occupied Shanghai

a. *Sorrows Left at Spring River,* 1944. A
drama of the Taiping Rebellion, directed by
Hiroshi Inagaki and Yueh Feng.
b. *Chu Hai-tang,* 1943.

Plate 19
Japanese Productions in Occupied Shanghai

a. *Sorrows Left at Spring River*, 1944.
b. *Ten Thousand Violets and One Thousand Red Blossoms.*

Plate 20

Lan Ma in *Lights of Ten Thousand Homes,*
Shanghai 1948, written by Yang Han-sheng
and Shen Fu.

Plate 21

a. Chang Jui-fang and the carters in *Along the Sungari River,* 1947, written and directed by Chin Shan.
b. *Winter of Three-Hairs,* 1949, a satirical film based on a newspaper comic strip (see page 175).

Plate 22
Films made in Hong Kong

Refugee Song, 1941.

Plate 23
Films made in Hong Kong

a. *Secret History of the Ch'ing Court,* 1948, directed by Chu Shih-ling. The Dowager Empress takes the Boxers as allies in her war against the foreigners.
b. Pai Yang and Tao Chin in *Child Husband,* 1949.

Plate 24

a. *Far Away Love,* 1947, with Chin Yi and
Chao Tan. "Pygmalion" encounters his
uniformed and fully independent "Galatea."
b. *Crows and Sparrows,* 1949, with Wu Yin
and Chao Tan. Produced by the Kun Lun
Studio, directed by Cheng Chun-li.

Plate 25

Daughters of China, 1949. Trapped by
Japanese soldiers, and ready for martyrdom.

Plate 26

a. *New Heroes and Heroines,* 1950, scenario
and direction by Shih Tung-shan.
b. *Steeled Fighter,* 1950, with Chang Ping
(resisting the enemy's temptation). Cheng
Yin's first fictional film.

Plate 27

Letter with Feather, 1953, by Chang
Chun-hsiang and Shih Hui. Bottom: trick-
ing the enemy clowns.

Plate 28
United for Tomorrow

a. Printed lyrics for each song are provided for spectators of different Chinese nationalities.
b. The obligatory scene of defiance.

c. Tragic simplicity.

Plate 29

United for Tomorrow, 1951, on a strike in a Shanghai textile mill. Directed by Chao Ming.

Plate 30

Victory of the Chinese People, 1950, a
Soviet-Chinese co-production directed
by Leonid Varlamov.

Plate 31

Red Banner on Green Rock, 1950, directed
by Chang Chun-hsiang.

Plate 32
The Minorities

a. The Miao people: *Caravan,* 1955.
b. The Mongolian people: *People of the Grasslands,* 1954, from a story by Malasinfu.

Plate 33

Wei Ho-ling and Pai Yang in *New Year Offering,* 1956, adapted by Hsia Yen from a story by Lu Hsun, directed by Sang Hu.

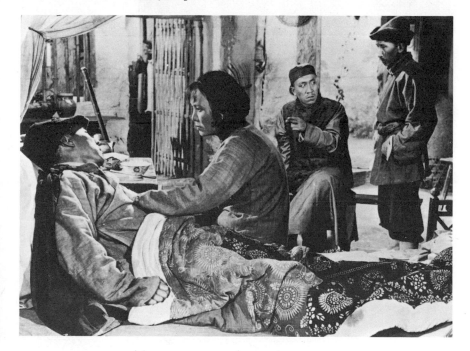

Plate 34
Pa Chin's *Family*, 1957.

a. Wang Tan-feng.
b. Wei Ho-ling and Chang Hui.

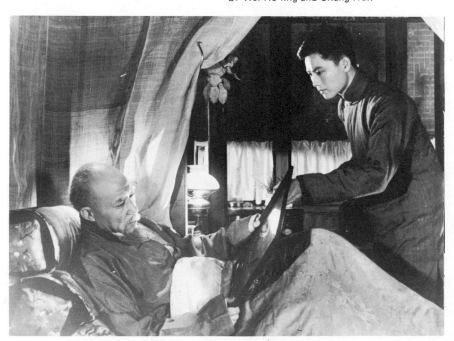

Plate 35

Joris Ivens welcomed in 1957 by Hsia Yen
(center) and Ssutu Hui-min (left).

Plate 36

a. Chang Jui-fang in *By the March 8 Canal*,
1958.
b. Tien Hua in *Daughters of the Party*,
1958.

Plate 37

a. *Girl Basketball Player No. 5*, written and
directed by Hsieh Chin (1957).
b. *My Day Off*, 1959, directed by Lu Han.
Chung Hsing-hua as the busy Shanghai
policeman.

Plate 38
Storm, 1959; written and directed by Chin
Shan.

a. Shih Yu in the role of political advisor to
the warlord Wu Pei-fu.

b. Filming the tragic conclusion.

Plate 39
Storm, 1959.

a. Capture of the strikers' lawyer (Chin Shan).
b. Shih Yu (left) and Gerald Tannebaum (right) as the British Consul in Hankow.

Plate 40

Where Is Mama?, a cartoon animating the style and motifs of Chi Pai-shih's paintings.

Plate 41
Lin Tse-hsu, 1959.

a. The Emperor (Han Fei) plays with his collection of clocks.
b. An appeal to Lin Tse-hsu, in spite of the imperial withdrawal of Lin's authority. Lin is played by Chao Tan.

Plate 42

a. *The Magic Lotus Lantern*, 1959, a danced film with Chao Ching.

b. During the filming of the 3-dimensional comedy, *Wondrous Encounters of a Magician*, 1962. The comedian Han Fei holds the parasol; in the center is the director, Sang Hu.

Plate 43

a. *Revolutionary Family*, 1960, with Yu
Lan (in foreground).
b. A landlord's family's war conference —
Hurricane, 1960, directed by Hsieh Tieh-li
from the novel by Chou Li-po.

Plate 44

a. A children's film, *Little Ding-dong*, 1963, directed by Hsieh Tien and Cheng Fang-chien; the bus conductor is played by Chin Yi.

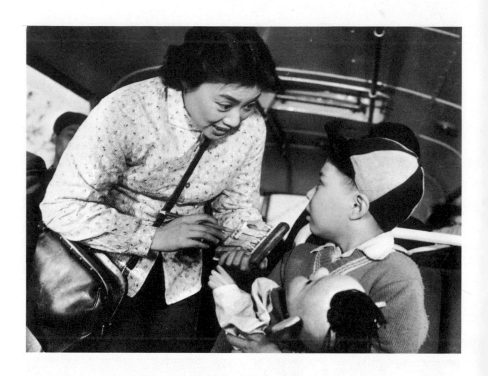

b. *Girl Divers*, 1964. The heroine, played by Chen Hsiao-hung, is studying the example of Lei Feng.

A Miscellany

1915?
The sale of stereopticon views to schools and clubs in the United States was a profitable business in the latter half of the nineteenth century. More than information was sold; attitudes also came, with lasting effects on popular prejudice. Below is an extract from the text supplied to the teacher with this photograph:

"Here is a crowd of yellow people. They are coolies, Chinese of the lowest class. You can tell by their faces that they are not a thinking lot. The lower class of Chinese are not very intelligent. The better class look very different from these people . . .

"Years ago these laborers from China flocked to the United States in great numbers. They can live more cheaply than other men because their standard of living is lower; that is, their homes, food and clothing are poorer and they do not demand education. United States workmen will not live that way and could not compete with the Chinese cheap labor. Laws were passed forbidding the Chinese to come to America."

1917? [an Italian sculptor tries films]
[Remo Bufano] went to China during World War I with a film company. His Chinese cameraman fled when revolution broke out and Mr. Bufano lived for months as a coolie on the Canton docks and later wandered off with a band of Buddhist monks. He lived for four months with Dr. Sun [Yat-sen] and made statues of him.
—obituary in *New York Times* 20 August 1970.

1925 [a prophecy]
... it is certain that in China the native theater has a much firmer grasp on the masses than in any other Asiatic country and will withstand the Europeanized theater and the motion-picture much longer.
—A. E. Zucker, "The Changing Theaters of Asia," *Asia* (New York), March 1926.

1928 [Lu Hsun comes to Shanghai to live]
By the time I came to Shanghai and saw films there, we had become "low-class Chinese." We saw white men and rich men sitting upstairs — and downstairs were the middle-class and low-class Chinese. On the screen white soldiers fought, white lords made money, white young ladies got married, and white heroes had adventures, filling the audience with admiration, envy, fear, and the feeling that all this was beyond us. However, when white heroes went to danger spots in Africa, there were always some black, loyal servants to guide them, work for them, fight for them, die for them, so that white masters could return home safely. When the white hero prepares for another adventure, he misses his loyal servant. He remembers his dead slave and his face falls. Then on the screen his memory brings to view a Negro's face, and in the faint glimmer of the theater's light we yellow-faced spectators let our faces fall. We are moved.
—translated from Lu Hsun, "Lessons from Films," September 1933 in *Pseudo-Frivolous Talk* (Shanghai, 1934).

1930 [ethnological footage?]
[The Japanese] followed me into China, perhaps because they were afraid I would give installations secrets to the Chinese; in China I travelled fourth class on a train; you can imagine the filthy stench. I shot and shot, and sneaked the film out. I got stuff on China you can't imagine; if they'd found out I would have been strung up.
—Leon Shamroy, interviewed by Charles Higham for *Hollywood Cameramen* (1970)

1934 [film-going tastes]
The most popular cinema actress now or ever, hitherto, in China is Janet Gaynor ... If Miss Gaynor were to come to China now, she would have a more queenly reception than would be given to any other woman of the western world ...

Perhaps, of all western screen celebrities, the one with fewest admirers in China is that distinguished actor George Arliss, who fails to draw a good audience even in the Crown Colony of Hongkong ...
—Wilbur Burton, "Chinese Reactions to the Cinema," *Asia* (New York), October 1934.

1934 [a Japanese ritual in occupied Shanghai]
With a solemn countenance the highest personage present proceeds to the sacrifice. . . . He has assumed this air of solemnity because he is thinking of his poor
soldiers who have fallen and because his face is almost touching the movie
camera. Have we forgotten to mention that the films are taking part in the funeral rites, having arrived opportunely on a lorry? Buddha plus military movies.

In face of the camera the lines of sorrow on this face deepen. Sorrow must make
an effective picture. . . . .
—Egon Erwin Kisch, *Secret China*, translated by Michael Davidson (London: John
Lane The Bodley Head, 1935), p. 42.

1935 [on forbidden subjects in Chinese films]
As in all other forms of creative work, the moving picture companies are unable
to find material for dramatic purposes, because all reference to poverty, youth
disaffection, rural conditions, or to any of the vital social problems of the day, is
forbidden. . . .
—Nym Wales [Helen Snow] , *Notes on the Left-Wing Painters and Modern Art in
China*.

1939 [a footnote on the taking of Nanking]
The German colleagues . . . included one prominent businessman, Herr John
Rabe, manager of the Siemens Company, who took moving pictures of Japanese
soldiers bayoneting prisoners and raping women. When he returned to Germany
with his films, he was immediately arrested and is still [1939] in a concentration
camp.
—Haldore Hanson, *Humane Endeavour* (New York: Toronto: Farrar and Rinehart, 1939), p. 142n.

1949 ["KMT Dumps Japanese Films"]
The controlling group of the KMT film-enterprise headed by KMT's ex-minister
of information Chang Tao-fan, have been attempting to dump into the interior,
the Pacific islands and foreign countries 150 films produced during the Japanese
occupation by the Japanese and the puppets. It is reported that 11 pictures have
already been sold to Philippine film merchants for $1,000 (US) each.

After the Japanese surrender, over 150 pictures were left by the Chinese United
Film Production Co., Ltd. which was established and run jointly by the Japanese, their puppet government and the film merchants. . . . Being produced under
the regime of the Japanese aggressor, it was natural that they were mainly propaganda for Japanese "New Order." The pictures were then taken over by the

KMT "Central Adjustment Committee for Film Enterprise," of which Lo Hsueh-lien and Chow Ke were chiefly responsible. These pictures were banned by exactly the same group which to-day is trying to dump them on distant markets.

The KMT group planned to change the titles of the pictures in order to avoid public attention. . . . They did not dare to sell the pictures openly but pretended to have sealed them up. However, in the meantime, they have secretly transported the poisonous pictures to the remote inland cities and the Pacific islands to make money. The ill-gotten gains have made broker Chow Ke a rich man.
— *China Digest* (Hong Kong), 5 April 1949, pp. 17–18.

1949 [a letter from the American wife of a Tientsin engineer]
I expected that American books and magazines would probably be banned and that surely no more American movies would be shown. . . . Our pre-liberation fears have not materialized and there's no change in our way of living so far.

American movies are still being shown, I saw Frank Sinatra and Jimmie Durante in *It Happened in Brooklyn* last week. Two rows of *Pa Lu* [Eighth Route] soldiers sat in front of us and enjoyed Jimmie Durante enormously. . . .
— Grace D. Liu's letter of 22 April 1949 to *The Saturday Evening Post.*

1951 [on film use]
When people were at first frightened of the rather painful anti-bubonic plague injections, short documentary films were shown in every cinema in the plague-affected areas, showing in a very realistic way how the disease originated, how the germs were carried by flea-bearing rats, the horrible effects and death agonies of the victims. The villagers were soon lining up for treatment and co-operating in the rat hunts.
—Wilfred G. Burchett, *China's Feet Unbound* (Melbourne: World Unity Publications, 1952), p. 311.

1951 [diary of 2 April 1951, Peking]
This [movie] was about Pearl River villagers in Kwangtung, a passionate story of revolt against unendurable village conditions, of flight to the city, and again extortion and persecution there. The typical three-way alliance of the city gangster, the KMT and the village landlord, is made brilliantly clear, as is the utter corruption of this group, despite the polite conversation, elegant manners, westernised habits and snappy clothes. The villagers learn that simplicity and honesty alone will not arm them against these heartless marauders. They become enlightened revolutionaries and learn how to fight and finally overthrow the despoilers of their livelihood.
—Rewi Alley, *Yo Banfa* (Shanghai, China Monthly Review, 1952), p. 36.

1953 [correcting some misconceptions]
In a social system which shows a very strong sense of purpose and direction,
people do not find the same need to escape, and the newspapers can use their
space for more constructive and creative purposes. The same is true of films. To
the outsider they may look dull and monotonous, but to the person committed
to that purpose they are full of valuable information on the principle and
method, which is just what he wants.
—E. R. Lapwood, "Some Misconceptions about New China," *China Monthly
Review* (Shanghai), May 1953, p. 41.

1954 [the spy film]
The spy, the saboteur, the counter-revolutionary agent: these were named objects of their fear. . . . This deliberate use of fear — the strongest mass emotion
and the cheapest to produce — as a sanction for extreme disciplinary actions is a
refinement of dictatorship.
—George Stafford Gale, *No Flies in China* (London: Allen and Unwin, 1955),
pp. 148, 165.

1957 [the hundred flowers]
[During the open criticism at the "Political College" in Shanghai] The first person to speak was a well-known mainland film star who said that the pictures she
had made since the Liberation were not at all popular with the public. She criticized the work of Party members in her sphere and supported her arguments
with the Marxist theories we had learned. I said very little, myself, because I had
been warned by a friend to be careful. . . . .
—*Out of China*, Francis Harper, ed. (Hong Kong: Dragonfly Books, 1964), p. 197.

1960 [an interview with Shih Wei, a film-actress]
. . . she said that an actor should not have too strong a personality.

"It is easier for the masses to identify themselves with a plain ordinary type. The
actor as a person should not attract too much attention. Individual performances
must not over-shadow the message of the film. . . ."
—Karl Eskelund, *The Red Mandarins* (New York: Taplinger Pub. Co., 1961),
Chap. V. Teacher of Virtue.

1965 [a staged newsreel]
Two Chinese students who took part in the protests outside the U.S. Embassy
[in Moscow] on March 4 and were treated as stretcher cases on their return to
Peking on March 14, had walked unaided on and off the plane at Omsk and
Irkutsk, Pravda reported today.

After the Embassy demonstration they had created scenes at a Moscow hospital, demanding treatment for "injuries" of which Soviet doctors could find no trace. . . .

Air steward Nikolai Kalganov, who served them with wine and vodka on the two-hour stage to Peking from Irkutsk, said the Soviet crew could not believe their eyes when Chinese [hospital] orderlies entered the plane and laid two "healthy lads" on stretchers.

Then, in front of newsreel cameras, the ambulances taking the students drove slowly past a 2,000-strong airport crowd from which anti-Soviet slogans were shouted.
—*Daily Worker* (London) correspondent, 22 March 1965.

1965 [an interpretation]
At Changchun they . . . showed me a new movie, in the style of local opera, which demonstrated the new priorities for women, at the same time seeming to reveal the unconscious tensions that result from sexual repression. Its subject was a young peasant girl, jealous of her brother since he was in the militia and had a rifle. Seizing his rifle, she first caressed it and then hugging it to her breast, did a dance. When her brother snatched it away, she did another dance with an equally symbolic broom handle, aiming it at apples on a tree, and singing that she was shooting at the head of Chiang Kai-shek. Any psychoanalyst would have been intrigued, but the Chinese movie makers, concerned only with the political moral, seemed unaware of any deeper implications.
—Charles Taylor, *Reporter in Red China* (New York: Random House, 1966), pp. 93—94.

1966 [an audience in June]
Now a dingy cinema, packed — this I wanted. The film [possibly *Stranger in Icy Mountains*, 1963] tells, in basic terms and technique, of good and bad people in pretty costumes of Sinkiang; of old regime plotters frustrated by a heroic Party Delegate; of a persecuted, nearly-dishonored girl-runaway who returns, a doctor, and finds her Commissar the victor. The audience is the noisiest, and they seem to laugh at the stilted gravity of the love scenes.
—Feliks Topolski, *Holy China* (London: Hutchinson, 1968).

1966 [hard to believe]
Napoleon seems to have exerted a strange fascination upon the Chinese leaders of modern times. . . . As for Mao Tse-tung's own admiration for "Na Po-liu," it seemed to be confirmed shortly before I left China, when it was announced that

French film producer Abel Gance was coming to Peking at the personal invitation of Chairman Mao. . . . Later, I heard, but this was not officially stated, that Abel Gance had been commissioned to do a film about Mao Tse-tung's life.
—Jacques Marcuse, *The Peking Papers* (New York: Dutton, 1967), p. 289.

1967 [a criticized film]
Two Families cooked up the story of an old poor peasant who after land reform managed to make a decent living as an individual farmer but went bankrupt as a result of the farm co-operative movement. In order to prepare public opinion for a capitalist come-back, it purposely misrepresented developments in China's countryside, vilified the co-operative movement and by insinuation attacked the rural people's communes.
—*Peking Review*, 1 September 1967.

1971 [two open minds]
The Chinese government has invited Rossellini to interview Chairman Mao Tse-tung and he hopes to go to China early in 1972. Regarding the projected interview Rossellini says, "I have no preconceptions; I go with an open mind."
—Introduction to "Roberto Rossellini," *Cinema* (Beverly Hills), Fall 1971, p. 14.

1971 [a review of *The Twelve Gold Medallions*, produced at the Shaw Brothers Studio, Hong Kong]
The Chinese warrior epic is as ritualized a film form as the American western and the plot almost invariably contains these non-referent intangibles as elements: national destiny, family unity, devotion to duty, self-honor, singleness of purpose, reverence [to] elders, and loyalty of classmates. Loyalty to classmates is especially big.

It is a shock to occidental viewers unschooled in Zen and mysticism suddenly to have actors levitate, fly, or catapult through the ceiling without apparent plot foundation. Characters can also split trees with their bare hands, stop waterfalls with a powerful stare, and cause instant death with a tap on the chest. (One such tap in "Medallions" left a bloody handprint on the wall behind where the character was standing.) Nevertheless one adjusts quickly.

The tempo of warrior epics is much faster than one is accustomed to in a Western action film. Shots used to denote the passing of time, such as a sunset, are held for no more than two or three seconds. Time passes very quickly, therefore, and there is little subplot romance present to encumber the forward movement. A quick trip to the john and you miss a whole massacre.

Warrior epics are technically quite competent. Special effects are elaborate and would be prohibitively expensive today in a Hollywood feature. . . . Cheng Kang,

director of "Medallions," makes frequent use of a "Zen zoom" shot in battle
sequences which is very effective.

The Shaw Brothers makeup department must buy Eastmancolor blood in the
handy 100-gallon vat: actors are shish kebabed with astonishing frequency.
Women's lib activists will be pleased to note that women warriors (there are
always women warriors) get equal treatment and are skewered as often and as
hideously as the gents. One luckless lady in "Medallions" gets strung up in a tree
and porcupined by arrows.

The audiences, predominantly Chinese, talk just as loudly through the feature as
do other New York audiences. Coming attractions at the Sun Sing are: "The
Invincible Fist," "Double Bliss" (an "LSD musical"), and "The Iron Buddha."
—Tom Costner, "One Wonton, Two Eggdrop," in *The Village Voice*, 15 April
1971.

1971 [film problems in Taiwan]
Each year thousands of filmgoers in Southeast Asia crowd cinemas to see Taiwan-
made motion pictures. But few realise how much of the original footage of each
film they miss. That footage ends up on the cutting room floor not because of
the director's discretion but at the insistence of the censor. The Nationalist
government controls films carefully because, since it considers itself still at war
with the mainland, even movie-making must be bent to the ultimate purpose of
defeating the communists and retaking the mainland.

This has created one of the world's most complex censorship systems. The
government — directly or indirectly — owns three of Taiwan's biggest film companies. The Kuomintang runs the most prolific company, the Central Motion
Picture Corporation. China Film Studio is affiliated with the defence ministry's
general political warfare department. And Taiwan Film Studio belongs to the
provincial government. The output of private companies pales in comparison.

Two years ago the government added another safeguard, the Cultural Bureau, a
branch of the education ministry. The bureau's film section screens locally-
produced films first in script stage, then again before distribution. Bureau policy,
in the words of Director Paul Wong, is that "there can never be enough censorship." This, coupled with box office commercial considerations, makes it clear
why Taiwan films rarely reach international standards.

Today, however, changes are in the air: a new generation of film makers is
emerging, the foremost of whom is Mou Tun-pei who produced his first film two
years ago at 27. Film makers such as Mou are aware of the numerous problems
inherent in making films here. But unlike the older and more seasoned film
directors, they are less easily discouraged; they are unimpressed by the "star"

system or the prestige of big film companies. They are willing to stand alone if necessary to ensure their products' integrity. Mou's first film is "I Didn't Dare Tell You" – "Pu Kan Ken Ni Chiang" — a simple story of misunderstanding between a widower and his 10-year-old son. Its basis is people's inability to communicate . . . from the boy and his father to the boy's schoolteacher and her fiance. The black and white film was financed privately by a group of retired navy men, all mainland-born. Mou kept costs under US$10,000 by using himself and other non-professionals as actors – something new for this part of the world.

At its 1969 preview, critics compared the photography and lighting to that of Ingmar Bergman; they compared Mou's sensitive portrayal of the son to DiSica's work. The younger members of the Cultural Bureau began to exert pressure to have the film voted best of the year for 1970.

Even film company owners who had not seen the preview became interested. Some who attended private showings received the film warmly. But the fanfare was shortlived. Older members of the bureau said certain changes would have to be made before the film could be distributed.

Then the unexpected happened: Mou was given a permit, but no local cinema owner would distribute the film. Although many agreed it was good, they argued it was an "art" film. A trial run in the provincial city of Changhua was arranged. It confirmed expectations: audiences were small. The film could not compete with the colourful, glossy swordplay pictures and musical comedies.

Another blow came when the film was refused an export permit on the ground that it showed too much poverty and would create the wrong impression abroad. Mou left the island to investigate an offer from Hongkong's Cathay organisation. It seemed Taiwan had lost a promising young director; one man who was not surprised was veteran director Pai Chingjui, Mou's former teacher. Trained in Italy, Pai returned to Taiwan in the mid-Sixties and has made several films since then. Financially successful Pai nonetheless is artistically discouraged. "The Chinese want stars, glamour, melodrama," said Pai. "This is the way it is. So I decided I would try to make each of my films a little more sophisticated. But it doesn't work. Now I'm famous. I make money. But I'm still not satisfied. I don't make enough money to make my own films and big producers won't back the kind of films I want to make."

Pai's films could be called "Chinese Hollywood" — melodrama or comedy. All but one have been financial successes. Pai considers his single flop — "Goodbye, Darling" — his first success in non-commercial film-making.

When Mou returned to Taiwan from Hongkong early in 1970, it seemed he would follow in Pai's footsteps; he signed a contract with a local film company to produce "The Fallen Woman." But he produced the film under his daughter's name, playing down his involvement. He was waiting for a chance to produce a privately-backed film.

Over a year after his return Mou got that opportunity. A group of young intellectuals — US-educated offspring of Kuomintang members, far more progressive than their parents — saw Mou's first movie. They decided to put up the money for another Mou film, and by April the young director was hard at work. Now "The End of the Runway" — "P'au Tao Chung Tien" is almost finished.

It is too soon to predict whether Mou will be able to create a good film which still appeals to a relatively unsophisticated audience. One thing is certain: he is one of the few in Taiwan today with the talent — and enough knowledge of the local motion picture bureaucracy — to do it.
—April Klimley, "Can Art Conquer Audiences?" *Far Eastern Economic Review,* 25 September 1971, p. 34.

A group of relevant documents that should not be overlooked, by John H. Weakland:

An analysis of seven Cantonese films. In M. Mead and R. Metraux (eds.), *The Study of Culture at a Distance* (Chicago: University of Chicago Press, 1953).

Themes in Chinese Communist Films, *American Anthropologist,* April 1966.
Chinese Film Images of Invasion and Resistance, *The China Quarterly,* July—September 1971.
Conflicts Between Love and Family Relationships in Chinese Films, available from Group Psychological Branch, Office of Naval Research.

Sources

Epigraphs on title-page

André Malraux, *La condition humaine,* translated by Alastair Macdonald as *Man's Estate* (London: Penguin Books, 1968).

P'u Sung-ling, a story entitled by the translator, Herbert A. Giles, "Joining the Immortals," *Strange Stories from a Chinese Studio* (Shanghai: Kelly and Walsh, 1916), p. 36.

Sources for Chapter 1 — Preliminaries 1896—1911

Epigraph: quoted in A. C. Scott, *Mei Lan-fang: Leader of the Pear Garden* (Hong Kong: Hong Kong University Press, 1959), p. 59.

1.　Translated advertisements in *Shen Bao,* 10 and 14 August 1896; quoted by Cheng Chi-hua, *History of the Development of Chinese Cinema* (Peking, 1963), vol. 1, p. 8.

2.　Georges Sadoul, *Louis Lumière* (Paris: Seghers, 1964).

3.　Translated from advertisement in *Shen Bao,* 27 July 1897; quoted by Cheng, *Chinese Cinema,* vol. 1, p. 8. The identification of James Ricalton is by Norman R. Speiden, Curator of the Edison National Historic Site.

4.　Translated from *Yo-shi Bao,* 5 September 1897; quoted by Cheng, *Chinese Cinema,* vol. 1, pp. 8—9.

5.　Chang Pei-hai, "Motion Pictures," in *Chinese Year Book* (Shanghai, 1937), p. 1111.

6.　[Tung Chi-ming] , *An Outline History of China* (Peking: Foreign Languages Press, 1958), pp. 267—269. This was the "orthodox" account of the Boxers in 1958; it soon became unthinkable to link the Boxers with the Dowager Empress.

7.　*National Film Archive Catalogue,* Part II: Silent Non-Fiction Films 1895—1934 (catalogued by David Grenfell, London 1960), p. 25.

8.　*Catalogue of the Charles Urban Trading Co., Ltd.* (London, November 1903) quoting Williamson catalogues of January 1901 and September 1902.

9.　William Basil Courtney, "History of Vitagraph" [chap. 7] , *Motion Picture News,* 21 March 1925, p. 1221.

10.　"Much travelled cinematographer," *Moving Picture World* (New York), 8 May 1909, p. 591.

11.　*National Film Archive Catalogue,* Part I: Silent News Films 1895—1933 (compiled by Joan Fulford and Diana Waller, London 1951).

12.　Mutoscope copyrights in *Motion Pictures, 1894—1912* (Washington, D.C.: Library of Congress, 1953).

13. Oscar B. Depue, "My First Fifty Years in Motion Pictures," *Journal of the Society of Motion Picture Engineers*, December 1947; reprinted in Raymond Fielding, *A Technological History of Motion Pictures and Television* (Berkeley: University of California Press, 1967), p. 61. The earliest footage shown in the January 1967 television program, *China: The Roots of Madness*, may be Depue's.

14. Listed in Cheng, *Chinese Cinema*, vol. 1, p. 636.

15. Translated from Hsiao [pseud.], "Development of Film Business in Peking," *Film Weekly* (Peking), 1 November 1921; quoted by Cheng, *Chinese Cinema*, vol. 1, p. 10. J. R. Kaim, "Chinese Films," *China Journal* (Shanghai), August 1939.

16. *Chicago Daily News*, 16 September 1914; Holmes' Hong Kong conversation took place in the summer of 1913.

17. Translated regulations as quoted by Cheng, *Chinese Cinema*, vol. 1, p. 11.

18. *Outline History of China,* p. 278.

19. Translated from Mei Lan-fang, *Forty Years on the Stage* (Peking: 1954), vol. 2.

20. Preface to "Call to Arms," in *Selected Works of Lu Hsun*, trans. Yang Hsien-yi and Gladys Yang (Peking: Foreign Languages Press, 1956), vol. 1.

Sources for Chapter 2 – In the Treaty Ports 1912–1927

Epigraphs: William Plomer, *Turbott Wolfe* (London: Hogarth Press, 1925 and 1965); *Motion Picture News*, 4 August 1923, p. 521 (see page 25).

1. Translated from *Lichtbild Bühne* (Berlin), 1914, Nr. 5 (31 January), p. 70.

2. Translated from Chang Shih-chuan, "My Experience as a Film Director," *Min Hsing Fortnightly*, 16 May 1933; quoted by Cheng Chi-hua, *History of the Development of Chinese Cinema* (Peking, 1963), vol. 1, p. 17.

3. Listed in Cheng, *Chinese Cinema*, vol. 1, pp. 520–521.

4. Synopsis translated from Cheng, *Chinese Cinema*, vol. 1, pp. 24–25.

5. Mei Lan-fang, *The Filming of a Tradition*, translated in *Eastern Horizon*, July 1965 (the final paragraph does not appear in the English translation).

6. "Plan Special Pictures for Orient," *Moving Picture World* (New York), 8 March 1919, p. 1324.

7. Mei Lan-fang, *Filming of a Tradition* (last two sentences omitted in published translation).

8. Synopsis from "China Takes to the Motion Picture," *The Chinese Economic Monthly* (Shanghai), August 1924 (reprinted in *China Weekly Review* (Shanghai), 13 September 1924)); the illustrations to the article are from this film.

9. [Giuliano Bertuccioli] , article on Chinese cinema in *Enciclopedia dello spettacolo* (Rome, 1956), vol. 3.

10. Joseph Needham, "The Past in China's Present," *Cambridge Opinion 26: China* (1962); also in *Arts and Sciences in China* (London), April-June 1963, p. 5.

11. William J. Reilly, "China Kicks in With a Champion [F. Marshall Sanderson] ," *Moving Picture World* (New York), 26 April 1919, pp. 499–500.

12. A. C. Scott, *Literature and the Arts in Twentieth Century China* (London: Allen and Unwin, 1965), p. 87.

13. *Motion Picture News*, 4 August 1923, p. 521.

14. "Europeans in China Patronize Pictures in Modern British-Controlled Theaters," *Moving Picture World* (New York), 14 August 1920, p. 923.

15. "Talks of Conditions in the Orient" [interview with J. W. Allen] , *Moving Picture World* (New York), 1 February 1919, p. 631.

16. C. J. North, *The Chinese Motion Picture Market* (Washington, D.C.: 1927), Trade Information Bulletin No. 467, United States Department of Commerce, p. 1.

17. *Ibid.*, pp. 32–33.

18. Major S. P. Rudinger de Rodyen Ko, "American Pictures Are Unjust to China, Which Is Potentially Great Film Market," *Moving Picture World* (New York), 21 May 1921, pp. 263–264.

19. Valentia Steer, *The Romance of the Cinema* (London: C. Arthur Pearson, 1913), p. 61.

20. Joseph L. Anderson and Donald Richie, *The Japanese Film* (Rutland, Vt.: Charles E. Tuttle, 1959; New York: Grove Press, Evergreen, 1960), p. 151.

21. *Illustrierte Film Woche* (Berlin), 1920. Nr. 43.

22. *Moving Picture World* (New York), 22 March 1919, p. 1643.

23. Translated from *Lichtbild Bühne* (Berlin), 1921, Nr. 2, p. 30.

24. Major S. P. Rudinger de Rodyen Ko, "American Pictures Are Unjust to China."

25. *Moving Picture World* (New York), 14 May 1921, p. 189.

26. Richard Griffith and Arthur Mayer, *The Movies* (New York: Simon and Schuster, 1957), p. 109.

27. Translated from A. J. W. Harloff, in *Le Monde Nouveau* (Paris), année 14, no. 2, 1934.

28. Sir Hesketh Bell, *Foreign Colonial Administration in the Far East* (London: E. Arnold, 1928), pp. 121–123.

29. Translated from M. Legendre, *L'Asie contre l'Europe* (Paris, 1933), pp. 288–289.

30. *Moving Picture World* (New York), 17 May 1924, p. 273.

31. Report by Lynn W. Meekins, *Moving Picture World* (New York), 13 May 1922, p. 150.

32. *Moving Picture World* (New York), 11 February 1922, p. 625.

33. Synopsis translated from Cheng, *Chinese Cinema*, vol. 1, p. 60.

34. *The Chinese Economic Monthly* (Shanghai), August 1924.

35. Henry McAleavy, *A Dream of Tartary: The Origins and Misfortunes of Henry P'u Yi* (London: Allen and Unwin, 1963), p. 133.

36. "Far East Exhibitors Are Having Troubles" interview with Kenneth McGaffey, *Motion Picture News*, 2 September 1922, p. 1125.

37. [Interview with H. W. Ray] *Moving Picture World* (New York), 16 August 1924, p. 558.

38. Translated from the list of Min Hsin newsreels in Cheng, *Chinese Cinema*, vol. 1, pp. 640—641.

39. Ouyang Yu-chien, *In the Midst of Life Comes the Vocation of Cinema* (Peking, 1962), pp. 1—2.

40. W. H. Jansen, "Eight Years Pioneering in China," *American Cinematographer* (Hollywood), February 1931, p. 11.

41. *Kinematograph Weekly* (London) 28 January 1926, and information from W. Slade Bungey, June 1966.

42. "Movies Big Aid in Chinese Unity," *New York World*, 1927 (undated clipping in files of Museum of Modern Art, New York).

43. Synopsis translated from Cheng, *Chinese Cinema*, vol. 1, pp. 92—93.

44. Translated from Hou Yao, "The Sadness of Farewells," in *Spirit of Peace*, 25 September 1926; quoted by Cheng, *Chinese Cinema*, vol. 1.

45. Synopsis translated from Cheng, *Chinese Cinema*, vol. 1, p. 100.

46. Translated from *Cinema Annals*, No. 11 (10 May 1925); quoted by Cheng, *Chinese Cinema*, vol. 1, p. 124.

47. Translated from Hung Shen, "Introduction to Modern Drama," dated 23 April 1935; quoted by Cheng, *Chinese Cinema*, vol. 1, p. 72.

48. Translated from Ouyang, *In the Midst of Life.*

49. Translated from Yang Hsiao-tsun, in *Talk of the Past* (Peking, 1962), pp. 14—15.

50. Synopses translated from Cheng, *Chinese Cinema*, vol. 1, pp. 76—77.

51. *Exhibitors Herald* (Chicago), 27 November 1926, p. 25.

52. *Exhibitors Herald* (Chicago), 2 April 1927.

53. This newsreel is preserved at the National Film Archive, London.

54. Translated from T'ien Han, "Memoirs of My Career in Films," *Zhungguo Dianying* (Peking), June 1958.

55. Felix Greene, *The Wall Has Two Sides* (London: Jonathan Cape, 1962).

56. *American Cinematographer* (Hollywood), August 1931, p. 27.

57. T'ien Han, "Memoirs of My Career in Films."

58. The scenario outlines by Sergei Tretyakov for *Zhung-guo* are preserved with the Eisenstein archive at the Central State Archive of Literature and Art, Moscow, to which institution I am grateful for photostats of all relevant documents; the only published reference by Eisenstein to this project is in his interview with Joseph Freeman, in *An American Testament* (New York: Farrar and Rinehart, 1938); see also Tretyakov, "China on the Screen," *Sovietskoye Kino* (Moscow), No. 5–6, 1927. The unpublished draft scenario of *Zhung-guo* should not be confused with a published work by Tretyakov, also entitled *Zhung-guo* (Moscow, 1927), a factual account of his stay in China.

Sources for Chapter 3 – Above and Under Ground 1928–1937

1. Robert Aura Smith, "Film Fate in China Hangs on Winning Interior," *Exhibitors Herald-World* (Chicago), 19 July 1930, p. 25.

2. Translated from *Jahrbuch der Filmindustrie*, ed. Karl Wolffsohn (Berlin, 1930), p. 625.

3. Translated from Lu Hsun's collection of essays, *Two Hearts* (Shanghai, 1932).

4. Statistics from Cheng Chi-hua, *History of the Development of Chinese Cinema* (Peking, 1963), vol. 1, p. 133.

5. *China Reconstructs* (Peking), April 1962; original Chinese text (in *Talk of the Past*, 1962) is more detailed.

6. Information on the first Chinese sound-films chiefly from Hsu Bi-ho, "The Beginnings of the Chinese Sound Film," in *Talk of the Past* (Peking, 1962).

7. Synopsis from A. C. Scott, *Literature and the Arts in Twentieth Century China* (London: Allen and Unwin, 1965), p. 68.

8. Synopsis translated from Cheng, *Chinese Cinema*, vol. 1, p. 150.

9. Synopses of the two German films translated from *Illustrierte Film Woche* (Berlin), No. 40, 1927; No. 24, 1928.

10. *The China Critic* (Shanghai), 6 March 1930.

11. Translated from Freddy Chevalley, *Close Up* (Territet), March 1929, p. 87; another review of *La Rose* appears in *Cinéopse*.

12. Emily Hahn, *China Only Yesterday* (Garden City, N.Y.: Doubleday, 1963), p. 296.

13. Translated from Alessandro Sardi, *Scenario* (Rome), April 1932, pp. 44–47.

14. Translated from Hsia Yen, "In Memory of Ch'u Chiu-pei," *Wen Yi Bao* (Peking), No. 12, 1955.

15. Translated from Cheng, *Chinese Cinema*, vol. 1, p. 185.

16. *International Literature* (Moscow), 1933, No. 3, p. 159.

17. Wang Pin-chi's review of Cheng Chi-hua's history, in *Chinese Literature* (Peking), No. 6, 1963.

18. T'ien Han, "The Composer Nieh Erh," *Chinese Literature* (Peking), No. 11, 1959; other details from Chang Wen-kang, "Two Pioneer Composers," *China Reconstructs* (Peking), December 1955.

19. Translated from Li Chi-ye, "Lu Hsun and Youth," in *Remember Mr. Lu Hsun* (Shanghai, October 1956), p. 26.

20. Translated from Lu Hsun's last collection of essays, *Pseudo-Frivolous Talk* ("Lessons from Films"), Shanghai, 1934.

21. Hsia Yen's reportage and postscript in *Chinese Literature* (Peking), No. 8, 1960.

22. Synopsis and censor's document translated from Cheng, *Chinese Cinema*, vol. 1, pp. 217—219.

23. Ida Treat, "China Makes Its Own Movies," *Travel* (New York), June 1936.

24. On the censorship of *Welcome Danger*, see also "China wert sich gegen Verunglimpfung im Film," in *Lichtbild Bühne* (Berlin), 31 May 1930.

25. Synopses in Cheng, *Chinese Cinema*, vol. 1, pp. 222—225.

26. "Fate" (1933), in *Pseudo-Frivolous Talk*.

27. Translated from vol. 4 of the works of Hung Shen (Peking, 1963).

28. Document translated from Cheng, *Chinese Cinema*, vol. 1, pp. 292—293, 296—297.

29. Bela Balázs, "Der Film such seinen Stoff," *"Die Abenteuer eines Zehnmark-scheins"*; quoted by Siegfried Kracauer, *From Caligari to Hitler: A Psychological History of the German Film* (Princeton, N.J.: Princeton University Press, 1966), p. 181.

30. Translated from Hsia Yen, "History of Chinese Films and Party Leadership," *Zhungguo Dianying* (Peking) No. 11—12, November-December 1967.

31. Freely translated from synopsis in Cheng, *Chinese Cinema*, vol. 1, pp. 334—335.

32. Translated from Sun Yu, "Recalling the Making of Big Road," *Dianying Yishu* (Peking), No. 5, 1960.

33. *Selected Works of Lu Hsun*, translated by Yang Hsien-yi and Gladys Yang (Peking: Foreign Languages Press, 1960), vol. 4.

34. Mei Lan-fang, *The Filming of a Tradition*, translated in *Eastern Horizon*, July, 1965.

35. Chen Lee's review of Cheng Chi-hua's history, in *Arts and Sciences in China* (London), No. 4, October-December 1963.

36. Translated from Chen Hsian-hsing, in *Talk of the Past* (Peking, 1962), pp. 98–99.

37. Translated from Ouyang Yu-chien, *In the Midst of Life Comes the Vocation of Cinema* (Peking, 1962), p. 20.

38. C. P. Fitzgerald, *The Birth of Communist China* (London: Harmondsworth, 1964), p. 81.

39. Translated from Pierre Lasserre, *Pour Vous*, 1 March 1934; quoted in Lapierre, *Les cent visages du cinéma* (Paris, 1948).

40. *Chinese Year Book* (Shanghai, 1937).

41. Translated from Ouyang, *In the Midst of Life,* p. 30.

42. Yao Hsing-nung, "Chinese Movies," *T'ien Hsia Monthly* (Shanghai), April 1937.

43. Synopsis in Cheng, *Chinese Cinema*, vol. 1, p. 495; after her success in *Crossroads*, Pai Yang refused leading role in *Miss Change-Body.*

44. News story from Chinese Central News Agency, 24 April 1937, on the eve of *The Good Earth's* Shanghai release; reprinted in Dorothy B. Jones, *The Portrayal of China and India on the American Screen*, 1896–1955 (Cambridge, Mass.; Massachusetts Institute of Technology, Center for International Studies, Communications Program, 1955), pp. 44–45.

45. Charles G. Clarke, "China Photographically Ideal," *American Cinematographer* (Hollywood), September 1934.

46. Bosley Crowther, *The Lion's Share* (New York: E. P. Dutton, 1957), pp. 234–235.

47. Ibid., p. 235.

48. Jones, *Portrayal of China*, p. 47.

49. *Ibid.*, p. 40.

50. This and following citations are from an unpublished diary kept by Joris Ivens during the filming of *The Four Hundred Million.* Sections of this diary can now be found in the autobiography of Joris Ivens, *The Camera and I* (Berlin: Seven Seas; and New York: International Publishers, 1969), pp. 141–179.

Sources for Chapter 4 — War: The Film Industry Moves Up River 1938–1945

Epigraph: Lao Shê's preface to his novel, *Cremation* (1944); translated in *A History of Modern Chinese Fiction*, by C. T. Hsia (New Haven, Conn.: Yale University Press, 1961), p. 367.

1.   These details of the "Doomed Battalion" are in W. H. Auden and Christopher Isherwood, *Journey to a War* (London: Faber and Faber, 1939), pp. 242–243.

2.   [Tung Chi-ming], *An Outline History of China* (Peking: Foreign Languages Press, 1958), p. 386. A more credible but no less vivid account of this battle was translated in *Chinese Literature* (Peking), No. 11, 1965, pp. 75—88; credit for the battle's strategy is variously awarded to Ho Lung and Lin Piao.

3.   Robert Payne, *Chungking Diary* (London: Hatchards, 1945), p. 201, entry for 19 May 1942.

4.   Ivens, *The Camera and I* (Berlin: Seven Seas; New York: International Publishers, 1969).

5.   Auden and Isherwood, *Journey to a War*, pp. 166- 167.

6.   Harrison Forman, "China Films Its Struggle," in *The Star Weekly* (Toronto), 19 September 1942, p. 7.

7.   Agnes Smedley, *China Fights Back* (New York: Vanguard Press, 1938).

8.   Violet Cressy-Marcks (Fisher), *Journey Into China* (London: Hodder and Stoughton, 1940), pp. 82—83.

9.   Tu Heng, "Cinema Chronicle," *T'ien Hsia Monthly*, vol. 9, no. 4 (November 1939).

10. Synopsis translated from Cheng Chi-hua, *History of the Development of Chinese Cinema* (Peking, 1963), vol. 2, p. 49.

11. Chinese translation and film were based on the U.S. edition of 1938, *Secret Agent of Japan*, by Amleto Vespa (Boston: Little, Brown).

12. Theodore H. White and Annalee W. Jacoby, *Thunder Out of China* (New York: William Sloane Associates, 1946), p. 127.

13. Synopsis and the history of the Northwest Film Company translated from Cheng, *Chinese Cinema*, vol. 2, pp. 66—71.

14. Yao Hsing-nung, "Chinese Movies," *T'ien Hsia Monthly* (Shanghai), April 1937.

15. Synopsis from A. C. Scott, *Literature and the Arts in Twentieth Century China* (London: Allen and Unwin, 1965), p. 75.

16. Synopsis translated from Cheng, *Chinese Cinema*, vol. 2, pp. 130—131.

17. Auden and Isherwood, *Journey to a War*, p. 184; the sonnet (XVI), quoted below, is on p. 274; the lines here are as later revised by Auden.

Sources for Chapter 5 – Fictions and Realities 1932—1945

Epigraph: Ilya Ehrenburg, *Men, Years-Life:* vol. 3, *Truce: 1921—1933*, translated by Tatiana Shebunina and Yvonne Kapp (London, 1963), p. 130.

1. Changchun

1.   Henry McAleavy, *A Dream of Tartary: The Origins of Henry P'u Yi* (London: Allen and Unwin, 1963), p. 199; see also Muto Tomo, *The Career of Amakasu Masahiko* (Tokyo, 1956).

2.   McAleavy, *A Dream of Tartary* pp. 216–217.

3.   *Ibid.*, p. 224.

4.   Joseph L. Anderson and Donald Richie, *The Japanese Film* (Rutland, Vt.: Charles E. Tuttle, 1959; New York: Grove Press, Evergreen, 1960), p. 152.

5.   *Ibid.*, pp. 151–152.

6.   *Ibid.*, p. 152; see also *Manchuria*, 20 July 1939 (Special Number: Motion Pictures in Manchoukuo): contains a detailed historical sketch by Liu Wenghua, with photos and full synopses of twelve films produced in Manchoukuo; also a complete scenario ("now being produced"), *Good Mother.*

7.   *Ibid.*, p. 154.

8.   McAleavy, *A Dream of Tartary,* p. 259.

2. Peking

9.   Anderson and Richie, *Japanese Film*, p. 153.

10. McAleavy, *A Dream of Tartary,* pp. 244–245.

3. Shanghai

11. Cheng Chi-hua to JL, 17 July 1963.

12. Translated from Ouyang Yu-Chien, *In the Midst of Life Comes the Vocation of Cinema* (Peking, 1962), pp. 38–39.

13. J. R. Kaim, "Chinese Films," *China Journal* (Shanghai), August 1939, p. 74.

14. Anderson and Richie, *Japanese Film*, p. 154.

15. *Ibid.*

16. Translated from Georges Sadoul, *Le Cinéma Français* (Paris, 1962), p. 90.

4. Yenan

17. See discussion of Lenin's position, in Allen S. Whiting, *Soviet Policies in China, 1917–1924* (New York: Columbia University Press, 1954).

18. Harrison Forman, *Report from Red China* (New York: Henry Holt, 1946).

19. Karmen's published diary, *Year in China* (Moscow, 1941); an English translation of excerpts from Karmen's book can be found in *International Literature*, No. 3, 1941.

20. Listed in Cheng Chi-hua, *History of the Development of Chinese Cinema* (Peking, 1963), vol. 2, pp. 497–498.

21. T. A. Hsia, "Twenty Years After the Yenan Forum," *China Quarterly* (London), January–March 1963.

22. This and the following quotations are from "Talks at the Yenan Forum on Art and Literature," in *Mao Tse-tung on Art and Literature* (Peking, 1960); this anonymous translation of the "Talks" first appeared in February 1956.

23. Forman, *Report from Red China*, pp. 88—89.

24. Edgar Snow, *Red Star Over China* (New York: Random House, 1937), p. 115.

25. Agnes Smedley, *China Fights Back* (New York: Vanguard Press, 1938), pp. 7, 143. The most detailed account of the new left theater was in a chapter cut by the publishers of Nym Wales' *Inside Red China*; this chapter, "A Living Theater at Work in Yenan," was finally published by Mrs. Snow in *My Yenan Notebooks* (Madison, Conn.: Snow, 1961), pp. 204—210.

26. In Raymond J. de Jaegher and Irene Corbally, *The Enemy Within* (New York: Doubleday, 1952), pp. 162—163.

27. Forman, *Report from Red China*, p. 41.

28. Gunther Stein, *The Challenge of Red China* (New York: McGraw-Hill, 1945), pp. 173—174.

29. Robert Payne, *Journey to Red China* (London: William Heinemann, 1947), and *China Awake* (New York: Dodd, Mead and Co., 1947).

30. Ho Ching-chih, "How 'The White-haired Girl' Was Written and Produced," in *The White-haired Girl* (Peking: Foreign Languages Press, 1954), pp. v, vii.

31. *Ibid.*, p. vii.

32. Ma Ko, "From 'Yangko' Opera to 'The White-haired Girl'," *Peking Review*, 25 May 1962.

33. Ho Ching-chih, "The White-haired Girl."

34. *The White-haired Girl*, an opera in five acts by Ho Ching-chih and Ting Yi, translated by Yang Hsien-yi and Gladys Yang (Peking: Foreign Languages Press, 1954).

35. Ting Ling's stories, "New Belief" (1939), "When I Was in Hsia Village" (1940), and "In the Hospital" (1941).

Sources for Chapter 6 — Between Victories 1945—1949

1. Chia Chi, "Making Films for Today," *China Reconstructs* (Peking), March 1958, pp. 6—9.

2. Oliver Edmund Clubb, *Twentieth Century China* (New York: Columbia University Press, 1964), p. 268.

3. *Ibid.*, p. 252.

4. *Thirty Years of Chinese Cinema*, published by Realist Film Association, Melbourne, 1952 (from materials furnished by Akira Iwasaki), p. 7.

5. Cheng Chi-hua, *History of the Development of Chinese Cinema* (Peking, 1963), vol. 2, p. 159.

6. Clubb, *Twentieth Century China*, p. 274.

7. Emily Hahn, *China Only Yesterday, 1850—1950* (Garden City, N.Y.: Doubleday, 1963), p. 321.

8. Translated from Shih Tung-shan, "Part of the Preparation for *Eight Thousand Li*," in the Art and Culture supplement, *Shanghai Newspaper*, 1947 (quoted by Cheng, *Chinese Cinema*, vol. 2).

9. Translated from Hsia Yen, "Were Those Eight Years Lived in Vain?, an open letter to Tung-shan and other friends," *Nan Chao Daily* (Singapore), 27 April 1947 (quoted by Cheng, *Chinese Cinema*, vol. 2); for Hsia Yen's review and synopsis of *Eight Thousand Li*, see *China Digest* (Hong Kong), 9 September 1947, pp. 17–18.

10. *China Digest* (Hong Kong), 9 February 1948, pp. 18–19 (English title was *Tears of the Yangtse*).

11. Translated from Shih Tung-shan, "Learn Hard and Reform Yourself Diligently," in *Why Culture and Art Workers Reform Their Ideas* (Peking, March 1952); quoted by Cheng, *Chinese Cinema*, vol. 2.

12. Translated from Cheng, *Chinese Cinema*, vol. 2.

13. Translated from Yang Han-sheng, in the Theatre and Film Weekly Supplement of *Ta Kung Bao*, 28 July 1948; quoted by Cheng, *Chinese Cinema*, vol. 2.

14. Mei Lan-fang, *The Filming of a Tradition,* translated in *Eastern Horizon*, August 1965.

15. A. C. Scott, *Mei Lan-fang: Leader of the Pear Garden* (Hong Kong: Hong Kong University Press, 1959), p. 126.

16. This and following quotations translated from Ōuyang Yu-chien, *In the Midst of Life Comes the Vocation of Cinema* (Peking, 1962), pp. 40, 45–46, 50, 52–53.

17. C. P. Fitzgerald, *The Birth of Communist China* (London: Harmondsworth, 1964), p. 91.

18. Cheng Ching-tze, "From Yenan Studio to Northwest Film Study Team," *Dianying Yishu* (Peking), No. 3, 1959.

19. *Motion Picture Herald* (New York), 1 February 1947; a copy of Grant McLean's film has been preserved in Canada.

20. This summarizes the detailed analysis of the civil war period in Chapter IV of Fitzgerald's history, *The Birth of Communist China*.

21. Quotations of the scenario, *Crows and Sparrows*, are translated from *Films of the May Fourth Movement* (Peking, 1961); this volume also contains the scenarios of *Eight Thousand Li, Spring River Flows East, Lights of Ten Thousand Homes,* and T'ien Han's *Martyr of the Pear Orchard*: a later volume (1962) contains earlier scenarios of this movement, from *Wild Torrent* to *Street Angel*.

22. Translated from Ugo Casiraghi, *Il cinema cinese, questo sconosciuto* (Turin, 1960), p. 24.

23. This and following documents are quoted by Dorothy B. Jones, *The Portrayal of China and India on the American Screen* (Cambridge, Mass.: Massachusetts Institute of Technology. Center for International Studies, Communications

Program, 1955) where a fuller account of the production of *The Keys of the Kingdom* is given.

24. *The Healthy Village* (Paris: UNESCO, 1952).

Sources for Chapter 7 – Between Wars 1949—1951

Epigraph from Agnes Smedley, *The Great Road* (New York: Monthly Review Press, 1956), p. 348.

1.   A. C. Scott, *Literature and the Arts in Twentieth Century China* (London: Allen and Unwin, 1965), p. 78.

2.   Tsai Chu-sheng, "The Chinese Film Industry." English translations of this essay appeared in varying versions, in *People's China*, 16 June 1950; in *The Cine-Technician* (London), September-October 1950; and in *Culture and Education in New China* (Peking, October 1951); the last is quoted here.

3.   Translated from "Der neue chinesische Film," *Neue Film Welt* (Berlin), No. 1, 1951; details on the action of the film in *Daily News Release*, 10 June 1949; a fuller, hostile description in Liu Shaw-tong's *Out of Red China*, trans. Jack Chia and Henry Walter (New York: Duell, Sloan, and Pearce, 1953), pp. 193—197.

4.   Chang Chun-hsiang, "Films for the Millions," *China Reconstructs* (Peking), January-February 1954.

5.   Rita Barisse, "The Chinese Way," *Films and Filming* (London), March 1955.

6.   *Daily News Release*, 26 May 1952, pp. 175—176.

7.   Wilfred Burchett, *China's Feet Unbound* (Melbourne: World Unity Publications, 1952), pp. 101—102.

8.   Claude Roy, *Into China* (London: McKibbon & Kee, 1955), pp. 283—284. A translation by Mervyn Savill of Roy's *Clefs pour la Chine* (Paris, 1953).

9.   Georges Sadoul, *Dictionnaire des films* (Paris, 1965), p. 148.

10. Tsai Chu-sheng, "The Chinese Film Industry," in *Culture and Education in New China.*

11. Kuo Mo-jo, "Report on Culture and Education," in *The First Year of Victory* (Peking, 1951), pp. 40, 37.

12. This and the following quotations from Sergei Gerasimov, "Film Story of Liberated China," *New Times* (Moscow), No. 50, 1950, pp. 22—24.

13. Sergei Yutkevich, *In the Theatres and Cinemas of Liberated China* (Moscow, 1953), from which the following extracts are translated.

14. Ivor Montagu, "Films and Film Makers in Communist China," *The Cine-Technician* (London), January-February 1953.

15. Yao Hua [pseud. of Jack Chen], "New China's Films," *People's China* (Peking), 16 April 1951 (condensed Russian translation in *Iskusstvo Kino* (Moscow), September-October 1951).

16. This and following quotations translated from Jerzy Toeplitz, "VII Festiwal Filmowy w Karlovych Varach," *Kwartalnik filmowy* (Warsaw), No. 7, 1952.

17. Chang Chun-hsiang, "Films for the Millions."

18. Yao Hua, "New China's Films."

19. "Introducing 'Wen Yi Pao'," in *Chinese Literature* (Peking), No. 4, 1955.

20. C. T. Hsia, *A History of Modern Chinese Fiction* (New Haven, Conn.: Yale University Press, 1961), p. 475; see also Merle Goldman, *Literary Dissent in Communist China* (Cambridge, Mass.: Harvard University Press, 1967), pp. 90—93.

21. Quoted in *Chinese Literature* (Peking), No. 4, 1955.

22. Translated from Dovzhenko's notebooks, *Iskusstvo Kino* (Moscow), No. 4, 1963, p. 110.

Sources for Chapter 8 — Open Door — See Mountain 1952—1957

Epigraph: The manifesto against Ts'ao Ts'ao in Chapter 22 of *Romance of Three Kingdoms*, trans. C. H. Brewitt-Taylor (Shanghai: Kelly and Walsh, 1925; Rutland, Vt.: Charles E. Tuttle, 1959).

1. *Motion Picture News*, 28 July 1923, p. 466.

2. Interview with H. W. Ray, president of Hong Kong Amusements, Ltd., *Moving Picture World* (New York), 16 August 1924, p. 558.

3. Siao-Yu [Siao Shu-tung] , *Mao Tse-tung and I Were Beggars* (Syracuse, N.Y.: Syracuse University Press, 1959), pp. 24—25.

4. BBC Third Programme talk by Michael Sullivan, "Some Thoughts on Chinese Painting," printed in *The Listener,* 8 July 1965.

5. Frederick T. C. Yu, *Mass Persuasion in Communist China* (New York: Praeger, 1964), pp. 143—145.

6. *Daily News Release*, 16 June 1952, p. 105.

7. *Daily News Release*, 4 December 1951, p. 24.

8. *Daily News Release*, 31 January 1953, p. 176.

9. *Catalogue of Chinese Films*, China Film Distribution & Exhibition Corporation (Peking, 1961), p. 12.

10. S.T.W. in *China Reconstructs* (Peking), May-June 1954.

11. Nicholas Guillen, "My Second Visit to Peking," *China Reconstructs* (Peking), January-February 1954.

12. Translated from Lu Hsun, "Lessons from Films," in *Pseudo-Frivolous Talk* (see p. 78).

13. Simone de Beauvoir, *The Long March* , translated by Austryn Wainhouse (Cleveland, Ohio: World Publishing, 1958), p. 44.

14. *Ibid.*, p. 78.

15. Translated from V. Petrov, "Impressions and Meetings," *Iskusstvo Kino* (Moscow), No. 6, 1953; an English translation of Lao Shê's play was published in 1958 (Peking: Foreign Languages Press).

16. *Daily News Release*, 6 September 1951, p. 31.

17. *Daily News Release*, 12 January 1953, p. 70.

18. de Beauvoir, *The Long March*, p. 129.

19. Gavin Lambert, in *The Observer* (London), 29 May 1955.

20. Ivor Montagu, "Films and Film Makers in Communist China," *The Cine-Technician* (London), January-February 1953.

21. R. J. Minney, "Film Making in China," *Film and TV Technician* (London), January 1957.

22. *Ibid.*

23. Jean Painlevé, "Scientific and Documentary Films in China: Some Observations," *Science and Film* (London), September 1957, p. 15.

24. N.A.N.A. dispatch from Berlin, in *New York Times*, 13 September 1956.

25. Proposals . . . (Adopted on 27 September 1956), p. 28.

26. Proceedings . . . (Peking, 1956).

27. Mu Fu-sheng [pseud.], *The Wilting of the Hundred Flowers* (New York: Praeger, 1962), p. 170.

28. Wilfred Burchett, *China's Feet Unbound* (Melbourne: World Unity Publications, 1952), p. 92.

29. Liu Yi-fang, "Old Plays: A Treasury Reopened," *China Reconstructs* (Peking), February 1957.

30. Translated from Ting Chien, "Tao Chin and Fifteen Strings of Cash," *Dazhong Dianying* (Peking), No. 6, 1957.

31. C. T. Hsia, *A History of Modern Chinese Fiction* (New Haven, Conn.: Yale University Press, 1961).

32. *Catalogue: A Selection of Art Films* (Peking, 1956), pp. 65–66.

33. *China Reconstructs* (Peking), December 1956.

34. Hsia Yen's report of 2 February 1960 is more fully quoted and described in Chapter 10.

35. *Dazhong Dianying* (Peking), No. 18, 1957, pp. 5–6; the attack is signed with a pseudonym.

36. *Cinema Nuovo* (Milan), March/April 1962; this translation published in *Atlas* (New York), April 1963.

Sources for Chapter 9 — Leap 1957—1959
Epigraph: Mao Tse-tung's article on co-operatives in first number (1 June 1958) of *Hong Qi* (*Red Flag*, translated in *Peking Review*, 10 June 1958, p. 6).

1.   Chou Yang, "Answers to *Wen Wei Pao* Correspondent's Questions," translated in *Chinese Literature* (Peking), No. 3, 1957; translation also published in *People's China* (Peking), 16 May 1957.

2.   Yang Yu, "New Films," *People's China* (Peking), September 1957, p. 19.

3.   *Ibid.*, p. 20.

4.   Translated from Ugo Casiraghi, *Il cinema cinese questo sconosciuto* (Turin, 1960), p. 57.

5.   *Ibid.*, p. 61. (Ko Ling's scenario for *For Peace*, under the title of *Professor Chiang's Family*, is the first in a Russian collection, *Scenarios of the Chinese Cinema* [Moscow, 1959]).

6.   Yang Yu, "New Films," p. 25.

7.   Chia Chi, "Making Films for Today," *China Reconstructs* (Peking), March 1958. In 1966 there was more serious criticism of Hsu Chang-lin for his 1962 comedy, *Football Fans*.

8.   *Selected Works of Lu Hsun*, trans. Yang Hsien-yi and Gladys Yang (Peking: Foreign Languages Press, 1956), vol. 1.

9.   *Peking Review*, 4 March 1958, p. 20.

10. *Peking Review*, 8 July 1958, pp. 15—16.

11. *Ibid.*, p. 16.

12. *Peking Review*, 30 December 1958, p. 20.

13. Translated from *Zhungguo Dianying* (Peking), No. 11, 1958.

14. Translated from Chin Shan, "Making the *Thirteen Hill Reservoir*," *Dazhong Dianying* (Peking), No. 21, 1958, pp. 11—12.

15. Yo Shih, *Dazhong Dianying* (Peking), No. 19, 1958.

16. Translated from Ching Lo-chu, *Zhungguo Dianying* (Peking), No. 12, 1958.

17. Lin Tieh, "The Spirit of Progress," *Peking Review*, 20 May 1958, p. 8 (originally published in *Renmin Ribao* as "The Great Leap Forward of Communist Ideas").

18. Translated from *Zhungguo Dianying* (Peking), No. 6, 1959, pp. 8—9.

Sources for Chapter 10 — Anniversary Year 1959
Epigraph: E. M. Forster, "India Again" (1946), in *Two Cheers for Democracy* (New York: Harcourt, 1951).

1.   Hsiung Deh-ta, "The Chinese Cinema Today," *The China Quarterly* (London), No. 4, October-December 1960.

2. Translated from *Zhungguo Dianying* (Peking), No. 12, 1958, p. 5.

3. *Catalogue of Chinese Films* (Peking, 1961), p. 102.

4. "New Plays," in *Chinese Literature* (Peking), No. 3, 1955.

5. Translated from *Zhungguo Dianying* (Peking), No. 4, 1959.

6. Yeh Yuan and Cheng Chun-li, "Commissioner Lin Tse-hsu," trans. Yang Hsien-yi and Gladys Yang, *Chinese Literature* (Peking), April 1961, p. 30; this is one of the few modern Chinese scenarios (in the form of a "treatment") available in English. See also *Guerrillas of the Plains* and *Serfs.*

7. Entitled "Strive for a Further Big Leap in the Film Industry," this was published in *Renmin Ribao* (Peking), 2 February 1960; two English translations are available: one circulated from Peking in June 1960; the other, a condensation, was published in *Survey of China Mainland Press*, and in *The China Quarterly*. My quotations are from the official and fuller Peking translation.

8. Translated from *Dazhong Dianying* (Peking), No. 4, 1959.

9. Hsia Yen, "Strive for a Further Big Leap . . ."

10. Translated by Derek Bryan, as *Red Storm* (Peking: Foreign Languages Press, 1965).

Sources for Chapter 11 — Hong Kong

1. Joseph L. Anderson and Donald Richie, *The Japanese Film* (Rutland, Vt.: Charles E. Tuttle, 1959; New York: Grove Press, Evergreen, 1960).

2. *China Digest* (Hong Kong), 14 January 1947.

3. An English translation in *China Digest* (Hong Kong), 1948.

4. Chi Pen-yu, "Patriotism or National Betrayal? — On the Reactionary Film *Inside Story of the Ching Court*," translated from *Red Flag* in *Peking Review*, 7 April 1967.

5. Mao Tse-tung's letter of 16 October 1954, quoted in *ibid*.

6. See Guido Aristarco in *Cinema* (Padua), 30 July 1950, and Ugo Casiraghi, *Il cinema cinese questo sconosciuto* (Turin, 1960), p. 77.

7. Casiraghi, *Il cinema cinese*, pp. 79—80.

8. Ezra Goodman, *The Fifty-Year Decline and Fall of Hollywood* (New York: Simon and Schuster, 1961), pp. 198—199.

9 Trishla Goyal, *The Marketing of Films* (Calcutta, n.d.), p. 314.

10. "H. K. Mandarin Movie Industry," *South China Morning Post* (Hong Kong), 29 December 1955.

11. William Stevenson, *The Yellow Wind* (Boston: Houghton-Mifflin, 1957).

12. Morando Morandini in *Inquadratura*, July-September 1958 (quoted in Casiraghi, *Il cinema cinese*, p. 88).

13. Casiraghi, *Il cinema cinese*, p. 86.

14. George C. Shen, letter to the Editor, *Sight & Sound* (London), Spring 1964.

15. Ian Jarvie, "Hong Kong Notes," *Sight & Sound* (London), Winter 1963/64, p. 22.

16. Photos taken during these productions, in *Life* (New York), 20 December 1963, p. 176.

17. Eileen Chang, lecture notes, University of Indiana, 1966.

18. *Variety* (New York), 14 August 1963, p. 4.

19. R. E. Durgnat, "Oriental Notebook," *Sight & Sound* (London), October-December 1954, pp. 81, 84.

20. *Eastern Horizon* (Hong Kong), November 1965, pp. 2—3.

21. *New York Herald Tribune* (Paris), 26 October 1966.

22. *Movie/TV Marketing* (Tokyo), June 1967.

23. *Time* (New York), 8 September 1967, p. 46.

Sources for Chapter 12 – A Chinese People's Cinema? 1960–1967
Epigraph: Chou En-lai quoted in Hsia Yen, "Strive for a Further Big Leap . . .," p. 6.

1. *Films and Filming* (London), October 1962, p. 26; an abridged translation of Chang Kuang-nien's attack was published in *Peking Review*, No. 50, 1963.

2. Tung Chi-ping and Humphrey Evans, *The Thought Revolution* (New York: Coward, 1966), p. 99.

3. Mikhail A. Klochko, *Soviet Scientist in Red China* (New York: Praeger, 1964), pp. 142—143.

4. Hsia Yen, "A Fine Working Style . . .," in *China's Screen* (Peking), No. 1, 1961.

5. Kuo Mo-jo's address to the Afro-Asian Writers' Emergency Meeting, translated in *Chinese Literature* (Peking), No. 9, 1966, p. 59.

6. The text of this collectively written opera was translated by Yang Hsien-yi and Gladys Yang in *Chinese Literature* (Peking), No. 2, 1961.

7. Translated from Hsi Chun, "History of the Yenan Film Team," *Dianying Yishu* (Peking), No. 1, 1960.

8. "Serving the Peasants," *Peking Review*, 26 February 1965, pp. 30-31.

9. *Ibid.,* p. 31.

10. Yang Chieh-ai, "More Peasants Enjoy More Films," *China Reconstructs* (Peking), September 1965; there is a "collectively written" story about a projection team, "Wall of Bronze," translated in *Chinese Literature* (Peking), No. 4, 1967.

11. Jan Myrdal, *Report from a Chinese Village*, translated by M. Michael (New York: Pantheon, 1965).

12. *Daily News Release*, 22 November 1952, pp. 139—140.

13. *Daily News Release*, 2 November 1953, p. 6.

14. Extracts from Lei Feng's diary translated from *Dazhong Dianying* (Peking), No. 3, 1963, p. 22.

15. *Daily News Release*, 3 November 1949.

16. A translation of "Sowing the Clouds" was published in *Chinese Literature* (Peking), No. 1, 1961; an English translation of *Hurricane* was published by the Foreign Languages Press, Peking, 1955.

17. [J. L.], "After *Storm — Hurricane*," *Iskusstvo Kino* (Moscow), No. 9, 1962.

18. Merle Goldman, "The Fall of Chou Yang," *The China Quarterly* (London), July-September 1966, p. 142.

19. Translated from *Dianying Yishu* (Peking), No. 10, 1960.

20. *Dazhong Dianying* (Peking), No. 2, 1959.

21. A translation of "The Story of Li Shuang-shuang" appeared in *Chinese Literature* (Peking), June 1960.

22. Agnes Smedley, *The Great Road* (New York: Monthly Review Press, 1956), pp. 290—291; Edgar Snow, *Journey to the Beginning* (New York: Random House, 1958), p. 87.

23. Edward B. Behr, "Impressions of Red China," *Weekend Telegraph* (London), 18 December 1964.

24. K. S. Karol, *China: The Other Communism*, trans. Tom Baistow (New York: Hill and Wang, 1967), p. 248.

25. Novel by Chin Ching-mai, translated in *Chinese Literature* (Peking), No. 7, 1966, pp. 116—118.

26. Lorenz Stucki, *Behind the Great Wall*, trans. Jean Steinberg (New York: Praeger, 1965), pp. 87—88.

27. Karol, *China*, pp. 126—127.

28. *Ibid.*, p. 129.

29. Peking *Kung-ren Ribao*, 4 December 1963 (translated in *Survey of Mainland China Press*, No. 3137).

30. Sophia Knight, *Window on Shanghai* (London: Deutsch, 1967), p. 105.

31. Josef von Sternberg, *Fun in a Chinese Laundry* (New York: Macmillan, 1965), pp. 82—83.

32. Hsinhua news-release, 16 April 1964.

33. Wangdui, "How I Acted the Part of Jampa," *Chinese Literature* (Peking), No. 1, 1965.

34. Huang Tsung-chiang's script for *Serfs* is translated in *Chinese Literature* (Peking), No. 1, 1965; in 1965 an unprecedented (for China) and detailed book on the production of *Serfs* was published. *Nung nu-ts'ung chü pên tao ying p'ien* includes the script, shooting script, and statements by most of this film's makers (no English translation yet announced).

35. Yeh Yuan and Cheng Chun-li, "Commissioner Lin Tse-hsu," *Chinese Literature* (Peking), April 1961.

36. Huang Tsung-Chiang, *Serfs*.

37. Sergei Eisenstein, "The Cinematographic Principle and the Ideogram," in *Film Form* (New York: Harcourt, Brace, and Co., 1949); see also p. 97.

38. Princess Der Ling (Mrs. Thaddeus C. White), *Two Years in the Forbidden City* (New York: Moffat, Yard, and Co., 1912), p. 35.

39. *Ibid.*, pp. 349–350.

40. *Ibid.*, pp. 28–35.

41. Translation from Ching Tzun [pseud.], in *Film Production* (Peking), No. 1, 1962; a new translation of "The Battle at Red Cliff" appeared in *Chinese Literature* (Peking), Nos. 1 & 2, 1962.

42. From chapters VIII and IX of *San Kuo, or Romance of the Three Kingdoms,* trans. by C. H. Brewitt-Taylor (Shanghai: Kelly and Walsh, 1916). Rutland, Vt.: Oharles E. Tuttle, 1959).

43. From Pearl Buck's translation, *All Men Are Brothers* (New York: John Day, 1937).

44. P'u Sung-ling, trans. Herbert A. Giles, in *Strange Stories from a Chinese Studio* (Shanghai: Kelly and Walsh, 1916).

45. *Ibid.*, p. 308.

46. Lu Hsun, *Old Tales Retold*, trans. Yang Hsien-yi and Gladys Yang (Peking: Foreign Languages Press, 1961).

47. Translation by Sidney Shapiro in *Chinese Literature* (Peking), August 1961.

48. Two good translations: by Ching Yi and Robert Payne in *The Chinese Earth* (London: Allen and Unwin, 1947), and by Gladys Yang in *Chinese Literature* (Peking), October-November 1962.

49. Yang Shuo, "Three Thousand Li of Rivers and Mountains" (Peking, 1953), trans. Li Chi, in *The China Quarterly* (London), January-March 1963.

50. Translation by Sidney Shapiro, *Chinese Literature* (Peking), May 1962, pp. 13–14; an English translation of the entire novel was also published that year by the Foreign Languages Press, Peking.

51. Agnes Smedley, *China Fights Back* (New York: Vanguard Press, 1938), pp. 104–105.

52. *Renmin Ribao* (Peking), 29 May, 9 June, 13 June, 1965.

53. Translated from *Renmin Ribao* (Peking), 29 May 1965.

54. Translated from *Renmin Ribao* (Peking), 9 June 1965.

55. Quoted in *Renmin Ribao* (Peking), 13 June 1965.

56. A.Zhelakhovtsev, "Chinese Cinema at the Service of the 'Cultural Revolution'," *Sovietskii Ekran* (Moscow), No. 8, 1967; also translated by Steven P. Hill in *Film Comment* (New York), Fall 1968.

57. Sophia Knight, *Window on Shanghai* (London: Deutsch, 1967), p. 226.

58. *Literaturnaya Gazeta* (Moscow), 13 November 1968, p. 14; see also *Sovietskaya Kultura* (Moscow), 16 January 1969.

59. This translation of *Guerrillas Sweep the Plains* was published, without naming its authors, in *Chinese Literature* (Peking), No. 6, 1969.

60. *Chinese Literature* (Peking), August 1966.

61. *Chinese Literature* (Peking), October 1966.

62. *People's China* (Peking), 16 August 1957, p. 38.

63. "Reactionary Films Criticized," *Peking Review*, 1 September 1967.

Sources for Illustrations in the Text
page

title-page, calligraphy by Chang Ch'ung-ho.

12. Newspaper advertisement for *War in Wuhan*'s revival in 1913, as reproduced in *Zhungguo Dianying*, No. 1, October 1956.

23. Advertisement for *Yen Rei-hsun*, as reproduced in *Zhungguo Dianying*, No. 1, October 1956.

28. Chinese posters for Pathé Films, ca. 1909, in the private collection of Gerhard Lamprecht, now deposited in the Deutsches Filmarchiv, Berlin.

43. Poster for *Resurrection of the Rose*, 1927; from the collection of the Nederlands Filmmuseum, Amsterdam.

47. Paper scissor-cut of a foreign plane (the pilot has a big nose) as reproduced in Tretyakov's *Zhung-guo* (Moscow, 1927).

59. Drawing by Liao Ch'eng-chih given to Helen Snow, as reproduced in *Inside Red China*, (New York: Doubleday, Doran, and Company, 1939), by Nym Wales [Mrs. Snow], p. 226.

97. Woodcut by G. Yecheistov from the cover of *Mei Lan-fang and the Chinese Theater* (Moscow and Leningrad, 1935).

109. Newspaper cartoon of "Mr. Wang" by Yeh Chen-yu, reproduced from A. C. Scott, *Literature and the Arts in Twentieth Century China* (Garden City, N.Y.: Doubleday Anchor, 1963).

113. Poster for Hearst Metrotone News (M-G-M) reproduced in *Motion Picture Herald*, 5 March 1932.

144. Drawing from *Dazhong Dianying*, No. 11, 1962, p. 33.

175. Newspaper cartoon of "Three-Hairs," by Chang Lo-pin, as reproduced in *Dazhong Dianying*, No. 23, 1957.

180. Norman McLaren's experiment in minimum animation, in West China, 1948 (film strip from National Film Board); scissor-cut paper animation, *Red Army Bridge*, 1964, from *Dazhong Dianying*, Nos. 10–11, 1964, p. 60.

214. Cartoon from *Dazhong Dianying*, No. 4, 1956. The film advertised is *Guerrillas Sweep the Plains* (1955).

221. Caricature of Liu Pan, from *Dazhong Dianying*, No. 18, 1957, p. 6.

253. Drawing by Yu Yen, during production of *Sisters on the Stage*, in *Dazhong Dianying*, No. 6, 1964, p. 26.

262. Footnote. From the picture-book based on the film *The Lin Family's Shop*, plate 18 (Peking, 1962).

289. A drawing for *Third Sister Liu*, by Li Ke-yu, *Chinese Literature*, No. 2, 1961, p. 88.

292–293. Scissor-cut animation, *When We Work Together We Have More Than Enough* (1963), by Ho Yu-men, from *Dazhong Dianying*, No. 7, 1963, p. 20; *A Dream of Gold*, 1962, designed by Tzu Ching-ta, from *Dazhong Dianying*, 26 October 1962, p. 29, and No. 4, 1963, p. 20.

297. Woodcut in *Dazhong Dianying*, No. 12, 1963.

299. Color woodcut by Wu Ching-hsun and Yu Chin-ku, "Introducing the Story Before the Film Starts."

311. Seal designed by Hsuei Li-tze for *Li Shuang-shuang*, from *Dazhong Dianying*, Nos. 5–6, 1963, p. 24.

312. Advertising for *Better and Better*, from *Dazhong Dianying*, No. 2, 1963, p. 6.

322. Illustration by Fa Nai-guang to a reportage in *Renmin Ribao* (28 December 1965) about Shanghai filmmakers in a naval engagement on the Fukien front.

326. Decor designed for *Serfs*, in the book of its production (Peking, 1965), opposite p. 236; poster for *Serfs*.

334. From the picture-book based on the film, *Nieh Erh* (Peking, 1962), plates 256–257.

335. From *Renmin Ribao*, 30 March 1966, a collective work by students in the Department of Wood Engraving, at the Art Institute: "The Family of the Hospital Helper."

354. Photograph of Chin Shan, 1959, courtesy of Ted Brake.

359. Drawing of Hsieh Tien, from *Dazhong Dianying*, No. 1, 1954, p. 7.

361. Drawing of Hung Shen, from *Chinese Literature*.

367. Photograph of Mei Lan-fang, 1935; photo by author.

374. Drawing of Shih Mei, from *Dazhong Dianying*, No. 1, 1954, p. 7.

380. Photograph of Ting Ling, 1937; photo by Helen Snow.

390. Drawing of Yu Ming, from *Dazhong Dianying*, No. 1, 1954, p. 4.

463. Stereopticon slide, Keystone Views.

Sources for the Plates
plates

1. Reproduced from *Asia*, March 1933, p. 186; courtesy Harvard University Library.

2. Frame enlargements, Library of Congress, Films Division.

3a. National Film Archive, London;

3b. Frame enlargement, Library of Congress.

4a. Frame enlargement, National Archives, Washington;

4b. Museum of Modern Art, Department of Film, New York.

5a. From Eisenstein Archive, Moscow.

5b, 6a, 7b. Copied from illustrations to Ida Treat's article in *Travel*, June 1936.

6b. Reproduced from *Asia*, October 1934; courtesy Toronto Public Library.

7a. Reproduced from *Asia*, September 1935.

8a. Photograph by the author;

8b. Staatliches Filmarchiv der DDR, Berlin.

9. Film Archive of China, Peking.

10. Nederlands Filmmuseum, Amsterdam.

11. Copied from illustrations to *Journey to a War*, by W. H. Auden and Christopher Isherwood (London, 1938); courtesy Faber & Faber, London.

12, 13. Museum of Modern Art, Department of Film, New York.

14. National Film Board of Canada, Montreal.

15, 16, 17. Museum of Modern Art, Department of Film, New York.

18, 19. Courtesy of Akira Iwasaki, Tokyo.

20. Reproduced from *Sight & Sound* (London), Spring 1949, p. 12; courtesy British Film Institute.

21a. National Film Archive, London;

21b. Pacific Film Archive, University of California, Berkeley, California.

22. Picture Collection, New York Public Library.

23. Cinématheque de Belgique, Brussels.

24. Film Archive of China, Peking.

25 to 34 (including frame enlargements). Progress-Film, Berlin.

35. Nederlands Filmmuseum, Amsterdam.

36a. Copied from *Catalogue of Chinese Films* (Peking, 1961);

36b. Contemporary Films, London.

37a. Contemporary Films, London;

37b. Haiyen Film Studio, Shanghai.

38, 39. Courtesy of Ted Brake, London.

40. Copied from *Catalogue of Chinese Films* (Peking, 1961).

41. Contemporary Films, London.

42a. Contemporary Films, London;

42b. Haiyen Film Studio, Shanghai.

43. Peking Film Studio, Peking.

44. Contemporary Films, London.

Index